THE EARLY ISLAMIC CONQUESTS

THE EARLY ISLAMIC CONQUESTS

BY FRED McGRAW DONNER

PRINCETON UNIVERSITY PRESS
PRINCETON, NEW JERSEY

Published by Princeton University Press, Princeton, New Jersey
IN THE UNITED KINGDOM:
Princeton University Press, Guildford, Surrey

Library of Congress Cataloging in Publication Data will be found on the last printed page of this book

Publication of this book has been aided by the Whitney Darrow Publication Reserve Fund of Princeton University Press
The maps have been prepared with the assistance of the Frederick W. Hilles Publication Fund of Yale University

This book has been composed in Linotron Bembo

Clothbound editions of Princeton University Press books are printed on acid-free paper, and binding materials are chosen for strength and durability

Printed in the United States of America by Princeton University Press, Princeton, New Jersey *to my parents*

GEORGE ROBERT DONNER

MYRTILLA McGRAW DONNER

in gratitude for
their guidance, encouragement,
and love

CONTENTS

PREFACE

This book presents a description and interpretation of the early Islamic conquest movement, from its beginnings under the Prophet Muḥammad (ca. A.D. 570-632) through the conquest of the Fertile Crescent. It attempts to do two things: first, to provide a new interpretation of the origins and nature of the Islamic conquest movement, and second, to establish as definitively as the sources will allow the course of two chapters in the early conquests, those of Syria and Iraq. For a general summary of the interpretive thesis to be presented, I refer the reader to the Introduction. It may, however, be useful to provide here a few remarks on some of the methods used to construct the interpretation presented and to reconstruct the course of certain episodes, since these methods are not always those used by other students of the conquests.

One way in which the present work differs from earlier studies of the conquests is in its approach to the sources. In using the written records—almost entirely chronicles and other literary sources in Arabic—I have assessed the reliability of pieces of evidence on the basis of my own understanding of the very complex process by which separate accounts were collected, synthesized, and transmitted by the early Arabic historians. This view of the sources has to a great extent freed me of the exaggerated and, in my opinion, unwarranted skepticism toward the Arabic sources shown by some recent authors. It is an approach, however, that usually remains implicit rather than explicit, although at times (notably in Chapter III) it proved impossible to keep such purely methodological issues quietly in the background. For a full and explicit statement of this view of the sources, I shall have to refer the reader to my study of early Islamic historiography currently in preparation.

This book also parts company with many of its predecessors in its attempt to use ethnographic literature, much of it of quite recent origin, to help elucidate economic, social, and political structures that flourished over thirteen centuries ago. Not all readers will agree with this approach, and I myself would be the first to warn against the wholesale transfer of anachronistic material across so many centuries. In this case, however, I feel that the judicious and selective use of later evidence in reconstructing earlier conditions is both defensible and, indeed, necessary. In the first place, certain fundamental aspects of Arabian life, such as the nomadic economy, have functioned historically within very narrow ecological and technological constraints, and there is little to suggest that these constraints themselves underwent serious modification in the intervening years, at least up to the first decades of this century. Thus the assumption that some aspects of Arabian life may have undergone very little change is not entirely unwarranted. In the second place, I am not proposing the reconstruction of entire dimensions of Arabian life, solely on the basis of modern evidence, when no ancient evidence exists. I attempt, rather, to describe certain relationships or institutions mentioned in the ancient sources on the basis of our fuller knowledge of what appear to be very similar relationships or institutions existing in more recent times. The ancient evidence, although limited in extent, thus provides the vital means for determining when an historical parallel between ancient and recent conditions should, or should not, be drawn. Finally, and perhaps most compelling, is the fact that the early sources are themselves limited and incomplete. Thus, if we wish to venture any meaningful interpretation at all, we are forced to draw, albeit cautiously, on later materials to explain certain early conditions. What we attempt to do, in short, is to use the known to shed light on the unknown. It is a process that involves certain risks, to be sure, but such risks are still preferable, in my opinion, to a perfectly secure, but perfectly uninformative, silence.

In general, I have tried to make as much of the book as possible accessible to nonspecialists (especially non-Arabists), particularly the sections that present the main points of my interpretation—the Introduction and Chapters I, II, and VI. On the other hand, the interpretation itself rests on an analysis that is of necessity complicated and detailed. Even in the more detailed chapters on the conquests of Syria and Iraq, however, I have tried to summarize in a clear and uninvolved way the general results of my analysis; these summaries can be found in the sections of Chapters III and IV entitled "The Course of the Conquest." I will confess, however, my hope that the text throughout will prove straightforward enough to be understood by the dedicated nonspecialist.

Any work of this kind, involving a considerable amount of synthesis, must rely heavily on the work of others, and I trust that my indebtedness to my scholarly predecessors is amply revealed in the notes. I wish, however, to single out three in particular—W. Montgomery Watt, for his careful work on the life of Muḥammad, Elias S. Shoufani, for his study of the *ridda* wars, and the late Werner Caskel, for his work on Arab tribal genealogies—who have most significantly facilitated my own research. Although my own interpretations differ from theirs on many points, it was nevertheless possible to refer to their studies constantly for verification of points of fact, which saved me countless months of labor in the primary sources.

I am also grateful to the many colleagues and friends who enriched my understanding with their discussion, criticized earlier drafts, and in various other ways helped me on the way. First and foremost, I wish to thank Professor Roy Mottahedeh of Princeton University, whose encouragement and thoughtful criticism have consistently been sources of aid and inspiration. Very helpful comments on parts or all of this work have been offered by Bernard Lewis and Avram Udovitch, of Princeton University; by Paul Bushkovitch, Deno Geanakoplos, Robert Good, Robert Harding, Robert Lopez, and Ramsay MacMullen, of Yale University; by David Robinson, of Michigan State University; by Walter Kaegi, Jr., of the University of Chicago; by Michael Morony, of the University of California, Los Angeles; by Richard Bulliet, of Columbia University; and by Father Albert Jamme, of the Catholic University of America. Collectively they alerted me to many errors of fact, infelicities of style, and uncertainties in my interpretation and thus strengthened the book greatly through their care. I would also like to express my gratitude to the Whitney A. Griswold Faculty Research Fund of Yale University, which generously supported travel undertaken while researching this book; to the Frederick W. Hilles Publication Fund of Yale University, for financial aid in preparing the maps; and to the Whitney Darrow Reserve Fund of Princeton University Press, for supporting publication costs. I am indebted, furthermore, to the Macmillan Publishing Co., Inc., and to George Allen and Unwin Ltd., for granting permission to quote passages from Arthur J. Arberry's *The Koran Interpreted*, and to Dr. Robert Lee Williams for his excellent cartographic work. Finally, I wish to offer special thanks to my editors at Princeton University Press, Margaret Case and Margaret Riccardi, for their admirable professionalism, sensitivity, and patience in dealing with a long and complicated manuscript; they are in many ways the quiet heroes behind an enterprise such as this one, and all readers owe them an immense debt of gratitude.

F.M.D.

NOTE ON TRANSLITERATIONS

The system adopted for rendering Arabic names and terms in Latin characters is, with insignificant modifications, the same as that now used in many English-language periodicals (for example, *International Journal of Middle East Studies*). I have followed this system strictly in the case of technical terms and personal names. In the case of place-names, however, I have followed a double system. Many have been given in strict transliteration, particularly when little known; but certain well-established localities have been designated by their common names, for example, "Damascus" (rather than "Dimashq"). In one instance, I have exploited this double system to differentiate two very similar place-names, namely, "al-Baṣra" (in Iraq) and "al-Buṣrā" (in Syria), by giving the former in strict transliteration and the latter in the Latin form, "Bostra." Finally, in mentioning certain Syrian towns I sometimes give both the Arabic and the Roman names, for example, "Ḥimṣ (Emesa)."

ABBREVIATIONS

The Arabic sources on which this study is largely based were the products of a scholastic system that preserved and transmitted a vast number of short, often fragmentary accounts about specific events. Since the sources now extant usually include accounts deriving from several different historiographical traditions, it is clearly necessary to indicate in references not only where the material is to be found (i.e., book title and page number), but also the historiographical tradition to which it belongs, since it is only the latter that can enable us to assess the account's significance as historical evidence. In order to facilitate such a process, a set of abbreviations has been developed for reference to commonly cited transmitters and means of transmission; these are used to represent at least the earlier links in the *isnād* or chain of transmitters that prefaces each account in some historical collections. A citation in the form "Tab. i/1234 (Sayf<MT)," for example, would indicate that the account under consideration, which could be found at the indicated volume and page of al-Ṭabarī's chronicle, was transmitted on the authority of the Kufan transmitter Sayf b. 'Umar (d. ca. A.D. 800), who received it by a specific method of transmission (referred to in the Arabic sources by the term *'an*, here represented by <) from the older authorities Muḥammad b. 'Abdullāh and Ṭalḥa b. al-'A'lam al-Ḥanafī (represented by MT).

Although this technique is admittedly somewhat cumbersome, it nevertheless provides for much greater historiographical precision than has been common in works on early Islamic history; and it is, I think, only in this way that we will ever be able to dispel the mists that still shroud so much of that history.

Those readers who wish to know the technical details concerning the various means of transmission should refer to Fuat Sezgin's *Geschichte des arabischen Schrifttums* I (Leiden: E. J. Brill, 1967), pp. 53-84.

FOR WORKS CITED

Aghani	al-Iṣfahānī, 'Alī b. al-Ḥusayn Abū l-Faraj. *Kitāb al-aghānī*. 22 vols. Būlāq and Leiden: E. J. Brill, 1867-1900.
Amwal	Abū 'Ubayd al-Qāsim b. Sallām. *Kitāb al-amwāl*. Edited by Muḥammad Khalīl Harrās. Cairo: Maktabat al-Kulliyāt al-Azhariyya, 1968.
Azdi	al-Baṣrī, Muḥammad b. 'Abdullāh al-Azdī. *Ta'rīkh futūḥ al-Shām*. Cairo: Mu'assasa Sÿill al-'Arab, 1970.
Azraqi	al-Azraqī, Abū l-Walīd Muḥammad b. 'Abdullāh. *Kitāb akhbār Makka*. Edited by Ferdinand Wüstenfeld. Leipzig: F. A. Brockhaus, 1858 (*Chroniken der Stadt Mekka*, 1).

Bal. *Ansab* I, etc.	al-Balādhurī, Aḥmad b. Yaḥyā. *Ansāb al-ashrāf.* vol. I. Edited by Muḥammad Ḥamīdullāh. Cairo: Dār al-Ma'ārif, 1959; vol. IVA. Edited by Max Schloessinger and M. J. Kister. Jerusalem: Magnes Press, 1971; vol. V. Edited by Shlomo D. F. Goitein. Jerusalem: University Press, 1936.
Bal. *Ansab* Reis. 597 etc.	al-Balādhurī, Aḥmad b. Yaḥyā. *Ansāb al-ashrāf.* MS, Reisülkuttap no. 597 and 598, housed in Süleymaniye Kütüphanesi, Istanbul.
Bal. *Fut.*	al-Balādhurī, Aḥmad B. Yaḥyā. *Futūḥ al-buldān.* Edited by Michael Jan de Goeje. Leiden: E. J. Brill, 1866.
Caetani, *Annali*	Caetani, Leone. *Annali dell'Islam.* 10 vols. Milan: U. Hoepli, 1905-1926.
C.S.C.O.	*Corpus Scriptorum Christianorum Orientalium*
Din.	al-Dīnawarī, Abū Ḥanīfa Aḥmad b. Dāūd. *al-Akhbār al-ṭiwāl.* Cairo: Dār Iḥyā' al-Kutub al-'Arabiyya, 1960.
EI(1), *EI*(2)	*Encyclopaedia of Islam*, 1st ed. Edited by M. T. Houtsma et al. Leiden: E. J. Brill, 1913-1934, with supplement, 1938; 2nd ed. Edited by H.A.R. Gibb et al. Leiden: E. J. Brill, 1960-.
I. D.	Ibn Durayd, Abū Bakr Muḥammad b. al-Ḥasan. *al-Ishtiqāq.* Edited by Ferdinand Wüstenfeld. Göttingen: Dieterischen Buchhandlung, 1854.
I. H.	Ibn Hishām, 'Abd al-Malik. *al-Sīra al-nabawiyya.* Edited by Ferdinand Wüstenfeld, *Das Leben Muhammads.* 2 vols. Göttingen: Dieterischen Buchhandlung, 1858-1860.
I.H.J.	Ibn Ḥazm al-Andalusī, Abū Muḥammad 'Alī b. Aḥmad b. Sa'īd. *Jamharat ansāb al-'Arab.* Edited by 'Abd al-Salām Muḥammad Hārūn. Cairo: Dār al-Ma'ārif, 1971.
I. K./Caskel	Ibn al-Kalbī, Hishām b. Muḥammad. *Jamharat al-nasab.* Edited by Werner Caskel and G. Strenziok. 2 vols. Leiden: E. J. Brill, 1966.
Iqd	Ibn 'Abd Rabbihi, Aḥmad b. Muḥammad. *al-'Iqd al-farīd.* Edited by Muḥammad Sa'īd al-'Iryān. 8 vols. Beirut: Dār al-Fikr, 1953.
I.S.	Ibn Sa'd, Muḥammad. *Kitāb al-ṭabaqāt al-kabīr.* Edited by Eduard Sachau et al. 9 vols. Leiden: E. J. Brill, 1904-1940.
Isaba	Ibn Ḥajar al-'Asqualānī Aḥmad b. 'Alī. *al-Iṣāba fī tamyīz al-ṣaḥāba.* 4 vols. Cairo: Maṭba'at al-Sa'āda, A.H. 1328 (A.D. 1910).

JAOS	*Journal of the American Oriental Society*
JESHO	*Journal of the Economic and Social History of the Orient*
JRAS	*Journal of the Royal Asiatic Society*
JRCAS	*Journal of the Royal Central Asian Society*
Khalifa	Khalīfa b. Khayyāṭ al-ʿUsfūrī, Abū ʿUmar Shabāb. *Ta'rikh*. Edited by Akram Ḍiyā' al-ʿUmarī. 2 vols. al-Najaf, 1967.
Kufi	Ibn Aʿtham al-Kūfī, Abū Muḥammad Aḥmad. *Kitāb al-futuḥ*. Edited by Muḥammad ʿAbd al-Muʿīd Khān et al. 8 vols. Hyderabad; Dā'irat al-Maʿārif al-ʿUthmāniyya, 1968-1975.
Masʿudi, *Tanbih*	al-Masʿūdī, ʿAlī b. Ḥusayn. *al-Tanbīh wa l-ishrāf*. Edited by M. J. de Goeje. Leiden: E. J. Brill, 1894. Reprinted Beirut, 1965.
Muhabbar	Ibn Ḥabīb, Muḥammad. *Kitāb al-muḥabbar*. Edited by Ilse Lichtenstadter. Hyderabad: Dā'irat al-Maʿārif al-ʿUthmāniyya, 1942.
Muruj	al-Masʿūdī, ʿAlī b. Ḥusayn. *Murūj al-dhahab wa maʿādin al-jawhar*. Edited by Yūsuf Asʿad Dāghir. 4 vols. Beirut: Dār Ṣādir, 1965-1966.
Q.	Qur'ān
Shoufani, *Al-Riddah*	Shoufani, Elias S. *Al-Riddah and the Muslim Conquest of Arabia*. Toronto: University of Toronto Press, and Beirut: Arab Institute for Research and Publishing, 1972.
Tab.	al-Ṭabarī, Muḥammad b. Jarīr. *Ta'rīkh al-rusul wa l-mulūk*. Edited by M. J. de Goeje et al. 15 vols. Leiden: E. J. Brill, 1879-1901.
Theophanes (de Boor)	Theophanes, *Chronographia*. Edited by Carolus de Boor. Leipzig: B. G. Teubner, 1883.
TMD I	Ibn ʿAsākir. *Ta'rīkh madīnat Dimashq*, I. Edited by Ṣalāḥ al-Dīn al-Munajjid. Damascus: Al-Majmaʿ al-ʿIlmī al-ʿArabī, 1951.
TMD (Leningrad)	Ibn ʿAsākir, Abū l-Qāsim ʿAli b. al-Ḥasan b. Hibatullāh. *Ta'rīkh madīnat Dimashq*. MS, Asiatic Museum, Leningrad, Arabic no. 202.
TMD (Zah.)	Ibn ʿAsākir, Abū l-Qāsim ʿAli b. al-Ḥasan b. Hibatullāh. *Ta'rīkh madinat Dimashq*. MS, Ẓāhiriyya Library, Damascus. 19 vols. (*Ta'rikh* l-*Ta'rikh* 18 and *Ta'rikh* 113).
Waq.	al-Wāqidī, Muḥammad b. ʿUmar. *Kitāb al-maghāzī*. Edited by Marsden Jones. 3 vols. Oxford: Oxford University Press, 1966.
Watt, *Medina*	Watt, William Montgomery. *Muhammad at Medina*. Oxford: Clarendon Press, 1956.

Ya'qubi	al-Ya'qūbī, Aḥmad b. Abī Ya'qūb. *Ta'rikh al-Ya'qūbī*. 2 vols. Beirut: Dār Ṣādir and Dār Bayrūt, 1960.
Yaqut	Yāqūt al-Ḥamawī, Shihāb al-Dīn Abū 'Abdullāh. *Mu'jam al-buldān*. 5 vols. Beirut: Dār Ṣādir and Dār Bayrūt, 1957.
ZDMG	*Zeitschrift der Deutschen Morgenländischen Gesellschaft*

FOR *ISNĀDS*

Means of Transmission:

a—	*anba'a-nī, anba'a-nā*
ak—	*akhbara-nī, akhbara-nā*
h—	*ḥaddatha-nī, ḥaddatha-nā, ḥuddithtu 'an*
q—	*qāla, qālū, qīla*
s—	*sami'tu 'an*
<	*'an*

Transmitters:

A	see MTZMAS
AH	Abū Ḥāritha
AM	Abū Mikhnaf
AU	Abū 'Uthmān Yazīd b. Asīd al-Ghassānī
I.I.	Ibn Isḥāq
I.K.	Ibn al-Kalbī
IL	Ibn Lahī'a
I.S.	Ibn Sa'd
K	Khālid b. Ma'dan al-Kalā'ī
KU	Khālid and 'Ubāda
M	see MTZMAS
Mad	al-Madā'inī
MbA	Muḥammad b. 'Ā'idh al-Dimashqī al-Qurashī
MTZMAS	Muḥammad b. 'Abdullāh, Ṭalḥa b. al-'A'lam al-Ḥanafī, Ziyād b. Sarjīs al-Aḥmarī, al-Muhallab b. 'Uqba al-Asadī, 'Amr. b. Muḥammad, Sa'īd b. al-Marzubān. When only one "M" is used, it stands for Muḥammad b. 'Abdullāh.
R	al-Rabī'a
S	see MTZMAS
Sayf	Sayf b. 'Umar al-Usayyidī al-Tamīmī
SbA	Sa'īd b. 'Abd al-'Azīz al-Tanūkhī
T	see MTZMAS
U	'Ubāda b. Nusayy
Waq	al-Wāqidī
WbM	al-Walīd b. Muslim al-Umawī al-Dimashqī
Z	see MTZMAS
Zuhri	al-Zuhrī

LIST OF MAPS

CHRONOLOGICAL TABLE

First Day of Islamic Month	A.H. 10	A.H. 11	A.H. 12	A.H. 13	A.H. 14	A.H. 15
Muharram	9 Apr 631	29 Mar 632*	18 Mar 633	7 Mar 634	25 Feb 635	14 Feb 636*
Ṣafar	9 May 631	28 Apr 632*	17 Apr 633	6 Apr 634	27 Mar 635	15 Mar 636*
Rabīʿ I	7 Jun 631	27 May 632*	16 May 633	5 May 634	25 Apr 635	13 Apr 636*
Rabīʿ II	7 Jul 631	26 Jun 632*	15 Jun 633	4 Jun 634	25 May 635	13 May 636*
Jumāda I	5 Aug 631	25 Jul 632*	14 Jul 633	3 Jul 634	23 Jun 635	11 Jun 636*
Jumāda II	4 Sep 631	24 Aug 632*	13 Aug 633	2 Aug 634	23 Jul 635	11 Jul 636*
Rajab	3 Oct 631	22 Sep 632*	11 Sep 633	31 Aug 634	21 Aug 635	9 Aug 636*
Shaʿbān	2 Nov 631	22 Oct 632*	11 Oct 633	30 Sep 634	20 Sep 635	8 Sep 636*
Ramaḍān	1 Dec 631	20 Nov 632*	9 Nov 633	29 Oct 634	19 Oct 635	7 Oct 636*
Shawwāl	31 Dec 631	20 Dec 632*	9 Dec 633	28 Nov 634	18 Nov 635	6 Nov 636*
Dhū l-Qaʿda	29 Jan 632*	18 Jan 633	7 Jan 634	27 Dec 634	17 Dec 635	5 Dec 636*
Dhū l-Ḥijja	28 Feb 632*	17 Feb 633	6 Feb 634	26 Jan 635	16 Jan 636*	5 Jan 637

* Leap Year

First Day of Islamic Month	A.H. 16	A.H. 17	A.H. 18	A.H. 19	A.H. 20
Muharram	2 Feb 637	23 Jan 638	12 Jan 639	2 Jan 640*	21 Dec 640*
Ṣafar	4 Mar 637	22 Feb 638	11 Feb 639	1 Feb 640*	21 Jan 641
Rabīʿ I	2 Apr 637	23 Mar 638	12 Mar 639	1 Mar 640*	19 Feb 641
Rabīʿ II	2 May 637	22 Apr 638	11 Apr 639	31 Mar 640*	21 Mar 641
Jumāda I	31 May 637	21 May 638	10 May 639	29 Apr 640*	19 Apr 641
Jumāda II	30 Jun 637	20 Jun 638	9 Jun 639	29 May 640*	19 May 641
Rajab	29 Jul 637	19 Jul 638	8 Jul 639	27 Jun 640*	17 Jun 641
Shaʿbān	28 Aug 637	18 Aug 638	7 Aug 639	27 Jul 640*	17 Jul 641
Ramaḍān	26 Sep 637	16 Sep 638	5 Sep 639	25 Aug 640*	15 Aug 641
Shawwāl	26 Oct 637	16 Oct 638	5 Oct 639	24 Sep 640*	14 Sep 641
Dhū l-Qaʿda	24 Nov 637	14 Nov 638	3 Nov 639	23 Oct 640*	13 Oct 641
Dhū l-Ḥijja	24 Dec 637	14 Dec 638	3 Dec 639	22 Nov 640*	12 Nov 641

* Leap Year

THE EARLY ISLAMIC CONQUESTS

INTRODUCTION

Few events in human history have transformed the face of such a large part of the globe as rapidly and as decisively as did the expansion of early Islam and the conquest by Muslims of much of the ancient world. Indeed, the Islamic conquest forms one of those rare turning points in history whose importance is unanimously accepted by all students of man's past. It is therefore hardly surprising that numerous scholars should have focused their attention on the conquest in an effort to explain what it represented, why it occurred, and what impact it had. What is surprising is that a phenomenon of this magnitude should appear to defy definitive analysis, for it can safely be said that, although everyone agrees on the paramount importance of the conquest as an historical phenomenon, few authors are in full agreement about its nature and, in particular, its causes.

The oldest view of the Islamic conquest is, of course, that of the Islamic community itself, which traditionally saw the conquest as the result of religious zeal for the new faith and as a truly miraculous demonstration of the divine favor that Islam is supposed to enjoy. Western scholars found this explanation unsatisfactory, however, and have tried to understand the conquests in terms quite different from those accepted by Muslims themselves.

One of the first Western interpretations of the Islamic conquest movement linked it to a mass migration of Arab tribesmen. Sir William Muir, for example, understood the conquest as the result of a mass migration of Arabs, which was in turn caused mainly by the cupidity of the tribesmen and their "love of rapine." Thus, in 1898 he wrote the following description of the conquest: "Warrior after warrior, column after column, whole tribes in endless succession with their women and children, issued forth to fight. And ever, at the marvellous tale of cities conquered: of rapine rich beyond compute; . . . fresh tribes arose and went. Onward and still onward, like swarms from the hive, or flights of locusts darkening the land, tribe after tribe issued forth and hastening northward, spread in great masses to the East and to the West."[1]

This view of the conquest was soon to be challenged, however. In

1911, Leone Caetani stressed the fact that the Muslims did not enjoy numerical superiority in their battles with Byzantium and Sasanid Persia and showed that the forces employed by all three contestants were in fact quite small.[2] Yet Caetani shared with Muir the view that the conquest was in some way generated by, or driven by, a migration of Arabs. The real reasons for the irresistible impulse of the Arabs, he wrote, were of a "practical and material nature, due in great part to profound economic distress, the final product . . . of the impoverishment of Arabia." Arabia's impoverishment was, for him, the result of a gradual process of desiccation in the peninsula—a theory borrowed from Hugo Winckler that Caetani developed in considerable detail.[3]

In 1914, Henri Lammens attempted to show that the theory of desiccation that Caetani saw as the cause of an Arab migration and of the conquest could not be defended. Instead, he felt, the Islamic expansion "was born of the irresistible penchant for the raid, which animates all the Arabs. The success of these tumultuous incursions, due to a superior military organization, suggested to them as an afterthought the idea of occupation and of conquest, absent at the outset."[4] Lammens thus rejected Caetani's main argument, that of desiccation, but introduced a new factor, that of superior military organization on the battlefield. He also attempted to explain the participation by bedouin—whom he called "more quarrelsome than warlike"—in the Islamic expansion as a reflection of the bedouin character, marked in his judgment by an oscillation between extremes of passivity and violence;[5] passivity in obedience to the Muslims' commanders, violence in relation to those being fought.

In 1924 Carl Heinrich Becker wrote an essay on the Islamic expansion in which for the first time attention was called to the fact that the great migration of Arabs took place only after the decisive victories of the conquest had been won by the Muslims in Syria and Iraq.[6] That is, the conquest of these areas preceded and unleashed the Arab migrations, not the reverse. These migrations were, he felt, stimulated by the promise of wealth and of land in the conquered domains. Becker was of the opinion, however, that the first conquests were essentially accidental, and that it was only after these decisive early victories that the further Islamic conquests became regular, planned operations. Following earlier writers such as Caetani, moreover, Becker felt that religion was a force of secondary importance in stimulating the expansion; rather, hunger and greed provided the driving force behind the migrations.[7] Becker's interpretation was more sophisticated and more firmly based in the available source material than earlier views and was widely accepted. Max von Oppenheim, for example, appears to have adopted Becker's understanding of the conquests when he wrote, in 1939, that "The most significant migratory movement [of Arabian bedouins] was released by early Islam."[8]

The old theory that the Islamic conquest was "explained"—that is, caused—by an Arab migration due to starvation or other economic pressures continued to enjoy some popularity.[9] But more recent writers have generally attempted to combine elements of several different earlier interpretations, making various modifications in content or in emphasis. In an essay published in 1957, for example, K. W. Butzer rejected the notion of long-term desiccation in Arabia but tried to show that there may have been a shorter period of severe drought between about A.D. 591 and 640, that is, on the eve of the Islamic conquest. There is reason to think that Butzer's analysis of the significance of short-term desiccations is greatly exaggerated,[10] but he was careful to draw a distinction between the spread of Islam and the Arab migrations—and perhaps the first to seek separate causes for the two phenomena. As he saw it, "The Arab migration was mainly conditioned by economic factors, by the poor living conditions of the bedouin in the inhospitable steppes of Arabia. . . . The bedouin emigration was mainly *caused* by economic factors, [but] was *rendered possible* by social and surrounding political events." Once the conquests—which were in his opinion unplanned—had been successfully completed, the bedouin undertook a mass migration to the new "promised land."[11]

Meanwhile, in 1956 G. H. Bousquet had published a statement in which he drew a sharp distinction between the nature of the conquests and the causes for their success. In discussing the nature of the conquests (by which he appears to mean the motivations behind them), he admitted that economic factors such as the attraction of booty had some importance, but only of a subordinate kind. The really important factor, he felt, was the religious commitment, for even those initially lured on by promises of booty became caught up in the religious enthusiasm of the new faith once on the battlefield. As for the causes of the conquest's success, he cited the general weakness of Byzantium and of Sasanid Persia due to their prolonged wars, and the fortuitous presence of a large number of good generals and administrators on the Arab side.[12]

The notion that the Islamic conquests were largely the result of fortuitous weakness among the Muslims' adversaries was also voiced by Marius Canard. In an article appearing in 1965, Canard rejected on various grounds those arguments that "explain" the Islamic conquests in terms of numerical superiority, superior weaponry, or superior military organization. Furthermore, he felt that those advantages that the Arabs enjoyed with regard to valor in battle, familiarity with the desert, inner lines of communication, and the stimulant provided by religious enthusiasm and the attraction of booty, were offset by the Arabs' inferior weaponry, poor military organization, unsophisticated tactics, and inferior numbers. Military factors, he concluded, could not explain the Arab successes, which he, like Bousquet, attributed to the general weakness of their opponents and to the disaffection of much of the subject population of Syria and Iraq. He also rejected the idea that the Arabs were driven out of Arabia by misery; booty may have had some importance in luring men to the front, but he doubted that economic factors played a primary role in the Arab expansion, otherwise it would have stopped in Syria and Iraq and not pushed beyond these areas.[13]

In a general study appearing in 1968, Francesco Gabrieli reviewed the factors contributing to the Islamic conquests. In his opinion religion was important, not because it unified the Arab tribesmen, but because it unified the elite, mainly companions of the Prophet, who led the campaigns of conquest. But, echoing Butzer, he concluded that material motives for expansion caused by short-term variations in climate—"the need for food, pastureland, and booty"—also played an important role in encouraging emigration from Arabia. As he put it, Arabia, after the *ridda* wars in which the regime in Medina put down the rebellious tribes, "was seething with arms and armed men: the victors, no less than the vanquished, needed an outlet for their surplus energies. . . . Certainly one of the major incentives for external conquest may have lain in this explosive internal situation, with its unchained passions, and in the desperate need for plunder and 'living space.' "[14] Military factors remained, in Gabrieli's opinion, a puzzle.

Most recently, M. A. Shaban proposed (1971) that the conquests were originally the product of another kind of economic pressure. In his view, the disruption of trade in Arabia by the *ridda* wars placed the nomadic tribesmen of the peninsula in such dire straits that they were greatly tempted to launch raids into the Fertile Crescent—raids that by chance succeeded and grew into the conquest movement. Shaban thus felt—as did many writers before him—that the conquests had an essentially accidental beginning; that is, the first conquests were the serendipitous result of disorganized raids launched mainly for reasons of economic necessity by Arab tribesmen, only some of whom were Muslims.[15]

Numerous other studies of the early Islamic period have briefly treated the conquests, usually discussing them in terms of the factors already discussed. Laura Veccia-Vaglieri, for example, considered many factors but saw Islam as the decisive one, both because it was "the coordinating element behind the efforts of the bedouin" and because of the religious enthusiasm it inspired.[16] Claude Cahen combined most of the factors mentioned by other scholars, stressing especially the disaffection of the former Byzantine and Sasanian subject populations and the impetus provided by religious faith and the thirst for booty.[17] Gustav Von Grunebaum made a selection of the factors usually introduced to account for the sweeping success of the conquest, without placing particular emphasis on any of them.[18] John J. Saunders tried to understand the conquest in terms of the impact of a religious ideology upon nomadic leadership.[19]

This brief (and incomplete) review of the literature is sufficient to reveal the general lack of consensus over the nature and causes of the Islamic conquest movement. This lack of agreement stems in part from the failure of many writers to distinguish clearly between two discrete but related phenomena. The first of these is the *Islamic conquest*—that is, the extension of the hegemony of the Islamic state from Medina over vast new domains in western Asia and North Africa. The second, related phenomenon is an *Arab migration*—the movement of Arabic-speaking individuals and tribal groups, some nomadic and some sedentary in their way of life, from various parts of the Arabian peninsula into new areas within the domains conquered by the Islamic state, and their settlement there. This confusion was compounded by the failure of some writers to make yet another vital distinction: that between the causes of the conquest movement itself and the causes for its success. The prevalence of such logical confusions has beclouded the scholarly debate immensely, because factors relating to one category were sometimes discussed as if they belonged to another. Any examination of the Islamic conquests that aims at bringing a measure of clarity to the subject, then, must rigorously distinguish the causes of the Islamic conquest itself, the causes for its success, and the causes of the Arab migrations that immediately followed it.

A closer look at the received interpretations of the Islamic conquests reveals an even more fundamental problem, however. For we find on examination that most of them view the conquest either as the result of some deterministic historical process, such as the pressure of increasing population in Arabia, or as the result of a fortuitous combination of historical accidents, such as the raids of undisciplined Arab tribesmen into the Fertile Crescent at a moment of temporary weakness in the Byzantine and Sasanian empires. In either case, these interpretations deny, in effect, that the "Arab conquest" was in any organic way related to the appearance of Islam. The deterministic interpretations, by explaining the historical events as the result of inexorable forces, imply that the Islamic conquests, or something very much like them, would have occurred whether or not Islam appeared on the scene; whereas the theories based on "accident" suggest that an empire was dropped, half-conquered, into the unsuspecting hands of the early Islamic leaders, who merely finished a conquest they had never dreamed of starting. In short, Western scholarship has proceeded on the basis of the unspoken assumption that the Islamic conquests could not "really" have been caused by Islam—an assumption that was, doubtless, made less obvious by the logical confusions discussed in the preceding paragraph. So pervasive has this assumption been, in fact, that Western scholars have never felt the need to justify it; instead, they have concentrated on scrutinizing those other factors that, given their assumption, "must" have been among the "real" causes of the conquests. Hence we find, in the extensive literature on the conquests, detailed discussions of Arabia's desiccation, population pressure, the thirst for booty, the "inherent" tendency of the bedouin to launch raids, the need for pasturelands, the Arabs' military technology and tactics, the military and financial weakness of the Byzantines and Sasanians, the disaffection of native populations under Byzantine and Sasanian rule, and the relative importance of religious fervor in spurring men to fight valiantly, but only exceptional recognition (and no detailed examination) of the notion that the appearance of Islam might itself have been of some importance in generating the Islamic conquests.[20] The idea that the conquests were the product of a definable movement having a powerful internal dynamic of its own, and traceable to a new religious ideology, was simply not deemed worthy of serious consideration.

The present book takes a rather different approach. It presents the thesis that Muḥammad's career and the doctrines of Islam revolutionized both the ideological bases and the political structures of Arabian society, giving rise for the first time to a state capable of organizing and executing an expansionist movement. There is still much room in such an interpretation for an element of historical accident; the fortuitous weakness of the Byzantines and Sasanians just when the Muslims began their expansion might be cited as a case in point—although even here, one wonders whether the mighty empires were not weaker in the eyes of scholars baffled by the astounding success of the conquests than they were in actual fact. In any case, it should not be assumed that Islam and the Islamic conquests were predestined to succeed, or even to happen at all; the accidents of history undoubtedly helped shape this chapter of man's past, as they helped shape all others. But, as the following pages will attempt to show, the Islamic conquests must be seen as more than a mere accident of history; they stand, rather, as a remarkable testament to the power of human action mobilized by ideological commitment as a force in human affairs.

Such a view requires that we undertake a careful examination of social and political organization in the Arabian peninsula on the eve of Islam and at the ways in which the rise of Islam affected these realities of Arabian life. It is to these issues, then, that we must now turn.

CHAPTER I

STATE AND SOCIETY IN PRE-ISLAMIC ARABIA

1. ARABIA VARIATA

Arabia was named after its nomads. It was, as the borders assigned to it by classical geographers suggest,[1] the land of the *'arab* or bedouin. But, although the very name "Arabia" may call forth in many minds images of a vast desert occupied exclusively by nomads, it is unlikely that nomadic peoples have ever formed more than a small fraction of its population. Settled peoples have far outnumbered the nomads in all historical periods, and there are very few districts in which no sedentary communities are to be found, areas that can be said to be the exclusive domain of nomadic peoples.[2] Most Arabians, then, are, and have been, settled people.

The way of life of these many sedentary communities in Arabia was far from uniform. It varied radically with differing local conditions—climate, terrain, and, especially, water resources—over the length and breadth of this vast peninsula. One form of settled life relied for its existence primarily on dry-farming (that is, farming supported by rainfall), augmented by irrigation works designed to capture, store, and distribute limited seasonal rains. Rainfall of sufficient quantity, and adequate predictability, is not, of course, to be found in all parts of Arabia. It occurs only in that region known in antiquity as *Arabia Felix*, "Happy Arabia": the mountainous districts of the Yemen, Ḥaḍramawt, and 'Asīr in southwestern Arabia, which because of their altitude and relative proximity to moist air from the Indian Ocean are blessed with fairly predictable rain in spring and fall, at the change of the monsoon.[3] Even here, the total annual rainfall is meager by comparison with that which falls in most of the northern hemisphere; to the European visitor, it seems an arid land indeed. But the ancient inhabitants of these districts developed, over the course of many centuries, irrigation techniques that exploited the terrain and such rain as did fall to maximum advantage for agriculture. The famed dam at Ma'rib in the northern Yemen—an impressive masonry structure over fifteen meters in height and more than five hundred meters long, whose remains are still clearly visible—is only the most widely known product of this technology, which covered appropriate districts of the Yemen with dams, cisterns, channels, and the like beginning, perhaps, as early as the second millennium B.C.[4]

Because of its relatively favorable climate, and because of the industry of the inhabitants in building irrigation works, parts of South Arabia were able to support intensive agriculture, though it seems unlikely that the region ever exported significant quantities of foodstuffs.[5] This agricultural productivity, in turn, supported a fairly dense population[6] and provided scope for the rise of a highly differentiated, stratified society in South Arabia.[7] To be sure, simple farmers (and, to a lesser extent, herdsmen) made up the vast majority of the local populace, but their productivity was great enough to free some members of their society to pursue artisantry and commerce, or to serve as a religious or political elite. And it was precisely these people who created the range of utilitarian goods and works of art, public and private, that fill modern museums, who conducted the long-distance trade about which we read in ancient texts, and who perfected the complex irrigation systems and erected the marvelous tower cities of the Yemen. It was these people, too, who organized South Arabia into the ancient kingdoms of Maʿīn, Qatabān, Sabā', Awsān, and Ḥimyar, which grew and struggled with one another for political dominance and control of the key trade routes. Although other economic factors, especially the booming trade in incense and spices for the Mediterranean market, doubtless contributed to the region's great prosperity during its heyday, the enduring strength of the region was primarily rooted in its basic agricultural productivity. The frankincense trade may have provided the glitter at times, but it was the yield from the gardens and fields of the Yemen and Ḥaḍramawt that supported the substance of the vigorous South Arabian civilization. In short, agricultural prosperity provided the foundation for an independent South Arabian civilization, and mercantile prosperity provided the means to elaborate that civilization to a high level of sophistication.

It was a unified culture. Although the Yemen was usually divided into several separate kingdoms, each ancient kingdom has left behind inscriptions that prove to be essentially dialects of the same language, written in variations of the same script. Similarly, the South Arabian kingdoms shared a common religious tradition, based on a pantheon of astral deities

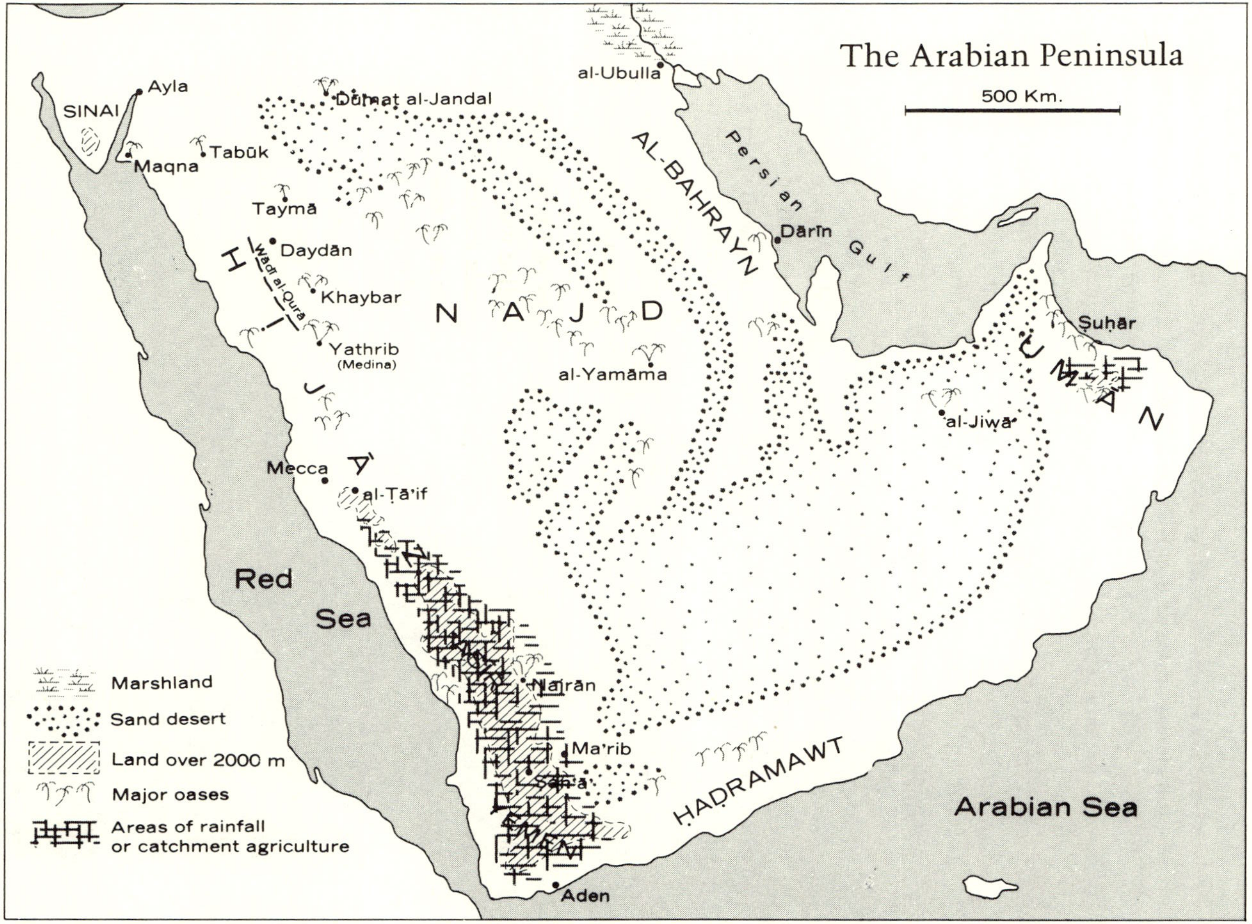
The Arabian Peninsula
500 Km.
Persian Gulf
al-Ubulla
AL-BAHRAYN
Dārīn
Ṣuḥār
'UMĀN
al-Jiwā'
Ayla
SINAI
Maqna
Tabūk
Dūmat al-Jandal
Taymā
Daydān
Wādī al-Qurā
Khaybar
Yathrib
(Medina)
NAJD
al-Yamāma
ḤIJĀZ
Mecca
al-Ṭā'if
Najrān
Ma'rib
Ṣan'ā'
YEMEN
Aden
ḤAḌRAMAWT
Red Sea
Arabian Sea
Marshland
Sand desert
Land over 2000 m
Major oases
Areas of rainfall
or catchment agriculture

in which the moon god, sun goddess, and fertility god identified with Venus were paramount; the presence of a myriad of lesser deities that varied from kingdom to kingdom hardly obscures the basic uniformity. What little is known of South Arabian political institutions suggests that they underwent a common course of evolution throughout the whole region, passing from a theocracy of priest-kings called *mukarribs* through secular kingships advised by representative councils to a decentralized system in which the power of the kings was attenuated by the virtual independence of tribal groups within the kingdom. Likewise, we find that art and building styles, and of course irrigation technology, were essentially uniform throughout the whole region. Finally, the area appears to have shared a single social order, in which "nobles" (*ashrāf*), that is, people from noble tribes, lorded it over lesser tribes.[8]

Arabia Felix was, then, an area unlike any other in Arabia. It was the only region whose productivity was sufficient to permit the development of an indigenous civilization with a distinctively Arabian stamp—a civilization that radiated out from its South Arabian centers over most of the Arabian peninsula.

In other areas of Arabia, rainfall, though far from rare, is (and for millennia has been) too meager and erratic to sustain dry-farming such as was practiced in South Arabia. Throughout most of the peninsula agriculture depended, in the absence of regular rainfall, on the presence of perennial springs or of reliable subterranean water that could be tapped by digging wells. Settlements in these regions therefore normally took the form of oases, pockets of relatively intensive cultivation (often devoted predominantly to date culture) supported by a permanent water source, which were surrounded by extensive areas of agriculturally useless desert, steppe, or stony mountains. In many cases these oases, which were scattered over most of the Arabian peninsula,[9] were too small to support more than a handful of peasants and a few artisans or small merchants near the level of bare subsistence. But in some spots the water supply was sufficient to irrigate enormous palm groves containing millions of trees, as well as other crops, and such centers were inhabited by a fairly sizable population. These large oases, because of their relative prosperity, were sometimes able to support a considerable number of artisans, merchants, religious leaders, and others who were not directly a part of the agricultural labor force. Such were, for example, the great oasis towns of the Ḥijāz region of western and northwestern Arabia: Yathrib (Medina), Taymā, Fadak, Dūmat al-Jandal, Khaybar, al-Ṭā'if, and the string of villages in Wādī al-Qurā. Similarly, the enormous oasis centers of al-Yamāma and al-Qaṭīf in eastern Arabia flourished in the midst of barren country because of their unusual subterranean water supplies. Oases of more modest size formed a broad band stretching from east to west across the Najd or uplands of northern central Arabia.[10]

Although the size and character of these oasis towns was primarily a function of the available water resources, their prosperity was at times affected by other factors, such as prevailing trade patterns or cultic practices. The town of Daydān in the northern Ḥijāz, for example, flourished in a relatively barren area because it served as a trading outpost for the South Arabian kingdom of Maʿīn until the second century B.C. Likewise, the efflorescence of Petra, just north of the Gulf of ʿAqaba, and the meteoric brilliance of Palmyra in the midst of the Syrian desert, were linked to their role in the caravan trade of their day. The rise of Muḥammad's native town of Mecca to a position of great importance in Arabia during the sixth century was also partly the result of the skill with which the Meccan tribe of Quraysh organized a network of trade contacts spreading over the whole peninsula.[11] The presence of important religious shrines could also cause a settlement to grow, as is again illustrated by Mecca; it became the metropolis of western Arabia on the eve of Islam partly because of its role as a *ḥaram*, or sacred enclave, and center of a religious cult.[12] Indeed, stripped of its functions as trade entrepôt and cultic center, Mecca would have remained a very small settlement, for it is located in an area ill suited to agriculture.[13]

Despite their marketing, trading, cultic, and social functions, however, the vast majority of the oasis towns in northern and central Arabia remained small and relatively poor. Even the larger oasis settlements were not sufficiently productive economically to support more than a modest number of people in nonagricultural pursuits. These limitations, and the fact that such settlements were scattered thinly over a vast area, meant that northern and central Arabia were not areas that could support the rise of an elaborate, independent civilization. There were simply too few people who could devote their time to the generation of new cultural forms to permit the rise of an indigenous civilization there. Thus northern and central Arabia remained culturally dependent upon the centers of civilization nearest it: such elements of high culture as were found there were merely bits of luster borrowed from the civilization of *Arabia Felix*, or from one of its rivals to the north: ancient Egypt, the great Semitic civilizations of the Fertile Crescent, the Hellenistic world, or ancient Iran.

Interspersed throughout the Arabian peninsula, from the Taurus mountains, across the Syrian steppe, to the shores of the Indian Ocean, living beside the settled communities we have described, were the nomads—herders of goats, sheep, or camels. They were ubiquitous in Arabia, and it is doubtless for this reason that the region came to be named after them. Although they were to be found in every corner of the peninsula, however, they were relatively few in number. The difficult steppe and desert environment that they had learned to exploit by continuous, regular migration from one seasonal pasture to another and from one well to another simply would not support a dense population. Their occupation of the land was, then, periodic, rhythmic, and extensive; ubiquitous they were indeed, but very thinly spread over this vast area. It is for this reason that the nomadic peoples of Arabia, despite the enormous territories they occupied, were always far outnumbered by the settled population, densely clustered in its compact oases and rich mountain valleys.[14]

Like the sedentary peoples, the nomads were themselves a diverse lot. Their normal way of life varied with the kind of terrain they occupied, with the kind of animals they herded, and with the political setting in which they found themselves. Indeed, the sharp distinction that we draw between nomadic and sedentary life is itself misleading, for there was in fact a continuum of ways of life in Arabia, of which the fully nomadic and the fully sedentary were only the two ends of the spectrum. In between these two extremes, as we shall presently see, there was a sizable population of "seminomads" who practiced both settled local agriculture and nomadic pastoralism in varying degrees depending upon the conditions under which they had to live.[15]

Indeed, even among the pastoral peoples of Arabia it was but a small fraction who could be called fully nomadic, that is, who were engaged in pastoralism exclusively throughout the year. Such full nomads as did exist were of two kinds. One kind embraced those who usually herded flocks of camels and were most prominent in the steppe-desert of the Najd, or on the fringes of the Empty Quarter, although they were also found in other regions suitable for their flocks. Among the examples of this kind were some of the groups in the Bakr b. Wā'il confederation of northeastern Arabia, or some groups among the Ṭayyi', Asad, and Tamīm of the Najd and northeastern Arabia. Similarly, in the Ḥijāz, the Muzayna, Ghifār, and Fazāra roamed pasturing districts between the oases and market towns. In adapting their lives to the harsh conditions of the Arabian desert, these full nomads came to live in small, cohesive tenting groups consisting of perhaps five to twenty people. These small tenting groups congregated with others (usually other groups of near kinsmen) at certain seasons of the year,[16] certainly, but many months were passed in the small herding units; for, since they lived off their flocks, too large a tenting group required flocks too large to be grazed in one place, at least during the seasons of meager pasturage. In addition, a large group would hamper the ready mobility that their way of life demanded. Hence they tended to roam for much of the year in groups just large enough to provide some measure of mutual defense against the few intruders who might pass their way.[17]

The camel pastoralists often lived very close to the level of bare subsistence, surviving solely on the milk of their camels and on those staples (especially dates) they were able to exchange for the few items they could produce themselves—hides, leather, cloth woven from camel or goat hair, and, especially, livestock. In some cases, goods or livestock seized in raids on other groups also contributed to their well-being. The pastoral economy rarely produced much of a surplus, however, and so virtually every member of these small herding groups was directly concerned with the herding process in some way. There was little place in their life for specialization in activities other than those related to herding, and hence no class of full-time merchants, artisans, or cultural or religious specialists could arise among them.[18] All men in such groups were herdsmen and, although one or another of them might gain some recognition as a political spokesman or military chief or religious leader, such distinctions were decidedly avocational and, frequently, of fleeting duration. It was, then, a society that displayed little stratification of wealth or specialization of function from person to person. Of necessity unencumbered by any but the most rudimentary and portable material possessions, the nomads evolved only such higher culture as they could carry easily with them—in particular, the orally transmitted arts of singing, storytelling, genealogy, and poetry, all of which they developed to a very refined level, and in which they took great pride. Their culture was characterized also by a great pride in martial virtues and in the exploits of their tribes in raiding other nomads or settled peoples—an activity that seems to have been partly of political significance (the assertion of dominance over rival groups), partly of economic significance (the redistribution of wealth), and partly, perhaps, a form of entertainment, a challenging and exciting game, seldom lethal, that reduced the monotony of desert life.[19]

Other groups of full nomads kept large herds of sheep and goats along with some camels. Such flocks moved much more slowly and needed water far more regularly than did herds of camels. As a result, these groups were required to remain near reliable sources of water and could never penetrate the interior of the peninsula. They tended to roam a band on the fringes of the desert, staying close to their permanent summer watering-points and encampments along the Euphrates or on the fringes of Syria, and penetrating only a limited distance into the desert in the winter and spring grazing season, when grazing was lush and water available from seasonal wells and pools of rainwater. Culturally, these people resembled the camel-herding tribes; in particular, they shared with the camel nomads a commitment to the warrior virtues. Because of their decreased mobility, however, they were much more vulnerable than were the camel nomads to control by nearby states or by other nomads.[20]

Far more numerous than the full nomads were the seminomadic peoples. Their exact annual migratory cycle depended on many factors, but a common pattern was for groups to establish settled villages on the fringes of the Syrian plain or of Mesopotamia, which they would farm in the manner common among peasants of the region; in winter, however, they would drive their flocks some distance into the desert to graze on the lush grasses that appear there during the winter and spring rains. In some cases, the whole group participated in these migrations, abandoning the settlement they had constructed and establishing a new one when they returned from the desert in the late spring; in other cases, only part of the group followed the herds, while others remained in the settlement for the whole year, waiting for the return of the herdsmen. As they sometimes had flocks consisting primarily of sheep and goats, they usually shared the pattern of relatively short migrations described for the fully nomadic shepherding groups. In other cases, their short migrations were the result of their inability to enter certain pastures because they were occupied by the more powerful full nomads.[21]

It is probable that many of the fully nomadic shepherding groups and the seminomadic groups had once been fully nomadic camel-herders but had since been edged out of better grazing grounds by more powerful nomads. They were thus forced by these circumstances to settle, hire themselves out as laborers, or even to begin farming—for the nomad, the most despised of professions!—for part of the year in order to survive. Such groups, even if they still herded camels exclusively, were clearly in no position to return to their former desert pasturelands, at least not until the power of stronger groups in the desert was broken. In around A.D. 600, for example, it appears that many pastoralists living along the Euphrates—the Tanūkh, Iyād, al-Namir b. Qāsiṭ, Taghlib, and several other groups—were either full-time shepherding groups, or were seminomads who occupied riverside villages but also engaged in considerable herding. Traditional accounts of the history of these groups, however, reveal that they had, at an earlier date, lived in the Najd and in eastern Arabia, presumably as full nomads, but had been edged out of these regions by the more powerful Tamīm, Asad, Ṭayyi', and by the nomads of the Bakr b. Wā'il confederation. Likewise, the Madhḥij and Kinda are recorded to have lived in central Arabia, where they almost certainly led a nomadic existence, but both were defeated and driven south by a rival confederation from North Arabia. As a consequence they entered the territories of the Ḥimyarite state, in about the mid-fourth century A.D., where they were employed as mercenaries and were settled partly, if not fully, on the land.[22]

There was, of course, considerable variation from the pattern of seminomadic life just described, not only from group to group, but also within a single group from year to year, in response to changes in local conditions. Shifts in the balance of power among nomadic groups deep in the heart of the peninsula might, for example, lead to increasing competition for pastures occupied by certain seminomadic herdsmen, who would find themselves gradually deprived of some of their grazing lands, temporarily or permanently. In such a situation, some of the herdsmen in the group would be forced to remain in the settlement for the entire year and would hire themselves out to nearby sedentary peoples or begin farming for themselves, at least until conditions changed. Conversely, several years of good rains and good pastures might permit a group to increase the size of its flocks, drawing more of the group into pastoral life, or allowing them to remain in pasture for a longer period. Conditions that had an adverse effect on the practice of agriculture and the establishment of settlements by the seminomads (which were, usually, located in marginal agricultural land in any case) could drive them back to the desert. Such conditions included pestilence, crop failure, or the imposition of high taxes by a state.

The seminomadic population of Arabia was, then, in a continuous state of flux, as individuals and sometimes entire groups moved back and forth between a more nomadic and a more settled way of life in response to climatic and political fluctuations. They fell somewhere on the continuum between fully nomadic peoples, especially the shepherding groups, and the fully settled village and oasis communities we have already described, and for that reason they partook of some aspects of the way of life of both. Like the nomads, their pastoral life demanded that they live, for the most part, in small, cohesive groups, although these groups could congregate during the rainy season when rich pasturage permitted it. Less powerful militarily than the full nomads, they nonetheless retained a martial pride and prowess that distinguished them from the passive, long-suffering peasantry. They derived their existence both from marginal agriculture and from the herding of flocks, and, like both peasant cultivators and fully nomadic pastoralists, their life was normally close to the minimum subsistence level, so that their communities showed little functional specialization and little disparity in wealth from person to person. Finally, their high cultural life was, like that of the full nomads, restricted to portable forms such as poetry and song.

2. A TRIBAL SOCIETY

Despite this great diversity in the economic basis and cultural patterning of Arabian life, there was a striking uniformity to Arabian social organization. For everywhere, it appears, Arabian society on the eve of Islam was tribal. The individual in such a society saw himself as belonging to several interrelated groups that expressed membership in terms of real or supposed kinship in the paternal line.[23] These groups provided the individual with varying degrees of support in social situations and were correspondingly the focus of the individual's loyalty. The smallest and most immediate of such groups was, of course, the family, which formed the ultimate focus of an individual's feelings of solidarity. But the individual also felt himself to be a member of a somewhat broader group that included several closely related families (those of his paternal uncles, for example) as well as his own. Beyond this were yet broader groups of increasingly distant "relatives," real or presumed—groups that also could serve as sources of solidarity at times. The largest solidarity group of this kind that provided the individual with effective social support was what we can call, arbitrarily, the "tribe." The "tribe," then, was essentially seen as a body of blood relations and was normally defined as being all those people descended in the male line from some eponymous ancestor: thus the tribe of Ḥanīfa was the Banū Ḥanīfa (B. Ḥanīfa), literally,

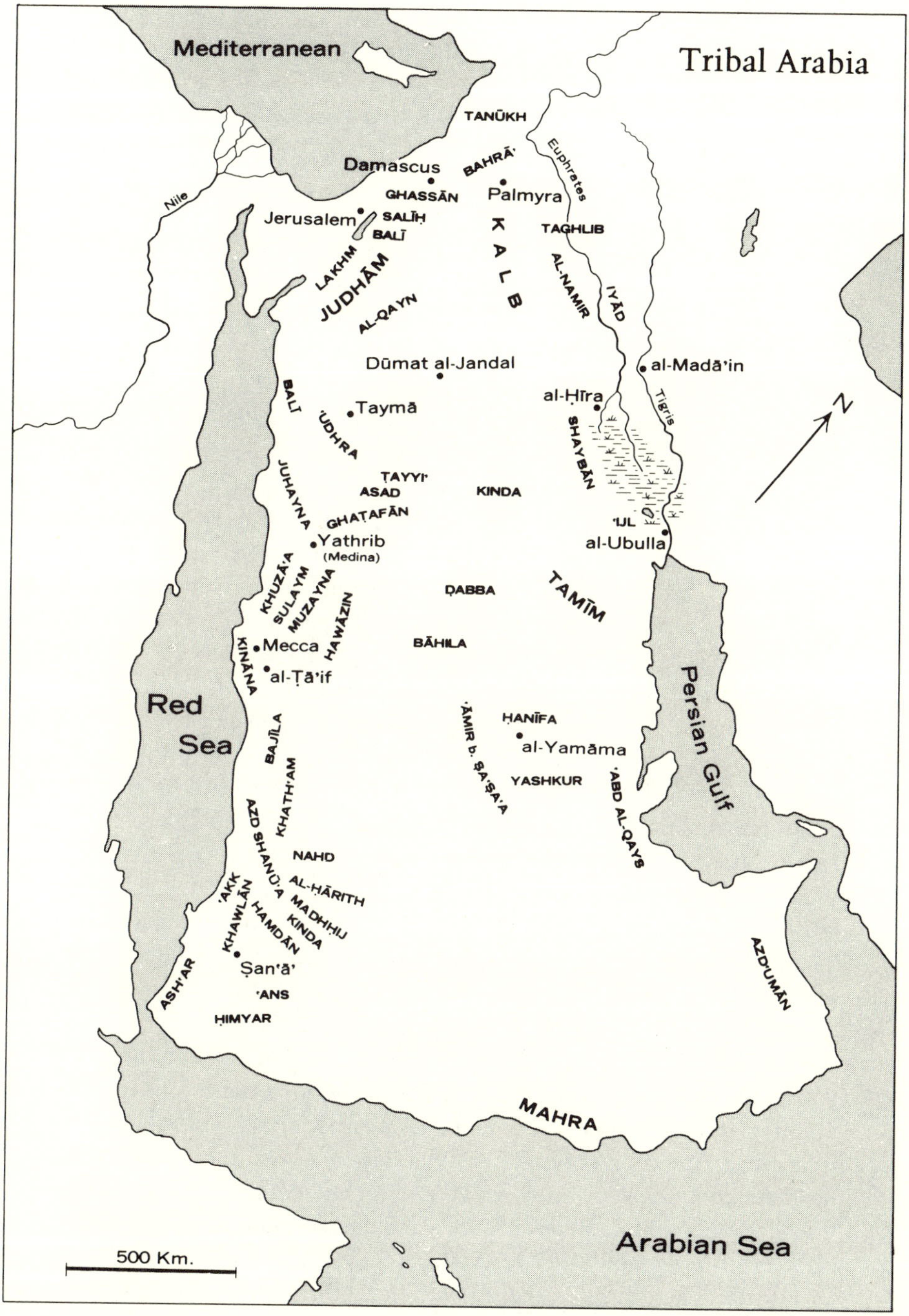
Tribal Arabia
Mediterranean
TANŪKH
Damascus
BAHRĀ'
GHASSĀN
Palmyra
Euphrates
Nile
Jerusalem
SALĪḤ
BALĪ
TAGHLIB
KALB
LAKHM
JUDHĀM
AL-QAYN
AL-NAMIR
IYĀD
Dūmat al-Jandal
al-Madā'in
al-Ḥīra
Tigris
BALĪ
Taymā
'UDHRA
SHAYBĀN
N
JUHAYNA
ṬAYYI'
ASAD
KINDA
GHAṬAFĀN
'IJL
Yathrib
(Medina)
al-Ubulla
KHUZĀ'A
SULAYM
MUZAYNA
ḌABBA
TAMĪM
HAWĀZIN
KINĀNA
Mecca
BĀHILA
al-Ṭā'if
Red
Sea
Persian Gulf
'ĀMIR b. ṢA'ṢA'A
ḤANĪFA
al-Yamāma
BAJĪLA
YASHKUR
'ABD AL-QAYS
KHATH'AM
AZD SHANŪ'A
NAHD
AL-ḤĀRITH
'AKK
MADHHIJ
KHAWLĀN
KINDA
HAMDĀN
Ṣan'ā'
ASH'AR
'ANS
AZD 'UMĀN
ḤIMYAR
MAHRA
Arabian Sea
500 Km.

the "Sons of Ḥanīfa." Fellow tribesmen, being in theory relatives, were supposed to stand together against the outsider.

There was, of course, no structural difference between the "tribe" and its component subgroups. Like the "tribe", the subgroups were the "sons of" an eponymous ancestor: the B. Ḥanīfa, for example, comprised several groups, including the B. 'Āmir ("Sons of 'Āmir"), B. al-Dūl, and B. 'Adī, where 'Āmir, al-Dūl, and 'Adī were viewed as three sons, or other descendants, of their common ancestor, Ḥanīfa. Thus the notion of the "tribe" was simply the extension to a higher plane of generalization of the same concept of group identification and solidarity, expressed in terms of kinship, that was used to define the subgroups right down to the level of the family. Presumably it was a concept that could be extended upward indefinitely, to embrace the whole human race—an exercise in the systematization of a world-view that medieval Arab genealogists pursued with great enthusiasm. In the Arabian setting, however, it is convenient to use the term "tribe" to refer to the many large solidarity groups of considerable stability that are mentioned constantly in the sources, and that in many cases seem to function as cohesive and virtually autonomous social (and sometimes political) units.[24]

The whole Arabian population, then, was divided into such tribes, and it was to his tribe and to the increasingly narrow subdivisions within the tribe that an individual felt his primary loyalty. The tribe, or one of its subgroups, was the individual's only defense against insult or injury in his dealings with society as a whole; if a man broke with his tribe, as a few pre-Islamic heroic poets apparently did, he had no choice but to face life alone and in virtual isolation—that is, to withdraw from Arabian society.[25] Whatever his way of life, the Arabian was first and foremost a tribesman—identified with his tribe, loyal to it, and secured as much as possible against abuse by it. This was as true of the fully settled populations of South Arabia or the oasis towns scattered through the peninsula, as it was of the nomadic peoples of Arabia.[26]

Our understanding of the tribe's role as a solidarity unit must be tempered, however, by an appreciation of the importance of inner divisions within the tribe. These inner divisions were also traceable to the tribe's character as a group of descendants of a common ancestor; for the main divisions were those between different lineages within the tribe, that is, between different lines of descent from the eponymous ancestor—between, for example, the B. 'Āmir and B. al-Dūl within the tribe of B. Ḥanīfa. These lineages were, of course, themselves internally subdivided into sublineages, which were in turn also subdivided, and so on until the smallest unit within the tribe was reached—the family and the individuals in it. Group solidarity was, to be sure, vitally important to tribal life, but feelings of solidarity within the lineage (against another lineage) could keep the members of different lineages within a tribe at odds with one another, just as feelings of solidarity within the tribe could, at other times, pull the different lineages together in the face of a common threat to the tribe as a whole. The strongest feelings of solidarity existed in the lowest levels of the tribal organization; among members of a single family or tenting group, for example, solidarity and loyalty of members was absolute and binding.[27] As one moved up to levels of broader group identification, the solidarity feelings became correspondingly weaker. Thus there was rarely open conflict within a single family, whereas rivalries between different lineages within a large tribe were quite commonplace and sometimes very bitter.[28]

The individual tribesman thus drew social support in different situations from different levels in his network of kinsmen. If he became involved in a dispute with another family closely related to his own, he could rely only on his own family to back him; but if the family or individual with whom he came into conflict belonged to a distantly related lineage, he might have the support of his entire lineage in the dispute, while his opponent would also enjoy lineage backing (presuming that the larger groups felt the issue to be of sufficient importance). The tribe, then, always brought social solidarity to its members, but it did not always provide the same degree of social support in all situations.

It is important to note, furthermore, that the assemblage of groups that we call a tribe was not a static entity but was continually evolving. Some lineages or sublineages within the tribe dwindled away, merged into others, or otherwise disappeared. Other lineages grew and underwent mitosis as their size became too large for effective contact and solidarity to be maintained among all members. New groups with no previous relationship to the tribe sometimes attached themselves to it, first perhaps as allies or clients, to be incorporated into the tribe as "relatives"—that is, granted a place in the tribal genealogy—with the passage of time. If the tribe existed in fairly stable circumstances and did not undergo rapid expansion or other drastic alteration, the overall tribal identification may likewise have remained stable over long periods; the tribesmen would still have considered themselves members of the Banū Ḥanīfa, let us say, despite many realignments and emergence of new loyalties that may have occurred among the subgroups making up the Banū Ḥanīfa. But if the tribe underwent steady expansion due to the absorption of outside groups and natural increase, the overall tribal identification became inflated and tended to fade, being replaced eventually by subordinate identifications (usually, those of the lineages that made up the tribe). Thus lineages within the tribe "graduated" to the status of being essentially independent tribes, and, although the old tribal identification and name was remembered for some time—usually as an "ancestor" of the new tribes that emerged—it no longer formed an effective focus of group solidarity and communal action.[29] This was, of course, a gradual process. The fact that the tribal organization was always in a state of flux meant, however, that it is usually impossible to determine exactly when a given group first emerged as an independent focus of loyalty and ceased being simply an important subdivision (lineage) of a larger tribe, or when a tribe lost its importance as an effective focus of loyalty and was replaced in this function by its former lineages.

Thus, for example, we find that on the eve of Islam, around A.D. 600, northeastern Arabia was dominated by a large tribal grouping called Bakr b. Wā'il.[30] This grouping included many separate tribes, of which the most prominent in the sources are the B. Shaybān, B. 'Ijl, B. Qays b. Tha'laba, B. Dhuhl, B. Taymallāt, B. Yashkur, and B. Ḥanīfa. Within each of these tribes were a large number of separate lineages; the B. Shaybān, for example, contained dozens of lineages, of which the B. Abū Rabī'a, B. Muḥallim, and the B. Murra b. Dhuhl (itself with many important sublineages) appear to have been the most prominent. The many tribes of Bakr b. Wā'il included both nomadic and sedentary peoples; the bulk of the B. Shaybān, for example, were nomadic tribesmen, whereas most if not all of the B. Ḥanīfa were settled tribesmen occupying the fertile grain-growing region of al-Yamāma in eastern Arabia. Other groups, such as possibly the B. Yashkur were presumably seminomads. All of these groups probably thought of themselves as branches of Bakr b. Wā'il, but the critical question is what level of identification in this tribal hierarchy corresponded to a significant group solidarity in terms of social functions like protection. The B. Shaybān, for example, may have functioned as an effective group in some situations (e.g., a clash with a totally separate tribe, such as their nearby rivals, the B. Tamīm nomads), but there is ample evidence to show that rivalries among various lineages within Shaybān were very common and quite sharp at times. When we move up the hierarchy to the next level of inclusion, however, it seems unlikely that the Bakr b. Wā'il as a whole functioned as a unified group at this time, despite the fact that the genealogists clearly considered the various tribes (Shaybān, etc.) to be lineages of the Bakr b. Wā'il. Bakr b. Wā'il may in fact once have been an effective solidarity group, but by A.D. 600, its importance seems to have faded, perhaps due to its growth. The Bakr b. Wā'il tribal identification was still remembered, in that Bakr was considered to have been an ancestor of the functioning tribal group of Shaybān, etc., but by this time it was not the whole Bakr b. Wā'il group, but the smaller groups within it, that formed the effective foci of group loyalty.

This system, then, placed the individual within a set of increasingly large groups upon whose memberships he could draw for support in appropriate circumstances. The relationships between these groups were conceived in terms of kinship and recorded in the form of genealogies. It should be clear, then, that the genealogical description of a given tribe cannot be seen as a true record of the "blood history" or actual descent of the various tribal groups. The genealogy is, rather, primarily a representation of political realities within the tribe, a record of power relationships among the various groups. This is not to say that the genealogies (at least those of the North Arabian tribes, which have been recorded for us in overwhelming detail) have no truly genealogical content; on the contrary, the materials from the most recent strata of the genealogies (i.e., material bearing on the generations just before the genealogy was recorded) do contain much accurate data on actual blood relationships between historical individuals. But the higher one moves up the genealogical "tree," the more the genealogy becomes a history, not of individuals, but of whole groups. Thus a tribal group *A* may have existed for many generations before subdividing into two groups, *X*, and *Y*; but the genealogy will remember such events in the distant past merely as a man, *A*, who had two sons, *X* and *Y*. The names of all those in the intervening generations will be dropped, because they are irrelevant to the purpose of the genealogies, which is to record the affiliations between various groups and thus provide a framework for solidarity alignments in case of a dispute. Similarly forgotten will be the names of all those groups that had the misfortune to die out or that were eventually absorbed by another group with whom, for one reason or another, they had taken up residence. It is clear, furthermore, that the genealogies, especially on the upper levels, will at times be "reconstructed" to reflect more accurately the power relationships that circumstances have created;

two groups that have established a close, lasting alliance will be brought closer together in the genealogical tree, as the Quḍā'a tribes were transferred from the 'Adnāni to the Qaḥṭāni side of the genealogy of Arabian tribes at the time of the second civil war (A.D. 680-684), when they sided with the Kalb coalition of Qaḥṭani tribes. Finally, the genealogies were used by rival lineages as a means of justifying their claim to tribal leadership and hence had in many cases a clear political purpose.[31]

Economic and Social Relations

The population of Arabia was, then, a mosaic of separate and largely independent tribes. All Arabians were, in social terms, tribesmen. But as we have seen, not all these tribesmen led the same way of life in economic terms; there was, rather, a great variety of life-styles ranging across the spectrum from fully nomadic, through partly nomadic, to several different kinds of fully settled life in villages or towns. We should not, however, picture the various economic patterns as being isolated from one another. Not only did nomadic, seminomadic, and settled peoples often live in close proximity to one another; they also had very important ties—economic, social, and political—that bound them inextricably together.

On the economic level, for instance, nomads, seminomads, and sedentary peoples in Arabia were normally interdependent; that is to say, each group needed the others to survive, or at least to survive in the manner to which it had become accustomed. The nomads and seminomads were, in all areas and at all times, dependent on settled communities for many essential items that they themselves could not produce: foodstuffs such as dates or grains, cloth, virtually all metal products including weapons, and so forth. What little income the nomads received above bare subsistence they derived mainly from the sale of livestock, milk and milk products, hides, and hair to the villages and towns in their midst. They also received payments from the settled merchants in exchange for their service as guides and guards for the merchants' caravans, plying the ancient routes that crisscrossed the peninsula. In a less constructive vein, they derived a significant component of their wealth from settled communities by plundering them, or—far more frequently—by extracting from them "brotherhood" payments (*khuwwa*), which can be considered as either protection money or taxation in return for defending the settlement from other tribes. Conversely, the settled peoples were also in some degree dependent on the nomads around them. As we have seen, they obtained livestock and other products from the pastoral economy and benefited from specific services that the nomads and their animals performed for them—notably manuring fields (in return for the privilege of letting flocks graze on the stubble) and, especially, transporting goods. Indeed, since trade within the peninsula was almost totally dependent upon the nomads, it is clear that all settled life in Arabia would have been considerably more isolated without them. There was, then, a symbiotic aspect to relations between the nomadic and sedentary peoples of Arabia.[32]

This symbiosis was far from perfect, of course. It was often marred by intense economic competition between sedentaries and nomads; seminomadic herders might drive settled cultivators off lands they wished to use as pasture; pastoralists in search of plunder might launch a devastating raid against an oasis or village, or even a fairly large town, or extract the *khuwwa* in return for sparing it; a state might organize punitive campaigns against nomads and seminomads in order to protect taxable settlements, or might levy taxes on them, or might deprive them of their share in the transit trade on which some nomadic groups were quite dependent for their livelihood. But this competition, though more apparent in the chronicles, was perhaps less important to the rhythms of day-to-day life in Arabia than were the symbiotic aspects of nomad-sedentary relations; at any rate, both aspects must be grasped to appreciate the patterns of economic interaction in the peninsula. Life was not all raids, protection money, and an endless struggle between desert and sown; the quiet exchange of livestock for dates and the hubbub of an arriving caravan had their place as well.

Nomads, seminomads, and sedentary folk were also bound together by important social ties. There was, in the first place, the possibility that a given tribe or lineage might include both nomadic groups and sedentary groups. It was not unusual for some members of a tribe that was basically nomadic to reside more or less permanently in one of the market towns frequented by the nomadic sections of the tribe. In such a case the nomadic tribesman making an occasional visit to town would stay with his urban kinsmen and subsist on their hospitality; the utility of such an arrangement for the tribe as a whole, guaranteeing as it did a secure lodging for the tribe's members when in town, explains why it was almost certainly very widely practiced.[33] Presumably the nomadic tribesman relied on his "city cousins," with their knowledge of and connections in the town, for help in whatever business he may have come for, whereas the urban kinsman could rely on the support of his nomadic relatives if trouble arose for him in town. Thus the existence of a tribe spanning the gap between nomadic and sedentary (town) life meant the closest possible ties between the two. Considering the usual deep-rooted disdain of the nomads for farming, however, it seems unlikely that a proud fully nomadic tribe would have deposited members as farmers in small villages; the presence of tribesmen resident in such villages and engaged perhaps in small-scale carrying trade is more likely.

In addition, the seminomadic groups, which practiced both herding and agriculture, provided an important point of contact between the nomadic life and the fully settled life of peasants; as we have seen, there was always a movement of individuals or groups from one way of life to the other as conditions varied from year to year. This, and the tendency of seminomadic groups gradually to become absorbed into the peasant or village populations near which they lived, assured many social ties between the pastoral and the peasant life.[34]

The nomads, seminomads, and sedentary peoples were bound socially in other ways as well. Many nomadic or seminomadic groups adhered to religious cults whose shrines were located in important settlements. This not only brought them into contact with the residents of these settlements, but also bound them to other worshipers, nomadic and sedentary.[35] Similarly, markets and fairs frequented by both sedentary and nomadic tribesmen provided the setting for the creation of many important social ties. Economic exchanges were not impersonal; routine trading contacts and cooperation in complex undertakings such as caravans not only welded nomadic and sedentary participants together in common economic interest, but doubtless caused them to establish important social ties as well. Thus on the eve of Islam, the merchants of the Meccan tribe of Quraysh had established close ties with the nomadic tribe of Tamīm, who cooperated in the organization of Meccan caravans. This economic link was reinforced both by binding the Tamīm to Mecca's pagan cult (by granting them certain functions in the performance of the cultic rituals) and by establishing marriage ties with the Tamīm.[36] Thus economic and cultic ties created social bonds that increased not only the intimacy, but also the stability, of relations among nomads, seminomads, and settled populations.

3. POLITICAL LIFE IN NORTHERN AND CENTRAL ARABIA

It will be readily appreciated in view of the foregoing material that power relationships among the various groups resident in the northern and central portions of the Arabian peninsula were normally very complex. The existence of nomadic and sedentary ways of life, the constant flux between them, the existence of varieties of social and cultic ties, economic interdependence and rivalry—all affected the forms of political life.

Generally, however, the dominance of one tribal group over others assumed one of two forms. A tribe could dominate others directly by virtue of its sheer military prowess, forming a kind of warrior aristocracy among them, or it could dominate others indirectly by serving as a religious aristocracy.[37]

From about the first century A.D. until recent times, northern and central Arabia were usually dominated by tribal confederations headed by a warrior aristocracy composed of powerful groups of nomadic camel pastoralists.[38] The power of these nomads was sometimes augmented by the use of a few horses—a luxury that, although expensive and difficult to maintain in Arabian conditions, could give the owners the advantage in certain military situations, such as quick, surprise raiding. But their continued power, besides resting in their own toughness, was also in part the product of their great mobility and consequent ability to evade pursuit by better organized but less mobile forces. These warrior nomads were able to subject the less powerful (because less mobile?) shepherding groups, seminomads, and the ever vulnerable peasantry and small merchants of the oases in their vicinity, extracting from them payment of the *khuwwa* tax. In return for this, the nomads refrained from plundering their "subjects" and, at times, defended them against interference by other powerful nomads. We should not, of course, picture the settled communities, especially the larger ones, as completely defenseless. In the first place, the wealthier towns—like the more powerful nomadic groups—might keep, at considerable cost, a certain number of horses. In addition, some of the larger oases or mountain towns appear to have been walled, and the residents of all oases of any size had constructed tower forts (*uṭum*) amid the palm groves, in which they could take refuge when danger threatened.[39] Some larger settlements even appear to have been able to raise militias for self-defense in cases of exceptional need—assuming, of course, that the rivalries among contending groups residing in the oasis could be composed long enough to present a united front against the attackers.[40] But these militias were, presumably, mainly composed of foot-soldiers (less effective warriors than mounted cameleers), and were decidedly limited to defensive operations; they could hardly be employed far from their home base without facing insurmountable problems of transport and supply. Similarly, the tower forts, fine though they may have been as refuges, did not protect the palm groves and fields upon which the oasis dwellers depended. Indeed, it was normal procedure for nomads wishing to subject an oasis to resort to a process of psychological warfare; they invested the whole settlement, and then gradually cut down palm trees a few at a time until the residents, watching the destruction of the town's livelihood from the safety of their towers, finally agreed to pay tribute before too much damage was done.[41]

In general, then, the nomadic groups formed the focus of real power in the region and became the core of the dominant warrior aristocracies. The organization of society along tribal lines, however, meant that it was not merely the strong nomadic groups themselves, but rather the tribes to which they belonged, that were powerful. Within such tribes even those individuals or groups who were not themselves physically powerful—the settled "city cousins" of a tribe the bulk of which was nomadic, for example—exercised considerable social power, because their tribal support was intimidating. Indeed, although the nomadic portion of the tribe was the ultimate source of the tribe's power, it was commonly from the oases or other settlements controlled by the tribe that this power was exercised and directed. It was quite usual for the leadership of a tribe that had subjected an oasis, for example, to take up more or less permanent residence in the town. There they served both as the dominant dynasty in the oasis and as the chiefs of their tribe, most of whom remained in the surrounding desert. In fact, most of their subjects in the oasis had, or claimed to have, a similar desert ancestry, had ties to other groups in the desert, and perhaps represented the descendants of earlier conquering dynasties that had settled in similar fashion in the oasis.[42] It was, indeed, in just this manner that many towns in the Fertile Crescent—Edessa, Ḥarrān, Hatra, Emesa (Ḥimṣ), Palmyra, al-Ḥīra, and others—acquired ruling dynasties of "Arab," that is nomadic, origin.[43]

There were, then, great disparities in power among the tribes of northern and central Arabia, and these disparities in power were reflected as disparities in honor (*sharaf, majd*) among them. Tribes that over several generations consistently proved themselves more powerful than their neighbors and rivals, and that imposed their will on them or extracted payments from them, came to be recognized as *sharīf*, "noble," and formed a kind of warrior aristocracy among the tribes.[44] In essence, this warrior aristocracy consisted of those tribes that were politically independent and could offer effective protection to weaker groups that might choose to attach themselves to them on a short-term or a long-term basis. Such arrangements were often used by artisans or merchants needing protection, for example, or by weaker or isolated nomadic groups, which might attach themselves permanently to the protecting tribe and ultimately be absorbed by it.[45] Groups such as these, which habitually needed the protection of the warrior aristocracy, or were normally subject to it, were known as "*ḍaʿīf*" (literally, "weak")—that is, nonnoble, politically dependent tribes. The hallmark of the noble tribes composing the warrior aristocracy was, then, their political independence. They paid tribute to no one, prided themselves on their independence and power, behaved defiantly toward their rivals or peers, bullied individuals of submissive groups, and boasted of the "purity" of their descent from some great chief whom they claimed, by means of their oft-manipulated genealogies, as a direct ancestor.[46] Arabian tradition expressed this dual basis of noble status in the terms *nasab* (noble lineage, i.e., descent from noble ancestors) and *ḥasab* (noble behavior).[47]

Despite their domineering behavior and pride of lineage, however, the tribes of the warrior aristocracy did not have a monopoly in the use of force even among groups dependent upon them. There were numerous groups that, although dependent on the warrior tribes and hence not "noble" in the same way, were nevertheless able to subject weaker groups. Such, for example, were the shepherding tribes (as well as many less powerful camel-herding groups). These paid the *khuwwa* to the warrior tribes from deep in the desert when the latter met them at the summer wells, but they were themselves quite powerful and normally extorted the *khuwwa* from seminomads and villages in the vicinity of their grazing grounds on the desert fringes.[48] Because they were constrained to pay tribute to the warrior tribes, they could not claim the same aristocratic bearing or descent as these; yet they did enjoy considerable status by virtue of their demonstrated tribal strength, and they ranked socially far above some other groups that were disdained for their weakness and "impure" descent. These latter, at the bottom of the political and social hierarchy, included not only the peasantry, but also certain "pariah" tribes. Some of these pariah groups roamed the desert serving as itinerant tinkers; others herded camels or other livestock among the more powerful tribes, from whom they were distinguished only by their servile behavior, greater poverty, and total defenselessness. They were, of course, taxed and generally abused by the stronger tribes among whom they lived.

This ranking of tribal groups according to their greater or lesser "nobility" was most clearly reflected in their marriage arrangements. Great emphasis was placed on assuring equality of status (*kafā'a*) between the bride and groom, that is, between the groups of which they were members. Group endogamy within tribal lineages was common and encouraged and tribesmen wishing to marry outside their tribe were careful to avoid marrying below their status. Women of the pariah tribes, for example, were refused in marriage by members of most nomadic groups, who considered them base and would not entertain the thought of sullying their purer tribal blood with them. This situation has suggested to some observers a virtual caste system among the Arabian tribes.[49]

As noted, the aristocratic status of the warrior tribes and the relatively higher status of some nonnoble tribes vis-à-vis others seem to be linked more or less directly to their actual military prowess. That is, the presumed purity of blood is concocted by inventing an appropriate genealogy for the tribe after it rises to dominance. The status of a tribe sometimes assumed a life of its own, however, and survived some time after the tribe's actual situation had changed. Upon the breakup and dispersion of a once powerful aristocratic tribe, for example, the scattered families may be shown great respect because of their recognized "noble lineage," even though they may have been reduced by circumstances to political dependence on another tribe. Further, tribes of recognized nobility sometimes provided ruling families for other tribes—even, in some cases, for the new tribe that had just supplanted the ruling family's former tribe.[50]

Thus far we have considered the power relationships between different tribes dominated by a warrior aristocracy, viewing the individual tribes themselves as homogeneous units. As already noted, however, a tribe is marked as much by internal divisions into lineages, sublineages, and so on, as it is marked by overall cohesiveness. It is therefore hardly surprising to find that distinctions in status existed between various lineages within a single tribe. Certain lineages or sublineages became recognized as its "ruling house" (*ahl al-bayt*), that is, as the segment of the tribe from which the tribal chiefs were drawn. The competition among different lineages for this position of pre-eminence within the tribe was continuous and often quite sharp, for recognition as the chief of one's tribe brought considerable esteem upon one's lineage. The greater "nobility" of the ruling house within the tribe was not immediately effaced, in the event that the dominant lineage was replaced by another; the humbled lineage continued to enjoy a certain prestige, was considered as having greater potential to provide tribal leadership than most other groups in the tribe, and attempted to recapture the dominant position from its rival. But the longer a group was "out of power," the weaker its claim to special status associated with tribal leadership became, and the lower its potential as a source of chiefs was deemed to be. Conversely, the more generations of leaders a group provided for its tribe, the more its leadership potential was reinforced in the eyes of its fellow tribesmen, and the greater became its leadership status in comparison with other groups. Every tribe—even the weakest and least "noble"—had its *ahl al-bayt* or "ruling house," which usually occupied a correspondingly dominant position in the tribe's genealogy.

The powerful, "noble" tribes forming the warrior aristocracy, then, provided one focus for political consolidation in northern and central Arabia; and the considerations of power and status just outlined provided the structural principles of hierarchization operative in these confederations. Such confederations had limited potential for political integration, however. The various subordinate groups were not bound to one another but had in common only their subjection by the warrior nobility. Furthermore, the fact that two tribal groups were both subordinate to a common warrior nobility had no necessary impact on their relationship with one another; they were, rather, left free to work out for themselves their relative positions in the hierarchy of power. Thus, although a warrior aristocracy might control (i.e., tax) a large number of lesser groups, concerted action by these groups was something the aristocracy could rarely engineer. In addition, these confederations were quite fragile and were subject to sudden dissolution, for there was no tie binding a subject group to the confederation should the real power of the dominant nomadic group falter. "I used to travel about my tribe for the quarter [of flocks payable as tax]," boasted the chief of the nomadic B. Ṭayyi', 'Adī b. Ḥātim;[51] but his very words suggest the degree to which his domination was a personal one, dependent upon his physical presence and the armed might of those immediate kinsmen who traveled with him.

Besides such imposed confederation, it was possible for tribal groups to join one another in alliance (*ḥilf*) against some common threat, or for some common purpose. In certain cases, these alliances grew to great size and displayed considerable stability. They were, however, purely cooperative ventures, lacking any centralized direction (not to mention centralized institutions). Component groups belonged to the alliance only as long as it served their purposes, and, even while belonging to it, each group remained completely independent and master of its own internal affairs.[52]

Religious Aristocracies

Although, in general, sedentary populations of northern and central Arabia were, because of their military weakness and immobility, vulnerable to interference by powerful warrior tribes and were often subdued by the latter, it was yet possible for sedentary groups to exercise considerable power under certain conditions. It has already been noted that some towns served as market centers and cultic centers for nomadic groups (and lesser settlements) in their vicinity, forming an area that was called a *ḥaram* or sacred enclave.[53] Each *ḥaram* was dominated by a "holy family," often descendants of some pious person who had first established the *ḥaram* as a cult site by delineating its borders. The holy family claimed to be the servants or priests of the god or goddess who resided there and the guardian of his or her shrine (a special spring, rock, or tree, for example). Those who adhered to the cult of that god recognized the sanctity of the shrine and of the sacred enclave around it, agreeing to observe a number of regulations imposed by the holy family. These regulations pertained in part to the cultic practices at the shrine, but also included others that had important social and political implications. In particular, murder was always forbidden in the *ḥaram*, which meant that a tribesman could enter it without fear of molestation by even his bitterest enemy.[54] The *ḥaram* thus became important as neutral ground where feuding tribes could send representatives to engage in negotiations, and it is in part the need that tribes felt for such neutral territories that explains the willingness of even the most powerful tribes to leave a *ḥaram* settlement unmolested and to put up with its sometimes irksome regulations. For the same reason, the *ḥaram* frequently thrived as a market town, both because merchants and artisans could rely on the security it provided them, and because tribesmen could go there to market without fear of encountering trouble. There were thus important economic and social reasons why a powerful tribe might agree to respect the *ḥaram*—particularly if the *ḥaram* was associated with the only important market center in an entire region. In addition, the willingness of powerful nomadic groups to respect the *ḥaram* was also rooted in their fear that disobedience to the holy family or infringement of the *ḥaram's* regulations would result in supernatural punishment by the god worshiped at the *ḥaram's* shrine.

Thus the sacred enclaves had not only cultic, but also economic and social importance.

Within such a setting, it was possible for the holy family to acquire great power. Some members of the family, notably the *manṣib* or head of the cult, were frequently called upon to adjudicate disputes among the tribes. In order to ensure that his decisions in such cases were observed, however, the *manṣib* frequently tried to secure agreements from tribes around the *ḥaram* that they would assist him in enforcing his judgment in case one of the litigants refused to accept it. These agreements were normally couched as expressions of willingness by the tribes to support the *manṣib* in any dispute, which provided an ambitious *manṣib* with the means to use the power of some tribes against others to consolidate his influence or control over them all, or to use their combined power to coerce new tribal groups to recognize the *ḥaram*. An uncooperative tribesman or tribal group could, for example, be banned from the *ḥaram* and its associated market—which, if he had access to no other market center, was a serious sanction indeed.

The *ḥaram* could, then, function as a focus for political consolidation, enabling the holy family and its *manṣib* to acquire considerable political power. Like the warrior aristocracy, the holy families in Arabia—who formed a kind of religious aristocracy—were considered noble (*sharīf*), primarily because they could provide real security for weaker tribesmen and groups who sought protection within the confines of the *ḥaram*. The nobility of the holy families was also partly rooted in the fact that a *ḥaram* was, normally, independent; that is, it paid no tax or *khuwwa* to any other group—exemption from such payment being the first concession a *manṣib* would extract from allied tribal groups.

Thus under appropriate conditions a religious aristocracy centered on a *ḥaram* could, by exercising cultic, economic, and social power, achieve what the warrior aristocracy achieved by means of superior fighting ability: a measure of political integration extending significantly beyond the limits of a single tribe.[55] An effective *manṣib* (especially one operating from a large market center on which many tribes were dependent) was sometimes able to construct a sizable political coalition, tying some tribes of proven martial ability firmly in his service, and bringing other tribes into a looser kind of confederation with the *ḥaram*.

Many examples of such *ḥaram* shrines, dominated by holy families, are known. The tribe of Thaqīf in al-Ṭā'if (which had a cultic center to al-Lāt) appears to have had special ties to the nomadic B. Hawāzin who roamed the western fringes of the Najd near al-Ṭā'if, and as we shall see, the rise of Mecca had much to do with the tribal ties associated with its cult of the Ka'ba, a templelike building containing the black stone considered to be the dwelling place of the god Hubal. Although far less well known, similar *ḥarams* (probably much more modest in their political consolidation in most cases) seem to have existed all over Arabia. The village of Nakhla, near Mecca, for example, had a shrine to al-'Uzzā; the Yemeni towns of Najrān (before its conversion to Christianity, at any rate) and Ṣan'ā' served as pagan cultic centers; and other shrines are known to have existed in the region of the mountains Salmā and Aja' in the northern Najd, in the vicinity of al-Ḥīra on the fringes of Iraq, and in many other districts.[56] Some of these *ḥarams* could, of course, be rivals, with rival families administering them, and—particularly if close together—they sometimes fought one another bitterly with the help of their tribal following. In addition, as centers of political consolidation, the *ḥarams* sometimes found themselves in competition with powerful warrior tribes for control over weaker tribal groups or settlements. Hence the political history of northern and central Arabia consisted essentially of the rise and fall of small polities, centered on competing warrior nomads or holy families, which tried to subject the myriad tribal groups around them, or to bring them into alliance against rivals.

The domination imposed by religious aristocracies was therefore in some ways similar to that of the warrior aristocracy. But there were also very significant differences between them. First, the domination of the warrior aristocracy rested almost exclusively on its greater fighting ability, whereas that of the religious aristocracy relied not only on the judicious use of force, but also on economic and cultic power to maintain its control. Thus the tribes subject to a religious aristocracy were bound more effectively to the dominant tribal group than were those subject to a warrior aristocracy, because the cultic and economic ties of the former could not be so readily replaced. Even though the warrior-nomad confederations normally appear to have been larger and more powerful than those of the religious aristocracy, they were thus subject to more rapid and total collapse. The more modest consolidation of power by a religious aristocracy, on the other hand, was likely to be far more enduring. Further, the stability of the religious aristocracy could generate a virtual concept of legitimacy.

A second difference was tied to the *manṣib's* role as adjudicator of intertribal disputes. Though this does not, in itself, imply a prevailing concept of law as the basis on which society is to be ordered, it is a first step in that direction.[57]

Third, the religious aristocracy in some cases had the advantage of a stronger economic base than did the warrior nomads, because the former were often located in agricultural centers and had important markets associated with their sacred enclaves. Under suitable economic conditions (admittedly not a frequent occurrence) there could thus develop within the settled society of the *ḥaram* classes of nonagricultural specialists: artisans, merchants, and perhaps even businessmen with managerial skills. Considered together, these three factors—the germ of a concept of legitimacy and of rule by law associated with the confederation and its rulers, and the potential to support a class of administrators—meant that the sacred enclaves had the potential to develop into a more thoroughly integrated, statelike structure[58] than did the nomadic confederations, which perforce remained at a very rudimentary organizational level.

4. TRIBE AND STATE IN ARABIA: FIRST ESSAY

The complexity and fragmentation of political life in northern and central Arabia was in part due to the absence of the state there,[59] a fact that can be most easily appreciated by considering briefly the situation in South Arabia, where the state did exist. Each South Arabian kingdom was controlled by, and named for, a dominant tribe that had imposed its rule over other tribes in a certain area. This ruling tribal nobility (*ashrāf*, "nobles")[60] was, like all tribes, subdivided into lineages, the leading lineage providing the kingdom's royal dynasty. The royal house and the other lineages of the nobility ruled as large landholders, each lineage or sublineage controlling certain districts and the nonnoble, settled tribes that occupied those districts. The nobles in each district collected from their subjects various taxes and required them to perform military service and corvée (particularly on roads and irrigation works) on demand. Furthermore, the state required that the peasantry sell them its entire crop, so that the agrarian sector of the economy was essentially a state-controlled monopoly.[61]

The scattered branches of the nobility, each in its own district, were not of course totally independent, but themselves had definite obligations (financial and military) to fulfill for the state. The exact nature and restrictiveness of these obligations varied, for the relations between the nobility and the monarchy underwent considerable evolution during the fifteen centuries in which the South Arabian kingdoms flourished. An early theocracy of priest-kings (*mukarribs*) developed into a more secular and centralized rule under a strong monarchy supported by an assembly of nobles; this, in turn, gave way after the first century A.D. to a less centralized arrangement, with a much weaker monarchy and greater power and autonomy in the hands of the tribal dukes (*qayls*), that is, heads of the separate branches of the nobility entrenched in their respective domains and ruling the tribe or tribes resident there. It is fair to say, however, that in general the kingdoms demanded and received from the nobles taxes and certain services. The nobles were held responsible by the king and the assembly for the proper supervision of the districts under their charge and were expected to safeguard agricultural productivity by, for example, maintaining and extending irrigation works. They were also required to see that the kingdom's laws (the decrees of the king and assembly of nobles) were enforced in their districts. In fulfilling the last requirement, the nobles appear to have relied upon the services of a hereditary class of administrators called *kabīrs*, who were appointed by them from a specific clan of the local tribe. Likewise, in providing military forces for the king, the nobles seem to have relied on a caste of warriors (*qsd* in the South Arabian inscriptions), which, along with the clan of *kabīrs*, formed the upper social level of the subject tribe. Although the military and administrative personnel were drawn from the subject tribes themselves, however, they owed their positions of considerable status within their tribe to the fact that they served the nobility. Thus their interests were bound to those of the nobility, for which reason they were willing to carry out those policies the nobility demanded.[62]

Furthermore, the ascendancy of the state appears to have been in some measure independent of the actual power of a given king; that is, kings were recognized as rightful rulers not merely because they were powerful, but because the abstract notion of kingship (and, consequently, of the kingdom or monarchial state) appears to have been commonly accepted, at least from the period of the consolidation of the monarchy in the first century A.D.[63] Even after the decline of the strongly centralized monarchy and the emergence of virtually independent *qayls* in the fourth and fifth centuries A.D., the notion of membership in a larger state survived;[64] and, although the king was now no longer in a position to make such regular demands of the nobles, he was still able to rely on their sense of duty to the state and monarchy in extraordinary circumstances. Thus he could still rally large forces in case of war and could call on the nobles to provide labor for repairing the huge Ma'rib dam after its collapse, in A.D. 450 and 543. There existed, in short, a "state mentality" in South Arabia, an acceptance *in principle* of a political and judicial authority higher than the tribe. The settled tribes were, in fact, administered by the state. Their economic and political life was shaped in accordance with the needs of the state and its noble caste, and the state applied its laws and claimed the right to adjudicate disputes within the tribes. The military resources of the kingdoms were also normally sufficient to keep the nomadic groups permanently resident in the region under strict state control. Nomads (*a'rāb*) show up in inscriptions as subordinate groups dependent on the various South Arabian kingdoms, and probably performing military service for the state. In contradistinction to northern and central Arabia, where powerful nomads formed a warrior aristocracy, the South Arabian nomadic groups thus appear to have been of an inferior political status compared with the South Arabian nobility.[65] In general, then, tribal groups in the South Arabian kingdoms were firmly under the control of the state.

In northern and central Arabia, on the other hand, there was no state. The subsistence-level economy and nearly undifferentiated society found among both nomadic and sedentary groups in this region forestalled the rise of classes of political, military, or administrative specialists; yet without these, no effective state control can exist. Troops to put down opposition and enforce judgments and regulations, administrators to assess and collect the taxes on which the state relies (among other things, to pay its troops and other officials), legal specialists to elaborate and enforce the state's law—this is the stuff of which states are made; and northern and central Arabia had none of them.[66]

The absence of the state in North Arabia is visible not only in the absence of administrative classes, but also—perhaps most strikingly—in the absence of any overriding concept of a law binding beyond, or even within, the limits of the tribe. Power relationships were simply a question of the strength of one individual or group against another, and they were hardly affected by notions of justice enshrined in a system of laws. That is to say, there was no law in the sense of an abstract principle of justice against which one should judge the individual claim, nor any acceptance of the notion that such a generalized set of regulations could be binding on the individual. It is for this reason that the tribe, the great network of kinship ties that provided the individual with a ready reserve of social support, assumed such importance in day-to-day life. For in the absence of any notion of an overriding law or authority to judge disputes, the individual's only defense was simply to be stronger than his opponent, and his only insurance against abuse, as we have seen, was the ability of his tribe to retaliate.

It is often claimed that Arabian society did operate under an accepted customary law, based on the *lex talionis* or law of retaliation. But the *lex talionis*, however well developed the customary procedures associated with it, contained no implicit concept of a higher authority to judge disputes, nor was there the slightest concern with the justice of one's case in seeking retaliation. Retaliation was sought, rather, to restore the tribe's honor—which was itself merely the ideological expression of the tribe's physical strength and ability to defend itself. Further, the fact that in, for example, a blood-feud the aggrieved party retaliated against the offending tribe[67] and not against some other was not due to any mutual acceptance of an abstract principle of reciprocity as constituting justice, but merely to the need to restore the group's honor, which could only be done by demonstrating the aggrieved tribe's ability to avenge itself on the offending tribe.[68] Indeed, in some cases retaliation was more effective as a means of restoring tribal honor when reciprocity was *not* observed, and in such cases the murderer (a half-wit or known coward, let us say) was ignored by the aggrieved tribesmen, who sought to strike down instead a more prestigious member of the offending group.[69]

The adjudication of disputes by means of *ḥakams* or arbiters was, of course, much practiced in Arabia. But the use of such referees in a dispute was totally optional; the disputants were free to ignore adjudication and seek vengeance if they desired, and the arbiter had no power or authority to ask them to do otherwise. Thus the resort to referees was essentially rooted not in any concept of an overriding law or higher authority according to which cases should be decided, but rather in the need[70] for some practical way to end the cycle of retaliation in a blood-feud by means of a neutral or disinterested referee. It is not, then, a concept of law; for any "law" that individuals are free to obey or to disobey at will is not a law. The focus of the system of *lex talionis* was, then, not justice according to law, but rather the restoration of tribal honor—that is, of social power.[71]

The tribe, then, provided for that security of person in northern and central Arabia which was in part supplied by the state and its law in

South Arabia. The tribe (and its subdivisions) was thus not only the basic social unit, but also the basic political grouping around which relationships of power were ordered—that is, politics was essentially a question of intertribal relations. Even within the framework of a large confederation, the tribe remained an autonomous unit with complete control over its internal affairs.

There was, then, no state in northern Arabia to impose its control over the tribes, so that society was dominated by the most powerful tribal groups—which were, as we have seen, those focused around warrior nomads or holy families. Despite the fact that confederations headed by warrior nomads as well as those headed by holy families lacked the administrative and legal features that we associate with the state, however, they did resemble the state in one respect: they functioned as sovereign entities, independent of external political control and desiring to extend their domination over new groups and areas. This meant not only that they acted as rivals to one another, as we have seen, but also that in those regions where confederations came into contact with established states on the peripheries of northern and central Arabia, the two tended to clash. Independent tribes and true states were, simply, competitors for political domination—in particular, for the privilege of drawing on the economic resources of the areas in dispute by means of taxation. This competition involved, for the most part, warrior-nomad confederations that frequented the fringes of the states in question, for the confederations of the sedentary religious aristocracy seem to have been of more strictly local significance, and were furthermore more vulnerable to retaliation by the state than were the nomadic groups. In this rivalry between nomadic tribal confederations and states, the states—Byzantine, Sasanian, or South Arabian—certainly had superior resources to draw upon, as well as an organizational advantage. They could muster considerably larger forces than warrior nomadic groups could raise (even in the unusual event that the dominant warrior nomads received significant military assistance from some of the other tribes subject to them). But these advantages in resources and organization were offset, and perhaps more than offset, by the great mobility and fighting skill of nomadic warriors, and by their ability to withdraw into arid regions that the cumbersome infantry and cavalry of the states found difficult to traverse—regions with which these armies were usually unfamiliar, but where precise knowledge of watering-points and grazing grounds spelled the difference between life and death. Thus the states on the periphery of the peninsula generally found it impossible to establish direct state control over northern and central Arabia.

Because they could not control central and northern Arabia directly, the South Arabian, Byzantine, and Sasanian states relied primarily on policies of alliance to keep the nomads of that region from interfering too seriously in their domains. These alliances assumed one of two forms, corresponding to the two kinds of tribal confederation that existed in northern and central Arabia: alliances directly with tribal confederations dominated by warrior nomads, who then served the state as "policemen"; and alliances with settled dynasties of nobles, which dominated confederations of tribes in the same manner as the religious aristocracy.

The last great South Arabian state, the kingdom of Ḥimyar, appears to have made an alliance of the first sort with the central Arabian tribes of Kinda and Madhḥij. Both of these tribes, which were powerful "warrior nobility," provided the Ḥimyarites with auxiliary mounted warriors on camelback (*a'rāb*) during their campaigns in central and eastern Arabia. They were not strong enough to prevent a raid on the town of Najrān in northern Yemen by the great North Arabian chief Imru' al-Qays in about A.D. 300, however, and in fact the latter dealt the Kinda and Madhḥij a crushing defeat and forced them to flee their home territory around Jabal Ṭuwayq. The Ḥimyarites must have considered them still valuable as warriors, however, for they took in the fugitives and installed them as "nobles" and landlords in certain districts in South Arabia, which ultimately came to be called after them. The central Arabian tribe of Murād appears to have had a similar history.[72] These central Arabian warrior tribes presumably continued to provide military service for the Ḥimyarite kings after their settlement in the Yemen, and eventually became integrated into the Ḥimyarite kingdom among the ruling caste; they had been, after all, part of the warrior aristocracy and were seen as *sharīf*. Later, in the fifth century A.D., the Ḥimyarites attempted to re-establish the Kinda tribe in central Arabia; clearly they still felt the need for a satellite confederation of nomadic groups serving them as allies in that region.[73]

Although the connection between the Ḥimyarite kingdom and the central Arabian tribes of Kinda, Madhḥij, and Murād was thus very intimate, it must be seen as an alliance. The desert tribes providing *a'rāb* for the Ḥimyarites were not fully integrated into the kingdom[74] as were the settled South Arabian tribes ruled by the Ḥimyarites, but were rather allied with it more or less as equals. We have, unfortunately, no details about the ties that bound the Kinda and other central Arabian tribes to the Ḥimyarites, but it seems plausible to assume that these tribes were essentially autonomous and not subject to Ḥimyarite administration, law, or even perhaps taxation. We can obtain some idea of what these ties might have been like, however, by examining similar relationships between the Byzantine and Sasanian Empires and the principally nomadic tribes in the Fertile Crescent.

Considerably more is known about the policy of the Byzantines toward the nomadic tribes of northern Arabia that impinged on the fringes of Syria. Like the Ḥimyarites, the Byzantines appear to have favored a policy of direct alliance with a powerful tribe of warrior nobility. Thus, in the fourth century A.D. they established an alliance with a tribe called Salīḥ, who probably served as military auxiliaries for the Byzantines.[75] In A.D. 502 the Salīḥ were superseded as Byzantine vassals by the Banū Ghassān, a tribe that had immigrated into Syria around A.D. 400 and built up a powerful confederation in the Syrian steppe roughly a century later.[76]

The Ghassānid confederation was a typical example of the kind of entity assembled by groups of aristocratic warrior tribesmen in Arabia. It bears all the surface characteristics of such confederations: emphasis on the "nobility" of the ruling house, absence of a clear cultic center, habitat and mobility suitable to warrior nomads, and fighting prowess of the ruling group. As Byzantine vassals, the Ghassānid chiefs (who were honored with the designation of "*phylarch*" or independently allied "tribal ruler" by the Byzantines) provided mounted auxiliary troops for their overlords and often campaigned with the Byzantine army against the Sasanians or the Sasanians' tribal allies. They also appear to have been used by the Byzantines to control internal disturbances, such as the Samaritan rebellion of 529.[77] But their main function was probably to keep the nomadic groups living within or near the Byzantine Empire under control—a function reflected, perhaps, in the very title of "*phylarch*." The Byzantines appear, indeed, to have created the alliance with the Ghassānid dynasty partly with a view to preventing nomadic raids such as those on Palestine around A.D. 500. The many nomadic and partly nomadic groups living within the Byzantine provinces of Palaestina II, Palaestina III, Arabia, Phoenicia ad Libanum, and perhaps northern Syria were, then, under the control of the Ghassānids,[78] who were presumably held responsible for the good behavior of these tribes and had the military power to chasten those who erred. They served, in short, as a kind of "tribal police" for the Byzantines. It seems likely that their predecessors, the Salīḥ, had served in the same way.

In its heyday, the Ghassānid confederation was very powerful. It is known, for instance, that they were able to launch successful campaigns into the territory of the B. Sulaym and B. Judhām in the northern Ḥijāz, and they are reported to have handed out harsh treatment to the powerful nomadic tribes of Asad and Tamīm in the Najd and to branches of Bakr b. Wā'il in northeastern Arabia[79]—all localities that lay well over 800 km. from the Ghassānids' "capital" (presumably their favored summer encampment) at al-Jābiya in the Golan. It was, of course, this tremendous power that made them desirable to the Byzantines as allies, but it was a power that could also be a threat to the Byzantines if turned against them. Hence the Byzantines were careful to tie the Ghassānid chiefs to themselves by granting them regular subsidies in exchange for their loyal service and effective control over the tribes.[80] In addition, the Ghassānid *phylarchs* were honored by being elevated to the rank of patrician, and one of them was even taken to Constantinople and crowned "king" by the emperor. The degree to which these measures increased the prestige of the Ghassānid chiefs is clear from the continued reference to them as *al-biṭrīq*, "the patrician," in Arabic sources. It was quite clearly a title that made a grand impression.

Indeed, it is likely that the power of the Ghassānid confederation was not only the cause of their favored position vis-à-vis the Byzantines, but also in part a result of it. Byzantine subsidies were probably used by the *phylarchs* to keep allies content, and the weapons and horses that the Byzantines may have provided them would clearly augment their military capacity. Unfortunately, we have little detailed information on how the Ghassānid confederation itself was put together. Members of the ruling family appear to have been in charge of different parts of the territories dominated by them,[81] but nothing is known about their relations to the many tribes that must have come under their sway.

In contrast to the Ḥimyarites and Byzantines, who made alliances directly with powerful groups of warrior nomads, the Sasanian Great Kings favored alliances with sedentary dynasties of "noble" status, the rulers of which elaborated a tribal policy of their own much in the manner of the "holy families" of Arabia's sacred enclaves. The Sasanians' backing undoubtedly gave these allied dynasties a nucleus of power that most "holy families" did not enjoy, however, and this may explain why these dynasties and the confederations that grew up around them were so much more prominent (even, it appears, without the benefits of religious sanctions) than those of most Arabian *ḥarams*.

Several dynasties were bound in this way to the Sasanians, reflecting the Sasanians' greater concern, as a major Indian Ocean power, with the Arabian peninsula when compared to the Byzantines. Most of these dynasties that were allied to the Sasanians are, however, very poorly known. The Great Kings appear to have supported a dynasty of the B. Ḥanīfa ruling in the rich district of al-Yamāma in eastern Arabia, for example, and it is reported that one of them was even crowned "king" by the Sasanians; presumably they were deemed important because of their role in the long-distance trade that passed through their oasis capital. Likewise, starting in the middle of the sixth century A.D., the Sasanians supported a vassal dynasty of *Julandās* (kings) in 'Umān.[82]

The most famous, and by far the best known of the Sasanian vassal kingdoms, however, was that of the Lakhmid dynasty in al-Ḥīra, on the fringes of the Iraqi alluvium.[83] Like the Ghassānids, the Lakhmids received from their overlords honored treatment (they, too, were crowned as "kings"), cash subsidies, and weapons, and they were provided as well with a garrison of Sasanian cavalry to bolster their power in al-Ḥīra and among the surrounding tribes. The result of this support was to make them one of the main factors shaping the political life of northern Arabia through much of the sixth century A.D., an honor for which they competed avidly with their Ghassānid rivals. Not being themselves nomadic warriors, however, their ability to control nomadic groups in their area depended—as with "holy families"—upon factors other than sheer force of arms; in particular, it rested upon the elaboration of a successful tribal diplomacy.

The nature of the ties that the Lakhmids established with tribes in northern and eastern Arabia depended partly on the tribes themselves and the kind of life various tribal groups led.[84] Directly along the west bank of the Euphrates from central Iraq to the Persian Gulf there was a string of settlements inhabited by sedentary agriculturalists and townsmen, most of them Arabic speaking, or by seminomadic herders of mixed flocks. Many Arab tribes of the Syrian desert and Najd were represented in the first group, whereas the second appears to have consisted of the bulk of the tribe of Tanūkh.[85] Immediately to the west of this band of settlement, between the river and the heart of the Syrian desert and Najd, lay an area that was especially suitable for shepherding nomads. They used pastures as far as perhaps 50 km. from the rivers in winter and spring for grazing their large mixed flocks of sheep and goats and returned to the banks of the Euphrates during the dry summer months.[86] Among these shepherding groups appear to have been many from the tribes of Iyād and al-Namir b. Qāsiṭ and, perhaps, Taghlib.[87] Yet farther to the west, in the Syrian desert and Najd proper, lay the winter and spring pastures of the camel-herding nomadic groups from B. Shaybān, 'Ijl, Qays b. Tha'laba, Taymallāt b. Tha'laba, Tamīm, Ḍabba, Ṭayyi', Asad, Dhubyān, and others. Some of these had summer encampments at perennial wells in the central Najd, others summered at wells in eastern Arabia or on the fringes of Iraq along the Euphrates, but all had some contact with nearby towns as market centers, and not a few of these groups had tribal kinsmen resident in al-Ḥīra or other towns along the river—al-Ubulla, al-Anbār, Hīt, 'Anāt, or (slightly inland) 'Ayn al-Tamr.

Not surprisingly, the Sasanians and their Lakhmid clients proved able to dominate the seminomadic Tanūkh in much the same manner that the Arab towns along the Euphrates were dominated, and for much the same reasons: located near the centers of Sasanian power in Iraq, and lacking both great power and great mobility, there was no effective way for these groups to resist or to escape Sasanian tax collectors. Similarly, the shepherding tribes, although more powerful, were also vulnerable to Sasanian control since they needed to return each summer to permanent watering places along the Euphrates. The Sasanians, in some cases through their Lakhmid clients, thus collected a tax (*itāwa*) on these tribes. The warrior virtues of the shepherding tribes led the Sasanians to rely on them also for auxiliary troops; hence at battles such as the famous clash at Dhū Qār (ca. A.D. 611), contingents of troops from the B. al-Namir, Iyād, and Taghlib fought alongside the Sasanians.

The Sasanians and their Lakhmid vassals were not able to dominate the camel-herding nomadic groups quite so easily, however. At most times the Lakhmids could boast a fairly impressive network of alliances with these powerful nomadic groups; the alliances tended to be somewhat unstable, however, and the coalition of tribal groups of which the Lakhmids were the focus was always shifting, as tensions between tribes or between lineages within a tribe led various groups to establish or break ties with the Lakhmids. The ability of these groups to escape effective control by the Sasanians was largely due to their great mobility, the location of their grazing grounds (well outside the direct reach of al-Ḥīra's forces), the availability of alternate summer watering-places some distance from al-Ḥīra, and the great fighting ability they displayed. Some of these tribal groups were totally independent (*laqāḥ*) of the Lakhmids' authority; they paid no taxes to al-Ḥīra and provided no contingents of warriors for them.[88] Above all others, it was these groups that were willing and able to exact taxes of their own (*khuwwa*) from settled groups or weaker nomads in the Sasanian domains, or to plunder villages and towns if they sensed weakness in the Sasanian defenses.

The threat posed by such *laqāḥ* tribal groups could only be countered by an effective coalition of other powerful nomadic groups under the Lakhmid's direction. Thus al-Ḥīra's tribal policy sought to bind chiefs of powerful groups as effectively as possible to an alliance with the Lakhmids. In some cases, for example, the Lakhmid kings were able to make commercial pacts with the tribes—even with distant tribes, such as the B. Sulaym and B. Hawāzin in the Ḥijāz and western Najd. In other cases purely military alliances for specific military campaigns were made, as the Lakhmids sought to take advantage of rivalries between tribal groups to prosecute a policy of *divide et impera*. The Lakhmids also attempted to win tribal chiefs over by means of various blandishments. Some chiefs were granted estates (or the revenue from them, perhaps) on the fringes of the fertile Iraqi alluvium to be held as private benefices; others were associated with the splendor of the Lakhmid court as a kind of honored companion (*ridf*) of the Lakhmid ruler, a measure that enhanced the chief's status and entitled him to a share in the ruler's portion of booty and taxes. The chief in return agreed to submit a certain amount of tax to be collected from his tribe, to provide some military contingents, and to keep his tribe under control. It is likely, too, that tribal groups allied to the Lakhmids may have received weapons and perhaps cash subsidies in return for their loyalty.[89] Finally, difficult tribes that had been brought into the network of al-Ḥīra's alliances could be controlled by holding hostages from the tribe in a kind of "house arrest" in al-Ḥīra as a guarantee of the tribe's good behavior.

Thus the Sasanians, through their Lakhmid vassal "kings," attempted to establish a network of alliances with the tribes in much of northern and northeastern Arabia as a means of keeping these tribes under control—in particular, to keep them from plundering or taxing settled districts in the Iraqi alluvium, or from plundering or disrupting the caravan trade. It is reasonable to assume that the purpose, and the functioning, of the Sasanians' other vassal princes, in al-Yamāma and in 'Umān, was much the same.

The Byzantines, Sasanians, and South Arabian kingdoms, then, all dominated certain tribal groups that lay within their ready control and attempted to extend their domination as much as possible over more elusive groups living deeper in the desert heartland of the Arabian peninsula. At times of internal weakness in any of these states, however, when for one reason or another the barrier of defenses they had erected against the nomads collapsed, nomadic groups were able to indulge in destructive raids on settlements usually far outside the realm of their control. Since the areas being pillaged were not normally contacted by the nomads, they were not areas upon which the nomads felt themselves economically dependent, and there was consequently little reason for them to spare them. It was not usually worthwhile to attempt to subject such regions to *khuwwa*, for example, because it was recognized that eventually the state would recuperate and once more bar the nomads from the area. Hence raids of this kind tended to be seen as one-of-a-kind operations, with emphasis on gathering as much loot in the single visit as possible. This pattern can be seen in the area around the river Jordan in the second decade of the seventh century when, during the political confusion in the wake of the Sasanian invasion of Syria and Palestine in A.D. 611, nomadic groups launched raids penetrating nearly to the walls of Jerusalem.[90]

Northern and central Arabia was, then, for centuries the arena of two kinds of political struggle. Within the region itself, there was an ongoing competition among tribal confederations built either around sedentary religious aristocracies or around nomadic warrior aristocracies, any of which could function as an independent center of power. The history of this struggle in most periods shows that various confederations rose to prominence for a time, but generally collapsed before being able to consolidate control over more than a few of the tribes of the region. The second political struggle was one between the powerful tribal confederations headed by warrior nomads and the great states surrounding northern and central Arabia—the South Arabian kingdoms and the Byzantine and Sasanian Empires. It was a struggle that tended to be played out most intensely on the peripheries of the region, where these independent tribal confederations came into direct contact with the domains of the various states. Historically, it proceeded in cycles. When the state was strong, it could dominate the nomads and prevent them from disrupting state domains, by means of careful patterns of tribal alliance; but when these defenses collapsed, usually due to some internal turbulence in the state, the nomadic warriors undertook campaigns of raiding, sometimes deep inside the territories normally held by the state. At no time before the rise of Islam did either side win a complete victory in this struggle. No state ever subjected tribal Arabia completely—partly due to the difficulty of penetrating the region—and the nomadic tribal confederations, because of their organizational limitations, could raid, but could never conquer and hold the great states of the periphery. Thus the struggle between tribe and state in northern Arabia see-sawed back and forth, but essentially remained a stalemate.

With the rise of Islam, however, the long struggle between the tribe and the state would be resolved, for once, definitively, in favor of the state. It marked the one period in history when a state successfully brought all of Arabia—nomadic and sedentary peoples alike—firmly under its control, an episode unique in the history of Arabia until recent times. The fact that the state destined to subject tribal Arabia so completely was not one of the established states on the periphery of the peninsula but was, rather, a new state that would emerge from a sacred enclave within central Arabia itself was a development that no contemporary observer could have foreseen.

CHAPTER II

THE FOUNDATIONS OF THE ISLAMIC CONQUEST

1. MUḤAMMAD AND THE ISLAMIC STATE

The West Arabian town of Mecca appears to have functioned for centuries as a typical *ḥaram*, a combination of pilgrimage center and marketplace. Because it supported no agriculture, it is probable that the residents of the town were from its earliest settlement active in the pursuit of trade, at least on a local scale, and it was from this trade and from the economic benefits associated with pilgrimage to its shrine, the Ka'ba, that the Meccans were able to live.

By the end of the sixth century A.D., however, Mecca had undergone an economic and social development that set it apart from other towns in northern and central Arabia. The Meccan tribe of Quraysh, or at least certain branches of Quraysh (notably the clans of B. Umayya ['Abd Shams] and Makhzūm) had come to dominate the lucrative West Arabian transit trade in luxuries such as slaves and spices. They maintained a far-flung network of commercial contacts stretching from the Syrian entrepôts of Bostra, Gaza, and al-'Arīsh to the Yemen; they concluded economic, and sometimes political, alliances with numerous nomadic groups in the deserts of northern and central Arabia, whose consent and assistance were needed to facilitate the passage of Meccan caravans; and they controlled large amounts of capital, invested in their trading ventures not only by themselves, but also, it seems, by virtually every resident of Mecca. The trade they worked was thriving, and the clans of Umayya and Makhzūm in particular had grown wealthy and influential in Meccan politics. Furthermore, by associating allied tribes with their commercial ventures by means of profit sharing, they were able to translate some of their economic influence in western Arabia into a measure of political influence as well.

The cause of this tremendous burst of economic activity in Mecca remains obscure, despite the considerable attention it has received. We cannot be certain whether Mecca's booming commerce resulted primarily from the decline of trading ventures organized by South Arabian competitors, from a shift in trade routes that brought more trade to the West Arabian land route at the expense of the Red Sea or other routes, from the development of superior organizational methods by the Meccan merchants, or from other factors. What is clear is that Meccan commerce was flourishing as never before, and that the leaders in this trade had developed from mere merchants into true financiers. They were no longer concerned only with "buying cheap and selling dear," but also with organizing money and men to realize their commercial objectives. There was emerging, in short, a class of men with well-developed managerial and organizational skills. It was a development unheralded, and almost unique, in central Arabia.[1]

It was in this environment that Muḥammad was born and raised.[2] Although he was from the B. Hāshim, one of the lesser clans of Quraysh, he grew up to be one of the most promising young men of Mecca. He was active in the caravan trade and renowned for his self-control and diplomatic tact—that *ḥilm* on which the Meccans prided themselves and which was in no small measure responsible for the successful spread of their commercial and political influence. As a person, he appears to have been deliberate and reflective, sensitive to the feelings of others and to the increasing tensions of a society in which extremes of wealth and poverty were becoming more apparent. He was also, it seems, given to serious contemplation, and in his mature years he came to devote considerable time to solitary retreats for this purpose.

It was during such a retreat, undertaken in about his fortieth year (ca. A.D. 610) that Muḥammad first experienced the religious visions that ended his promising future as a merchant and respected tribesman of Quraysh and forced him to embark on a new path in life. In these visions he received revelations of the word of God, brought to him by a figure who came to be identified as the archangel Gabriel, and which contained the germ of that system of religious and ethical teachings that would come to be known as Islam. Henceforth he saw his mission in life as being that of a prophet—the last in a long line of prophets beginning with Adam, and including Abraham, Moses, and Jesus—whose duty it was to bring God's word to his fellows and to lead them from the error of their ways: polytheism, avarice, and pride. There was but one God, and the greatest sin was therefore the denial of God's oneness and the setting of some other being as equal to Him. God was all-powerful and had created all human life from dust; it was therefore man's duty to give thanks to God for life itself and for all of the bounties, great and small, that accompanied it. All men were equally creatures of God; oppression of the poor and weak by the rich and powerful was therefore an affront against God's creation and hence against God Himself. Man was responsible for his deeds and would pay or be rewarded at the last judgment; therefore it was imperative that each show his faith and humility before God through prayer and almsgiving. Muḥammad was the Prophet, the bearer of this final dispensation from God to man; to disbelieve in his preaching was, therefore, to disbelieve in God. Such was the kernel of Muḥammad's teaching in the first years after the revelation began to come to him.

The Quraysh rebuffed these admonitions from their Maker with all the scorn and arrogance that one would expect from a society of self-made men. Many of them found Muḥammad's talk of the resurrection of the dead, the last judgment, and an afterlife in heaven or hell simply ludicrous; others were offended by his condemnation of the tribe's ancestors as polytheists and his insistence that they were paying for their impiety in hellfire; still others seem to have felt that they could not accept his claim to prophethood without according too much honor to a man from a rival clan of Quraysh.[3] His first followers were mostly poor or socially undistinguished individuals (though there were some notable exceptions), and he and his small following were the object first of derision by, and then of the open hostility of, the Meccans. Indeed, it was only the protection offered by his uncle Abū Ṭālib, head of the B. Hāshim, that permitted Muḥammad to continue his teaching. It was a protection based, however, not in any great concern for Muḥammad's teachings, but rather in a desire to avoid the ignominy of seeing one's kinsman abused in public. After the death of Abū Ṭālib, Muḥammad and his followers suffered increasingly from the threats and abuses of the Quraysh, and he therefore began to seek new sources of support and protection outside of Mecca. He approached some of the chiefs of the B. Thaqīf of al-Ṭā'if, and also groups of nomadic tribesmen when they came to market, hoping to convince them to protect him so that he could continue his preaching, but to no avail. He finally succeeded, however, in winning over to Islam a small group of men from Medina who were in Mecca looking for an arbiter to help them resolve the bitter feuds that had long divided them; and in the following year a much larger delegation of Medinese came to Mecca and agreed not only to embrace Islam, but also to grant the Prophet and his followers their protection. Shortly thereafter, in A.D. 622, Muḥammad and the Muslims of Mecca emigrated to Medina.

It is not clear in what role Muḥammad came to Medina at the outset—whether he was considered to be the political chief of all Medina, or whether, as seems more likely, he was at first viewed merely as the head of the small group of Muslims in Medina and an arbiter to help the Medinese resolve their long-standing feuds. Whatever his initial position, however, it is clear that Muḥammad rather quickly consolidated power in the city and soon emerged as the dominant political chief of Medina.

With his *hijra*, or emigration to Medina, and his ordinances there—particularly those contained in a group of documents collectively known as the "Constitution of Medina"—Muḥammad established a new *ḥaram*.[4] His consolidation of political power was in fact similar to that undertaken by the *manṣib* in any Arabian *ḥaram*, at least in method, but Muḥammad's political consolidation went far beyond that of the usual Arabian *manṣib*. We have seen that the tribal confederations constructed around sacred enclaves, although having the potential to develop into state-like polities, did not normally do so. They could never successfully grow beyond a limited size. The traditional difficulty in Arabian politics was not so much in building up a powerful coalition (although that was itself no easy task), but in maintaining it. It was not the means of extending dominance that were lacking, but the means of giving the tribal confederation, once built, a measure of cohesiveness. Yet without this cohesion, a confederation could grow only to a limited size before cracks began to appear within it. Muḥammad's new polity based in Medina, however, was able in some measure to overcome this difficulty. It displayed a cohesiveness far in advance of that found in the usual tribal confederation centered on a *ḥaram*—a cohesiveness that resulted both from a new ideology and from the gradual rise of new institutional and organizational arrangements. It grew, in short, into a true state.

The transition to state organization was, of course, a gradual process; one cannot isolate any specific moment at which the Islamic state can be said to have come into existence. But it is clear that Muḥammad, by the end of his career, controlled a polity that had in some measure acquired the main characteristics of a state: a relatively high degree of centralization, a concept of the primacy of law or centralized higher authority in the settlement of disputes, and institutions to perform administrative functions for the state existing independent of particular incumbents. For want of a precise moment, we can select the *hijra* in A.D. 622 and the start of Muḥammad's political consolidation in Medina as the point at which the rise of the new Islamic state begins.[5]

The appearance of the Islamic state in western Arabia was an event unparalleled in the history of the peninsula, and it had unparalleled consequences. It was the integrative power of the new state, acting on the raw material of Arabian society, that unleashed the expansive military potential of the peninsula and generated the Islamic conquest—a phenomenon that transformed the face of the ancient world profoundly and irrevocably. In order to appreciate the integrative power of the Islamic state and to see why it provided greater cohesion than had hitherto existed in Arabia, however, it is necessary to examine somewhat more closely specific ideological and organizational aspects of the developing new state.

2. MUḤAMMAD'S TEACHINGS

Already in the Meccan phase of Muḥammad's career, and even more after the Islamic state began to emerge in Medina, the Prophet elaborated a set of concepts that helped bolster ideologically the cohesion of the new state. These social and political concepts were largely inseparable from Muḥammad's religious teachings; that is, certain ideas that Muḥammad put forth had, as the Western observer would see it, both religious and sociopolitical content. They pertained simultaneously to relations between the believer and God, and to relations between the believer and the rest of mankind, and therefore contributed not only to the rise of a new theological system, but to the rise of a new state as well. Three such concepts were especially important to the rise of the Islamic state: the concept of a unique, separate, and unified Islamic community or *umma*, the concept of an absolute higher authority, and the concept of the centralization of authority within the *umma*. All three are clearly interrelated, but it will be convenient for the moment to consider each of them separately.

The notion of the *umma* or community of believers would, once it had been fully elaborated, have a revolutionary import in the context of Arabian society.[6] To be sure, the concept of a community of men was thoroughly familiar in Arabia. There was the tribe, for example, with which the *umma* is commonly compared, and with which it shares some characteristics.[7] And, although it is usually stated that the *umma* differed from the tribe in that it was based on ties of religion rather than of kinship, it seems clear that even the notion of religious ties extending across tribal groups was not unknown in pre-Islamic Arabia. Several different tribes might participate, for instance, in a common cult associated with a *ḥaram* they all frequented; and, although we might hesitate to see in such an association a true "community," self-contained and self-defending, such as the *umma* seems to have been, it nonetheless clearly represents a situation in which members of different tribes were linked to one another on the basis of religious affiliation.[8] What was unique in the concept of the *umma* was, then, not the idea of community, or even the idea of a community defined by religion, but rather the uncompromising monotheism of the Islamic community that, by its active rejection of paganism, in essence laid claim for the *umma* to the souls and bodies of the whole pagan population. The *umma* claimed to be the universal community of believers, reflecting its character as the body of worshipers of the one and universal God. The notion that the *umma* could, and indeed must, expand to include the entire pagan population (if not the whole of mankind) was thus implicit in it. It is hardly necessary to point out that the general acceptance, consciously or unconsciously, of such a notion by members of the *umma* could ultimately prove most supportive of an extended conquest movement having a political, as well as a religious, character.

Another unusual aspect of the *umma* concept was the intensity of its grip on the individual believer. In the first place, the uniqueness of the *umma* and its character as a monotheistic religious community transformed the act of breaking with the community from a social act into a moral one. Such a break was not merely unfortunate or undesirable, but positively evil, because there was only one Islamic *umma*. To break ties with the *umma* was to break with both God and man; it was both a sin and a crime.[9] It is difficult to assess the degree to which this shift in the interpretation of such an act created greater cohesion in the Islamic community and prevented attrition of its membership. But it was a situation new to Arabia. Even the Arabian Jew, and even more the worshiper of al-'Uzzā or some other pagan deity, could break with his particular community and join another that worshiped in the same way; but since there was only one Islamic *umma*, to break with it even politically brought down the full moral charge of apostasy on the individual, as appears to have happened during the *ridda* wars after Muḥammad's death.[10]

Even more important, however, was the way in which Islam required believers to stand united against unbelievers:

> O believers, take not for your intimates outside yourselves; such men spare nothing to ruin you; they yearn for you to suffer.[11]

> Leave alone those who take their religion for a sport and a diversion, and whom the present life has deluded.[12]

This emphasis on the separateness of the *umma* greatly reinforced its cohesion and the degree to which it could evolve toward social and political centralization. Indeed, not even in Judaism or Christianity as practiced in Arabia was the nexus between religious doctrine and community cohesion so close. The regulations of the *umma* demanded that the tribal ties of believers be transcended, whereas Judaism and Christianity made no such demand; in principle nothing prevented the Arabian Jew or Christian from having close ties with pagans, but in the *umma* this became impossible for Muslims. Members of the *umma* were to sever ties with the tainted society of pagans, even if they were one's closest kinsmen—and failure to do so endangered the believer's soul.[13]

Thus the *umma* was very different in its political and social implications from other Arabian religious communities, whether pagan, Jewish, or Christian. It not only facilitated, it demanded the breaking of tribal ties. The *umma*, rather than the tribe, thus became the focus of a Muslim's social concern. Indeed, it was the insistence on rupturing the traditional ties of kinship in favor of the *umma* that apparently most enraged some of Muḥammad's opponents among Quraysh.[14] But it was exactly this emphasis on the broader, supratribal character of the *umma* that allowed it to expand.

A second aspect of the teachings of early Islam that contributed to the political consolidation of the Islamic community was the concept of an absolute higher authority in the form of divine law. Islam stressed not only God's omnipotence and omniscience, but also His function as the ultimate lawgiver and judge of all human action:

> Say: "My Lord has commanded justice. Set your faces in every place of worship and call on Him, making your religion sincerely His.[15]

> So set thy face to the true religion before there comes a day from God that cannot be turned back; on that day they shall be sundered

> apart. Whoso disbelieves, his unbelief shall be charged against him; and whosoever does righteousness—for themselves they are making provision, . . .[16]
>
> And whatever you are at variance on, the judgement thereof belongs to God.[17]
>
> Judgement belongs to God, the All-high, the All-great."[18]

The believer was thus provided with the notion of a divine law against which all human action was to be measured—a concept of an absolute higher authority the like of which was, as we have seen, hitherto unknown in Arabia. Man was now seen to be answerable for his deeds in a manner that transcended mere responsibility to one's kinsmen. Furthermore, the content of the revelation contained in the Qur'ān included many practical rulings on matters of day-to-day concern, so that this divine law became not only a set of abstract moral guidelines, but a true social (and political) legislation with a divine basis that was to be applied and observed in the *umma*, regulating such matters as inheritance, marriage, slavery, and the like. This meant that the *umma*, as a political and social community, not only regulated the lives of its members—any tribe, after all, did that—but that it did so according to a set of rules that transcended the boundaries of tribal identity and claimed universal validity.

As we have seen, it was the absence of any notion of law or higher authority in pre-Islamic northern and central Arabia that allowed the *lex talionis*—a system of justice based solely on the relative power of different groups—to control social relations.[19] The advent of Islam and the notion of a divine law that it brought did not mark the sudden end of the *lex talionis*; the retaliatory system was too deeply rooted in Arabian society to be plucked out with ease, and indeed the Qur'ān even condoned retaliation. But it would be mistaken to conclude from this that the new notion of an absolute higher authority was ineffective or had no impact. For the retaliatory system, although it continued, was now brought within the framework of an overriding higher authority. Certain strict limitations were introduced into the system: believers were instructed, for example, to be satisfied with a single retaliation, to prefer blood-money to retaliation when the former was offered, and so on:

> O believers, prescribed for you is retaliation, touching the slain; freeman for freeman, slave for slave, female for female. But if aught

> is pardoned a man by his brother, let the pursuing be honorable, and let the payment be with kindliness.[20]
>
> And slay not the soul God has forbidden, except by right. Whosoever is slain unjustly, We have appointed to his next-of-kin authority; but let him not exceed in slaying; he shall be helped.[21]
>
> It belongs not to a believer to slay a believer, except it be by error. If any slays a believer by error, then let him set free a believing slave, and bloodwit is to be paid to his family unless they forgo it as a freewill offering. If he belong to a people at enmity with you and is a believer, let the slayer set free a believing slave. If he belong to a people joined with you by a compact, then bloodwit is to be paid to his family and the slayer shall set free a believing slave. But if he finds not the means, let him fast two successive months—God's turning; God is All-knowing, All-wise. And whoso slays a believer wilfully, his recompense is Gehenna. . . .[22]

Thus although retaliation continued, it was now the divine law that gave the believer permission to secure justice for himself, and even then, only under specified conditions that were laid out in the injunctions cited above and in similar passages. Furthermore, although Islam could not eliminate the vengeance system entirely, it did attempt to eliminate feuding, the endless and (from the point of view of divine law) unjustified pursuit of blood vengeance, which was the most pernicious aspect of the retaliatory system. The absence in Muḥammad's day of a specialized police force to punish offenders and maintain order undoubtedly had much to do with the continuation of the retaliatory system, since there was no personnel to bring an offender to justice unless the aggrieved himself performed this duty.[23] But the principle of a higher authority clearly stood behind and regulated the retaliatory system in a manner that was completely new. Although the limitations introduced may appear to be but minor rectifications of the retaliatory system (and in terms of actual practice they were), they nonetheless reflected a radical shift in the way disputes were to be viewed by society. Retaliation was now to be sought not because it was necessary to re-establish the potency of the aggrieved group, but because God had ordained that justice should be done and the wicked punished.[24] Thus in accepting Islam the believer was also required to accept the idea that feuding within the *umma* was not to be tolerated—an act that contributed much to the cohesiveness of the Islamic community.

The existence of a concept of an absolute higher authority is also reflected in the utterance "no confederacy in Islam" (*lā ḥilfa fī l-islām*) ascribed to Muḥammad. This phrase probably meant that special political alliances between smaller groups or individuals within the *umma* were no longer to be tolerated.[25] Rather, an individual's or group's political ties were now to be determined by the *umma* and its regulations: "The peace of the believers is one; no believer shall make peace separately from [another] believer, while fighting in God's way."[26] Thus, in principle at least, the *umma* eliminated conflicting political associations as it had eliminated internal feuding, insisting on the primacy of the absolute authority in establishing such relations. It need hardly be stressed that this would greatly augment the cohesiveness of the new state.

The advent of a notion of divine law that was the duty of believers to obey, then, set the stage for a more orderly approach to social and political relations. It may, furthermore, have eased the way for the rise of a state bureaucracy—so necessary to the functioning of a state, yet alien to the pre-Islamic political scene in northern and central Arabia. For with the acceptance of the idea of a supreme authority transcending tribal affiliations, it became possible for believers to accept administrators who were representatives of that authority. It was a situation in marked contrast to the pre-Islamic setting, in which only representatives of one's own tribe, or of a dominant tribe, would have been heeded.[27]

A third notion implicit in the new faith that proved of great importance for the consolidation of the *umma* and, ultimately, for the conquest movement, was the notion of centralization of authority. Islam's strict monotheism—the idea that there was but one locus of divine power in the universe—may have made it easier for Muslims to accept as well the idea of a single locus of political authority in the realm of worldly affairs. But more important in securing acceptance for the idea of centralized authority was Muḥammad's claim to prophethood, which made Muḥammad the only (or at least the only contemporary) channel of communication between the realm of the divine and the mundane world of the *umma*, the only link between the hot, dusty palm groves and barren crags of the Ḥijāz and the lush gardens of paradise. If one accepted the notion of God's oneness and Muḥammad's claim to be the Apostle of God—and this was the very minimum demanded of all Muslims—then it followed logically that all religious authority radiated from God *through Muḥammad*, that in the *umma* the absolute and all-embracing law of God was to be applied *by Muḥammad*, and that the guidance God provided to believers was to come *from Muḥammad*. Thus we find that some of the separate documents making up the "Constitution of Medina" conclude with the phrase: "Whenever you differ about a matter it must be referred to God and to Muḥammad."[28] Implicitly, then, Muḥammad was in a position to claim absolute religious and political authority in the *umma*, and, indeed, over the whole world.

Especially when linked with the prohibition of internal feuding within the *umma* and with the claim of the *umma* to control the political relations of its membership, Islam thus provided a very strong impetus for the centralization of political power in Muḥammad's hands. And yet this was not simply the creation of a great deal of personal power. Undoubtedly Muḥammad's personal appeal—his "charisma"—greatly helped his consolidation of power. But Muḥammad accrued power not merely because he was Muḥammad, but also—especially, it seems—because he was the leader of the new Islamic community. However strong a Muslim's personal attachment to Muḥammad may have been, his primary tie was not to Muḥammad at all, but to Islam, to God and His authority as enshrined in the laws of the *umma*, to the *umma* itself as the political manifestation of God's will for man. This meant that the consolidation of power in the *umma* and the centralization of that power in Muḥammad's hands, although greatly augmented in Muḥammad's lifetime by his position as God's apostle, did not prevent the ultimate transfer of authority after his death, because the real vehicle of authority was not in fact Muḥammad, but rather the community as a whole and the divine law that guided it. As the Qur'ān expressed it, "Those who swear fealty to thee swear fealty in truth to God. . . ."[29] Thus, from the point of view of the believer, the centralization of authority in the *umma* was both irresistible as long as Muḥammad lived and heritable by his successors after his death.[30]

Conversion to Islam thus opened the minds of converts to the acceptance of several social and political ideas that had the potential for revolutionizing the political life of seventh-century North Arabia.[31] The formulation of the *umma*, the concept of an overriding higher authority, and the strong tendency toward centralization of that authority provided powerful ideological underpinning for the rise of state institutions hitherto unknown in the region. A law providing the state with the justification for interfering, in principle, in a broad range of community affairs, a basis of definition for the community that extended beyond the tribe, a powerful centralized leadership, even the notion of administrators—all became somewhat more acceptable once the believer accepted Islam. The simple statement "There is no God but God, and Muḥammad is the apostle of God," which became the cornerstone of the Islamic faith, contained concepts that chipped away at the social and political particularism of pre-Islamic Arabian life and set the stage for the great process of integration and expansion that we call the Islamic conquests.

3. MUḤAMMAD'S CONSOLIDATION

Muḥammad's career was remarkable not only for his religious teachings, but also for his highly successful pursuit of political power. It was, indeed, the conjunction of new ideological factors with the growth of a new polity under Muḥammad's leadership that gave rise to the Islamic state. It is therefore important that we consider selected aspects of Muḥammad's political consolidation, although we cannot trace his political career in detail.

Three main themes can be discerned in Muḥammad's rise to power in Medina. The first was his struggle to establish himself firmly as ruler of Medina against the opposition of various powerful groups resident in the oasis—notably, the Jewish clans of Qaynuqā', al-Naḍīr, and Qurayẓa. He was ultimately able to consolidate his control over Medina, but only at the cost of exiling the first two and liquidating the last of the Jewish clans after earlier attempts to secure their support had been rebuffed.[32]

The second theme in Muḥammad's political career was his long struggle to humble the Quraysh in his native city, Mecca. His plundering of Meccan caravans and an early victory against the Meccans at the battle of Badr (A.H. 2/ A.D. 624) prompted the Meccans to respond with a campaign ending in the defeat of Muḥammad's forces at Uḥud (A.H. 3/ A.D. 625), and with an unsuccessful attempt to subdue Medina by siege at the battle of the Trench (A.H. 5/ A.D. 627). The struggle, which to this point appears to have been a stalemate, began to go increasingly in Muḥammad's favor only after a period of truce reached with the Meccans at al-Ḥudaybiya in A.H. 6/ A.D. 628. Eventually, Muḥammad was able to conquer Mecca (A.H. 8/ A.D. 630), partly because of increased tribal support and partly because of a famine in Mecca that Muḥammad exacerbated by means of a blockade of the city's food supplies.[33] The Meccans were treated leniently and incorporated as full partners in the now flourishing Islamic enterprise, only a handful of Muḥammad's bitterest opponents in Mecca being executed. With the support and participation of Quraysh, the Islamic state proceeded to expand at a rapid rate in the final few years of Muḥammad's life.

The third theme in Muḥammad's consolidation was the course of his relations with nomadic groups, first in the immediate vicinity of Medina, and then, as his power grew, increasingly far afield. At the outset he had little if any effective support from nomadic groups (at Badr, for example, no nomadic allies seem to have fought with the Muslims), but by the time of the conquest of Mecca he was backed by contingents from several nomadic tribes of the Ḥijāz. As he entered the last years of his career, nomadic groups increasingly found that they had to come to terms with the Islamic state, in part because it controlled the main agricultural and market centers in the Ḥijāz, upon which the nomads depended: Medina, Khaybar (conquered A.H. 7/ A.D. 628), Mecca (A.H. 8/ A.D. 630), al-Ṭā'if (A.H. 8/ A.D. 630). Indeed, it was after the defeat of the last powerful coalition in the Ḥijāz at Ḥunayn (A.H. 8/ A.D. 630) and the subsequent fall of al-Ṭā'if that there occurred the so-called "Year of Delegations" in which, if we are to credit our sources, tribal groups from as far away as 'Umān, al-Yamāma, and the Yemen came to Muḥammad seeking alliance.[34]

These three themes were pursued simultaneously and were to a considerable degree interdependent; success (or failure) in one domain had repercussions in the others. Thus the success against the Meccans at Badr appears to have strengthened Muḥammad's hand enough to allow him to exile the B. Qaynuqā', and the collapse of the Meccan siege of Medina at the battle of the Trench led to a swift and ghastly reckoning for the B. Qurayẓa, who had tried to help the Meccans during the siege. Similarly, Muḥammad's struggle with Mecca increasingly took the form of a race by each of the two parties to gain the support of nomadic allies in order to construct a coalition large enough to overpower the other.[35]

Muḥammad's consolidation of power in western Arabia was pursued in part by traditional means familiar to ambitious chieftains in the Arabian milieu. First of all, it seems that he was viewed as a paragon of the traditional virtues of leadership, as a poet of the Thaqīf made clear:

> I have neither seen nor heard of anyone like Muḥammad in the whole of mankind;
> Most faithful [is he], and generous to abundance when asked for a gift . . .
> Amid the dust [of battle] he is like a lion, [Standing] over its cubs in the den.[36]

Nor did Muḥammad himself object to using an appeal to traditional values to bolster his position, despite the fact that his teachings tore away at certain aspects of that very value system. Thus, Muḥammad's representatives held an oratorical and poetical "duel" with the orator and the poet from a delegation of B. Tamīm, after which the Tamīmīs marveled, "By God, his orator is more eloquent than ours, and his poet more skilled in poetry than ours. . . ."[37] Although the practice of such poetic and oratorical competitions hailed directly from the age of paganism (*jāhiliyya*), Muḥammad was willing and able to use them to his advantage. Muḥammad's poet, Ḥassān b. Thābit, consistently heaped scorn on Muḥammad's enemies not only for their stiff-necked opposition to God's will, but also for their failure to live up to traditional virtues. Thus we hear him berating 'Ikrima b. Abī Jahl, one of Muḥammad's bitterest opponents, after the battle of the Trench, in the following terms:

> As he cast his spear at us, he was already in flight.
> Perhaps, 'Ikrima, you have not had such an experience before!
> As you turned away to run like an ostrich,
> You certainly did not stray from the most direct way out!
> Nor did you turn your back in the manner of men—
> Rather, your nape was like that of a hyena.[38]

These and other verses fall nicely into the old Arabian tradition of *hijā'*, or satiric poetry intended to bolster one's own prestige and the prestige of one's tribe at the expense of one's enemies.

Muḥammad also knew how to bolster his own growing polity in traditional fashion by means of marriages. Thus we find that after the defeat of the obstreperous B. al-Muṣṭaliq (formerly among the *aḥābīsh* or tribal allies of Quraysh), from whom many captives were taken by the Muslims, Muḥammad married Juwayriyya bint al-Ḥārith b. Abī Ḍirār, the daughter of the tribe's chief, and paid off her ransom-money. As a result, not only was she freed from captivity, but the whole B. al-Muṣṭaliq was then considered to be related to Muḥammad by marriage, so that one hundred families of the tribe were also released from bondage.[39] The effect was to tie both the chief of the B. al-Muṣṭaliq and the bulk of the tribe to Muḥammad both through marriage and gratitude. Similarly, Muḥammad married the Jewess Ṣāfiyya bint Ḥuyayy b. Akhṭab, daughter of the "king" of Khaybar, after the capture of that city.[40] This in effect made Muḥammad the heir to political leadership in the town. In like manner, he appears to have married the sister-in-law of the man of B. Kilāb who was responsible for collecting the tax (*ṣadaqa*) on his tribe, although he divorced her before the marriage was consummated.[41]

Muḥammad also showed himself to be adept at using the promise of material gain, or the granting of gifts outright, in order to bolster the allegiance of important individuals. One such practice was the award of a share in the spoils seized after a battle or raid. Military successes by Muḥammad's forces, especially major victories such as that at Ḥunayn, from which there was a great deal of booty, meant an increased ability to attract and hold individuals who took occasion to think about their position in this world, as well as in the next.[42] Sometimes, too, leadership of a raiding party would be promised to a convert whose resolve needed reinforcement. When the influential Meccan ʿAmr b. al-ʿĀṣ embraced Islam after the truce of al-Ḥudaybiya, Muḥammad sent him to lead the raid on Dhāt al-Salāsil, which promised to be lucrative for the leader.[43]

In other cases, gifts were granted that were not directly related to military service, that is, they represented not merely a participant's normal share of booty, but a special gift granted from the Prophet's share of the booty, from tax revenues, or from other properties. His faithful follower Abū Bakr, for example, was given a house in Medina.[44] The best-known case of this kind involved large gifts assigned after the battle of Ḥunayn to certain prominent recent converts as a means of "conciliation of hearts," (*ta'līf al-qulūb*).[45] Important members of the Quraysh, along with the chiefs of the powerful B. Fazāra, B. Tamīm, and B. Naṣr nomads, were given gifts of one hundred camels apiece, to which a quantity of silver was sometimes added—a windfall far in excess of the normal share of booty.[46] Lesser grants of a similar nature were given to less influential recent converts at the same time.[47] Likewise, when the tribal delegations began to come to Muḥammad in the year after Ḥunayn (the so-called "Year of Delegations"), he rewarded those in the delegations who embraced Islam with "prizes" (*jawā'iz*),[48] presumably to bolster their pious resolve. At other times Muḥammad offered, not single grants, but income-bearing properties, as a financial reward. He is said to have given lands in Khaybar bearing 100 loads of dates annually to a group of allies from the Syrian tribe of Lakm called the Dāriyūn, to the Sabā'iyūn (a group from the South Arabian tribe of Sabā'?), to the Ruhāwiyūn (a group from Madhḥij who had settled in Medina), and to the Ashʿariyūn (a South Arabian tribe).[49] He rewarded Zayd al-Khayl, a chief among the Najdi warrior tribe of B. Ṭayyi', by giving him an oasis called Fayd,[50] and a convert of the B. Ja'da b. Kalb by awarding him an estate (*ḍay'a*) called al-Falj.[51] Most interesting of all, perhaps, was his award of tax incomes paid by certain tribes to a clan of the Balī tribe of the northern Ḥijāz as a means of winning them over to Islam.[52]

The use of wealth for political ends was, of course, nothing new in Arabia. It was a method open to use by any and all who could acquire enough wealth to buy support in this way. Indeed, the prevalence and importance of such material inducements in undertaking political consolidation are visible in the tradition that Muḥammad praised the delegation of the 'Abd al-Qays tribe as "the best people of the East" because "they came to me without asking for money."[53] The account implies that the distribution of largesse was seen as normal behavior, and even as obligatory, for a political chieftain. The importance of this factor in Muḥammad's efforts to build a political base, however, is to some extent a reflection of the great efflorescence of Meccan trade on the eve of Islam, which very probably made the populations of western Arabia (at least) more conscious of the uses to which wealth could be put and more familiar with its manipulation, and which certainly led to the accumulation of large amounts of wealth in Mecca itself. Both these considerations would have led Muḥammad to rely more heavily on the use of wealth in his political career than would have been likely, or even possible, a century earlier: first because West Arabians were in general more susceptible to the attraction of wealth than before, and may even have expected to receive some economic incentive in return for their support,[54] and second, because the Quraysh would undoubtedly use wealth in this way, making it difficult for Muḥammad to avoid doing so as well if he wished to continue his struggle with them. Besides, Muḥammad was himself a Meccan, so that the use of largesse would seem perfectly natural to him. Muḥammad was even able to profit somewhat from the fortunes that had been amassed in Mecca before Islam, through the wealth of a few of his early supporters (notably Abū Bakr and 'Umar b. al-Khaṭṭāb). He is reported to have said no man's wealth profited him as did that of Abū Bakr, and he apparently drew upon it as if it were his own.[55] Wealthy followers, especially 'Uthmān b. 'Affān, are said to have provided money and mounts to outfit the force that Muḥammad sent against Tabūk in the northern Ḥijāz in A.H. 9/ A.D. 630.[56] The great bulk of Mecca's wealth undoubtedly remained in Mecca, however, and it is therefore not surprising that the opposition of the wealthy Quraysh was viewed by Muḥammad as the main threat to his rising power.

Similar to the use of material inducements was the use of promises of participation in the affairs of the new Islamic regime. These we can expect to have been most effective in tying men of affairs to Muḥammad's state, since they naturally would have wanted to find scope for their talents and ambitions in the new political setting. Indeed, they seem to have been used mainly to win over the Quraysh, who came from the most sophisticated society in western Arabia. Despite their long opposition and late conversion to Islam, Muḥammad appointed a number of prominent Qurashis to important positions as military commanders, governors, or close advisers.[57] Not only were they, because of their skills, the natural pool of talent to tap for these positions, but their exclusion from such posts would have left them with a strong sense of grievance against the state that had taken from them their previously active role in Arabian politics. They may, in fact, have agreed to embrace Islam partly in return for a direct commitment from Muḥammad to admit them to the upper echelons of the circles of power in the Islamic state. Thus in a striking passage, we are informed that ʿAmr b. al-ʿĀṣ swore allegiance to Muḥammad "on the condition that my past sins be pardoned and that he [Muḥammad] give me an active part in affairs; and he did so."[58]

Muḥammad's consolidation of power was traditional also in that it relied upon a precise knowledge of the political and economic situation among the many tribal groups that he contacted. Only such an understanding of intertribal and intratribal rivalries could serve as a guide in building a coalition of many tribal groups. It was hardly an accident, for example, that, after his arrival in Medina, Muḥammad made early contact with the B. Mudlij and B. Ḍamra branches of Bakr b. ʿAbd Manāt b. Kināna; we can be sure that their history of enmity to the Quraysh was well known to him.[59] Likewise, Muḥammad's success in breaking the Meccan coalition that besieged Medina at the battle of the Trench was rooted in a lively awareness of the disparate interests of various groups in the coalition.[60] In other cases, rivalries over leadership within a given tribe allowed Muḥammad to gain first a foothold, and then a sizable following in the tribe as he played one faction off against another. This appears to have been the case with the Ḥijāzi tribe of B. Sulaym, who moved from an attitude of outright hostility to Muḥammad (most clearly seen in their ambush of his missionaries at Biʾr Maʿūna in A.H. 4/ A.D. 625) to one of support for Muḥammad (reflected in their contribution of a contingent of one thousand men to Muḥammad's force at the conquest of Mecca in A.H. 8/ A.D. 630). This growing support seems to have been linked in part to Muḥammad's ties to one of the many rival leaders in Sulaym, al-'Abbās b. Mirdās; some factions of the tribe probably remained lukewarm to Islam, however, and one of them[61] rebelled during the *ridda* wars after Muḥammad's death. It is possible that al-'Abbās b. Mirdās was able to rise to prominence in his tribe because of the backing he had from the Islamic state.[62] In a somewhat different vein, we see that if Muḥammad was able to break into existing political constellations, he was then able to use one part of the grouping to persuade or coerce others into the Islamic protection system. An example of this is provided by the course of relations between Muḥammad and the tribes of Bajīla and Khath'am. Both these tribes, along with a number of others, reportedly worshiped an idol called Dhū l-Khalaṣa in the Sarāt region;[63] that is, presumably these groups were part of a tribal confederation centered on the *ḥaram* of Dhū l-Khalaṣa, and participated in the kind of mutual security arrangements usually associated with such *ḥarams*. When one part of the B. Bajīla made a pact with Muḥammad, he sent the chief Jarīr b. 'Abdullāh al-Bajalī to smash the pagan idol his tribe had previously worshiped. In the course of his campaign, Jarīr—no longer, since his conversion to Islam, bound by the protection system of the *ḥaram* of Dhū l-Khalaṣa—attacked and killed some members of the tribe of Khath'am, his former allies. This ultimately forced the Khath'am, too, to enter Muḥammad's defense arrangements in order to ward off further attacks by the B. Bajīla; hence they sent a delegation to Muḥammad asking him to "secure us through God and his Apostle," which he did.[64]

Although the general tactics of such a tribal policy were undoubtedly familiar to most Arabians, the precise knowledge of the political situation among far-flung tribal groups in diverse corners of the peninsula upon which it rested was not something most Arabians would have possessed. It was a kind of knowledge, however, that could have been acquired in Mecca, which through its commerce had contact with tribes from all over the peninsula. Once again, we can see in Muḥammad's Meccan upbringing an important contribution to his later political success. As members of Quraysh, he and some of his early followers—such as Abū Bakr—had the specialized knowledge needed to work out the subtle details of assembling a tribal coalition.

Thus Muḥammad's political consolidation relied from the start on many methods traditionally employed in Arabia to build a base of power. He played one tribe against another and one clan within a tribe against others in order to isolate and weaken powerful rivals; he bound important followers to him and to his *umma* by marriage; and he used gifts of money, goods, lands, or influence when it was efficacious to do so. Most important, perhaps, was his fine political sense, which allowed him to judge whether an opponent was implacable and had to be ruthlessly crushed, or whether his loyalty could eventually be won; and, though he did not shrink from using force directly when it served his purposes,[65] he understood when leniency and restraint were more powerful than brute force itself. In short, not only did he use traditional means to build up his political base, but he used them exceedingly well. In this respect much of his success was due, of course, to his Meccan background. But the fact that he was ultimately able to overpower his teachers and arch-rivals in the art of political consolidation, the Quraysh in Mecca, despite their greater wealth, greater prestige, and broader range of tribal contacts throughout Arabia, is perhaps the greatest testament to his personal genius as politician and strategist. It is not every player, after all, who can beat his masters at their own game.[66]

From the point of view of the present discussion these traditional methods are significant because they led to Muḥammad's consolidation and because they would be resorted to again by Muḥammad's immediate successors during the *ridda* wars and the Islamic conquests, in order to preserve Medina's growing hegemony over the tribes of Arabia. As we noted earlier, however, it was not the extension of political control, but the maintenance of political cohesion, that was the perennial problem in Arabian political life. It is therefore essential to note that the embryonic Islamic state created by Muḥammad displayed certain features giving it considerably more cohesiveness and a more thoroughly centralized structure than was found in normal Arabian tribal confederations. It is in these novel features that the impact of the new ideology of Islam upon the solid political accomplishments of Muḥammad's career is most clearly visible—indeed, it was the new ideology that gave those accomplishments durability and made of them the foundation of the conquest movement. It is also in these features that the institutions of the state, as defined above, can first be discerned.

There was, first of all, apparently a more systematic approach to taxation in the new Islamic state than had hitherto prevailed in northern Arabia. Certainly the exaction of tribute or taxes by dominant groups was nothing new to the region, and it would be natural to expect that like earlier Arabian polities the Islamic state made regular demands for taxes on the various groups under its protection. Although the injunctions in the Qur'ān refer for the most part to voluntary almsgiving, the Qur'ān does berate, in the strongest terms, those who withhold their "voluntary" alms:

> Those who treasure up gold and silver, and do not expend them in the way of God—give them the good tidings of a painful chastisement, the day they shall be heated in the fire of Gehenna. . . .[67]

Indeed, those who are guilty of "hypocrisy," paying lip service to Islam but lacking true faith, should have a "freewill offering" (*ṣadaqa*) levied from them:

> And other[s] have confessed their sins; they have mixed a righteous deed with another evil. . . . Take of their wealth a freewill offering, to purify them and to cleanse them thereby, and pray for them; thy prayers are a comfort for them: God is All-hearing, All-knowing.[68]

There is, then, reason to think, both from the weight of traditional Arabian practice and from the Qur'anic injunctions, that tax payments, at least in the form of alms, were virtually required of all Muslims.[69] There was, however, an important distinction between the alms-tax to be levied by Muḥammad or by his agents, and taxes levied by pre-Islamic nobilities: namely, the fact that the alms of Muslims was restricted in incidence and in use in ways that may have made groups and individuals within the *umma* more willing to acquiesce to such financial demands. In the first place, those who were destitute were specifically exempted from paying the alms tax:

> O believers, . . . advance a freewill offering; that is better for you and purer. Yet if you find not means, God is All-forgiving, All-compassionate.[70]
>
> There is no fault in the weak and the sick and those who find nothing to expend, if they are true to God and to His Messenger.[71]

The freewill offerings (*ṣadaqāt*) were, furthermore, to be used for certain purposes only—in contrast to the way alms were abused by Jewish and Christian religious leaders:

> O believers, many of the rabbis and monks indeed consume the goods of the people in vanity and bar from God's way.[72]
>
> The freewill offerings (*ṣadaqāt*) are for the poor and needy, those who work to collect them, those whose hearts are brought together

(*al-mu'allafa qulūbu-hum*), the ransoming of slaves, debtors, in God's way, and the traveller; so God ordains; God is All-knowing, All-wise.[73]

The mention here of "those who work to collect" the freewill offerings is interesting and provides a hint as to how these collectors—presumably the same as Muḥammad's agents (*'ummāl*)—were paid.

Thus, what can be gleaned from the Qur'ān about the principles of the taxation system established by Muḥammad suggests that it was in theory regulated to prevent extortion, that all who were able were practically required to pay, and that the use of revenues collected was strictly defined. But the actual practice of taxation under Muḥammad is much more difficult to assess because only the most fragmentary evidence exists.[74] It seems clear that some communities of non-Muslims subject to the Islamic state, such as the Jewish colony at Khaybar, were required to pay a fixed tribute;[75] but the collection of taxes from groups of Muslims, or from those groups that appear to have included both Muslims and non-Muslims, is less clear. Various passages suggest that some nomadic groups may have been required to pay a form of tax even before they had converted to Islam,[76] whereas other nomadic groups—perhaps those that were more powerful—were able to remain exempt from taxation even after some of their chiefs had entered into alliance with Muḥammad.[77] It seems, however, that the disparity in these arrangements reflects the difficult conditions of the beginning and middle of Muḥammad's career, and that toward the end of his life he began to impose a more uniform and centralized control in his relations with these groups. Thus the earlier, purely "secular" alliances with tribal chiefs appear to have given way in the last few years to alliances that required formal submission to the *umma* and acceptance of Islam.[78] In the realm of taxation, Muḥammad made a broad effort to collect taxes from many tribal groups (which may hitherto have been merely allies supporting him in battle but not paying tax) at the time of the campaign to Tabūk in A.H. 9/ A.D. 630; the tribes of Aslam, Ghifār, Layth, Ḍamra, Juhayna, Ashja', Ka'b b. 'Amr, and Sulaym were taxed at this time.[79] The final stage in the process of systematization appears to have been taken in the beginning of A.H. 11/ A.D. March 632, when Muḥammad sent representatives to collect taxes from all tribes that were aligned with Medina.[80] He was to die shortly thereafter, leaving to his successor Abū Bakr the difficult task of coping with the tribes' efforts to evade this most unwelcome domination by the new Islamic state. But, though he was not to see its effective implementation, it seems clear that the creation of a centralized tax regime formed the culmination of Muḥammad's long and successful process of political consolidation.

Less spectacular and less well known than the centralization of taxation, but equally significant, are hints about the extension of a centralized legal authority over those areas controlled by Muḥammad and the *umma*. This imposition of the overriding legal authority of Islam, which we have seen to be inherent in Muḥammad's teachings, would have come as part of the political expansion of the Islamic state; the many treaties that Muḥammad drew up with various tribal groups, in which they are obligated to observe the regulations of Islam, almost certainly refer to regulations involving inheritance, torts, and the like, as well as ritual observance.[81] The centralization of legal authority is also reflected, in another way, in the following incident. The town of Jurash in the northern Yemen sent a delegation to Muḥammad and embraced Islam. In return for their submission, Muḥammad "gave them a special reserve (*ḥimā*) round their town with definite marks for horses, riding camels, and ploughing oxen. The cattle of any (other) man who pastured there could be siezed with impunity. . . ."[82] The creation of such a reserve affected, of course, not only the people of Jurash, but also all other inhabitants of the region who may, in the past, have pastured cattle in the vicinity of the new *ḥimā*. In effect it was an assertion by the Islamic state of absolute jurisdiction over grazing rights. It thus suggests both the centralization of legal authority, and (since such an ordinance would hardly have been set where it could not have been enforced) the effectiveness of that centralization.[83] Also interesting in this respect is the treaty made with the people of Najrān, a predominantly Christian community in northern Yemen. This document, if we can accept it as authentic, abolished at one stroke all blood-feuds dating from before Islam, made clear that those guilty of usury would not be protected by Muḥammad, and required that litigations between Najrānīs and other parties be decided "with equity without giving the people of Najrān the advantage over the other party, or giving the other party the advantage over them."[84] Thus, although it did not explicitly claim for Muḥammad or his representatives the exclusive right to adjudicate disputes, it did impose upon the community in question certain judicial principles to be followed in case of litigation. There also exists a group of accounts that suggest that Muḥammad verified the rights of many groups to occupy the districts in which they traditionally lived. A typical example is the pact with B. Ṭayyi': "The Apostle of God wrote [a document] for 'Āmir b. al-Aswad b. 'Āmir b. Juqayn al-Ṭā'ī [to the effect] that those lands and sources of water that he and his tribe, Ṭayyi', had possessed at the time of their conversion to Islam should remain theirs, as long as they performed prayer, brought the alms-tax (*zakāt*), and forsook the polytheists. Al-Mughīra was the scribe."[85] These brief documents are somewhat similar to those awarding estates or other tracts of land that we have already discussed. But in these cases they do not appear to be grants of new lands to individuals, but rather the registration of rights to lands long occupied by specific groups. The great number of such documents that survive suggests that Muḥammad was making an effort to eradicate the lawlessness of existing land tenure arrangements in favor of a much stricter regime of land rights. No longer would possession of certain districts be determined solely by the relative power of the different tribal groups contending for them; rather, a tribe's claim to certain territories was validated by Muḥammad and backed by the power of the Islamic state. Presumably, it was, then, the Islamic state that was responsible for adjudication of all disputes over land and water rights.

The implementation of a more centralized system of taxation and of justice than had hitherto existed was carried out mainly by agents (*'ummāl*) appointed by Muḥammad to oversee various tribal groups that had submitted to Islamic rule.[86] The appointment of agents was of course not completely unknown in northern and central Arabia; the states of the peripheries of the peninsula—Byzantines, Sasanians, and South Arabians—had at times installed agents or governors among various northern and central Arabian groups. But these had usually been sent to oasis settlements, whereas nomadic groups had been supervised by means of alliances with their own chiefs.[87] Muḥammad also used the latter approach at first in dealing with powerful nomadic tribes of the Najd such as sections of B. Tamīm; these appear to have initially concluded "secular" alliances (that is, alliances that did not require them to embrace Islam or to pay tax) with Muḥammad through their chiefs.[88] But in some other areas, especially throughout the Ḥijāz where his control was most firm, Muḥammad sent out trusted associates to supervise, it seems, both the settled communities and the nomadic tribal groups. Sometimes the agent was a relative or former ally of the group being administered, but even in such cases he was not necessarily one of the leaders within the group; rather, he might be chosen for his zeal for Islam. Exactly this seems to have occurred, for example, in the case of 'Uthmān b. Abī l-'Āṣ of

Thaqīf; although he was the youngest of the delegation of Thaqīf that came to Muḥammad, he was appointed governor of al-Ṭā'if by Muḥammad because of his zeal for Islam and knowledge of the Qur'ān.[89] In other cases, the administrator was unrelated to the group to which he was sent, whether nomadic or settled, although such agents probably worked with the active cooperation of the chief of the group. In appointing agents—direct representatives of his authority—to serve among various tribal groups, Muḥammad thus adopted a practice long used by the states on the Arabian fringes, but he modified it by extending it to nomadic as well as sedentary groups. It stood in marked contrast to the usual practice among tribal confederations in northern Arabia, which relied almost completely on alliances established through the tribal chieftains of the subordinated groups, and it also moved beyond the essentially personal tie that had hitherto marked much of Arabian politics.[90]

The duties of these agents probably varied from place to place, depending upon the terms under which the groups they supervised belonged to the *umma*,[91] but in general they were responsible for overseeing the collection and forwarding of taxes to Medina, and for rallying tribesmen when needed for military campaigns.[92] They may also have been responsible for providing religious instruction, such as teaching the Qur'ān and ritual prayer, in some cases.[93] As Muḥammad's direct representatives, they seem also to have been the persons to whom new Muslims took an oath of allegiance.[94] It is natural to assume that these agents also adjudicated disputes, or at least advised the person who actually performed the adjudication to assure that settlements were in accord with the general guidelines laid down by Muḥammad or the Qur'ān;[95] however, solid evidence for this function is not found in the sources. One passage does suggest that the agent had certain judicial powers; it states that the agent sent to 'Umān reports that the rulers there had accepted Islam and "have given me a free hand in matters of taxation and adjudication."[96] A clearer example of the adjudicating powers of the governor or agent comes only from the period of the Islamic conquests, thus, about five years after Muḥammad's death. In this incident a man of Muzayna who slapped the Ghassānid chief Jabala b. al-Ayham is hauled off to the Muslims' commander, Abū 'Ubayda, for judgment.[97]

The network of administrative agents created by Muḥammad corresponded roughly in extent to the limits of the Islamic state's control—itself a much debated point.[98] They were certainly widespread in the Ḥijāz, however, and probably in certain parts of the Yemen and the Najd as well. It is undoubtedly correct to say that they were "not officials of an impersonal state" and that they "worked more by persuasion than by coercion."[99] Yet their presence marks a key step in the transition from a purely personal kind of bond, such as had existed between tribal chiefs in earlier North Arabian confederations, to a more thorough political integration. For the primary loyalty of the agents—unlike that of subjected or allied tribal chieftains—was not to the group being administered, but to Muḥammad, to God, and to the *umma*. Their presence throughout much of the Islamic state represents, therefore, a considerable advance toward more fully centralized control.

Thus by the end of his career, Muḥammad had established a new state in western Arabia. Though constructed largely by traditional means, it was bound together by novel ideological and institutional factors that allowed it to transcend the usual forms of political organization in tribal confederations. The prevalance of an overriding concept of law, the focusing of political authority in God, the *umma*, and Muḥammad, the systematization of taxation and justice, the establishment of a network of administrative agents to supervise member groups—all these helped lend the new Islamic state a durability and a degree of centralized control over its subjects hitherto unknown to the area.

4. THE NEW RULING ELITE

The new state that Muḥammad had created began to transcend the tribal particularisms of Arabian life. Tribes and tribal loyalties continued to exist, of course, but there had been imposed on them a broader order that bound individuals and groups within the Islamic state to one another in ways that cut across tribal lines—through ideology (common faith and legal authority) and through practical measures (taxation, administration, and military service).

If the growth of Muḥammad's state was marked by the gradual transcendence of tribal particularisms, however, it was equally marked by the emergence of an increasingly distinct ruling elite within the Islamic state. Indeed, the rise of the state and the emergence of the ruling elite within the state appear to have been so intimately connected that it is impossible to envisage one process without the other. As the institutions of state control and centralization gradually became more evident, the new ruling elite became more sharply defined—and vice versa.

At the outset of Muḥammad's career in Medina, the Islamic community was very small—embracing only Muḥammad and a few loyal followers, mainly from Mecca and Medina—and, it seems, quite homogeneous. All Muslims were, both in theory and in fact, more or less equal in status within the early community. To be sure, some were closer to Muḥammad than others, but essentially the small, cohesive early *umma* was a highly egalitarian group. As the community grew gradually into a state, however, this situation changed. In the first place, the Islamic state was able to conquer several sizable settlements of Christians and Jews resident in Arabia, and these communities of non-Muslims were brought into the Islamic state and its protection system as subject communities, exchanging the payment of regular tribute for guarantees of protection and decent treatment by their new overlords.

The best-known cases of this tributary system involved the predominantly Jewish oasis of Khaybar in the northern Ḥijāz and the large Christian community at Najrān in the northern Yemen. The Jews of Khaybar capitulated to Muḥammad when he besieged the place in A.H. 7/ A.D. 628, and agreed to pay to the Muslims one-half the produce of the oasis annually as their tribute. This agreement was supervised by an administrator appointed by Muḥammad to act as assessor and assure that the crop was justly divided between the Islamic state and the Jews of Khaybar.[100] The Christians of Najrān may have made a similar kind of arrangement, although no army was ever sent by Muḥammad against them. Conflicting traditions exist regarding the terms of their submission, at least one of which outlines the rights and privileges guaranteed to the people of Najrān by the "protection (*jiwār*) of God and His Apostle" but makes no mention of any tribute to be paid by them.[101] Other accounts make it clear, however, that a certain share of the produce of Najrān was to be turned over to the Islamic state,[102] and we can assume that Muḥammad's agent to Najrān, his nephew and son-in-law 'Alī b. Abī Ṭālib,[103] was charged with supervising its assessment and collection, as his counterpart in Khaybar had been. These two examples probably reflect the situation of the many other less known communities of non-Muslims under the control of the Islamic state during Muḥammad's lifetime. Presumably the Jewish communities of Fadak, Wādī al-Qurā, Taymā, and elsewhere in the peninsula, as well as the many Christian communities (some of them nomadic groups) scattered throughout Arabia were reduced to the status of protected tributaries. The state that began to emerge was thus truly an Islamic state; any Muslim was identified with the state and its aspirations in a way that non-Muslims were not, and in a sense any Muslim, however humble, was superior in status to any non-Muslim, however wealthy or powerful.

The expansion of the state also meant, besides the absorption of such communities of non-Muslims, the inclusion of many new groups within the Islamic community itself. As the early community began to expand beyond the confines of Medina, bringing more and more outlying tribal groups under the shelter of the new state and into membership in the community, the earliest companions of Muḥammad—the Meccan Emigrants (*muhājirūn*) and the Medinese Helpers (*anṣār*) became more and more clearly the dominant group in the state.[104] It was the leaders of the *muhājirūn* and *anṣār* whom Muḥammad consulted on important matters. By comparison, somewhat later converts from outside Medina, even those drawn in at a relatively early date such as the tribes of the Tihāma coastal plain, held a somewhat lower position. In principle equals, they never could enjoy the prestige of having been among Muḥammad's supporters during those dark first months in Medina, or of having fought alongside Muḥammad at the critical early battles of Badr, Uḥud, or the Trench. Though their chiefs may have been consulted by Muḥammad—ever the consummate diplomat!—when decisions were to be made regarding military campaigns in their territory or in which their participation was important, it is not likely that even these chiefs held the position of honored advisers occupied by the leaders of the *muhājirūn* and chiefs of the *anṣār*.[105]

With the conquest of Mecca in A.H. 8/ A.D. 630 and the subsequent conversion of the Quraysh to Islam, the makeup and solidity of the ruling elite underwent a radical and rather sudden transformation. Muḥammad may have seen the utility of winning over this powerful group in order to further the process of consolidation on which he had embarked; at any rate, he used many means to win them over, including, as we have seen, special gifts to "reconcile their hearts" and promises of participation and influence. Despite their long opposition to Muḥammad, then, the Quraysh were thus brought into the Islamic state, not as subjected and despised enemies, but more as partners in an ongoing enterprise and members of the elite, through Muḥammad's conciliatory policy. Prominent members of Quraysh were, as we have seen, placed in important positions as agents of the state and seem to have been consulted by the Prophet in making policy. Their inclusion in the ruling elite of the Islamic state was very probably responsible for what appears to be the more carefully organized and systematic approach to statesmanship practiced by Muḥammad in the closing years of his life, as the organizational skills of the Quraysh were put to use in the service of Islam. To a lesser extent, the same policy seems to have been followed with respect to the Thaqīf of al-Ṭā'if, who may have been relieved of the usual burden of taxes (*zakāt*) imposed on most Muslims.[106]

Needless to say, the *muhājirūn* and *anṣār*, as early converts, tended to look askance at the favors bestowed upon the Meccan "upstarts" and viewed them with suspicion and hostility. But the result of this policy of inclusion was to create within the growing Islamic state a ruling elite that included not simply the earliest converts to Islam, but—more significantly, perhaps—all the sophisticated mercantile and managerial groups in the Ḥijāz. To the extent that the emerging elite was truly dominant in the state, then, the rise of the state represented the domination of the talented merchants and financiers of the Ḥijāz over other groups in the Ḥijāz and beyond. This hard distinction was, of course, somewhat blurred by the presence of certain allies of Quraysh or of the earliest Muslims who, by virtue of their alliances, appear to have occupied positions at least on the fringes of the ruling elite. There were present in Medina, for instance, a number of tribesmen who had been converted to Islam at an early date and had taken up residence there although they hailed originally from elsewhere in Arabia.[107] Similarly, the Quraysh appear to have had close allies, especially among the tribes of the Yemen, some of whom appear to have become prominent in affairs of state in the last year or so of Muḥammad's life. The tribes of Bajīla, Madhḥij, and perhaps Kinda, Ash'ar, and Azd fell into this category, although the exact nature of their relationships with the Islamic state remains poorly understood.[108] They would emerge later, however, as significant supporters of the Islamic state after the *ridda* wars and during the Islamic conquests. Despite the presence of these other groups on the fringes of the ruling elite, however, the elite was essentially composed of the early converts, the late converts from al-Ṭā'if, and, especially, the Quraysh. The degree to which the Quraysh had become identified with Islamic domination is neatly reflected in a traditional account about Maslama (Musaylima), a man of the B. Ḥanīfa in the Yamāma district of eastern Arabia who during Muḥammad's lifetime claimed also to be a prophet. At one point he is reported to have written to Muḥammad as follows: "From Musailima the apostle of God to Muḥammad the apostle of God: Peace upon you. I have been made partner with you in [this] affair; half the earth belongs to us, and half to Quraysh. . . ."[109] It is noteworthy that the account represents the Quraysh as being the dominant group, and, though it doubtless gives an exaggerated notion of their position, it nevertheless suggests clearly that the Quraysh were full partners—we might say senior partners—in the direction of the new Islamic state.

The rise of such a Ḥijāzi ruling elite exercising a measure of direct dominance over other tribal groups in the Islamic state implied, of course, the subordination of nomadic groups within the state to those sedentary groups that made up the elite. This in itself marked a significant shift from the normal pattern of power relationships prevailing between nomadic and sedentary segments of the population in northern and central Arabia, for, as we have seen, nomadic groups were usually the source of much real power in the region, or were at least potent enough to preserve their own autonomy. This situation was not, however, simply a fortuitous outgrowth of Muḥammad's consolidation; it was, rather, a conscious policy of Muḥammad's to bring nomadic groups firmly under the control of the Islamic state. Indeed, it seems that at first Muḥammad may have required any nomadic peoples who embraced Islam to abandon their nomadic way of life and to settle permanently in Medina or elsewhere—to make, that is, a *hijra* (literally, "settling") of their own. Thus when a delegation from the nomadic tribe of Muzayna came to Muḥammad in A.H. 5, they were instructed by the Prophet to make the *hijra* in their own tribal territory (*dār*). The term "*muhājirūn*," which was applied to them by Muḥammad, was not, furthermore merely a symbolic gesture granting them an honorary status as equals of Emigrants from Mecca (*muhājirūn*), but must be taken literally to mean that the Muzayna Muslims had in fact made a *hijra* themselves—that is, they had given up the nomadic life for permanent settlement.[110] Even more explicit was a pact that Muḥammad made with some early converts, which stated, "I grant to whoever of you settles (*hājara*) the same [duties and privileges] as I have taken for myself, whether he settles his [own] territory or resides in Mecca or [comes] to it as a pilgrim. . . ."[111] What is striking in this passage is the tacit exclusion of anyone who does not settle—who persists in the nomadic life—from the duties and privileges of full membership in the Islamic community; that is to say, one could not be a Muslim without being settled. The nomads could take one of two kinds of oath of allegiance to the state: the nomads' pledge (*bay'a 'arabiyya*) or the pledge of settlement (*bay'at hijra*). Only those who agreed to settle were promised full rights with other Muslims, whereas those nomads who, though Muslims, chose to remain in their own territories were to be as the *a'rāb* (nomadic allies) of the Muslims, subject to God's jurisdiction but having no share in any booty gathered.[112] In another passage, it again becomes evident that the term "*muhājirūn*" is not simply an honorific applied to early converts, but refers to actual sedentarization (*hijra*) in Medina or elsewhere. In this case, nine men of the B. 'Abs came to Muḥammad; they were, we are told, among the earliest *muhājirūn*. The Prophet told them that if they could locate one more man so that they would total ten in number, he would honor them with their own battle-standard (*liwā'*). At this point Ṭalḥa b. 'Ubaydallāh—an early convert from Quraysh and definitely a townsman—entered and joined them, so they received their standard and were made a military unit whose battle-slogan became, we are told, "Oh ten!"[113] It is difficult to see in what way the ten could have been deemed a unit if nine of them had been perpetually absent from Medina tending their flocks. It is therefore fair to assume that, since the ten fought together as a unit, the nine from B. 'Abs were truly settlers in Medina, where the tenth man, Ṭalḥa, was resident. Yet another passage reveals that at an early stage in Muḥammad's career, he preached that nomadic life was incompatible with Islam. Three men of the B. 'Abs came to him and declared, "Our Qur'ān reciters[114] have come to us and informed us that there can be no Islam to anyone who has not taken up a permanent settlement.[115] Now, we have flocks and herds that form our livelihood; if there is indeed no Islam to those who do not settle, [tell us] and we shall sell them and settle."[116] Again, the import is clear: to be a Muslim, one had to lead a settled life.

Thus there seems to have been, at least at an early stage in Muḥammad's career, a definite policy of requiring Muslims to be—or to become—settled people. As the number of converts from nomadic groups rose, however, this policy became increasingly difficult to implement. The Prophet appears to have changed his tack already by the time that the three men of B. 'Abs came to him, in fact, for he is said to have instructed them to "believe in God wherever they were" and seems to have permitted them to remain nomads. It is clear, too, that by the end of his career the Islamic community included both sedentary peoples and a great many nomadic groups. But the nomadic groups remained virtual subjects of the Islamic ruling elite composed of sedentary peoples; though Muslims, they remained essentially outside the circles of influence in Medina. An interesting passage mirrors how firmly Muḥammad barred even powerful nomadic chieftains from the emerging elite. When the nomadic B. 'Āmir b. Ṣa'ṣa'a sent a delegation to Muḥammad, their chief (the famous poet 'Āmir b. al-Ṭufayl) asked the Prophet what he would give him if he embraced Islam. The Prophet replied that if he became a Muslim, he would have the same rights and duties as any other Muslim. 'Āmir pressed the Prophet with "Won't you give me authority after you?" to which Muḥammad responded, "That is not for you nor for your tribe." 'Āmir then asked the Prophet to let him be in command of the nomadic peoples, with Muḥammad in command of the settled peoples, an offer that Muḥammad similarly refused.[117] This reluctance on Muḥammad's part to grant the B. 'Āmir too much authority because they were the wrong tribe (i.e., a nomadic tribe?) is quite striking when contrasted with the relatively free access to positions of authority enjoyed by the Quraysh, the Thaqīf, and the Medinese *anṣār*.

The accession of Quraysh and, perhaps, certain other sedentarized groups to the ruling elite after the conquest of Mecca and the conversion of the B. Thaqīf of al-Ṭā'if strengthened, if anything, the state's tone of dominance toward the nomadic peoples. The Quraysh, after all, were the most cultivated society of western Arabia and would have held the bedouin to be boorish and crude. Whereas the Quraysh prided themselves on their *ḥilm*—self control, firmness mingled with compassion—the bedouin were seen by them as "wild men," excitable, boisterous, and impulsive; in short, marked by behavior that was precisely the reverse of the Meccans' ideal.[118] Their general attitude toward the bedouin can be seen in an episode that took place before their conversion to Islam, at the time of the truce of al-Ḥudaybiya, when a man of B. Kināna whom they had sent out to spy on Muḥammad's activities returned with a glowing account of the Muslims' preparations for ritual sacrifice. This report the Quraysh dismissed with the comment, "Sit down! You are only a nomad, you know nothing."[119] Like Muḥammad himself, the proud Quraysh were certainly not of a mind to let the turbulent nomadic groups slip out of their control or to allow them to acquire much influence in ruling the state—a task for which the sedentary peoples of the elite doubtless considered the nomads totally unqualified.

In sum, the simultaneous rise of the Islamic state and of a ruling elite within the Islamic state represented the emergence of three kinds of domination. First, it marked the hegemony of Muslims over non-Muslims; second, the dominance of an essentially Ḥijāzi ruling elite over other tribal groups; and third, it marked the hegemony of a sophisticated sedentary elite and their state over nomadic groups. These divisions were not absolutely rigid, of course. In the first place, they overlapped. Further, there were numerous exceptions, some more readily explainable than others, to the pattern described. Finally, the structure of the Islamic state and nature of its hegemony were, at the time of Muḥammad's death, still very much in the process of crystallizing out of the mother-liquor of Arabian society. But to the degree that we can speak of the hegemony of the Islamic state at the end of Muḥammad's career, we must describe it in these terms.

5. ABŪ BAKR AND THE *RIDDA* WARS

Muḥammad's death in A.H. 11/ A.D. 632 plunged the Islamic state into a period of intense crisis. It raised the question of leadership of the Islamic community, and even of the political unity of the community, in the most pointed way; and it also encouraged movements of opposition to the Islamic state in many parts of the Arabian peninsula, some of which had been under Islamic domination, others of which had merely been watching with increasing concern the growing might of Muḥammad's new state.

Before facing the threat posed by these opposition movements, however, it was necessary for the ruling elite itself to decide how the state was to be led after Muḥammad's death, and, indeed, whether the polity assembled by Muḥammad could and should remain politically unified. Had the emerging elite been thoroughly cohesive, the second issue might never have arisen, and the first might have been easily settled. But, as we have seen, the elite had come by the end of Muḥammad's career to include several different groups that felt a rivalry toward one another. With Muḥammad no longer present to act as arbiter, the smoldering antagonisms among the *anṣār*, the *muhājirūn*, and the new converts of Quraysh and Thaqīf burst into full flame. The *anṣār*, in particular, appear to have been on the verge of choosing their own chief (or chiefs), and they urged the Quraysh (both the *muhājirūn* and the recent converts) to do the same; "let there be one ruler among us, and one among you, Oh Quraysh,"[120] they told a small delegation of *muhājirūn* who came to discuss the question of the succession with them. Clearly the *anṣār* were disenchanted enough with the position enjoyed by the Quraysh that they yearned for a return to "home rule." Besides, many of them may have questioned the whole concept of a succession to Muḥammad's unified authority; after all, had he not taught that he—alone—was the apostle chosen to bring mankind the final revelation of God's will? Was he not the "seal of the prophets," the last in the series that began with Adam? In what way, then, could he have a successor? Let the separate tribal groups in the Islamic state remain faithful to Islam, then, but let them choose their own chieftains. It was the stiffest challenge that the deep-rooted tradition of Arabian political particularism was to raise to the integrative principles of the Islamic state for many decades.

That this challenge was ultimately met, that the notion of an integrated and relatively centralized Islamic political unit ultimately triumphed in the form of Abū Bakr's election as Muḥammad's caliph (*khalīfa*, "successor"), was not inevitable. The traditional accounts make the tumultuous character of the debate over the succession quite clear and suggest that Abū Bakr's election was the result both of the persuasive rhetoric of the *muhājirūn* and of the decisiveness of 'Umar b. al-Khaṭṭāb, who boldly swore allegiance to Abū Bakr in the thick of the deliberations and thereby galvanized the whole assembly into concurrence.[121] Had the *muhājirūn* arrived at the deliberations too late, or had they said or done the wrong thing, the *anṣār* might have chosen their own leaders and rejected the notion of political unification with the Meccans. There were, however, several factors at play that contributed to Abū Bakr's recognition as the heir to Muḥammad's political functions and that made him the obvious candidate for the succession once it had been generally agreed that there should in fact be a successor.[122] First, he was universally respected for the depth of his attachment to Islam and for his loyalty to Muḥammad. One of the earliest converts, he is said to have been a friend of Muḥammad's even before Islam,[123] and he continued to be one of the Prophet's most intimate companions throughout his life. When Muḥammad instructed his persecuted followers in Mecca to make their way to safety in Medina, it was Abū Bakr whom he asked to remain behind with him in Mecca until the last moment, and who then made the dangerous passage to Medina alone with him. Abū Bakr it was also who, when the Prophet instituted the general tax late in his career, chose to contribute, not half his fortune (as several other prominent companions had done), but the whole of it, to the state treasury. When Muḥammad asked him what he had left his family, he responded simply, "I left them God and his Apostle."[124] On grounds of piety and loyalty to the interests of Islam, then, his credentials were impeccable.

A second factor in his favor was his acceptability to all parties in the elite. He appears to have been simple and direct in his manner, and so enjoyed the confidence of each group. Raised a Meccan, he seems to have been able to assure the late converts of Quraysh that he would continue to give them a significant role to play in affairs of state, as the Prophet had done before him—a promise he indeed kept. At the same time, however, he was, because of his long and close association with Muḥammad, both familiar to and trusted by the *anṣār*, and he was evidently able to convince them that they would not be dominated by the Quraysh.

Finally, Abū Bakr was the natural choice to be Muḥammad's political successor because he seems to have had special talents in this sphere of activity and may in fact have been instrumental in the formulation of tribal policy during Muḥammad's lifetime. He was, we are told, one of the two men of Quraysh who were specially renowned for their political sagacity (*ḍāhiya*).[125] Furthermore, he was famed as an expert in tribal genealogies[126] and seems to have served as Muḥammad's adviser on genealogy. This function is revealed, for example, in an episode reported to have taken place when Muḥammad was establishing contact with the bedouin tribes and calling them to Islam. Muḥammad and his followers came upon a bedouin tribal council (*majlis min majālis al-'arab*), but it was Abū Bakr who was singled out by Muḥammad to engage the gathering in conversation, and to identify them, which he did by means of a lengthy cross-examination showing clearly his great knowledge of the various tribes and their subordinate groups.[127] The account, even if a later fabrication, shows that Abū Bakr enjoyed the reputation of being very knowledgeable in genealogies and reveals that he was remembered as the companion of Muḥammad responsible for handling the Apostle's contacts with the tribes. Nor was this genealogical expertise merely an academic accomplishment; the tribal basis of Arabian political life meant that to have a precise knowledge of a tribe's genealogy—which, we must recall, was at heart an expression of alliances and rivalries within the tribe—was to have important insights into the political structure of the tribe. The genealogist was, then, a kind of political specialist; he understood not only lines of filiation, but something of the power structure of tribal groups. Abū Bakr was, then, eminently suited to be Muḥammad's adviser on tribal policy, which he probably helped to shape. For the same reason he became a logical choice for the succession. At the time, the main task facing the Islamic state and the ruling elite was to overcome the tribal opposition to Islamic domination that had sprung up all over the peninsula—that is, to prosecute a successful tribal policy that could coax, cajole, or coerce the tribes of Arabia into the state. What more natural choice for the succession than Abū Bakr, who by knowledge and experience was the acknowledged master of this subtle kind of diplomacy?[128]

Once the succession had been agreed upon, Abū Bakr turned his attention to the difficult task of consolidating the Islamic state's power in Arabia. The opposition movements that had arisen took one of two forms. One group challenged both the political control of Medina and the religious claims of Islam by proposing rival ideologies; the leaders of these movements posed as prophets and political leaders much in the manner of Muḥammad himself. This category included the rebellion of B. Asad in the Najd, led by the "false prophet" Ṭalḥa b. Khālid,[129] the opposition of the B. Ḥanīfa in al-Yamāma, led by the "false prophet" Maslama b. Ḥabīb,[130] the movement of parts of B. Tamīm and B. Taghlib in northeastern Arabia, led by the "false prophetess" Sajāḥ, who ultimately joined forces with Maslama and the B. Ḥanīfa, and the rising of the B. 'Ans in the Yemen, led by al-Aswad al-'Ansī, who also claimed prophethood. There was, in addition, a second class of movements that had a more strictly political character. In some cases it took the form of a tax rebellion against the Islamic state, such as among the B. Fazāra, the branches of B. Asad,[131] and among parts of the B. Tamīm,[132] all in the Najd and all groups that had earlier been brought within the state. In other cases, such as among the Rabī'a tribes led by al-Huṭam in al-Baḥrayn, among the Azd in 'Umān, among the B. Kinda led by al-Ash'ath b. Qays in Yemen, and among the Khawlān, also in the Yemen, a struggle arose among local factions, some of whom were allies to the Islamic regime whereas others, encouraged by Muḥammad's death, tried to prevent the spread of Islamic control. None of these movements seem to have involved an outright rejection of Muḥammad's prophetic mission, as the movements led by "false prophets" did, but they did oppose the extension of the political control of the Islamic state.[133]

The Arabic sources call all these movements collectively the *ridda*, "apostasy" or "repudiation" (of Islam) and thus at least imply that all were equally acts of blasphemy that deserved military supression by the new state. Recent scholarship has taken exception to the traditional Islamic view and argued that not all the movements can truly be called *ridda*—some because they involved no rejection of the religious teachings of Islam (e.g., in al-Baḥrayn, 'Umān, or among the B. Fazāra), others because the group in question had never made any agreement to recognize Muḥammad as prophet or to embrace Islam (e.g., the B. Hanīfa).[134] For those concerned with the political consolidation of the early Islamic state, however, these distinctions are less significant than they are for students of religious aspects of Islamic rule. From the political point of view, every *ridda* movement represented at heart an attempt to oppose the hegemony of the Islamic state based in Medina. This was as true of those movements whose members declared themselves loyal to Islam but refused to pay the tax to Medina as it was of those movements that rejected as well Muḥammad's claim to prophecy, and it applied as much to movements arising in areas once under direct Islamic rule (e.g., in the Najd) as to those arising in areas never under Islamic rule (e.g., in al-Yamāma) that wanted to remain free thereof. The term "*ridda*," as a general term to identify all these movements, thus retains some usefulness. The *ridda* itself represented a massive challenge to Islamic domination of the Arabian peninsula, and the *ridda* wars saw the completion of that process of political consolidation by the Islamic state that had begun under Muḥammad's leadership. Seen in this light, it is really of secondary importance whether a specific group or area was subjected by Muḥammad and had to be reconquered by Abū Bakr, or whether it was subjected for the first time by Abū Bakr.[135] What is significant is that the political consolidation begun by Muḥammad continued with but slight interruption under Abū Bakr, so that by the time of the latter's death the new Islamic state had successfully conquered the entire Arabian peninsula.

Abū Bakr's objective was very simple: to extend the hegemony of the Islamic state over the entire population of Arabia and, in particular, over all the nomadic tribal groups—for we can be fairly certain that he understood the importance of maintaining firm control over powerful nomadic groups if the state was to survive. His response to the various *ridda* movements was, in part, to send troops to subdue them. Khālid b. al-Walīd of Makhzūm (Quraysh) was dispatched with a force of *muhājirūn* and *ansār* to suppress the various risings in the Najd and to counter the most serious of all the opposition movements, that of the B. Ḥanīfa in al-Yamāma. At about the same time, Shuraḥbīl b. Ḥasana (of Kinda, but raised in Mecca as an ally of the B. Zuhra of Quraysh)[136] was sent to the Najd and appears to have joined forces with Khālid. Al-'Alā' b. al-Ḥaḍramī (from Ḥaḍramawt, but an ally of the B. Umayya of Quraysh)[137] was directed to go to al-Baḥrayn (eastern Arabia), where he fought the rebellion among the Bakr tribes. 'Ikrima b. Abī Jahl and Ḥudhayfa b. Miḥṣan, both of the B. Makhzūm (Quraysh), and 'Arfaja b. Harthama al-Bāriqī (from the 'Asīr?),[138] were sent to conquer 'Umān and the Mahra country in southeastern Arabia, and al-Muhājir b. Abī Umayya of Makhzūm (Quraysh) and Khālid b. Asīd of B. Umayya (Quraysh) were sent against the Yemen, to help Medina's governor there, Ziyād b. Labīd al-Anṣārī, in bringing it under firm control. Closer to home, Ṭurayfa b. Ḥājiza al-Sulamī was dispatched to put down a minor rising among part of his tribe of Sulaym, near Medina, and Suwayd b. al-Muqarrin al-Muzanī was sent to the Tihāma coastal strip, where he was, perhaps, responsible for maintaining order among the nomadic tribes.[139]

In addition to these military measures, Abū Bakr also resorted to diplomacy to accomplish his aim of bringing all of Arabia under Islamic control. He seems to have reached some kind of agreement with one section of the powerful B. Shaybān on the fringes of Iraq, resulting in a cooperative military venture between the leader of this section, al-Muthannā b. Ḥāritha, and Khālid b. al-Walīd, who was sent there after the repression of the rising in al-Yamāma. This episode marked the beginning of the extension of Islamic control to the Arab tribes and Arab towns along the Euphrates—and simultaneously initiated a clash with the Sasanian Empire. In a similar way, he sent 'Amr b. al-'Āṣ and Khālid b. Sa'īd north to the tribes on the fringes of Syria, some of whom had embraced Islam before Muḥammad's death, others of whom were persuaded to join the Islamic state for the first time.[140]

The careers of Muḥammad and of Abū Bakr thus together form a single phase in the continuing story of the rise of the Islamic state to power in Arabia. This continuity is marked not only in the process of consolidation itself, but also in the methods employed—a fact that need hardly surprise us in view of the important role Abū Bakr had played in the formulation of Muḥammad's tribal policy. Like Muḥammad, Abū Bakr used wealth and marriage—in addition to force—to win over former enemies and to tie them, with their sometimes important skills or large tribal followings, to the new state. We find, for example, that a member of the B. Ḥanīfa who sided with the Muslims when the bulk of his tribe backed the "false prophet," Maslama, was rewarded by Abū Bakr with the grant of an estate (*aqṭa'a-hu*) in a place called al-Khiḍrima.[141] Similarly, it is reported that the rebel al-Ash'ath b. Qays al-Kindī repented and came once again to pay allegiance to Islam; later, Abū Bakr agreed to let him settle in Medina and agreed to let him marry his sister, Umm Farwa. Later, in the caliphate of Abū Bakr's successor, 'Umar b. al-Khaṭṭāb, al-Ash'ath joined the Muslim forces sent to conquer Iraq.[142]

The *ridda* wars thus formed an extension of Muḥammad's career in that they continued the consolidation of the Islamic state's rule over Arabia; but they also represented the continuation of the second theme in the emergence of the new state, namely, the rise of a ruling elite within the Islamic state itself. By the end of the *ridda* wars, the Islamic ruling elite was more firmly entrenched than ever before. The sedentary elements from the Ḥijāz—Medinese, Meccans, and Thaqafis from al-Ṭā'if—had remained a united bloc once the succession crisis had been resolved by Abū Bakr's election; and, together with a few nomadic allies from the Ḥijāz and certain segments of other tribes whose leaders had allied themselves firmly with Muḥammad at an early date, they formed the hard kernel of Islamic supremacy, which was able to reassert itself through their efforts. All the major campaigns of the *ridda* wars were led by generals drawn from this ruling elite of sedentary townsmen, and the core of the force sent to the Najd and al-Yamāma, at least, appears to have been drawn from the *muhājirūn, anṣār*, Quraysh, and Thaqīf.

At the completion of the *ridda* wars, then, Arabian society consisted of three rather clear-cut political strata. On the top was the Islamic ruling elite—within which, we might note, the Quraysh appear to have been occupying a more and more prominent place. Just under them were those nonelite tribesmen who had backed Medina during the *ridda* wars and had participated in the Islamic conquest of Arabia. These seem to have included the B. Aslam, B. Ghifār, B. Muzayna, B. Ashja', B. Juhayna, B. Ka'b b. 'Amr, parts of the B. Sulaym (all essentially nomadic groups from near Medina in the Ḥijāz), parts of the B. Ṭayyi' (perhaps only the branches of Jadīla and al-Ghawth), parts of the B. Tamīm, and perhaps sections of the B. Asad and B. Ghaṭafān, all from the Najd, and probably the B. Bajīla and various sections of Yemeni tribal groups that remained loyal to Medina, such as the B. Sakūn of Kinda.[143] In addition, the northern Ḥijāzi or Syrian tribes that did not rebel against Medina were probably in this category, although they also did not participate in the *ridda* wars; they included the B. Bali, B. 'Udhra, and parts, perhaps, of the B. Quḍā'a, such as the B. Kalb.[144] These tribal allies of the Islamic ruling elite certainly played an important role in military ventures, but they were seldom if ever seen in positions of authority; though part of the Islamic regime, they were certainly not part of the ruling elite that shaped policy.

Beneath these two groups was what we can call the class of conquered Arabs—those tribesmen who had unsuccessfully resisted the spread of

Medina's hegemony and had been subdued in the *ridda* wars. The conquered or subject Arab tribes (e.g., the B. Ḥanīfa, probably most of the B. Asad, etc.) remained, for the time being, in their traditional territories and pursued their usual way of life (be it pastoralism, agriculture, artisanry, or trade), but played no active part whatsoever in the Islamic state. They formed, simply, the administered population of Arabia, subject to the Islamic ruling class, to which they paid taxes in return for the regime's protection against external interference and its services in adjudicating their tribal disputes. As former rebels, they were deemed untrustworthy, and in order to keep them under control Abū Bakr appears to have taken prisoners from these subjected tribes to hold hostage as a guarantee of the tribes' continued good behavior.[145] Thus, after the siege of the fortress of al-Nujayr in the Yemen, the Muslims took captives from the B. Kinda; these were ransomed by the repentant Kindite chief, al-Ash'ath b. Qays, only some time later.[146] Nor was this merely an isolated incident; the practice of taking captives was generally applied to the rebel tribes, as is indicated by a passage informing us that the first act taken by 'Umar b. al-Khaṭṭāb upon becoming caliph (in A.H. 13/ A.D. 634) was "to return the prisoners of the people of the *ridda* to their tribes."[147]

The *ridda* wars thus represent the culmination of that general process of political consolidation begun by Muḥammad by which an Islamic ruling elite established full control over the tribal population of the whole Arabian peninsula. They represent, too, the culmination of that process by which the new state, run by sedentary tribesmen, attained virtually complete control over the nomadic sector of the Arabian population, which had traditionally been able to avoid such domination. This control was expressed most clearly in the annual tax paid by the Arabian tribes to the Islamic state—the imposition of which seems to have been instrumental in sparking some of the *ridda* rebellions.[148]

If the period of the *ridda* wars formed the culmination of those processes begun in Muḥammad's career, however, it was simultaneously the beginning of something new—the Islamic conquest movement that so transformed the face of the ancient world. It was, first of all, the efforts of the Islamic state to extend its domination to all Arab tribal groups—including those in the steppes and towns of Iraq and Syria—that led to the first direct clashes between the new Islamic state and the Byzantine and Sasanian Empires. But the conquests also developed from the events of the *ridda* wars in a more integral way. For it was the firm subjugation of the nomadic warrior tribesmen of Arabia by the Islamic state that put into the hands of the new ruling elite the means to undertake an expansionist movement of unparalleled proportions. We shall turn to the structure of this expansionist movement into Syria and Iraq in subsequent chapters, but we must never forget that the conquest of those regions was preceded and made possible by the Islamic conquest of Arabia.

The Islamic conquest of the Near East cannot be viewed, then, as something separate from the career of Muḥammad the Apostle or from the conquest of Arabia during the *ridda* wars. It must be seen as an organic outgrowth of Muḥammad's teachings and their impact on Arabian society, of Muḥammad's political consolidation, pursued by traditional and novel means, and especially of his efforts to bring nomadic groups firmly under state control, and of the extension of that process of consolidation by the Islamic state and its emerging elite under the leadership of Abū Bakr. These elements, together, formed the foundations on which the Islamic conquest movement rested.

CHAPTER III

THE CONQUEST OF SYRIA

1. THE LAND BETWEEN TWO SEAS

Syria is a geographical extension of Arabia.[1] The topographical configurations that characterize the Arabian peninsula—that great slab of limestone, lifted up at its western and southern edges to form the steep coastal ranges of the Ḥijāz and the Yemen, and sloping gradually down toward sea level at the Persian Gulf—are repeated in Syria's parallel ranges of mountains, running along the Mediterranean coast, and in the flatter expanses of the Syrian steppe, sloping gradually downward toward Iraq. Within this basic topographical pattern there is, of course, considerable local variation. The Mediterranean coastal range, which rears up along the central Syrian littoral to form the towering barrier of Mount Lebanon, is much lower along the northern coast of Syria in the Jabal Ansariyya area and becomes little more than a set of rolling hills in Palestine. In general, however, the mountain folds become lower and less dramatic as one moves inland from the Mediterranean coast, across the Lebanon range, the Anti-Lebanon, the Jabal al-Ruwāq, and so on, until the ridges finally give way to form the essentially level Syrian steppe. The main exception to this pattern, the massive pyramid known as Mt. Hermon that rises out of the southern end of the Anti-Lebanon, does not alter the general picture.

Though Syria's topography continues that of Arabia, however, its landscapes are tempered and made more gentle than Arabia's by their more northerly location and, particularly, by the proximity of the Mediterranean Sea, whose moist breezes leave rain in quantities unknown to the Arabian Peninsula itself. This gift of moisture is not bestowed equally on all parts of Syria, of course. As the prevailing westerly winds carry the moisture-laden clouds eastward, over the successive chains of mountains and hills, the water is increasingly coaxed out of them, so that by the time they reach the central Syrian steppe there is relatively little moisture left. Thus the coastal ranges receive several months of heavy rainfall, mainly during the winter and spring, whereas the central steppe is favored only with a few inches during the course of the year and begins to display, during the driest summer months, the truly desert conditions found farther south in Arabia proper. In areas where rainfall is sufficient, however, it has permitted the cultivation of crops by dry-farming, something virtually unknown in northern and central Arabia (though practiced in limited measure in the Yemen, as we have seen). The green hills of Palestine, the tangled thickets and dense, wooded ravines of Lebanon, the fertile open basins of the Litani, Orontes, and Jordan rivers, carrying the runoff of mountain springs and seasonal rain and snow, all give Syria a general aspect of verdure and moisture unknown to Arabia. It is little wonder that Arabians viewed Syria as a kind of paradise on earth, a land of prosperity and plenty and of blessed relief from the heat and aridity of the peninsula.[2]

Syria has, over the centuries, derived more than mere vital moisture from the Mediterranean, however. Its location on the Mediterranean's eastern shore meant that it was also reached by the larger currents of various Mediterranean civilizations. By the time of the rise of Islam, Syria had been exposed to, and dominated by, Hellenistic culture from the days of Alexander and his successors through the long centuries of Roman and Byzantine rule.[3] Coming by sea, or by land to these shores familiar to them because of earlier contacts by sea, the various bearers of Greek language and Greco-Roman culture established themselves in Syria, especially in the towns and cities ranged up and down the coast and in the fertile, rain-fed districts a short distance inland. These towns, which drew their economic support from the high productivity of Syria's valleys and cultivated hillsides, received cultural sustenance from a steady flow of intellectual currents and stylistic tastes that pulsated from the West together with more mundane articles of commerce along the arteries of international maritime trade. Thus many of these urban centers were not only major Syrian cities; they were also great centers of Greco-Roman civilization. Antioch gave birth to the orator Libanius and his pupil Chrysostom; Beirut (Berytus) was one of the main centers for the study of Roman law; Gaza and its school produced the famous sophist Procopius.

The Hellenistic impact on Syria was, however, always a bit artificial, and Hellenistic culture always something imposed on Syria from above. Even after nearly ten centuries of exposure to Greek language and Greco-Roman culture, the great mass of the Syrian populace remained thoroughly Semitic. Syrians never embraced the Greek tongue or Greek

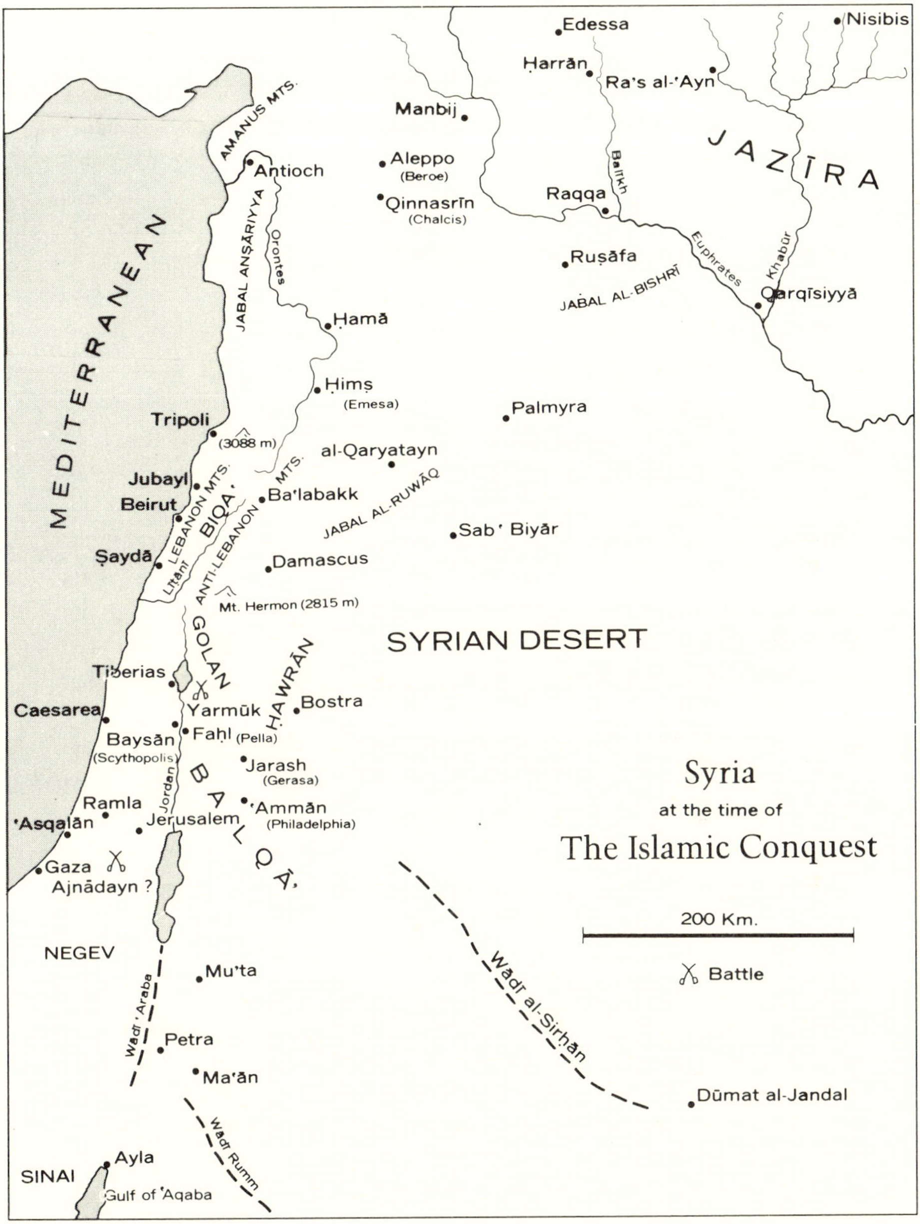
Syria
at the time of
The Islamic Conquest
200 Km.
Battle
Edessa
Nisibis
Ḥarrān
Ra's al-'Ayn
Manbij
JAZĪRA
AMANUS MTS.
Antioch
Aleppo
(Beroe)
Qinnasrīn
(Chalcis)
Raqqa
Balīkh
MEDITERRANEAN
JABAL ANṢĀRIYYA
Orontes
Ruṣāfa
Euphrates
Khabūr
JABAL AL-BISHRĪ
Qarqīsiyyā
Ḥamā
Ḥimṣ
(Emesa)
Palmyra
Tripoli
(3088 m)
al-Qaryatayn
Jubayl
Beirut
LEBANON MTS.
BIQĀ'
Ba'labakk
ANTI-LEBANON MTS.
JABAL AL-RUWĀQ
Sab' Biyār
Ṣaydā
Līṭānī
Damascus
Mt. Hermon (2815 m)
GOLAN
ḤAWRĀN
SYRIAN DESERT
Tiberias
Yarmūk
Bostra
Caesarea
Baysān
(Scythopolis)
Faḥl (Pella)
Jarash
(Gerasa)
BALQĀ'
Jordan
Ramla
'Ammān
(Philadelphia)
'Asqalān
Jerusalem
Gaza
Ajnādayn ?
NEGEV
Wādī 'Araba
Mu'ta
Wādī al-Sirḥān
Petra
Ma'ān
Dūmat al-Jandal
Wādī Rumm
Ayla
SINAI
Gulf of 'Aqaba

culture to the extent that some other groups—the diverse peoples of Asia Minor, for example—certainly had. With the exception of a city elite, settled Syrians in A.D. 600 still spoke some form of Aramaic, the language of Jesus and of the Palestinian Talmud; and one dialect of this language, Syriac, had become by this time the medium for an extensive and growing Christian literature. Syriac literature was deeply indebted to Hellenistic civilization in many ways, of course, an indebtedness that is most clearly seen in the heavy borrowing of Greek religious and philosophical terms where Aramaic had none of its own, and in the interest evinced in the rational categories and burning issues of Greek Christian theology. But if the form and expression of this literature were perceptibly Hellenized, its spirit remained peculiarly Syrian, with its devotion to ascetic ideals and its passion for the didactic value of the lives of the Eastern saints, those models for the attainment of personal sanctity and salvation whose biographies, filled with the miraculous evidence of divine intervention in human affairs, make up a good part of the Syriac tradition. And among the great masses in Syria who could neither read nor write, Hellenism had sent down only very shallow roots before striking the solid Semitic bedrock. Christianity had been almost universally adopted by Syrians, of course, and this in an age when Christianity had been profoundly shaped by the traditions of Greek thought.[4] But Christianity itself was, after all, a Syrian export, not an alien creed. In any case, most Syrians chose to espouse, not Byzantine orthodoxy, which attempted to keep God and man from mingling too closely by confining each to a separate nature in Christ, but, rather, the heretical Monophysite creed, which forced the divine and the human in Christ into a most intimate fusion. To Monophysites, Christ had had but a single nature; he was not merely man and God, as the Greek theologians insisted, but a Man-God. The Byzantine church in Syria was, then, essentially restricted to the Greek-speaking urban elite, whereas the bulk of the population clung to its Aramaic tongue and to its characteristically Syrian view of the interaction of the human and the divine. The Hellenistic veneer in Syria was very thin indeed. A peasant or townsman might disguise himself as Titus or Julius in an inscription, but his father or son would often still bear a Semitic name.[5]

The Aramaic-speaking settled population of Syria had thus avoided thorough Hellenization, but there was another element of the Syrian populace that was even less touched by Hellenism: the nomadic and seminomadic pastoralists, roaming the Syrian steppe and the deserts of northern Arabia, of whom we have already had occasion to speak.[6] These people spoke another Semitic language, Arabic, and culturally had more in common with the tribal society of the Arabian peninsula than they did with the settled communities of Syria. Like the latter they had for the most part adopted Monophysite Christianity, but they were distinct from the settled people of Syria both in language and in their way of life, the rigors of which left little room for the adoption of those elements of high culture (literature and art) that we call Hellenism.

As in Arabia proper, however, there was continuous interaction—economic, social, and political—between these nomadic peoples and the Aramaic-speaking villagers and townsmen of Syria.[7] Nomads and semi-nomads traded with the merchants of Syria's towns and summered at wells on the outskirts of Syrian settlements. Indeed, it seems that these Arabic-speaking pastoral peoples were, on the eve of Islam, nearly as ubiquitous (if not as numerous) in many inland districts of Syria as they were in the Arabian peninsula itself. They had long dominated southernmost Syria, where the Nabataean Arabs had once established their mercantile capital at Petra. They occupied at times the valleys between the mountain folds in central Syria, such as the rich plain of Coele-Syria (the Biqā'), which with the headwaters of the Litani and Orontes rivers lay between the Lebanon and Anti-Lebanon ranges, and certain regions of Palestine.[8] Even in northern Syria, they had been able to conquer and establish dynasties in many towns on the fringes of the steppe: Ḥimṣ (Emesa), Ḥarrān, Edessa, Hatra. A Byzantine official inscription in Greek, Syriac, and Arabic, found near Ḥarrān in the Taurus foothills and dating to the latter part of sixth century A.D[9]—an era before Arabic had any written literature—reveals that speakers of Arabic were regular enough residents there to warrant the great effort that writing a hitherto unwritten language must have entailed. As for the Syrian steppe itself, of course, it had been dominated by Arabic-speaking peoples for centuries; the kingdom of Palmyra was only their most sensational political accomplishment.

Syria was, then, a land between two cultural seas. The language and unwritten cultural ways of Arabia washed against urban and rural Syrian society from the east and south, just as Greek and Greco-Roman culture washed against it from the north and west. The cities situated along the "coastline" of this inland cultural sea, whose heart was the steppe-desert of Syria and northern Arabia—cities such as Edessa, Aleppo, Ḥimṣ, Damascus, and Bostra—were as profoundly affected by Arabian cultural patterns as the Mediterranean coastal towns were by Greco-Roman ones, albeit in very different ways. The arid sea of the Syrian steppe, furthermore, hemmed in the average Syrian townsman or villager just as effectively from the east as the Mediterranean did from the west; certainly he could no more contemplate walking eastward across its expanses than the coastal villager could hope to walk toward the setting sun across the waters of the Mediterranean. The seas could only be navigated by those who were properly equipped and who knew their ways—be they mariners or the nomadic pastoralists who called the Syrian steppe home.

2. THE MUSLIMS' ASPIRATIONS IN SYRIA

This land, Syria, seems to have been a goal of the Muslims' expansionist ambitions from a very early date. Only Arabia itself, with its holy cities of Mecca and Medina, seems to have been of greater importance to them. Once Muḥammad's consolidation of power in western Arabia made possible the extension of Islamic political influence to distant areas,[10] Muḥammad and the first Muslims turned their attention especially to establishing their control over the northern Ḥijāz and even over southern Syria itself.

The reasons for this overriding interest in expansion toward Syria were numerous. It was, first of all, an area with which Muḥammad and the settled tribesmen of Mecca, Medina, and al-Ṭā'if who made up the new Islamic ruling elite were familiar because of commercial contacts they had had with Syria before Islam. Not only did Aramaic-speaking merchants from Syria regularly come to sell foodstuffs in the markets of Medina (and presumably elsewhere in the Ḥijāz);[11] the merchants of Quraysh and Thaqīf themselves made frequent visits to Gaza, al-'Arīsh, Bostra, and probably many other commercial centers in southern Syria.[12] They had seen Syria first-hand, and had witnessed the economic prosperity of southern Syria—an area that, like the Ḥijāz itself, was thriving on the eve of Islam due to the vigor of the caravan trade that passed through it.[13] Some members of Quraysh even owned property in Syria: Abū Sufyān, for example, owned land near Damascus before Islam.[14] There was, then, significant economic attraction to draw the attention of the early Muslims to Syria. It seems likely, furthermore, that this was especially the case after the Muslims had conquered Mecca and the tribe of Quraysh had been included in the new Islamic ruling elite as full partners, for of all groups in the Ḥijāz elite, it was undoubtedly the great merchants of Quraysh who had the closest ties to Syria and would have been most eager to bring it under their control. We can surmise, then, that once they had been swept up by the consolidation of the Islamic state, the Quraysh used all their considerable influence with Muḥammad to persuade him and his closest advisers of the desirability of expansion toward the north—if indeed he needed to be persuaded. For it has also been suggested that Muḥammad saw expansion to the north as a means of providing a livelihood—in the form of booty and captured lands—for the many new Muslims with little or no means of support who flocked to Medina during his last years.[15]

There were other factors that made Syria loom large in the minds of the early Muslims of the Ḥijāz, however, and it would be mistaken to assume that economic interests were the only reasons for Muḥammad's or his followers' interest in Syria. One such factor was Syria's place in the cultic or religious dimension of Islam itself. Jerusalem was, after all, a Syrian city. It had been the first *qibla*, or focus toward which Muslims faced when performing ritual prayer; and, though the *qibla* was later changed to the Ka'ba in Mecca, Jerusalem doubtless remained important in the minds of the faithful. Though no longer the *qibla*, it was still revered as the place where Jesus and other prophets mentioned in the Qur'ān had lived and preached—and we must remember that they were thought to have preached Islam, the same message of strict monotheism and human humility before God and one's fellows that Muḥammad preached. No matter that these earlier bearers of Islam to mankind had had their message corrupted by later religious hierarchs; the fact remained that there was a rather special connection between Syria and the religion of Islam itself, for the simple reason that God had several times chosen Syria as the place where Islam was to be revealed. Jerusalem, indeed, came to be revered as the location from which Muḥammad had made his miraculous nocturnal ascent to heaven, or *mi'rāj*.[16]

We may find an echo of the importance Muḥammad attached to Syria in his grant of lands to the B. al-Dār clan of the Syrian tribe of Lakhm. Among the places granted, according to some texts, was the town of Hebron in Palestine, some twenty-five kilometers south of Jerusalem.[17] This town was clearly outside Muḥammad's political control at the time the "grant" was made;[18] but it was the traditional site of the tomb of Abraham, one of the most important links mentioned in the Qur'ān in the chain of prophets leading up to Muḥammad, and, if the accounts are authentic, it is possible that the "grant" of Hebron was intended as a symbol of Islam's claim to be the culmination, or at least the continuation, of the message brought by such earlier prophets.

Thus we must add to the purely economic factors certain religious or ideological inducements that may have helped make Syria the focus of the early Muslims' aspirations. In addition to the economic and religious factors, however, there were also practical political reasons why Muḥammad and his followers should have viewed expansion toward Syria as a matter of considerable importance. As we have seen, a central aspect of the consolidation of the Islamic state was the subjection of nomadic groups to control by a ruling elite of settled people from the Ḥijāz. The political importance of securing the backing of the nomads had become clear to Muḥammad and his advisers during his struggle with the Quraysh, and from the time of the treaty of al-Ḥudaybiya he had been able to build up his following among nomadic tribes of the Ḥijāz to the extent that he was able to conquer Mecca and, shortly thereafter, al-Ṭā'if.[19] The continued political consolidation of the Islamic state beyond the confines of western Arabia would of course have involved further efforts to subdue nomadic groups that remained independent of the state. That is, one of the obectives of the new ruling elite was simply to expand the state—to extend its political control until it embraced all nomadic groups in the Arabian and Syrian desert and steppe (and, of course, all those settled communities that lived in the nomads' midst). Establishing Islamic control over the tribes to the north of Medina may have been seen as especially crucial, however, because it was only in the north that the Islamic state faced serious competition from another state for the allegiance of the tribesmen—competition from the Byzantine state, which was attempting to create (or to re-create) a firm coalition of tribal allies, and to extend its influence among the tribes of Syria and the northern Ḥijāz from the north, just as the Muslims were attempting to do so from the south.

Of the two states, the Byzantine was of course the older, with institutions and ruling traditions that stretched back hundreds of years; by contrast the governing institutions of the fledgling Islamic state were, as we have seen, just beginning to take shape in the matrix of a tribally organized society. In addition, the Byzantines had had long-standing alliances with certain Syrian nomadic tribes such as the Ghassānids. The latter were responsible, as we have seen, for keeping other tribal groups under control. They defended the southern and eastern flanks of Byzantine Syria against random plundering raids launched by nomadic groups and against concerted offensives launched by coalitions of tribesmen organized by Byzantium's mortal enemy, Sasanid Persia. Under normal circumstances, it seems likely that the Islamic state would have had little success in breaching such a well-established system of tribal alliances. Indeed, under normal circumstances it is possible that Muḥammad's political consolidation never would have proceeded as far as it did without sparking some Byzantine intervention to cut it short. For the Byzantines would certainly have known what was afoot in the Ḥijāz from the news that came up the trade routes along with tangible commodities; and once Muḥammad's consolidation had begun to seem a threat, they would have very likely interfered with that consolidation through the agency of their tribal allies, just as the long arm of Byzantine diplomacy had engineered an invasion of the distant Yemen through their Axumite allies nearly a century before. Indeed, as we shall see, there is some evidence to suggest that the Byzantines belatedly attempted to make contact with disaffected parties in Muḥammad's following, presumably with just such disruptive intent.[20]

But as fate would have it, political conditions in Syria were not at all normal for the Byzantines during Muḥammad's career. The most recent and most disastrous of Byzantium's Persian Wars had resulted in the loss of Syria and Egypt to the Sasanians; Persian armies had entered northern Syria in the spring of A.D. 611, and by the beginning of A.D. 617 had marched into Egypt. When in 622 Muḥammad fled his native city as an outcast in order to take refuge in Medina, therefore, Syria was no longer a Byzantine province. Thus Muḥammad's consolidation of power, which began to advance rapidly after the treaty of al-Ḥudaybiya (A.D. 628), took place under the shadow of a Sasanian occupation of Syria; and the culmination of his political career occurred while Heraclius was leading the Byzantine army victoriously into the heart of Sasanian Iraq, and while Byzantine control was first being restored in Syria after the departure of the Sasanians in A.D. 629 or 630.[21]

Byzantium was once more in control of Syria, but the decade and more of Sasanian occupation had seriously shaken the foundations of Byzantine supremacy in Syria. The long continuity of Byzantine (i.e., Roman) rule, stretching back five hundred years, had been decisively ruptured. Before the Persian occupation, Syrians would naturally have thought of their land as a Byzantine province because to them it seemed that it had always been one; but as the months of occupation stretched into years, this assumption of Syria's Byzantine affiliation surely grew dimmer. In an area where the Persian occupation lasted fifteen years, for example, a whole generation up to and including young adults—in an era of short life-spans, perhaps half the total population—would never have experienced Byzantine rule at all, and might be expected more naturally to think of Sasanid Persia as the relevant imperial power in Syria.[22] In addition, the Sasanian occupation had without question destroyed institutional arrangements of all kinds that had been characteristic of Byzantine rule. The Ghassānid kingdom, among other things, had been destroyed.[23] We can assume that this included the alliances that the Byzantines had so painstakingly built up with nomadic groups in the Syrian steppe; and in this domain especially, reconstructing the alliances was bound to be especially difficult because changes had taken place among the tribes of Syria themselves. In the turbulence of the years of occupation and strife, it is certain that some tribal groups had migrated—taking advantage of the temporary collapse of central authority to press in on the rich cultivated districts. New tribal alignments and coalitions had probably emerged under the changed conditions, although it is impossible to describe the details of these changes, which will remain forever lost to history.

The Byzantine restoration in about A.D. 630 was thus followed by a period during which the Byzantine authorities tried to reassemble the pieces of their shattered political presence in Syria. The southern limits of Byzantine control, which had formerly extended to Ayla, now seem to have come no farther south than the Dead Sea.[24] In particular, it was a time when the Byzantines seems to have been reconsidering their strategic needs and tribal alliances, perhaps with a view to establishing them on a new basis. On the one hand, some sources suggest that they decided to drop the subsidies they had once paid to some tribal groups,[25] perhaps because they felt that the financial expenditure was less necessary in the aftermath of their total victory over the Sasanians. On the other hand, they seem to have been trying to reconstruct their tribal alliances from the ground up, extending their ties among the Syrian and northern Ḥijāzī nomadic groups in order to form the defensive coalitions needed to guard Syria from the southeast. It was, as we have noted, just this effort to extend their political control over these tribes that made the Byzantines appear such a threat to the Muslims, who also aspired to bring the tribes under control. The Persian occupation meant, however, that the Byzantines and Muslims were much more evenly matched in this competition for tribal support than the disparity in the ages of their respective states would suggest. Twenty years earlier, the Byzantines would have had great institutional advantages over the Muslims in such a struggle; but those advantages, especially the patterns of traditional alliances with powerful tribes, had been partly swept away, and the two contestants were more or less on an equal footing—both were starting essentially from scratch on the path of political consolidation among the tribes.

From the point of view of the Muslims, the task of subjecting and unifying the tribes of Arabia under a new Islamic ruling elite was difficult enough in its own right; the efforts of a rival state to organize the tribes could only make it even more difficult for them to attain their objectives. Hence it became imperative for the Islamic state to assert its influence in the direction of Syria as soon as possible, before the Byzantines could make too much headway in their efforts to organize the tribes to the north. Rapid expansion toward Syria was, then, not only attractive to the ruling elite of the early Islamic state for economic reasons, and desirable for religious reasons, it was also perhaps seen as necessary for straightforward political and strategic reasons.

3. EARLY CONTACTS WITH SYRIA AND THE NORTHERN ḤIJĀZ

Muḥammad's interest in Syria and the route leading to it can clearly be seen in his military activities. Toward the end of his career he devoted increasing attention to the tribes and towns of the northern Ḥijāz and fringes of southern Syria, and he appears to have contemplated an invasion of southern Syria itself.[26] Among his most far-reaching raids were those to Dhāt al-Aṭlāḥ (Rabīʿ I, A.H. 8/July, A.D. 629), to Mu'ta in the Balqā' region of Syria (Jumāda I, A.H. 8/September, A.D. 629), to Dhāt al-Salāsil, probably in the northern Ḥijāz (perhaps Jumāda II, A.H. 8/October, A.D. 629), and to Tabūk in the northern Ḥijāz, with the associated raid on Dūmat al-Jandal (probably Rajab, A.H. 9/October, A.D. 630). At the time of his death, furthermore, he had just dispatched an expedition to the north under Usāma B. Zayd.[27] Certain episodes in the accounts of the Tabūk campaign suggest that the Prophet was originally considering an invasion or raid on Syria. He tried to persuade a Muslim to join the expedition by tempting him with the possibility that, if he went, he might be able to raise up offspring from among the women of Syria.[28] The expedition to Tabūk a bit later is termed a raid on the Syrians (Banū Aṣfar).[29] The raid on Dhāt al-Salāsil, which was perhaps launched to break up a gathering of hostile tribal groups to the north of Medina (gathering, perhaps, with Byzantine backing?) saw the commander, 'Amr b. al-'Āṣ, being sent out to rally the bedouin "to make war on Syria."[30] There is, furthermore, a persistence to Muḥammad's campaigning in the north even in the face of failure, and a care in making preparations for some campaigns (particularly for Tabūk), that suggest the great importance of expansion toward the north in Muḥammad's plans. This is not to say that Muḥammad was planning the conquest of all of Syria and its inclusion in the Islamic state, or even that he foresaw the possibility of such a conquest, much less the details of its course. Although, like every great politician, he doubtless left his ultimate objectives open to modification in the light of new opportunities, he probably had as his immediate objective in the north the subjection of Arabic-speaking nomadic tribes living in the northern Ḥijāz and southern Syria, or at least the extension of Medina's influence sufficiently to bring these tribes into alliance with the Islamic state.[31] This much at least was probably seen as necessary if the Islamic state was to survive: for its survival depended on a friendly attitude among these tribes, with which Medina, Mecca, and other places in the Ḥijāz had regular contact through commerce and in other ways. Settled communities such as Tabūk, which were surrounded by nomadic groups, would also be absorbed, of course, not only because of their location, but especially perhaps because they were occupied and in some cases controlled by branches of various surrounding tribes, the bulk of which were nomadic. In addition, such towns were essential as bases from which the Islamic state could attempt to observe and to control neighboring nomadic groups; their integration along with the nomads was necessary to ensure that the new state would successfully prevent the aggregation of too much power by the warrior tribes, in which lay the greatest potential threat to the survival of Islamic control in this part of Arabia.

B. 'Udhra and B. Sa'd Hudhaym

Among the many tribal groups living on the route through the northern Ḥijāz to Syria that Muḥammad contacted in his career were the B. 'Udhra and B. Sa'd Hudhaym. They appear to have had nomadic sections roaming from Wādī al-Qurā northward as far as Taymā' and other settlements as well.[32] Little is known of Muḥammad's relations with the B. 'Udhra; a few individuals from this tribe are said to have been or to have become Muslims during the Tabūk campaign,[33] and one commander among the Muslims in the Mu'ta campaign was from 'Udhra[34] (presumably leading a considerable number of fellow tribesmen). Further, a delegation of some members of 'Udhra is said to have come to Muḥammad in Ṣafar of A.H. 9/May-June, A.D. 630, and another from Sa'd Hudhaym at an unspecified date, and both delegations reportedly embraced Islam.[35] Muḥammad is reported to have sent agents to collect the *ṣadaqa* from the tribes of Sa'd Hudhaym and 'Udhra,[36] which suggests that the two tribes (or at least sections of them) were fairly firmly within Medina's sphere of influence by the time the agents were sent.[37] But in general, the B. 'Udhra and B. Sa'd Hudhaym are mentioned very little in the accounts of Muḥammad's political consolidation or in those of the *ridda* wars, which suggests that they were too weak to figure significantly in the tribal politics of the Ḥijāz at the time and probably had to come to terms with the new Islamic state at an early date without stubborn resistance.

Balī

Somewhat more is known about Muḥammad's contacts with the tribe of Balī. Part of this tribe occupied districts in the Ḥijāz and al-Tihāma near the Red Sea coast, to the west of Wādī al-Qurā and al-Ḥijr, but the bulk of one important section of the tribe, the B. Irāsha, resided farther north, in the Balqā' region of Syria[38] and was thus in close contact with the Byzantines. The northerly parts of the tribe took a firm stand against Muḥammad at an early date. They were part of a large number of tribal auxiliaries for the Byzantines that destroyed at Mu'ta the army of Muslims sent into Syria in A.H. 8/ A.D. 629; indeed, it was a man of B. Irāsha of Balī who commanded the Byzantines' Arab allies.[39] Likewise, it was a gathering of Quḍā'a tribesmen, including men of the Balī (presumably again of the B. Irāshā sections) that threatened to encroach on the Prophet's territory almost immediately after Mu'ta. This challenge, perhaps part of a Byzantine effort to consolidate power among the tribes after the Mu'ta victory, sparked the Muslims' campaign to Dhāt al-Salāsil (A.H. 8/ A.D. 629).[40]

If the northern sections of the Balī were fairly consistently opposed to Muḥammad, the sections of the Balī that resided in the Ḥijāz appear to have been better disposed to him. A considerable number of Balī tribesmen had established ties of alliance with various occupants of Medina before Islam, and when the Medinese embraced Islam, these allies (some of whom had probably taken up residence in Medina) appear to have done so as well; at any rate, a considerable number of Balawīs are listed among the early companions of the Prophet, including several who fought on the side of the Muslims as early as Badr.[41] The bulk of the southern part of the Balī doubtless continued to pursue their nomadic way of life in the Ḥijāz and did not have the intimate ties to early Islam that their Medinese kinsmen had acquired, but at worst they assumed an attitude of neutrality (or noninvolvement) vis-à-vis Muḥammad—there is, at least, no surviving evidence from Muḥammad's early career to suggest any opposition to him (or even any significant contact with him) by these groups. When the first reports of contact between the Muslims and the Ḥijāzi Balī do appear, furthermore, during the raid on Dhāt al-Salāsil, they suggest that the Muslims expected the Balī to be cooperative. For when Muḥammad sent out the force of three hundred men to move against the concentration of Quḍā'a tribesmen (including, we should remember, some men of the northern branches of the Balī), he instructed the force to conscript additional troops among the nomadic tribes whom they contacted in the territories of the Balī (i.e., the southern Balī), B. 'Udhra, and Bal-Qayn; and in fact the Muslims were able to raise an additional two hundred troops in this way. Although all three tribes may have contributed men to the campaign, Muḥammad clearly hoped especially to raise levies from the Balī, for he appointed as commander of the expedition 'Amr b. al-'Āṣ, a Qurayshite whose mother was from the Balī, and who therefore presumably had ties that could assist him in conscripting troops.[42] 'Amr sought levies, we are told, among the B. Sa'dullāh and other branches of the Balī.[43] Thus the southern branches of the Balī appear to have included individuals with early ties to the Prophet and in general seem to have been favorably disposed to him. It was not long after the raid to Dhāt al-Salāsil, in A.H. 9, that a delegation of men from the Balī—again, presumably from the southern branch—came to Muḥammad to join his growing polity; an initiative for which they were rewarded, as we have already seen, by being granted the tax revenues from some other tribes.[44] Despite these ties, it is not clear whether or not all of the southern parts of the Balī remained loyal to the new regime in Medina upon Muḥammad's death. Abū Bakr is said to have sent 'Amr b. al-'Āṣ against those tribesmen of Quḍā'a who had opposed Medinese control during the *ridda* wars,[45] and although the account does not specify that the Balī were among these Quḍā'a tribes, another account informs us that 'Amr at this time raided the Balī and the B. Sa'd (i.e., the B. Sa'dullāh of Balī, or the B. Sa'd Hudhaym).[46] Thus some of the Balī may have attempted to break free of the Islamic state after the death of Muḥammad.

Judhām and Lakhm

The region from roughly Tabūk in the northern Ḥijāz extending northward to the east of the Wādī 'Araba and the Dead Sea as far as the Balqā' region around 'Ammān was occupied by the Judhām and, living among them, by branches of the old Syrian tribe of Lakhm. The latter were also found in Palestine, to the west of the Dead Sea and Jordan River.[47] Muḥammad had contact with both tribes during the later years of his career. Both Judhām and Lakhm were among the Byzantine allies that defeated the Muslims at Mu'ta in A.H. 8/A.D. 629,[48] and the campaign against Tabūk in A.H. 9/ A.D. 630 was partly in response to a report that the Byzantines, again with allies from Judhām and Lakhm, were massing in the Balqā' district.[49] Thus it appears that, right up to the time of Muḥammad's death, parts of Judhām and Lakhm remained in the Byzantine camp and opposed the rise of the Islamic state. Nor do we find mention of significant numbers of early converts from either tribe.[50]

There were, however, a few people from Lakhm and Judhām who embraced Islam or came to terms with the Islamic state in the years just before Muḥammad's death. In the case of Lakhm, there were ten men of the B. al-Dār section who reportedly embraced Islam in A.H. 10 and were rewarded by Muḥammad with grants of land.[51] There was also a branch of the B. Ghanm of Lakhm called B. Ḥadas that is said to have separated itself from the rest of Lakhm and held back from fighting the Muslims at Mu'ta.[52] But in general there is little to suggest that much of Lakhm had allied itself to the Islamic state; the case of the B. Ghanm is poorly known, and the ten men of al-Dār who embraced Islam seem to have severed themselves from the rest of their tribe by settling in Medina. In the case of Judhām, it seems that Muḥammad's growing power included some groups to come to terms with him. The incident of Farwa b. 'Amr al-Judhāmī, a Byzantine governor over the tribes around 'Ammān or Ma'ān, who embraced Islam and was then crucified by the Byzantines, may be merely a pious legend.[53] Another set of incidents, however, suggests that at least part of the B. al-Ḍubayb branch of Judhām formed an alliance with the Prophet, probably shortly after the truce of al-Ḥudaybiya, and some may have embraced Islam.[54]

Muḥammad sent 'Amr b. al-'Āṣ to collect the *ṣadaqa* on Judhām (i.e., presumably only the B. al-Ḍubayb of Judhām) as well as on the B. Ḥadas (of Lakhm) and on the B. 'Udhra and Sa'd Hudhaym.[55] It appears, however, that the B. al-Ḍubayb broke with the Islamic state upon Muḥammad's death, for Usāma b. Zayd is said to have attacked them during his campaign early in the caliphate of Abū Bakr.[56]

B. al-Qayn (or Bal-Qayn)

To the east of the tribes just considered, extending from the Wādī Thajr north of Taymā', along the Wadi al-Sirḥān and up to the fringes of the Ḥawrān, lived the tribe of al-Qayn or Bal-Qayn.[57] The raid on Dhāt al-Salāsil apparently got as far as their territory,[58] but they were among the tribal allies of the Byzantines at Mu'ta according to some sources,[59] and there is little evidence that any members of al-Qayn were among the early companions of the Prophet.[60] One set of traditions does suggest that at least a fraction of the B. al-Qayn had been incorporated into the Islamic state by the time of Muḥammad's death and had been under the supervision of a "governor" named 'Amr b. Ḥakam. Even over those sections of B. al-Qayn, however, Muḥammad's control was slight, for the same account relates that on the Prophet's death part of the tribe rebelled under a leader named Zumayl b. Quṭba al-Qaynī.[61] Thus Muḥammad may have been able to draw a few sections of al-Qayn into alliance with him (probably the southernmost sections of the tribe); but this attraction among al-Qayn was neither very extensive nor very strong. The bulk of the tribe probably remained either loosely allied with the Byzantines or otherwise independent of the Islamic state.

B. Kalb

Even farther to the east, stretching from the oasis town of Dūmat al-Jandal southward into the Nafūd desert of the Najd and northward into the heart of the Syrian steppe, lay the territory of the B. Kalb.[62] They thus lived just to the east of the B. al-Qayn, who were among their main rivals in the decades before the rise of Islam.[63] Though a few converts to Islam from the B. Kalb are known,[64] details of contacts between Muḥammad and this tribe as a whole are few, and, as most have to do with the confused accounts of the Prophet's expeditions—whether real or supposed—against Dūmat al-Jandal, it is difficult to arrive at a clear picture of his relations to the tribe. In general, the accounts suggest that Muḥammad raided Dūmat al-Jandal several times and succeeded in bringing the ruler of Dūma and part of B. Kalb into some form of alliance with Medina.[65] These accounts have been criticized as unreliable,[66] but there is other information that suggests that the Muslims made contact with branches of the B. Kalb. According to this account, one of the groups sent on the raid to Dhāt al-Salāsil (against the "Quḍā'a" tribes) was dispatched to campaign among pagan tribes of the B. Kalb in the Syrian highlands (*mashārif al-Shām*).[67] This account provides some added support for those that assert that parts of Kalb were brought under the supervision of an Islamic agent during Muḥammad's lifetime. But it is clear that the bulk of the B. Kalb remained outside the Islamic state during Muḥammad's day, and even those parts that may have been brought into alliance with Muḥammad appear to have turned away from Medina after the Prophet's death.[68]

B. Ghassān

There are a few accounts describing contacts between the early Islamic state in Medina and the tribe of Ghassān. Though the Ghassānid chiefs' special relationship as *phylarchs* of the Byzantines was probably destroyed by the Sasanian occupation, much of the tribe seems to have kept up its ties with the Byzantines even after the buffer state had collapsed.[69] Most of the tribe resided in the Ḥawrān and near Damascus in central Syria,[70] and it was doubtless these groups of Ghassān that are mentioned among Heraclius's tribal allies (along with Lakhm, Judhām, and 'Āmila, a tribe resident in the Balqā' region)[71] who gathered in central Syria, causing Muḥammad to put together the campaign against Tabūk in response to this threat.[72] Indeed, by some accounts it was a man of Ghassān, Ibn Abī Sabra, who led the Byzantines' tribal allies at Mu'ta.[73] The Ghassānid "king," al-Ḥārith b. Abī Shamir, reportedly received a messenger from Muḥammad who summoned him to embrace Islam, but he rejected this overture and stayed firm in his alignment with the Byzantines.[74] Another account relates that the same chieftain, al-Ḥārith b. Abī Shamir, himself sent envoys to disaffected parties in Muḥammad's following at the time of the Tabūk campaign, offering an alliance with them against Muḥammad.[75] This reveals that these Ghassānids were still (or were once again) closely tied to the Byzantines; it also suggests that the Ghassānids (and hence the Byzantines) were sufficiently aware of, and concerned about, Muḥammad's political consolidation in the Ḥijāz to attempt disrupting it by diplomatic means. We can draw similar conclusions from another account, in which a man of Ghassān was sent to the Ḥijāz by the Byzantines to assess Muḥammad's situation.[76] The branches of Ghassān residing in Syria thus appear to have in general remained aligned with the Byzantines and to have been hostile to the efforts of the new state in Medina to expand northward. Evidently a column of warriors sent out to B. Ghassān in the Syrian highlands during the raid on Dhāt al-Salāsil[77] was unable to bring any significant number of them under Muḥammad's control. Yet there were also some branches of Ghassān that lived not in Syria, but farther south, in Taymā' and perhaps in Medina itself.[78] It is possible that the individuals who formed the delegation from Ghassān that came to the Prophet in Ramaḍān, A.H. 10/ December, A.D. 631[79] were from these southern branches of Ghassān, which because of their location can be expected to have pursued a policy more independent of Byzantine influence than that of their Syrian cousins.

Other Northern Tribes

Many other tribes inhabited Syria, but they were generally located too far north and east to be in contact with the Islamic state during Muḥammad's lifetime, or were too weak to figure prominently in the sources. The Tanūkh lived as seminomadic or settled groups in many areas of central and northern Syria, along the western fringes of the Syrian steppe at least as far north as Qinnasrīn and Aleppo.[80] They were apparently among the tribes on the Byzantine side at Mu'ta,[81] but otherwise Muḥammad seems to have had no contact with them. The tribe of Salīḥ, one branch of which (the B. Ḍaj'am) had once been Byzantine *phylarchs* before the Ghassānids assumed that role, seems to have occupied the Ḥawrān[82] but evidently had no contact with the early Muslims.[83] The important tribe of Bahrā', which occupied central and eastern parts of the Syrian steppe as far as the Euphrates,[84] provided at least one companion of the Prophet[85] but generally seems to have had no contact with the Muslims before the Islamic conquests that followed Muḥammad's death. They remained politically close to the Byzantines, and members of their tribe were among the Byzantines' tribal allies at Mu'ta.[86] In addition to these tribes, the bulk of which lived in Syria, there were probably resident in Syria small sections of many other tribes the majority of whom lived elsewhere.[87]

We may summarize our findings as follows. Muḥammad's political consolidation, which among other things aimed at the subjection of nomadic tribal groups by the Islamic state's ruling elite of settled folk from the Ḥijāz, involved sustained and partly successful efforts to bring the tribes of the northern Ḥijāz and of southern Syria into Muḥammad's sphere of influence, or, better yet, under his firm control. Though the campaigns to Dhāt al-Aṭlāḥ and Mu'ta were disastrous defeats for the Muslims, the raid on Dhāt al-Salāsil appears to have bolstered Medina's influence in the Wādī al-Qurā and northern Ḥijāz, and the Tabūk campaign brought several towns in the northern Ḥijāz and southern Syria under Muḥammad's control, as well as establishing his influence over local nomadic groups. The nature of the ties Muḥammad was able to make with the tribes varied from group to group. Some tribal groups may have been merely informal allies who had concluded a kind of nonaggression pact with Muḥammad but who otherwise enjoyed complete independence; others, however, appear to have embraced Islam and agreed to adopt a settled life;[88] still others, whatever else they may have agreed to, were at least subjected to the *ṣadaqa* tax that Muḥammad levied on nomadic groups in the last years of his life.

Although the nature and degree of Medina's control varied from place to place, toward the end of Muḥammad's lifetime his influence appears to have been quite pervasive among the nomadic groups at least as far north as the northern tip of the Gulf of Aqaba and Wādī Rumm. The Sa'd Hudhaym, the 'Udhra, southern sections of the Balī, the Ḍubayb branch of Judhām, the B. al-Dār and B. Ḥadas branches of Lakhm, parts of the al-Qayn, perhaps part of the Kalb, and isolated southern branches of the Ghassān, who lived in this part of the Ḥijāz, all appear to have become allied to Muḥammad for a time, and the main towns of this region, Taymā', Tabūk, and the settlements in Wādī al-Qurā, were the object of successful campaigns by forces from Medina. It seems, however, that Muḥammad's control of the nomadic groups in this region preceded his control over the towns: as one chronicle puts it, "Dūmat [al-Jandal], Ayla, and Taymā' became afraid of the Prophet when they saw that the nomads (*al-'arab*) had embraced Islam."[89] It was probably for this reason that the Byzantine governor ("king" in the sources) of Ayla, Yuḥannā b. Ru'ba, made contact with the Prophet when he was at Tabūk, requesting terms like those imposed on Dūmat al-Jandal; and the residents of Jarbā', Adhruḥ, and Maqnā—all, apparently, towns near Ayla—did the same.[90] Presumably, if the account is trustworthy, the same factors persuaded the Byzantine governor (*'āmil*) over Ma'ān, a bit north of Ayla, to embrace Islam.[91] It was the same logic that had won over the stubborn citizens of al-Ṭā'if a short time before: no Arabian town can long prosper if all the nomads of the surrounding countryside are hostile to it.

Farther to the north, however, the Islamic state was never accepted in Muḥammad's day. The tribes of Bahrā', most of Judhām, most of Lakhm, most of al-Qayn, most or all of Kalb, Tanūkh, Salīḥ, 'Āmila, and those sections of Ghassān and Balī that lived in Syria all showed themselves hostile to Muḥammad or were too far away to come into contact with him. It was not, furthermore, simply hostility engineered by the Byzantines; there seems to have been a measure of popular sentiment involved. When Zayd b. Ḥāritha marched with his army of Muslims through the hilly region between al-Sharāt and the Balqā' on his way to Mu'ta, the villagers of the Jabal Akthab district—reportedly Christians of Lakhm, Judhām, and al-Qayn—attacked the Muslims' infantrymen as they passed, wounding some and killing one.[92] Clearly these settled or partly settled tribesmen were openly antagonistic to the new state in Medina.

Indeed, Medina's control was not very firm, even in the northern Ḥijāz, for on Muḥammad's death several groups in this region appear to have broken their ties with the state. In the distant Syrian steppe, the branches of al-Qayn and Kalb that had become affiliated with Muḥammad appear to have repudiated their ties to Medina, and in the Ḥijāz the B. Ḍubayb of Judhām and the B. Sa'dullāh (and other branches?) of the Ḥijāzī Balī appear to have done likewise. This meant that at the beginning of Abū Bakr's caliphate, he had the support only of those tribes occupying the central Ḥijāz, around Mecca and Medina, and as far north as the Wādī al-Qurā and Taymā', but that whatever influence the Muslims had built up in the northern Ḥijāz and southern Syria was lost.[93]

The re-establishment of Medina's control over the northern Ḥijāz seems to have proceeded without great difficulty, however. Even the few accounts that suggest that some of the tribes in this region tried to break away make no mention of any important fighting or serious resistance there;[94] the tribes involved do not seem to have been particularly powerful, and they probably submitted with little or no resistance once new representatives of Medina's authority appeared in their neighborhood. Muḥammad had planned to send an expedition under Usāma b. Zayd toward Syria, perhaps to raid some of the Quḍā'a tribes;[95] and Usāma, who set out on the eve of the Prophet's death and was ordered by Abū Bakr to proceed in accordance with Muḥammad's instructions, apparently received delegations of leaders from some of the Quḍā'a tribes during his campaign.[96] Presumably these groups—which Quḍā'a tribes were involved is, unfortunately, not specified—came to submit to Medina without fighting. Abū Bakr reportedly also appointed 'Amr b. al-'Āṣ and al-Walīd b. 'Uqba to serve as agents over Quḍā'a tribes,[97] and

'Amr was responsible for raiding among the Quḍā'a that had broken with the Islamic state, including the B. Sa'd (presumably B. Sa'dullāh of Balī) and perhaps other groups from Balī and Kalb, as we have seen.[98] 'Amr was aided in his raids on these tribes by Shuraḥbīl b. Ḥasana, a commander whom Abū Bakr sent from al-Yamāma to the northern Ḥijāz after the Muslims' victory at 'Aqrabā'.[99] This limited military campaigning appears to have been sufficient to restore Medina's hegemony to the north as far as the southern borders of Syria.

4. THE COURSE OF CONQUEST IN SYRIA

Well over a dozen discrete sets of accounts about the dispatch of the Islamic armies to Syria are preserved in the Arabic sources. The separate accounts communicate much contradictory information and are consequently impossible to reconcile in many respects. The contradictions are most evident in matters of relative chronology, reflecting the fact that the authorities who transmitted these traditional accounts were themselves relying on extremely fragmentary bits of information, coming from diverse sources, which each of them attempted to piece together to form a more or less coherent narrative.[100] It is therefore hardly surprising to find that different authorities will sometimes describe the same episodes but in different sequences, or that at other times, when different sources of information have been consulted, there is considerable variety in the events mentioned by individual authorities.

It is, nevertheless, possible to reconstruct the broad outlines of the conquest of Syria by the Muslims, even if many details remain obscure. The conquest can be divided into three main phases. The first phase embraced all the early military campaigning in southern Syria from the departure of the first troops in A.H. 12/ A.D. 633 until the arrival of a group of reinforcements from Iraq, commanded by one of the tactical geniuses of the early Islamic period, Khālid b. al-Walīd of the B. Makhzūm (Quraysh). During this phase a few minor engagements occurred in southern Syria, mainly with local garrison forces, and reinforcements appear to have been sent north continually from Arabia to the Islamic armies, but no major confrontations with the Byzantines developed. It was a phase in which the Muslims came to dominate the open countryside of southern Syria, but in which the towns remained outside their control.

The second phase began with Khālid b. al-Walīd's arrival in Syria in A.H. 13/ A.D. 634 and was one of concerted Byzantine resistance. During this phase, the Muslims began to extend their control in southern Syria from the tribal countryside to the important towns;[101] selected towns were put to siege and occupied: Bostra (Buṣrā), Gaza, Faḥl (Pella), Baysān (Scythopolis), Damascus, and, briefly, Ḥimṣ (Emesa) and Baʿlabakk (Heliopolis). This process naturally elicited an increasingly strong reaction from the Byzantine authorities; the Byzantine emperor Heraclius, realizing that local Byzantine city garrisons were inadequate to repel the attacks, dispatched successive portions of the imperial army to combat the invaders. This in turn resulted in the main encounters between the Byzantine and Islamic armies, at Ajnādayn, Faḥl, Marj al-Ṣuffar, and the Yarmūk. These battles (about A.H. 13-15/ A.D. 634-636) saw the decisive defeat of the Byzantine army in Syria, and, although many towns in southern Syria and all of northern Syria still remained outside the Muslims' control, the defeats suffered broke the ability of the Byzantines to offer organized resistance to the Muslims' advance.

The third phase of the conquest of Syria, extending from roughly A.H. 16/ A.D. 637 until roughly A.H. 27/ A.D. 647-648, was one of consolidation in the aftermath of the victories at the Yarmūk, Ajnādayn, and so forth. It involved the rapid conquest of the remaining countryside not under the Muslims' control, especially in northern Syria, and the piecemeal reduction of individual Syrian towns, which had been left alone to resist the advancing Muslims by the collapse of the Byzantine military presence in Syria. Among these towns were some in central Syria that may have been conquered once but had slipped out of the Muslims' control or been abandoned by them during the final Byzantine offensives of the second phase: Damascus (again?), Ḥimṣ (again?), Baʿlabakk (again?), Ḥamā, Qinnasrīn, Aleppo (Beroe), Jerusalem, Caesarea, Tyre, Sidon, Beirut, Antioch, and others. It was marked by the return to Iraq of at least some of the Iraqi reinforcements that had come to Syria after the first phase, accompanied perhaps by some who had never been to the Iraqi front, and also by the opening of offensives into Egypt and into the Jazīra region lying between the upper reaches of the Euphrates and the Tigris.

These are the general outlines of the Islamic conquest of Syria. Let us now consider the conquest in more detail.

5. PHASE I: THE INVASION OF SYRIA

The great military campaigns into Syria that resulted in the definitive conquest of this much-desired area were initiated by Abū Bakr upon the completion of the Islamic conquest of Arabia. The earlier campaigns sent toward Syria, especially the activities of Usāma b. Zayd in al-ʻAraba, ʻAmr b. al-ʻĀṣ, and al-Walīd b. ʻUqba, doubtless prepared the way for the conquests that followed, but the invasion itself begins with the dispatch of several sizable armies by Abū Bakr. This event is traditionally dated to the beginning of A.H. 13, but there is good reason to believe that it actually occurred in the autumn of A.D. 633/Rajab, A.H. 12.[102]

The decision to launch the invasion was certainly not reached without careful deliberation and consultation with prominent members of the ruling elite in Medina, and we may accept the numerous descriptions of these consultations as efforts to flesh out the vague recollections of the actual discussions that must have taken place, even though we must view with skepticism the too precise details of "eyewitnesses" who provide for us verbatim the supposed words of advice delivered to Abū Bakr by various individuals.[103] Once the decision to invade had been made and a call for volunteers sent out, Abū Bakr appointed several commanders. The first to be appointed was probably Khālid b. Saʻīd b. al-ʻĀṣ. His career is shrouded in mystery as the sources are very contradictory regarding his activities, but it seems that he was appointed very early,[104] and that Abū Bakr soon removed him from his command on the urgings of ʻUmar, supposedly because he had refused to take the oath of allegiance to Abū Bakr for some months following Muḥammad's death.[105] Some sources state that Khālid was dismissed even before he could leave Medina with his army,[106] but others describe him marching as an independent commander and place his dismissal only after his departure. According to one account, Abū Bakr sent Khālid b. Saʻīd toward Syria with instructions similar to those given to Khālid b. al-Walīd in Iraq—that is, presumably, to bring the Arabic-speaking tribal groups with whom he made contact under control.[107] To this end he seems to have been sent to Taymā' and told to remain there.[108] His immediate objective was probably to serve as a protective barrier (*rid'*) against a large concentration of tribes being assembled by the Byzantines, to prevent them from striking southward in the Muslims' territory in the Ḥijāz.[109] He appears to have received considerable reinforcement there before being dismissed, for Abū Bakr had made contact with his governors among various tribes, to see if they might volunteer for campaigning in Syria, and some of these volunteers were sent to Khālid b. Saʻīd's force[110]—among them al-Walīd b. ʻUqba, who had been Medina's agent (*ʻāmil*) over part of Quḍāʻa but who had agreed to serve with Khālid and is reported to have reached him as a reinforcement.[111]

It seems unlikely, however, that Khālid b. Saʻīd actually did any significant campaigning in this area before being removed from his command. The tales of his disastrous defeat by the Byzantine army at Marj al-Ṣuffar, which some old authorities place at this time, are almost certainly misplaced accounts about a later battle that took place at Marj al-Ṣuffar after the Muslims had seized Faḥl (Pella).[112] It is possible, however, that Khālid may have had some minor contacts with the Byzantines or, more probably, with their tribal allies. There are no accounts providing information about such contact,[113] but there are allusions in the sources to the defeat of the "*jaysh al-bidāl*," that is, the army of reinforcements that had come to Khālid b. Sa'īd's assistance, and Khālid b. Sa'īd and al-Walīd b. 'Uqba are said to have withdrawn to Dhū l-Marwa, a place in Wādī al-Qurā, thereafter.[114] It thus seems that Khālid advanced to Taymā', was reinforced by al-Walīd and others making up the "*jaysh al-bidāl*," was defeated or driven back by tribesmen allied to the Byzantines in a relatively minor skirmish, withdrew to Dhū l-Marwa, and was then replaced as commander.

With regard to the activities of the other commanders in Syria during the first phase of the conquests we are on more secure ground. Most sources agree that four commanders took a leading part in the initial invasion and in the campaigning of the first phase—'Amr b. al-'Āṣ, Yazīd b. Abī Sufyān (replacing Khālid b. Sa'īd), Shuraḥbīl b. Ḥasana, and Abū 'Ubayda b. al-Jarrāḥ. What cannot be determined from the traditional accounts is which of these commanders was dispatched first, and which ones went later as independent commanders or as reinforcements for one of the forces sent out earlier. On such questions of timing and interrelationship, the early authorities are in sharp conflict: thus al-Madā'inī states that Yazīd's army was the first to depart, followed after a few days by Shuraḥbīl and then by Abū 'Ubayda, and that 'Amr b. al-'Āṣ was sent last as a reinforcement to the other three;[115] al-Wāqidī, on the other hand, states that 'Amr b. al-'Āṣ was the first to depart, followed by Shuraḥbīl and Yazīd,[116] and makes no mention whatsoever of a force under Abū 'Ubayda at this time.[117] Other sources give even less consistent information.[118] As the divergent accounts of various authorities cannot be harmonized, and as there is no particular reason to favor the relative chronology of any one authority over those of others,[119] it is necessary to conclude simply that the four commanders were sent out, probably at roughly the same time, but in an order that cannot be determined.

Nor is there any more consensus in the sources over the relationship among the various commanders. Most consider the commanders to have been independent, but some say that 'Amr b. al-'Āṣ was to be in charge of joint operations,[120] whereas others ascribe the supreme command to Abū 'Ubayda[121] or to Yazīd b. Abī Sufyān.[122]

There is considerably more agreement among the sources, however, over the general direction in which the four commanders marched. 'Amr b. al-'Āṣ, according to most accounts, was directed toward Palestine. This was an area with which he was familiar from his commercial travels before the rise of Islam.[123] He seems to have proceeded from Medina along the coastal caravan route known as the Mu'riqa road as far as Ayla, at the head of the Gulf of 'Aqaba.[124] Ultimately he passed across the Negev (or perhaps even into the Sinai)[125] and reached the villages of Dāthin and Bādan in the vicinity of Gaza, where he held negotiations with the military commander (*biṭrīq, patricius*) of Gaza. When the negotiations broke down, the Muslims became engaged in a skirmish with local forces in which the Muslims were victorious.[126] 'Amr's forces camped at a place called Ghamr al-'Arabāt during this early campaigning;[127] it was located in the middle of the Wādī 'Araba, between the Dead Sea and the Gulf of 'Aqaba.

The other commanders were dispatched to Syria, that is, to areas east of the Wādī 'Araba and the Jordan valley. Ibn Isḥāq states that Yazīd b. Abī Sufyān, Shuraḥbīl b. Ḥasana, and Abū 'Ubayda marched via the Tabūk road toward the Balqā' district.[128] Shuraḥbīl had been in al-Yamāma, in eastern Arabia, with Khālid b. al-Walīd during the *ridda* wars and upon his return to Medina was sent out toward Syria by Abū Bakr;[129] al-Madā'ini and al-Wāqidī claim that he was sent to Jordan (that is, to the region south of the Balqā' and east of Wādī 'Araba).[130] Sayf's authorities, on the other hand, state that he was appointed to al-Walīd b. 'Uqba's former governorship over the outlying Quḍā'a tribes.[131] This may be consistent with the opinion of al-Madā'inī and al-Wāqidī if we assume that the tribes al-Walīd b. 'Uqba had governed resided in southern Jordan. Nothing more is heard of Shuraḥbīl's activities during the first phase of the conquests, however, so it is impossible to verify his whereabouts.

Yazīd b. Abī Sufyān appears to have been sent to the region of the Balqā', east and northeast of the Dead Sea.[132] His route thither is not specified. At some point—whether on the way to the Balqā' or after he had reached it—he is reported to have sent a column of Muslims, commanded by Abū Umāma al-Ṣudayya b. 'Ajlān al-Bāhilī, to a place called 'Araba in Palestine in order to break up a force of 5,000 Byzantine troops commanded by a certain Sergius, who appears to have come from Caesarea. In the resulting skirmish, Abū Umāma's detachment was victorious and, according to Abū Mikhnaf, Abū Umāma pursued the Byzantines to a place called al-Dābiya or al-Dubbiya where he again defeated them.[133] The episode is rather obscure and seems to have been of minor importance.

As for Abū 'Ubayda, he was active in the Golan region to the east of Lake Tiberias and south of Damascus.[134] It may have been during this first phase of campaigning that Abū 'Ubayda fought the inhabitants of a place in the Balqā' called Ma'āb, which then capitulated in return for a treaty with the Muslims.[135]

In sum, the great mass of textual material dealing with the first phase of the conquest in Syria reduces itself to a few very general facts. The activities of Khālid b. Sa'īd cannot be ascertained, but we can feel certain that after Khālid b. Sa'īd's appointment and dismissal as commander, four main commanders were active in Syria: 'Amr b. al-'Āṣ in southern Palestine, Shuraḥbīl b. Ḥasana in Jordan, Yazīd b. Abī Sufyān in the Balqā', and Abū 'Ubayda in the Golan. Which of them was in overall command, if any was at this stage, cannot be determined. 'Amr became engaged in some small skirmishes around Gaza, Yazīd's forces, in some around 'Araba in Palestine, and Abū 'Ubayda, in some around Ma'āb in the Balqā'. At some point, furthermore, 'Amr b. al-'Āṣ took up a position at Ghamr al-'Arabāt. But the relative chronology of the departure and campaigning of these commanders remains completely outside our grasp, and the general picture of the campaigning in the first phase of the conquests is a very spare one indeed.

We can, however, yet draw some conclusions on the essential objectives of the campaigning in this first phase of the conquest. It is evident that the main field of activity of the four commanders was not around the major cities of Syria, nor was it in the key agricultural and settled districts of central Palestine, the Ḥawrān, and the like. They appear instead to have been sent to those areas where Arabic-speaking nomadic and seminomadic tribes would have been the dominant elements in the population. Thus 'Amr was sent via Ayla through the Negev as far as Gaza, and, although it is his raids on a few villages near Gaza that are recorded in the sources, these were clearly limited in extent, and it is probable that most of his energy was devoted to bringing the seminomadic tribes of the Negev under his control. This may have been his primary occupation while camped at Ghamr al-'Arabāt. Shuraḥbīl, as we have seen, was sent to Jordan, perhaps to govern and supervise some of the Quḍā'a tribes. Yazīd b. Abī Sufyān was active in and around the Balqā'—some of which was certainly of agricultural importance. It was, however, also a region where seminomadic tribes would have played a prominent role in local life. Abū 'Ubayda, for his part, was sent to the former "capital" in the Golan of the Byzantines' Ghassānid allies, that is, to the dominant nomadic group in the western Syrian steppe. All four commanders, in short, were sent to regions on Syria's desert fringe.

We should note, furthermore, that at this stage the Muslims were not concerned with reducing major cities. Abū Bakr is even said to have instructed Abū 'Ubayda to restrict himself to raiding the open countryside and not to attack the cities of Syria—at least not until the order to do so should be given.[136] The main cities of Syria—Damascus, Jerusalem, Gaza, Bostra, Pella, Philadelphia ('Ammān), Gerasa, not to mention many others on the coast or farther north—appear to have been ignored, at least for the time being. This may explain in part why the Byzantine Greek and Syriac sources make so little mention of the Islamic armies at this stage: the Muslims were not yet fully perceived as a threat, because they had not launched concerted attacks on the towns.

This pattern of evidence suggests that in the first stage the Muslims were concerned with establishing their control over the Arabic-speaking nomadic, seminomadic, and settled tribesmen living on the fringes of the Syrian steppe. If the urban populations of Syria were not yet "Arab," that is, Arabic speaking, there can be no serious doubt that the nomadic and seminomadic tribes in this area were. The settled rural population, on the other hand, was probably linguistically mixed. Peasants living in areas near the coast, in the mountains, and in such districts where the nomadic population was generally insignificant, certainly spoke various dialects of Aramaic, but in those areas along the fringes of the Syrian steppe and in southern Palestine, many villages had regular contact with Arabic-speaking nomadic groups, and a good number of peasants may indeed have been related by blood or marriage to tribal kinsmen who led a nomadic way of life. It is thus fair to assume that in the settled districts raided during the first phase of the Islamic conquest in Syria, a good proportion of the settled villagers already spoke Arabic. They were, in short, already "Arab" tribesmen, leading a sedentary way of life.

It may, of course, be merely a coincidence that the Muslims' sphere of activity in the first phase of the conquest of Syria corresponded roughly to the area occupied by Arabic-speaking tribal groups of southern Syria. But it is suggestive to read that the first commander appointed by Abū Bakr, Khālid b. Sa'īd, was sent to Syria at the same time that Khālid b. al-Walīd was sent to Iraq, and with similar instructions.[137] As we shall see, Khālid b. al-Walīd seems to have been concerned with conquering those parts of Iraq that were occupied by Arabs, that is, by Arabic-speaking tribesmen.[138]

It thus appears that in Syria, as in Iraq, Abū Bakr was determined first to bring the nomadic and seminomadic groups, and the tribes to which they belonged, under the control of the Islamic state. The first phase of the conquest in Syria was thus an effort to extend further the process of political consolidation that had been begun by Muḥammad and continued during the *ridda* wars, a key element in which had been the subjection of the nomadic Arab tribes whose power was always a potential threat to the power of the state. By reducing to subject status the tribes of southern Syria, the Islamic state eventually reached the point at which it could unleash the series of concentrated assaults on cities and armies that was destined to bring all of Byzantine Syria firmly under Islamic rule. These campaigns, which formed the start of the Islamic conquest of Syria in earnest, appear in the Byzantine sources as a sudden explosion from the desert, but, as we see, they were in fact the fruit of a long and deliberate process of political consolidation.

Whatever their disagreements on chronology, the sources are in fairly close agreement over the composition and size of the forces involved during the first phase of the conquest of Syria. Abū Bakr's general call for volunteers for the Syrian campaign was directed, we are told, specifically to the settled people of Mecca and al-Ṭā'if, to the people of the Yemen, and to the nomads (*al-'arab*) of the Ḥijāz and the Najd.[139] It appears that he first summoned only the *muhājirūn* and the *anṣār*, but when the army that formed appeared too small, he summoned the people of the Yemen to join in the invasion of Syria as well.[140] In fact, the various accounts of the first phase of the conquest make it clear that, after the dispatch of the four commanders, new groups of soldiers—Yemeni tribesmen, nomadic people from the Najd, and others—gradually arrived in Medina and were sent out to one or another of the armies in Syria as they arrived.[141] The forces in Syria were thus continually being augmented with new reinforcements.

Various accounts provide us with some further details on the size and composition of these forces. The overall size of the combined armies during the first phase appears to have been about 24,000 men.[142] Shuraḥbīl b. Ḥasana, Yazīd b. Abī Sufyān, and Abū 'Ubayda, according to al-Madā'inī, marched with 7,000 men each,[143] and 'Amr b. al-'Āṣ, according to al-Wāqidī, marched with 3,000 men.[144] Al-Balādhurī, on the other hand, mentions only 'Amr, Yazīd, and Shuraḥbīl and states that each marched with about 3,000 men, but he reports that with continuous reinforcements each army grew to about 7,500 men and then to an overall total of 24,000.[145]

Particularly important in the forces in Syria were tribesmen from the Ḥijāz and the Yemen. 'Amr b. al-'Āṣ's force of 3,000, according to al-Wāqidī, included many *muhājirūn* and *anṣār*, that is, settled Medinese and Meccans,[146] whereas Ibn A'tham states that it contained 3,300 cavalry from Quraysh and their clients, 1,700 horsemen led by chieftains of the Ḥijāzī nomadic tribe of Sulaym, and 200 horsemen under a commander from the Yemeni tribe of Murād (a branch of Madhḥij).[147] Another group of 3,000 men marched as reinforcements to Abū 'Ubayda under the command of Hāshim b. 'Utba b. Abī Waqqāṣ, a prominent Qurayshite, and consisted of tribesmen of Hamdān, Murād, and Azd (all Yemeni tribes) along with Aslam, Ghifār, and Muzayna (nomadic groups from the Ḥijāz).[148] Another passage informs us that 4,000 Yemenis arrived, led by Qays b. Hubayra al-Murādī, and were sent to join Abū 'Ubayda, Shuraḥbīl, and Yazīd b. Abī Sufyān,[149] while another group of 2,000 men led by Sa'īd b. 'Amr b. Khidhyam was sent to join Abū 'Ubayda.[150] One account, however, suggests that there may have been a few Najdi tribesmen among the forces active in Syria, for according to it the tribesmen of 'Abs, Ṭayyi', and Asad who had fought alongside Khālid b. al-Walīd during the *ridda* wars returned to their home territories thereafter and remained there until the call to fight in Syria was issued, at which time they came to Medina.[151] We also learn that the armies were accompanied to Syria by some women and dependents as well as by horses and arms, but not by donkeys or sheep.[152]

All considered, then, our sources provide a fairly coherent picture of the forces dispatched by the Islamic state to Syria during the first phase of the conquests: 24,000 strong, they consisted mainly of settled people from the Ḥijāz, nomads from the Ḥijāz, and tribesmen (probably mostly settled) from the Yemen.

6. KHĀLID B. AL-WALĪD'S MARCH TO SYRIA AND THE CHRONOLOGY OF THE EARLY CAMPAIGNS

Before the onset of the Muslims' offensives against the urban centers of Syria, the four main forces of Muslims in Syria were reinforced by a

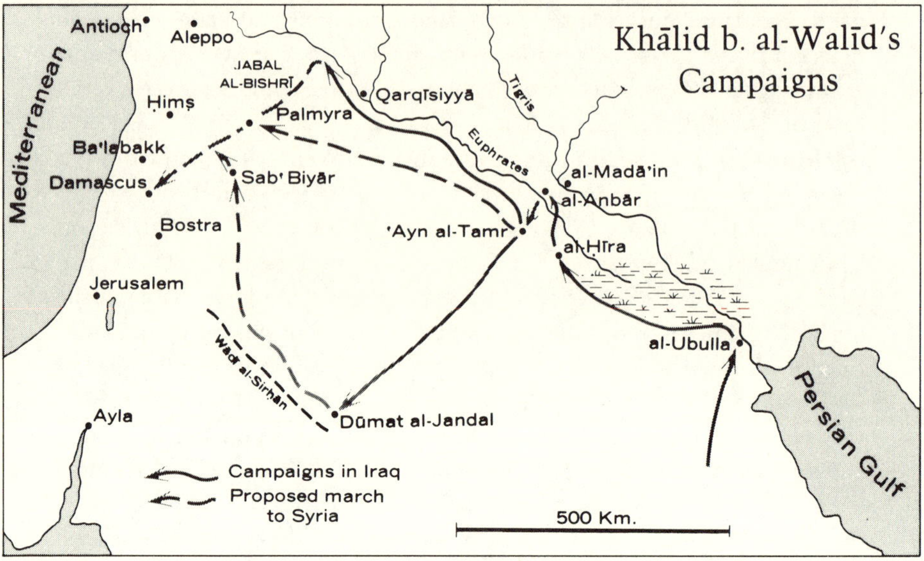

Khālid b. al-Walīd's Campaigns

small fifth force led by Khālid b. al-Walīd, a member of the Makhzūm clan of Quraysh and by all odds one of the best of the Muslims' military tacticians. Unlike the other reinforcements coming to Syria, however, which marched there from Medina, Khālid and his troops arrived in Syria from Iraq, where they had been sent by Abū Bakr after completing the subjugation of the rebellious B. Ḥanīfa in al-Yamāma during the *ridda* wars.[153]

The story of Khālid's march from Iraq across the Syrian desert to Syria fired the imagination of the chroniclers, who almost without exception include some version of it in their accounts of the conquests.[154] Most versions agree that Khālid and his men set out from al-Ḥīra,[155] which had served as his base of operations in Iraq, and emerged in Syria proper at a point near Damascus. But there is much disagreement in the sources over what places Khālid passed through on his route of march,[156] and this has generated considerable difference of opinion among those more recent scholars who have tried to reconstruct Khālid's itinerary.[157]

One of the difficulties in using the traditional accounts to establish Khālid's route of march is that the medieval authors included in his march to Syria references to incidents and locations that belong to his earlier campaigning in Iraq.[158] Into this category fall the reports of Khālid's campaigns against tribes and towns located on or near the west bank of the Euphrates as far north as Jabal al-Bishrī—in particular, the expeditions to al-Anbār, 'Ayn al-Tamr, Ṣandawdā', and a number of other places the location of which is less certain,[159] as well as his campaigns to subdue parts of the nomadic tribes of al-Namir b. al-Qāsiṭ and Taghlib. Likewise, the references to Khālid's activities at Dūmat al-Jandal may stem, entirely or in part, from his earlier campaigning there as part of his consolidation of control over the fringes of Iraq from his base at al-Ḥīra. The assumption that this material has been misplaced not only simplifies the task of determining Khālid's itinerary, but also restores a measure of agreement between the descriptions of his march to Syria and the general statements provided in the sources as to the purpose of his march. The latter suggest that Abū Bakr ordered Khālid to march to Syria as quickly as possible, and emphasize the urgency with which Khālid proceeded.[160] Under such circumstances it is difficult to see why Khālid would have struck out through hostile territory and become embroiled in many campaigns against unsubdued towns and tribes, the successful completion of which would have required months. For this reason it is most plausible to conclude that many of the episodes usually included as part of Khālid's march to Syria in fact belong to earlier campaigning in Iraq, before Abū Bakr's urgent request for reinforcements in Syria reached him.[161]

Eliminating this material from the accounts of Khālid's march to Syria does not by any means resolve all the difficulties that arise in establishing his itinerary, however. The basic problem is the impossibility of reconciling those accounts that suggest that Khālid's force marched via Palmyra (Tadmur) with those that suggest that he marched via Dūmat al-Jandal. A choice must be made between one or the other, but there are various episodes in the traditional accounts that support each of the proposed itineraries, making it impossible to make a choice that is definitive and not merely personal preference. In order to appreciate this problem, however, it is necessary to look briefly at some of the incidents that—whatever we decide with regard to the itinerary—are reported to have taken place during the march.

Perhaps the most famous episode in the march to Syria, and indeed in all of the early conquest literature, is the account of Khālid's "desert march." According to most traditions, Khālid and his men came at some point on their way to a place called Qurāqir. From there they had to make a march of five nights (six days) through totally waterless country before reaching the next watering-point, at a place called Suwā, but the troop did not have enough waterskins and could not carry sufficient water to take the men, camels, and horses that far. On the advice of his guide, a man named Rāfi' b. 'Amr of the Ṭayyi' tribe, Khālid forced twenty of the camels to drink great quantities of water, tied their mouths (to prevent them from eating or chewing their cud and thereby spoiling the water), and then set out across the desert, slaughtering some of the camels daily and using the water in their stomachs. On the sixth day, with the water at an end, the party managed to locate with some difficulty the water-point at Suwā.[162]

Another episode that appears to have taken place during the march to Syria was a raid on the Bahrā' tribe; most sources place this event either at Suwā or nearby, shortly after the completion of the desert march.[163]

A third episode mentioned in many sources describes Khālid's activities at Palmyra, where he reportedly surrounded the town, which then capitulated in return for a treaty.[164]

With these facts in mind, it is possible to reconsider the problem of Khālid's itinerary. One proposed solution would have Khālid march up the Euphrates as far as Jabal al-Bishrī, through localities already conquered during his earlier campaigns in Iraq, and then march southwest to Palmyra and on via al-Qaryatayn and Ḥuwwārīn to the environs of Damascus. The assumptions in this case are, first, that medieval chroniclers lumped together with Khālid's itinerary the accounts about his earlier conquests in this area, since the same localities were mentioned in both sets of traditions; and second, that the references to Dūmat al-Jandal as a point on the itinerary are simply misplaced data properly belonging to Khālid's earlier campaigns from al-Ḥīra. These assumptions are, as we have seen, fully defensible. The main difficulty with this itinerary is that it forces us to locate the desert march from Qurāqir to Suwā in the stretch between Jabal al-Bishrī and Palmyra, which is neither sufficient distance to warrant a six days' march nor devoid of good watering places.[165] Some sources, furthermore, state that Qurāqir was a well of the B. Kalb, and most suggest that Suwā was closely identified with the B. Bahrā', as Khālid's skirmish with Bahrā' took place at Suwā or near it.[166] But, though the presence of Bahrā' between Palmyra and the Euphrates is plausible, it seems very unlikely that the B. Kalb controlled wells this far north before the rise of Islam.[167]

A second possible itinerary would have Khālid march from al-Ḥīra toward Palmyra more or less directly, passing perhaps through 'Ayn al-Tamr and then striking out across the desert.[168] This would be the most direct route from al-Ḥīra to Syria and might be a logical choice, as there were ancient caravan routes that connected Palmyra with the middle Euphrates district, along one of which Khālid might have marched.[169] In this case, the assumptions are that in the traditional accounts of Khālid's march the references to Dūmat al-Jandal and to most of the sites near the Euphrates are misplaced and belong in fact to his earlier campaigns—once again, assumptions that can be defended. The desert march from Qurāqir to Suwā would then fall somewhere in the stretch between 'Ayn al-Tamr and Palmyra. This is territory that could have been associated with the Kalb and Bahrā' tribes, as Qurāqir and Suwā seem to have been, and the distance is sufficient to warrant a six-days' march.[170] But, although it is an area where water is scarcer than around Jabal al-Bishrī, it is not altogether devoid of important watering-points,[171] and there seem to be no likely sites that might be identified with either Qurāqir or Suwā on toponymic grounds.

The third possible itinerary, proposed by A. Musil, would have Khālid march from al-Ḥīra west southwestward to Dūmat al-Jandal in northern Arabia, and thence to Qurāqir, which could be identified with Qulbān Qurājir on the eastern edge of the Wādī al-Sirḥān. From there, he marched six days straight northward, across very arid country, until reaching Suwā, which could be identified with modern Sab' Biyār, one hundred fifty kilometers east of Damascus.[172] This solution assumes that the references to locations along the Euphrates belong to Khālid's earlier campaigning, which is acceptable enough; and the identification of Qurāqir with Qulbān Qurājir seems plausible on toponymic grounds. In addition, Qulbān Qurājir is located in the heart of territory once controlled by the B. Kalb, and Sab' Biyār could from its location have been associated with either the Kalb or Bahrā'. But the solution proposed is not without its difficulties. First, it forces us to assume also that the references to Khālid's activity at Palmyra are erroneous or misplaced, an assumption that is unsatisfactory because so many sources mention Khālid's activity at Palmyra (making it capricious simply to reject these references as errors), and because there are no references to any other visits by Khālid to Palmyra, either before or after the period of the march to Syria (making it difficult to assume that the material is misplaced).[173] In addition, it is not easy to explain why Khālid should have chosen to make the difficult desert march from Qulbān Qurājir when he could have simply marched from there to Bostra to join the other commanders, via a route that is well watered and half the distance of the desert march.[174]

The first proposed itinerary thus seems unlikely on topographical grounds, but both the second and third seem plausible as routes Khālid's army may have taken on its way to Syria. Whether one prefers the route via Palmyra or that via Dūmat al-Jandal will depend on whether one attaches more importance to the accounts of Khālid's activity at Palmyra, or to the similarity between place-names given in accounts of his march and modern toponyms in the Syrian desert. Neither itinerary can, however, be decisively ruled out.

The further course of Khālid's march, once he had reached a point in the Syrian desert near Jabal al-Ruwāq, is not without its difficulties, but by comparison with the earlier portion of his march it is less troublesome. A number of sources mention that as Khālid approached the cultivated and settled portion of Syria, he became engaged in raids at al-Qaryatayn and Ḥuwwārīn, both of which lie between Palmyra and Damascus, as well as at a place called al-Quṣam, which was evidently nearby. According to al-Balādhurī, there were skirmishes with the inhabitants of both al-Qaryatayn and Ḥuwwārīn, and the defenders at the latter were reinforced by people from Ba'labakk and Bostra. At al-Quṣam (which al-Balādhurī places before Palmyra) Khālid is reported to have made terms with the B. Mashja'a b. al-Taym of Quḍā'a. Much the same is reported by al Ṭabarī's anonymous sources, except that al-Quṣam is placed after Qaryatayn and Ḥuwwārīn. Ibn Isḥāq also mentions a skirmish at Ḥuwwārīn.[175]

Nearly all traditions, however much they may differ on the route of Khālid's march, agree that Khālid emerged in Syria proper at a point near Damascus. He is reported to have fallen upon the B. Ghassān at Marj Rāhiṭ (near Damascus) as they were celebrating Easter (i.e., April 24, A.D. 634/19 Ṣafar, A.H. 13), and he or his lieutenants raided several localities in the famous Ghūṭa, the rich cultivated district that supports the city of Damascus.[176] According to some accounts, Khālid and his men then proceeded toward Bostra (Buṣrā or Qanāt Buṣrā), where they joined the other Islamic armies already in Syria; according to others, they joined forces at Marj Rāhiṭ and proceeded together to Bostra.

Like the topographical problems surrounding Khālid's march to Syria, the chronological ones are complex, but they prove less difficult to resolve, and they have a more general importance because they help establish the chronology of the entire first phase of the Islamic conquest in Syria. The basic data relating to the timing of Khālid's march and its relation to the conquests in Syria are the following. First, there is a general consensus among the various authorities that the Islamic armies in Syria were dispatched from Medina in the first months of the year A.H. 13/early spring of A.D. 634.[177] Second, virtually all accounts of Khālid's march agree that Abū Bakr instructed Khālid to proceed from Iraq to Syria in order to reinforce the Muslims' forces there. The earliest that he could have written Khālid in this vein, then, was roughly at the time the armies were to set out from Medina for Syria, and many accounts state that Abū Bakr only asked Khālid to make his march after the Syrian commanders had requested the caliph to send them reinforcements—that is, after the first phase of operations in Syria was already well underway,[178] or several months into the year A.H. 13/roughly summer of A.D. 634 at the earliest. A third group of accounts conforms to this chronology; these assert that Khālid left al-Ḥīra in Rabī' II of A.H. 13/June, A.D. 634, or that he arrived in Syria in Rabī'. These accounts are reinforced by a statement implying that the "desert march" from Qurāqir to Suwā was made in hot weather.[179] The fourth piece of evidence creates difficulties for this otherwise consistent chronology, however; it states that Khālid reached Marj Rāhiṭ, near Damascus and raided the B. Ghassān there as they were celebrating Easter (*fī yawm fiṣḥi-him*),[180] which in A.D. 634 fell on April 24/19 Ṣafar, A.H. 13. This places Khālid's arrival in Syria nearly two months before other accounts state he left Iraq, and only about a month after the departure of the Muslims' armies from Medina for Syria—hardly enough time for those armies to have reached Syria, campaigned there, requested reinforcements from Abū Bakr, and seen Khālid arrive in response to their request.

This chronological dilemma can be resolved in one of two ways. One is to assume that the notice claiming that Khālid arrived in Damascus at Easter is mistaken or misplaced. We would then be free to accept the somewhat later chronology that the other evidence seems consistently to support. The difficulty with this approach is that there is no particular reason to consider the notice erroneous or misplaced; indeed, it is just this kind of evidence, providing a precise dating that is not part of the early historians' chronological schemes, that can be expected to be most reliable.

The other solution is to assume that the chronological scheme elaborated by the early authorities is too late by at least several months, and the statement that Khālid arrived in Damascus at Easter is correct. Since the weakest point of the traditional Arabic sources is precisely their chronology, this approach seems plausible enough; we can simply move the events of Khālid's march, as well as the departure of Islamic troops for Syria, several months back to allow enough time for everything to take place and permit Khālid to arrive in Syria at Easter. There is, in addition, one further piece of evidence that supports the earlier chronology: a passage in an anonymous Syriac chronicle of A.D. 724 that dates the first clash of the Muslims' armies with the Byzantines near Gaza to February of the year 945 of the Seleucid era,[181] that is to February, A.D. 634/Dhū l-Qa'da, A.H. 12. This, too, at once requires that the departure of Islamic armies for Syria be set back several months. It is therefore plausible to conclude that these forces left Medina for Syria in the autumn of A.D. 633, first clashed with the Byzantines near Gaza in February of 634, demanded reinforcements from Abū Bakr shortly thereafter, and were reinforced by Khālid, who left Iraq in early April and reached the environs of Damascus at Easter, April 24, A.D. 634.[182]

The composition of the force that marched to Syria with Khālid can be determined only to the extent that we can ascertain the composition of the forces that fought with him in Iraq—itself not an easy task.[183] Khālid was apparently instructed by Abū Bakr to march with the fighting men (*ahl al-quwwa*), at least those who had come with him from the Ḥijāz and the campaign to al-Yamāma during the *ridda* wars, and to leave behind the women and the weak (who were to return to Medina), and also, it seems, most of the tribesmen native to Iraq who had joined forces with Khālid's army when the Muslims first arrived there. We can surmise that Khālid's force contained a considerable number of *muhājirūn* and *anṣār* and probably some members of nomadic groups from the Ḥijāz and Najd that had remained loyal to Medina during the *ridda*, such as sections of Muzayna, since these appear to have accompanied Khālid during his campaigning in al-Yamāma. Though most of the Iraqi tribesmen are said to have remained in Iraq, not all stayed behind—to judge, at least, from an account of the action at Palmyra, in which four men of the B. Sadūs (a section of the Iraqi tribe of Dhuhl) are reported to have been killed.[184]

Reports vary greatly on the size of Khālid's force, as is usual in accounts of this type. There is no way to resolve these disparities, but it is likely that the lower figures, which place the size of the force marching from Iraq to Syria at between 500 and 800, are more realistic than the much higher figures provided by some sources.[185]

Despite the manifest difficulties that the material raises, it is nonetheless possible to draw a few general conclusions about the Islamic conquests from the accounts of Khālid's march. They suggest the small size of the forces involved in much of the conquest, since even if the most inflated figures are accepted it is difficult to see that the added manpower brought by Khālid's force could have been decisive. They suggest also the importance, in this early stage of the conquests, of the tribal groups that had early allied themselves to the Islamic state and stood by it during the *ridda* wars—notably Meccans, Medinese, and some nomadic tribesmen mostly from the Ḥijāz. Both these conclusions are more firmly bolstered by evidence from other phases of the conquest in Syria and from the evidence about the conquests in Iraq.

But Khālid's desert march also bears some further, and rather unique, implications for the conquest movement. One is that his march reveals the extent to which Islamic control was being imposed over the Arabian and Syrian deserts, the hitherto inaccessible refuge of powerful nomadic groups. Whether we view his march as an undertaking made possible by the successful completion of this process by which the Islamic state brought the desert under its control, or whether we view it rather as the last phase of the process by which the central parts of the Syrian desert were finally subjugated, it is clear that the new Islamic state had neared the completion of its consolidation over Arabia. Certainly Khālid would not have marched his modest force through such territory if the Muslims still faced significant resistance (a few skirmishes aside) from the nomads of the central districts of the Syrian steppe.

A second implication of Khālid's march is that it reflects the degree to which the rulers of the new Islamic state in Medina could coordinate the activities of their armies in the field. Given the means of communication existent in that day and the great distances involved, it is obvious that individual commanders must have had a great deal of freedom to act on their own initiative, and many tactical decisions were doubtless made by them as situations arose. But the ability of Abū Bakr to order an army—even a very small army—operating in Iraq to join other forces of Muslims in Syria in response to strategic needs there reveals that the Muslims' commanders were not simply engaged in haphazard campaigning. However great the individual commanders' discretionary powers, it seems clear that the general guidelines on matters of policy and strategy to be followed in the conquest were drawn up in Medina, by the ruling elite, and that the commanders were merely given the liberty to implement those policies as best they could.

7. PHASE II: THE DEFEAT OF THE BYZANTINES

With Khālid's arrival in Syria the second phase of the Islamic conquest of Syria can be said to have begun—a phase in which the Muslims turned their full attention to the conquest of some important Syrian towns, faced increasingly stiff organized resistance from the Byzantines, and eventually broke that resistance in several major confrontations with the Byzantine army.

Unfortunately, the course of events during this second phase of the conquest cannot be established with any confidence. The many accounts of the conquest generally make reference to the same incidents and often provide a considerable amount of detail in describing these incidents; but different early systematizers of historical traditions assembled fragmentary accounts in different ways, resulting in several contradictory sequential schemes, and it is virtually impossible to accept one sequential or chronological arrangement of the material and to reject another except on grounds that are essentially arbitrary.[186] All of these chronological schemes are at heart later efforts to bring order to a mass of fragmentary accounts (*akhbār*) about the conquests in Syria, and though one such scheme may appear to be more plausible than another, all are essentially guesswork and none has any real claim to validity. In view of this situation, it is necessary to summarize each of the main traditional reconstructions separately, and then to conclude by making some general observations on the nature of the second phase of the conquest by drawing on all reconstructions as appropriate.

The Reconstruction of Ibn Isḥāq, al-Wāqidī, and others

One chronological reconstruction of the conquest of Syria is provided in more or less complete form in traditions of Ibn Isḥāq (d. 150/767), al-Wāqidī (d. 207/823), and the Syrian scholar Sa'īd b. 'Abd al-'Azīz al-Tanūkhī (fl. ca. A.D. 800?), with but minor variations among them as regards the sequence of events,[187] and this reconstruction formed the basis of the later account of al-Ya'qūbī (d. 284/897). The main characteristics of this chronological reconstruction are that it places the battle of Ajnādayn roughly at the time of Abū Bakr's death in about Jumāda I, A.H. 13/July, A.D. 634; the battle of Faḥl in about Dhū l-Qa'da 13/January 635; the fall of Damascus in Rajab 14/August-September 635; and the battle of Yarmūk in Rajab 15/August-September 636. It seems likely that Ibn Isḥāq was initially responsible for creating this systematization, in view of the fact that he was active much earlier than the other scholars, but it is possible that he drew up only the sequence of events and that the efforts to assign a firm date to each event in the sequence were made by al-Wāqidī or one of the other transmitters who adopted Ibn Isḥāq's sequential scheme.

According to this reconstruction the first Syrian city to fall to the Muslims was Bostra. It was taken when Khālid b. al-Walīd, who had just arrived in Syria at a point near Damascus after his desert march from Iraq, proceeded south to Bostra (Buṣrā or Qanāt Buṣrā) and met up with Abū 'Ubayda, Shuraḥbīl b. Ḥasana, and Yazīd b. Abī Sufyān, who had already gathered at or near the city. After a siege, the town submitted to the Muslims in exchange for a pact (*ṣulḥ*) requiring it to pay an annual tax (*jizya*). This occurred, according to one miscellaneous tradition, five days before the end of Rabī' I, A.H. 13/late May, A.D. 634.[188]

After completing the conquest of Bostra, the commanders marched together toward Palestine, where they joined 'Amr b. al-'Āṣ, who was facing a large concentration of Byzantine troops commanded by "al-Qubuqlār" (*cubicularius*, chamberlain) at a place called Ajnādayn, described as lying between Ramla and Bayt Jibrīn. The location has been identified by modern researchers with the ancient Yarmūth near Wādī al-Simṭ, twenty-five kilometers west-southwest of Jerusalem.[189] The Byzantines reportedly sent out a bedouin of the B. Quḍā'a, probably a Christian, to serve as a spy on the Muslims—a perfectly plausible happening, even if the tale of his findings and his report to the Byzantine commanders is filled with legendary or imaginative devices designed to make it a better story. The battle at Ajnādayn—according to this reconstruction the first major one between the Muslims and a Byzantine army—was bitterly fought, and although the Byzantines were apparently routed and the Byzantine *cubicularius* himself reportedly killed, the Muslims' victory did not come easily, for several sources list the names of prominent early Muslims who fell as martyrs on the field of battle.[190] The Muslims, who numbered about twenty thousand according to one source, were commanded by 'Amr b. al-'Āṣ, whereas the other generals active in Syria (Yazīd b. Abī Sufyān, Shuraḥbīl b. Ḥasana, and Khālid b. al-Walīd) were evidently present as subordinates.[191] The battle took place, according to most accounts, on the 27th or 28th of Jumāda I, A.H. 13/29 or 30 July, A.D. 634, according to others around 18 Jumāda I, in

Jumāda II, or even in Dhū 'l-Qa'da of A.H. 13/January, A.D. 635. In any case but the last, it is generally supposed to have occurred during the last months of Abū Bakr's caliphate, and the news of the Muslims' victory is supposed to have reached him on his deathbed, in Jumāda II, 13/August 634.[192]

From Ajnādayn, the defeated Byzantines apparently fled in disorder to the town of Faḥl (Pella), on the east bank of the Jordan just across from Baysān (Beth Shan, Scythopolis), where there appears to have been a Byzantine garrison. The Muslims therefore marched from Ajnādayn and pursued them there. The Muslims' advance was impeded, according to one account, by the Byzantines' tactic of breaking the river banks and causing a large area to become flooded; but despite the muddy conditions the Muslims were able to score another important victory over the Byzantine forces and to occupy Faḥl. A variant account states that in a battle near Faḥl an enormous number of Byzantines—the source provides the figure of 100,000—was killed, after which the survivors fled to the city for refuge, were besieged in it by the Muslims for four months, and ultimately agreed to capitulate in exchange for a treaty.[193] The defeated Byzantines then retreated toward Damascus. Some sources claim that 'Amr b. al-'Āṣ commanded at Faḥl, but others put the command in the hands of Khālid b. al-Walīd or of Abū 'Ubayda b. al-Jarrāḥ; Shuraḥbīl b. Ḥasana is also said to have been present, apparently as a subordinate commander.[194] It was when the Muslims were encamped before Faḥl, according to some of these transmitters, that the news of Abū Bakr's death and of the accession of 'Umar b. al-Khaṭṭāb as the second caliph is said to have reached the Islamic armies in Syria. 'Umar is reported to have removed Khālid b. al-Walīd from the position of commander-in-chief of the forces in Syria and to have placed Abū 'Ubayda b. al-Jarrāḥ in his stead.[195] Generally this reconstruction dates the battle of Faḥl to Dhū l-Qa'da, A.H. 13/December, A.D. 634-January, A.D. 635.[196]

The purveyors of this reconstruction generally place at about this point some notice of another engagement with the Byzantines at a place called Marj al-Ṣuffar, the location of which is uncertain.[197] There is, however, sharp disagreement among them over its dating, and in some cases a tendency to confuse the engagement at Marj al-Ṣuffar with that at Ajnādayn can be detected. Al-Wāqidī placed this episode after the battle of Faḥl, in Muharram of A.H. 14/March, A.D. 635, and states that after the encounter the Muslims marched on to Damascus, which they reached in the same month.[198] Ibn Isḥāq, on the other hand, dates the battle at

Marj al-Ṣuffar to Jumāda I of A.H. 13/July, A.D. 634, that is, about the same time as the battle of Ajnādayn and thus before Faḥl,[199] whereas Sa'īd b. 'Abd al-'Azīz places Marj al-Ṣuffar before Ajnādayn.[200] Those sources that provide any information about the battle other than its ostensible date state that Khālid b. al-Walīd commanded the Muslims and suggest that their losses were very considerable, perhaps as many as four thousand men, but that the engagement was a victory for Khālid. Other accounts describe the battle as having taken place on a river near a mill, which was made to turn from the blood of the slaughtered Byzantines.[201] Basically, however, it seems clear that the battle was poorly known to the authors of this reconstruction; they provide little information about it, and its chronological placement evidently posed great problems for them.

After Faḥl and Marj al-Ṣuffar, the Muslims are portrayed as advancing on Damascus, where the remnants of the Byzantine armies from Ajnādayn and Faḥl had taken refuge. The Byzantine commander is said by some sources following this reconstruction to have been a certain Bāhān.[202] The Muslims placed the city under siege for an extended period, with each of the Muslims' generals taking up a position at one of the city gates: Khālid b. al-Walīd at the East Gate, 'Amr b. al-'Āṣ at Bāb Tūmā, Abū 'Ubayda at the Jābiya Gate, Shuraḥbīl b. Ḥasana at the Paradise Gate, and Yazīd b. Abī Sufyān at the Little Gate and Kaysān Gate. In addition, there seems to have been an outlying garrison (*maslaḥa*) under either Abū l-Dardā' or his lieutenant 'Uwaymir b. 'Āmir al-Khazrajī, located at a village called Barza in the Ghūṭa five kilometers north of Damascus.[203] The defenders of Damascus evidently sent to the Byzantine emperor Heraclius asking for reinforcements, but a Byzantine column that was sent to relieve the city was defeated by a troop of Muslims between Bayt Lihyā and Thaniyyat, east of Damascus. According to most accounts in this reconstruction, the end of the siege came when one of the Muslims' commanders succeeded in breaking the city gate on one side of Damascus, just at the moment when the Damascenes were negotiating a treaty and opening their gates to another commander on the other side of town; but there are conflicting opinions on which commander—Khālid, Abū 'Ubayda, or Yazīd b. Abī Sufyān—played which role. In any case, the two forces of Muslims are said to have converged at a place called *al-maqsallāṭ*, plausibly identified with the *macella* or covered market in the middle of the city,[204] and there the commanders conferred and agreed to treat the entire city as if it had submitted under a pact. Although all authorities in this group agree that the city was conquered in Rajab, A.H. 14/August-September, A.D. 635, there is far less unanimity on the length of the siege; some state that it lasted four months, whereas others say it lasted six months, a year, or fourteen months. Similarly, there are differences of opinion over who was commander-in-chief during the siege, some claiming that Abū 'Ubayda held this position since the time of Faḥl, others claiming that news of Abū Bakr's death and 'Umar's replacement of Khālid by Abū 'Ubayda as commander-in-chief only reached the Muslims at Damascus, and that Abū 'Ubayda hid the news from Khālid until the siege was over.[205]

After the conquest of Damascus, Abū 'Ubayda is said by some to have left Yazīd b. Abī Sufyān in charge of the city, while he himself advanced toward Ba'labakk, which capitulated, and then to Ḥimṣ (Emesa). According to other traditions, the force that defeated the Byzantine column intending to relieve Damascus pursued them as far as Ḥimṣ, which capitulated to the commander of that force, al-Simṭ b. al-Aswad al-Kindī; only later, after completing the siege of Damascus, did Abū 'Ubayda come via Ba'labakk to Ḥimṣ. Yet other traditions claim that Abū 'Ubayda sent ahead a column under Khālid b. al-Walīd and Milḥān b. Zayyār al-Ṭā'ī, which proceeded via Ba'labakk and the Biqā' (Coele-Syria) to Ḥimṣ, where they were joined later by Abū 'Ubayda; the commanders then reduced Ḥimṣ in joint action. The conquest of Ḥimṣ is dated by this reconstruction to Dhū l-Qa'da, A.H. 14/December, A.D. 635-January, A.D. 636.[206]

In response to the Muslims' victories at Ajnādayn and Faḥl and their occupation of Damascus, Ba'labakk, and Ḥimṣ, the Byzantine emperor Heraclius, who was watching these developments from Antioch, is said to have organized an enormous force, usually described as numbering 100,000 or more. It apparently consisted not only of regular Byzantine army units, but also of contingents from Antioch, Qinnasrīn, Aleppo (Beroe), Mesopotamia, and Ḥimṣ, as well as a contingent of 12,000 Armenians commanded by a certain Jaraja (George). In addition, it included 12,000 Syrian Arab tribesmen led by the Ghassānid chieftain Jabala b. al-Ayham; among them, we are told, were tribesmen from the Lakhm, Judhām, Bal-Qayn, Balī, 'Āmila, Ghassān, and other tribes of the Quḍā'a group. The supreme commanders of this colossal Byzantine force were a eunuch called al-Ṣaqallār (*sacellarius*, bursar) by the Arabic sources, and the general Bāhān, a Persian Christian who had joined the Byzantine army. As the Byzantine force began to march south from Antioch, Abū 'Ubayda and the Muslims' other commanders concluded that it was necessary to reunite their forces. Abū 'Ubayda and his men therefore abandoned Ḥimṣ and withdrew to join his cohorts in Damascus. Meanwhile the Byzantine force entered Ḥimṣ, proceeded to Ba'labakk and the Biqā', and neared the outskirts of Damascus. The Muslims, apparently fearing that they might become caught between the approaching army and other Byzantine forces stationed in northern Palestine,[207] which could too easily cut off the Muslims' lines of communication or retreat southward toward the Ḥijāz, decided to abandon Damascus as well and withdrew to al-Jābiya in the Golan. The massive Byzantine army also proceeded to the Golan region and set up camp along the Nahr al-Ruqqād; the combined forces of Muslims then maneuvered into a position along the Yarmūk valley adjoining Nahr al-Ruqqād, and the stage was set for what was by all accounts the largest single military encounter between the Byzantines and the Muslims in Syria. The Muslims were far outnumbered by the Byzantine force; most accounts put the Muslims' army at about 24,000. Even if the figures provided for both sides are greatly inflated, they suggest that the Muslims' army was only about one-fourth the size of the Byzantine force at Yarmūk. The composition of the Muslims' force at Yarmūk is described in one account as follows: roughly one-third consisted of men of the Azd tribe, in addition to which there were tribesmen from Ḥimyar, Hamdān, Madhḥij (including five hundred of B. Zubayd), Khawlān, Khath'am, Kinda, and Ḥaḍramawt (all Yemeni tribes), as well as groups from Kināna, Lakhm, Judhām, and others from Quḍā'a (all Ḥijāzī or Syrian tribes). Tribesmen from Najrān are also said to have participated.[208] The descriptions of the battle of Yarmūk in this reconstruction are few, but, if the details provided can be believed, the Muslims, after some initial difficulties that forced even the women to fight, succeeded in driving the Byzantines back decisively. Many Byzantine troops were killed in the fighting, but many more seem to have perished by plunging over the banks of a ravine that adjoined the battlefield in the course of their retreat at night. The sources in this reconstruction date the Muslims' victory at Yarmūk to Rajab, A.H. 15/August-September, A.D. 636.[209]

The Muslims then pursued the remnants of the Byzantine army, which fled northward. This brought the Muslims once again before Damascus and Ḥimṣ, which according to this reconstruction readily agreed to submit on the same terms they had been granted when the Muslims first reduced these towns before the battle of the Yarmūk.[210]

With the destruction of the Byzantine army at Yarmūk, the second phase of the conquest of Syria, as presented by this reconstruction, came to an end. Thereafter the Islamic forces are portrayed as spreading out over various parts of Syria and forcing the capitulation of those towns and districts that were not already under the Muslims' control, without facing any organized resistance from a Byzantine army—a process of consolidation that can be said to form the third phase of the conquest of Syria.

The Reconstruction of Abū ʿUthmān Yazīd b. Asīd al-Ghassānī and others.

In addition to the reconstruction just described, there exists in more or less complete form another, very different reconstruction of the events during the second stage of the conquest of Syria. This reconstruction was transmitted by the Kufan scholar Sayf b. ʿUmar (d. between A.H. 170 and 193/A.D. 786 and 809) from Abū ʿUthmān Yazīd b. Asīd al-Ghassānī, Abū Ḥāritha al-ʿAbshamī, and a few other authorities, who in turn seem to have derived their information mainly from two early collectors of historical traditions who were named Khālid and ʿUbada.[211] The basic characteristic of this reconstruction is that it places the main events in the conquest of Syria in the following sequence: Yarmūk; sieges of Damascus and Faḥl simultaneously by separate armies; fall of Damascus; battle of Faḥl; simultaneous activity at Baysān and Tiberias by one force and at Marj al-Rūm and Ḥimṣ by another; activity in Palestine (Caesarea, Gaza); Ajnādayn. It also provides fewer precise datings than does the reconstruction of Ibn Isḥāq and al-Wāqidī; Yarmūk is dated to A.H. 13, around the time of Abū Bakr's death, and the fall of Damascus is dated to A.H. 14, but other events are undated.[212]

According to this reconstruction, the Byzantine emperor Heraclius became alarmed by the activities of the Muslims in southern Palestine and southern Syria during the first phase of the conquest and therefore marched with his army to Ḥimṣ, where he organized his forces. He dispatched separate armies to confront each of the Muslims' four commanders active in Syria: against ʿAmr b. al-ʿĀṣ he sent a large force (put at 90,000 men) commanded by his full brother Theodore (Tadhāriq), who camped at Jilliq;[213] against Yazīd b. Abī Sufyān, he sent a force under Jaraja b. Tūdharā; against Shuraḥbīl b. Ḥasana, he dispatched Durāqiṣ;[214] and against Abū ʿUbayda he sent al-Fīqār (*vicarius*, lieutenant commander?) b. Naṣṭūs with an army said to have been 60,000 strong. The Muslims' commanders became concerned because of the advance of the Byzantine armies and decided to consolidate their forces at the Yarmūk. The Byzantine forces also gathered in the vicinity, at a place called al-Wāqūṣa on the banks of the Yarmūk. There the forces under ʿAmr b. al-ʿĀṣ were apparently able to hem the Byzantines in on one side, as the ravine of the Yarmūk prevented them from withdrawing in another direction. The Byzantines remained trapped in this way for the months of Ṣafar and part of Rabīʿ I, A.H. 13/April-May, A.D. 634. The combined armies of ʿAmr, Yazīd, Shuraḥbīl, and Abū ʿUbayda numbered, we are told, 21,000 to 27,000 men, in addition to which there was a reserve force of 6,000 men under the command of ʿIkrima b. Abī Jahl, which brought the Muslims' total forces to 27,000-33,000 men. There was also a group of 3,000 men who had been part of Khālid b. Saʿīd's army, but it is not clear whether these are already included in the above figures or are to be considered separately. The Muslims were, in any case, seriously outnumbered by the Byzantines, and the commanders sent to Abū Bakr requesting reinforcements. It was at this time, according to this reconstruction, that Abū Bakr wrote to Khālid b. al-Walīd to march from Iraq to Syria; and when Khālid reached Syria, he proceeded with his army to Bostra, which he and his men alone reduced, and then continued his march to join the other commanders gathered at the Yarmūk. As he came with a force of about 10,000, according to these sources,[215] the total strength of the Muslims' armies at Yarmūk was now about 37,000-43,000. When Khālid arrived, furthermore, he was apparently accepted as commander-in-chief, whereas until this time we are told that each of the Muslims' commanders had operated more or less independently. Eventually the Muslims and Byzantines closed battle, and the ensuing fighting was apparently difficult, with considerable casualties in dead and wounded among the Muslims.[216] As in the preceding reconstruction, in this one there are accounts describing how it was necessary at a critical juncture in the battle for women to participate in the fighting.[217] Eventually, however, the battle went in favor of the Muslims, and the huge Byzantine force was decimated, with more casualties falling victim to the precipitous ravines that penned the Byzantines in than were actually killed by the Muslims themselves. Unfortunately, the reconstruction provides almost no general information about the composition of the Islamic army at Yarmūk. One passage informs us that 1,000 companions of the Prophet were present at the battle, including 100 who were already aligned with Muḥammad at the time of his first major encounter with the Quraysh at Badr.[218] There are no further references, however, suggesting which tribal groups may have taken part on the Islamic side, and even the collected names of those individuals mentioned as participants in the battle provide little more than a verification of the importance of the early companions and the names of a few non-Quraysh tribesmen. One poem, reputedly by ʿAmr b. al-ʿĀṣ, suggests that the Lakhm and Judhām tribes fought (poorly) in the Muslims' ranks at the Yarmūk.[219] It is worthy of note, however, that, although the number of members of Quraysh mentioned as participants is fairly great, very few members of the *anṣār* are mentioned.[220]

After the victory of Yarmūk, according to this reconstruction, Abū ʿUbayda left a certain Bashīr b. Kaʿb b. Ubayy al-Ḥimyarī with a force to hold the locality and to prevent the return there of Byzantine troops who might threaten the Muslims' lines of communication and reinforcement from the south; Abū ʿUbayda himself proceeded to al-Ṣuffar[221] to pursue the remnants of the Byzantine army. There he learned that the fugitives from the Yarmūk army had taken refuge at Faḥl and that Damascus had been reinforced by Byzantine troops coming from Ḥimṣ. Abū ʿUbayda is reported to have written to ʿUmar, who had in the meantime acceded as caliph, asking his advice. ʿUmar instructed Abū ʿUbayda to go to Damascus first, but to send other commanders against the Byzantine garrisons at Faḥl, in Palestine, and at Ḥimṣ. He also ordered that all the commanders who had served in Syria for Abū Bakr be confirmed in their commands, with the exception of Khālid b. al-Walīd, who was not to be under Abū ʿUbayda's orders; he also instructed that ʿAmr b. al-ʿĀṣ be made commander for Palestine.[222] Abū ʿUbayda accordingly drew up, under ten leaders headed by Abū l-Aʿwar, a force that was dispatched to Faḥl. Abū ʿUbayda then marched on Damascus, sending a force under Dhū Kalāʿ[223] to serve as a barrier (*ridʾ*) between Damascus and Ḥimṣ, and sending other troops under ʿAlqama b. Ḥakīm and Masrūq to serve as a barrier between Damascus and Palestine. His own force numbered among its subordinate commanders Khālid b. al-Walīd; ʿAmr b. al-ʿĀṣ, who like Abū ʿUbayda was given charge of one of the two wings; ʿIyāḍ b. Ghanm, who had come with Khālid from Iraq; Shuraḥbīl b. Ḥasana, who commanded the infantry (*rajl*); Yazīd b. Abī Sufyān; and Abū l-Dardāʾ, who during the action at Damascus fell on a Byzantine garrison at Barza, just north of the city. The field commander (*amīr*), we are told, was Khālid b. al-Walīd. These forces surrounded Damascus and put it to siege; the inhabitants' efforts to secure reinforcements from Heraclius in Ḥimṣ were foiled by Dhū Kalāʿ's detachment, which blocked the passage of the Byzantine relief force. The siege of Damascus lasted, according to these sources, about seventy days, after which the city seems to have made a treaty with one commander just as Khālid's troops were breaching the city walls in another place. The fall of Damascus to the Muslims is dated by Sayf, or his authorities, to Shawwāl, A.H. 14/November-December, A.D. 635.[224]

Once Damascus has fallen, 'Umar ordered Abū 'Ubayda to send the Iraqi contingent back to Iraq, where their services were needed for the impending clash with the Sasanians, so they marched off under Hāshim b. 'Utba leaving their former commander Khālid b. al-Walīd behind in Syria. Abū 'Ubayda then placed Yazīd b. Abī Sufyān in charge of a garrison of Muslims in Damascus that included a number of Yemeni chiefs. Yazīd seems to have lost no time in sending out small detachments on his own initiative; he is said to have dispatched Diḥya b. Khalīfa al-Kalbī to Palmyra and al-Zahrā' al-Qushayrī to al-Bathaniyya and the Ḥawrān district south of Damascus, both of which made treaties on the same terms as Damascus.[225] For his part, Abū 'Ubayda proceeded southwest with most of the other commanders to join the other Islamic forces that had, in the interim, invested the Byzantines near Faḥl. When the Muslims under Abū l-A'war and the ten commanders approached Faḥl, the Byzantines apparently blocked wells and took refuge across the Jordan in Baysān, which put the swampy low ground along the river between the Muslims and the Byzantines and impeded the Muslims' cavalry. In addition the Byzantine forces at Faḥl/Baysān are said to have been very numerous,[226] so Abū l-A'war made little headway against them. When Abū 'Ubayda reached the area with his large army coming from Damascus, he took up the position near Faḥl and sent Abū l-A'war to besiege the town of Tiberias.[227] The Muslims at Faḥl were still prevented from attacking because of the swampy ground, but eventually the Byzantines themselves, commanded by Saqallār b. Mikhraq (*sacellarius*), launched a surprise attack. This was not only repulsed by the Muslims, but converted by them into a crushing defeat of the Byzantine forces; the Byzantine commander himself was among the casualties and was succeeded as commander by one Naṣṭūrus.[228]

After the victory at Faḥl, according to this reconstruction, Abū 'Ubayda again divided his forces. Shuraḥbīl b. Ḥasana, 'Amr. b. al-'Āṣ, and their men were left in charge of Faḥl and besieged Baysān, but after several days of siege and a number of minor engagements in which sorties by the defenders were repulsed by the Muslims, the town capitulated on terms similar to those granted to Damascus. Abū l-Aʻwar, who had been sent against Tiberias, met with similar fortune there: the town capitulated on terms like those of Damascus when the inhabitants learned that Damascus and Faḥl had fallen.[229]

Meanwhile, Abū ʻUbayda marched with the remainder of his army to Ḥimṣ. He was accompanied by Khālid b. al-Walīd, and the two commanders were joined on the way by the detachment that had been left at the Yarmūk under Bashīr b. Kaʻb,[230] and by the forces under Dhū Kalāʻ that had been stationed between Damascus and Ḥimṣ. The approach of the combined Islamic army caused Heraclius, who was at the time in Ḥimṣ, to respond by sending two forces, under Tūdharā al-Biṭrīq (Theodore the *patricius*) and Shanas al-Rūmī. The two Byzantine forces seem at first to have positioned themselves so as to block the Muslims' advance on Ḥimṣ, but the force under Theodore then apparently moved toward Damascus. Khālid b. al-Walīd was accordingly dispatched with part of the Muslims' army to pursue Theodore's force. In the meantime Yazīd b. Abī Sufyān, who had been left in command of the garrison in Damascus, came out and engaged Theodore's troops as they approached Damascus. After battle was joined, we are told, Khālid's forces arrived on the scene, with the result that the Byzantine army was completely destroyed at a place called Marj Dimashq or Marj al-Rūm; Theodore himself was reportedly killed, and only scattered remnants of his army escaped. Yazīd b. Abī Sufyān then returned to Damascus, while Khālid moved to rejoin Abū ʻUbayda, who in the meantime had engaged and destroyed the other Byzantine force, killing its commander Shanas.[231]

As a result of these disasters Heraclius himself withdrew from Ḥimṣ to Edessa, leaving a Byzantine garrison to defend Ḥimṣ. Abū ʻUbayda and Khālid then moved up and invested the city. The siege seems to have taken place during the winter months, for we are told that the Byzantines hoped that the cold would discourage the Muslims (many of whom were barefoot) and thought that they would withdraw before summer. Despite the rigors of the weather, however, the Muslims kept up the siege through the winter, and even prepared to take the city by assault. At this the inhabitants of Ḥimṣ finally agreed to a treaty in which considerable latitude was allowed for the relative prosperity of various citizens, the richer paying a higher rate of tribute. After the town had capitulated, Abū ʻUbayda occupied it himself with a garrison force. He is said to have sent out several subordinate commanders against unspecified objectives, perhaps mainly to reduce the villages of the countryside surrounding Ḥimṣ: al-Simṭ b. al-Aswad al-Kindī with the B. Mu'āwiya of Kinda;[232] al-Ash'ath b. Minas with the Yemeni tribe of al-Sakūn, closely related to Kinda;[233] Bilāl and Khālid (b. al-Walīd?) "with the army (*al-jaysh*)"; and three other men who were evidently assigned to garrison Ḥimṣ itself.[234]

Meanwhile the Muslims' other forces that had under 'Amr b. al-'Āṣ and Shuraḥbīl b. Ḥasana successfully reduced Baysān, extended their activity to Palestine proper; there the remaining Byzantine forces (probably consisting for the most part of city garrisons from this region) attempted to re-form at Gaza and at Ajnādayn. According to these sources, 'Umar directed 'Amr and Shuraḥbīl to march against the Byzantines who had gathered at Ajnādayn under a commander named Arṭabūn, and sent 'Alqama b. Mujazziz to besiege the Byzantines gathered at Gaza under their leader al-Fīqār (*vicarius*). In addition, Mu'āwiya b. Abī Sufyān was sent to besiege Caesarea and thereby to prevent it from sending reinforcements to the other Byzantine concentrations. Arṭabūn was supported, it is said, by large garrisons at Jerusalem and Ramla, so 'Amr sent 'Alqama b. Ḥakīm al-Farāsī and Masrūq b. Fūlān al-'Akkī to keep the force at Jerusalem occupied, and Abū Ayyūb al-Mālikī to Ramla to tie down the Byzantine force there, said to have been commanded by Tadhāriq.[235] This allowed 'Amr to concentrate on the force led by Arṭabūn; and after receiving some additional reinforcements sent by 'Umar, he engaged the enemy and defeated them decisively at Ajnādayn. The remnants of the Byzantine army fled to Jerusalem, so 'Amr's army moved toward that city and joined up with the other commanders whom he had sent in that direction. According to this reconstruction, the encounter at Ajnādayn marked the end of concerted efforts by the Byzantines to resist the advance of the Muslims.[236]

The Reconstruction of 'Amr b. Muḥammad and others

In addition to the two more or less complete reconstructions of the events of the second stage of the conquest of Syria so far described, there exist fragments of several other early reconstructions. Of these one of the more important appears to have been assembled by several traditionists whose accounts are transmitted only by Sayf b. 'Umar: 'Amr b. Muḥammad, Muḥammad b. 'Abdullāh, Ṭalḥa b. al-A'lam al-Ḥanafī, al-Muhallab b. 'Uqba al-Asadī, Ziyād b. Sarjīs al-Aḥmarī, and Sa'īd b. al-Marzubān. Sayf appears to have consulted the works of these authorities and harmonized them to form a synthetic account, which makes it difficult to trace the provenance of various elements in the synthesis. It is possible, furthermore, that this sequential reconstruction was partly dependent on that of Abū 'Uthmān Yazīd b. Asīd al-Ghassānī, since in at least one instance Muḥammad b. 'Abdullāh cites the latter as his source.[237] The elements of this reconstruction that survive place the engagement at the Yarmūk very early, immediately after the seizure of Bostra, and they describe also a major battle at Ḥimṣ that is evidently later. Unfortunately no information from this reconstruction bearing on Faḥl, Damascus, or Ajnādayn seems to survive, whereas al-Ṣuffar is placed very early in Phase I.

According to this reconstruction, the Byzantines gathered at Yarmūk very early—already in the time of Abū Bakr—and it was this fact that caused the Muslims' commanders, 'Amr b. al-'Āṣ, Abū 'Ubayda, Yazīd b. Abī Sufyān, and Shuraḥbīl b. Ḥasana, to request reinforcements. Abū Bakr accordingly ordered Khālid b. al-Walīd to march from Iraq; and Khālid, after his arrival in Syria near Damascus, marched to Qanāt Bostra, the first city in Syria conquered by him and his troops, and then proceeded to al-Wāqūṣa (Yarmūk) to join the other commanders, bringing 7,000 or 9,000 men. The Muslims, it is said, totaled 36,000 men, and the Byzantines, commanded by their general Bāhān, numbered 240,000. The reconstruction includes dramatized accounts of the mission of a man from the Syrian bedouin (*min 'arab al-Shām*) sent by the Byzantines to spy on the Muslims before the battle. When battle was finally joined, the Byzantines were routed and many of them perished when they plunged into a ravine near the battleground during their flight. The reconstruction itself seems to date the battle of Yarmūk to Jumāda II, A.H. 13/August, A.D. 634, at about the time of Abū Bakr's death, as the news of the Yarmūk victory is said to have reached Medina twenty days after 'Umar's accession. But Sayf b. 'Umar appears to favor a date some weeks later, in early Rajab of A.H. 13/early September, A.D. 634.[238]

This reconstruction also describes an encounter between the Muslims and Byzantines at Ḥimṣ, which from the circumstances described in it clearly belongs to the third phase of the conquest of Syria.[239]

Other Reconstructions

A number of other reconstructions also survive only in fragmentary or incomplete form. Among them can be mentioned that of Abū 'Uthmān al-Ṣan'ānī; in addition to having a totally different account of Khālid's activities on the way to Syria, it places the conquest of Damascus shortly after Khālid's arrival there from Iraq. Though the placement of this event is very different, however, many of the details of the siege of Damascus itself are comparable to those described in other reconstructions.[240]

Another reconstruction of which only scraps are extant is that of the great scholar al-Madā'inī (d. 238/850). It likewise places the conquest of Damascus immediately after Khālid b. al-Walīd's arrival in Syria from Iraq, and follows it with the battle of Ajnādayn and then of al-Wāqūṣa or al-Yāqūṣa (Yarmūk). The last is said to have taken place in Rajab of A.H. 13/September, A.D. 634.[241]

Especially noteworthy is the later reconstruction provided by Ibn A'tham al-Kūfī (d. 314/926), which survives in complete form. This synthesis, though apparently based at least in part on the reconstruction of Ibn Isḥaq and al-Wāqidī,[242] presents a sequence of events that agrees with their reconstruction only partly; in addition, the account of Ibn A'tham shows considerable internal confusion, suggesting that it was created by combining traditions from a variety of sources not all of which were in agreement. After describing how Abū 'Ubayda gathered a force at al-Jābiya, Ibn A'tham's reconstruction of the second phase of the conquest of Syria begins with Khālid's arrival near Damascus in response to Abū Bakr's request that he march from Iraq to reinforce the Muslims in Syria. At Damascus Khālid joined Abū 'Ubayda and the other commanders, and together they are said to have conquered the city. Thereafter, subordinate commanders were dispatched against Bostra, Ba'labakk, the Balqā' district, Palestine, Ḥimṣ, and the Ḥawrān. A bit later a Byzantine force gathered at Ajnādayn, but when the Muslims, led by Khālid b. al-Walīd, set out to meet them, the Damascenes rose in rebellion behind them and forced them to return and again conquer the city. Then the Muslims again marched toward Ajnādayn to confront the Byzantines who, aided by the Christian bedouin, had assembled a force numbering 40,000 under a general called Qalfaṭ. The Muslims were victorious there, totally destroying the Byzantine force and killing its commander. The Muslims then returned to Damascus; at this point in the narrative is described a siege of the city that lasted thirteen months, a battle at Marj al-Ṣuffar in which 20,000 Byzantines were soundly defeated, and at least three different conquests of Damascus itself by the Muslims (which, as noted above, is said to have been conquered at least twice already). The death of Abū Bakr and accession of 'Umar are said to have taken place at the time of the siege of Damascus, the fall of which is dated to Rajab,

A.H. 14/August-September, A.H. 635 as in the reconstruction of Ibn Isḥāq and al-Wāqidī.[243]

Alarmed by the fall of Damascus, the Byzantines are said to have drawn up a large force including many Christian tribesmen. This troop, which numbered 100,000, gathered at Faḥl and was confronted by the Muslims, who numbered 20,000. Khālid was dispatched to Ba'labakk to break up another Byzantine force that had gathered there, after which he marched into Palestine. Meanwhile, the Byzantine force at Faḥl was defeated by the rest of the Muslims.[244]

After the victory at Faḥl, Abū 'Ubayda advanced on Ḥimṣ with Khālid, 'Amr b. al-'Āṣ, and Yazīd b. Abī Sufyān. The city capitulated after a siege, and subordinate commanders were sent out as far as Aleppo. In the meantime, however, the Byzantines assembled another mammoth force, commanded by a general named Māhān, which began to march south to engage the invading Muslims. As it approached, the Muslims withdrew from Ḥimṣ to Damascus, and eventually the two sides squared off for battle near the Yarmūk. Māhān's army is said to have numbered 400,000, whereas the Muslims under Abū 'Ubayda were 43,000. The composition of the Muslims' forces is described in such a way as to make clear that Ibn A'tham relied on the traditions of Sa'īd b. 'Abd al-'Azīz al-Tanūkhī for his information.[245] Despite the great disparity in the size of the armies, the Muslims scored a signal victory; Māhān and his shattered forces were required to flee, leaving behind great numbers of casualties. Eventually Khālid pursued Māhān and the remnants of his army as far as Ḥimṣ, where he engaged them and delivered another defeat to them in which Māhān himself was killed. Khālid then camped at Ḥimṣ, and Abū 'Ubayda turned his attention to the region of northern Palestine ("al-Urdunn") around Jerusalem.[246]

The Non-Arabic Sources and the Chronology of the Second Phase of the Conquest

A consideration of the various reconstructions of the conquest of Syria found in the Arabic sources, as well as of many isolated traditions that do not appear to be part of any major synthesis, leads to the conclusion that the actual sequence of events in the second phase of the conquest in Syria cannot be definitely determined on the basis of the Arabic sources. Since each of the reconstructions represents an attempt by early systematizers to provide a reasonable sequential (and ultimately, chronological) framework on which the fragmentary accounts of the conquest that came down to them could be hung, it is pointless to consider the plausibility of a specific reconstruction as a measure of its historical reliability. The whole purpose of these reconstructions was, after all, to create a plausible context for events about which information was available after the true context had been forgotten. In fact, each of the main reconstructions has strengths and weaknesses from the point of view of plausibility. The reconstruction of Ibn Isḥāq and al-Wāqidī, for example, places events in a strictly linear sequence, one after the other, and provides a plausible chronology for these events; but in so doing it raises the question of the relationship among the various Islamic armies in Syria, since all of them seem to be present at all events. The reconstruction of Abū 'Uthmān, on the other hand, seems to crowd events together in the years A.H. 13 and A.H. 14, but it provides a much more satisfying account of the way in which separate but coordinated Islamic armies may have worked simultaneously at reducing different localities, now joining forces to meet some special situation, now breaking up into smaller units to tackle more modest objectives. It is of course possible that one or another of the several reconstructions previously discussed is in fact more accurate than the others, or that part of one and part of another, considered together, would correspond most closely to "what actually happened"; but there is no way, working on the basis of the Arabic sources alone, that we can determine which of these conflicting reconstructions is to be preferred.

This difficulty, which arises directly from the way in which the Arabic sources for the conquests were assembled and the fragmentary nature of the material upon which they drew, could only be overcome if there existed an independent source of historical information that could provide secure datings for some of the events involved, or that could at least offer independent verification of one of the sequences propounded by the various reconstructions. It has, in fact, long been assumed that the Christian sources in Greek and Syriac provided just such an independent historiographical tradition. These sources, although few in number and very niggardly in their information about the conquests, seemed to provide support for the chronological scheme proposed by Ibn Isḥāq and al-Wāqidī, which led many researchers to conclude that only their reconstruction could be considered reliable. The result was a series of studies that attempted to unravel the conquest of Syria simply by rejecting as wrong all those accounts that could not be harmonized with the reconstruction of Ibn Isḥāq and al-Wāqidī. In this manner it was possible to generate what appeared to be a very precise picture of the course of the conquest in Syria, in which in some cases even the very day on which an event transpired could be established.[247]

The assumption that the Greek and Syriac sources represent an historiographical tradition independent of the Arabic tradition is not, however, one that can be accepted without hesitation. The only Byzantine Greek source of any importance for understanding the events of the second phase of the conquest of Syria—the *Chronographia* of Theophanes (d. A.D. 817)[248]—contains material about the events of early Islam that could only have been derived from the Arabic historiographical tradition, such as a description (albeit brief) of Arab genealogy.[249] The assumption that the Greek sources were not familiar with the reconstructions being generated by Arab historians cannot, then, be maintained. As for the Syriac sources, the later ones such as the chronicles of Michael the Syrian (d. after A.D. 1200) and of Elias, Archbishop of Nisibis (d. 11th century A.D.) are quite clearly familiar with the Arabic chronological schemes. Elias of Nisibis betrays his indebtedness to the reconstruction of al-Wāqidī and others not only by giving the same basic sequence of events, but by dating the events in Islamic dates (e.g., the fall of Damascus after a six-month siege is dated to Rajab, A.H. 14). His dependence on Arabic sources is also visible from the fact that he provides specific information about commanders active on the Iraqi front, which is not the kind of data that an independent local Syrian tradition would have known about or preserved.[250] Michael the Syrian is not so clearly dependent on the reconstruction of al-Wāqidī and company, but he also provides datings in the "years of the Ṭayyāyē (bedouin)" and knows about events in Iraq.[251] The only remaining Syriac source of any importance is a fragment that states explicitly that the Byzantines gathered at Gabīthā (= al-Jābiya/Yarmūk?) on 20 Āb 947 of the Seleucid era, which corresponds to 12 Rajab, A.H. 15/20 August, A.D. 636, and were then overwhelmingly defeated by the Muslims in a battle that cost 50,000 Byzantine lives.[252] This valuable fragment thus supports al-Wāqidī's dating of the battle of Yarmūk exactly, but unfortunately the date of the fragment cannot be established and it is therefore impossible simply to assume that its dating was not also derived from al-Wāqidī's chronology, either directly or indirectly via later Syrian chronicles.[253] As we shall see, the Christian sources (whether in Greek, Syriac, or Arabic) usually provide in any case only a very sketchy description of the events of the conquest. Indeed, one would expect that writers in the Islamic tradition would naturally have had much more interest than their Christian counterparts in reconstructing the events of the conquest, which must have been after all a rather painful subject for the latter to deal with. It is therefore reasonable to suggest that the Islamic writers were in fact the first to try to assemble a coherent picture of the conquest, and that it was from the attempted reconstruction by Islamic scholars writing in Arabic that the Christian writers in part drew their material.

In addition, the non-Arabic sources can hardly be taken as decisive in matters of chronology even if one assumes that they were elaborated independently of the Arabic historiographical tradition, because taken as a group they provide only a rather sketchy and in some ways inconsistent picture of the conquest of Syria. The most detailed account among the non-Arabic authors is by far that of Theophanes. According to his reconstruction, the first city in Syria to fall to the Muslims was Bostra, but unlike the Arabic chroniclers he places this event already in the reign of the caliph ʿUmar. The Muslims[254] then invaded as far as Gabitha (al-Jābiya), where they engaged and defeated Theodore, the brother of the emperor Heraclius. After his defeat Theodore withdrew to Edessa, and Heraclius appointed as generals Baanes[255] and Theodore the *sacellarius*.[256] In coordinated actions, they are said to have encountered the Muslims near Edessa (an error for Emesa/Ḥimṣ?)[257] and to have driven them back as far as Damascus. Heraclius at this time abandoned Syria in despair and returned to Constantinople. All of this, according to Theophanes, occurred in one year.[258]

In the following year[259] Baanes and Theodore the *sacellarius* joined forces to counter a massive Arab invasion of the region around Damascus; but in a battle on the 23rd of July, Theodore's force was defeated. The army of Baanes then mutinied against the emperor Heraclius, declaring Baanes to be emperor, and the forces of Theodore the *sacellarius* withdrew. Subsequently the Muslims were able to engage the remaining Byzantine forces and to defeat them soundly at the Yarmūk. The Muslims were aided in the battle by a southerly wind that blew dust in the faces of the Byzantines, and by the ravine in which many Byzantines met their death. Both armies at the Yarmūk are said to have numbered 40,000. After the victory at Yarmūk, the Muslims seized Damascus and then continued on to seize "Phoenicia" (Palestine and Lebanon).

The essential feature of Theophanes's reconstruction is thus the following sequence: Bostra; defeat of Theodore (brother of Heraclius); penetration by the Muslims as far as Edessa (i.e., Emesa/Ḥimṣ?); repulse of

Muslims to region of Damascus; defeat of Theodore (*sacellarius*) in July and withdrawal of his army; mutiny in Baanes's army; battle of Yarmūk; fall of Damascus.

Elias of Nisibis, on the other hand, who as we have seen presents a picture very similar to that of al-Wāqidī and Ibn Isḥāq, places the fall of Damascus after a six-month siege in Rajab, A.H. 14/August-September, A.D. 635, followed by the fall of Ba'labakk and Ḥimṣ four months later, and puts the battle of Yarmūk in the following year.[260] Michael the Syrian states that after the seizure of Bostra, the Muslims had overrun all of Syria as far as the Euphrates a full two years before the battle at the Yarmūk. But he also states that Baanes came to Damascus the year before Yarmūk, implying either that it had not fallen to the Muslims or that it had fallen but was retaken by Baanes.[261] The anonymous Syriac fragment mentions a pact with Ḥimṣ preceding the battle of Gabīthā (Yarmūk?), but says nothing definite about Damascus.[262] Thus the non-Arabic sources for the second phase of the conquest of Syria, because of the very sketchy picture of events they provide, the vagueness with which they present the sequence of events, and their probable dependence on the Arabic sources, are not decisive in establishing a secure chronology of the events in this phase.

The Character of the Second Phase of the Conquest in Syria

Our analysis of the sources reveals that it is unrealistic to attempt the construction of a precise chronological scheme for the events of the second phase of the conquest of Syria. We must, rather, settle for a relatively greater element of uncertainty, at least in matters of chronology, than did earlier scholars who operated on the basis of different assumptions about the sources.

This is not to say, however, that the information contained in the sources is fabricated.[263] The sources do in fact allow us to view, sometimes in considerable detail, specific incidents in the Islamic conquest of Syria; what they do not allow us to do is to ascertain the order in which many of these events occurred. It remains clear that the Islamic armies engaged elements of the Byzantine army several times and delivered serious defeats to them at the Yarmūk, at Ajnādayn, and at Faḥl. It is also clear that during this stage several important cities in Syria—namely, Bostra, Damascus, Faḥl, Baysān, Ba'labakk, and Ḥimṣ—were put to siege and ultimately conquered by the Muslims. Much of the detail about these battles or sieges has been recounted above, and there is little reason to cast doubt upon its veracity, even though the timing of these events relative to one another remains obscure. On the basis of this information, however, it is evident that the engagements in the second phase of the conquest of Syria were fundamentally different from those of the first phase, when the Muslims were active mainly in the open countryside of Syria and clashed with what appear to have been local Byzantine garrison troops, but seem to have held back from important towns and cities and avoided contact with the regular Byzantine army. In the second phase they evidently embarked on a new policy, at once more aggressive toward the cities of Syria and more willing to challenge the Byzantine authorities in direct confrontations with their army. There is no way to ascertain what might have caused this shift in the Muslims' policy in Syria, but it is reasonable to propose that the change might have resulted from the Muslims' success in bringing a number of the nomadic and seminomadic tribes of Palestine and southern Syria under their control during the first phase. Having done so, they might have felt secure enough to risk the head-on collision with the Byzantines.

The sources for the second phase of the conquest in Syria also allow us to draw some general conclusions about the tribal composition of the Islamic armies in Syria, and about the attitude of Syrian nomadic tribes toward the Muslims at this time. Besides great numbers of the Quraysh, various Yemeni tribes appear to have been prominent in the armies sent to Syria, in particular the Azd, who are said to have made up one-third of the army at Yarmūk, as well as the Ḥimyar, Hamdān, Madhḥij (including 500 from the B. Zubayd of Madhḥij), Khawlān, Khath'am, Kinda and Sakūn, and Ḥaḍramawt. Tribesmen from Najrān also participated, and there are also mentioned at Yarmūk some tribesmen from the Ḥijāzī and Syrian tribes of Kināna, Lakhm, Judhām, Balī, and other unspecified Quḍā'a tribesmen, and a hint that the B. Sulaym participated at Marj al-Ṣuffar.[264] Unfortunately, the sources do not allow a more detailed analysis of the tribal composition of the forces involved in various incidents during the conquest, but it is significant that the general picture of the composition of the armies in the second phase agrees with that seen during the first phase, that is, many tribesmen of Quraysh and many Yemeni tribesmen, along with some basically nomadic tribesmen from the Ḥijāz. It is also noteworthy that, although many Quraysh are mentioned as participants in the second phase of the conquest of Syria, relatively few of the Medinese *anṣār* appear to have been present.[265]

The presence of some Syrian tribesman (e.g., Lakhm, perhaps Judhām and Balī) among the Muslims should not be taken as an indication that the Syrian tribes in general had joined the Muslims, however. There are repeated references throughout the sources to Christian bedouin tribesmen providing assistance to the Byzantines,[266] and, as we have seen, the Byzantine army that was ultimately defeated at the Yarmūk included tribesmen from the Ghassān, Lakhm, Judhām, Bal-Qayn, Balī, ʿĀmila, and others of Quḍāʿa.[267] These probably represent nomadic and semi-nomadic groups that traditionally had been part of the Ghassānid confederation in alliance with Byzantium.[268] In the case of tribes such as Lakhm, Balī, and Judhām that are said to have been on both sides, it is likely that existing political divisions within the tribes were important in determining whether a group aligned itself with the Muslims or the Byzantines, but the dearth of evidence does not permit us to clarify this intratribal politics enough to explain the alignments.[269] What is clear, however, is that a considerable number of Syrian tribesmen continued to back the Byzantines even at the end of the second phase of the conquest, or at the very least had refused to join the Muslims. Hence the leadership of the Islamic state continued to attach great importance, in Syria as in Arabia, to subduing the nomadic tribes who were the most dangerous source of potential resistance to their state's control; and, as in Arabia, they seem to have considered subjection of the nomads to be the prerequisite for the conquest of other areas occupied mainly by sedentary peoples. Thus, after the conquest of Ḥimṣ, ʿUmar is said to have written to Abū ʿUbayda to "remain in your city [Ḥimṣ] and [concentrate on] winning over the powerful, tough, Syrian bedouin."[270] Even in the context of such distant campaigning, the early Islamic ruling elite clear-sightedly recognized the fundamental importance of the struggle between state power and nomadic power.

8. PHASE III: THE OCCUPATION OF SYRIA

As in the second phase of the conquest of Syria, the events of the third phase are sometimes described inconsistently by the Arabic and other sources. Fortunately, the conflicts among the sources are fairly limited, so that to a certain extent it is possible to construct a composite picture of the main actions in this phase by harmonizing various accounts.

With the decisive defeat of the Byzantine armies in the second phase, the ability of the Byzantines to offer coordinated resistance to the Muslims virtually collapsed. Henceforth the Muslims faced, with few exceptions, no standing Byzantine armies as they swept across Syria, but only isolated resistance from local garrisons or militias resident in the main towns they wished to reduce. Syria was open to occupation by the Muslims, and the events of the third phase are merely the course of that occupation. Because of the collapse of Byzantine power, it was furthermore no longer necessary for all the Muslims' forces in Syria to join together as one army. Hence they separated into smaller forces that were active in different localities at the same time. For this reason the course of events in this phase is best discussed in terms of specific episodes and locales.

The Conquest of Ḥimṣ, Qinnasrīn, Aleppo, and other Towns of Northern Syria

After the defeat of the main Byzantine forces in the second phase of the conquest, Abū 'Ubayda and his subordinate commanders moved northward into the power vacuum left by the Byzantine collapse. The city of Ḥimṣ was occupied and became, it seems, Abū 'Ubayda's headquarters,[271] from which the Muslims sent troops to take the important town of Qinnasrīn (Chalcis). It is not clear, however, who led the forces against Qinnasrīn or other towns in northern Syria. Some sources say that Abū 'Ubayda himself conquered Qinnasrīn, Antioch, Aleppo, Qūruṣ (Cyrrhus), and other places; others claim that Abū 'Ubayda sent 'Amr b. al-'Āṣ, who made treaties with Qinnasrīn, Aleppo, Manbij, and Antioch; still others state that Abū 'Ubayda sent Khālid b. al-Walīd to reduce Qinnasrīn and Aleppo, after which he was joined by Abū 'Ubayda; and one other tradition states that Qinnasrīn was taken by troops from al-Kūfa in Iraq.[272] In any case, Abū 'Ubayda appears to have been the main commander for operations in northern Syria for a time, and he clearly sent out small forces under subordinates to establish garrisons in several areas adjacent to the main region of the Muslims' activity.[273]

There is some mention of organized Byzantine resistance in this region. According to some sources Heraclius had left Qinnasrīn under a general named Mīnās, and it was necessary for the Muslims to defeat his army before occupying the area. Others claim that Abū 'Ubayda was threatened by a Byzantine force while he was in Ḥimṣ, but only after certain spots farther north such as Qinnasrīn had been taken by the Muslims.

The Byzantines, according to this account, marched with conscripts from the Jazīra in order to drive the Muslims out of northern Syria. Abū 'Ubayda requested his lieutenants to return to Ḥimṣ to reinforce him with their garrisons (*masāliḥ*), among them Khālid b. al-Walīd who came with his men from Qinnasrīn. Once assembled, they decided to remain in their fortified position in Ḥimṣ rather than to engage the Byzantine force; they also wrote to 'Umar to send reinforcements. The caliph accordingly ordered the Muslims on various fronts to send whatever cavalry they could spare to aid Abū 'Ubayda, as a result of which a force of 4,000 cavalry was reportedly sent from Iraq to Syria under the Tamīmī chieftain al-Qa'qā' b. 'Amr, and other forces were dispatched against Raqqa (commanded by Suhayl b. 'Adī), against Nisibis (commanded by 'Abdullāh b. 'Itbān), and against the nomads (*'arab*) of Rabī'a and Tanūkh in the Jazīra (commanded by al-Walīd b. 'Uqba). Much of the Byzantine force threatening Ḥimṣ then melted away when the troops from the Jazīra learned that the Muslims were advancing on their home districts, as they wished to be there to defend them. This enabled Khālid b. al-Walīd to defeat the remaining Byzantine force. According to other traditions, Abū 'Ubayda himself defeated a Byzantine force between Ma'arrat Miṣrīn and Aleppo.[274]

Despite the fragmentary or partly contradictory evidence, it is clear that the entire area around Qinnasrīn, Aleppo, and Antioch and as far east as the Euphrates submitted rather quickly to the Muslims at the outset of the third stage of the conquests. The sources also provide many isolated details of the events in this area: for example, Antioch is said to have rebelled after making its treaty, and Abū 'Ubayda was forced to send Ḥabīb b. Maslama al-Fihrī or other lieutenants against the town. Similarly, Qinnasrīn is said to have rebelled and been reconquered by al-Simṭ b. al-Aswad; in other cases, the reduction of villages and monasteries in the countryside surrounding various towns is described.[275] But these details are too fragmented to contribute much to the general outlines of the conquest in this region. It seems, however, that Heraclius finally abandoned Syria at about this time, leaving Edessa for Shimshāṭ (Samosata) when the Muslims occupied the Qinnasrīn-Aleppo-Antioch area, and eventually departing for Constantinople.[276] When he withdrew, according to one source, he stripped the area between Alexandretta and Tarsus of its garrisons—the personnel of which appear also to have been the local cultivators—so that the Muslims found only barren country there; and he broke up the fortifications in this region as well.[277]

Although Abū 'Ubayda thus seems to have commanded the Muslims at the outset of their conquest of northern Syria, it is not clear how long he was personally active in that area. He is said to have returned to Palestine fairly early in order to invest Jerusalem,[278] but he presumably retained formal command over the forces in the north. The traditional datings for the Muslims' siege of Jerusalem imply, however, that Abū 'Ubayda's activity in northern Syria must have occurred in about A.H. 15-16/A.D. 636-637.[279]

The Conquest of Jerusalem and 'Umar's Visit to Syria

One of the Muslims' first objectives in the third phase of the conquest appears to have been Jerusalem. As noted, at least one of the reconstructions of the course of events in the second phase described the beginnings of an advance on Jerusalem by some of the troops led by 'Amr b. al-'Āṣ to Ajnādayn.[280] It seems, however, that the real siege of Jerusalem was undertaken by troops under Abū 'Ubayda after his activity in the north around Qinnasrīn. In addition, Yazīd b. Abī Sufyān, Mu'ādh b. Jabal, Khālid b. al-Walīd, 'Amr b. al-'Āṣ, and other commanders may have participated in the siege. The siege was a prolonged affair, partly because the defenders refused to make a pact with Abū 'Ubayda, demanding instead that the caliph 'Umar himself conclude a treaty with them.[281] It may have been at about this time that Abū 'Ubayda concluded a treaty with the Samaritans in which they agreed to pay a head-tax but were freed from taxes on their lands in exchange for their services as guides and spies.[282]

According to traditional sources, 'Umar came from Medina to al-Jābiya[283] in Syria in A.H. 16 or 17/A.D. 637-638. The reasons for his trip are not entirely clear. Perhaps he came partly to conclude the treaty with the people of Jerusalem. Other sources suggest that he came in response to Abū 'Ubayda's request for reinforcements at the time of the Byzantine offensive against Ḥimṣ.[284] But he also had other business to transact at al-Jābiya, such as dividing the booty (much of it from the battle of the Yarmūk?), supervising the judicious distribution of properties and dwellings taken by the Muslims, organizing the military commands (*junūd*) and border posts (*furūj*) in Syria, making arrangements for the stipends paid to troops (*'aṭā'*) and for their rations (*rizq*), which seem to have been allotments of bread, oil, and vinegar for each man, as well as settling the inheritances of those martyred in battle.[285] That is, 'Umar appears to have had a number of administrative matters to attend to in the wake of the Muslims' victories and of their occupation of much of the Syrian steppe and the settled areas of southern Syria.

The question of 'Umar's interest in Syria is complicated by the fact that various sources disagree on how many times he visited the area, some stating that he came only once (usually dated to A.H. 16), others that he came two, three, or four times between A.H. 16 and 18. One of these visits evidently coincided with the famous "Year of Ashes," a nine-month drought during which occurred the devastating 'Amwās plague that claimed the lives of many of the heroes of the conquest of Syria, including Abū 'Ubayda, Mu'ādh b. Jabal, Yazīd b. Abī Sufyān, and Shuraḥbīl b. Ḥasana.[286]

'Umar did negotiate a treaty with the people of Jerusalem at al-Jābiya, however, although it remains unclear whether this was done on the urgings of Syrian Jews, as some sources maintain, or through the Christians of the city who made a treaty forbidding Jews to live in Jerusalem, as other sources state.[287] Eventually the caliph came to Jerusalem in person to pray and evidently to make some administrative arrangements as well.[288] In any case, it is hardly surprising that he should have shown an interest in Jerusalem, given the importance it held in the early Islamic cult; indeed, Theophanes reports that one of 'Umar's activities was to begin building a temple (i.e., mosque) in Jerusalem.[289]

The Occupation of Palestine

The conquest of the remaining parts of Palestine[290] west of Jerusalem is not clearly presented in the sources. Divergent opinions are found regarding who commanded the Muslims at the conquest of major towns. What is clear, however, is that the reduction of this area was accomplished by several different forces, and it is doubtless the fact that many troops were present in Palestine and were probably constantly moving about there that led to the confusion in the sources.

One set of accounts ascribes the conquest of much of northern Palestine ("Jordan") to Shuraḥbīl b. Ḥasana, and of much of southern Palestine to 'Amr b. al-'Āṣ. According to these accounts, 'Amr and a bevy of lesser commanders set out against southern Palestine at the end of the second phase of the conquests, or at the start of the third phase,[291] and held the whole area around Ramla and Gaza after defeating the Byzantine forces in these places. From the few references to his activity, however, it appears that 'Amr and his subordinates (such as 'Alqama b. Mujazziz, sent against Gaza) may have made repeated incursions into southern

Palestine from some more secure area, perhaps east of the river Jordan, so that reconstructing the exact course of their activities there is impossible.[292] It was, finally, from southern Palestine that 'Amr b. al-'Āṣ set out on his offensive against Egypt—whether on his own initiative or on the request of 'Umar, again being a matter of dispute in the sources. It is possible, however, that 'Amr decided to go (or was sent) to Egypt to pursue the Byzantine forces evacuating Palestine after their defeat by the Muslims; for some sources state that the Byzantine commanders in Palestine, Arṭabūn and Tadhāriq, withdrew to Egypt at the time of 'Umar's arrival in al-Jābiya, that is at about the time 'Amr appears to have moved against Egypt.[293] Similarly, Shuraḥbīl b. Ḥasana, whose activity may have begun at the end of the second phase, is said to have conquered all of northern Palestine except for Caesarea and Tiberias, although few details are provided.[294]

Since the Byzantine forces in Palestine seem to have withdrawn to Egypt, most of the localities in Palestine capitulated to the Muslims with little resistance—doubtless part of the reason why so little is said about them in the conquest accounts. The exceptions were provided by Gaza, already mentioned, and especially by Caesarea. The latter was subjected to a long siege by the Muslims; some sources say that it lasted seven years, but there is no agreement on the date of its fall, which is placed in A.H. 18, 19, or 20/A.D. 639, 640, or 641 by different authorities. Most sources state that the siege was conducted by Mu'āwiya b. Abī Sufyān (who is also said by some to have conquered 'Asqalān),[295] beginning already at the end of the second phase of the conquests.[296] But others claim that the siege of Caesarea was begun, or that the city was conquered, not by Mu'āwiya but rather by 'Iyāḍ b. Ghanm, 'Amr b. al-'Āṣ, or 'Abdullāh b. 'Amr. b. al-'Āṣ, or that the siege was begun by Yazīd b. Abī Sufyān and concluded after his death by his brother Mu'āwiya. In addition, several other prominent commanders are said to have been present at the siege of Caesarea as subordinates, including Ḥabīb b. Maslama al-Fihrī, al-Ashtar al-Nakha'ī, Daḥḥāk b. Qays al-Fihrī, and 'Ubāda b. al-Ṣāmit.[297]

The Occupation of the Coastal Regions

The last parts of Syria to be brought under the Muslims' control were the coastal strip of Lebanon and northern Syria, and the mountainous districts lying just inland from the coast in these regions. There are, in fact, very few notices of any campaigning into the rugged mountain districts, which were always difficult of access and marked by a considerable measure of local autonomy in any case. It can be safely assumed that the day-to-day life of the mountain districts was not greatly affected by the early conquests, and that the area remained essentially beyond the practical control of the Muslims for many years.[298]

The numerous important towns along the Syrian littoral, on the other hand, were the object of definite campaigns by several commanders and eventually were brought under firm control by the Islamic state. But even in those cases where the Muslims made fairly early contact with the coastal towns, such as at Caesarea, it was often a considerable time before the towns could be conquered definitively. The reason for the Muslims' difficulties in controlling the coast was simply the ease with which the Byzantines could maintain contact with the coasts by sea, allowing them to raid and reestablish their lost authority there even though the Muslims may have set up small garrisons in previously conquered towns.[299] We can be certain, too, that Caesarea's long resistance was made possible by regular Byzantine supplies reaching it by sea.

Most of the Muslims' campaigns to the Syrian coast appear to have been relatively minor affairs, carried out by smaller subordinate forces rather than by one of the main armies. Thus one of Abū 'Ubayda's lieutenants, 'Ubāda b. al-Ṣāmit al-Anṣārī, was sent from Ḥimṣ to reduce al-Lādhiqiyya, 'Anṭarṭūs, and other towns along the northern coast.[300] Similarly, Yazīd and Mu'āwiya b. Abī Sufyān were dispatched against the Lebanese coast and seized Ṣaydā (Sidon), Beirut, Jubayl, and other towns.[301] The city of Tripoli, on the other hand, was put to siege by a commander named Sufyān b. Mujīb al-Azdī, but only in the days of the caliph 'Uthmān, that is, after his accession in A.H. 24/A.D. 644.[302]

Through the confusion of conflicting accounts of the third stage, what emerges is the picture of a mopping-up operation—the gradual occupation or reduction, without significant Byzantine opposition, of all of Syria that remained outside Islamic control. It was not that the Byzantines had lost their local support entirely. Many towns resisted the Muslims for a time, only to give up their resistance as hopeless; others, such as Antioch, submitted to the Muslims readily, but rose in rebellion a short time later; and from various accounts it seems that some of the Arabic-speaking tribesmen of Syria, such as parts of the B. Ghassān, B. Tanūkh, B. Iyād, and B. Salīḥ, remained Christian and attempted to follow the Byzantine emperor Heraclius as he withdrew from Syria—they did not all join the Muslims voluntarily, even at the bitter end.[303] The Islamic occupation of Syria in the third stage was possible, first and foremost, because the ability of the Byzantines to resist had been decisively shattered in the second phase. Thereafter, those in Syria who wished to resist the Muslims found that they had to do so on their own, as there was no Byzantine power to back them. Fortunate indeed was the town that, like Tripoli, was in close enough touch with the Byzantines by sea to call on them for aid when the Muslims came to besiege it—and even then the Byzantines provided, not relief, but only ships to evacuate the inhabitants, abandoning the town to be occupied by the victorious Muslims. Putting up serious resistance to the Muslims in Syria was, it seems, by this time beyond the realm of the practical. Indeed, the main focus of the Islamic conquest movement had already begun to shift elsewhere. The Jazīra and Egypt were being occupied, and from northern Syria the Muslims were beginning to launch regular raids into the Anatolian heartland of the Byzantine empire; hence the focus of Byzantine resistance naturally had to shift to these new areas as well. Syria had become a land under Islamic rule.

CHAPTER IV

THE CONQUEST OF IRAQ

1. LOWLANDS

Much of Iraq[1] is a low-lying basin covered with the alluvial deposits of the great and lesser rivers that flow through it: the Tigris and the Euphrates entering it from the north and northwest, and the numerous smaller tributaries of the Tigris feeding into it from the east. It is, in most places, a tiresomely flat plain, and one so nearly level that the rivers hardly know in which direction to flow and have more than a few times changed their minds on the matter. Flat, then, and locked in a uniformly arid climate; rainfall averages only between ten and eighteen centimeters per year, mostly falling between November and April, and becomes only slightly more abundant toward the eastern edge of the basin. Even the colors of the country can be hypnotically uniform, especially in summer, when the northwest wind raises the dry, tan silt to hang heavily in beige clouds over the tawny rivers. At such times all objects appear blurred, and everything in the landscape blends together into a haze of muffled whitish-brown.

Behind this facade of uniformity, however, lies a set of sharp contrasts that have determined many aspects of Iraq's character as a land. On the one hand, Iraq is dry—nearly devoid of meaningful rainfall, boasting few indigenous sources of water, spending half the year under parching heat. On the other hand, Iraq is a land of water—the abundant waters of the Tigris and Euphrates, augmented by numerous smaller tributaries, rivers that have been throughout history exploited by a net of canals to spread their precious moisture over a broad area, rivers that, if untended, collect themselves in the south to form enormous marshes. Despite its aridity, Iraq is a land that can be virtually submerged during the late spring floods under a shallow, wind-rippled sea. This dichotomy between dry and wet generates other contrasts, no less striking. One tract of land supports lush gardens; the next, beyond the end of an irrigation ditch and separated from the first only by a low hillock, is barren dust. To one side a level horizon, scorching heat, blinding brightness; to the other a wall of nodding palms, deep shade, cool dark pools. In August, a sunbaked dusty lot; in April, a rain-pelted sheet of water; in June, pasturage and grazing flocks.[2]

The Rivers and Marshes

The course of the Euphrates during the early seventh century was roughly the same as it is today, at least as far south as the beginning of the great marshes a bit below al-Ḥīra. Of the two channels that formed when the river split not far above the present site of al-Ḥilla, however, the eastern channel (today the main channel) appears to have been less important at the time of the Islamic conquest than was the western channel, which passed by the town of al-Ḥīra. This western watercourse, apparently first opened only in the third century A.D., had grown increasingly important as al-Ḥīra developed under the Sasanians into a major military and mercantile center.[3] Both the eastern and western channels flowed southward into the marshes and lost themselves there.

Similarly, the Tigris followed roughly the same course at the time of the Islamic conquest that it follows today, at least as far south as the town of Mādharāyā (modern Kūt al-Imāra), except for a one hundred-kilometer stretch just north of the Sasanian capital at al-Madā'in (Ctesiphon), where it lay eight to fifteen kilometers west of its present course, and excepting also a vastly different pattern of meanders, ever subject to change, notably around al-Madā'in and Dayr al-'Aqūl.[4] Below Mādharāyā, however, the modern (eastern) channel—which had been the main channel in ancient times and during the first centuries of Sasanian rule—became silted up and impassable during the last years of the Sasanian empire; the bulk of the Tigris waters flowed south, not east, from Mādharāyā, entering the great swamps. This shift in the lower Tigris is described by the Arab historian al-Balādhurī as being the result of a massive flood that in A.D. 629 swept away the bunds and irrigation works and created the new (western) channel.[5] Thus, at the time of the Islamic conquest the Tigris flowed south from Mādharāyā, passing the site on which Wāsiṭ would be built (Zandaward; Kashkar) in the later seventh century and eventually dispersing its waters into the marshes of southern Iraq.

Some distance below the sites of al-Kūfa and Wāsiṭ, then, both the Euphrates and Tigris fed into the enormous region of marshes and interconnected lakes, or al-Baṭīḥa, which was and is today (although in different configuration) the dominant feature of the landscape in southern

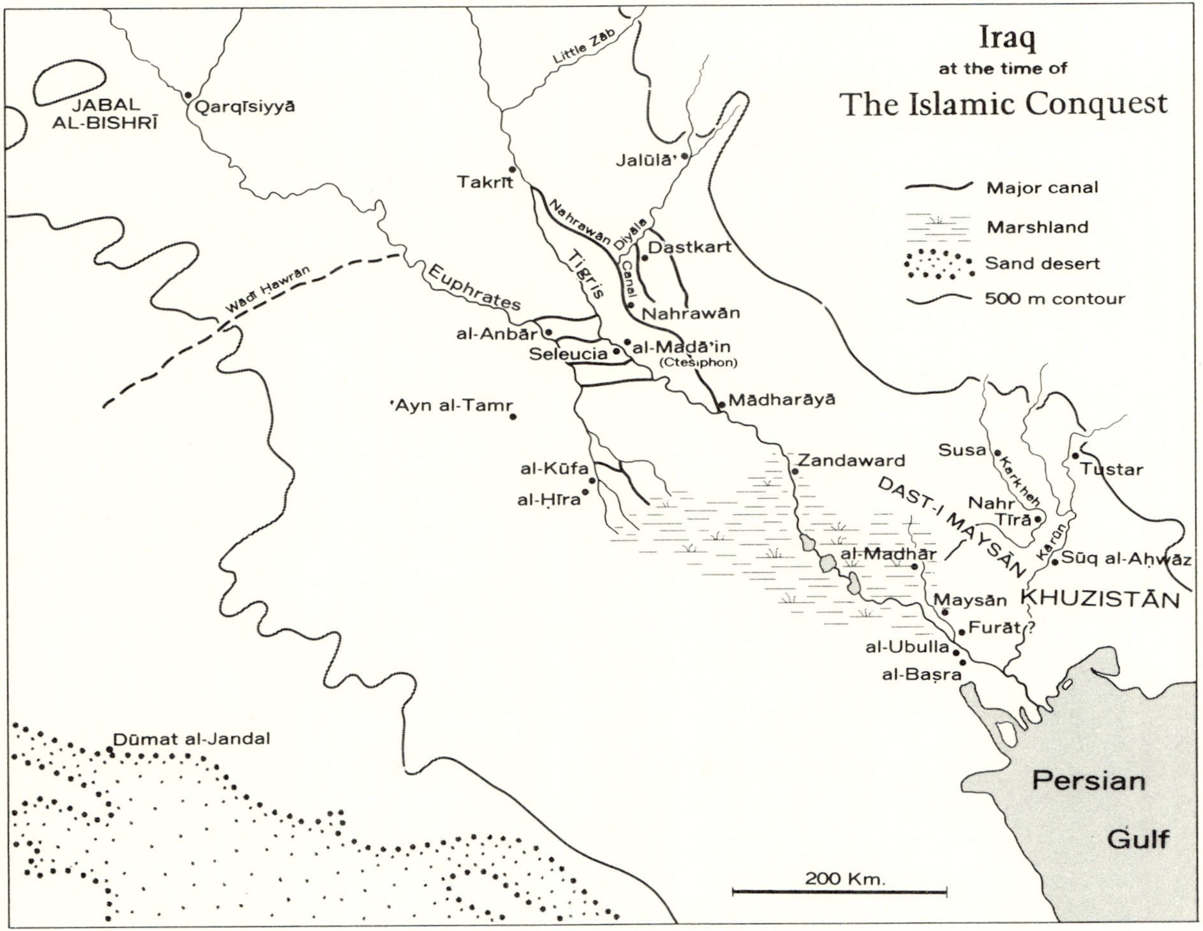
Iraq
at the time of
The Islamic Conquest
Major canal
Marshland
Sand desert
500 m contour
JABAL
AL-BISHRĪ
Qarqīsiyyā
Little Zāb
Jalūlā'
Takrīt
Nahrawān
Diyāla
Dastkart
Tigris
Canal
Nahrawān
Euphrates
Wādī Ḥawrān
al-Anbār
Seleucia
al-Madā'in
(Ctesiphon)
Mādharāyā
'Ayn al-Tamr
al-Kūfa
al-Ḥīra
Zandaward
Susa
Karkheh
Tustar
DAST-I MAYSĀN
Nahr
Tīrā
Kārūn
al-Madhār
Sūq al-Aḥwāz
Maysān
KHUZISTĀN
Furāt?
al-Ubulla
al-Baṣra
Dūmat al-Jandal
Persian
Gulf
200 Km.

Iraq. The marshland in this region was gradually encroaching on irrigated agricultural districts from roughly the end of the Parthian period (ca. A.D. 200) up to and through the Islamic period.[6] The sudden shift in the course of the Tigris in A.D. 629, which introduced more water into the western half of the southern plain, greatly augmented this gradual process of marsh formation and resulted in the almost total inundation of that area. At the same time, the diversion of Tigris waters to the west caused the area farther east, formerly watered by the river, to become largely barren desert.[7]

The exact limits of the marshes in the seventh century are difficult to determine, but they appear to have lain considerably to the west of the present marshes. Classical sources refer to continuous swampland in this region, extending as far as the "borders of Arabia," which we can reasonably equate with the southern limit of the present Hawr al-Ḥammār marshes and their medieval counterpart.[8] In the west, the marshes appear to have extended all the way up the Euphrates to just below al-Kūfa. The northern border probably ran in an irregular line east from below al-Kūfa to somewhat below Wāsiṭ, with the eastern border of the marshes near or to the west of the modern Hawr al-Sa'diyya.

The marshes probably released their waters into the Persian Gulf through a mass of small channels, but there was certainly one navigable main channel connecting the Gulf with the seaport of al-Ubulla and later al-Baṣra. Recent investigations[9] suggest that this channel divided not far upstream of al-Ubulla to form the two channels known in medieval geographical works as the Abū l-Asad canal and the One-Eyed Tigris. The former in fact drained the waters of both the Tigris and Euphrates from the marshes; the latter, which followed the older course of the Tigris before its change of course in A.D. 629, was a "dead end," at least for navigational purposes, since the former Tigris bed had gone dry roughly above the town of al-Madhār. This channel still retained some importance at the time of the Islamic conquest, however, because not only al-Madhār but also the towns of Maysān (Charax) and Furāt appear to have been located near its banks.

It is not clear to what degree the channels of the Tigris and Euphrates through the marshes were open and navigable at the time of the conquests. Below Wāsiṭ, the Tigris divided into numerous branches that, as described, flowed into the northern limit of the marshes. It does not appear, however, that the Tigris had a single deep channel that was navigable all the way through the marshes. Instead, canal-like openings through the reeds joined the shallow, open bodies of water to create a network of small passages. Goods were transported by means of shallow-drafted skiffs that could negotiate the lakes and the courses through the reeds, ultimately leading to the Abū l-Asad canal.[10] As for the Euphrates, its course through the marshes during this period is unknown; indeed, it is possible that the river had no open channel from where it entered the marshes until the beginning of the Abū l-Asad canal, but that it flowed instead through a diffuse maze of small rivulets or seeped through the reedbeds.[11] It is noteworthy, in this context, that the maps of Iraq that have been transmitted in Arabic geographical works of the tenth to twelfth centuries A.D. show no clear Euphrates channel, although the larger canals linking the Euphrates and the Tigris are shown. Instead, the Euphrates is depicted as flowing into the "marshes of al-Kūfa" just below that city; the drawings are done in such a way that the absence of a navigable channel is apparent.[12] Much of the area covered by the marshes was thus a dense forest of reeds, laced with narrow channels and giving place occasionally to shallow bodies of open water. Scattered through the midst of the marsh were small mounds of dry land that had either been built up or lay behind weirs and on which the inhabitants of the region built their houses and raised what crops they could; but these dry places must have been quite small in view of the almost perfect flatness of the alluvium in this area.[13]

Although no tributaries augment the flow of the Euphrates during its course through Iraq, a number of rivers flowing southwest out of the Zagros mountains join the left bank of the Tigris. These include the 'Uẓaym (Adhaim), Diyāla, Chankula Gala, and Karkheh, as well as smaller streams. Of these Tigris tributaries, by far the most important is the Diyāla. It carries a large quantity of silt into the Tigris system[14] and its waters support a large district of irrigated fields in the plain through which it flows before reaching the Tigris. The lower course of the Diyāla lay a bit to the east of, and parallel to, its present course in the seventh century, and it flowed into the extensive network of irrigation channels that existed east of the Tigris at the time. The 'Uẓaym is much smaller than the Diyāla, and although its flow can be torrential during the winter and spring, it dwindles to a mere brook in summer.[15] Its importance to irrigation is therefore slight. Other tributaries of the Tigris are also of limited importance.

The third major river flowing into Iraq is the Kārūn, which at the time of the Islamic conquest was called the Dujayl.[16] Flowing almost due west off the Iranian plateau, it enters its delta near Shustar (Tustar) and brings with it great quantities of silt, which are deposited farther downstream, near the head of the Persian Gulf.[17] Along its course it receives a number of tributaries, notably the Diz, entering the Kārūn's right bank about forty kilometers above al-Aḥwāz, and the Jarrāḥī, entering its left bank near the Kārūn's estuary. Today the lower course of the Kārūn runs directly into the Shaṭṭ al-'Arab, making it strictly speaking a tributary of the Tigris-Euphrates system, but in the seventh century, the river drained directly into the Persian Gulf via the Hawr 'Abdullāh, that is, to the east of the present Shaṭṭ al-'Arab estuary. Its lower course was flanked on both sides by large areas of marshland, which drained into the Gulf and stood contiguous to the great marshes at the lower reaches of the Tigris-Euphrates system.[18]

Irrigation and Land Use

The rivers themselves, however, comprised but a part of Iraq's hydraulic picture. Perhaps more important from the point of view of agricultural exploitation were the countless canals and irrigation channels that for several thousand years had been a prominent feature of the countryside. For the rivers, left to themselves, would permit the cultivation only of the narrow strips of land along their banks and would probably destroy much of what was planted in the course of uncontrolled spring flooding. The hydraulic network elaborated in Iraq aimed both at improving water transport and at putting the available water to better use in order to increase the amount of land under cultivation.[19] In addition, there were drainage canals that helped dry out low-lying, marshy lands in order to make them cultivable and flood channels that diverted some of the torrential flow in flood season in order to prevent ruination of dykes and cultivated areas by scouring.[20]

One very important set of main canals drew water from the left bank of the Euphrates and conducted it eastward across the alluvium into the Tigris in the region of northern Iraq where the two rivers flow closest to one another. The head of this canal network lay in the vicinity of al-Anbār on the Euphrates. This series of main channels, made possible by the somewhat lower level of the Tigris at this point, dated back to Babylonian times. Besides being navigable by boat and therefore important to commerce and communication, each canal was the spine of a maze of branching side-channels that irrigated whole districts that would otherwise have lain barren. This raised agricultural output in the region enough to support the urban centers so long found there—the representatives at the time of the Islamic conquest being the cluster of cities called al-Madā'in (Seleucia-Ctesiphon). The main channels operative in this system were the Dujayl canal, the Ṣarṣar canal, the al-Malik canal, and the Kūthā canal, which, with their subsidiary channels, irrigated the districts of Maskin, Qaṭrabbul, Nahr al-Malik, Kūthā, Nahr Jawbar, and others.

Farther down the Euphrates was located another group of canals. In Islamic times, the eastern channel of the Euphrates, which flowed past al-Jāmi'ayn (Ḥilla) and the ruins of Babylon, was called the Ṣūrā canal. Whether it was originally a canal or simply a natural channel matters little; its waters were tapped by numerous side channels to irrigate the districts of Ṣūrā, Barbīsamā, Bārusmā, Bābil, Khuṭarniya, al-Jāmi'ayn, and Upper and Lower Fallūja. From its right bank flowed the Nars canal; this joined with the Badāt canal, which flowed from the left bank of the Euphrates. These channels watered parts of the *sawād* of Kufa and then lost themselves, like the two (or more?) branches of the Euphrates, in the great marshes south of al-Kūfa.

Like the Euphrates, the Tigris and its tributaries provided the water for an extensive irrigation network. The most important developed area lay in the Diyāla plain, where large irrigation channels with smaller branch canals had existed for centuries. Because the water of the Diyāla alone is insufficient to irrigate such a large region, a large feeder canal called the Qāṭūl al-A'lā or Qāṭūl al-Kisrawī branched off the left bank of the Tigris below Takrīt and flowed into the Diyāla near Ba'quba. The course of the Diyāla from this point as far as the town of Nahrawān was called the Tāmarrā canal. At Nahrawān an enormous trunk canal branched from the left bank of the Tāmarrā and flowed southeast, parallel to the course of the Tigris, as far as Jarjarāyā, a distance of about 125 kilometers, where it rejoined the Tigris. This trunk canal, called the Nahrawān canal, watered the vast area that lay between it and the Tigris and extended as far as Mādharāyā (modern Kūt al-Imāra). The Qāṭūl-Nahrawān system appears to have been the work of the Sasanian dynasty.

Farther up the Diyāla, several other main irrigation canals branched off the left bank, notably the Rūz and Mehrūt canals (to call them by the names they bore in the Islamic period). Taken together, this vast complex of main channels and the many small canals that radiated from them irrigated much of the Diyāla plain.[21]

Such, at least, was the situation until late Sasanian times. Evidence from the Diyāla region, however, indicates a massive abandonment of this region at the end of the Sasanian period. This abandonment has been ascribed to a combination of factors: political instability, increasing salinity of the soil in certain districts (notably around Nahrawān), silting, and perhaps changes in the course of the lower reaches of the Nahrawān canal generated by the massive shift in the course of the lower Tigris in A.D. 629, described above. Although certain areas were subsequently resettled in early Islamic times, the fact that villages of the Sasanian period were abandoned and new settlements were established by the Muslims implies a major breach in the continuity of local life.[22] It is therefore likely that considerable areas lay vacant in the Diyāla region on the eve of the Islamic conquest, and that the canal system, although still basically operable, was in poor repair due to recent neglect.

The canals branching from the Tigris below Mādharāyā at the time of the Islamic conquest are as poorly known as the course of the river itself. It appears, however, that the generally high level of development that marked the irrigation system of the upper half of Iraq was not matched in the south, where much potentially useful agricultural land lay under marshes at this time due to recent flooding.[23] Still farther south, the region around al-Ubulla and its successor city, al-Baṣra, may have been irrigated by canals; at any rate, the existence of canals for navigation is well attested.[24]

The Kārūn river sytem was also the focus of an impressive irrigation network, which appears to have been started during the Parthian period and was most thoroughly elaborated during the last years of Sasanian rule. In this case the irrigation procedure was not so simple as elsewhere in Iraq, for the terrain of the main developed area—the district lying between the Karkheh and the upper Kārūn—is not as flat as is, for example, the Diyāla floodplain. The construction of this network along the Kārūn consequently involved the excavation not only of long feeder canals and the usual maze of distributing channels, but also of weirs and barrages to raise the river level enough to carry water up to higher areas, as well as of occasional tunnels to carry water under or through insurmountable natural obstacles. The lower course of the Kārūn saw no such engineering projects in Sasanian times, perhaps because of the salinity of the soil. Here as in other areas of Iraq the evidence of settlement patterns reveals a disruption at the time of the Islamic conquest, although it is impossible to determine whether this disruption preceded or was subsequent to the Islamic invasion.[25]

We can conclude, then, that at the time of the Islamic conquests the following areas were the primary agricultural districts in Iraq: (1) The banks of the Euphrates, Tigris, Kārūn, and other rivers from the points where they enter the Iraqi plain to their entry into the swamps; (2) The region between the Euphrates and Tigris that was irrigated by the Dujayl, Ṣarṣar, Malik, and Kūthā canals; (3) the region lying northeast of al-Ḥīra; (4) the 'Uẓaym-Diyāla plains, watered by the Nahrawān canal system; and (5) the upper reaches of the Kārūn valley and the land between the Kārūn and the upper Karkheh. With the exception of the areas watered by the Kārūn, the great bulk of agriculturally productive land appears to have been located in the northern half of our region, whereas much of the southern half was either covered by marshland or, having only recently been covered by marsh, was barren plain.

This impression of a contrast between conditions in central and southern Iraq is strengthened by a few references to the superior character of the land surrounding al-Kūfa when compared with that around al-Baṣra shortly after the foundation of the two cities. We are told that a delegation of Basrans complained to the caliph 'Umar in the following terms: "Our brethren the Kufans settled in the residences of Chosroes, amid sweet springs and luxuriant gardens . . . but we, the people of al-Baṣra, came to settle in a crusty salt-flat that soaks up water;[26] its soggy ground does not dry up, and no pasturage grows in it. One side of it is in the desert, and the other in a sea of brackish water. . . . "[27] The status of the land for taxation corroborates the view that the area around al-Baṣra was desolate in comparison with al-Kūfa; for although al-Kūfa was in land that paid the *kharāj* tax, al-Baṣra was legally on "dead land" (*mawāt*), that is, land that was not under cultivation.[28] Southern Iraq, then, does not appear to have been a flourishing agricultural district at the time of the Islamic conquest; central Iraq, on the other hand, appears to have been quite prosperous.

Scattered throughout both northern and southern Iraq were in all probability small areas supporting limited agriculture; these would have been found, for instance, on occasional high spots within the confines of the great marshes, as well as around the scattered permanent springs or wells located in the midst of otherwise barren areas. But their agricultural importance, in comparison with the five districts suggested above, must have been slight.

On these agricultural lands grew a selection of the various crops that prosper in Iraq's climate—dates, olives, and fruit trees, sugar, vegetables of many varieties, wheat, barley, and rice.[29] Except for the absence of date palms in the northernmost area, around Takrīt, due to the more rigorous winters, variations in crops grown within Iraq depended, not on climatic differences (which are slight), but on local conditions and choice; the date palm predominates in southern Iraq, for example, because it tolerates the highly saline soil of this region far better than other trees that accept Iraq's climate.[30]

In the marshes, of course, very different styles of life prevailed. Then as now, the populace was probably composed mainly of villagers who cultivated some rice and maintained a few water buffaloes, but who relied heavily also on fishing to supply their food. Among them lived semi-nomads herding flocks of water buffaloes. These people, less numerous than their settled neighbors, very likely wintered in the middle of the marshes and migrated in summer to the banks of the major watercourses passing through or on the edge of the marshland.[31] As already shown, large-scale agriculture was not feasible in this area.

We cannot assume, however, that even the irrigated districts of the Iraqi alluvium were comprehensively cultivated. Some areas probably lay fallow in any given year, or were planted not in vegetables or grain but in fodder. In addition, the prevailing practice of harvesting fields before the arrival of the full heat of summer left much of the alluvium open in the summer months. Tucked amid intensively cultivated plots, these areas could be visited during the summer by pastoralists with flocks of sheep, goats, and camels—visits the agriculturalists themselves might well have encouraged, as the dung left behind by the livestock would improve the crop in following years. The patterns of land use within the irrigated districts themselves were, clearly, more varied than might at first appear; they were in a continuous state of flux, and, perhaps most important, they provided the setting for a constant interaction between settled peasants and migratory herdsmen, not only on the desert fringes, but throughout the heartland of the alluvium itself

The Foothills and the Steppe[32]

The alluvial lowland just described is edged by districts with somewhat different characteristics. These border districts are, on the east, the foothills of the Zagros mountains, and on the north, west, and southwest, the desert steppe of northern Mesopotamia (the Jazīra), Syria, and Arabia. All these districts are of interest partly because of the contrast that exists between them and the lowlands in land use.

The foothill region is especially interesting in this respect. The rivers that run through the region make irrigation possible in theory, but as one moves gradually to higher elevations and the first gentle undulations of the plain give way to real hills, the construction of large-scale irrigation works requires ever larger investments of labor to overcome the increasing unevenness of the terrain. Eventually, irrigation becomes impractical. As one moves into the hills, however, rainfall gradually increases until it becomes sufficient to support dry-farming. The region of foothills thus divides into three zones. The lowest is suitable for irrigation-based agriculture; the highest for rainfall agriculture. In the middle lies a transitional zone in which dry-farming is only marginally productive, but where large-scale irrigation can be undertaken only at great expense—an investment such as that made by the Parthians and Sasanians in the region near Susa, for example. In the absence of such investment, the middle zone generally becomes, in the rainy season, lush pastureland. Hence it often serves as the winter grazing ground for pastoralists who, in summer, could be expected to take their flocks either up into the cooler summer pasturelands in the mountains, or down into the irrigated alluvium with its certain supplies of water.

The steppe areas bounding the lowlands have no permanent rivers and receive insufficient rainfall for dry-farming. As a consequence, these broad areas are exploited almost solely by pastoralists, who find in the steppes winter and spring grazing for their flocks. The aridity of the steppe forces these migratory herdsmen to seek permanent sources of water during the summer months. These are, occasionally, perennial wells located in the midst of the steppe, but more usually the banks of the great rivers of Iraq are visited as summer campsites. Thence the migrants can set out in small groups to graze on fallow lands within the alluvium.

The patterns of land use that are found in the area here defined as Iraq are, thus, diverse. They include the most land-intensive, such as irrigation-based agriculture, as well as the most land-extensive, such as pastoral nomadism, which moreover exist virtually atop one another. It is therefore hardly surprising that the population of this monotonous flatland should have reflected a corresponding diversity.

2. ARAB AND NON-ARAB IN IRAQ

Just as the level but complex landscape of Iraq was internally divided by countless rivers and channels, so its population was internally divided by barriers of language, religion, social class, and way of life. As in Syria, so also in the alluvial plains of Iraq the great bulk of the population spoke some dialect of Aramaic. They were in many cases doubtless the direct or indirect descendants of the peasantry that had, centuries in the past, supported the ancient civilization of Sumer and Babylon. But though Aramaic was widely spoken among them and served as the area's lingua franca, other languages were also represented. Above all, there was Persian; centuries of Iranian rule had brought into the population sizable numbers of people who spoke some brand of Persian, and the presence of nomads who spoke Iranian dialects in the foothills of the Zagros, immediately adjoining Iraq on the east, enhanced this trend. Persian speakers were found in every city of any importance in Iraq, particularly in the roles of soldiers or administrators, but they were also found scattered throughout the countryside, occupying their *dastkart* or landed estates. Near the port cities of the south, which served as termini for the maritime trade with India, Ceylon, and East Africa that the Sasanians had come to dominate, there may well have been colonies of Indians and Africans, speaking their languages. Some of the ancient languages of Iraq, such as late Babylonian, may even have survived as spoken dialects among isolated groups living in the depths of the marshes. And in many places, especially near the Euphrates, there was Arabic.[33]

Each of these linguistic communities, furthermore, carried with it a special set of identifications; speakers of the same language felt an affinity not only because they could understand one another, but also because they all identified with certain glorious episodes in the distant past and saw themselves as descendants and heirs of the heroes of those days. Thus speakers of Persian harked back to the great deeds of the Achaemenids, whereas speakers of Aramaic viewed themselves as descendants of those who had participated in the grandeur of Nebuchadnezzar's kingdom.

In religion, too, Iraq's population was diverse. Zoroastrianism was the official faith of the Sasanian state, but it seems likely that it was observed mainly by the Persian ruling elite in Iraq and therefore restricted mainly to the larger towns. If the fire temple dominated the urban scene, however (at least officially), it was certainly the church or the synagogue that shaped the faith of most of Iraq's rural inhabitants and of many town dwellers as well.[34]

The Nestorian Christian community may have been the largest single religious community in Iraq on the eve of the Islamic conquest, and it seems to have had a great following throughout the country; we read of Nestorian monks resident in al-Anbār, of a prominent Nestorian preacher serving in al-Ḥīra, of monasteries in Khūzistān, and of a Nestorian patriarch in Ctesiphon with subordinate clerics in Kaskar, Jundayshāpūr (Beth Lapaṭ), Furāt al-Baṣra (Prāth d-Mayshān), Dastumaysān, Susa, and doubtless many other places as well. The vigor of the community is attested by the existence of numerous Nestorian religious schools in Iraq, the most important of which was that of Seluceia in al-Madā'in, near the Patriarchate.[35]

By comparison with the Nestorian, the Jacobite, or West Syrian, church was only weakly represented in Iraq. Indeed, it was only in the wake of Heraclius's campaign in Mesopotamia and Iraq, and the subsequent decade of Byzantine rule in Mesopotamia (A.D. 627-637), that a Jacobite metropolitan was established in Takrīt in A.D. 629, to direct his flock under the protective gaze of the Byzantine authorities in Mesopotamia, and the community that he was sent to supervise does not appear to go back much before the middle of the sixth century A.D. The Jacobites thus seem to have had few followers in the heart of Iraq, and those in Takrīt always looked north to the powerful Jacobite communities in Mesopotamia, such as the monastery of Mār Mattay near the ancient Nineveh. There were, however, Monophysite churches and a school in al-Madā'in, so the creed was not completely unknown even in central Iraq.[36]

The Jewish community of Iraq was second in size only to the Nestorian and seems to have been well organized under its *gaon* or exilarch, who resided in Veh-Ardashīr, a district of al-Madā'in.[37] The main Jewish settlements lay by the waters of Babylon, in the area traversed by the great canals that connected the Euphrates with the Tigris, and along the Euphrates toward Syria. In these areas too, as well as around al-Madā'in, were located the numerous rabbinical schools, echoes of whose fame still reverberate in the tomes of the Babylonian Talmud.[38] There were, however, smaller Jewish communities to be found in all parts of Iraq, even in Maysān in the south and in the Zagros foothills to the east.[39]

Other religious communities also existed in Iraq; besides the Manichaeans and Mazdakites, driven underground by Sasanian persecution during the fifth and sixth centuries, there were the Mandaeans, a gnostic baptismal sect living mainly in Maysān in the south of Iraq. But these communities were dwarfed in numbers by the Christians, Jews, and Zoroastrians.

In addition to these linguistic and religious divisions, there were also the important, if predictable, class distinctions that separated soldiers from slaves, peasants from priests, merchants from gentry, and courtiers from kings. To some extent these divisions may have corresponded to linguistic and religious distinctions; most of the high-level administrators, court attendants, and soldiers, for example, were probably Zoroastrians and Persian speaking, whereas most of the free or slave peasantry was probably Jewish or Christian and spoke Aramaic. Likewise, the class of landed nobles (*dahāqīn*), who provided an elite cavalry for the Great Kings and appears to have dominated much of the Iraqi countryside on the eve of the Islamic conquest, probably consisted of Zoroastrian Persians.[40]

There remains to be considered one more element in Iraq's population, and indeed a very important one: namely, the many tribesmen whose native language was Arabic. The Syrian desert had been Arab for centuries before the rise of Islam, and Arabic-speaking tribal groups had long been in close contact with the western fringes of the settled alluvium of Iraq. Indeed, various Arab tribes—consisting mainly of nomadic or seminomadic groups, but sometimes including significant sedentarized populations—dominated the desert fringes of Iraq right up to the Euphrates on the eve of Islam. Even members of those nomadic groups that lived a considerable distance into the desert had at least occasional contact with the settlements along the Euphrates, because of their need for agricultural produce and manufactured articles that only the sedentary population could produce; and in many cases such "desert" tribes had sections that resided more or less permanently in the riverain towns.

Many tribes were represented in this Arab population on the eve of Islam. The B. Tanūkh were certainly among the more prominent of them; they appear to have consisted mainly of seminomadic or recently sedentarized groups living in hair tents along the Euphrates between al-Ḥīra and al-Anbār and probably farther upstream as well. From the fact that they are not mentioned in military activities at this time it appears that they were no longer essentially a nomadic people. Near them roamed the nomadic shepherds from the tribes of al-Namir b. Qāsiṭ, Iyād, and Taghlib—more mobile and more militarily capable than the Tanūkh, and hence more suitable for service as Sasanian auxiliaries. Farther south, to the south and west of the great marshes from near al-Ḥīra to the head of the Persian Gulf, Iraq abutted on the home territories of various branches of the Bakr b. Wā'il confederation, a loose grouping of tribes that dominated the whole region from the marshes southward to the district of al-Yamāma in eastern Arabia. Certain tribes of the Bakr b. Wā'il consisted mainly of powerful camel nomads who had regular contact with Iraq during the decades before the rise of Islam: the B. Shaybān, B. 'Ijl, B. Taymallāt b. Tha'laba, B. Qays b. Tha'laba, and the B. Dhuhl. In addition there were other powerful nomadic groups that lived considerably farther from Iraq but seem to have had frequent contact with the towns and peoples along the Euphrates. Among them were groups such as the B. Tamīm, who lived in northern and eastern Arabia, generally to the west of the territories held by the Bakr b. Wā'il tribes, the B. Ṭayyi', whose home territory was in the northern Najd around the mountains that bore their name,[41] and the B. Kalb, who dominated the oasis of Dūmat al-Jandal and the surrounding steppe of the northern Najd and the southern reaches of the Syrian desert. Though mainly nomadic, furthermore, each of these tribes had members resident in various towns along the Euphrates, the populations of which can be reconstructed from accounts of the early campaigns of conquest there.[42]

There can be little doubt, then, that there was significant contact between Arab and non-Arab at least in the districts of Iraq bordering the Euphrates. As there were many Arab tribes in the Jazīra, furthermore, it is very likely that the Arab element was also very strong in the northernmost districts of Iraq, north of the great transverse canals of central Babylonia. It appears, in fact, that there were nomadic tribes in the area just south of Takrīt that were being converted to Christianity in the sixth century by the zealous Jacobite missionaries of that town.[43] The degree to which Arabs had penetrated into the Iraqi alluvium before the rise of Islam is, however, more difficult to determine. But the fact that the alluvium is called, during the Islamic conquest, *arḍ al-'ajam*—"the land of those who do not speak Arabic"—and the fact that surveyors during the early days of Islamic dominion placed the edge of Arab land[44] at the Euphrates lowlands (*asfal al-Furāt*) suggests that the bulk of the alluvium was still predominantly non-Arab, even if sometimes visited by Arabic-speaking bedouin.

As noted above, the sizable nomadic population that lived on the fringes of Iraq presented a problem for the Sasanian authorities.[45] They had to take special precautions to secure the rich agricultural lands of the Iraqi alluvium against sporadic raiding or the levying of "taxes" on the peasants by powerful nomadic groups. The system of defenses they constructed consisted, as we have seen, of a variety of elements: a string of Sasanian garrisons, mostly of modest size, along the desert fringes;

the incorporation of certain nomadic tribes as auxiliary contingents in the Sasanian army; and in particular the elaboration by their client-kings, the Lakhmids, of a complex set of alliances with powerful nomadic groups roaming the Najd and northeastern Arabia. The Sasanians employed all of these techniques in order to stabilize the desert frontier, in the hope of preventing unwanted disruption of their tax base.

On the eve of the Islamic conquest, however, this complex system of defenses was no longer fully operative, and the Sasanian state had in general fallen on hard times. In A.D. 602 the Sasanians had suddenly abolished their Lakhmid client-kingdom in al-Ḥīra, perhaps because they felt that other methods of controlling the nomadic groups were proving more efficacious. It is plausible to assume, however, that this act created a kind of diplomatic crisis among many tribes whose relations to one another had formerly been clearly defined by the Lakhmids' policy; many of these tribes were doubtless now looking in new directions for support in the political struggles in which they became involved.[46] In addition to the crisis created by the massive floods of the late 620s, the Sasanians had suffered military defeats. The lengthy war with the Byzantines on which the Sasanians embarked in A.D. 611 turned out to be a disaster for the Persians; the Sasanian armies were driven out of Egypt and Syria, and in 628 the Byzantine emperor Heraclius even marched his army to the very heart of the Sasanian domains, sacking the Great King's estates at Dastkart and threatening to occupy Ctesiphon. The result was a change of government in the empire, followed by a sustained succession crisis during which effective Sasanian government was virtually nonexistent. This, too, doubtless had repercussions among the nomadic groups on the fringes of Iraq, who must have come increasingly to question the utility of alliance with (or the reasons for fear of) an empire whose fortunes seemed so dim.

When the first Islamic armies appeared on the fringes of Iraq in A.H. 12/A.D. 633, then, they faced a Persian empire that was financially and physically exhausted by years of war; that had lost northern Mesopotamia and its tax revenues to the Byzantines; that was burdened by an annual indemnity to the Byzantines as part of the peace settlement; that was just emerging from a period of factional strife within the royal house; that had seen important agricultural districts ravaged by Byzantine armies or by massive floods; and that had, finally, severed its ties with its main agents of stability on the desert frontier. The most surprising aspect of the Islamic conquest of Iraq is not that it succeeded, but that under these circumstances the Sasanians could still put up very stiff resistance to the invading Muslims; it suggests the degree to which the Sasanian claim to legitimacy had struck deep roots in the minds of many groups in Iraq.

3. THE COURSE OF THE CONQUEST IN IRAQ

The conquest of Iraq by the Muslims actually involved two separate arenas of activity. One was in central Iraq, around the city of al-Ḥīra and, farther into the alluvium, near al-Madā'in; the other was in southern Iraq, around the city of al-Ubulla and in the Khuzistān district around the city of al-Aḥwāz. The Muslims' armies in these two areas of Iraq, effectively separated from one another by the great marshes, had for the most part very little contact with one another. The ruling elite of the state in Medina seems to have viewed the two regions as independent fronts, and the course and character of the conquest in each region was quite distinct.

The sources for the first phase of the conquest in Iraq pose many of the same problems as do the sources for the conquest of Syria: in particular, difficulties in establishing the sequence in which various episodes occurred. Fortunately, however, the sources for the later stages of the conquest of Iraq are much clearer on these matters. All authorities give essentially the same sequence of events for the conquest of central Iraq. For the conquest of southern Iraq the question of phasing is not so critical because no major engagements were fought there. The essentials of both the character and the course of the conquest are thus much clearer in the case of Iraq than for Syria. Although the absolute chronology—the actual year in which specific events took place—is no more certain for many events in Iraq than for those in Syria, the vexing problems of the relative chronology that are so much at issue in discussions of the Syrian conquests simply do not arise for Iraq in the same way. In addition, the sources for Iraq provide much more detailed information about the tribal composition of the armies active there than do the sources for Syria.

Although central and southern Iraq really formed two independent fronts during the conquest, both areas shared a common first phase, during which the Islamic state first began to extend its control to the Arab tribes living on the fringes of Iraq. The first phase began with the arrival in Iraq of Khālid b. al-Walīd, the victorious general who had suppressed the rebels of the *ridda* in the Najd and in al-Yamāma. Khālid marched into Iraq from the south and campaigned in the districts lying west of the Euphrates, on the desert fringes of the alluvium. His activity there lasted from about the early months of A.H. 12/late spring of A.D. 633 until Muharram, A.D. 13/April, A.D. 634. During this time he imposed the rule of the Islamic state not only over the nomadic groups that lived on the desert fringes of Iraq, but also over the heavily Arabized towns along the right bank of the Euphrates: al-Ubulla, al-Ḥīra, and others. He then departed for Syria in April of 634 in order to reinforce the Muslims there, leaving in al-Ḥīra a garrison of Muslims and local tribesmen allied to them under the command of al-Muthannā b. Ḥāritha of the B. Shaybān. With Khālid's departure for Syria, the first phase of the conquest in Iraq ended. There was little or no penetration of the alluvium itself by the Muslims during this phase, nor any contact with a major Sasanian army, and in general the first phase represented a continuation of the process of state consolidation over the Arab tribes that had been pursued during the *ridda* wars. It was, in short, less a part of the conquest of Iraq itself than a preparation for the conquest.

The second phase of the conquest in central Iraq began some time after the death of Abū Bakr and the accession of 'Umar b. al-Khaṭṭāb (A.H. 13-23/A.D. 634-644), when the new caliph organized an army under the command of Abū 'Ubayd al-Thaqafī and sent it to join al-Muthannā in central Iraq. This joint force undertook sporadic raiding into the alluvium of Iraq. Eventually, the Muslims were engaged by a sizable Persian army, which defeated them soundly at the battle of the Bridge, causing great losses among the Muslims; the Muslims' commander Abū 'Ubayd, was even killed in the debacle. Al-Muthannā, himself wounded, reassembled the shattered remnants of the army—those who had not fled—and bided his time. He appears to have withdrawn to the desert fringes of Iraq, and may have undertaken periodic raids while new recruits were being sent to aid him by the high command in Medina. The traditional accounts include at this time a description of an overwhelming military victory by the Muslims at the "battle of Buwayb," but there is reason to suspect that much of this description is exaggerated and that no such major battle ever took place. All of this activity—the raids before and after the battle of the Bridge, and the battle itself—can be considered to make up the second phase of the conquest in central Iraq. It was a phase in which offensives against Iraq were mounted by the Muslims and effectively contained by the Sasanians.

The third stage of the conquest in central Iraq began some time after the disaster at the battle of the Bridge and the withdrawal of the Muslims' remaining forces under al-Muthannā. The defeat at the Bridge appears to have convinced 'Umar that a major force had to be sent to central Iraq. He accordingly sent out a call for more troops and eventually was able to dispatch two new armies to central Iraq. The first of these was a group of tribesmen of the Bajīla tribe led by Jarīr b. 'Abdullāh al-Bajalī; this force reached central Iraq quickly and may have participated with al-Muthannā's followers in desultory raiding, but its presence does not seem to have altered the strategic situation in Iraq markedly. It was followed, however, by a second and much larger army that had assembled in Medina and marched toward central Iraq under the command of Sa'd b. Abī Waqqāṣ. Additional troops were sent to join Sa'd's army as they became available, and Sa'd himself raised other levies from the tribes through whose territories he and his army passed en route to Iraq. It is not clear exactly how the Iraqi campaigns meshed with the Muslims' military activities in Syria at this time, but apparently some troops—among them those men who had earlier fought with Khālid's army in Iraq and then marched to Syria with him—were ordered to proceed from Syria to Iraq to reinforce Sa'd's army. A limited number of reinforcements also arrived in central Iraq from the southern Iraqi front.

Sa'd's army, after spending the winter in the Najd, moved to the fringes of central Iraq, where it took up a position at al-Qādisiyya (not far from al-Ḥīra) and awaited the arrival of the Persians. The Sasanians' army was very large and far outnumbered the Muslims, but after several days of intense fighting, and considerable loss of men, the Muslims managed to rout their adversaries. The defeat of the Persians at al-Qādisiyya was the turning point in the struggle for control of the rich alluvium of central Iraq; for, despite stiff resistance from isolated Persian garrisons, units of Sa'd's army were rapidly able to reduce central Iraq in its entirety. The Sasanians at first fell back to their capital at al-Madā'in but soon abandoned it and retreated to the less accessible Zagros range in order to re-form their ranks. The Muslims occupied al-Madā'in, which then served for some time as their base of operations in central and northern Iraq, and were able to seal their conquest of the area by wresting a solid victory from the reformed Sasanian forces at Jalūlā' in the Zagros foothills. The Muslims were henceforth the undisputed masters of northern and central Iraq.

Although the sequence of events in the third stage of the conquest in central Iraq is fairly clear, the chronology of these events is uncertain;

the battle of al-Qādisiyya, for example, is dated variously to A.H. 14, A.H. 15, or A.H. 16, depending on the authority consulted. Whatever the dating, however, the third stage involved the decisive defeat of the Sasanians' main army and the rapid consolidation of the Muslims' control over central Iraq.

The conquest of southern Iraq is not so easily subdivided into phases as is the conquest in central Iraq. Upon Khālid's departure from this region, sections of the indigenous tribe of B. ʿIjl that were loyal to Medina seem to have been the only guardians of the Muslims' interests there. The leader of B. ʿIjl, Suwayd b. Quṭba, was apparently encouraged by al-Muthannā's raids farther north and, realizing the weak condition of Persian defenses in southern Iraq, wrote to ʿUmar requesting that he send an army to the area. ʿUmar dispatched a force under ʿUtba b. Ghazwān, which joined Suwayd. Together they reportedly raided the countryside in southern Iraq, eventually capturing (or recapturing?) al-Ubulla and penetrating into the Aḥwāz district at the head of the Persian Gulf. ʿUtba returned to Medina, leaving lieutenants in charge until he should return; but when he died during his trip, he was replaced by al-Mughīra b. Shuʿba al-Thaqafī, who prosecuted the raids and consolidated campaigns until his replacement. His successor, Abū Mūsā al-Ashʿarī, completed the conquest of southern Iraq and the Zagros foothills, receiving at a critical moment before the siege of Tustar some reinforcements from the northern Iraqi front. The conquest of southern Iraq thus involved the reduction of a sequence of Persian strongholds; no major Sasanian army appeared in the area to oppose the Muslims' advance.

Such, then, are the rough outlines of the conquest of Iraq. Let us now consider the conquest in more detail.

4. PHASE I: KHĀLID B. AL-WALĪD'S CAMPAIGN

Unlike Syria, Iraq was a region that had not particularly attracted the attention of the early Islamic leadership. There is no evidence to suggest that Muḥammad or the early Muslims had any special ambitions in Iraq, whether rooted in religious tradition or in commercial interest, comparable to their aspirations in Syria. Even the great merchants of Quraysh, for all their far-flung commercial interests on the eve of Islam, seem to have had only indirect trading relations with the main entrepôts of Iraq.[47] Abū Bakr's decision to interfere in the political affairs of Iraq, by sending forces under Khālid b. al-Walīd and other generals there, sprang from his desire to complete the process of state consolidation over the tribes of Arabia that had been undertaken during the *ridda* wars, rather than from some specific commercial, religious, or even military interest in Iraq itself. Indeed, the whole first phase of the Muslims' operations in Iraq was directed, not against the rich Iraqi alluvium, but rather against the Arab tribes that inhabited the steppe and riverain towns along the western bank of the Euphrates. The first phase of the conquest of Iraq was, in short, merely a continuation of the *ridda* wars—the subjection by the Islamic state of the Arab tribes.[48]

Abū Bakr appears to have sent two commanders toward Iraq in order to establish the control of the Islamic state over the tribes there. One, 'Iyāḍ b. Ghanm of the Qurashī clan of Fihr, was to proceed with a force to the important oasis town of Dūmat al-Jandal in northern Arabia; having subdued it, he would than be able to march easily to the fringes of Iraq along the well-worn caravan route that connected Dūmat al-Jandal with al-Ḥīra, the main town of the middle Euphrates district.[49] At roughly the same time, Abū Bakr instructed Khālid b. al-Walīd, the victorious commander whose army had subdued the main rebellions in the Najd and al-Yamāma during the *ridda* wars, to march on Iraq from his position in eastern Arabia, so that the two commanders would be approaching from different sides and meet there.[50] But as matters developed, 'Iyāḍ was unable to proceed beyond Dūmat al-Jandal because of stiff resistance there, which forced him to undertake a lengthy siege of the town. And, despite reinforcements that appear to have been sent to him, he remained engaged at Dūmat al-Jandal, unable to reduce it, until finally Khālid had to join him from Iraq somewhat later to help him finish the siege.[51]

Khālid, for his part, had greater success. After receiving orders to proceed to Iraq, Khālid set out—directly from al-Yamāma, according to most authorities, although some suggest that he first returned to Medina briefly before marching to Iraq, or that he was in the interim engaged in fighting the rebellion of tribes in al-Baḥrayn.[52] The date of his departure cannot be exactly determined, but it must have fallen sometime between the battle of 'Aqrabā', around the beginning of A.H. 12/February-March, A.D. 633, and Muharram, A.H. 13/early April, A.D. 634, when Khālid left Iraq to march to Syria. We are told, furthermore, that Khālid had already sent his first booty from the Iraqi campaigns to Abū Bakr in Medina before the caliph wrote to the people of Mecca, al-Ṭā'if, and the Yemen asking them to join an expedition against Syria.[53] As the armies left Medina for Syria in the middle of A.H. 12/autumn of A.D. 633, Khālid must have been in Iraq some time before this. We can, therefore, tentatively date his departure for Iraq to the late spring or very early summer of A.D. 633, or about Rabīʿ I or Rabīʿ II of A.H. 12.[54]

The composition of the force that Khālid led to Iraq can only be roughly determined; there are unfortunately but few statements in the sources that reveal what groups may have made up the core of his army. If Khālid went directly from al-Yamāma to Iraq, we can perhaps assume that the core of his army in Iraq was essentially the same in its makeup as that of the army in al-Yamāma, but the composition of the latter is itself rather uncertain; it appears to have included, besides Medinese (*muhājirūn* and *anṣār*), large numbers of bedouin, some of whom were apparently from the tribes of the Najd—B. Ghaṭafān, B. Asad, B. Tamīm, and B. Ṭayyi'. The bulk of each of these tribes had thrown off Medina's hegemony at the beginning of the *ridda*, but a fraction of each had apparently remained loyal to Medina and, under Khālid's leadership, had helped the Muslims overpower their fellow tribesmen.[55] But we read also that Khālid's army for Iraq was reinforced by 500 men of the B. Ṭayyi' and by a contingent from B. Tamīm,[56] and one account describes how Khālid divided his army into contingents for the march to Iraq, placing one group under the supervision of ʿAdī b. Ḥātim, a chief from B. Ṭayyi', and another under ʿĀṣim b. ʿAmr of Tamīm.[57] Although there is no guarantee that these contingents were tribal units, the choice of commanders suggests that both ʿAdī and ʿĀṣim had a considerable following of their fellow tribesmen of Ṭayyi' and Tamīm. It is also claimed that Jarīr b. ʿAbdullāh al-Bajalī was sent to Khālid at the head of the reinforcements from the B. Bajīla, but this appears to be a misplaced reference to slightly later events, when Jarīr was sent to Iraq during the caliphate of ʿUmar.[58] A statement to the effect that Khālid's army of 2,000 men was augmented by 8,000 tribesmen of Rabīʿa and Muḍar is, numbers aside, perfectly reasonable but too vague to be helpful.[59] By considering the individuals who are mentioned as participants in the many episodes during Khālid's campaigning in Iraq, however, it is possible to obtain a slightly fuller picture of the tribal composition of the army.[60] All considered, it seems probable that Khālid's force (exclusive of the tribesmen of B. Dhuhl, ʿIjl, and Shaybān who aligned themselves with him in Iraq) consisted of a core of Medinese (*anṣār*) and Quraysh, and contingents from at least the B. Tamīm, B. Ṭayyi', and probably from B. Muzayna. The precise composition of these contingents is not clear, but we can surmise that the force from B. Ṭayyi' represented only those portions of the tribe (the B. Ghawth and B. Jadīla) that had been persuaded by 'Adi b. Ḥātim to join the Muslims and desert the "false prophet" Ṭalḥa during the *ridda*.[61] It seems probable that the members of B. Tamīm in Khālid's army were also from sections of the tribe that had remained loyal to Medina during the *ridda* wars. The B. Muzayna was entirely loyal to Medina during this period, and it is possible that the army included groups from other Ḥijāzī tribes that, like Muzayna, had not participated in the *ridda*.

As for the size of Khālid's force, we can only guess: an estimate of about 1,000 or somewhat more for the main force (excluding Iraqi tribal allies, but including some dependents) squares fairly well with the figure of 2,000 mentioned earlier, and also fits with statements that Khālid marched from Iraq to Syria with a force of 500 to 800, which represented half of his army in Iraq.[62]

The general course of Khālid's progress in the first part of his campaigning in Iraq can be quite clearly traced, despite very great confusion in the sources on specific details.[63] His first real engagement in Iraq was, according to several accounts, at the town of al-Ubulla (Apologos) and the nearby village of Khurayba, but other sources claim that al-Ubulla was first conquered only later by 'Utba b. Ghazwān.[64] Khālid campaigned around al-Ubulla and then proceeded to march along the west bank of the Euphrates, where he became embroiled several times with Persian forces, presumably small local garrisons maintained by the Sasanians to guard the edge of the alluvium from incursions by nomadic groups. Encounters are reported at places called Dhāt al-Salāsil, against a Persian commander named Hurmuz; at Nahr al-Mar'a; at al-Madhār, against a commander named Qārin; at al-Walaja, against the commander al-Andarzaghar; and at Ullays, against Jābān.[65] Of these localities, several can be identified. Nahr al-Mar'a was a canal that led into the Tigris from the west a little north of al-Ubulla, and al-Madhār was a town located several days' march up the Tigris from al-Ubulla. Ullays, on the other hand, was farther north; it appears to be the old town of Vologesias, once a great trading center, located just south of al-Ḥīra on the west bank of the Euphrates. Al-Walaja also appears to have been near al-Ḥīra.[66]

At the Arab town of al-Ḥīra, an important commercial center and the focus of Sasanian political authority in the middle Euphrates region, Khālid seems to have had the greatest engagement of his Iraqi campaign.

The town was a Sasanian strong-point and had a garrison of Persian cavalry under the command of al-Azādhbih, who may also have been the town's governor.[67] But Khālid was able to invest the city, and the town's Arab notables, after first taking refuge in several castles, eventually agreed to surrender and made a covenant with the Muslims in which they agreed to pay a tax.[68] At about the same time, Khālid's forces were reducing a number of villages that appear to have been located near al-Ḥīra. The sources describe how the small gentry (*dahāqīn*) of the Milṭāṭayn region near al-Ḥīra, and the villagers of Bāniqyā, Basmā, Quṣṣ al-Nāṭif (?), Furāt Siryā, the villages of middle and lower Bihqubād, and other villages were subjected by Khālid's force or, more frequently, made terms with them and submitted to a tax.[69]

From al-Ḥīra, Khālid's army moved against al-Anbār, located farther upstream on the east bank of the Euphrates. It, too, was an Arab town under a Persian commander (*shirzād*). After making terms with it, he apparently raided market towns in its vicinity that were gathering places for the nomads of B. Bakr b. Wā'il, B. Kalb, and other Quḍā'a tribes. But his next major engagement was at 'Ayn al-Tamr, which lay about ninety kilometers south of al-Anbār and some distance west of the Euphrates; there, considerable resistance was raised by tribesmen of the B. al-Namir b. Qāsiṭ, and it was necessary for Khālid to put the town's fortress to siege as he had at al-Ḥīra. After it was thus forcibly reduced, Khālid seems to have conquered also another nearby town named al-Ṣandawdā'.[70]

Khālid had by this time brought the whole west bank of the Euphrates bordering on the rich alluvial districts of central Iraq under the control of the Islamic state, reducing in particular the key Arab towns in this region: al-Ḥīra, al-Anbār, 'Ayn al-Tamr, and other less well-known sites. But he had also managed to subdue the Arab tribes that lived in the desert along the Euphrates. Fortunately the sources, which are frequently so much in conflict over details of chronology and topography, prove unusually full on the subject of Khālid's contacts with various tribal groups in this region. Before proceeding to a description of the remainder of Khālid's campaigning in Iraq, therefore, it is worth examining the relationships Khālid was able to establish with the tribes of southern and central Iraq, especially since these relationships were of the utmost importance to the success of the campaign itself.

At the time of Khālid's entry into southern Iraq, the political situation there, especially among the Arab tribes along the Euphrates, was very fluid. The near collapse of Sasanian political power, and with it the slow crumbling of the Sasanians' network of tribal alliances, had encouraged groups from some of the powerful nomadic tribes of northeastern Arabia to press in on the settled districts along the Euphrates in search of ready plunder. Particularly active in this way were a chieftain of the B. Shaybān named al-Muthannā b. Ḥāritha; a chieftain of the B. 'Ijl named al-Madh'ūr b. 'Adī; and a chieftain of the Sadūs branch of the B. Dhuhl named Quṭba b. Qatāda.[71] The former seems to have been raiding in the vicinity of al-Ḥīra, and the latter two in the vicinity of al-Ubulla, towns that they probably hoped to reduce to tributary status.

The early relations between these nomadic groups and the Islamic state are difficult to discern. Most sources suggest that the raiding around al-Ḥīra led by al-Muthannā had been underway for some time—perhaps as long as a year—before Khālid's arrival in Iraq[72] and give no hint that this activity had any relation to the rise of Islam. Other sources, however, suggest that al-Muthannā and the chieftains of B. Dhuhl or B. 'Ijl who were active around al-Ubulla did have ties to the Islamic state before Khālid's arrival. Some state that the raids launched by al-Muthannā and Suwayd b. Quṭba of Dhuhl angered Abū Bakr at first, but that the caliph decided to coopt al-Muthannā by recognizing him as the leader of his tribe and by sending him a robe of investiture, a standard, and orders to fight the Persians. Only when a Persian counteroffensive threatened to drive al-Muthannā and Suwayd back, according to these sources, did Abū Bakr decide to send Khālid b. al-Walīd to Iraq.[73] Another authority claims that al-Muthannā went to Medina himself and asked Abū Bakr to appoint him commander of raids on the Persians.[74] Other sources state merely that al-Muthannā and al-Madh'ūr (of 'Ijl) or Quṭba (of Dhuhl) had campaigned in Iraq before Khālid's arrival and were induced by Abū Bakr to join forces with Khālid and to accept him as supreme commander.[75]

Once Khālid and his army arrived in Iraq, however, the relations between the Muslims and various tribal groups along the Euphrates become much more clearly visible in the sources. Certain groups of tribesmen from Iraq already raiding the Sasanians seem to have joined Khālid's force as allies or auxiliaries. Quṭba b. Qatāda,[76] backed presumably by a following from the B. Sadūs of Dhuhl, is said to have assisted Khālid in taking al-Ubulla; al-Madh'ūr b. 'Adī and other chieftains of B. 'Ijl are listed among Khālid's allies at al-Walaja and Ullays, whereas al-Muthannā b. Ḥāritha of Shaybān and his following were prominent in Khālid's offensives at and near al-Ḥīra.[77] In the campaigning north of al-Ḥīra, however, Khālid's army seems to have been on its own. Neither al-Muthannā b. Ḥāritha nor any of the other allies so important to Khālid's victories between al-Ubulla and al-Ḥīra are mentioned in the campaigns against al-Anbār, 'Ayn al-Tamr, or the villages raided nearby.[78] This suggests that these local tribal allies assisted Khālid's army when he was in their own tribal territory, but that they were not incorporated into his army and remained behind at home when he marched on to campaign in other regions.

There were, on the other hand, very important tribal groups that put up bitter resistance to the Islamic forces. In some cases, such as that of B. Shaybān and B. 'Ijl, these opponents of Islamic rule were members of the same groups that provided some of Khālid's staunchest backers; that is, the group was divided into a faction that supported Khālid and one that did not. This inner division, it appears, sometimes ran along lineage lines, sometimes along religious lines, and sometimes along lines that cannot be ascertained. At the battle of al-Walaja, for example, the Muslims faced, in addition to a Persian garrison, ranks of landed gentry (*dahāqīn*) and of bedouin from the fringes of the settled districts (that is, seminomadic tribesmen?) who had been collected by the Persians between al-Ḥīra and Kaskar to reinforce their own forces.[79] It is clear that the Arab tribesmen who aided the Persian forces at al-Walaja included Christian tribesmen, for we learn that the defeat at al-Walaja filled other Christian tribesmen from the tribes of Bakr b. Wā'il with a desire to avenge the deaths of their kinsmen killed by the Muslims, and led them to force Khālid to do battle at Ullays. The pro-Persian force that Khālid defeated at Ullays likewise included a contingent of Christian Arab tribesmen. In addition to Christian tribesmen from B. 'Ijl, led by 'Abd al-Aswad al-'Ijli and Jābir b. Bujayr, the Persians were backed by men from B. Ḍubay'a, B. Taymallāt, and "bedouin of the outskirts of the people of al-Ḥīra"; and we are told that when the Christian tribesmen (including those of B. 'Ijl) lined up to do battle at Ullays, "the people in strongest opposition to them were the Muslims of B. 'Ijl," among whom are listed 'Utayba b. al-Nahhās, Sa'īd b. Murra, Furāt b. Ḥayyān, al-Muthannā b. Lāhiq, and Madh'ūr b. 'Adī.[80] In the case of B. 'Ijl, then, it seems that there was a rift between those who had embraced Islam, or at least aligned themselves with Khālid, and those who had retained their Christian faith and consequently sided with the Sasanians in opposition to the Muslims' advance. The other tribes of the Lahāzim confederation, which appear to have been Christianized, also opposed Khālid.

A slightly different basis for inner division within a given tribal group appears in the case of the B. Shaybān. The chief who backed Khālid so zealously at al-Ḥīra, al-Muthannā b. Ḥāritha, was certainly of Shaybān and presumably led a following of warriors from that tribe, but he was not from the previously dominant lineage of Shaybān, the B. Hammām b. Murra; he was, rather, from an obscure lineage, the B. Sa'd b. Murra. It appears, furthermore, that the old dominant lineage of Shaybān, the B. Hammām, had backed the rebellion of the "false prophetess" Sajāh against Islamic domination during the *ridda*. All considered, this suggests that the Muslims were exploiting a case of lineage rivalry within B. Shaybān, backing the ambitious chieftain of a minor lineage who aspired to supplant the leaders from the old dominant lineage and, in so doing, undermining the latter's power to resist absorption into the Islamic state.[81] Al-Muthannā was amply rewarded for his services in support of Khālid's conquests by being left in practical control of al-Ḥīra and environs when Khālid departed.

The accounts of Khālid's siege of al-Ḥīra reveal that the Arab population of this town also opposed the Muslims' advance, and the identity of the town's notables who represented it when requesting a treaty from Khālid suggests the diversity of the Muslims' tribal opposition in Iraq. One of these spokesmen was Iyās b. Qabīṣa, a member of B. Ṭayyi' and of a family that had served the Sasanians as governors and military commanders;[82] another was 'Amr b. 'Abd al-Masīḥ, from his name evidently a Christian, of the B. Buqayla, a branch of the B. Azd;[83] a third was Hāni' b. Qabīṣa b. Mas'ūd of the B. 'Ā'ish, a section of the B. Shaybān;[84] a fourth was 'Adī b. 'Adī, who was apparently related to 'Amr b. 'Adī b. Zayd al-'Ibādī, the former Christian scribe, Arabic translator, and specialist in affairs concerning the nomads for the Sasanian king.[85] Another representative, Ḥayrī (or Jabrī?) b. Akkāl, is mentioned but little can be ascertained about him.[86] There were, furthermore, yet other tribes represented in the population of al-Ḥīra. One source states that the inhabitants of al-Ḥīra in Abū Bakr's day were "mixed people from splinter groups of Tamīm, Ṭayyi', Ghassān, Tanūkh, and others."[87] Some of the B. Lakhm, who had formerly provided the ruling dynasty for the city, were certainly still to be found there as well.[88] It is also probable that there were members of the B. Kalb in the town; some are known to have occupied Dūmat al-Ḥīra (in or near al-Ḥīra?), and as one of the castles in the city was called Qaṣr al-ʿAdasiyīn (a branch of Kalb) we can speculate that they may have occupied part of the town around this fortification.[89] Finally, it seems probable that groups such as B. Iyād, who had provided tribesmen for the armies of the former kings of al-Ḥīra,[90] would also have had some members resident in the town.

In his campaigning around al-Anbār and ʿAyn al-Tamr Khālid also faced the opposition of local Arab tribal groups. The population of al-Anbār was probably mostly Arab, for after it capitulated Khālid is said to have found in it a group of men writing in Arabic.[91] Unfortunately no mention is made of the tribes living in al-Anbār itself, but there is some reason to suspect that they were largely the same ones found in al-Ḥīra. The traditional accounts of the first settlement of the two towns and of their subsequent history up to the Islamic period portray them as being founded at the same time and for the same reasons. They were, furthermore, supposedly settled by the same people and had even had their populations consolidated in the distant past after the death of Bakht-naṣṣar (Nebuchadnezzar).[92] Although these pseudohistorical accounts cannot be accepted at face value, they nonetheless suggest that close similarities had long existed between the two towns and their inhabitants. The raids Khālid launched against market towns near al-Anbār reveal that the B. Kalb, other branches of Quḍāʿa, and branches of B. Bakr that frequented them were hardly friendly to the Muslims. From the names of the many captives taken by the Muslims at ʿAyn al-Tamr, furthermore, it can be seen that this town too had an Arab population that opposed Khālid's advance.[93] The tribal composition of the town's population cannot be determined. It is worthy of note, however, that Iyās b. Qabīṣa of B. Ṭayyi'—mentioned above as the spokesman and former governor of al-Ḥīra—had once served as an administrator for the Sasanians in ʿAyn al-Tamr.[94] It therefore seems likely that the B. Ṭayyi' occupied an important position in the town. Without doubt the most prominent tribe mentioned in connection with the defense of ʿAyn al-Tamr, however, is the B. al-Namir b. Qāsiṭ. Their leader, Hilāl b. ʿAqqa b. Qays b. al-Bishr, a Christian, joined forces with the Persian troops sent out by the Sasanians to hold Khālid at bay. When the battle was over, Khālid had him crucified for his actions.[95] Although it is not clear whether he resided in ʿAyn al-Tamr, it seems likely that his tribe, the B. al-Namir, were the dominant nomadic group in the vicinity of the town and hence were probably represented in the town's population. The same might be said of other tribal groups that formed part of Hilāl b. 'Aqqa's army, for it reportedly included tribesmen of the B. Taghlib and the B. Iyād.[96] As for the town of al-Ṣandawdā', it was inhabited by non-Arabs and by Arabs of the tribes of Iyād and Kinda.[97]

In sum, it is clear that Khālid had some support from local tribal groups during the first part of his campaigning in Iraq, but it appears that the vast majority of the nomadic, seminomadic, and settled Arab tribal groups living along the Euphrates opposed the spread of Islam there. In the region around al-Ubulla, Khālid had the backing of the B. Sadūs of Dhuhl, it seems, and farther north he was assisted by part of the B. 'Ijl and a relatively insignificant group from B. Shaybān. But against him there was aligned a vast array of tribes, including the Christian tribesmen from B. 'Ijl, Ḍubay'a and Taymallāt. The dominant lineage of the powerful B. Shaybān seems to have opposed the spread of Islam, the settled tribesmen, from many tribes, living in al-Ḥīra, al-Anbār, 'Ayn al-Tamr, and other towns resisted his advance or, at least, showed no eagerness to join him, and the nomadic parts of al-Namir, Iyād, Taghlib, and probably Kalb and many other tribes living in the region west and north of al-Ḥīra likewise seem to have opposed his march. It was the reduction of these Arab tribes that proved to be his main task during the first part of his campaigning in Iraq, and we can suggest that it was probably his primary objective in going to Iraq as well. The clashes with Sasanian garrisons were unavoidable, particularly because these tribal groups were politically aligned with the Sasanians, but at this stage they were essentially incidental.

If an analysis of the first part of Khālid's campaigning in Iraq suggests that his main objective was the subjection of the Arab population of the Euphrates districts to Islamic rule, an analysis of the second part of his campaigning shows this point even more clearly. This part of his activity (that is, after the reduction of the middle Euphrates district around al-Ḥīra, al-Anbār, and 'Ayn al-Tamr) included two main operations. One was a march to the town of Dūmat al-Jandal in northern Arabia to assist his comrade 'Iyaḍ b. Ghanm in the siege of that town, possession of which would give the Muslims a strategic position dominating the southern parts of the Syrian desert and the approaches from northern Arabia to both Syria and Iraq.[98] The other operation was a march northward from the middle Euphrates district, already under his control, along the west bank of the Euphrates as far as Jabal al-Bishrī near the mouth of the Balikh river. The usual chronological limitations of the sources prevent us from knowing which of these operations took place first; the confusion in relative chronology or sequence is in this case unusually great because many sources combined accounts of incidents that occurred in these two separate operations with accounts of Khālid's later march across the desert to join the Muslims in Syria. The product was a synthetic narrative describing Khālid's march from al-Ḥīra to Syria and mentioning as stages in the march localities both around Dūmat al-Jandal in the south and along the upper Euphrates in the north.[99] But although we cannot determine which came first, it can readily be seen that in both Khālid's campaign on the upper Euphrates and his operations against Dūmat al-Jandal his primary objective was the reduction of the still-independent Arab tribal groups, mostly nomadic, that occupied these respective regions.

Khālid's campaign against Dūmat al-Jandal grew out of the continued difficulties faced by 'Iyāḍ b. Ghanm in his effort to conquer the town.[100] 'Iyāḍ's inability to reduce the town had apparently already caused Abū Bakr to dispatch at least two troops of reinforcements to him under the command of 'Abd b. 'Awf al-Ḥimyarī and al-Walīd b. 'Uqba,[101] but these may have been relatively small forces, as they receive virtually no comment in most sources. They were, at any rate, insufficient to turn the tide in the Muslims' favor. It seems that some of the tribes of Syria who opposed the Muslims' encroachments—probably, in fact, nomadic groups from the Byzantine-backed confederation led by the B. Ghassān—had rallied to aid the defenders of Dūmat al-Jandal. Their reasons for doing so were probably in part strategic, for if they could prevent 'Iyāḍ from taking the oasis the Muslims' further advances both into Syria and Iraq would be made much more difficult; but it is also possible that some of them owned property (buildings, gardens, or date palms) in Dūmat al-Jandal and hence had a personal stake in the affairs of the town. The attempt to occupy Dūmat al-Jandal, which the Muslims apparently expected to be a fairly minor undertaking, thus evolved into a major strategic confrontation upon which hinged the political future not only of the oasis itself but of the heart of the Syrian desert as well. Khālid's force in Iraq was the closest to Dūmat al-Jandal and hence the logical one to serve as reinforcement there.[102] Accordingly Khālid was notified of the situation in Dūma—either directly by letter from Abū Bakr, or indirectly by al-Walīd b. 'Uqba, who came as messenger to Khālid from Dūma itself—and persuaded to march there from 'Ayn al-Tamr where, by all accounts, he received the news.[103]

By the time Khālid joined 'Iyāḍ at Dūma, the opposition had assembled a powerful coalition of tribes to resist the Muslims. There appear to have been two leaders of this coalition. One was Ukaydir b. 'Abd al-Malik, a chieftain of the B. Kinda who seems to have been the local ruler of Dūmat al-Jandal; a Christian, he had once made a treaty with Muḥammad and agreed to pay a tax to him, but had apparently broken with the Islamic state after the Prophet's death.[104] The other leader was al-Jūdī b. Rabī'a of Ghassān, who may have been the military commander during the siege.[105] He was probably a Christian, but it is not certain whether he lived in Dūmat al-Jandal (perhaps as the local representative of the Ghassānids, who may have brought the town of Dūma into their pro-Byzantine tribal confederation) or whether he was there merely as an ally of Ukaydir.

When Khālid and his forces set out for Dūma, the inhabitants are said to have summoned their tribal allies (*aḥzāb*) to aid them. These allies, who were apparently mostly Christian tribesmen, were drawn from several tribes living in the Syrian desert: Bahrā', Kalb, Ghassān, Tanūkh, and Ḍaj'am (the last a branch of B. Salīḥ).[106] It is possible that these allies were raised through the agency of al-Jūdī of Ghassān and they may represent the main nomadic groups (i.e., those of military importance) that formed part of the Ghassānids' pro-Byzantine tribal coalition on the eve of the Islamic conquests. Whatever their political attachments, however, it is clear that all could unite in their opposition to the spread of Medina's hegemony over northern Arabia and the Syrian steppe.

Despite the size of the coalition, however, the presence of Khālid's force proved sufficient to tip the scales in the Muslims' favor. After a pitched battle the Muslims were victorious, reportedly killing the chief Ukaydir and taking many captives, including the Kalbī chief Wadī'a and the daughter of al-Jūdī, Laylā bint al-Jūdī.[107] Many of the combatants who were taken captive by the Muslims were apparently killed, excepting those of B. Kalb, for whom a Tamīmī chief in Khālid's army is said to have interceded because the Kalb had been allies (*ḥulafā'*) of the Tamīm before Islam.[108] Then, according to those sources that do not combine the campaign against Dūma with Khālid's march to Syria, he returned to al-Ḥīra.[109]

The other operation in the latter part of Khālid's campaigning in Iraq involved a march with his forces along the west bank of the Euphrates. The details of this campaign can be sorted out only with partial success because localities and groups contacted are generally woven into accounts of Khālid's march to Syria, which probably occurred later as a separate undertaking.[110] Several episodes can, however, be isolated from various, often conflicting, accounts. There are references to a raid on a church or synagogue, evidently near 'Ayn al-Tamr, where a group of students was learning to write Arabic, during which many captives were taken;[111] and there is also a reference to a clash with a Persian force under the command of Rūzbih and Zarmihr.[112] But most frequently described as part of Khālid's activities along the upper Euphrates are a raid made against the B. al-Namir b. Qāsiṭ[113] and another made against some of the B. Taghlib under the chieftains Hudhayl b. 'Imrān and Rabī'a b. Bujayr, which appears to have occurred at a place called al-Ḥuṣayd. As one source puts it, Khālid planned "to surprise Taghlib in their territory" (*dār*).[114] Finally, there are references that suggest that Khālid's raiding activity against al-Namir and Taghlib may have extended as far north as the area around Qarqīsiyā' and Jabal al-Bishrī.[115] After completing his raiding operations on the upper Euphrates, Khālid presumably returned to his headquarters around al-Ḥīra although the sources, which always consider these operations as part of his march to Syria, never mention his return. It was in al-Ḥīra, finally, that Khālid received Abū Bakr's instructions to proceed to Syria to assist the Muslims there, and from it he set out on his famous desert march, which has already been described.[116]

Khālid's campaigning thus completed in Iraq the process of establishing Medina's authority over the Arab tribes that had begun with Muḥammad and had been continued during the *ridda* wars in Arabia. The first part of his activity in Iraq saw the successful reduction of several powerful, heavily Christianized tribal groups of the Bakr b. Wā'il confederation (Shaybān, 'Ijl, Taymallāt, Ḍubay'a) that lived along the lower and middle Euphrates, as well as the towns of the desert fringes in these regions, which had sizable Arab populations. The latter part of his campaigning resulted in the defeat of at least parts of the tribes of al-Namir b. Qāsiṭ and B. Taghlib along the middle and upper Euphrates banks, and of a powerful coalition of tribes (perhaps part of the confederation headed by B. Ghassān) that contested at Dūmat al-Jandal the Muslims' efforts to dominate the central reaches of the Syrian desert and the northern Najd. Thus the first phase of the Islamic conquest in Iraq was really an extension of the *ridda* wars.

This is not to say that the Muslims had no local tribal support. We have seen that certain groups of tribesmen provided important assistance for Khālid's forces, especially in the lower and middle Euphrates districts.

But it is important to avoid the conclusion, too often drawn, that the Muslims were merely capitalizing on that antagonism of local tribesmen toward the Sasanians that had been so furiously vented at the battle of Dhū Qār in A.D. 610—an outlook that suggests that the conquest of Iraq had already begun before the Muslims arrived and implies that perhaps it might have succeeded even had the Muslims not appeared on the scene, due to the weakness of the Persians. In the first place, in the case of the B. Shaybān at least, the powerful lineages that had defeated the Persians some thirty years earlier at Dhū Qār were by the time of Khālid's arrival once more firmly in the Sasanian camp and are seen to have opposed the Muslims' advance, whereas the Shaybānī tribesmen who backed Khālid were led by al-Muthannā b. Ḥāritha, a chieftain from a hitherto obscure lineage. The tribesmen who resisted the spread of Islam, furthermore, appear to have been far more numerous than those who backed the Muslims. What backing the Muslims did receive from Iraqi tribesmen was probably the product, not of a widespread desire among the tribes to throw off Persian rule—for which there is no evidence—but rather of a skillful tribal policy, exercised by Abū Bakr, Khālid b. al-Walīd, and others of the new Islamic ruling elite, that took full advantage of lineage rivalries and religious differences within the tribes contacted. Finally, it should be noted that al-Muthannā's raids and Khālid's conquests were of a radically different character from the point of view of the local tribes involved in them, despite a similarity of objective (i.e., the conquest of al-Ḥīra). Khālid and al-Muthannā were both interested in attacking the town and could thus form a convenient military alliance, but the main ambition of al-Muthannā and his followers in their early raids in this area had probably been to free themselves of state control and to establish their position as an independent, dominant lineage within the B. Shaybān. The Muslims, on the other hand, were concerned with precisely the opposite task: their ambition was to extend the power of the state—the new Islamic state—over the Arab tribes, including of course the B. Shaybān. Al-Muthannā and his followers thus secured Khālid's tactical "support" for their campaign to reduce al-Ḥīra only at the cost of placing themselves under the authority of the Islamic state and its generals.

In comparison with the opposition Khālid faced from the Arab tribes of Iraq, the resistance that could be offered by Sasanian forces was for the moment relatively insignificant; the Sasanians had in any case traditionally relied on their tribal allies to keep the peace for them in this region, strengthening the tribesmen's allegiance to the Great King by the judicious placement of Sasanian garrisons of limited size (just how limited, the battle of Dhū Qār had once made painfully clear). Although Khālid's campaigning in Iraq was punctuated by periodic collisions with such Sasanian garrison troops, his main objective was the extension of the authority of the Islamic state over all Arabic-speaking tribesmen, whether nomadic or sedentary, who lived along or adjacent to the Euphrates. The clashes with the Sasanians were, at this stage, more or less accidental byproducts of the drive to consolidate control over the tribes. The conquest of Iraq, properly so called, was yet to come.

5. PHASE II: FIRST OFFENSIVES IN CENTRAL IRAQ

Upon his departure for Syria, Khālid left several garrisons of Muslims in various places in central Iraq. At the same time, he sent the women and other noncombatants who had evidently accompanied his army to Iraq back to Medina under the guidance of one of the *anṣār*.[117] One set of sources claims that a member of the B. Tamīm was left in charge of almost every important outpost in Iraq at this time. These accounts derive, however, from transmitters who appear to have collected cycles of tribal oral traditions in circulation among the tribes that later settled in Iraq, especially the B. Tamīm; and as the accounts display all the exaggerated tribal chauvinism associated with such oral traditions, it is reasonable to set them aside as documents having more polemical than historical significance.[118] More plausible, especially in view of the Islamic regime's concern with bringing all Arab tribesmen under its control, are reports that one of the *anṣār*—that is, someone who, as an early Medinese supporter of Muḥammad, was close to the regime in Medina—was left to supervise affairs in al-Ḥīra upon Khālid's departure for Syria. But it is not clear whether this person, 'Amr b. Ḥarām al-Anṣārī, was left behind by himself and instructed to rely upon local allies such as al-Muthannā b. Ḥāritha and his followers from the B. Shaybān, or whether he was left with a small contingent of troops from Khālid's army to serve as a garrison.[119] Most sources, however, agree that the supreme commander in Iraq after Khālid's departure (at least in military affairs) was al-Muthannā b. Ḥāritha, who had assisted Khālid so greatly in his conquest of al-Ḥīra and environs; he was appointed commander over those tribesmen, mainly of Rabī'a, who had embraced Islam. This appointment may have been little more than a recognition of his long-standing aspiration to control al-Ḥīra, however, and his real authority may not have extended far beyond the borders of the territory already controlled by his sections of the B. Shaybān. This conclusion is supported by the notice that Khālid left al-Muthannā in charge of the area around the (future) site of al-Kūfa, that is, the district near al-Ḥīra.[120]

The fullest account of al-Muthannā's activity in Iraq after Khālid's departure is provided by one tradition that describes how al-Muthannā placed his brothers al-Sayb, al-Madh'ūr, and Mas'ūd in charge of some garrison posts and put other tribal chieftains such as 'Utayba b. al-Nahhās al-'Ijlī over other posts. By this account, the Persians then sent an army of 10,000 men under the command of Hurmuz Jādhwayh against the Muslims; al-Muthannā, however, set out from al-Ḥīra and engaged the Persians at Bābil, defeating them utterly even though they had elephants in their army and greatly outnumbered the Muslims. The Muslims then reportedly pursued the fleeing Persians as far as al-Madā'in, seizing Sasanian garrisons in the alluvium all the way to the Tigris.[121] No other early source mentions any such battle or indeed any significant raiding at this time by al-Muthannā, however, and it seems likely that much of the content of this tradition may belong to a later phase of the conquests, after the defeat of the Sasanians at al-Qādisiyya or at least after the arrival of the army of Abū 'Ubayd al-Thaqafī, when the Muslims could more plausibly be expected to have raided as far as the Tigris.[122]

After 'Umar's accession as caliph in A.H. 13/A.D. 634, he decided to send a modest force from Medina to reinforce the Muslims in Iraq, who naturally had been weakened by the departure of Khālid and his troops. It is possible that his main objective in doing so was to assure that the tribes on the fringes of Iraq remained firmly under the control of the Islamic state; but many sources claim that the army was sent when al-Muthannā himself came to Medina and asked for aid against the Persians.[123] There are, however, other traditions that imply that al-Muthannā remained in Iraq and was joined there by the new army.[124]

Whatever the reasons, the new army was sent out to Iraq. 'Umar chose Abū 'Ubayd b. Mas'ūd al-Thaqafī to lead the force, acting over the objections of many who wished him to appoint one of the *muhājirūn* or *anṣār*, and although the ostensible reason for his choice was that Abū 'Ubayd had been the first to respond to his call for volunteers to make up an army, it seems more likely that he was chosen to lead because the army included many members of his tribe of Thaqīf. As an early Muslim and respected leader from that tribe, he would thus have had a special effectiveness as the army's commander.[125] He set out with the army from Medina and marched to Iraq, raising levies from the tribes (unfortunately not named) through whose territory he passed en route.[126]

Upon reaching Iraq, Abū 'Ubayd and al-Muthannā joined forces under the overall command of Abū 'Ubayd. This combined force proceeded to make raids into the agricultural heartland of central Iraq, overcoming what appear to have been small Sasanian outposts near al-Ḥīra and fanning out to reduce settlements or Sasanian forces at al-Namāriq, al-Saqāṭiya, Bārusmā, Nahr Jawbar, al-Zawābī, and Zandaward, in the alluvium between al-Madā'in, Kaskar, and al-Ḥīra.[127] The exact sequence of these raids cannot, and for our purposes need not, be reconstructed with any precision, but they seem to have ended in a pitched battle at al-Qarqas, the so-called battle of the Bridge, in which the Muslims were severely defeated by a large Persian force. Four thousand of Abū 'Ubayd's army were killed (1,000 in battle, the remainder by drowning), including Abū 'Ubayd himself, and 2,000 fled, leaving 3,000 who remained with al-Muthannā.[128] The battle is dated variously to A.H. 13 or A.H. 14.[129]

After its defeat by the Persians at the battle of the Bridge, the army appears to have disintegrated and fled in disorder. All elements that survived the battle appear to have taken part in this retreat; those traditions that state that the *muhājirūn* and *anṣār* fled while al-Muthannā took up a position near al-Ullays,[130] neatly gloss over the fact that both groups were doing in essence the same thing—retreating to the safety of their home territory. Thus the *anṣār* and *muhājirūn* headed for Medina and the Ḥijāz, and al-Muthannā and his tribesmen returned to the desert fringes of Iraq near al-Ḥīra, where they had their home.

Composition of the Army

The tribal composition of Abū 'Ubayd's army in Iraq is suggested in general terms by the groups that are said to have contributed volunteers or levies to it. As noted above, it contained three separate elements: first, a core of volunteers from Medina and environs, led by Abū 'Ubayd; second, tribal levies collected en route to Iraq; and third, al-Muthannā's forces. We can be fairly sure that the last-named element was primarily made up of sections of the B. Shaybān, al-Muthannā's tribe. We can speculate that the second element probably contained men from the tribes of the Najd, such as Ṭayyi' and Asad. We can also speculate that the first group contained members of the *anṣār*, and perhaps men of Sulaym, who lived near Medina.

We need not be content with speculation, however, as there are several passages that describe the composition of all or part of these forces in at least general terms. One states that Abū 'Ubayd's army had a core of 1,000 men from Medina and vicinity selected by 'Umar. Another states that the army consisted of 5,000 cavalry, but this may refer to the entire force including the tribal levies. A third source states that Abū 'Ubayd's army was originally 4,000 men of the *muhājirūn, anṣār*, slaves (*'abīd*), and clients (*mawālī*), to whom about 1,000 Rabī'a tribesmen who had joined al-Muthannā's force were added, making a total of about 5,000. Although the figures are difficult to reconcile, these general statements provide a tentative picture of the makeup of this force.[131]

A still more detailed picture can be obtained by examining two further sources of information. One is a list of all individuals mentioned in the conquest accounts themselves as participants in the battle of the Bridge;[132] the other is a list of individuals mentioned in a wide variety of sources who are reported to have died as martyrs in the battle of the Bridge or other engagements during the second phase.[133] We must first consider, however, what information these lists can be expected to yield. The basic assumption in working with them, is, of course, that a tribal group that was heavily represented in the campaign would also be heavily represented among the participants and martyrs of that campaign. This correspondence will be far from perfect, however, because Islamic writers tended to show great interest in the fate of the Meccans, the Medinese, and the early companions of the Prophet, but much less interest in the fate of other tribesmen who came to be allied to the Islamic regime.[134] Hence we can expect that the Quraysh and the *anṣār* will in general occupy a disproportionately prominent position in these lists in comparison with other tribal groups. The lists can, nevertheless, provide us with some additional clues about the composition of the armies fighting in Iraq at this time.

The assemblage of individual participants at the battle of the Bridge corroborates some of the impressions about the composition of Abū 'Ubayd's army gained from the general statements already discussed, but also suggests considerably more. We find that many of the *anṣār* are mentioned among the participants,[135] but that there are no individuals who can be identified with any certainty as being among the *muhājirūn* or other Quraysh. We can tentatively suggest, then, that the *anṣār* far outnumbered the *muhājirūn* in the contingent of Medinese who marched to Iraq in this force.

The general statements mention that the core force that marched from Medina included people from the vicinity of Medina as well as Medinese, and the list of individual participants suggests who these other groups might have been. By far the most important among them were the B. Thaqīf, the tribe of al-Ṭā'if to which Abū 'Ubayd himself belonged. The great number of Thaqafīs mentioned[136] suggests that the Thaqīf may have been the most important single tribal group in Abū 'Ubayd's army. This conclusion is also suggested by the fact that most traditions present various Thaqafīs as having held a virtual monopoly over the command posts during the campaign. In addition to the numerous Thaqafīs, the core force may have included some members of the B. Sulaym, who resided near Medina.[137]

Unfortunately, the list of individual participants provides little information on the identity of the tribes from which Abū 'Ubayd raised levies on his way to Iraq. The presence of a few men of Tamīm, Ṭayyi', and Ḍabba[138] suggests that these tribes, which had their territory near Abū 'Ubayd's route through the Najd, may have contributed levies. Similarly, the list of participants provides few clues to the precise composition of al-Muthannā's force, as only al-Muthannā and his brother al-Madh'ūr are mentioned at the battle of the Bridge.

The list of martyrs who fell at the battle of the Bridge is most revealing, however. Over thirty-five martyrs from the *anṣār* are listed, and six members of Thaqīf are also named, along with one man of Fazāra, two from Tha'laba, and several whose tribal identity or place of martyrdom is not certain.[139] The great predominance of *anṣār* in this list may reflect the traditionists' special interest in them or a real predominance of the *anṣār* in the army at the battle of the Bridge; but in the latter case one would expect that at least some of the commanders of the army would have been from the *anṣār*. The absence of any members of the Quraysh or *muhājirūn*, in whom the traditionists would also have been interested, confirms the conclusion that few of them participated in the second phase of the conquests in central Iraq. The presence of men of Fazāra and Tha'laba (parts of Ghaṭafān, living on the eastern fringes of the Ḥijāz) suggests that these tribes may, like Sulaym, have contributed to the core force that marched from Medina.

We can summarize the evidence of various sources as follows. The army sent out by 'Umar under Abū 'Ubayd's command appears to have been composed of a large contingent from B. Thaqīf and of numerous *anṣār*, and probably also included some men from B. Sulaym, B. Fazāra, and B. Tha'laba, all of whom lived in the vicinity of Medina. In addition, these tribesmen probably brought with them a number of people of dependent status—clients or slaves. The dominant position of the B. Thaqīf in this army is reflected in the commanders named, most of whom were Thaqafīs. There may have been some *muhājirūn* in this force, as a few general statements suggest, but the presence of large numbers of them or of other members of Quraysh is unlikely.

This army marched across northern Arabia toward Iraq, picking up tribal levies where it could—the B. Ḍabba, B. Ṭayyi', and B. Tamīm being the most likely to have contributed them. Once in Iraq, the army joined forces with al-Muthannā and his force, presumably composed of men from B. Shaybān, and other tribal groups native to the desert fringes of Iraq, such as B. 'Ijl.[140]

6. TRANSITIONAL PHASE: REINFORCEMENTS AND RAIDS IN CENTRAL IRAQ

After his withdrawal from the battle of the Bridge, al-Muthannā and his following began to launch raids on the Iraqi alluvium from his position along the desert fringes of Iraq. At the same time, 'Umar ordered that groups of reinforcements be sent to Iraq to assist al-Muthannā and the Muslims remaining with him. These new reinforcements were evidently dispatched to Iraq as they became available to the caliph for service, and were drawn from many different tribal groups. The chieftain 'Iṣma b. 'Abdullāh of B. Ḍabba, a tribe of the Najd, went with members of his tribe to assist al-Muthannā, and two other groups from B. Ḍabba also responded to 'Umar's call for troops and were sent out under the command of Ibn al-Hawbar and al-Mundhir b. Ḥassān. Several branches of the B. Tamīm also contributed troops—a group of the B. Ḥanẓala of Tamīm under a chief named Rib'ī, another from the B. 'Amr of Tamīm led by Rib'ī b. 'Āmir b. Khālid of the Usayyid clan, and 1,000 men from unspecified parts of Tamīm led by al-Ḥusayn b. Ma'bad b. Zurāra of the B. Dārim section of Tamīm. Also from the Najd came a group of B. Ṭayyi', led by the chief 'Adī b. Ḥātim al-Ṭā'ī, who had been a steadfast backer of the Islamic state during the *ridda* wars. From eastern Arabia came forth a chieftain named Qurṭ b. Jammāḥ with a group of his tribe of 'Abd al-Qays. Likewise, some tribesmen from the B. Khath'am, who resided in the Sarāt region south of Mecca, presented themselves under a certain 'Abdullāh b. Dhī l-Sahmayn and were sent to Iraq.[141]

The most important contingents to join the central Iraqi campaigns at this time, however, appear to have been drawn from the B. Bajīla and Azd. Most of the B. Bajīla had been driven out of their former home districts in the Sarāt region shortly before the rise of Islam, and had taken refuge among other tribal groups, notably the B. 'Āmir b. Ṣa'ṣa'a (who lived in central and western Arabia between al-Ṭā'if and Jabal Ṭuwayq) and the B. Jadīla of Qays b. 'Aylān (who lived in the Sarāt region south of al-Ṭā'if).[142] A group of tribesmen from those sections of the B. Bajīla that had remained in the Sarāt, or perhaps a mixed group of Bajīila and Azd tribesmen, came to Medina in response to 'Umar's call for reinforcements. Their leader at this time was 'Arfaja b. Harthama, of the B. Bāriq section of Azd, who had once fled his tribe because of a homicide and had attached himself to the B. Bajīla, among whom he rose to become their leader. Upon their arrival, 'Umar ordered that further tribesmen be levied from those branches of Bajīla that had taken up residence with the 'Āmir b. Ṣa'ṣa'a and Jadīla, and that these additional troops be joined to those from the south under 'Arfaja's command. Some of the Bajīla tribesmen, however, led by a man named Jarīr b. 'Abdullāh al-Bajalī of the B. Qasr of Bajīla (one of the sections that had remained in the Sarāt) protested the appointment over them of a commander who was not, after all, of their tribe, but rather of the Azd; the caliph therefore removed 'Arfaja from his command and placed Jarīr b. 'Abdullāh in charge of the Bajīla tribesmen instead. Under Jarīr's leadership the army of Bajīla tribesmen then set out for Iraq.[143] One source puts the size of this force at 700 men, but others indicate that the B. Bajīla eventually made up one-quarter of the Muslims fighting at al-Qādisiyya, which implies a force of at least 1,500 men and perhaps considerably more.[144] Indeed, the Bajīla force was evidently large enough to make 'Umar feel that it was worth a special effort to assure its support, for he is said to have rewarded Jarīr for his cooperation by promising him one-fourth of the fifth of spoils from the Iraqi campaigns normally reserved for the caliph and the state treasury.[145] Jarīr was clearly in a position to drive a hard bargain, which suggests that his tribal force was sizable.

The subsequent activities of 'Arfaja b. Harthama al-Bāriqī after his dismissal from command of the Bajīla force are harder to ascertain. According to one report, he went to Syria; according to another, he ultimately settled in southern Iraq and no mention is made of his going to Syria or to central Iraq; according to yet another, a group of 700 men of Azd and Kināna were sent to central Iraq by 'Umar, who appointed 'Arfaja commander of the Azdī tribesmen among them.[146] But another account states that the 700 Azd who went to central Iraq at this time were under the command of a different chief, Mikhnaf b. Sulaym al-Azdī of the B. Ghāmid of Azd.[147] It thus seems likely that a considerable number of tribesmen of Azd hailing from the Sarāt district[148] made their way to central Iraq to reinforce al-Muthannā and the Muslims there, but whether 'Arfaja b. Harthama led or accompanied them cannot be determined.

There were, then, many separate groups of tribesmen that went as reinforcements to central Iraq after the defeat of the Muslims at the battle of the Bridge. The route of march taken by these groups on their way to Iraq is not described except in the case of Jarīr b. 'Abdullāh's force of Bajīla tribesmen, and this instance is problematic. Some traditions state that Jarīr was headed first for southern Iraq, where he defeated a Persian force at al-Madhār, and only then marched on central Iraq—in the direction of al-Madā'in—after which he reached the vicinity of al-Ḥīra and joined forces with al-Muthannā.[149] It is, however, difficult to credit these accounts, which require Jarīr to have passed with a small army through unpacified territory, several hundred miles from any possible reinforcements by the Muslims' other forces in Iraq, and without any evident object. As noted above, traditions regarding Jarīr's activities were sometimes misplaced and viewed as part of Khālid's campaigning during the first phase of the conquest in Iraq.[150] It is possible that a similar displacement may have occurred here, and that the raids made by Jarīr into lower and central Iraq during the third phase of the conquests, after the battle of al-Qādisiyya, when he accompanied a force from al-Kūfa to southern Iraq to reinforce the Muslims there, have been mistakenly presented as part of his activities in this earlier transitional phase. It thus seems likely that Jarīr and his army marched directly from Medina toward the central Iraqi front.

Upon the arrival of these new forces in Iraq, a dispute broke out between al-Muthannā and Jarīr over who was to be in overall command of the Muslims there. Some accounts describe Jarīr merely as a reinforcement serving under al-Muthannā's command, but others claim that he refused to recognize al-Muthannā as his superior.[151] Whoever was in command, different groups of troops appear to have undertaken raids on various localities in the Persian-controlled alluvium and along the

Euphrates such as al-Anbār and al-Nukhayla, as far south as Kaskar and as far north as 'Ayn al-Tamr. The tribes of al-Namir and Taghlib were also raided.[152]

Many sources, furthermore, describe at this time an episode in which al-Muthannā rallied the Muslims and led them to a stunning victory against a sizable Persian army at a place called Buwayb.[153] In this battle the Muslims are even said to have killed the Persian commander, Mihrān. There are, however, numerous reasons to question the historicity of this traditional presentation of the material. In the first place, the accounts of the battle of Buwayb display a strong tendency to glorify the role of al-Muthannā as leader of this campaign. He is, for example, represented as calling other tribal leaders to join him in making a decisive attack, and in leading this attack.[154] Similarly, the events after the battle, when nearby towns were raided by al-Muthannā and his men, are described in such glowing terms[155] that we begin to wonder whether we may not be dealing with a kind of "al-Muthannā Saga"—especially since it is reported by the sources that Muthannā died some months afterward of wounds he had suffered at the battle of the Bridge. Personal valor is certainly a trait well attested among Arab nomadic leaders of the time, but the laudatory reports of al-Muthannā's prowess and leadership at a time when he is known to have been nursing fatal injuries do not inspire our confidence.

We may, in addition, question the way in which the traditions under scrutiny present al-Muthannā as supreme commander and portray the battle of Buwayb as a clash between two sizable armies. According to their view, al-Muthannā led a force organized into wings, and he enjoyed the support of reinforcements from various tribes. Among his subordinates were, reportedly, Jarīr b. 'Abdullāh al-Bajalī and 'Iṣma b. 'Abdullāh al-Ḍabbī who had recently arrived in Iraq.[156] As noted above, however, some accounts state that Jarīr refused to subordinate himself to al-Muthannā, which tends to cast some doubt on the notion that al-Muthannā had sweeping powers of command as portrayed in the traditions about Buwayb. Indeed, one account notes that when al-Muthannā complained to 'Umar about Jarīr's insubordination, the caliph replied that he would not place al-Muthannā in command over a companion of the Prophet (i.e., over Jarīr). Other accounts state flatly that when 'Umar became caliph he removed al-Muthannā from his command.[157] This tends to generate further suspicion that the accounts about Buwayb are unduly favorable to al-Muthannā.

It should be noted, finally, that most of the accounts about the battle of Buwayb that ascribe improbable deeds of valor or powers of command to al-Muthannā are derived from traditionists who may have obtained their information from tribal oral traditions, the purpose of which was to celebrate the tribe's glorious history—in this case, that of the B. Shaybān and of the Rabī'a faction of which Shaybān was, in the decades after the conquest, an important part. This suggests that the accounts of the battle of Buwayb were designed to enhance the reputation of al-Muthannā and of his tribe among later generations and to counter the disgrace of his humiliating defeat at the battle of the Bridge.[158]

We may conclude, then, that the "battle of Buwayb" probably never occurred in the grand form in which it is usually described and may not have occurred at all. The accounts of it that have come down to us appear to be a kind of tribal epic, evidently based on oral traditions that circulated among the B. Shaybān, designed to restore the reputation of al-Muthannā and his tribe after their resounding defeat at the battle of the Bridge. This cycle was elaborated in the manner of the "*ayyām al-'arab*" tales by piecing together numerous accounts of small skirmishes to create a synthesized "major battle."[159] The apologetic tendencies of this cycle explain the unlikely accounts of al-Muthannā's exploits at a time when he was seriously wounded, and of what appear to be inflated notions of his powers of command. It seems that, to a core of material provided by tribal traditions of the B. Shaybān, there were added bits of oral traditions current among other tribes of the Rabī'a group. We find, for example, traces of a "Euphrates Arab" (B. Namir and B. Taghlib—both of Rabī'a), tradition[160] designed to give these tribes, well known for their stubborn resistance to the spread of Islam, some positive credit in the conquest of Iraq.

All considered, it seems most reasonable to conclude that after the battle of the Bridge, al-Muthannā withdrew to the safety of the desert to nurse his wounds, both military and physical. After this defeat, 'Umar sent reinforcements including those under Jarīr b. 'Abdullāh al-Bajalī to bolster the central Iraqi front. These forces probably undertook only small-scale raids and fleeting skirmishes with the Persians[161]—one of which, as one tradition suggests, may have occurred at a place called al-Buwayb, although we cannot definitely deduce whether al-Muthannā's force, Jarīr's force, or both were involved. Major confrontations with the enemy were, however, avoided. Perhaps some, even much, of the information included in the "Buwayb cycle" is valid data about these small raids that have been transplanted into the context of a larger battle, but it is impossible to distinguish factual material from the strands of fiction with which it is interwoven.

Although we may reject the notion of a major battle such as that described in the Buwayb epic, however, there is little reason to doubt the occurrence of raids from the accounts of which the epic was later constructed. The accounts of Buwayb and other raids of the transitional phase can, then, be scrutinized to provide further hints about the relative importance of various tribal groups in the Muslims' armies by collecting the names of individual participants.[162] This data can be used to verify the general descriptions of the composition of forces earlier discussed that were either sent to Iraq or already active there. Such an analysis confirms the importance of the Azd, B. Ḍabba, and B. 'Ijl in the campaigning of the transitional phase. The B. 'Ijl, who were native to the fringes of Iraq, doubtless formed part of al-Muthannā's army, whereas the Azd and B. Ḍabba originally came from the Sarāt region and the Najd respectively, as we have seen. The list of individual participants also suggests that the B. Ṭayyi' (Najd) and, perhaps, the B. al-Namir b. Qāsiṭ (upper Euphrates) may have contributed some tribesmen to the Muslims' forces. But various accounts reveal that the majority of these two tribes remained Christian and aligned with the Sasanians, and even those who joined the Muslims appear to have remained Christian.[163]

In sum, the following picture emerges of the armies active in central Iraq on behalf of the Islamic state during the transitional phase of the conquests there. Al-Muthannā b. Ḥāritha led tribesmen who had retreated with him after the disaster at the battle of the Bridge, including mainly members of his own tribe of B. Shaybān and of another Iraqi tribe, the B. 'Ijl. Many groups of reinforcements were sent to Iraq by 'Umar, of which the most important appear to have been the B. Bajīla contingent commanded by Jarīr b. 'Abdullāh al-Bajalī, troops from the Azd (probably from the clans of Bāriq and Ghāmid), and troops from the B. Ḍabba. Other groups who seem to have been active in Iraq during the transitional phase but whose importance in the Islamic armies there cannot be clearly established include the B. Kināna (perhaps attached to the Azd), the Khath'am, B. 'Abd al-Qays, B. Ṭayyi', the clans of 'Amr, Ḥanẓala, and perhaps Dārim of Tamīm and possibly some tribesmen from B. Taghlib and B. al-Namir b. Qāsiṭ.

It is noteworthy that the bulk of the new reinforcements sent to Iraq at this time hailed from the Najd or the Sarāt district, rather than from the Ḥijāz. The loyal groups that had provided the backbone of the armies during the first and second phases of the conquest in Iraq—tribesmen from Medina, Mecca, al-Ṭā'if, and from nomadic groups living in the vicinity of these cities, such as the Muzayna and B. Sulaym—are conspicuous by their absence from the Islamic armies in central Iraq during the transitional phase. As in phases I and II, however, the ruling elite may still have been trying to draw primarily on tribal groups that had not participated in the rebellions against the Islamic state during the *ridda* wars. Most of the new tribes that provided contingents (Azd, Ḍabba, Kināna, Khath'am) do not appear to have played much of a role on either side during the *ridda*; they had probably been too weak to wish to become involved in the struggle between Medina and the rebel tribes and hence had remained on correct terms with the Islamic state. Early support for the Islamic state by the Azd is suggested by the fact that at least one Azdī is said to have fought with the Muslims against the B. Ḥanīfa of al-Yamāma during the *ridda*, although it is possible that this was merely an isolated individual.[164] The B. Ṭayyi' had been split during the *ridda*, with part of the tribe rising against the Islamic state and another part siding with Medina; but the contingent from B. Ṭayyi' that participated in the activities of the transitional phase was commanded by 'Adī b. Ḥātim, who had been the leader of the loyalist section of the tribe during the *ridda*. The 'Abd al-Qays tribe was also split during the *ridda*, so it is possible that those who came to central Iraq during the transitional phase likewise represented the branches of the tribe that had remained loyal to Medina during the *ridda*. As for the Bajīla, the situation is more difficult to ascertain. The leader of the Bajīla tribesmen, Jarīr b. 'Abdullāh, had embraced Islam with a following of 150 men some years before the Prophet's death and had been sent by Muḥammad to subdue and, evidently, to serve as governor in districts in the northern Yemen where the Bajīla tribe resided. He also appears to have played some part in the *ridda* wars on the side of Medina and may have been sent by Abū Bakr to help subdue the Bajīla and other tribes in the Yemen once again, as the majority of them had cast off their allegiance to Medina upon Muḥammad's death.[165] Certainly he was loyal to the regime in Medina, but whether his following had also been entirely loyal is less clear. Since many of his followers came, not from the sections of Bajīla resident in the Sarāt district of northern Yemen, but rather from sections resident among other tribes in the Najd, it is possible that they represented parts of Bajīla that had not rebelled during the *ridda*.

Nevertheless, the transitional phase marked the beginning of a shift away from exclusive reliance by the new regime in Medina on those tribal groups from the Ḥijāz whose interests had been, since Muḥammad's conquest of Mecca and al-Ṭā'if, closely linked to those of the Islamic state. This shift toward a broader base of military support was doubtless the result of the Muslims' defeat at the battle of the Bridge during the second phase, as well as of building pressure on the Syrian front, all of which created a military manpower crisis that forced 'Umar to turn to new tribal groups for military support, even if their loyalty to the Islamic state had not been clearly demonstrated during the *ridda* wars. Indeed, 'Umar is even said to have ordered that former rebel tribesmen should be recruited into the army at this time to assist the Muslims in central Iraq.[166] The execution of this policy was, however, something that developed fully only during the third phase of the conquests in central Iraq.

7. PHASE III: THE CONQUEST AND OCCUPATION OF CENTRAL IRAQ

The buildup of troops in central Iraq that had begun with the dispatch of many groups of tribesmen during the transitional phase found its culmination during the third phase. The continued massing of Persian forces in central Iraq, and the disagreement between al-Muthannā and Jarīr over who was to command the Muslims there, seem to have convinced 'Umar that more troops should be sent out and that he should go to Iraq himself to settle the question of who was to command. He was dissuaded from going in person by some of his advisers, however, who pointed out that assigning an early companion of the Prophet as commander-in-chief in central Iraq would resolve the problem, since both Jarīr and al-Muthannā would willingly submit to his authority.[167]

'Umar consequently placed Sa'd b. Abī Waqqāṣ, one of the *muhajirūn* from Quraysh and a veteran of the battle of Badr and of other early engagements with the Prophet, in command of the groups of tribesmen who were still gathering near Medina in response to 'Umar's call for reinforcements to go to Iraq. Sa'd had been tax agent among the Hawāzin tribe in the Najd for Abū Bakr and 'Umar and had come to Medina at the head of 1,000 men of this tribe when 'Umar issued his call for troops. He now found himself in charge of the largest single force the Islamic state had sent to Iraq and designated the commander-in-chief of military operations on the central Iraqi front.[168]

Sa'd marched with this army across the Najd to a place called Zarūd in the Shaqīq sands between the Najd and Iraq, where he apparently camped for the winter and solicited levies from the tribes of the Najd.[169] Some of these levies joined him at Zarūd; others, on Sa'd's instructions, gathered at Sharāf or other points between the Najd and Iraq to await Sa'd's arrival. Additional contingents were also being sent to Sa'd by 'Umar as they became available in Medina. When spring came Sa'd appears to have set out for Sharāf, where the tribal levies joined his army, and the greatly augmented force proceeded to Iraq. Sa'd camped his army at al-'Udhayb, on the edge on the alluvium not far from al-Ḥīra and the site of the battle of al-Qādisiyya.[170]

In the interim, al-Muthannā b. Ḥāritha had died while Sa'd was camped at Zarūd, leaving in command of his men a prominent member of the important clan of Sadūs in the B. Shaybān, Bashīr b. al-Khaṣāṣiyya, who had the support of other chieftains of Iraqi orgin.[171] Other important Iraqi chiefs, including Furāt b. Ḥayyān and 'Utayba b. al-Nahhās of B. 'Ijl, apparently went as a deputation to 'Umar upon al-Muthannā's death, probably to tender their continued allegiance and to clarify the question of who should succeed as commander, and these seem to have joined Sa'd on their way back to Iraq. Sa'd was also joined by al-Muthannā's widow, Salmā bint Khaṣafa, and his brother, al-Mu'annā b. Ḥāritha, perhaps only after he had reached Iraq, and Sa'd married al-Muthannā's widow, probably to bolster his ties to the tribesmen of Shaybān whom al-Muthannā had once led.[172]

By the time of Sa'd's arrival in Iraq, the Persian Great King Yazdegird III had finally managed to consolidate his power and end the chaos that had afflicted the Sasanian royal house since the Byzantine invasion a decade earlier. He now proceeded to summon together a massive army intended to put an end to the raids and occupation of towns in Iraq by the Muslims. This army, under the command of the Persian general Rustam, crossed the Euphrates and took up a position at al-Saylaḥān, facing Sa'd's force.[173] The size of the Sasanian army is said to have been anything from 30,000 men to 210,000 men according to various sources.[174] At this time may have occurred the dispatch of envoys from Sa'd's camp to the Persian leaders, an episode presented in much embroidered form in the Arabic sources, which depict the rebuff of the Muslims' ambassadors by Rustam in very dramatic and heavily symbolic terms.[175] Sa'd also seems to have sent out small groups to do reconnaissance, to raid and harrass the Sasanian troops, and to collect food and fodder for his army.[176]

Eventually, however, the two armies drew up in battle order at al-Qādisiyya, southwest of al-Ḥīra on the fringes of the desert, and made ready for combat. 'Umar ordered additional reinforcements from Syria and southern Iraq to bolster Sa'd's army, and also sent camels and sheep to Sa'd's force for food.[177] Some sources give detailed descriptions of the way in which Sa'd organized his army in marching into battle, with various contingents (wings, vanguard, cavalry and infantry units, etc.) under specified commanders, but as few of these descriptions agree it is impossible to draw definite conclusions about the actual organization of the army. It seems very likely, however, that the army was carefully organized and was not simply a horde of warriors led by their tribal chieftains.[178]

Similarly, little can be said with certainty about the actual course of the fighting at the battle of al-Qādisiyya. The sources provide very full descriptions of many incidents in the battle, but little in the way of an overall picture of the evolving tactical situation, and many of the incidents described appear to be accounts drawn from tribal oral traditions that portray in glowing terms the deeds of valor performed by the tribes' heroes.[179] Many of these episodes may in fact have occurred, but there is in most cases no way to establish the historicity of specific accounts or incidents. What emerges from the mass of accounts about the battle, then, is a very sketchy outline. The battle is said by many sources to have lasted three days, with especially bitter fighting on the second and third days and fighting continuing into the night after the third day. The Sasanians evidently had elephants in the army, which caused some consternation among the Muslims' cavalry at first; and there is much mention of individual combats between champions from the two sides while most of their cohorts watched and cheered on their contender. On the second or third day, the cavalry reinforcements from Syria are said to have arrived. Other sources do not mention the length of the battle's duration.[180]

Whatever its course, however, the battle of al-Qādisiyya was clearly a victory for the Muslims. Sa'd's troops appear to have defeated the Sasanian forces totally. His army pursued the shattered enemy to the Euphrates and the al-Ṣarāt canal running eastward from the Euphrates near Bābil, and ultimately the Persians were constrained to flee to al-

Madā'in.[181] The Muslims had broken the back of Persian resistance in central Iraq, and the rich alluvium lay open to them.

Size and Composition of the Army at al-Qādisiyya

For all its importance, the battle of al-Qādisiyya appears to have been a clash between two rather small armies. Figures for the Sasanian army have been noted above. Figures for Sa'd's army vary greatly from source to source, but the enormous numbers given in later sources[182] appear to be much exaggerated, for there is a persistent tendency in earlier sources to place the total number in Sa'd's army at between 6,000 and 12,000 men.[183] It is not usually stated whether these totals include the forces from southern Iraq and from Syria that came to Sa'd's assistance; these might therefore account for some of the variation in the figures provided.

It is, however, possible to establish the tribal composition of the army Sa'd commanded at al-Qādisiyya. The army consisted, as described above, of six groups: (1) a core force that marched with Sa'd from Medina to the Najd; (2) tribal levies raised from tribes whose grazing grounds were in or near the Najd; (3) the remainder of al-Muthannā's and Jarīr's forces in Iraq; (4) a number of tribal groups that responded to 'Umar's summons too late to march from Medina with Sa'd, but that were sent along later by 'Umar to join Sa'd's army in the field; (5) a group of reinforcements from southern Iraq; (6) a group of reinforcements from Syria. Of these groups, the third has already been described.[184] It remains to analyze the other groups in turn.

The few accounts offering detailed descriptions of the core force that marched with Sa'd from Medina put it at 4,000 men. One account states that Sa'd brought 1,000 warriors of Hawāzin to Medina and that he was joined there by 3,000 people (not all fighting men; women and children are mentioned) from the Yemen and al-Sarāt. Over the people of al-Sarāt was Humayḍa b. al-Nu'mān b. Hurayḍa al-Bāriqī; they numbered 700 and came from the Bāriq, Alma', and Ghāmid sections of Azd, and "others of their brethren." The Yemenis on the other hand are said to have numbered 2,300 including al-Nakha' b. 'Amr (of Madhḥij).[185]

Another tradition states that there were 1,300 from Madhḥij under three tribal leaders: 'Amr b. Ma'dīkarib over B. Munabbih (i.e., "Munabbih the elder" = B. Zubayd, as 'Amr is commonly called "al-Zubaydī"); Abū Sabra b. Dhu'ayb over B. Ju'fī and those habitually joined to them who were allied to Ju'fī; and Yazīd b. al-Ḥārith al-Ṣudā'ī over

Ṣudā', al-Janb, and Musliya, who numbered 300. With Sa'd also marched 1,000 of Qays b. 'Aylān, under Bishr b. 'Abdullāh al-Hilālī, and 600 from Ḥaḍramawt and al-Ṣadif (both places in southern Arabia) under Shaddād b. Ḍam'aj. The total for the army is not given[186] but two other traditions state that the total force that left Medina numbered 4,000.[187]

It is possible to harmonize all these traditions fairly convincingly if we assume that the 1,000 Qays b. 'Aylān of the second tradition are the same as the 1,000 Hawāzin of the first. Hawāzin was one of the largest subdivisions of Qays b. 'Aylān, but it included the tribe of 'Āmir b. Ṣa'ṣa'a, an important group usually given almost independent stature by the genealogists. If the Hawāzin contingent included members of B. 'Āmir—and the lineage of Hilāl, to which Bishr b. 'Abdullāh belonged, may have been a subsection of 'Āmir—traditionists might have felt more comfortable calling the contingent by the looser term "Qays" rather than Hawāzin, from which the B. 'Āmir were perhaps beginning to differentiate themselves even though they were, strictly speaking, part of Hawāzin.[188]

The core force that left Medina under Sa'd therefore appears to have been composed of the following tribal groups: about 1,000 men of Hawāzin (perhaps including men of 'Āmir b. Ṣa'ṣa'a); about 800 people of various branches of Azd who had come from al-Sarāt; about 600 coming from Ḥaḍramawt and al-Ṣadif (both in South Arabia); and a large number of people from different sections of Madhḥij, including Munabbih (the elder, = B. Zubayd), Ju'fī, Ṣudā', al-Janb, and others, apparently totaling about 1,300; this would place the size of the contingent from al-Nakha', mentioned in the first tradition but not in the second, at about 400 men. The total force would number about 4,000.

It is plausibly stated in one account that the tribal levies recruited in the Najd were drawn from the tribes of Tamīm and Asad, and from the coalition of al-Ribāb, allies of Tamīm, which included the B. Taym, B. 'Adī, B. 'Ukl, B. Thawr, B. Ḍabba, and others, all of which had territory in or adjacent to the Najd. Tamīm and Asad are said to have contributed 3,000 men each and al-Ribāb 1,000 men.[189] Another account, however, states that Tamīm provided 1,100 men under two chiefs, 'Āṣim b. 'Amr and 'Āṣim b. Zurāra, and that B. Asad provided 800 men under the leadership of the former rebel Ṭalḥa (Ṭulayḥa) b. Khuwaylid al-Asadī.[190]

'Umar is said to have sent successive reinforcements to Sa'd after his departure from Medina. One account mentions a contingent of 400 men of B. Sakūn, a branch of Kinda, led by Ḥusayn b. Numayr al-Sakūnī and Mu'āwiya b. Ḥudayj al-Sakūnī; also mentioned are unspecified tribesmen from the Yemen, and from B. Ghaṭafān and other branches of Qays from the Najd.[191] There is also mention of 1,000 tribesmen, presumably of B. Sulaym, which lived on the eastern fringes of the Ḥijāz between Mecca and Medina, led by Khath'am b. 'Abdullāh al-Sulamī.[192]

The reinforcements arriving from Syria are frequently mentioned; they seem to have involved two forces. One, commanded by Sa'd's nephew Hāshim b. 'Utba b. Abī Waqqāṣ, included a strong contingent from the B. Murād (a branch of Madhḥij) under Qays b. al-Makshūḥ al-Murādī, and from B. Hamdān under Sa'd b. Nimrān al-Hamdānī, as well as other "Yemeni" tribesmen from the Ḥijāz. They may also have included tribesmen from Kinda and al-Nakha' (another branch of Madhḥij) as al-Ash'ath b. Qays al-Kindī and Mālik al-Ashtar al-Nakha'ī are said to have been among them.[193] Figures for its size vary, however, from between 300 to 2,000 men. The other force appears to have been commanded by 'Iyāḍ b. Ghanm al-Fihrī (of Quraysh), who led back to Iraq the *ahl al-ayyām*, that is, the troops who had fought with Khālid b. al-Walīd in Iraq and had then made the "desert march" with him from Iraq to Syria in order to join the Muslims at the Yarmūk and the conquest of Damascus. This force is said to have numbered between 1,000 and 5,000 men of Rabī'a and Muḍar depending on the source consulted, and included such chieftains as al-Qa'qā' b. 'Amr al-Tamīmī and al-Hazhāz b. 'Amr al-'Ijlī.[194]

Little can be said of the reinforcements that came from southern Iraq to assist Sa'd at al-Qādisiyya. They were led by al-Mughīra b. Shu'ba al-Thaqafī and are said to have numbered anywhere from 400 to 1,500 men.[195] Nothing can be ascertained about their composition, but it is very likely that they reflected the composition of the forces sent to southern Iraq, which appear to have consisted of large numbers of tribesmen of Thaqīf, of nomadic tribesmen from the Ḥijāz from groups such as B. Sulaym, Balī, and Muzayna, and perhaps of some tribesmen from Tamīm and other tribes of the Najd.[196]

Other statements about the composition of forces at al-Qādisiyya are suggestive, notably the declaration that only 700 men of Kinda were at the battle, or that one-fourth of the Muslims at al-Qādisiyya were of the B. Bajīla.[197] Considered together, these general descriptions of the various contingents that made up the army at al-Qādisiyya provide some insight into the wide variety of tribal groups drawn upon by the Islamic state for military units at this time. It is noteworthy in particular that these accounts make little or no mention of Medinese (*anṣār*) or of Thaqafīs among the elements in the army at al-Qādisiyya, in marked contrast to the situation during the second phase of the conquest in Iraq. There are, however, certain problems with these general statements, since if we accept them all at face value the total size of the army at al-Qādisiyya becomes inflated considerably above the upper figure of about 12,000 men that the early sources appear to provide. It is therefore likely that some of the traditions cited above give exaggerated figures.

The names of martyrs reported to have fallen in battle at al-Qādisiyya supplement and to some extent clarify the accounts just discussed.[198] Of twenty-seven known martyrs, eight were of the *anṣār*, whereas only one was of Quraysh. This implies strongly that the *anṣār*, but not the Quraysh, took an active part in the battle, for had many prominent Qurashīs fallen their names would certainly have been recorded. Since few if any *anṣār* appear to have gone to Iraq as part of the buildup of forces there in the third phase, it is likely that the *anṣārī* participants in the battle were men who had come during the first or second phases of the conquest, survived the battle of the Bridge, and remained in Iraq when most of their fellows had retreated to Medina.

Others in the list of martyrs at al-Qādisiyya whose tribal affiliations can be established include one each from B. Ṭayyi' and Juhayna and seven members of al-Nakha', a clan of the Yemeni tribe of Madhḥij. This provides some support for those traditions that claim for the clan of al-Nakha', and perhaps for other branches of Madhḥij, an important role at al-Qādisiyya. Conspicuous by their absence are the B. Shaybān and other tribes native to the fringes of Iraq; the B. Tamīm, whose leaders are given such a prominent role in the battle by the Tamīmī tribal traditions; and the B. Bajīla, claimed by some accounts to have provided one-fourth of the army at al-Qādisiyya. This suggests that these tribes may have provided a more modest number of men for the army at al-Qādisiyya than some accounts claim.

It is also possible to gain some insight into the composition of Sa'd's army at al-Qādisiyya by considering as a body the names of individuals mentioned in various accounts of the battle.[199] It is first necessary, however, to weed out those traditions that display a clearly tendentious character. The presence of many tribal traditions that exaggerate the prowess of specific individuals in battle might suggest that little material of value will remain after this sifting process has been completed; yet the distortion is less significant than one might suppose. Many of the exaggerations do distort the role of specific individuals in the conquest (by making them appear more prominent than they probably were) but in most cases the presence of the individuals in question can hardly be doubted. In short, the distortions that were introduced tended to amplify details about individuals who did participate at al-Qādisiyya, but do not seem to have injected as actors individuals who were not present at all. There are a few cases in which we might question the very presence of an individual, but this is usually done on the assumption that a once ambiguous tradition has been misplaced in the context of the battle of al-Qādisiyya when it in fact belongs elsewhere. Such cases appear to be very few in number; more frequently, though it may be necessary to take the exploits of certain tribal leaders (for example, Ṭalḥa b. Khuwaylid al-Asadī) with a grain of salt, we can hardly doubt that they participated at al-Qādisiyya without flying in the face of evidence from a wide variety of sources.

The assemblage of individuals named in the accounts of al-Qādisiyya in general substantiates the conclusions about the composition of the army that have been drawn from other sources. The accounts of the battle give considerable prominence in numbers to the tribes of al-Nakha', Murād, and other branches of Madhḥij; to the Azd; to Sakūn and other sections of Kinda; to Tamīm; to Asad; and to the tribes of the confederation of al-Ribāb—Taym, Thawr, and 'Adī. The B. Bajīla, who arrived during the transitional phase, are also given a prominent role, as are the tribes of Shaybān, 'Ijl, and others of the desert fringes of Iraq.

Consolidation of the Muslims' Control in Central and Northern Iraq

After their victory at al-Qādisiyya, Sa'd's troops pursued the Persians into the cultivated alluvium (*sawād*) of central Iraq. Raiding parties—perhaps foraging parties—were sent out by Sa'd, and these appear to have covered much of the central Iraqi alluvium, reducing villages and eliminating the remains of scattered Sasanian garrisons throughout the area. These raids provided a convenient grafting-place for many tribal traditions with their usual hyperbole in describing the exploits of tribal leaders, notably at such encounters as the capture of Bābil. Sa'd also sent out a strong force that chased the remnants of the Sasanian army to al-Madā'in. The Muslims invested the city, or camped near it, for a considerable time (various sources say anywhere from two to twenty-eight months); there was some skirmishing, especially around the Bahurasīr (Veh-Ardashīr) quarter, but finally the Muslims were able to cross the Tigris and seize the city after Yazdegird and the bulk of his men had withdrawn from it.[200] From al-Madā'in the Muslims continued their raiding forays throughout the *sawād* and also sent forces up the Tigris and Euphrates to Takrīt and al-Qarqīsiyā'. The Persians attempted to re-form their ranks in the Zagros foothills, but Sa'd dispatched a sizable army to meet them there; the sources put the size of this army at 12,000 men. The two forces met at Jalūlā', at which battle the Muslims were again victorious, ending the possibility of a restoration of Sasanian control in central Iraq.[201]

There are no reports of any new contingents of troops being sent to the Muslims' army during the campaigns of al-Madā'in and Jalūlā'; the forces active in these campaigns therefore probably had roughly the same composition as at al-Qādisiyya, although some change would have been caused by the departure of the southern Iraqi contingent, which returned to the south after the battle of al-Qādisiyya, and of the Syrian contingent, some of which left either after al-Qādisiyya or after the capture of al-Madā'in.

The names of individuals listed as participants in the campaigns at al-Madā'in and Jalūlā' reflect, in general, this continuity. Most of the names—certainly all those of any importance—appear also in the accounts about al-Qādisiyya, reflecting the fact that the same forces were involved.

As in the accounts of al-Qādisiyya, the descriptions of the battle of Jalūlā' suggest that the Muslims were drawn up in a formal battle order comprising wings, infantry and cavalry units, and the like; but once again the various statements about this organization differ drastically on such basic matters as who commanded which unit. It is therefore impossible to state definitively anything more than the general observation that the Muslims appear to have gone into battle in a well-organized manner. Such, at least, is the impression conveyed by the great mass of traditional accounts, rooted no doubt in the assembled recollections of those individual participants or their contacts who transmitted personal accounts of the events to later collectors of historical traditions.

In sum, the armies sent to central Iraq during the third phase of the conquests there had a composition decidedly different from those of the first and second phases, and even from those of the transitional phase. During the third phase, a willingness on the part of the Medinese ruling elite to employ as military units contingents drawn from tribal groups that had once rebelled against Medina during the *ridda*—a tendency already faintly visible in the transitional phase—becomes for the first time clearly evident. This is not to say that "loyalist" tribal groups were passed over, of course. The Azd, who seem to have provided many tribesmen for Sa'd's army in Iraq, may have been among the early supporters of the Islamic state, and the Azdī leader, Humayḍa b. al-Nu'mān, had once been appointed over the Sarāt district by 'Umar.[202] The B. Sulaym, seen also among the Muslims active in the campaign of Abū 'Ubayd al-Thaqafī during the second phase of the conquests in Iraq, appears to have been split during the *ridda*, but at least part of the tribe backed Medina from the very beginning of Abū Bakr's caliphate.[203] But many of the new groups found in Sa'd's army had resisted the Islamic state following Muḥammad's death, in some cases even before. The tribesmen of B. Asad, for example, came to Iraq under their chief Ṭalḥa b. Khuwaylid, one of the leaders of the rebellion in the Najd. Some of the Kinda tribesmen arrived led by the former rebel al-Ash'ath b. Qays al-Kindī, and tribesmen of Murād (a section of Madhḥij) came forth led by Qays b. Makshūḥ al-Murādī, who appears to have been allied to al-Ash'ath during the *ridda*.[204] The chief of the B. Zubayd (another section of Madhḥij), 'Amr b. Ma'dikarib al-Zubaydī, appears to have been associated with the rebel al-Aswad al-'Ansī in the Yemen. The B. 'Āmir b. Ṣa'ṣa'a seem to have opposed the Islamic state (though not very vigorously) during the *ridda* wars, shortly after the battle of Buzākha in the Najd. The B. Ghaṭafān also opposed the Islamic state during the early stages of the *ridda*.[205] Other groups may also have been among the rebels of the *ridda*, but not enough is known about them to be certain; these include sections of Tamīm and of Madhḥij (Ju'fī, Jaz', Anas Allāt, Ṣudā', Janb, Musliya), the B. Hamdān, and the people of al-Ṣadif in South Arabia. The Ribāb tribes, which were closely allied to parts of B. Tamīm on the eve of Islam, fall in the same category. It is adequately clear, in any case, that 'Umar and the leadership of the Islamic state had, by the third phase of the conquests, begun to recruit former rebels of the *ridda* into the armies sent to central Iraq on a large scale. This reflects a fundamental shift in policy toward the former rebel tribesmen by the state when compared to its attitude during the first and second phases.

The broad agreement among various sources concerning the sequence of events in central Iraq stands in sharp contrast to the situation for Syria; but, though the relative chronology of events in Iraq is clearer than in Syria, the absolute chronology is no less vague. In some cases, events in central Iraq are dated in relation to events in Syria; thus one account states that the battle of the Bridge took place forty days after the battle of the Yarmūk[206]—the dating of which has been, as we have seen, a subject of some disagreement. In other cases, different authorities simply provide divergent datings for events in central Iraq. Thus the battle of al-Qādisiyya is dated variously to Muharram, A.H. 14/March, A.D. 635, to Ramaḍān or Shawwāl, A.H. 15/October or November, A.D. 636, or to A.H. 16/A.D. 637-638.[207] Similarly, the fall of al-Madā'in to the Muslims and the battle of Jalūlā' are dated variously. Some place the capture of al-Madā'in in A.H. 16, after a siege of two months, whereas others state that the siege lasted twenty-eight months.[208] The battle of Jalūlā', all agree, took place after the fall of al-Madā'in; but some feel that it occurred late in A.H. 16.[209] Others state that Sa'd b. Abī Waqqāṣ had occupied al-Madā'in for three years before sending troops to Jalūlā',[210] or date Jalūlā' (or even al-Madā'in and Jalūlā') to A.H. 19.[211] Given this kind of disagreement and the chronologically ambiguous nature of many of the accounts about the conquest, it is impossible to do more than guess at the true dates involved.

8. THE CONQUEST OF SOUTHERN IRAQ

The course of the conquest of southern Iraq by the Islamic state can be divided into a second and third phase following Khālid b. al-Walīd's action there, which formed the first phase; but such a subdivision, corresponding to the activity in southern Iraq of the successive commanders there, 'Utba b. Ghazwān on the one hand and al-Mughīra b. Shu'ba and Abū Mūsā al-Ash'arī on the other, turns out to be far less significant than in central Iraq because the composition of forces does not appear to have undergone appreciable change between the two later phases. The campaigns in southern Iraq are more confused in sequence than those in central Iraq, but the absence of any decisive battles with major Sasanian armies on this front made the exploits there less desirable as grafting-places for tendentious traditions. This in some measure simplifies the task of unraveling the course of events there and of establishing the tribal composition of the forces involved.

Khālid b. al-Walīd's contact with this region during the first phase of the conquest—if, indeed, he had any—was of little or no lasting importance. The raiding activity that local Arab tribes had undertaken against al-Ubulla (and, presumably, against other urban centers) even before Khālid's arrival was, however, of greater significance. The analysis of Khālid's campaign in Iraq performed above suggested that the main tribes active in this area during the first phase of the conquests were the B.

'Ijl and B. Dhuhl. After Khālid's departure, raiding activity appears to have continued, under the leadership of Suwayd b. Quṭba al-Dhuhlī or al-'Ijlī, as the various traditions give his name; that is, raiding continued led by a clan or clans of the B. Dhuhl or B. 'Ijl. According to one tradition, this group of raiding tribesmen included not only members of the B. Bakr (which included Dhuhl and 'Ijl), but also tribesmen of the B. Tamīm.[212]

'Umar was either requested by the leader of these raids, or decided on his own initiative, to send a force of Muslims to support this activity and, presumably, to insure that those involved always acted in the best interests of the Medinan regime. An initial force, sent out under Shurayḥ b. 'Āmir of the B. Sa'd b. Bakr of Hawāzin, was destroyed at an encounter with a Persian garrison at Dāris near al-Aḥwāz,[213] so 'Umar sent another force under 'Utba b. Ghazwān of the B. Māzin b. Manṣūr (a minor branch of Qays b. 'Aylān), an early companion of Muḥammad and an ally (*ḥalīf*) of the B. Nawfal b. 'Abd Manāf of Quraysh.[214] With the mission of 'Utba b. Ghazwān began the Islamic conquest of southern Iraq. According to some sources, 'Utba was sent by 'Umar with the objective of cutting the supply lines serving the Persian forces around al-Madā'in in central Iraq;[215] hence his campaign was, initially, seen as a part of the Muslims' overall strategy in their struggle with the Sasanian Empire.

The size of 'Utba's force was small. Although one source states that it numbered 2,000 men, another gives its size as 300, swollen to 500 by the addition of nomadic tribesmen (*a'rāb wa ahl al-bawādī*), a third puts the total at 800 men, and yet another tells us that 'Utba marched with a mere 40 men.[216] The small size of this army is underscored by accounts that place the number of those participating in the conquest of al-Ubulla at 270 or 300 men.[217] Joined by local tribesmen, also presumably in very limited numbers, 'Utba and his army moved against al-Ubulla, the main town of the region, which was defended by a Persian garrison including 500 cavalry (*asāwira*). 'Utba's army first camped at al-Khurayba, near al-Ubulla, and then managed to defeat the defenders and to occupy the town, taking much booty. 'Utba placed Nāfi' b. al-Ḥārith b. Kalada in charge of al-Ubulla for the time being, and proceeded with his lieutenants to use the city as a base of operations for contingents sent out against other localities until the Muslims established their new camp-city of al-Baṣra not far from the site of al-Ubulla.[218] The towns of al-Furāt, Maysān, and the districts of Abazqubādh and Dastumaysān, along with the areas along the banks of the lower Tigris were seized at this time, some by 'Utba himself and some by his subordinates Mujāshi' b. Mas'ūd al-Sulamī and al-Mughīra b. Shu'ba al-Thaqafī, although there is some disagreement on who seized which place. Generally, Mujāshi' is said to have taken al-Furāt on 'Utba's orders, but some place 'Utba himself in command there or state that Mujāshi' merely commanded the vanguard of a force led by 'Utba. Al-Mughīra, for his part, is sometimes said to have led a troop that conquered Maysān, Dastumaysān, Abazqubādh, and the banks of the Tigris, but other sources ascribe these conquests to 'Utba himself. The confusion arises partly because 'Utba decided to return to Medina at about this time, leaving Mujāshi' in command; but as Mujāshi' was absent on campaign, he instructed al-Mughīra to take charge of al-Ubulla until Mujāshi''s return. It seems to have been after 'Utba's departure that al-Mughīra went out against Maysān and Abazqubādh. In any case, it is clear that under 'Utba or his subordinates the Muslims conquered al-Ubulla and the nearby districts of southern Iraq.[219]

The composition of 'Utba's force can be glimpsed if we consider the names of individuals mentioned as participants in these early campaigns in southern Iraq.[220] By far the best-represented group was the Thaqīf of al-Ṭā'if, who appear to have been the dominant element in the army. Although the commander, 'Utba b. Ghazwān, was not a member of this tribe, he had close ties to it because he was married to a prominent woman of the tribe; and when he first came to southern Iraq he was accompanied by several of his in-laws who were soon to become key figures in the political life of the area, including Abū Bakra b. Kalada and Nāfi' b. al-Ḥārith b. Kalada.[221] It is noteworthy that only one other member of 'Utba's tribe of Māzin (Qays) is mentioned in the sources, and he in an insignificant role.[222] It does not appear, then, that 'Utba had significant backing from his own tribe, for had such supporters been present they would certainly have been placed in positions of some importance in order to bolster 'Utba's authority. 'Utba seems to have been selected as a leader of the expedition by virtue of his position as an early companion of the Prophet and committed Muslim and because of his close ties by marriage to the Thaqīf, rather than because of his own tribal affiliations.

The isolated individuals from many other tribes mentioned among the participants in these conquests in southern Iraq do not permit firm conclusions about the presence or absence of groups from these tribes in 'Utba's army, but a few observations can be made nevertheless. The B.

Bajīla does not appear to have contributed men to 'Utba's force except for Shibl b. Ma'bad al-Bajalī and his son, who are said to have been the only Bajīla tribesmen in al-Baṣra.[223] Shibl's presence was probably due to the fact that he was also an in-law of 'Utba b. Ghazwān.[224] A few members of the B. Tamīm mentioned among the participants may be the product of a pro-Tamīm tradition designed to establish the tribe's claim to have been among the early settlers in al-Baṣra,[225] but their presence cannot be rejected out of hand. The individuals from Sulaym, Muzayna, and Balī form a neat group, as all three tribes roamed the Ḥijāz and in other situations were among the early allies of the Islamic state.[226]

'Utba b. Ghazwān died and was replaced as commander on the southern Iraqi front by al-Mughīra b. Shu'ba, an early companion of the Prophet and member of Thaqīf. It was al-Mughīra who led a force of Muslims north to assist Sa'd b. Abī Waqqāṣ at the battle of al-Qādisiyya, although this may have occurred while al-Mughīra was still merely a subordinate commander under 'Utba b. Ghazwān. Sometime after al-Mughīra's return to southern Iraq, he was accused of adultery and, although acquitted, was replaced as commander on the southern front by Abū Mūsā al-Ash'arī, another early companion.[227] Under al-Mughīra and Abū Mūsā the remainder of southern Iraq and the Khūzistān district were conquered by the Muslims, and their activities can be taken to comprise the third stage of the conquest in southern Iraq.

It is, however, difficult to establish the exact timing or course of these later campaigns. It seems that the Sasanians, after their defeats at al-Qādisiyya and Jalūlā', decided to send forces to Khūzistān to resist the advance of the Muslims there. They consequently established their base of operations in al-Aḥwāz and from it raided the districts of Maysān and Dastumaysān that had fallen into the Muslims' hands.[228] Al-Mughīra appears to have taken Nahr Tīrā and the Persians' stronghold at al-Aḥwāz, perhaps some time before the Persian buildup of forces; but they were lost again and had to be retaken by Abū Mūsā.[229] The fall of al-Aḥwāz pushed the Persians back to four main strongholds: Manādhir, Tustar, Sūs, and Rāmhormuz. Manādhir seems to have fallen shortly after al-Aḥwāz and without stiff opposition,[230] but the others proved to be more serious operations. The Surraq district, located just south of al-Aḥwāz, probably was reduced at this time.[231]

The siege of Tustar seems to have been especially important, as the main Persian force regrouped there after the loss of al-Aḥwāz to the Muslims. In response to this opposition, Abū Mūsā is said to have requested reinforcements from 'Umar, who accordingly instructed the Muslims in central Iraq to send troops to assist in southern Iraq. Two groups of reinforcements were therefore sent, one from al-Kūfa under al-Nu'mān b. Muqarrin al-Muzanī, and the other from Jalūlā' under Jarīr b. 'Abdullāh al-Bajalī. According to one source, the former numbered 1,000 and the latter 2,000 men, and when more reinforcements were requested by Abū Mūsā, 'Ammār b. Yāsir marched to southern Iraq with half the garrison of al-Kūfa. The town of Tustar was put to siege by the combined forces from central and southern Iraq, and after stiff resistance and a pitched battle the city fell to the Muslims.[232] They followed up their victory by sending a contingent to Rāmhormuz, which agreed to a truce with the Muslims.[233]

The other main objective in Khūzistān after the fall of al-Ahwāz and Tustar was the city of Sūs (Susa). Abū Mūsā's army, commanded by himself or one of his lieutenants depending on the tradition consulted, came up to the town and forced it to submit under terms of a treaty, although the citizens may have tried to resist at first and only agreed to the treaty at the last moment. It is not clear whether the troops from al-Baṣra were assisted by the reinforcements from central Iraq, as some sources state, or whether the latter had returned to al-Kūfa after the fall of Tustar, as others claim. In any case, the seizure of Sūs was a relatively smooth operation for the Muslims, and they proceeded to dispatch contingents to reduce the remaining towns in the area, notably Jundāysābūr and Mihrajān Qadhaq.[234] With the conclusion of these campaigns, the conquest of the southern part of the Iraqi alluvium and the adjacent foothills of Khūzistān was essentially complete.

The composition of the forces active in these later campaigns in southern Iraq under the leadership of al-Mughīra b. Shu'ba and Abū Mūsā al-Ash'arī can, once again, be seen by considering the names of individual participants.[235] Reinforcements were sent, as noted above, from central Iraq, but they appear to have returned to al-Kūfa and hence did not affect the composition of the forces remaining in the south. Reinforcements are also said to have come from al-Baḥrayn (eastern Arabia), under the command of Harthama b. 'Arfaja al-Bāriqī of the Azd; the tribal composition of these reinforcements cannot be established, however, as virtually nothing is known about 'Arfaja's forces in al-Baḥrayn.[236] Nor are there clear references to the identity of reinforcements coming to assist the Muslims in southern Iraq, either from Medina or from the Najd. There is no question that such reinforcements were arriving, however;

one source states that 'Umar dispatched groups of 50 and 100 men to assist 'Utba as they became available, and others describe him as "throwing men at them." Thus, although no new major army was sent out, sizable numbers of new recruits were reaching southern Iraq, for by the time al-Mughīra b. Shu'ba reviewed his troops in al-Baṣra, they are said to have numbered 4,000 men—a considerable augmentation over 'Utba's modest force, even if the figure is exaggerated.[237] It appears, however, that the tribal composition of the forces active in the third phase of the conquest in southern Iraq was roughly identical to that of the preceding phase. The most important group continued to be the Thaqīf. Other important groups appear to have been the *anṣār*, the Iraqi tribe of B. Shaybān, and the B. Tamīm. The case of B. Tamīm is, however, complicated by the source of the accounts about them, most of which derive from traditionists who appear to have collected tribal oral traditions of the B. Tamīm that had a decidedly chauvinistic character.[238] As in the second phase, the forces of the final phase also appear to have included tribesmen from near Medina, such as Sulaym and Muzayna.

The usual chronological problems exist with regard to the campaigns in southern Iraq. One account states that al-Aḥwāz was raided by al-Mughīra at the end of A.H. 15 or beginning of A.H. 16/winter, A.D. 636-637,[239] and another informs us that al-Mughīra's governorship of al-Baṣra covered the years of A.H. 15 to 17/ A.D. 636 to 638,[240] but such uncontested statements are rare. Thus we find that several authorities date the conquest of al-Ubulla and the foundation of al-Baṣra to A.H. 14/A.D. 635-636, but that some place the latter as late as A.H. 16/A.D. 637-638.[241] Similarly, the campaigns to Tustar, Rāmhormuz, and Sūs are placed anywhere between A.H. 16 and A.H. 20 by various authorities.[242] The knowledge that the latter took place after the battles of al-Qādisiyya and Jalūlā' on the central Iraqi front is hardly of assistance since the date of events to the north is also very uncertain. We must, then, be content with a sequence of events and with the general understanding that the conquest of southern Iraq took place between A.D. 635 and 642. To seek greater chronological precision is to demand more of the sources than they can reasonably be expected to provide.

9. CONCLUSIONS

The aforegoing description of the conquests in Iraq makes it evident that the central and southern Iraqi fronts were essentially independent spheres of activity. There was, to be sure, some coordination of activity between the two fronts, just as there was some coordination of activity between Iraq and Syria, for, as we have seen, the army in the south and that in central Iraq each sent aid to the other at a critical juncture. But this cooperation was decidedly the exception; for the most part, the two fronts represented separate struggles fought against different opposing forces. We find nothing in Iraq to compare with the sustained close interaction of the several armies of Muslims in Syria in the face of unified Byzantine resistance there, or of the continuous shuffling of commanders and men from one force to another that marked the Muslims' activities on the Syrian front. Despite occasional mutual support, the arenas of operation in central and southern Iraq were independent—perhaps because of the presence of the great marshes in southern Iraq, newly augmented by a shift in the course of the Tigris, which may have hampered mobility between the Muslims in the two areas as they penetrated deeper into the Iraqi alluvium.

It also appears that the operations on the southern Iraqi front were far less elaborate than those in central Iraq and included fewer people. It seems unlikely that the forces sent to southern Iraq ever exceeded a few thousand men at this time, whereas we have seen that conservative estimates would place the number of men fighting under Sa'd b. Abī Waqqāṣ's command in central Iraq at several times that number. This is doubtless because it was in central Iraq, not in southern Iraq, that the Sasanians chose to make their main stand against the Muslims. Few major encounters are reported from the southern front, and these seem mainly to have involved the reduction of scattered Sasanian garrisons, usually of modest size, and the imposition of control by the Muslims over the towns and villages of the region. In the north, this kind of operation could only begin after bitter Sasanian resistance had been broken in several major military engagements, notably the battle of al-Qādisiyya.

As in the case of Syria, the conquests in Iraq can be subdivided into phases. But the sources for the conquests in Iraq are such that that composition of the armies active there in each phase can be established with far more precision than is possible for Syria. During the first phase, which was in essence a continuation of the *ridda* wars, the Islamic state was intent on subduing the Arabic-speaking tribesmen living on the fringes of Iraq and employed armies consisting of loyal groups from the Ḥijāz—*anṣār*, some Quraysh, and West-Arabian nomadic groups such as Muzayna—as well as loyal sections of tribes of the Najd and of Iraq itself—Shaybān, 'Ijl, and others. This phase, which consisted of Khālid b. al-Walīd's campaigns in Iraq, was common to both central and southern Iraq.

On the central Iraqi front, the army that was sent from Medina during the second phase seems to have been primarily made up of tribesmen from Medina and al-Ṭā'if (that is, of *anṣāris* and Thaqafīs), along with a certain number of clients or slaves from those places who were dependent on participants in the campaign. Levies were raised also from tribes passed along the way to Iraq—such as B. Ḍabba, B. Ṭayyi', and B. Tamīm—but they appear to have played a minor role in the campaigns of the second phase. On the southern front, the backbone of the forces sent out during the second phase appears to have been, once again, the Thaqīf, and contingents of B. Sulaym, Bali, and Muzayna—all tribes that had remained for the most part firmly aligned with Medina during the *ridda*—were also present in the forces there. In both central and southern Iraq, furthermore, the armies of the second phase were joined by local tribesmen who had early allied themselves with the Medina regime, notably parts of B. Shaybān, 'Ijl, and Dhuhl. Thus on both fronts, the core of the army during the second phase consisted predominantly of settled Ḥijāzī tribesmen (*anṣār* and Thaqīf) to which were added groups levied from the nomadic tribes of the Ḥijāz, Najd, and Iraq that were loyalist in sympathy.

In the south of Iraq, the composition of the forces appears to have changed little during the course of the conquests. In central Iraq, however, the composition of the forces was transformed radically with the arrival of the third phase, because the army sent during the second phase was destroyed at the battle of the Bridge and had to be replaced. The new armies sent to central Iraq during the transitional and third phases had core forces very different from those of the armies of the first and second phases, relying now, not on groups from the Ḥijāz, but on various contingents from tribes in the Yemen and al-Sarāt districts: Bajīla, Azd, Madhḥij, Kinda, and tribesmen from Ḥaḍramawt and al-Ṣadif in South Arabia. Furthermore, although the tribesmen drawn upon for the core force during the transitional phase (mainly Bajīla and Azd) appear to have been adjudged loyal by the regime in Medina and had not participated in the *ridda* rebellions against the Islamic state, by the third stage the state was clearly beginning to conscript former rebel tribesmen. Thus we find contingents in the core force at this time led by such people as al-Ash'ath b. Qays al-Kindī, leader of one of the movements of opposition to the Islamic state in the Yemen during the *ridda* wars. A similar tendency can be noted in the conscription of tribal levies from the nomadic tribes of the Najd through whose territory the core forces passed on their way from Medina to Iraq: by the third phase, even notorious former rebels such as Ṭalḥa b. Khuwaylid al-Asadī could join the Islamic armies with their following.

This analysis of the conquest of Iraq by phases sheds some light on the policy followed by the second caliph, ʿUmar b. al-Khaṭṭāb, toward the Arab tribesmen. The well-known statement that Abū Bakr barred former rebels from participating in the conquests, whereas ʿUmar allowed them to participate, is revealed to be true, but imprecise, because it only becomes true during the third, final stage of the conquests in Iraq. As we have seen, there is no evidence to suggest that ʿUmar raised troops from among the former rebels during the second phase or even during the transitional phase of the conquest of Iraq; it is therefore mistaken to conclude that his "first act was to reverse Abū Bakr's policy towards the ex-rebels."[243] In fact, ʿUmar tried at the outset of his caliphate to continue Abū Bakr's policy of excluding former rebels from the conquest campaigns (Phase II forces), but after the defeat at the battle of the Bridge, he was required to gather troops from some groups other than the stalwarts of the Ḥijāz (transitional phase forces), and ultimately he decided to abandon Abū Bakr's policy in order to secure the necessary fighting men—even if they were former rebels (Phase III forces). It was this change in policy that made possible the successful conquest of Iraq.

CHAPTER V

MILITARY ORGANIZATION, MIGRATION, AND SETTLEMENT

1. THE STRUCTURE OF THE ARMIES OF CONQUEST

Perhaps the most striking fact about the armies that carried out the Islamic conquest of the Fertile Crescent was their small size. As noted above, conservative estimates would place the number of *muqātila* ("fighting men") in the Islamic armies at the battle of al-Qādisiyya in central Iraq at between 6,000 and 12,000 men, the number active in southern Iraq at perhaps 2,000 to 4,000 men, and the number fighting at the battle of the Yarmūk in Syria at perhaps 20,000 to 40,000 men. These low figures are in themselves sufficient to lay forever to rest the notion that the Islamic conquest was actually the result of a mass migration of Arabian tribesmen, a view that implies the movement, not of any army, but rather of whole tribes, making their way northward complete with kith and kin.[1]

Nor was the progress of the conquering armies simply the wandering of a disorganized horde. In the first place, it is clear from an examination of the composition of the Islamic armies in Iraq and Syria that the state leadership in Medina raised troops by a process of recruitment. Volunteers were urged to present themselves, or tax agents among the tribes were instructed to send a contingent of tribesmen to serve in the armies, and these groups gathered at prearranged points—often, near Medina itself—to be formed into an army, or dispatched to join existing forces already in the field. They went, furthermore, not necessarily where they wanted to go themselves, but where the ruling elite in Medina felt they were needed; several groups of tribesmen, for example, including Bajīla, Azd, and Kināna, are said to have petitioned 'Umar to be sent to Syria, but they had their requests denied and were sent to Iraq instead.[2]

In addition, there is no mention of whole tribes migrating during the period in which the Fertile Crescent lands were being wrested from the Byzantines and Sasanians.[3] The presence of nonmilitary elements with the *muqātila* appears to have been in general quite limited. Certainly there were some women and children who accompanied the armies to Syria and Iraq, for we occasionally find accounts of the fighting men's families (*'iyālāt*), who were located in most instances safely behind the battlelines. These people may have performed important functions in support of the army, however, such as caring for the flocks that supplied milk and meat for the warriors, tending to the wounded, or even participating in the hostilities. At the battle of al-Qādisiyya, for example, women are said to have delivered the coups de grâce to wounded Persian soldiers left on the battlefield; and at the Yarmūk, women were instructed to stone and scold retreating Muslims in order to shame them from abandoning the field.[4] But in general, the indications are that these "family members" were not very numerous. "The tribes that had the most women at al-Qādisiyya," we are told, "were Bajīla and al-Nakha'." In the former were 1,000 unmarried women and in the latter 700, and most of them were married by men of other Arab tribes in the army—who evidently had few womenfolk from their own tribes available to them.[5] Indeed, one veteran is reported to have said that, after al-Qādisiyya, "we married women of the peoples of the book (i.e., Christians and Jews), as we did not find many Muslim women."[6] The army does not, then, appear to have been a collection of complete tribes or even of complete sections of tribes; it was, rather, a selection of people (mainly men) from various tribes who could effectively serve as part of a fairly well-organized army. The general impression of small numbers—not tribal hordes—is even supported explicitly in one passage, in which a veteran of al-Qādisiyya describes how, after the battle, the Muslims overran areas with desirable lands but could not take advantage of this situation because "the number of Muslims was few."[7]

The fragmentary nature of available evidence makes it impossible to draw a precise picture of the weaponry or composition of the Islamic forces. It is clear, however, that the Muslims had contingents both of infantry (swordsmen and archers) and of cavalry (lancers), with camels providing the main means of transport of men and materials. During the early phases of the conquests, however, horses—not normally abundant in Arabia—were doubtless in short supply among the Muslims; and, though the cavalry was of some importance in many tactical situations, the brunt of the fighting seems to have fallen upon the infantrymen, especially those from the settled districts of Arabia that provided so many contingents in the early armies. The Muslims' archers may have shielded their cohorts from the full force of the Byzantine and Sasanian heavy cavalry and thereby neutralized their superiority in this respect, but it is apparent that the Muslims had no special technological advantages over their enemies, other than the great mobility in desert terrain provided by camel transport.[8]

The fact that these small armies met with such sweeping successes in sustained campaigning against the two greatest powers of the late antique world suggests, furthermore, that the armies were well organized. Unfortunately, it is no easy matter to determine the way the *muqātila* were organized in battle, as the evidence provided by the sources is very skimpy and not always consistent. There are, on the one hand, many accounts that describe the army as if it were organized by tribal groups. When we read, for example, that al-Muthannā b. Ḥāritha and his tribesmen of B. Shaybān raided the Persians before Islam, that al-Muthannā was granted a robe of investiture and a battle-standard by Abū Bakr and ordered to continue his fighting, and that eventually he and his men joined forces with the armies of Khālid b. al-Walīd and then Abū 'Ubayd al-Thaqafī when they arrived in Iraq, the implication is very strong that the tribesmen of Shaybān, even when joined into the Islamic armies sent from Medina, were a separate contingent commanded by their tribal leader, al-Muthannā.[9] In many battles, furthermore, tribal groups appear to have fought as separate units, as for example at al-Qādisiyya, where we read of attacks launched by B. Tamīm, B. Asad, and B. Bajīla.[10] Indeed, separate tribal contingents had their own tribal standards (*liwā'*, *rāya*), the purpose of which was doubtless to serve as the rallying point for the tribesmen during battle. Abū Bakr is said to have ordered the commanders in Syria to assign a special standard for each tribe; elsewhere we learn that the *muhājirūn* had a standard that was yellow with white, green, and black markings, and other tribes had their standards each in specific colors.[11] When 'Umar went to Syria and reviewed the armies there, furthermore, the troops are said to have presented themselves to him "tribe by tribe."[12]

If all these statements suggest that the armies of the Islamic conquest were organized into tribal units, however, there are as many accounts that hint at the existence of army units organized along supratribal or nontribal lines. First, the army is often described as consisting of units that are either functional or that relate to tactical position on the battlefield, with no reference to tribal composition. Thus we sometimes read that the army was made up of ranks (*ṣufūf*) of archers, swordsmen, cavalrymen with lances, and the like; or we hear of tactical units such as the "heart" (*qalb*) or central brigade, the left and right flanks (*maysara, maymana*), the wings (*jināḥ*), advance guard (*ṭalīʿa*), vanguard (*muqaddima*) or rear guard (*sāqa*). Sometimes these two kinds of description are combined, so that we hear of a "heart" and flanks, along with units of cavalry (*khayl*), infantry (*rajl*), and the like. There are also vague references to units called the *kardūs* and the *katība*, but little can be deduced about their composition or function; they seem, however, to have been medium-sized units, smaller than a grouping such as the "heart," flanks, etc.[13]

The relationship between these tactical and functional units and the tribal groupings described earlier is hardly clear. It is possible that large tactical units were superimposed on tribal units, so that, for example, all the tribesmen of B. Azd would find themselves together as part of the *qalb* or *maymana*. It is more difficult to believe that the functional units could have been drawn up in this way, however; presumably most tribal groups included some individuals who were cavalrymen or lancers and others who were infantrymen or swordsmen, who would then end up in different units depending upon their weaponry. Indeed, there are enough references to multitribal units to make it seem likely that such arrangements were the rule rather than the exception.[14]

One account, however, suggests that the army that fought at al-Qādisiyya had a rather well-defined command structure. According to this account, the supreme commander of the army (*amīr*), Saʿd b. Abī Waqqāṣ, was responsible for appointing the commanders of various tactical divisions within his army. Thus he selected the commanders of the two wings, the advance guard, vanguard, cavalry, and other tactical units in the line of battle; these subordinate commanders appear to have been called "field commanders" (*umarāʾ al-taʿbiʾa*). The army also appears to have been divided into "tens" (*aʿshār*), but it is not clear whether this meant units of ten men each, or tenths of the army, or something else. These "tens" were commanded by "commanders of the tens" (*umarāʾ al-aʿshār*), who had to be men of good standing in Islam (*la-hum wasāʾil fī l-Islām*). Still other army leaders were the standard-bearers (*aṣḥāb al-rāyāt*), who had to be early adherents to Islam (*min ahl al-sābiqa*). In addition, the tribal leaders (*ruʾūs al-qabāʾil*) performed some leadership functions in the army.[15] The manner in which these various commanders and groups related to one another is not readily apparent, but one passage implies that a kind of chain of command existed, starting with the *amīr* at the top and running down through the field commanders, then the commanders of the "tens," then the standard-bearers and "leaders" (*quwwād*), and ending with the tribal chiefs.[16]

It appears from this description that tribal groups fighting under their tribal leaders were indeed part of the military arrangements, but only at a very low level. The entire organization of commands seems, in fact, to have been designed to ensure that the tribal leaders had direct control only over a small group of tribesmen, and that their ability to mobilize men independently would be held in check by a preponderance of higher commands outside their control and perhaps by army subdivisions that cut across tribal boundaries. It is also important to note that the higher and middle command posts, including the standard-bearers and the commanders of the "tens," could only be given to men whose allegiance to the Islamic state was unimpeachable. Most striking in this regard is the fact that the upper-level commands in both Syria and Iraq were assigned almost exclusively to members of the new Islamic ruling elite of settled people from Mecca, Medina, or al-Ṭā'if. It is, furthermore, indisputable that the ruling elite was consciously concerned with insuring adequate control over those tribesmen in the army whose allegiance to the state was not so certain; for we read that 'Umar, who first recruited former rebels of the *ridda* into the Islamic army, instructed his commanders in the field not to give them any command positions.[17] "Do not appoint the leaders of the former rebels over a hundred men," he wrote; and, at the time of the campaigns into the Iranian plateau, he instructed the commander to consult notorious rebel chiefs such as Ṭalḥa b. Khuwaylid al-Asadī on matters of military strategy, in which they were expert, but not to appoint them to command posts.[18]

In sum, the armies that undertook the Islamic conquest of the Fertile Crescent were more than simply collections of tribal contingents. Though various tribal contingents were the raw material out of which the armies were fashioned, it seems that they were organized so that the tribesmen of various tribes would be tied together and kept under the command of men whose loyalty to the regime in Medina was firm—if possible, under the command of a member of the new ruling elite dominated by the Quraysh, *anṣār*, and Thaqīf. In this way, the organization of the army reduced the possibility that tribal leaders could rally a group of supporters around themselves and "secede" from the Islamic state. It also provided sufficiently centralized control over each army by its commanders to permit the effective strategic planning underlying the conquest campaigns.

This relatively centralized organization of the armies of conquest is reflected in the establishment by the state of a fixed payroll, according to which the regime issued to its soldiers a regular stipend, called the *'aṭā'*. This military salary was graded according to the date the individual soldier had joined the conquest movement, with those who had served in the earliest campaigns receiving the highest stipends. The pay scale for Iraq, for example, awarded 3,000 dirhams yearly to the troops who had fought with Khālid b. al-Walīd in the earliest Iraqi campaigns (the so-called *ahl al-ayyām*), whereas troops who joined after that time but before the battle of al-Qādisiyya (the *ahl al-Qādisiyya*) received 2,000 dirhams per annum. Later contingents received lower stipends.[19] Clearly this kind of arrangement could only be instituted after the successful completion of the main conquests in Iraq and Syria, which yielded enough booty to give the treasury the means to issue regular payments. The *'aṭā'* system seems, however, to be already in place soon after the major conquests in Iraq and Syria, and its existence provides additional evidence of the centralized organization of the military and of the early conquest movement as a whole.

2. FIRST SETTLEMENTS IN IRAQ

Even before the successful completion of the military campaigns in Iraq, the forces in both central and southern Iraq established central camps that became the headquarters for further operations in Iraq and in the adjoining Iranian plateau. These new settlements became the focus of the Muslims' military and political activity in Iraq, and their settlement reveals something of the tribal composition of the armies active on the two Iraqi fronts.

In central Iraq, Sa'd b. Abi Waqqāṣ had adopted the abandoned Sasanian capital of al-Madā'in as his headquarters, and the Muslims in his force occupied houses in the town and settled there.[20] Some time later it was decided to move the Muslims' main garrison from al-Madā'in to a new site at al-Kūfa, near the old Arab town of al-Ḥīra. This move is variously attributed to the unhealthy climate of al-Madā'in, the desire for better communications with the desert and Arabia, or the need for pasturage for the bedouins' flocks, and in fact all these factors may have contributed to the decision.[21]

During their months in al-Madā'in, the army under Sa'd had consolidated its control over the alluvium (*sawād*) and had conquered Ḥulwān, Māsabadhān, Mosul, and Qarqīsiyā'. Under Sa'd's direction were four commanders, one at each of these frontier posts.[22] In addition, 'Umar ordered that those tribesmen from the Mesopotamian tribes of Taghlib, with allied sections of al-Namir and Iyād—now all subject to the Muslims—who agreed to adopt Islam should migrate and settle (*hājara*) with the Muslims at al-Madā'in. Those tribesmen who did not convert are reported to have remained in their home districts under Islamic rule.[23]

When the bulk of the Islamic force transferred from al-Madā'in to al-Kūfa, Sa'd allowed those who wished to remain in al-Madā'in to stay on there as a garrison. Those who opted to do so were groups of mixed origin (*aqwām min al-afnā'*), the majority being of B. 'Abs;[24] thus most of Sa'd's force, including those of Taghlib, Iyād, and al-Namir who had recently joined it, settled in al-Kūfa. The reinforcements from Syria who had reached Sa'd's army at the time of the battle of al-Qādisiyya had been ordered back to Syria to help the Muslims resist a Byzantine counteroffensive against Ḥimṣ,[25] and, as we hear of no additional reinforcements augmenting Sa'd's army while at al-Madā'in, we can safely assume that the group of Muslims that first settled al-Kūfa had roughly the same composition as the army of Sa'd at al-Qādisiyya, as analyzed above.[26] The date for the establishment of al-Kūfa is given variously as A.H. 15, 16, 17, or 18.

As noted above, the Muslims who overpowered the Sasanians in Iraq were an army, and not simply a mass of migrating tribal groups. It is therefore hardly surprising that al-Kūfa initially had the appearance of an army encampment, with temporary dwellings of reeds that were abandoned by their residents—fighting men and some dependents—when they marched on a campaign, and were rebuilt upon the army's return from the field.[27] Yet certain traditions suggest that the settlement of al-Kūfa may have been decided upon by 'Umar and the Islamic high command in order to settle the members of Sa'd's army who had come from a nomadic background, such as tribesmen from Asad, Tamīm, Taghlib, al-Namir, Iyād, and others. "Establish for the bedouin (*al-'arab*) who are with you a place of settlement (*dār al-hijra*)," 'Umar is said to have written to Sa'd.[28] This impression is reinforced by 'Umar's request, mentioned above, that Mesopotamian bedouin who converted should be settled in al-Madā'in; thus it may be that the move to al-Kūfa was dictated largely by the need for adequate fodder for the livestock that these bedouin brought with them. This need is further reflected in the many statements describing the Muslims' concern with the pasturage around the prospective site of al-Kūfa: "The only countryside that is good for the bedouin (*al-'arab*) is that which is good for sheep and camels," 'Umar reminded them, and they questioned bedouin leaders carefully about the quality of pasturelands in various districts before selecting the site of al-Kūfa for settlement.[29]

Whatever we take to be the objective for settling the garrison at al-Kūfa, however, it is clear that it functioned as the reserve of troops from which units were sent out on campaign in the east on a rotating basis, a process that had begun even at al-Madā'in.[30] It is also clear that the actual settlement of the site was a planned operation. We are even told that the settlement process (*tanzīl*) of al-Kūfa was under the direction of a certain Abū l-Hayyāj b. Mālik al-Asadī,[31] the first Islamic city-planner. Although we are entitled to be skeptical of such detailed information, and might be inclined to base our interpretation on certain passages that seem to imply a rather haphazard settlement of al-Kūfa,[32] excavations have uncovered early foundations that reflect clear efforts at planning,[33] and other passages in our sources also verify the organized nature of the earliest settlement of al-Kūfa. The first step was, apparently, the building of a mosque and assembly area (*masjid*) and commander's headquarters and residence (*dār al-imāra*).[34] These buildings were located in a large courtyard that was surrounded by residences (*dūr*) for the Muslims arranged according to their tribe, as follows:[35]

NORTH OF COURT:	Sulaym Thaqīf along court and along two roads Hamdān along another road Taym al-Lāt and Taghlib along another road
SOUTH OF COURT:	Asad along a road; between them and Nakha', a road; between them and Kinda, a road; between them and Azd, a road.
EAST OF COURT:	*Anṣār* Muzayna along a road Tamīm and Muḥārib along a road Asad and 'Āmir along a road
WEST OF COURT:	Bajāla and Bajīla along a road Jadīla and mixed groups along a road Juhayna and mixed groups along a road.

All of these groups adjoined the central courtyard. Around them, according to our text, were plotted off sections for the settlement of the "*ahl al-ayyām*" (those who had fought in Iraq with Khālid b. al-Walīd), the "*al-Qawādis*" (those who had fought at al-Qādisiyya), as well as for the frontier troops and troops in Mosul.[36]

The tribal groups that settled in al-Kūfa confirm some of our conclusions about the composition of the army at al-Qādisiyya. Although it is impossible to establish the number of tribesmen in each group represented, the description does provide some hints about the relative importance of certain groups. In particular, Thaqīf appears to have been more numerous than any other group, whereas other large tribes appear to have been Hamdān, Asad, Nakha', Kinda, Azd, Muzayna, and perhaps Sulaym and the *anṣār*—these deductions based on the assumption that the number of men needed to occupy both sides of a road or the area between the roads was roughly uniform from place to place around the courtyard. These remarks suggest that our picture of Sa'd's army is largely correct, if we adjust it by noting that the Hamdān and especially Thaqīf were more numerous than the analysis of the army at al-Qādisiyya would lead us to believe.

Figures for the size of the first settlement of al-Kūfa vary as widely as did figures for the Islamic army at al-Qādisiyya. Although one tradition puts the initial settlement at 100,000,[37] and another states that there were at this period 40,000 fighting men (*muqātila*),[38] the lowest figure, totaling 20,000 (12,000 of Yemen, 8,000 of Nizār or North Arabian stock)[39] seems most plausible, as it conforms fairly closely to the estimates made above for the size of the army at al-Qādisiyya (between 6,000 and 12,000), with allowances for several thousands of dependents who settled in al-Kūfa with the fighting tribesmen.

Our knowledge of the initial settlement of al-Baṣra and environs is much less complete than that for al-Kūfa. Like al-Kūfa in central Iraq, early al-Baṣra served as the Muslims' main camp in southern Iraq, from which raiding into the Zagros was organized. Its settlement is normally thought to have occurred in about A.H. 15, although there are some hints that it may have been established, not before, but after al-Kūfa.[40] The foundation of the city is usually ascribed to 'Utba b. Ghazwān.[41] Like al-Kūfa, it had a mosque and commander's residence, and at this early stage its houses were built of reeds, which those going on campaigns would bundle up and leave until their return.[42] Other accounts suggest that al-Baṣra was preceded by village-like settlements (*dasākir*) that were abandoned for al-Baṣra, or which may have simply grown into being the city of al-Baṣra as the population increased.[43] One account states that the Muslims initially settled on the shores of the Tigris and then withdrew bit by bit into the plain, digging a canal to provide water and lengthening it with each move.[44] In short, the accounts of al-Baṣra's early settlement are confused, and they provide no data concerning the composition of the first settling groups. One account states that al-Baṣra was built, not to house the army of 'Utba b. Ghazwān, but rather to provide a settlement for the Muslims raiding Fārs (Persis) from eastern Arabia (al-Baḥrayn).[45] Whereas the influx of Muslims from eastern Arabia to al-Baṣra was destined, shortly after the conquest, to become an important factor in its growth, it is not at all clear whether al-Baṣra's original settlers included any tribesmen from this region. The one detailed account of military cooperation between the troops of al-Baṣra and Muslims from Baḥrayn who were raiding Iṣṭakhr, furthermore, suggests that the troops from al-Baḥrayn (called "*ahl Hajar*") returned to their tribes after the campaigning, and that only a few of the 'Abd al-Qays tribe who had been saved by the arrival of the troops from al-Baṣra settled in the city on the army's return. The statement that al-Baṣra was originally "settled" by tribesmen from al-Baḥrayn may reflect this limited settlement and the larger migrations from that area that occurred before Islam, but it seems likely that the first Islamic settlement was undertaken by 'Utba's force, which had been sent to southern Iraq, and the composition of which has been analyzed above. The supervisor of the settlement of tribesmen at al-Baṣra was, we are told, 'Āṣim b. al-Dulaf Abū l-Jarbā', of the B. Ghaylān b. Mālik b. 'Amr b. Tamīm.[47]

Yet al-Baṣra was at this early stage very different from al-Kūfa because it was certainly very much smaller. Although the initial settlement of al-Baṣra was probably barely 1,000 people (based on the size of 'Utba's army), that at al-Kūfa was probably many, perhaps twenty, times larger. This relationship probably survived for some time because of the differing potential of the environs of the two cities to support large populations; for, whereas al-Kūfa lay adjacent to one of the richest agricultural regions in Iraq, al-Baṣra's surroundings appear to have been, at the time of the conquest, relatively infertile and unsuitable for grazing. The nearest really productive region that could supply al-Baṣra was probably the region around al-Aḥwaz.[48] This reality is reflected in the fact that the *sawād* (alluvium) of al-Kūfa is described as stretching from Kaskar to the Zāb and Ḥulwān to al-Qādisiyya, whereas the *sawad* of al-Baṣra included Aḥwāz, Dastumaysān, and Fārs—relatively distant regions.[49]

3. MIGRATIONS TO IRAQ UP TO THE FIRST CIVIL WAR

The Islamic conquest of the Iraqi alluvium and the destruction of Sasanian power were not caused by a mass migration of Arabian tribes from the peninsula, but the conquests appear to have stimulated a mass migration to Iraq once they were complete. These migrations occurred primarily between the conclusion of the conquest (A.H. 17/A.D. 638) and the outbreak of the First Civil War (A.H. 35/A.D. 656)—a period of roughly twenty years. Unfortunately, most of our sources display little interest in this migration process and say very little directly about it. We must, therefore, build up our picture of the migration from inference. One series of passages describes these migrants to al-Kūfa as *rawādif*, "those who come after."[50] In fact, the term "*rawādif*" is an administrative one, just as are such terms as "*ahl al-Qādisiyya*" or "*ahl al-ayyām*"; in each case the term designates a specific level of entitlement in the system of stipends or salaries (*'aṭā'*) paid by the state to its soldiers and officials. Much of what we know of the *rawādif*, therefore, relates to their position in the salary hierarchy. We learn, for example, that there were several groups of *rawādif*, called simply "first *rādifa*," "second *rādifa*," etc. The distinctions among the different *rawādif* groups relate to the pay that they were entitled to receive but also reflect, at least loosely, the order in which they arrived in Iraq and were integrated into the Islamic military and fiscal institutions established there. The earlier immigrants received stipends or salaries (*'aṭā'*) higher than those who arrived relatively later; thus the members of the first *rādifa* received a salary of 1,500 dirhams per year,[51] those in the second received 500, those in the third 300, the fourth 250, and those arriving after the fourth *rādifa* received 200 dirhams.[52] (These rates can be compared with the 3,000 and 2,000 dirhams paid to the *ahl al-ayyām* and *ahl al-Qādisiyya*, respectively). These *rawādif* tribesmen were clearly additional fighting men (*muqātila*), and not simply the families of the original settlers of al-Kūfa, for we are told that when 'Umar ordered the governor of al-Kūfa to march to Nihāwand and sent a message urging the city's *muqātila* to support this campaign by voluntary enlistment, the *rawādif* were the first to join up "in order to show valor in the religion and to attain a share [in the abandoned lands]."[53] The *rawādif* were, then, the new recruits who fought alongside the veterans of al-Kūfa.

Other sources pass over this period with little reference to the influx of tribesmen. Even in the many passages that deal with the assignment of pay (*'aṭā'*), there is no mention of the *rawādif* and little mention of the *ahl al-Qādisiyya* or others in Iraq.[54] There are, furthermore, descriptions that provide a radically different picture of how the payroll was arranged; one, in particular, states that the tribesmen of Yemen received 400 dirhams, those of Muḍar 300 dirhams, and those of Rabī'a 200 dirhams.[55] Nonetheless, it is clear even from these passages that the influx of tribesmen was considerable both in the area around al-Kūfa and near al-Baṣra, of which we are told that the situation was in many respects similar.[56] Even quite early on, during the governorship of 'Utba b. Ghazwān, we hear of overcrowding in al-Baṣra: "Due to 'Utba's successes in the field," we are told, "the tribes gathered to it [al-Baṣra] until they became numerous in it."[57] In al-Kūfa, as we shall see, the influx of *rawādif* caused crowding and necessitated the reorganization of quarters.[58] By the end of 'Uthmān's caliphate, (ca. A.H. 30), his governor in al-Kūfa, Sa'īd b. al-'Āṣ, could write to the caliph that "the affairs of the people of al-Kūfa are disturbed. Their notables and leading clans and people of priority and precedence have been overpowered, and the ones who are coming to predominate in the lands are *rawādif* who have come after [the first settlers] and nomads who have followed. . . ."[59] Despite the absence of detailed information on these migrations, therefore, it is nonetheless clear that the two decades between the conquest of Iraq and the outbreak of the First Civil War in A.H. 35/A.D. 656 witnessed a considerable influx of tribesmen into al-Kūfa and al-Baṣra.

We cannot, unfortunately, determine whether this influx was in the form of a steady trickle of new tribesmen over this period, or whether it occurred as the movement of a few large, discrete groups of tribesmen. The division of the *rawādif* into "first *rādifa*," "second *rādifa*," etc., seems to imply that the tribesmen came in a few large "waves" of migration. But we must remember that this sharp classification of tribesmen into *rawādif* groups was created for purposes of fiscal administration and not, or at least not necessarily, in order to describe the migrations themselves. Our suspicion that the classification of tribesmen into fiscal categories might not correspond perfectly to the priority of their arrival in Iraq is awakened, furthermore, by the following circumstances. It is reported that the *rawādif* tribesmen who fought valiantly at Nihāwand were rewarded by 'Umar for their bravery by being "joined to the *ahl al-Qādisiyya*," that is, by being granted the same high salary that the latter enjoyed and, presumably, by actually being classed among the *ahl al-*

Qādisiyya.[60] Although the people assigned in this manner to a different salary class were probably exceptional cases, the example makes it clear that membership in one or another salary classification, although loosely based in priority of migration to Iraq, was not rigorously so based. In particular, it becomes questionable whether it is possible to assume in all cases that the *ahl al-Qādisiyya* can be equated with the "early-comers."

In view of the scarcity of solid information about these important migrations, it is very difficult to know which tribes were involved in them. In many cases, as we shall see, the tribesmen migrating after the conquests belonged to the same tribes as those who had participated in the conquest movement itself.[61] In other cases, the new immigrants appear to have been from tribes that had taken little or no part in the original conquest process. We hear, for example, of the arrival of successive groups of the B. al-'Amī, who began to settle in al-Baṣra shortly after the conquest of southern Iraq around A.H. 17.[62] Likewise, we learn that among the latest immigrants arriving in al-Kūfa after the fourth *rādifa* were the *ahl Hajar* and *al-'Ibād*;[63] the former were probably from eastern Arabia (al-Baḥrayn),[64] whereas the latter may have been the Christian Arab inhabitants of al-Ḥīra, or perhaps of the 'Ibād branch of the Khuzā'a (of Azd) from the Ḥijāz.[65] Likewise, there were by 'Umar's time some of the B. 'Abs (Ghaṭafān) in al-Kūfa.[66] We also learn of a messenger of the tribe of 'Abd al-Qays who was sent to 'Umar by his governor in al-Kūfa, 'Abdullāh b. 'Ityān, in A.H. 21,[67] and by 'Uthman's time an 'Abd al-Qays quarter existed in al-Baṣra.[68]

In general, however, we learn little about the identity of the *rawādif* from the few direct statements about them. We can, fortunately, turn to several potential sources of information in order to clarify which tribes were represented in the migration of tribesmen between the conquest of Iraq and the First Civil War. These potential sources of data are (1) the changes that these migrations induced in the garrison cities, and (2) the identity of individuals participating in the campaigns that were sent out from Iraq to subdue the Iranian plateau.

The Evolution of al-Kūfa and al-Baṣra

The great migrations caused sweeping changes in the garrison cities of al-Kūfa and al-Baṣra, which grew and began to adopt a new character as both the number of fighting men and the noncombatant population increased. In al-Kūfa, besides the superficial change from houses of cane to those of mud brick,[69] important changes in the structure of the city itself can be traced. The initial arrangement of settlement quarters (*khiṭaṭ*) for various tribal groups, which has been described above, could not remain intact under the impact of the migrations. Some of the tribal contingents that had been settled along the central courtyard in the original settlement arrangement now found their numbers so swollen by the influx of *rawādif* immigrants of their tribe that their original quarter was insufficient to hold them all; they moved, accordingly, en masse to settlements established by the *rawādif* of their tribe (presumably on the edge of the town) and gave up their quarter adjoining the courtyard. Other contingents in the original settlement plan, which were among the more numerous ones at the time of the initial settlement and which were not flooded by the arrival of so many new tribesmen, settled the more moderate numbers of *rawādif* of their tribes in houses in the center of the city that had been left vacant by those original settlers who had had to move out and which were adjacent to their own quarters; or, if no vacancies were available nearby, they doubled themselves up within their own quarters in order to make room for their *rawādif*.[70] Thus the original settlement pattern of al-Kūfa became, as the migration of new tribesmen continued, somewhat modified. In general, those tribes that had contributed the largest contingents in the conquest movement and that had, relatively, fewer *rawādif* immigrants, remained in their original quarters and adjacent ones in the core of the city, whereas those in which the number of *rawādif* predominated over the original settlers of the tribe probably moved to the outskirts of town and started a new quarter.[71]

The way in which these rearrangements were calculated to preserve the contiguous, unified residence of all members of a given tribe who lived in al-Kūfa underlines the fact that unified tribal residence was considered to be essential, but it does not tell us why it was considered essential. It may be that unified tribal quarters were desired especially by the tribesmen themselves in order to facilitate the tribe's function as a defensive structure protecting its members, but it is equally possible that the placement of tribesmen in quarters unified by tribe was desired by the administrative leadership of the city (and army), because the tribe may have been viewed by these officials as the most convenient—indeed, perhaps the only—kind of administrative subdivision one could introduce among the tribesmen. It is possible that both motivations lay behind the clear desire to preserve "tribal unity." We can be sure, at least, that the city administration condoned, if it did not in fact generate, this settlement policy, for the "city-planner" of al-Kūfa, Abū Hayyāj al-Asadī, not only helped draw up the original settlement pattern for the town but was also in charge of settling the *rawādif.* In order to make their transition to city life a smooth one, he established a kind of "reception station" (*munākh*) for newly arriving tribesmen, in which they lived until he could look after them and grant them a tract "where they wished."[72]

Each tribal settlement in al-Kūfa had its own mosque (*masjid*), which served as the nerve center and gathering place for the quarter.[73] Not every Arabian tribe had residents in al-Kūfa, of course, so under 'Uthmān a guest house (*dār al-ḍiyāfa*) was instituted, where visitors to al-Kūfa from tribes that had no tribal settlement there could stay.[74]

Ultimately, the immigration of new tribesmen created such an imbalance in al-Kūfa that Sa'd asked 'Umar for permission to reorganize it. "Some of the tenths (? *a'shār*) became greatly preponderant over others, so Sa'd wrote to 'Umar about [the possibility of] making them equal. ['Umar] therefore wrote back that he should make them equal. So [Sa'd] sent to a number of genealogists of the Arabs and to those of judgment among them and to their learned men . . . and they made them equal in sevenths. . . ."[75] The new arrangement was as follows:[76]

FIRST SEVENTH:	Kināna and their allies (*ḥulafā'*) of the Aḥābīsh and others; Jadīla (= B. 'Amir b. Qays 'Aylān).
SECOND SEVENTH:	Quḍā'a—among them at that time was Ghassān b. Shibām—plus Bajīla, Khath'am, Kinda, Ḥaḍramawt, and Azd.
THIRD SEVENTH:	Madhḥij, Ḥimyar, Hamdān, and their allies.
FOURTH SEVENTH:	Tamīm, the rest of al-Ribāb, Hawāzin.
FIFTH SEVENTH:	Asad, Ghaṭafān, Muḥārib, al-Namir, Ḍubay'a, and Taghlib.
SIXTH SEVENTH:	Iyād, 'Akk, 'Abd al-Qays, Ahl Hajar, al-Ḥamrā'.
SEVENTH SEVENTH:	(not given)

This arrangement of tribesmen in al-Kūfa into "sevenths" remained in force, we are told, through the caliphates of 'Uthmān and 'Alī and into Mu'āwiya's time, when his governor, Ziyād b. Abī Sufyān, reorganized the city into quarters.

By the end of 'Umar's reign (A.H. 23/A.D. 644), the residents of al-Kūfa included not only Arabian Muslims, but others as well. Thus in the sixth division of the city listed above we find "al-Ḥamrā'," that is,

Persian infantry who had joined the Islamic armies early in the conquests.[77] We also learn that by this time certain members of the Persian landed gentry (*dahāqīn*) were residing in al-Kūfa.[78] Furthermore, under 'Umar the Jews of Najrān in South Arabia were expelled from the Arabian peninsula and settled in a place called "al-Najrāniyya" in al-Kūfa.[79]

Of the city of al-Baṣra during this period we know virtually nothing in detail. The sources seldom refer to events there, focusing instead on events in al-Kūfa, Medina, and the frontiers of conquest. It is evident that certain tribes, such as 'Abd al-Qays, settled in al-Baṣra in large numbers during this period, since they are seen to have large quarters in the city by early Umayyad times. But we are completely devoid of any specifics as to the course of settlement or of reorganizations in the city, and any attempt to describe al-Baṣra's organization in quarters must begin with the five divisions into which it was organized under the Umayyads.[80]

The Eastern Campaigns

The traditions describing the eastern campaigns in the Zagros during this period[81] are confused and difficult to reconcile. They fall into several groups: those relating to the battle of Nihāwand, those relating to the conquest of Iṣbahān and its surroundings, and those relating to the conquest of Hamadhān and other cities in north-central Iran usually associated with it in the conquest accounts, such as al-Rayy and Qūmis.

The accounts provided by various sources for the battle of Nihāwand present a fairly unified picture of certain general aspects of the campaign. The cadre of leaders is usually the same, although a great number of individuals are mentioned in each account, usually in connection with incidental events, who are not related in other accounts. It is thus possible to compile a list of participants named in the Nihāwand campaign, which reveals the predominance of individuals from al-Kūfa already familiar from the campaigns of conquest in central Iraq.[82] The list reveals, however, that tribesmen of 'Abd al-Qays, unknown in the earlier campaigns in Iraq, were present at Nihāwand, suggesting that this tribe had begun its migration to the garrisons of Iraq, including al-Kūfa, by this time (ca. A.H. 21/A.D. 642). Otherwise, however, there is little to suggest that the tribal complexion of the armies based in al-Kūfa had changed markedly since the conquest of central Iraq.

Accounts of the campaigns for Iṣbahān and for Hamadhān do not show the same consistency that those for Nihāwand display. Some sources state that the Iṣbahān campaign was directed from the garrison at al-Kūfa, others that it involved a force from al-Baṣra, and there is broad disagreement on the sequence of the campaigns after Nihāwand. It seems likely that, as a few traditions maintain, the Iṣbahān force contained contingents from both al-Kūfa and al-Baṣra, and that the compilers of traditions had, in many cases, only incomplete accounts of the campaign, which led them to attribute the force solely to one garrison or the other. It is also probable that certain traditions concerning Iṣbahān really refer to events in the Nihāwand campaign and have been misplaced, for the constellation of personal names in some of these accounts is strikingly similar to those found in the accounts for Nihāwand.[83] In view of such difficulties a clear unraveling of the historical traditions regarding these campaigns is impossible. An investigation of the personal names in these campaigns is not thereby ruled out, however, because the confusion probably stems, not from deliberate falsification, but from misplacement, synthesis, and successive summarization of what were originally accurate short reports. A collection of the names of individuals mentioned in various accounts as participants at Iṣbahān and Hamadhān reveals no striking change in the tribal composition of the armies coming from Iraq.[84]

We must conclude, then, that an investigation of the eastern campaigns does not suggest an influx of tribesmen from new tribal groups into the Iraqi garrison towns, with the exception of the 'Abd al-Qays tribe. The bulk of the *rawādif* tribesmen who poured into Iraq were, then, probably members of those tribes that had participated in the earlier campaigns of conquest in central and southern Iraq itself.

4. EARLY ADMINISTRATION IN IRAQ

The massive migration of tribesmen into the Iraqi garrison towns not only generated changes in the organization of the towns themselves, but also forced the representatives of the ruling elite in Iraq to develop a more sophisticated administration for the army. Unfortunately the sources are not very forthcoming on this issue. The little that is provided suggests that some of the tribesmen were organized into pay units, each of which was called an *'irāfa*. The *'irāfa* appears to have originated during the lifetime of Muḥammad as a unit of ten or fifteen men, and this type of organization survived intact into the early phase of the conquest; it gave way, however, when the *'aṭā'* or regular military pay was instituted.[85] By the time al-Kūfa had been settled in "sevenths," the *'irāfa* had evolved into a unit arranged by pay entitlement; there were now *'irāfas* of *ahl al-ayyām* (i.e., those who had fought with Khālid), of *ahl al-Qādisiyya*, and of the different *rawādif.* Furthermore, the *'irāfas* were no longer simply units of ten men but were of varying sizes so that the total payment each *'irāfa* received was the same—100,000 dirhams. This is clearly an arrangement designed to be of convenience to the paymaster distributing *'aṭā'* to each unit, rather than to the commander on the battlefield. According to one text, the military pay in al-Kūfa was handed over to the head of each of the seven divisions of the city and to the "standard-bearers" (*aṣḥāb al-rāyāt*), who in turn paid it out to the heads of the *'irāfas*, the *nuqabā'* and the *umanā'*; these then paid out the individual pay to "their people" in their homes.[86] Parenthetically, the text adds that the standards held by the "standard-bearers" were in the hands of the bedouin (*al-'arab*). It seems likely that the "standard-bearers" were generally the tribal leaders heading various contingents into battle. Thus from the point of view of pay, the *muqātila* (warriors) were organized by tribe and then subdivided into *'irāfa* units.

This passage bears other important implications for the organization of tribesmen in al-Kūfa. It states, for example, that the treasury issued pay (*'aṭā'*) to the "standard-bearers," whom it equates with key tribal leaders with command over their tribesmen in the military domain as well; but it also states that pay was issued to the "commanders of the sevenths" into which al-Kūfa was divided. The relationship between the "commanders of the sevenths" and the "standard-bearers" is not specified or patently obvious but is perhaps clarified by the groups among whom they in turn distribute the pay issued them: namely, the heads of the *'irāfas*, the *nuqabā'* and the *umanā'*. We have suggested that the "standard-bearers"—themselves tribal military leaders—were broadly responsible for distributing pay among the warriors within their tribe, who were organized for pay into *'irāfas*, and it seems plausible to suggest that the "commanders of sevenths" were responsible for issuing pay to what may have been nonmilitary sectors of the city's population, divided into units headed by *nuqabā'* and *umanā'*. In short, the "standard-bearers" were in charge of the military payroll, whereas the "commanders of the sevenths" were in charge of the civilian payroll, that is, of payments to tribesmen and their families who were performing services of a nonmilitary nature for the Islamic state. We have little evidence of what these nonmilitary services might have been; administration would have been a logical one, as would services such as organizing the supply of provisions—food, weapons, and mounts—which would have involved extensive trading and shipping operations and considerable contact with the bedouin of Arabia and Syria who provided fresh mounts and other supplies. If this interpretation of the brief text is correct, we catch a rare glimpse of the organization of al-Kūfa, evidence for fully half of which—the civilian half—has disappeared almost without trace, largely because of the predominantly military focus of the conquest accounts themselves.

5. SETTLEMENT IN IRAQ

It is clear from the aforegoing that a great number of the Arabian tribesmen who immigrated into Iraq during or shortly after the conquest settled in the two main garrison towns of al-Kūfa and al-Baṣra. In addition, the Muslims established subordinate garrison posts at various points in the Iraqi countryside. These smaller fortified points oversaw local conditions and presumably helped ensure the collection of taxes in their districts. Under the supervision of the governor of al-Baṣra, for example, were tax agents (singular *'āmil*) in the towns of al-Furāt, Surraq, Jundaysābūr, Manādhir, Sūq al-Aḥwāz, and Kuwar al-Dijla.[87] Likewise, in central Iraq there was a post over Kaskar,[88] which was a subordinate post under al-Kūfa's control, and it seems likely that similar posts existed in several other towns in central and northern Iraq, although no list of al-Kūfa's outposts (such as we have for al-Baṣra) has come down to us. Certainly there was an outpost, as we have seen, in al-Madā'in,[89] and it appears that Jalūlā' also had a garrison from the time it was captured at least until the time of the Nihāwand campaign.[90] Although the Arab troops on the four "frontier posts" (*thughūr*) to the north and east of Iraq—Mosul, Qarqīsiyā', Ḥulwān, and Māsabadhān—were reportedly withdrawn and settled in al-Kūfa, to be replaced by Persian troops who had joined the Muslims (*asāwira*)[91] it seems probable that a few Arab tribesmen stayed on in each place with the Arab deputies who remained there to direct affairs. Although it is possible to argue that the tax agents over a certain town or district might in fact have resided in al-Kūfa and merely have been responsible for supervising accounts of the tax, it seems more likely that such agents were actually dispatched to the districts for which they were responsible, as this was generally the practice followed by the appointment of tax agents on the provincial level by the Islamic regime. This interpretation finds some support by the wording of one instance, where the agent is said to be in charge of "collecting the tax" (*jibāyat al-kharāj*).[92] It thus seems plausible to conclude that, in addition to the main concentrations of Arab tribesmen in al-Kūfa and al-Baṣra, there were much smaller groups of tribesmen established, for military or administrative purposes, in many of the lesser towns of the region.

An investigation of where immigrant tribesmen settled in Iraq other than in such garrison towns leads directly into the complex problem of the legal status of lands in the conquered territories. In the two centuries following the conquest, Islamic legal scholars sought increasingly to categorize all lands according to how they had been conquered: whether by force (*'anwa*), by treaty with the inhabitants (*ṣulḥ*), or by abandonment and confiscation by the Islamic state, as in the case of the former Sasanian crown lands taken over by the new regime (*ṣawāfī*). According to this system, the legal status of the land in one of these categories determined not only the kind of tax the land paid in subsequent years, but also its availability for purchase or settlement by Muslims. Unfortunately, this systematization was projected back into the accounts of the conquest period itself, and it tended to distort records of the earlier state of affairs. Although there can be little doubt that some lands were in fact acquired by force, by treaty, or by abandonment, the contradictions that exist in various accounts dealing with the status of a particular tract of land reveal the degree to which the streamlined categories of the later systematization fail to accommodate the more complex realities of the actual arrangements made at the time of the conquest. This situation hinders greatly any effort to understand the actual process of settlement during the conquest period.[93]

It is clear from the general tenor of the conquest accounts for Iraq, however, that the primary objective of the Islamic regime in its expansion into Iraq was not the dispossession of the indigenous peasant populace and the settlement of Iraq by Arabs, but rather the seizure of political control over the country in order to draw off the tax revenues for the benefit of the Islamic state, that is, for the ruling elite. In order to ensure the continued inflow of taxes, the regime attempted to secure the general stability of the countryside and clearly realized that the productivity of the area depended upon the retention of most of the lands by the native peasantry. This reality is reflected both in the character of the peace terms made with various localities and in incidents and direct statements that reveal that the peasants continued to work their lands. "Divide the movable booty," 'Umar wrote to Sa'd, "but leave the land and the camels in the hands of those who work them. . . ."[94] The taxes that the peasants paid provided the funds that the Islamic regime needed to meet its payroll; they were the source of the *'aṭā'*.

Some of the lands of Iraq fell vacant upon the Islamic conquest, or were at least abandoned by their landlords. Such lands had usually been the possession of the Sasanian royal house or of noble families who had fled (or been killed) during the Islamic conquest. These lands formed only a portion of the agricultural land of Iraq, of course; when they were appropriated by the Muslims, they became known collectively as *ṣawāfī* or "state lands": "they became immovable booty (*fay'*) for those upon whom God had bestowed [them], whereas the rest of the alluvium was subject to protection (*dhimma*), and [the Muslims] levied upon them the tax (*kharāj*) of Kisrā."[95] Like all booty, these appropriated lands were divided up. The usual share of one-fifth was reserved for the caliph, to be used by him in the interests of the Islamic state; these became the "state lands" par excellence, and the meaning of the term "*ṣawāfī*" appears to have been rather quickly restricted to this portion of the abandoned lands only, and not to the bulk of them. The remainder of the abandoned lands—or the yields of these lands—were divided among the immigrant Muslims, that is, among the soldiers who had participated in the campaigns resulting in their seizure. The individual soldier's share of these lands was apparently called the *naṣīb* (literally, "share," "portion"). That the term "*naṣīb*" refers to shares of land and not to other kinds of booty becomes evident from an incident that occurred on the eve of the First Civil War. At that time, the rights of Quraysh to control tracts of land in the Iraqi alluvium was the subject of heated debate between the governor, Sa'īd b. al-'Āṣ, and a group of tribal leaders who had participated in the conquest of Iraq, led by al-Ashtar al-Nakha'ī (of Madhḥij), who objected to Quraysh's growing influence. When the governor declared that "the alluvium is a garden for Quraysh," al-Ashtar al-Nakha'ī and his followers flew into a rage that revealed that the focus of their concern was the use of the land: "Do you dare," he challenged the governor, "to make the target of our lances[96] and what God has bestowed upon us a garden for you and your clan?" Al-Ashtar followed this assertion of his rights with a threat. Then, to sum up his point of view, he uttered as a kind of rallying-cry the phrase "No *naṣīb* for Quraysh!"[97] The context establishes clearly that in this case "*naṣīb*" refers to land and not to other kinds of booty, although it is not clear whether the dispute is over the ownership of the land or merely over its usufruct. The word appears to have the weight of a technical term not only in this case but also in an account referring to the Nihāwand campaign, for which, as we have seen, the *rawādif* tribesmen volunteered eagerly in order to secure a *naṣīb* for themselves.[98] The latter passage makes it clear that, although a new recruit might begin to receive his pay (*'aṭā'*) as soon as he was entered in the army muster-rolls and took up training, he could not hope to secure a share in the abandoned lands (*naṣīb*) of the conquered territories without doing some campaigning on the frontiers. Although both *'aṭā'* and *naṣīb* served as inducements to take up military service, therefore, it can readily be seen that their appeal was quite different and probably each was most effective on a different group of people.

The simple fact that Arab tribesmen appear to have received a share in abandoned lands scattered about the empire does not, however, tell us how those lands were used. Some passages speak of the settlement of tribesmen on plots of land (*qaṭā'i'*). The word appears to refer in many cases to special grants of land made to individuals by the caliph, for personal or political reasons, from among his share of the state lands (*ṣawāfī*). The most famous of these assignments known to us from this period appears to be that which was awarded to the Bajīla tribe after the conquest of Iraq, in which they had played such an important part. In return for their services they were granted pieces of land by 'Umar—a reward the promise of which Jarīr, the leader of Bajīla, had exacted from the caliph as a condition for his participation in the campaigning in Iraq.[99] These lands were a "kind of gratuity [for them] from the fifth of that which God had provided as booty. . . ." Jarīr was to be given a plot (*qaṭī'a*) "sufficient to feed him, no less and no more."[100] The tribe of Bajīla together received one-fourth of the *sawād*, we are told, because they had made up one-fourth of the Islamic force at the battle of al-Qādisiyya.[101] Their grants may have lain in the region around al-Anbār and Hīt, an area that they had subdued at the time of the settlement of al-Kūfa.[102] Yet the Bajīla were convinced by 'Umar to relinquish their lands to the state in return for a regular stipend or cash gifts,[103] and purchases of additional land by them in this region were also declared void.[104]

Others are reported to have received grants of land from the caliph at the same time as the Bajīla tribe,[105] but it is not known whether they, too, were "reclaimed" by the caliph's change in policy. There are, however, so many references to individual land grants (presumably plots selected from the "state lands") made by the early caliphs, especially by

'Uthmān, that there can be little doubt that at least some of the alluvium was settled by immigrant Arabian tribesmen. We read, for example, of a grant of land made by 'Umar to Khawwāt b. Jubayr al-Anṣārī, and later bought from him by the family of 'Urwa b. al-Zubayr[106]; of date plantations established by 'Abdullāh b. 'Āmir b. Kurayẓ, 'Uthmān's governor over al-Baṣra, on the Mecca road;[107] of a village called Jubayrān that belonged to Jubayr b. Ḥayya, and of estates in both al-Kūfa and al-Baṣra.[108] The process of granting parcels of land in Iraq to private individuals reached its peak under 'Uthmān; indeed, one source states flatly that he was the first to assign such grants in Iraq. Ṭalḥa b. 'Ubaydallāh, Wā'il b. Ḥujr al-Ḥaḍramī, Khabbāb b. Aratt, 'Adī b. Ḥatīm al-Ṭā'ī, Khālid b. 'Urfuṭa, al-Ash'ath b. Qays al-Kindī, Jarīr b. 'Abdullāh al-Bajalī, 'Abdullāh b. Mas'ūd, 'Ammār b. Yāsir, Sa'd b. Abī Waqqāṣ, Usāma b. Zayd, Sa'd b. Mālik al-Zuhrī, al-Zubayr b. al-'Awwām, and Ibn Habbār are mentioned as being among those who received grants of land from 'Uthmān, most of which appear to have been villages or country estates in the vicinity of al-Kūfa.[109] A few grants were apparently made during 'Alī's caliphate (A.H. 35-40/A.D. 656-661); Kardūs b. Hāni' al-Kardūsiyya and Suwayd b. Ghafla al-Ju'fī received grants near al-Kūfa from him.[110] These instances do not include, of course, the many buildings or houses (*dūr*—perhaps houses with open land attached?), baths, and other pieces of land strictly within the urban setting of al-Kūfa or al-Baṣra.[111]

Regarding the bulk of the abandoned lands, which were divided up among the Arab tribesmen as their *naṣīb*, we know less than we do about the plots granted by the caliphs from their share in the abandoned lands. But there was evidently some reluctance among the tribesmen to settle on parcels scattered throughout the non-Arab alluvium, for we are told that the tribesmen preferred not to settle on the *ṣawāfī* (abandoned lands) in the non-Arab areas, but kept them as a kind of permanent benefice (*ḥabīs*); each year they would divide them and would then confer them (for the year) upon an agreed person, who was usually one of the commanders.[112] The meaning of this passage is less than obvious, but the intent may be that the lands were worked by slaves or peasants bound to the soil, and the person whom the tribesmen chose each year received the income from all plots and saw that it was justly distributed among the tribesmen.[113] The account indicates that this process began, in the northern Iraqi area, even while the Muslims were garrisoned in al-Madā'in, and before al-Kūfa was founded. The reluctance of tribesmen in central and northern Iraq to exploit the possibilities for settlement available to them, furthermore, is attributed there to their unwillingness to be cut off from other Arabian tribesmen by being in the *arḍ al-ʿajam*, "un-Arab" territory. Those individuals who received tracts of land from the caliph's share of the *ṣawāfī* may not have settled on them in person, but merely have drawn the income from them, but it seems plausible to assume that some did settle. They may have been more willing to settle on them than other tribesmen were on their *naṣīb* because the caliphal grants appear to have been located in the *rīf*, that is, in the portion of the alluvium situated on the edge of the desert and hence nearer to both al-Kūfa and to districts that were already Arabized. Such, as least, seems to be the import of the statement that, during the division of *ṣawāfī* lands, " 'Umar was content with the *sawād* of the *rīf*."[114]

The question of tribal settlement on lands in the alluvium of central and northern Iraq is, as we have seen, difficult to resolve. On the one hand, the tribesmen are reported to have been hesitant to occupy scattered tracts in this region. On the other hand, there must have been scattered outposts of tribesmen to support tax collection, or as local garrisons, and one would expect also that some tribesmen did indeed settle on their *naṣīb* even though the majority apparently did not. It seems probable that tribal settlement was limited, with few settlers establishing roots except near al-Kūfa and in the subordinate centers. Clearly the bulk of the fighting men (*muqātila*) were required to maintain their ties with the army in al-Kūfa, but if they spent only part of their time campaigning, it is reasonable to ask whether they could not have spent the remaining time on a private farm. In any case, regardless of their own commitments, the fighting men could have settled their families on such land as was available to them for settlement.

The possibility for settlement by tribesmen in the region of al-Baṣra was affected by the fact that the agricultural area immediately adjacent to al-Baṣra was, as we have seen, considerably smaller than that in the vicinity of al-Kūfa. Nonetheless, we read that the remainder of the lands of al-Baṣra that had belonged to the dynasty of Kisrā (that is, the abandoned lands around al-Baṣra) were of two different categories: half was divided among individuals (*maqsūm*), the other half being left for "the common welfare" ([*li-l-ijtimāʿ*] presumably of the army and society in al-Baṣra in general).[115] In view of this, it does not seem unreasonable to suggest that a similar situation existed around al-Kūfa, namely, that part of the *naṣīb* lands were settled by individuals, and the remainder held in common.

To summarize, it seems that the settlement of Arab tribesmen on lands in Iraq was slowly taking place after the conquest, although it was by no means the predominant tendency. Such settlement as did occur appears to have involved only a part of the abandoned lands that were taken over by the Muslims; the great bulk of the countryside appears to have remained, at least for the first few decades after the conquest, largely unaffected by Arab settlement.

6. MIGRATION AND SETTLEMENT IN SYRIA

In comparison with Iraq, much less is known about migration to Syria by Arabian tribesmen and their settlement there after the Islamic conquest, mainly because much of the data for the conquest period derives from traditions of Iraqi origin. It is possible, however, to make some general observations on the question of migration and settlement in Syria.

As in Iraq, the Islamic armies in Syria appear to have established a central military camp from which operations came to be directed. This was the encampment of al-Jābiya in the Golan, once the capital of the Ghassānid vassal kingdom. The Muslims also established a camp town at al-Ramla in Palestine after the conquest of this region was complete. Unlike al-Kūfa and al-Baṣra in Iraq, however, neither al-Jābiya nor al-Ramla developed into an important Islamic settlement. This was true for several reasons. First, it is possible that the settlement of al-Jābiya, at least, was disrupted, if not halted, by the severity of the ʿAmwās plague that struck Syria in about A.H. 18/A.D. 639. One account states that when the Muslims first came to al-Jābiya they numbered 24,000 (i.e., roughly the number that fought at the Yarmūk?), but after the plague only 4,000 remained[116]—although it is not clear whether the others died in the pestilence or merely fled and hence could have returned.

Another reason why al-Jābiya and al-Ramla never developed as did their Iraqi counterparts was that the Muslims in Syria seem to have preferred to reside in established Syrian towns. Whereas in central Iraq most Muslims gave up the camp at al-Madā'in for the new city of al-Kūfa, in Syria al-Jābiya was passed over as a place of settlement in favor of Damascus, Ḥimṣ, Aleppo, and other cities, where many, if not most, of the Arabian Muslims who came to Syria appear to have settled. This was possible in some cases because part of the urban population of Syria—especially those who spoke Greek, belonged to the Byzantine Orthodox church, and dominated Byzantine local administration and the economic resources of the area—fled upon the arrival of the Muslims, leaving considerable amounts of vacant property in the towns. When the Muslims seized Damascus, for example, many citizens fled to the Byzantine emperor Heraclius in Antioch.[117] Similarly, Abū 'Ubayda and the Muslims found Aleppo abandoned, according to some sources, because its inhabitants had fled to Antioch.[118] When Qāṣirīn and Bālis on the Euphrates in northern Syria capitulated to the Muslims, most of the inhabitants chose to evaculate them for Byzantine-held territory farther north.[119] The inhabitants of Tripoli, likewise, decided to abandon their city after the Muslims put it under siege and arranged to be evacuated by the Byzantine fleet from their beleaguered town, which then fell into the hands of the Muslims.[120] In al-Lādhiqiyya, some of the Christians (the Greek-speaking, Orthodox ones?) fled upon the arrival of the Muslims.[121] Doubtless these events were repeated in many other localities for which we have no record.[122]

Not all the vacant space in various Syrian towns was the result of headlong flight, however. There are many accounts that suggest that the Muslims made treaties with the inhabitants of some towns, among the terms of which was the stipulation that a certain amount of property within the city would be vacated by the citizens to make room for the Muslims. Frequently the text states that the townsmen were required to relinquish half of their houses and churches for use by the Muslims as dwellings and mosques.[123] Other frequently mentioned clauses include guarantees of security to the natives for their lives, children, dwellings, churches, and property, promises that the city walls would not be torn down, stipulations as to the amount and kind of tribute or tax the natives were required to pay the Muslims in cash or in kind, statements regarding service as guides and the like that the natives were pledged to provide for any Muslims who needed them, bans on the building of new churches, restrictions on whether and when Christians could ring church bells, restrictions on matters of personal attire and the use of transport animals (Christians, for examples, were sometimes forbidden to ride horses), and statements about many other similar matters. All of this, however, raises the difficult question of the historicity of the various treaty texts, or summaries of treaty contents, that are found in many sources. Although texts are sometimes given in very great detail, we find statements that cast doubt on their authenticity. Al-Wāqidī, for instance, states, "I have read Khālid b. al-Walīd's document to the people of Damascus and did not see in it any reference to 'half the homes and churches' [to be turned over to the Muslims], as has been reported. I do not know from where those who reported it got this information."[124] There is, furthermore, good reason to suspect that many of the details in the purported treaties, and in some cases even very simple statements to the effect that a certain area was conquered by force (*'anwa*) or by treaty (*ṣulḥ*), belong to the systematizations of subsequent generations of legal scholars seeking to rationalize later taxation or legislative measures.[125]

Whatever the ultimate cause of the abandonment—whether flight, voluntary evacuation, or dispossession—the urban properties left vacant were gradually settled by Muslims. In Ḥimṣ, we are told, the general who made terms with the city "divided it up among the Muslims in lots (*khiṭaṭ*), so that they might occupy them; and he settled them also in every place whose occupants had evacuated it and in every abandoned yard." Some of the citizens appear to have given up their houses to the Muslims and themselves resettled along the Orontes River.[126] In Tiberias, the leaders of the army and their cavalrymen are said to have settled in the town after the battle of Faḥl and the fall of Damascus, and reinforcements that arrived subsequently were scattered among the cities and villages of the surrounding area.[127] In Jerusalem, 'Umar settled the troops (i.e., those from al-Jābiya?) in the town once its inhabitants had concluded terms with him.[128] In exceptional cases it seems that the new settlers were not Muslims; this seems to have been the case in Tripoli, which Mu'āwiya, as governor of Syria for the caliph 'Uthmān (A.H. 23-35/ A.D. 644-656), settled with Jews.[129]

As a result of this settlement process, then, many Muslims came to hold grants of land (sg. *qaṭī'a*) or dwellings (sg. *dār*) in various Syrian cities, scattered references to a few of which survive to serve as examples. We are told, for instance, that 'Amr b. al-'Āṣ owned several residences in Damascus, one near the al-Jābiya gate, one by the *raḥbat al-zabīb* (raisin farms?), one known as *al-māristān al-awwal*, and so on.[130] Likewise, Ḥabīb b. Maslama al-Fihrī is said to have settled in Damascus, where he had a *dār* overlooking the river Baradā near the "mill of the Thaqafīs."[131] Under 'Umar and 'Uthmān tracts of land in 'Asqalān were given out to the Muslims.[132]

Despite much uncertainty over details, then, it is nevertheless clear that Muslims from Arabia began to settle in the towns of Syria immediately after the conquest. The conditions in the countryside, however, are less fully described in the sources.[133] A few references do suggest that there was some settlement in the countryside. As noted above, for example, the troops that reinforced the Muslims at Tiberias are said to have been scattered among the towns and villages of the districts around the river Jordan. Certain other passages speak of the distribution of what appear to have been abandoned agricultural lands (also called *qaṭīʿa*, "piece of land") to Muslims on the condition that they restore them to productivity and pay a tithe (*ʿushr*) on the produce.[134] Indeed, one of ʿUmar's objectives in coming to al-Jābiya immediately after the conquest of Syria is said to have been to supervise the division of captured lands among the Muslims.[135] Although it is possible that some of these agricultural lands were actually within major cities, it seems likely that most were in rural areas. In addition, a few scattered references suggest that some of the immigrants from Arabia may have had connections with rural areas in Syria; Saʿd b. ʿUbāda, for example, a leading chief of the Medinese tribe of Khazraj, apparently settled in Damascus but may also have had property in the Ḥawrān, where he is said to have died.[136] But perhaps most important of all is a passage that states that Muʿāwiya b. Abī Sufyān, as governor of Syria and the Jazīra, was instructed by ʿUthmān to settle nomads (*al-ʿarab*) in places far from the cities and villages and to let them use unclaimed or vacant lands. Hence he settled members of B. Tamīm at al-Rābiya, Qays and Asad and others at al-Māziḥīn and at al-Mudaibir, the last of which at least was located near al-Raqqa.[137]

These few hints suggest that there was some settlement by Muslims immigrating from Arabia on lands in the Syrian countryside during the first decades after the conquest of Syria. But there is reason to think that such settlement in rural areas was probably of very limited extent. In the first place, there is the question of how much rural land was available for settlement by the Muslims. The only references relating to the settlement of Muslims stipulate that they were to occupy abandoned or vacant lands. Although it is possible to argue that the Islamic state may intentionally have dispossessed Syrian peasants and handed their lands over to new settlers from Arabia, we have seen that in Iraq the policy of the state was to keep the peasantry on the land so that it could provide a tax base. Presumably the advantages of such a policy to the state were just as compelling in Syria as in Iraq; hence it seems likely that the rural lands available for settlement by Muslims in Syria would have been primarily those already abandoned by the peasantry. But it further seems likely that very few Syrian peasants fled at the time of the Islamic conquest. Although there were, as we have seen, a goodly number of Byzantine refugees from the cities of Syria, the conditions of the Syrian rural population were very different and made it less likely that they would follow their urban compatriots in flight. It was, first of all, not in accord with the economic interest of the Syrian peasant to flee. The wealthier urbanites may have had considerable movable wealth to take with them into exile, or may have owned properties outside Syria (e.g., in Constantinople itself) to sustain them after their flight, but the peasant's only tangible asset was the land he worked; to flee would have left him totally destitute. It seems probable, then, that the economic interests of the Syrian peasantry were best served by remaining steadfastly—if timorously—on their lands, and by humbly making their peace with the invaders and their new regime as best they could. There were, in addition, social and cultural reasons why the Syrian peasantry would have hesitated to join their urban neighbors in flight; the urbanite, with his Greek speech and Orthodox faith, could naturally see the Byzantine domains as a refuge, but the rural population of Syria, which was predominantly Syriac speaking and Monophysite in faith, would hardly have identified closely with the Byzantine Empire. Indeed, the new invaders from Arabia may actually have been more familiar and seemed less alien to them than their former Greek overlords. In general then, it seems probable that most of the refugees from Syria to Byzantium represented the Orthodox urban upper classes; the Syrian peasantry probably stayed on their lands. The rural lands available for settlement by the Muslims, therefore, were probably only those of peasants who had been killed in the wars of conquest or by the increase of brigandage that such unsettled times would unavoidably have encouraged.

A second reason why we may suspect that the settlement on rural lands in Syria was limited is that our sources say nothing about tribal migrations to Syria, suggesting that relatively few tribesmen migrated there immediately after the conquests. Although the argument from silence is perilous in view of the scarcity of source material in general, it is nonetheless striking that we find no single hint suggesting that there occurred in Syria anything like the great migrations of Arabian tribesmen, classified into *rawādif*, that flowed into Iraq in the decades following the conquests there. The cause of this low level of immigration into Syria by Arabian tribesmen, at least when compared with Iraq, is probably also a reflection of the ruling elite's settlement policy. It may be that Syria was viewed by the Quraysh, who increasingly dominated the elite, as their own special preserve; their long-standing commercial ties with Syria before Islam meant they were familiar with Syria and its commercial potential, and they may have wished to keep the province to themselves and relatively undisturbed by tribal immigration. Certainly it was to Syria that most of the Quraysh appear to have gone during the campaigns of conquest, whereas the two other main groups in the elite, the *anṣār* and the Thaqīf, went—or were sent—to Iraq. This predominance of the Quraysh in Syria is most strikingly visible in the lists of martyrs from various battlefronts during the conquest; many Quraysh fell in the engagements in Syria, but virtually no *anṣār* or Thaqīf, who are, however, heavily represented among the martyrs in the Iraqi campaigns. There were, of course, many other tribesmen, not of the ruling elite, who fought in the great battles against the Byzantines in Syria. Many of these tribesmen may not have settled in Syria (as their counterparts did in Iraq after its conquest), however, but may instead have moved on to new garrisons in Egypt or to districts such as Diyār Muḍar in the Jazīra before settling down. It is therefore not implausible to suggest that the settlement policy of the ruling elite was in large measure responsible for the apparent absence of large-scale settlement in Syria by Arabian tribesmen immediately after the conquests had been completed.

In sum, the general picture of migration to and settlement in Syria by Muslims of Arabian origin remains extremely sketchy. But it seems most probable that such immigration as did take place was quite limited in extent, involving mainly members of the original conquering armies; very few additional tribesmen appear to have immigrated in the few decades following the conquest itself. Those tribesmen who did immigrate, furthermore, appear to have settled mainly in abandoned quarters of established Syrian towns, rather than in newly created camp cities (as in Iraq) or in rural areas. There may, however, have been some settlement in rural areas by native Syrian nomads who had embraced Islam.

CHAPTER VI

CONCLUSIONS

1. TRIBE AND STATE IN ARABIA: SECOND ESSAY

As we have seen, the appearance of the unifying ideology of Islam, coupled with the skillful use of both traditional and novel means of political consolidation, resulted in the emergence under Muḥammad and Abū Bakr of a new state that was able to organize and dominate more effectively than ever before the different tribal groups of the Arabian peninsula.[1] In place of the extreme political fragmentation that had formerly existed in Arabia, with various tribal groups vying with one another for local dominance, there emerged a relatively centralized, unified, and unifying polity that integrated most of these tribes into itself and made them functioning parts of the larger whole.

It was this integration of the Arabian tribes into a single new Islamic state that set the stage for the conquests, which in fact represented the fruit of that integration. The process of state consolidation that began with Muḥammad continued unabated throughout the whole period of the early Islamic conquests. As under Muḥammad, each tribal group integrated into the state during the conquest period was administered by an agent (*'āmil*), often one of the Quraysh or the *anṣār*, who appears to have supervised the tribe and collected the taxes that were due from it. There were, as we have seen, such governors or agents over some of the tribes of Quḍā'a in southern Syria under Abū Bakr;[2] and we read that somewhat later, under 'Uthmān, a member of the Quraysh named al-Ḥakam b. Abī l-'Āṣ was appointed to collect taxes from the Quḍā'a.[3] Likewise, Sa'd b. Abī Waqqāṣ had served as 'Umar's agent in charge of collecting the *ṣadaqa* tax from the Hawāzin tribe in the Najd before being appointed commander of the army that marched to al-Qādisiyya; 'Utba b. Abī Sufyān was 'Umar's agent among the Kināna tribe; and the existence of the agents over other tribes in Arabia in 'Umar's day is well attested by numerous references.[4] Most notable are those passages that show how, under the early caliphs, the *ṣadaqa* or tax in camels was levied by the state on nomadic groups—traditionally the hardest groups to control. This was sometimes accomplished by sending agents to the wells to wait for a specific nomadic group to gather there for water, thereupon levying the tax on them.[5] Tribes outside the Arabian peninsula proper that were newly subjected by the Islamic state in the later phases of the conquest of the Fertile Crescent, furthermore, were reduced to paying taxes just as their counterparts in Arabia itself had been during the careers of Muḥammad and Abū Bakr. In the Jazīra, for example, the Islamic state seems to have dispatched two agents, one over the non-Arabs (*'ajam*) of the region—here approximately equivalent to the settled populace?—and another over the nomads (*al-'arab*) of the Jazīra.[6] In some cases, such as that of the B. Taghlib nomads who lived in northernmost Syria and Iraq, the terms for the tax levied on them depended upon whether they decided to embrace Islam or to remain Christians. Two terms for taxes are commonly used in the sources describing such situations: *ṣadaqa* and *jizya* (or *jazā'*). The former appears to mean specifically the tax or tribute levied by the state on nomadic groups, taxes paid usually in camels.[7] The *jizya*, "tax" or "tribute," appears to have been levied on sedentary populations that had chosen to adhere to their Jewish or Christian faith; presumably the sedentary population of Muslims paid *zakāt*, "alms." The existence of a separate term for the tax on nomads (whether they were Muslims or not) highlights the degree to which the state viewed the nomads as members of a different class from settled people—not a particularly surprising situation, since the ruling elite was, as we have seen, eager to bring the nomads under control by settling them if possible.[8] Indeed, this differential tax system could discomfort nomadic chiefs of considerable stature who preferred to remain Christian, as the case of Jabala b. al-Ayham of the B. Ghassān demonstrates. He is reported to have come to 'Umar and asked, "Will you levy *ṣadaqa* from me as you would from the [ordinary] bedouin (*al-'arab*)?" 'Umar replied that he would collect *jizya* from him instead, as he did from others of his religion.[9] Jabala's reluctance to pay the "nomads' tax," the *ṣadaqa*, however, hints at the negative overtones carried by this levy, itself a reflection of the inferior status that nomadic groups occupied in the new Islamic political order. The *jizya*, "tribute" or "tax," on the other hand, which was levied on settled peoples who were not Muslims and therefore were, strictly speaking, subjects and not allies of the Islamic ruling elite, could be waived if an individual or group performed some service for the Islamic state; thus 'Umar is said to have ordered that the Persian cavalrymen (*asāwira*) who had been in the Sasanian armies should be freed of the *jazā'* if they assisted the Muslims in the conquest of Iraq.[10] It is not specified, however, whether or not the *asāwira* embraced Islam in joining the Islamic armies. The entire discussion of taxes, however, is confused and betrays some meddling by later legal scholars who employed such accounts to provide precedents for their own systematizations of tax laws applying to non-Muslims. But though the details of terminology may have been corrupted, there is no question that some form of tax—whatever its name or rate of incidence—was levied on tribal groups such as the B. Taghlib that were newly absorbed by the expanding Islamic state only during the conquest period. This supports the view that the political integration begun during the careers of Muḥammad and Abū Bakr continued through the age of the early conquests.

Similarly, this continuing process of state integration can be seen in the fact that tribal groups subject to the state were liable to the recruitment of their members into the Islamic armies sent to fight on various fronts during the conquests. As already noted in describing the campaigns in Iraq, 'Umar drew up the armies of conquest by requesting his agents among the tribes to send contingents from the groups for which they were responsible. On the way to the front, the core forces so assembled were also able to raise further recruits as they passed through the territories of various tribes and could contact the tribesmen at the wells and towns they frequented.[11] These recruited tribesmen were not simply a horde wandering aimlessly toward the Fertile Crescent, furthermore, but were organized into contingents of a relatively well-coordinated army whose objectives and general movements were established by the ruling elite.[12] This provides yet further evidence that the process of state integration and the establishment of some meaningful control over the tribes of Arabia by the Islamic ruling elite continued through the conquest period. The various tribal groups, whether nomadic or settled, were no longer the virtually autonomous political entities they had once been. They were, rather, absorbed into the larger framework of a state, which taxed, recruited, and administered them in certain respects more or less at will.

If the conquest period saw the continuation of the process of state formation that had begun under Muḥammad and Abū Bakr, however, it also saw some changes in the political structure of the state. At the end of the *ridda*, as we have seen, Arabian society was divided into three fairly sharply defined political strata: the ruling elite on top, a small middle group of loyal tribesmen allied to the elite, and a large population of recently conquered (or reconquered) tribesmen beneath them. The elite itself was composed mainly of sedentary tribesmen from the Ḥijāz, notably the Quraysh of Mecca, the Medinese *anṣār*, and the Thaqīf of al-Ṭā'if, who had remained loyal during the *ridda* wars. The cohesiveness of the elite seems to have been reinforced by intermarriage.[13] Associated with the elite was the middle stratum, which consisted mainly of members of some tribes from the Sarāt or the Yemen, many of whom may have had close ties of long standing with the Meccans, Medinese, or Thaqīf, and may in some cases have been resident in one of the Ḥijāzī towns as allies of one or another group. The middle stratum also included some members of those nomadic groups of the Ḥijāz that had remained loyal to Medina during the *ridda*, such as Muzayna or parts of Sulaym; it is possible, however, that many of these individuals had also taken up residence in Mecca, Medina, or al-Ṭā'if as allies of one of the three main groups of the elite. The conquered tribesmen, who formed the lowest stratum, were integrated into the state in the sense that they paid taxes to it and were dominated by it, but they had no active share in the formulation or execution of state policy, which remained the exclusive domain of the elite.

This situation persisted into the caliphate of 'Umar and the beginning of the campaigns of conquest in Syria and Iraq. The ruling elite continued to dominate the conquered tribesmen of Arabia, and at the beginning of the conquest it was state policy that former rebels of the *ridda* should not be recruited into the Islamic armies, both because they were deemed unreliable and because they were, in view of their earlier opposition, not considered worthy to share the spoils of conquest with those groups and individuals that had remained loyal to the state. The former rebels were, then, still excluded from any active participation in the state's activities. The escalating conflicts of the conquest era, however, strained this simple arrangement of things to the breaking point. The ruling elite itself had provided a significant part of the military manpower for the *ridda* wars and for the campaigns for the first and second phases of the conquest of Iraq as well,[14] but their manpower resources were strictly limited, and when further hostilities demanded the raising of new and larger armies, a manpower crisis arose. It was resolved by a decision, made during the caliphate of 'Umar b. al-Khaṭṭāb, to begin recruiting former rebel tribesmen for military duty in the conquest armies. This decision, as we have seen, made available the manpower necessary to wrest victory in the transitional and third phases of the conquest in central Iraq, for unlike the armies of the first and second phases, the core of which had consisted mainly of the *anṣār*, Thaqīf, and some nomadic groups that had been consistently loyal to Medina, those of the transitional and third phases consisted mainly of former rebels of the *ridda*.[15] The recruitment of these former rebels greatly enlarged the intermediate political stratum that lay between the Islamic ruling elite and the conquered tribesmen of Arabia, namely, a class of tribesmen who were allied to, or associated with, the ruling elite, and who were literally employed by the ruling elite to help accomplish the state's goals.[16]

This shift in policy toward the former rebels of the *ridda*, and the growth of the intermediate stratum of tribesmen who were associated with the state but were not part of the elite, however, posed serious problems for the state leadership. There was considerable peril in bringing contingents of such tribesmen into the armies, for to do so meant putting men of dubious loyalty together in sizable groups and allowing them to bear arms—a situation that could all too easily be an invitation to foment another rebellion against the ruling elite. The fact that no such rebellion occurred during the conquest period is itself the strongest evidence demonstrating that the Islamic state and its ruling elite succeeded in integrating disparate tribal groups to itself. What remains to be considered, however, are the means by which this integration was effected. How did the elite manage to keep these conquered former rebels under control and prevent them from raising another rebellion once they were assembled in large groups as part of the Islamic armies? This becomes the central question around which revolves an understanding of the new Islamic regime's stability during the conquest period, and of the dynamism of the Islamic conquest movement itself.

Means of Integration

In fact, the means used by the state to integrate the tribal population of Arabia to itself during the conquests were highly varied, and some tended to be more effective than others in binding particular individuals or groups to the state. They ranged in character from the purely ideological or idealistic to the crassly venal, and it is no doubt the very breadth of this spectrum of inducements to loyalty, all tied up in one way or another with the Islamic regime, that made the integration process so successful.

On the purely ideological plane, the same factors that had assisted the process of political integration under Muḥammad continued to function during the conquest period, notably the impetus to political unification and centralization implicit in Islam's concepts of a universal, unique God, of an overriding moral authority established by God and expressed in revelations granted His Apostle and in the unity of the Islamic community. As under Muḥammad, these factors led those individuals who were, for whatever personal or psychological reasons, strongly attracted to the religious message of Islam also to the conviction that a thorough political and social unification under the guiding principles of Islam was desirable or even morally necessary.[17] Although Muḥammad's successors could not claim, like him, to be prophets blessed with a direct link to a God who was viewed as the ultimate source of all the validating precepts of Islam, the fact that they represented the communal leadership of the new polity that was guided by those precepts lent them great moral and political authority. The importance of a sincere belief in the religious precepts of early Islam, then, must not be underestimated when considering the rise of the Islamic state to supremacy in Arabia or the conquests that the expansion of that state generated. Because the impact of such beliefs depended so much on the frame of mind of individual believers, about which there remains no trace of documentary evidence (e.g., letters, memoirs, or the like), the religious motivation to political loyalty and unity is difficult to assess in individual cases. The historian, furthermore, here comes face to face with the impossible task of explaining in historical terms not what people believe, but *why* some should choose to believe in particular ideological systems even when to do so may at times threaten their material or other personal interests. Although we cannot hope to explain the mystery of human faith, however, we can point to its undeniable role in human affairs; and even if not every Muslim was so inspired, there can be little doubt that some Muslims, in their zeal to do well by the new religious and social dispensation of Islam, would have clung firm to the Islamic state and fought for its interests to the death. Depending on the individual, then, the ideology of Islam itself could serve as an important factor contributing to the successful integration of the Islamic state.

In addition to the ideological factors, however, there were also the many practical means by which the loyalty of various individuals was secured by the Islamic state. As under Muḥammad, for example, the promise of material gain in the form of booty or other rewards was doubtless still an effective inducement for many tribesmen to remain loyal. Indeed, the great scope of the conquests, and the relative success of some campaigns, could be expected to have made the prospects of securing considerable booty quite promising, at least for a time. But during the conquest period the granting of gifts, which had been practiced by Muḥammad, became more regularized and eventually institutionalized. In the first place, there was established a system of stipends or direct salary payments (*'aṭā'*) to warriors serving in the Islamic armies, at least by the time of 'Umar b. al-Khaṭṭāb. The stipend payments, because they were predictable, created a direct and enduring link between the interests of those recruited into the Islamic armies and the interests of the state and the ruling elite in a way that merely sharing in the distribution of booty from a successful campaign could not. Moreover, tribesmen in the Islamic armies who rebelled against the regime now did so at the cost of losing the stipends that the regime provided. The *'aṭā'* was graded in order to reflect the priority of an individual's adherence to Islam; in Iraq, as we have seen, the immigrant tribesmen were organized into pay units called *'irāfas*, according to the time of their arrival in Iraq. Those who had fought under Khālid b. al-Walīd in the first phase of the conquest there (the so-called *ahl al-ayyām*) received the highest stipends, those who came in the second phase somewhat less, and those who arrived only with the third phase (called the *ahl al-Qādisiyya*) or even later, in one of the *rawādif* migrations, received still less. This schedule was not rigidly tied to military performance or priority in joining Islam, however; sometimes an unusually generous stipend was awarded in recognition of the special status of the recipient—as in the case of the Prophet's widows and numerous early Muslims in Medina, who took no part in the military activity on the fronts—or to guarantee the loyalty of individuals or groups whose services seemed especially desirable. Most notable among the latter were some of the *asāwira* or Persian cavalry, once part of the Sasanian garrisons in Iraq, who appear to have changed sides at a fairly early date and joined the Islamic armies. They were rewarded by being granted the highest level of stipend (*sharaf al-'aṭā'*), two thousand dirhams per annum. They indeed proved useful allies and served beside the Muslims at al-Qādisiyya, Jalūlā', and in Khūzistān, as well as providing troops to guard the outlying garrisons the Muslims established at Ḥulwān, Māsabadhān, Mosul, and al-Qarqīsiyā'.[18] Similarly, stipends were granted to some Persian or Aramean petty nobles (*dihqāns*) who cooperated with the Muslims in Iraq.[19] In most cases, it appears that these individuals were required to embrace Islam in order to receive their stipend.[20]

Tribesmen also became bound to the state when they received shares in the *naṣīb* lands, that is, in the abandoned lands taken over by the Islamic state and offered to the tribesmen for settlement or exploitation. Since the benefits accruing to the tribesmen from such lands could only be enjoyed if the tribesmen remained loyal, such grants made it further in their interest to be politically quiescent.[21]

In addition, the organization of the army was itself a factor that weakened purely tribal ties and strengthened the bonds between the tribesmen and the state—a matter of considerable importance because at this early stage the army was in fact so much of the state apparatus. The existence of units (whether for pay or for combat) such as the hundreds or tens that cut across tribal lines by embracing individuals from many tribes doubtless helped to establish new lines of solidarity that helped transcend the narrow tribal identification.[22]

Ideologically and organizationally, then, the Islamic state had resources upon which it could draw to override the tribal loyalties that had traditionally been the stumbling block in the path of successful political integration in prestate Arabia. It would, however, be a serious mistake to conclude that the successful integration of the Islamic state from the time of Muḥammad through the early conquest period was solely the result of these means of transcending tribal ties. The methods outlined above did contribute much to the state's cohesion, above all by providing organizational goals that were supratribal in the context of a justifying ideology. But the day-to-day stability of the new regime, and the effectiveness with which the rulers were able to control the thousands of tribesmen now under their charge and to bring them to do their bidding, was also the result of the elite's keen awareness of the ingrained strength of tribal ties and of the ways in which these ties could be used to foster, rather than to obstruct, their consolidation of power. Themselves, after all, Arabian tribesmen, the members of the elite realized that the tribal identification was too well rooted in Arabian society simply to be abolished by decree or swept aside by a few measures that tended to transcend the exclusiveness of the tribal bond. The success of their integration of the tribesmen into a state, then, depended as much upon their ability to use tribal ties for their own ends as it did upon their ability to override those ties.

It was not simply by chance, for example, that the tribesmen settling in al-Kūfa were organized into quarters by tribe; the tribal identification provided a means—perhaps, in view of the tribesmen's background, the only means—by which the state could conveniently classify individuals for its administrative purposes related to pay, military organization, and the like. It is probably for this reason that tribal and nontribal arrangements for battle and pay appear to have existed simultaneously. The only way the ruling elite could keep track of the thousands of individual tribesmen serving it was by their tribal affiliation, however much it may have wanted eventually to submerge such affiliations in a greater loyalty to the state. After all, a tribesman could readily have deceived others about his membership in one or another military unit—who was to know, given the rudimentary character of the administrative apparatus at this early date?—but he could not very well lie about his tribal origins.

The tribal tie, furthermore, was even more vital to the state in cases where the elite needed a certain leverage over the tribesman. If, for example, a military unit's commander was held responsible for seeing that all the men in his unit—drawn, let us say, from many tribes—appeared in formation when the army marched to battle, what was to prevent the individual tribesman, not of the commander's tribe and perhaps disgruntled with the rigors of state service, from simply leaving and quietly returning to his kinsmen somewhere in Arabia? If, on the other hand, the individual warrior's tribal chief was held responsible for seeing that he showed up in his unit when expected, it became much more difficult for the warrior to vanish in the same fashion. His absence could be reported to the tribal chief, who would know the tribesman, his kin and therefore probably his whereabouts. The tribesman who wished to turn his back on his duties to the state could now do so only by breaking his ties with his fellow tribesmen, not a very inviting prospect.

The use in these ways of tribal ties thus helped the elite consolidate its control over the tribesmen to a considerable degree. Because such methods usually worked through the tribal chiefs or lineage heads, their allegiance was in several ways critical to the successful integration of the tribes into the state. These leaders could, if themselves strongly enough tied to the state, bring with them a sizable body of tribesmen over whom they had considerable influence or control. This possibility became attractive to the Islamic state, as we have seen, when it was faced with a pressing need for more manpower to carry out the large campaigns of the later phases of the conquests. On the other hand, these chieftains—particularly those who had once led rebellions against the Islamic state during the *ridda*—were themselves the most serious potential rivals of the state's power. It was just these tribal leaders, after all, who would be most likely and most able to break away from the state and to establish themselves as independent rivals; indeed, it was for this reason that the elite had, during the first phase of the conquests, barred the former rebels from any participation in the state's activities. The challenge facing the ruling elite, then, was to tie the interests of key tribal leaders firmly enough to the state that their loyalty, or at least their cooperation, was assured. This done, the elite could use the essentially tribal allegiance of these chieftains' followers to accomplish the ultimate objectives of the state.

We find, consequently, that the elite used on these tribal chiefs not only the methods applied to secure the loyalty of the average tribesman—stipends, appeals to their religious conscience, and the like—but also a number of additional, extraordinary incentives to make certain that the chiefs knew where their interests lay. The meager evidence available suggests that ʿUmar and the ruling elite during the conquest period resorted to a policy modeled after that pursued by Muḥammad in a similar situation: namely, "conciliation of hearts" (*ta'līf al-qulūb*). This policy is visible in the elite's arrangements with Jarīr b. ʿAbdullāh of the Bajīla tribe. In their moment of greatest need, after the severe setback the Muslims had suffered at the battle of the Bridge, the elite approached Jarīr in an effort to raise badly needed troops.[23] Jarīr drove a hard bargain; he agreed to put his sizable following of B. Bajīla at the service of the Islamic state, but only in return for a promise of extra booty over and above the normal share. Significantly, this extra booty is likened to *ta'līf al-qulūb*. The sources generally state that the extra booty was being granted to Jarīr himself, which makes it look as if Jarīr, rather than the Bajīla tribesmen, were being won over: "If Jarīr wants it understood that he and his tribe only fought for a pay like that of 'those whose hearts were reconciled' (*al-mu'allafa qulūbu-hum*), then give them their pay,"[24] ʿUmar wrote to the Muslims' commander, Saʿd b. Abī Waqqāṣ, after the Iraqi campaigns. Jarīr's allegiance to Islam was, however, fairly well assured, as his previous career indicates.[25] It seems probable, therefore, that his demand for extra pay was rooted in a realization that he would only be able to exercise meaningful authority over the tribesmen of Bajīla by himself holding out to them the promise of extra booty. Perhaps the regime felt that an added inducement to ensure the loyalty of Bajīla was well advised because the number of them that went to fight in Iraq was so great (according to some accounts, one-quarter of the Muslims at al-Qādisiyya). In any case, it is clear that at least in the case of Jarīr and the B. Bajīla, the ruling elite employed the policy of "conciliation of hearts" that Muḥammad had used in similar circumstances.[26]

In addition, the Islamic elite could tie important tribal leaders to the regime by means of marriages, which thereby cemented an alliance between an individual chieftain and some key figure in the elite itself. This use of marriage for political purposes, already practiced by Muḥammad and indeed quite frequent in pre-Islamic Arabia, was thus continued. We learn, for example, that the chief of Kinda, al-Ash'ath b. Qays, who had rebelled during the *ridda*, was eventually pardoned by Abū Bakr, who bound him to the regime by allowing him to marry his own sister, Umm Farwa. Thereafter, he witnessed the major confrontations in central Iraq and settled in al-Kūfa.[27] In other cases marriage may have functioned more indirectly to tie tribesmen to the regime, as in the case of Sa'd b. Abī Waqqāṣ, who married the widow of the Shaybānī chieftain al-Muthannā b. Ḥāritha; the objective was perhaps to bind al-Muthannā's former followers to Sa'd.[28]

Key tribal leaders could also be bound to the state by granting them special gifts of land to be held as private estates; these appear to have been larger tracts than the *naṣīb* lands distributed to the ordinary tribesmen. This phenomenon has been discussed within the context of migration and settlement.[29]

Finally, the ruling elite could bind important tribal leaders to the state by associating them in special ways with the elite itself. The process of currying favor with these leaders, by inviting them to attend a governor's audiences and to discuss with him affairs of government, functioned in this manner. The status of those chiefs who became the governor's intimates must have risen considerably in the eyes of the tribesmen who served under them. Tribal leaders in this category began to see their status enhanced and their enhanced status solidified by their evolving relationship with other tribal leaders; at the same time, they could see that their enhanced position was generated, not by their own actions, nor even by their actions together with others in this evolving group, but solely by virtue of their role as associates of the Islamic regime.[30] If the effective power of certain tribal leaders over their tribesmen was thus increased, it was increased by enhancing the leaders' status in ways peculiarly related to the state, so that it could not easily be used against the state. These leaders emerged from the conquest period as the *ashrāf*, the tribal notables of the garrison towns, who for decades showed themselves subservient to the state and its interests.[31]

The association of such key tribal figures with the Islamic state was strengthened by the organization of the military payroll. As noted above, the tribal leaders were apparently in charge of distributing pay for the warriors of their tribes to the *'arīf* or head of the *'irāfa.* This function, that of "distributor of surplus," must also have increased the status of the tribal leaders and their ability to command and control the tribesmen under them.[32]

In these ways, then, the ruling elite attempted to tie tribal leaders to the state by special acts of favoritism and to exploit the nexus of tribal allegiances focused on them to the advantage of the state. Yet we should not assume that the Islamic regime, once it had decided to employ former rebel tribesmen in its armies, would willy-nilly shower favors upon their leaders in order to bind them to the state. *Ridda* leaders were still viewed with suspicion by the ruling elite for obvious reasons, as is revealed by the example of the B. Asad. The predominant figure in the tribe was Ṭalḥa b. Khuwaylid, a notorious rebel leader who had once claimed prophethood and rallied a large following from the tribes of Asad, Ṭayyi', and Ghaṭafān in opposition to Medina. Only a small fraction of B. Asad had remained loyal to the Islamic state during the *ridda*, and, led by Ḍirār b. al-Azwar, had fought as part of Khālid b. al-Walīd's force during the *ridda* wars, and perhaps in Iraq and Syria as well. The great majority of B. Asad followed Ṭalḥa into rebellion; hence we find little indication that significant numbers of tribesmen from Asad participated in the Islamic armies in Iraq during the offensives of the first, second, or transitional phases there. In the third phase, however, a considerable number of Asadīs, including Ṭalḥa b. Khuwaylid himself, are found among the Muslims at al-Qādisiyya and in the later campaigns in western Iran. Yet traditional accounts record the considerable discomfort that the Islamic ruling elite felt in employing such rebel leaders as Ṭalḥa. When, during the eastern campaigns, Ṭalḥa was absent longer than expected on a reconnaissance mission and failed to return after the others who had been sent out had long been back, the Muslims feared that he had "apostasized" and joined the Persians.[33] Clearly, his loyalties were suspect. 'Umar instructed Sa'd b. Abī Waqqāṣ, commander of the Muslims at al-Qādisiyya, not to put any of the *ridda* leaders in command of a hundred men,[34] for the same reason—they could not be trusted. In accordance with this general order, we find that the chieftain 'Uyayna b. Ḥiṣn of the B. Fazāra, who had backed Ṭalḥa during the *ridda* and had been captured and sent to Medina, was later sent by 'Umar to Iraq with Sa'd b. Abī Waqqāṣ on the condition that the latter "not appoint him to a position of command."[35] Similarly, Qays b. Makshūḥ al-Murādī, whose political activities in the Yemen during the *ridda* had given Abū Bakr reason to doubt his intentions, was sent by the caliph to Iraq, with the proviso that he be consulted in matters of warfare and strategy but not put in command of anything.[36] "Abū Bakr did not ask the former rebels for help in the *ridda* or against the Persians," we are told; " 'Umar conscripted them but did not put a single one of them in a command post."[37] Passages such as these make it quite clear that the bulk of the former *ridda* rebels, and (despite the special favors granted them) even the key tribal chiefs among them, participated in the activities of the Islamic state not as members of the policy-making and governing elite, but primarily as simple employees of the state. These arrangements helped assure that the process of state integration would not be wrecked by the secession of powerful tribal chiefs, and that the elite's objectives for the state would not be too greatly distorted by the activities of these chiefs.

The State and the Nomads

If the essence of the Islamic state's accomplishment was the integration of all Arabian tribal groups into itself and their domination by the Islamic ruling elite, the real guarantee of the state's continuing ascendancy lay particularly in its ability to keep the nomadic tribesmen under control. As we have already seen, the early Islamic state and its ruling elite took an attitude quite hostile to the nomadic way of life.[38] Early Islam itself appears to have expressed, along with the more strictly religious and ethical notions of God's unity and power and mankind's duty to be faithful and just, the social ideals of the settled life. To a certain extent, this bias in favor of settled life may reflect simple cultural preference, since Muḥammad himself and the Islamic ruling elite were sedentary townsmen from the Ḥijāz. During the conquest period, this bias continued to be characteristic of the elite, despite the great numbers of nomadic tribesmen who eventually came to be associated with the state as employees of the army; it is reflected, for example, in an episode in which some nomads (*ahl al-bādiya*) asked 'Umar to provide them with rations, to which 'Umar replied, "By God, I will not supply you until I have supplied the settled people [*ahl al-ḥāḍira*]."[39] In a somewhat different vein, 'Uthmān is said to have dismissed the opinion of an important tribal chieftain, Ibn Zurāra, as the word of an "imbecile bedouin"—reflecting the general feeling of disdain the settled townsman held for the excitable, undisciplined nomad.[40]

But the ruling elite's bias against the nomad was rooted in more than mere disapproval of the nomadic way of life; it was ultimately founded in the keen awareness that the nomads, above all others, were a potential danger to the integration of the state and the political ascendancy of the elite. For it was the nomadic groups of the peninsula that were traditionally the ultimate source of power there; even in cases of conflict between two rival centers of settlement (as between Mecca and Medina during Muḥammad's rise to prominence), the outcome depended largely on which side could most successfully mobilize a coalition of nomadic allies. The new Islamic state's survival, then, depended directly on its continued domination of the nomadic elements in Arabian society.

The leadership of the Islamic state was thus very conscious of the nomads' power and of their ability to obstruct the centralizing tendencies of the state, and their suspicion and fear of the nomads is made quite plain in many instances. Many accounts, for example, make it clear that the challenge facing the fledgling Islamic state upon Muḥammad's death was to keep the nomads from rebelling; one of the *anṣār* is said to have announced at that time, "By God, I am afraid that the nomadic tribes [*qabā'il al-'arab*] may rebel against the jurisdiction of Islam [*dīn al-Islām*], and if some man of the B. Hāshim or [the rest of] Quraysh does not take charge of this affair, it will be the end [of it]."[41] During the conquest period, likewise, when the pious companion Abū Dharr (who originally hailed from the nomadic B. Ghifār of the Ḥijāz) took up residence, not in Medina, but in the isolated village of al-Rabadha, he was urged to make a pact with Medina so that he would not rebel "like the bedouin."[42]

The ruling elite's concern for controlling the nomads, and their disdain for the nomadic way of life, caused them to reserve command positions in the army, governorships, and other important posts in the evolving state apparatus whenever possible for settled people. The nomads seem to have been considered of dubious reliability or of inappropriate background, even if they had a history of loyalty to the Islamic regime. Thus, when 'Utba b. Ghazwān (a very early companion of the Prophet and resident of Mecca[43]) left his post as commander-in-chief and governor of al-Baṣra, placing Mujāshi' b. Mas'ūd of the nomadic tribe of Sulaym over al-Baṣra in his stead, 'Umar's reaction was a thoroughly negative one. Although his exact words are given differently in several accounts, the drift of them is the same in all cases: "Appoint the settled people over the nomads"; "the settled people are more suited to be made commander than are the nomads."[44] Even though Mujāshi' was a companion of the Prophet and of unquestionable loyalty, his nomadic background meant that he was deemed unsuited for such commands; 'Umar appointed al-Mughīra b. Shu'ba, of the sedentary Thaqīf, in his place.[45]

The elite's concern with controlling the nomads also had far more important repercussions, for it led the elite to elaborate a policy of settlement of the nomads during the conquest period that had a profound influence upon the subsequent history of the entire region. As in many other cases, the precedent or guiding principle for the elite's action seems to have been established by Muḥammad himself, for as we have seen, the Prophet placed great emphasis on the importance of settlement (*hijra*) and the abandonment of the nomadic life for those embracing Islam; it was considered impossible to remain a nomad and to be a Muslim in the true sense of the word.[46] The tax system of the early Islamic state, which had a special tax category (*ṣadaqa*) for nomadic tribesmen, appears to support this view; Muslims leading a settled life were subject to alms (*zakāt*), and sedentary non-Muslims were subject to some kind of tribute or tax (*jizya, jazā'*),[47] but the tax on nomads is always referred to as *ṣadaqa*. Although this may simply reflect administrative convenience, it may also suggest that even those nomads who had embraced the religious tenets of Islam were in some way not considered to be quite the same as settled Muslims—or were not really considered Muslims at all. With the completion of the *ridda* wars and the subjection of most of Arabia by the Islamic state, Abū Bakr, 'Umar, and the rest of the ruling elite found themselves faced with a "nomad problem" of unparalleled dimensions. The nomads were, for the moment, reduced to subject status and supervised by the tax agents sent out among them, but it must have been clear to the elite that something would have to be done to keep the nomads from again asserting their power against that of the state. The solution found by the elite was simple but bold and effective: recruitment of nomadic tribesmen into the Islamic armies and their settlement in garrison towns away from the desert and the home territories of their tribes. By encouraging the nomadic warrior tribesmen to join its armies, the Islamic state not only increased its own military strength, it also reduced the real power of nomadic groups remaining in the desert by skimming off the men of fighting age who would have been able to spearhead potential resistance to Islamic rule. The power of the state over the nomads was thus doubly augmented by this process. It is probable that one of the reasons why the attractions of state service—stipends, lands, shares of booty, etc.—were kept high was to assure that the Arabian and Syrian nomads felt it to be in their interest to leave their home territories. Indeed, one passage links the award of the stipend directly to the abandonment of the nomadic way of life, as if the *'aṭā'* was more a reward for deciding to settle down than it was a reimbursement for military services, for ʿUmar is reported to have said, "The sooner one settles, the sooner one receives a stipend."[48] The settlement of conscripted tribesmen, furthermore, was to take place preferably outside the Ḥijāz or other regions of Arabia where settlement was possible; ʿUmar reportedly encouraged some of the tribesmen gathered in Medina to settle in Iraq by reminding them that they were "in the Ḥijāz, not in a place of settlement. . . ."[49] From the accounts of the conquests in Syria, it is evident that the Syrian bedouin of B. Qays and other tribes who embraced Islam emigrated from the desert and were either sent to the frontiers to campaign or were settled as garrisons in towns such as Bālis on the Euphrates; likewise, ʿUthmān instructed his governor in Syria and the Jazīra, Muʿāwiya b. Abī Sufyān, to settle some of the nomads in places away from towns and villages where they could make use of empty lands (presumably as farmers?); others were granted stipends and assigned to the cities, towns, and frontier posts as garrison troops.[50] It was, then, a conscious policy of the early Islamic state through the conquest period to settle nomadic tribesmen. Recruited into the army and dispatched to garrison towns, the nomads became integrated into the state organization as employees and were gradually transformed into sedentary citizens, effectively cutting them off from their former desert life and from the opportunities for secluded opposition to Islamic rule it had allowed.

Indeed, the very placement of the garrison cites may be in part a product of the state's program to break the power of independent nomadic groups. It is generally agreed that the garrisons were established primarily to control the non-Arab populations of the conquered domains, to defend Arabia from invasion by either the Byzantines or the Sasanians, and to function as the springboards for further Islamic campaigns into yet unsubdued areas. Although these considerations are almost certainly valid ones, it is possible that the garrisons were also situated with yet another function in mind: namely, to keep a watchful eye on the Arabian and Syrian nomadic populations. Having reduced the possibilities of revolt among the nomads by winning some to state service and leaving those that remained in the desert weaker in numbers, the elite proceeded to ring the desert with a set of large garrisons. This may explain why the garrison in central Iraq was in al-Kūfa, on the desert fringe, and not in al-Madāʾin, the old Sasanian capital; the latter would have made supervision of the non-Arab population easier, but the former was more suited to keeping the nomadic tribes of northeastern Arabia under control. The garrisons in Iraq, Syria, and Egypt certainly had important functions as defense points against Sasanian or Byzantine aggression, and the garrison in the Yemen may have been for defense against Abyssinia; but the garrison in al-Yamāma ("al-Baḥrayn") looks suspiciously as if it were intended to keep a close check on the B. Ḥanīfa, who had been the bitterest opponents of the Islamic state during the *ridda* and who would ultimately be the first to raise a major rebellion against the state's rule some fifty years later. From this ring of strategic centers, the Muslims could control even the remote central Arabian nomads, many of whom had to move out of the pasturelands of the Najd to those of Iraq, Syria, East Arabia, or the Ḥijāz during the dry summer months.

2. THE CAUSES OF THE ISLAMIC CONQUEST

The age of the early Islamic conquests, then, saw the successful integration of the fragmented tribal society of Arabia, including the nomadic groups, into a relatively unified state dominated by a ruling elite that was committed to the doctrines of early Islam and to the settled way of life. An appreciation of this political integration suggests some new approaches to the debate over the causes of the Islamic conquest, the causes of its success, and the causes of the Arab migrations that accompanied it.

The Arab migrations to the Fertile Crescent and adjacent regions that took place during the decades of conquest can best be explained as a result of the state's policy toward tribesmen (especially nomadic tribesmen), whom it recruited and settled in garrison towns, where they could be more easily controlled and could themselves serve as instruments of state control and state expansion. The considerable attractions that the elite offered those tribesmen who joined the army were probably the primary reason why so many tribesmen chose to do so: they would be relatively prosperous because of their regular pay and shares in the revenues from *naṣīb* lands, their life would be interesting, and, as warriors for the most wildly successful enterprise Arabia had ever seen, they would be respected. Some, perhaps, were also swayed by the promise of booty to be gained in campaigning. But the realistic bedouin probably knew that booty was not guaranteed—and those who were really interested in plunder did not necessarily join the army to acquire it, but preferred to extort money from peasants in the provinces already safely under Islamic rule during the absence of the Islamic forces, whose charge included protecting the conquered peasantry from such brigands.[51] A few tribesmen may have wanted to migrate in order to settle on rich new lands, but as we have seen, there is little to suggest that this was a major cause of the migrations, as most emigrant tribesmen preferred to remain clustered in their new garrison towns or in the quarters of established towns that they came to occupy.[52] Nor is the migration to be explained as the result of some natural crisis—hunger, overpopulation, or the desiccation of pasturelands—that forced the tribesmen out of the peninsula; 'Umar is said to have complained that he had difficulty locating enough men to conscript into the armies during the third phase of the conquests,[53] which suggests that overpopulation was hardly a problem in the peninsula. How, after all, could any significant "surplus" population have managed to survive in an area of such precarious agricultural resources as were possessed by Arabia? The theories relating an Arab migration to long or short-term desiccation of the peninsula rest on evidence that is tenuous at best, and do not explain why the conquest and migration occurred as a sudden burst of expansive energy rather than as the gradual efflux of the most miserable in Arabian society. Theories relating the Arab migrations to the collapse of the Arabian luxury trade fail to explain why the bulk of Arabia's tribesmen, who played little direct part in this trade, should have been so directly and immediately affected by such a collapse. The collapse of commerce, however, may very well have created a crisis for certain groups that were heavily engaged in commerce—notably, the Quraysh, Thaqīf, and other townsmen—but in order to link this to a mass migration of tribesmen from all quarters of the peninsula, we must assume that these sedentary groups formed a ruling elite with enough control over the rest of Arabia's tribesmen to use them to "recapture" trade that had shifted to new routes; in short, we are brought back to the notion of a sweeping political integration led by these sedentary groups. It seems, then, that the Arab migrations took place mainly because the political and perhaps economic interests of the Islamic ruling elite were best served by a large-scale emigration of tribesmen into the conquered domains. The migrations were the result of state policy, planned in its general outlines by the state and implemented by the state's offer of various incentives to the emigrants. "The soonei one settles, the sooner one receives a stipend."

The many factors traditionally adduced to explain the military success of the Islamic conquest movement are generally quite plausible and can be accepted without much hesitation. The relative merits of the military organization of various contestants are difficult to assess since practically nothing is known about the tactical or strategic practices of any of them. It seems clear that the Muslims had no technological advantages over their opponents on the battlefield and were in fact inferior to their enemies in the use of cavalry. There can be little doubt, however, that the conquests were made easier by the exhaustion of the Byzantine and Sasanian Empires due to prolonged warfare, the confusion that reigned in the Sasanian ruling house, the disruption caused by recent enemy occupation in Syria and Iraq, the destruction wrought by immense floods in southern Iraq, the disaffection of many of the subjects of the two empires for religious or other reasons, the convenience of inner lines of communication that the Muslims enjoyed, and the like. But to these factors must be added one more that was perhaps the single most important one contributing to the success of the conquests: the remarkable degree to which a new Islamic state with an expansionist policy could harness for its purposes the rugged warriors of Arabia. The rise of the state made it possible to weld into an incredibly effective fighting force those tribesmen whose energies had hitherto been consumed by petty quarrels among themselves and whose political horizons had hitherto usually been limited to their own tribe and its affairs. The success of the conquests was, then, first and foremost the product of an organizational breakthrough of proportions unparalleled in the history of Arabian society until modern times. However important other factors may have been, it is difficult to believe that the conquests could have succeeded without the rise of a state with the capacity to integrate Arabia's fragmented society and draw on it to attain well-defined political and military objectives. It is not even too rash, perhaps, to suggest that the Islamic conquest might have met with great success even had the Byzantine and Sasanian Empires not been reeling from their recent quarrels. The Muslims succeeded, then, primarily because they were able to organize an effective conquest movement, and in this context the impact of the new religion of Islam, which provided the ideological underpinnings for this remarkable breakthrough in social organization, can be more fully appreciated. In this sense, the conquests were truly an *Islamic* movement. For it was Islam—the set of religious beliefs preached by Muḥammad, with its social and political ramifications—that ultimately sparked the whole integration process and hence was the ultimate cause of the conquests' success.

Most difficult of all to explain is what caused the conquest itself—that is, what it was that led the ruling elite of the new Islamic state to embrace an expansionist policy. Several factors can plausibly be suggested, however, any or all of which probably led specific individuals in the elite to think in terms of an expansionist movement. First, there is the possibility that the ideological message of Islam itself filled some or all of the ruling elite with the notion that they had an essentially religious duty to expand the political domain of the Islamic state as far as practically possible; that is, the elite may have organized the Islamic conquest movement because they saw it as their divinely ordained mission to do so. This view coincides closely with the traditional view adopted by Muslims themselves. Skeptical modern scholars have tended to discount the religious factor, but it must be borne in mind that as an ideological system early Islam came with great force onto the stage of Arabian society—we have seen how it appears to have laid the groundwork for a radical social and political transformation of that society. The pristine vigor of early Islam may be difficult to sense now, after the passage of so many centuries and in the context of an age dominated by social and political ideas very different from those of ancient Arabia, but its revolutionary impact on seventh-century Arabia can hardly be doubted. We should, therefore, be wary of recent attempts simply to dismiss as insignificant what was clearly felt by contemporaries to be a profoundly powerful movement. Furthermore, we must recognize that even in cases where other, more mundane factors were partly responsible for stirring an individual member of the elite to favor the idea of an expansionist movement, it was Islam that provided the ideological sanction for such a conviction. The precise degree to which the purely ideological element may have bolstered the practical resolve of the elite to embark on an expansion that was considered worthwhile for other reasons as well can hardly be estimated, but it would be unrealistic, indeed foolhardy, to dismiss ideology or faith as a factor altogether. Some of the ruling elite, then, may well have believed in expansion of the state and the conquest of new areas simply because they saw it as God's will, and many others were surely susceptible to the psychological comfort of having such legitimation for their actions.

Other factors, however, certainly contributed to the adoption of an expansionist policy by the state. Much of the elite—the Quraysh, Thaqīf, and many Medinese as well—may have wanted to expand the political boundaries of the new state in order to secure even more fully than before the trans-Arabian commerce they had plied for a century or more, or to recapture routes that had shifted north.[54] There is ample evidence that some members of the ruling elite retained a lively interest in commerce during the conquest period and wished to use wealth and influence accruing to them as governors or generals for new commercial ventures; ʿUtba b. Abī Sufyān, for example, who was ʿUmar's tax agent over the Kināna tribe, wanted to use the money he made from the post for trade.[55] The Quraysh in particular, perhaps because of their long-standing commercial contacts in Syria, may have been especially eager to see the state expand in that direction. There were also other financial advantages that would accrue to the elite from the expansion of the state: the acquisition of properties in the conquered areas, the ability of the state to levy taxes on conquered populations, the booty in wealth and slaves, at least some of which would reach the ruling elite even if they did not participate actively in the campaigns that seized them.

Finally, there is the possibility that members of the elite saw an expansion of the state as necessary in order to preserve their hard-won position at the top of the new political hierarchy. The policy of encouraging tribesmen to emigrate, upon which the continued dominance of the elite in part rested, was itself dependent on the successful conquest of new domains in which the emigrant tribesmen could be lodged. This view suggests that the conquest of Syria and Iraq was one of the objectives of the ruling elite from a fairly early date. On the other hand, it is also possible to argue that the conquest of Syria and Iraq were merely side effects of the state's drive to consolidate its power over all Arab tribes, including those living in the Syrian desert and on the fringes of Iraq. This process generated the direct clashes with the Byzantine and Sasanian Empires that ultimately led to the Islamic conquest of Syria and Iraq, but that does not necessarily imply that the conquest of Syria and Iraq was a conscious objective of the ruling elite from the start.

These considerations can serve as plausible guesses as to why the state and its dominant elite adopted an expansionist policy. In the absence of real primary sources that might illuminate for us the actual motivations of individuals and of the elite as a body, they will have to remain merely guesses. The true causes of the Islamic conquests—currents in the minds of men—will probably remain forever beyond the grasp of historical analysis.

EPILOGUE

The Islamic conquests had a profound impact on the Near East and on the general course of world history. Among other things, they carried the new faith of Islam to distant regions and created the political and social conditions that allowed it to strike deep roots there; they thus represent the practical starting point in the evolution of the great civilization of medieval Islam, as well as the beginning of the end of the late antique world. For a time, they also resulted in a dramatic change in the political patterns prevailing in the Near East; for this state that took Arabia as the very basis of its power, and used it to dominate the old cultural and political centers of the Fertile Crescent, Iran, and Egypt, was a development unheralded in the region's history, one that stood the usual geo-political realities on their heads.

Not all of the political changes that came with the rise of Islam proved to be of equal durability, of course. It is perhaps ironic, however, that of the two basic political developments that marked the rise of Islam—the integration of Arabian society including the nomads into a unified state, and the emergence of a ruling elite that dominated that state—the latter should prove more durable than the former; that is, the Islamic ruling elite (or a descendant of it) showed itself able to survive long after its original Arabian-Islamic state had disintegrated. Not even the elite weathered the first decades after the conquests completely unchanged, however. Soon after the opening of the conquests, the elite began to undergo a transformation that pitted one branch against another, so that it became increasingly narrowly defined as successive groups were eased out of positions of real influence. At the outset, as we have seen, the elite included tribesmen of Medina (the *anṣār*), the Meccan Quraysh, and the Thaqīf of al-Ṭā'if. But even Muḥammad himself had been hard put at times to control the rivalries among these groups, and after his death these rivalries became sharper and eventually broke out in open conflict. The selection of Abū Bakr to be Muḥammad's successor as head of state, for example, was made possible only by assuaging the fears of the *anṣār* that they might be overpowered by the Quraysh. Despite such assurances, however, the Quraysh seem in any case to have risen quickly to a position of practical dominance over other elements in the elite during the conquest period. The *anṣār*, in Abū Bakr's day, were already worried enough to demand of him, "Who is in charge of this affair? Do the *anṣār* have a share in it?"[1] A bit later, during the caliphate of 'Umar, the governor of southern Iraq, 'Utba b. Ghazwān (a man of B. Qays but a longtime resident of Mecca and ally of Quraysh) complained that the Qurashi commander in central Iraq, Sa'd b. Abī Waqqāṣ, ordered him about. 'Umar replied to his demand for an independent command by saying, "It is not for you, 'Utba, to be instated with authority over a man of Quraysh who is a companion of the Prophet and a man of honor." 'Utba reminded 'Umar that he, too, was a companion of Muḥammad and, as an ally of Quraysh, entitled to be treated as one of them, but 'Umar refused to alter his stand.[2] Similarly, the general Abū 'Ubayda b. al-Jarrāḥ is said to have opened an address to the Syrians whom he governed by stating, "Oh people, I am a man of Quraysh (appointed) over Syria"[3]—not a Muslim over Syria, we may note, but a man of Quraysh. His use of this phrase may have been related to the way in which conquered areas in Syria appear to have been "reserved" especially for the Quraysh, whereas the *anṣār* and Thaqīf were sent more frequently to Iraq.[4] But it is also probably reflective of the general rise of the Quraysh to real dominance within the ruling elite.

The Meccans thus seem to have nudged the *anṣār* out of real power during the period of the early conquests, until the two groups split openly during the First Civil War, when the *anṣār* tried to restore their faded fortunes by backing the faction around 'Alī b. Abī Ṭālib against two other factions representing rival groups within the Quraysh.[5] The *anṣār* lost the struggle, however, and after the First Civil War were for practical purposes no longer a part of the ruling elite. Certainly the caliphate seems to have become the unique preserve of the Quraysh by this time. As for the Thaqīf, they seem to have avoided a direct clash with the Quraysh, but then they never appear to have posed quite the same challenge to the Quraysh's domination of the elite as had the *anṣār*. Even at the start they seem to have been part of the elite mainly by virtue of their long and intimate affiliations with the Quraysh, and after the First Civil War they, too, slowly slipped into oblivion, retaining a vestige of their former importance, perhaps, in their accustomed tenure of certain governorships, notably in Iraq.

By the postconquest period, then, the struggle for dominance within the elite had become exclusively a question of which branch of the Quraysh was to rule. This issue was raised already in the First Civil War in the form of a struggle between the B. Umayya, led by Mu'āwiya

b. Abī Sufyān, the B. Hāshim, led by 'Alī b. Abī Ṭālib, and other branches of the Quraysh, led by Ṭalḥa b. 'Ubaydallāh and al-Zubayr b. al-'Awwām. The Second Civil War (A.H. 60-73/A.D. 680-692) saw a similar struggle between the Alids, branches of the B. Umayya, and an alliance of other Quraysh led by al-Zubayr's sons. The issue was raised yet again in the Abbasid coup of A.H. 132/A.D. 750, when the B. al-'Abbās (a lineage of B. Hāshim) ousted the B. Umayya from power and had most of them murdered, and yet again in the numerous rebellions of various Alid pretenders against the Abbasids—that is, in a protracted struggle between two rival factions within the B. Hāshim. The ruling elite had thus been successively narrowed to limit leadership of the state first to the Quraysh, and then to a few select lineages of the Quraysh. It is interesting to note that in later years the debate over who had the right to lead the Islamic community eventually emerged in a curiously Arabian formulation, even though the protagonists were by now only in the most attenuated sense Arabians. The arguments used by those groups that were the main rivals for power within the elite (notably the Alids and Abbasids) came increasingly to rest on considerations of genealogy, whereas those of groups outside the elite that wished to gain access to it (notably the pious and the Khawārij) relied increasingly on the importance of virtuous, properly Islamic behavior as justifications for holding power. This dichotomy contains a curious echo of the notions of *nasab* (nobility of descent) and *ḥasab* (nobility of action) current among the pre-Islamic Arabian aristocracy as the principles validating their claims to authority and noble status.

The decades immediately following the conquests, marked as they were by two civil wars, constituted a period of real political turmoil in the Islamic state. But these quarrels among members of the ruling elite and the turbulence they generated were not caused by the failure of the original process of consolidation by which the elite had integrated Arabia's tribesmen into the state. Indeed, the striking thing about the First and Second Civil Wars is the degree to which the tribesmen remained bound to the state throughout them, even though the leadership of the state was divided against itself. The tribesmen waited out these squabbles in the ruling elite, or plunged in on the side of one or another group in the elite, but it never seems to have occurred to most of them that they should or could raise the standard of revolt in their own name. With very few exceptions, they appear to have accepted their status as subjects or employees of the state and its elite without demur; those tribesmen who tried to evade state control by forming little bands of escapees from the garrison towns, and by raising havoc in the Iraqi and Iranian countryside as Khawārij, were a mere handful of Arabia's population. The victory of the Islamic state over the bodies and minds of Arabia could hardly have been more complete.

Yet, as noted above, this firm integration of the tribes of Arabia by the state was not to be long lived. Arabian society, so long politically fragmented and outside state control, was soon to revert to its original disunity. The Islamic state's victory over the tribes was thus to be a phenomenon unique in the history of the peninsula until modern times.

The ultimate disintegration of the Arabian-Islamic state should not be taken, however, as an indication of any decline in Islam's power as an integrating ideology. Indeed, the integrating power of Islam continued to work on an even more extensive scale after the conquests, as it wove disparate communities together to form the rich tapestry of medieval Islamic civilization, linking individuals and groups thousands of miles apart with a sense of common heritage, common values and beliefs, and common goals in life. Rather, the collapse of the Arabian state had more mundane causes. As we have seen, the political integration of Arabia by the early Islamic state was the product of two primary elements—the integrating concepts implicit in Islam and the vigorous and skillful pursuit of political consolidation by a group of leaders well versed in the techniques of traditional Arabian politics. It was the latter, not the former, that ultimately faltered. Ideologies are like the switch settings and signal lights that control the movement of trains. The signals must be green, the switches open, if a train is to proceed down a certain track; but simply opening the switches will not in itself move the train—one has also to undertake the difficult chore of firing up the engine and setting it in motion. The Islamic state, first established on the firm domination of Arabian society by the ruling elite, underwent a transformation because the focus of the state moved out of the Arabian milieu, and its rulers gradually lost sight of the fundamental principles of Arabian politics; they forgot, so to speak, how to fire the engine. The caliph Mu'āwiya b. Abī Sufyān (A.H. 41-60/A.D. 661-680), though ruling from Damascus, still clearly understood the principles of Arabian politics; he drew on all tribes as much as possible for his military backing, playing them off against one another when necessary, but keeping the interests of all tied in one way or another to the state that he ruled by means of his deft tribal diplomacy. His brilliant lieutenant and foster brother, Ziyād b. Abī Sufyān, kept a close rein on the turbulent tribesmen of Iraq in much the same way; by using one group to control another, and by using the tribal notables to control the masses of ordinary tribesmen, he managed to keep most groups of tribesmen from becoming too powerful and preserved among them at least a modicum of interest in serving the state. But then both Mu'āwiya and Ziyād had grown up in tribal Arabia and were familiar with its politics; Mu'āwiya, as a boy, had served Muḥammad himself as a scribe and participated in the conquest of Syria, and Ziyād had been raised in al-Ṭā'if by the family that led the conquests in southern Iraq.

As decades passed, however, the caliphs became less and less Arabian. Though descended from the Arabian Quraysh, they were usually raised in new capitals, Damascus or Baghdad, and hence did not grow up with the importance of controlling tribal particularism or nomadic power so constantly before their eyes. Shortly after the Second Civil War, a drastic shift in the basis of the Islamic state's power had already taken place as the result of an intentional change of policy; the caliph 'Abd al-Malik (A.H. 65-86/A.D. 685-705) constructed his new army primarily on tribes of Syrian origin, leaving the bulk of Arabia's tribesmen few ties to bind them to the state. Indeed, he demilitarized the great garrison towns of al-Kūfa and al-Baṣra in Iraq, erecting between them a new garrison at Wāsiṭ, which he manned with loyal Syrian troops whose charge was, as much as anything, to keep the Arabians of al-Kūfa and al-Baṣra under control. It marked the end of the process of integration by which the Islamic state had made Arabia's fragmented population a part of itself, and on which the original power of the state had rested. Later Umayyad caliphs, for various reasons, narrowed their base of support even further, relying not even on all Syrian tribesmen but only on one or another faction of Syrians. The integration of Arabia, concurrently, became ever more fragile, and the peninsula slipped slowly but steadily beyond the state's control. By the time of the Abbasid takeover (A.H. 132/A.D. 750), when the new dynasty replaced Syrian with settled Khurasani tribesmen as its base of military power, the Near East had returned to the geopolitical pattern that it has displayed in most historical periods, before the rise of Islam or after it: a powerful state or states centered in the Fertile Crescent and Egypt, supported especially by the rich taxes to be drawn from those regions, relying on standing armies made up of settled soldiers native to those regions—and struggling with variable success to extend its control over, or at least to keep at bay, the nomadic warriors of the Arabian peninsula who remained generally outside its firm grasp. Arabia reverted to being the land of the nomads. Islam and the Islamic state survived and thrived, to be sure, but the great experiment in the political integration of Arabia by the Islamic state had come to an end.

NOTES

INTRODUCTION

1. Sir William Muir, *The Caliphate: its Rise, Decline, and Fall*, p. 45.

2. Leone Caetani, *Studi di Storia Orientale* 1, pp. 369-371.

3. Ibid., p. 368; on desiccation, pp. 133-135, 136ff.

4. Henri Lammens, *Le Berceau de l'Islam. L'Arabie occidentale à la veille de l'Hégire*, p. 177.

5. Ibid., p. 332-333.

6. Carl Heinrich Becker, "Die Ausbreitung der Araber," pp. 89-90.

7. Ibid., p. 70.

8. Max Adrian Simon von Oppenheim, *Die Beduinen* 1, p. 24.

9. E.g., Bernard Lewis, *The Arabs in History*, p. 55.

10. Karl W. Butzer, "Der Umweltfaktor in der grossen arabischen Expansion." Butzer's argument rests heavily on an analysis of rainfall data from several successive years during the 1930s, which he tabulates and analyzes to demonstrate that annual fluctuations in rainfall are considerable, with rainfall in a given year being as much as 44 percent over or 58 percent under the annual mean. He introduces a serious distortion into the analysis, however, by choosing the calendar year (January-December) as his basis for analysis, rather than the seasonal year or annual wet season (midsummer to midsummer). From the point of view of the pastoralist concerned with rainfall for the fodder it produces, it is insignificant whether a heavy rain falls on December 31 of one calendar year or on January 1 of the next calendar year, as long as there is sufficient rain during every annual wet season; but the analysis based on calendar years makes such a difference in date statistically significant. When we reanalyze the data Butzer has tabulated according to wet seasons, the fluctuation in rainfall is seen to be much more modest, with the high and low figures falling at about 23 percent above and 13 percent below the mean.

11. Ibid., pp. 367-369.

12. Georges Henri Bousquet, "Observations sur la nature et causes de la conquête arabe," pp. 37-52.

13. Marius Canard, "L'expansion arabe: le problème militaire," pp. 37-63.

14. Francesco Gabrieli, *Muhammad and the Conquests of Islam*, pp. 110-115.

15. Muhammad Abdulhayy Shaban, *Islamic History, A.D. 600-750 (A.H. 132). A New Interpretation*, pp. 24-25.

16. In the *Cambridge History of Islam* 1, p. 60.

17. Claude Cahen, *Der Islam I: Vom Ursprung bis zu den Anfängen des Osmanenreiches*, pp. 22-23.

18. Gustav E. Von Grunebaum, *Classical Islam: A History, 600 A.D.-1258 A.D.*, p. 53.

19. John Joseph Saunders, "The Nomad as Empire Builder: A Comparison of the Arab and Mongol Conquests," pp. 79-103.

20. The few exceptions are, for the most part, quite recent. Veccia-Vaglieri and Gabrieli (notes 16 and 14 above) seem to be hinting at something like the interpretation to be proposed here in their brief accounts, summarized above. More direct is the bald statement by Maxime Rodinson, in an article entitled "The Life of Muḥammad and the Sociological Problem of the Beginnings of Islam," p. 29: "At the base of the Arab conquest is the preaching of the prophet Muḥammad." This remains, however, more a statement of faith than a developed argument.

CHAPTER I

1. E.g., Pliny, *Natural History*, VI. 32, where the borders of Arabia extend considerably beyond the Arabian peninsula proper and include much of Syria, Mesopotamia, and even the eastern desert of Egypt—all regions occupied by the bedouin or Scenitae of the classical texts. On the wide distribution of "Arabs" (nomadic speakers of Arabic?) by the fourth century A.D., see Franz Altheim and Ruth Stiehl, "Šāpūr II. und die Araber," in *Die Araber in der alten Welt*, 2, pp. 344-356.

2. The reason for this situation—the fact that nomads are in general economically dependent upon sedentary communities—will be treated in Section 2 below.

3. There are of course exceptions to this pattern. The Ẓufār province of South Arabia receives not rain but heavy mist for about one month each summer, giving rise to unusual flora—including the frankincense tree. But this region never developed into the center of an important independent culture, so the exception hardly affects the argument presented here.

4. On irrigation technology in ancient South Arabia, see Adolf Grohmann, *Arabien*, pp. 147ff.; Richard LeBaron Bowen, Jr., "Irrigation in Ancient Qatabân (Beihan)," in his *Archaeological Discoveries in South Arabia*, pp. 43-131, including excellent photographs of the Ma'rib dam; Gertrude Caton-Thompson and Elinor Wight Gardner, "Climate, Irrigation and Early Man in the Hadramawt."

5. See Wilfred H. Schoff (tr.), *The Periplus of the Erythraean Sea*, §24, §28, §32, on foodstuffs being imported to the Yemen during the first or second century A.D.

6. Modern population estimates demonstrate that the Yemen, despite its relatively small area, still supports a disproportionately large percentage of the population of the Arabian peninsula: 4 to 5 million out of an estimated total population of 10 to 13 million. Cf. P.G.N. Peppelenbosch, "Nomadism on the Arabian Peninsula—A General Appraisal," p. 341.

7. The use of this term will conform to that of Morton Fried, *The Evolution of Political Society*: egalitarian, ranked (differences in status but not in access to wealth), and stratified (differences in status and in access to wealth) societies comprise the three main types prior to the rise of the state according to this scheme.

8. The best general introductions to South Arabian civilization are Grohmann, *Arabien*, and (although dated) Ditlef Nielsen, *Handbuch der altarabischen Altertumskunde*; a readable survey in English is provided by Brian Doe, *Southern Arabia*.

The clearest essay on South Arabian religion is that of Nielsen in his *Handbuch*, but its conclusions must be modified along lines suggested by Albert Jamme, "Le panthéon sud-arabe préislamique d'après les sources épigraphiques." See also Werner Caskel, "Die alten semitischen Gottheiten in Arabien"; on irrigation, see note 4 above; on political and social institutions, see Jacques Ryckmans, *L'Institution monarchique en Arabie méridionale avant l'Islam* (*Ma'în et Saba*) and Maria Höfner, "War der sabäische Mukarrib ein 'Priesterfürst'?"; on cultural influences, see Carl Ratjens, "Kulturelle Einflüsse in Südwest-Arabien von den ältesten Zeiten bis zum Islam, unter besonderer Berücksichtigung des Hellenismus."

9. Even the desolate Empty Quarter is not totally devoid of oases; there is, for example, al-Liwā' (al-Jiwā') in the northern part of the great sands. For a description of this region see Wilfred Thesiger, *Arabian Sands*.

10. General descriptions of conditions in northern Arabia: Eldon Rutter, "The Habitability of the Arabian Desert"; William Bayne Fisher, *The Middle East. A Physical, Social, and Regional Geography*, pp. 456-480. More detailed descriptions are provided by Alois Musil, *The Northern Ḥeǧâz* and *The Northern Neǧd*. For descriptions of Medina and other large oases of the northern Ḥijāz on the eve of Islam, see Julius Wellhausen, *Medina vor dem Islam* (*Skizzen und Vorarbeiten*, 4, pp. 1-64); Henri Lammens, *Le Berceau de l'Islam*, esp. pp. 82ff.; and William Montgomery Watt, *Muhammad at Medina*, pp. 151ff. Charles M. Doughty's remarkable *Travels in Arabia Deserta* contains good descriptions of local life in Khaybar, Taymā', Hā'il, Burayda, and other north-Arabian oases. For the oases of eastern Arabia, somewhat different in character, see Charles H. V. Ebert, "Water Resources and Land Use in the Qaṭīf Oasis of Saudi Arabia," and Federico S. Vidal, *The Oasis of al-Hasa*. On the mountain towns of western Arabia on the eve of Islam see Henri Lammens, *La Cité arabe de Ṭāif à la veille de l'Hégire*.

11. On Mecca's trade on the eve of Islam, see Chapter II, Section 1 below; on the caravan cities of Petra and Palmyra, the study of René Dussaud, *La Pénétration des Arabes en Syrie avant l'Islam*, is most helpful in the present context; on Daydān, see Werner Caskel, *Lihyan und Lihyanisch*.

12. On the functioning of such *ḥarams*, see Section 3 below.

13. Evidence for difficulties in pursuing agriculture at Mecca is assembled in Fred McGraw Donner, "Mecca's Food Supplies and Muḥammad's Boycott."

14. Estimates of the nomadic population of the Arabian peninsula in modern times, and of the approximate proportion of the population that is nomadic or sedentary in different regions, are found in Peppelenbosch, "Nomadism on the Arabian Peninsula."

15. The existence of a spectrum of ways of life extending from fully nomadic to fully sedentary is noted in Christoffel Anthonie Olivier van Nieuwenhuijze, *Sociology of the Middle East*, pp. 51-52, 78. From the vast literature on pastoral nomads in Arabia and the Fertile Crescent region, the following proved most informative: for some theoretical approaches to the problem, see Elizabeth E. Bacon, "Types of Pastoral Nomadism"; the best general descriptions of Arabian nomadic groups are found in Robert Montagne, *La Civilisation du désert. Nomades d'Orient et d'Afrique*; Donald Powell Cole, *Nomads of the Nomads. The Āl Murrah*

Bedouin of the Empty Quarter; Alois Musil, *The Manners and Customs of the Rwala Bedouins*; Max von Oppenheim, *Die Beduinen*; Antonin Jaussen and Raphaël Savignac, *Coutumes des Fuqarâ* (*Mission archéologique en Arabie, supplément au volume II*); Robert Montagne, "Notes sur la vie sociale et politique de l'Arabie du Nord"; Harold R. P. Dickson, *The Arab of the Desert. A Glimpse into Badawin Life in Kuwait and Sau'di Arabia*; J. C. Glubb [read John Bagot Glubb], "The Bedouins of Northern 'Iraq [read Northern Arabia]"; Joseph Chelhod, *Le Droit dans la société bédouine*; and Doughty, *Travels*. On the bedouin on the eve of Islam, see Francesco Gabrieli (ed.), *L'Antica Società Beduina*; Georg Jacob, *Altarabisches Beduinenleben*; Erich Bräunlich, "Beiträge zur Gesellschaftsordnung der arabischen Beduinenstämme"; and Lammens, *Le Berceau de l'Islam*. For an attempt at an historical overview, see Werner Caskel, *Die Bedeutung der Beduinen in der Geschichte der Araber*. The works of M. B. Rowton deal primarily with the role of nomads on the fringes of the Fertile Crescent states but have some implications for the rather different conditions in the Arabian peninsula: see his "Autonomy and Nomadism in Western Asia"; "Urban Autonomy in a Nomadic Environment"; "Enclosed Nomadism."

16. This was usually during the hot summer months, when they congregated at permanent wells controlled by the tribe.

17. Cole, *Nomads of the Nomads*, p. 62ff., mentions very small tenting groups, suggesting that the need for defense did not weigh heavily on the nomads during their extended migrations, but this probably reflects the thorough pacification of the desert by the Saudi state—an abnormal situation in the historical perspective.

18. There did exist itinerant groups of tinkers and merchants, who visited the nomads periodically and performed services for them. They were never viewed as part of the groups they visited, however, and the former were in fact considered to be of inferior social status, belonging to the so-called "pariah" tribes (on which see below, Section 3). Furthermore, they moved from one tenting group to another, staying with each group perhaps only a few days. Hence the economic drain they imposed on any single tenting group was very slight. Cf. Musil, *Manners and Customs of the Rwala Bedouins*, pp. 269-270.

19. On the culture of camel pastoralists, see, in addition to the works cited in note 15 above, the following: on religion among the bedouin of pre-Islamic Arabia, Toufic Fahd, *Le Panthéon de l'Arabie centrale à la veille de l'Hégire*; Gonzague Ryckmans, *Les Réligions arabes préislamiques*; and Julius Wellhausen, *Reste Arabischen Heidentums* (*Skizzen und Vorarbeiten*, 3). On material culture, see Albert de Boucheman, *Matérial de la vie bédouine, recueilli dans le désert de Syrie* (*tribus des Arabes Sba'a*). The poetic traditions of pre-Islamic bedouins are well attested; for the importance of poetry as a means of recounting glorious events in a tribe's history and of expressing tribal honor among the recent bedouin, see Robert Montagne, "Contes poétiques bédouins (recueillis chez les Šammar de Ğezīré)." On raiding as a major source of income, see Peppelenbosch, "Nomadism on the Arabian Peninsula," pp. 342-344; for raiding as a method of redistributing wealth in camels, see Louise E. Sweet, "Camel Raiding of North Arabian Bedouin: A Mechanism of Ecological Adaptation"; raiding as opposite of potlatch, see Louise

E. Sweet, "Camel Pastoralism in North Arabia and the Minimal Camping Unit," in Anthony Leeds and Andrew P. Vayda (eds.), *Man, Culture, and Animals. The Role of Animals in Human Ecological Adjustments*, pp. 129-152; William Irons, "Livestock Raiding among Pastoralists: An Adaptive Interpretaion." Musil, *Manners and Customs of the Rwala Bedouins*, p. 540, distinguishes between raids for booty (called *ghazw*) and battles fought between two tribes because of competition for grazing territory (called *manākh*).

20. On shepherding groups, see Henri Charles, *Tribus moutonnières du Moyen-Euphrate*; Albert de Boucheman, "Note sur la rivalité de deux tribus moutonnières de Syrie. Les Mawâlî et les Ḥadîdyîn"; and Antonin Jaussen, *Coutumes des Arabes au Pays de Moab*. For tribes of the Euphrates region on the eve of Islam, see Henri Charles, *Le Christianisme des arabes nomades sur le limes et dans le désert syro-mésopotamien aux alentours de l'Hégire*.

21. On seminomads, see Touvia Ashkenazi, *Tribus semi-nomades de la Palestine du Nord*; Jaussen, *Coutumes*; Lothar Stein, *Die Šammar-Ǧerba. Beduinen im Übergang vom Nomadismus zur Sesshaftigkeit*; and the anonymous *Les Tribus nomades et semi-nomades des états du Levant placés sous mandat francais*.

22. On the movement of Iyād, Tanūkh, and other nomadic groups from the Ḥijāz or eastern Arabia to Iraq, see Tab. i/744ff.; Ferdinand Wüstenfeld, "Die Wohnsitze und Wanderungen der arabischen Stämme, aus der Vorrede des Abu 'Obeid el-Bekrí zu seinem geographischen Wörterbuche"; Bal. *Ansab* I, 26 (I.K.); Ibn Isḥāq, *Kitāb ḥurrāb al-Basūs bayna Bakr wa Taghlib*, fol. 202a-202b. On the history of Madhḥij and Kinda, see below, Section 4.

23. There has long been controversy over the degree to which matriarchal or matrilineal systems were prevalent in pre-Islamic Arabia. The case for matriarchy was eloquently stated by William Robertson Smith, *Kinship and Marriage in Early Arabia*; more recent discussions of the subject are provided by Robert F. Spencer, "The Arabian Matriarchate: An Old Controversy," and Watt, *Muhammad at Medina*, pp. 373-388. There is some evidence for the survival of matriliny (if not of matriarchy) into the early seventh century (see, for example, I.H. 953 involving the South Arabian tribe of Kinda), but in general the practice seems to have pretty well died out by Muḥammad's time.

24. Anthropologists have recently come to question the usefulness of the term "tribe"; see for example Morton H. Fried, "On the Concepts of 'Tribe' and 'Tribal Society.' " The difficulty with the term seems to arise from the apparent need to find a clear structural definition of the "tribe" that is both broad enough to include all those groups that are commonly called "tribes" the world over and narrow enough to provide some meaningful criteria to distinguish such "tribes" from other patterns of social organization. The fabulous diversity of these thousands of "tribal" societies, however, makes the search for an all-embracing structural definition a courageous undertaking at best. The matter is further complicated by attempts to fit the "tribe" into rigid evolutionary schemes in which it becomes a distinct stage in the development of human society, falling between simpler "bands" and more complex "chiefdoms," "states," or whatever the particular evolutionary theory decrees. Thus the term "tribe" is expected to embrace not only the many, diverse "tribal" societies themselves; it has also to

conform to the needs of evolutionary theory, that is, it must display greater complexity than that of "bands," but must lack those complexities that distinguish "chiefdoms," "states," and so forth. Certain theorists of social evolution have indeed developed concise and consistent definitions of the "tribe" that fit into the evolutionary scheme; see, for example, the appealing formulation by Marshall D. Sahlins, *Tribesmen*. But these "theoretical" definitions of the "tribe" increasingly lose breadth as they gain precision and consistency, so that a truly satisfactory definition from the standpoint of evolutionary theory excludes many of those groups that are commonly called "tribes"; yet it is precisely this narrowness of definition that makes the theory questionable, since the theoretical scheme claims, not specific, but general validity.

The definition proposed here is not intended to be a general definition of something called the "tribe"; it is rather intended to be a description of the main characteristics of the "Arabian tribe." That is, by restricting our attention to Arabia and the Fertile Crescent region, we find a fairly uniform set of social practices and social structures, the general outlines of which we set forth in the definition. Within the limits imposed, then, the term "tribe" as defined above remains useful as a descriptive symbol.

The difficulty that ensues when we try to extend the definition suggested here beyond the limits of our inquiry, even to a region as seemingly similar in culture and history as North Africa, can be seen by comparing Arabian conditions with those described by Jacques Berque, "Qu'est-ce qu'une 'tribu' nord africaine?"

25. The case of the man who, having committed a crime among his own tribe, was forced to flee and live in solitude, is exemplified by the story of al-Halqām b. al-Ḥārith al-Azdī: cf. Kufi, I/107. The account is legendary, but presented as if it were historical fact, and hence presumably was a realistic enough situation to seem plausible.

26. The casual manner in which tribesmen will kill those isolated individuals who are seen as unprotected by a tribe is noted by Wilfred Thesiger, "The Badu of Southern Arabia"; for an ancient example of how the realization that an individual was under the protection of a specific tribal group could dramatically and suddenly change the way he was treated in public, see I.H. 245-246 (case of Abū Bakr and Ibn al-Dughunna); I.H. 244-245; I.H. 301-302.

The South Arabian tribe was not an exact replica of the North Arabian; among other things, it was often named, not after an eponymous ancestor, but rather after the locality in which the tribe lived: cf. Werner Caskel, "Der arabische Stamm vor dem Islam und seine gesellschaftliche und juristische Organisation," pp. 139ff. Nevertheless, it seems likely that the basic definition of the tribe proposed here still applies to the South Arabian units. Nikolaus Rhodokanakis attempted to show that the "subject" tribes in the ancient South Arabian caste system were mainly administrative units imposed by the state for facilitating taxation and corvée and had absolutely no basis in real or fictive blood relationship. This point he developed in his article "Die Bodenwirtschaft im alten Südarabien," and pressed very hard in his chapter in Nielsen's *Handbuch*, esp. p. 119; it was subsequently adopted by Maria Höfner in "Die Kultur des vorislamischen Südarabien." There is, however, no reason why the South Arabian tribes could not have been both kinship-based identification groups providing a certain solidarity in local disputes and administrative units for the purposes of the state; the two are not mutually exclusive categories. Indeed, under Muḥammad and the first caliphs the Islamic state treated each tribe as an administrative unit, working sometimes through the tribal chiefs, although it is quite clear in the case of the North Arabian tribes at least that these were groups that defined themselves in terms of kinship. Nor does the position of ancient South Arabian tribes as groups having a special labor function (". . . die Wirtschafts-, Arbeits-, und Steuergemeinschaft, die eben Stamm heisst") necessarily imply the absence of a rationalizing kinship system. A social order resembling the ancient South Arabian "caste system," with a ruling tribe lording it over subject tribes, appears to have survived until recent times in the Ḥaḍramawt; the subject tribes, however, although restricted by custom to the pursuit of a certain trade or kind of work, were nonetheless viewed as kinship groups: cf. Christiaan Snouck Hurgronje, "Sa'd ès-Suwênî, ein Seltsamer Walî in Ḥadhramôt," p. 226. Finally, we may note that the partitioning of a tribe by the state, which Rhodokanakis takes as proof that the tribes of South Arabia were not kinship units, in fact proves no such thing. The Islamic state similarly dispatched groups of tribesmen from one tribe to different localities, especially during the Islamic conquests, but there is no question about the kinship basis of the tribes involved. Indeed, the kinship basis of the Arabian tribe, with its deep inner divisions along lineages, facilitates, rather than hinders, such partitions.

27. Although tenting groups among nomads were commonly composed of related families, this was not always the case. Unrelated families might join one another for a time to form a tenting group, and in case of attack they defended one another as fiercely as if they were immediate kinsmen. Cf. Cole, *Nomads of the Nomads*, pp. 42, 63-64; see also the incident in Thesiger, *Arabian Sands*, p. 193.

28. The model for this type of organization, known to anthropologists as segmentary lineage, was first proposed in an attempt to describe the structure of certain African "tribes" but seems to apply very closely to the Arabian setting (both to nomadic and sedentary groups). For theoretical formulations of the model, see Marshall Sahlins, "Segmentary Lineage: An Organization of Predatory Expansion," remembering that Sahlins attempts to fit this construction into his evolutionary scheme; and Georges Balandier, *Political Anthropology*, pp. 68-70, on lineage rivalries. For evidence that our description reflects the structure of recent and ancient Arabian tribes, see the sections dealing with social structure in the works cited in notes 15, 20, and 21 above; Caskel, "Der arabische Stamm vor dem Islam"; and Carlo Alfonso Nallino, "Sulla costituzione delle tribù arabe prima dell'islamismo." Examples of rivalries between different lineages within a single tribe are fairly common in early Arabic texts; for example, that between 'Abd al-Dār and 'Abd Manāf, two lineages of the Meccan tribe of Quraysh, visible in I.H. 84-85, 203-204. Anthropologists debate the extent to which marriage practices among bedouin, in particular, affect lineage differentiation; cf. Robert F. Murphy and Leonard Kasdan, "The Structure of Parallel Cousin Marriage," and the riposte by Raphael Patai, "The Structure of Endogamous Unilineal Descent Groups."

29. The tribes of Asad and Tanūkh are mentioned in Ptolemy, *Geography* VI.

7, §22, as living in central Arabia in the second century A.D. Five centuries later the Tanūkh had migrated to the Euphrates and were widely scattered, no longer a single political entity. They were apparently succeeded in central Arabia by the Nizār—which by the early Islamic period was no longer a functioning tribal unit and was remembered in the genealogies as the distant "ancestors" of numerous North Arabian tribes: cf. Caskel, *Bedeutung der Beduinen*, p. 8.

30. Cf. Fred McGraw Donner, "The Bakr b. Wā'il Tribes and Politics in Northeastern Arabia on the Eve of Islam."

31. Among the better studies of the political content of Arabian genealogies is Bräunlich, "Beiträge zur Gesellschaftsordnung der arabischen Beduinenstämme"; see also Emrys Peters, "The Proliferation of Segments in the Lineage of the Bedouin of Cyrenaica (Libya)." Ian G. Cunnison, "History and Genealogies in a Conquest State," discusses the "telescoping" of genealogies, albeit within the context of a nonsegmentary society. Balandier, *Political Anthropology*, pp. 68-70, gives a discussion of genealogical adjustment, and Bal. *Ansab* I, 25 provides an example of a pre-Islamic Arabian tribe—in this case, the Thaqīf—changing its "ancestry" to fit political realities.

32. On economic symbiosis of nomadic and sedentary groups: Dussaud, *Pénétration des Arabes*, pp. 14ff.; Chelhod, *Le Droit*, pp. 356ff.; Doughty, *Travels*, 2, pp. 113ff. On the *khuwwa* tax: Chelhod, *Le Droit*, pp. 384ff.; Jaussen, *Coutumes des Arabes*, pp. 162ff.; Jaussen and Savignac, *Coutumes des Fuqarâ*, p. 8; all stress that protection is provided by the stronger tribe in exchange for the payment of *khuwwa*.

33. For an example of a tribe that includes both nomadic and sedentary members, see the description of the population of al-Ḥīra, below, Chapter IV, Section 4; cf. the description of the 'Aqaydāt tribe in Charles, *Tribus moutonnières*, pp. 95ff.

34. A classic study of the slow process by which formerly nomadic families are absorbed into a village and ultimately into settled society as a whole is Albert de Boucheman's *Sukhné. Une petite cité caravanière*. On the process of sedentarization, see further: Sabatino Moscati, *The Semites in Ancient History. An inquiry into the settlement of the Beduin and their political establishment*, for an historical overview; Robert A. Fernea, *Shaykh and Effendi. Changing Patterns of Authority among the El Shabana of Southern Iraq*, stressing the changes in social structure that accompany sedentarization; Nafi N. al-Kasab, *Die Nomadenansiedlung in der Irakischen Jezira*; Stein, *Die Šammar-Ǧerba*; Mohamed Awad, "Settlement of Nomadic and Semi-Nomadic Tribal Groups in the Middle East"; Henri Charles, *La Sedentarisation entre Euphrate et Balik. Note d'ethno-sociologie*.

35. On nomadic and sedentary groups united by a common cult, the cult of the Ka'ba in Mecca can stand as a prime example; the Christianized bedouin who flocked to the sanctuaries of St. Sergius in Syria, or those who came to hear St. Simeon Stylite, provide material for another.

36. Meir J. Kister, "Mecca and Tamīm (Aspects of their Relations)."

37. The terms are those of Robert Bertram Serjeant, "Ḥaram and Ḥawṭah, the Sacred Enclave in Arabia," in Abdurrahman Badawi (ed.), *Mélanges Taha Hussain*, pp. 41-58.

38. The full military capacity of camel-herding nomads only developed in about the first century A.D. as a result of the adoption of a more secure type of riding saddle: cf. Walter Dostal, "The Evolution of Bedouin Life," in F. Gabrieli (ed.), *L'Antica Società Beduina*, pp. 11-34, and his "Zur Frage der Entwicklung des Beduinentums."

39. The towns of al-Ṭā'if and Jurash in the Ḥijāz and 'Asīr were apparently walled in Muḥammad's day: I.H. 869, 954 (Jurash); I.H. 869, 872 (al-Ṭā'if).

40. On the eve of Islam, the Jewish clans of Yathrib (Medina) were, for example, known for their fighting ability; and one of them, the B. Qaynuqā', was reportedly able to field on one occasion seven hundred men, three hundred of them wearing mail: I.H. 545-546.

41. E.g., I.H. 873: cutting palms and vineyards during the siege of al-Ṭā'if. For a modern example, see Alois Musil, *The Middle Euphrates*, p. 288.

42. Thus the chief of the nomadic B. Tamīm, Mālik b. Nuwayra, is said to have owned gardens on the eve of Islam: Kufi I/21. Montagne, "Notes," emphasizes that nomadic groups are the source of military power, although polities of any size are usually centered on a town. See also Chelhod, *Le Droit*, pp. 345-346; Henry L. Rosenfeld, "The Social Composition of the Military in the Process of State Formation in the Arabian Desert"; and modifications to the latter suggested by Talal Asad, "The Beduin as a Military Force: Notes on Some Aspects of Power Relations between Nomads and Sedentaries in Historical Perspective."

43. On these see, for example, Dussaud, *Pénétration des Arabes*, infra; Franz Altheim and Ruth Stiehl, "Odainat und Palmyra," in their *Die Araber in der alten Welt*, 2, pp. 251-273; their "Die Araber an der Oströmisch-Persischen Grenze im 4. Jahrhundert," in *Die Araber*, 2, pp. 312-332; Judah B. Segal, *Edessa and Harran*; Ernst Herzfeld, "Hatra"; Javier Teixidor, "Notes hatréennes"; and Javier Teixidor, "The Kingdom of Adiabene and Hatra."

44. We should not, however, think of the warrior aristocracy as full-time specialists in military matters. They were nomadic pastoralists and, like other groups, spent most of their time herding.

45. On the absorption of client groups, see Bräunlich, "Beiträge," pp. 191ff.; Chelhod, *Le Droit*, pp. 220ff.; Siegmund Fraenkel, "Das Schutzrecht der Araber." There exist a number of terms for various kinds of protection or clientship relations, but it is often not clear whether a single practice is meant by several terms, or whether different practices are involved; e.g., "clientship," (*walā'*) and "short-term protection" (*jiwār*). These are not the same as *ḥilf*, "alliance," however, on which see below, p. 33.

46. Cf. the poem by the Tamīmī chief, al-Zibriqān b. Badr, in I.H. 935-936:

> "We are the noble ones, and no other clan is our equal;
> From our number kings [are raised], and among us temples erected.
>
> How many clans we have overpowered during [our] raiding!
> It is [only] a surfeit of might [such as ours] that finds imitators . . ."

47. These ideals of nobility are evident in the description of a chief whose tribesmen "used to call him al-Kāmil [i.e., "the Perfect"] because of his toughness, his poetry, his honor (*sharaf*) and his lineage (*nasab*)": I.H. 284; Guillaume's

translation, p. 196. A similar description is found in a poem by 'Abīd; a true chief heeds wise counsel, defends the tribe in word and by fighting, stands up for the tribe in contests of praise and boasting, strikes down the enemy in defense of the tribe, etc.: Charles Lyall (ed. and tr.), *The Dīwāns of 'Abīd ibn al-Abras, of Asad, and 'Āmir ibn al-Ṭufail, of 'Āmir ibn Ṣa'ṣa'a*, XXX, verses 10-14.

48. An ancient example may be provided by the B. Fazāra, a tribe of the Ḥijāz composed primarily of nomads. The poet 'Āmir b. Ṭufayl of the B. 'Āmir b. Ṣa'ṣa'a mocked them because they "pasture their camels in the very midst of their homeland," that is not venturing far from it for fear of the B. 'Āmir and other surrounding tribes hostile to the Fazāra, and notes that they "pay their tribute (*kharj*) without any friendliness": Lyall, *The Dīwāns*, IX, verses 1-2. We can deduce, then, that the B. Fazāra were weaker than the B. 'Āmir and paid tribute to them. Yet, as the events of Muḥammad's career show, the B. Fazāra were a force to be respected, particularly by the residents of Medina: cf. I.H. 669-670 (Fazāra as part of coalition assembled by Quraysh that attacked Medina in A.H. 5/A.D. 627); I.H. 719ff., Waq. 537ff. (chieftain of Fazāra raids Muḥammad's flocks).

49. This caste-like society among recent bedouin tribes is noted by Cole, *Nomads of the Nomads*, pp. 71-72; Harold R. P. Dickson, *The Arab of the Desert*, p. 141; Musil, *The Manners and Customs of the Rwala Bedouins*, pp. 136-137. The strict customs regarding marriage—designed to preserve the tribe's honor—did not prevent tribesmen from indulging regularly in casual sexual relations with women; as long as the paternity of the child remained unknown so that the "half-breed" could not claim membership in the father's tribe, such sexual relations were permissible, even with women of the so-called "pariah" tribes, among some of which prostitution may have been an important source of income for many women: see Henry Field and John Bagot Glubb, *Yezidis, Sulubba and Other Tribes of Iraq and Adjacent Regions*, p. 14. Thesiger, *Arabian Sands*, p. 194, notes frequent cases of sexual relations out of wedlock, bastard children (not despised) living with their mothers, and even a whole tribal section composed of bastards. The concern with *kafā'a* among these groups, then, was not at all related to sexual mores, but rather derived from a desire to prevent the purity of the tribe's honor from being sullied by demonstrable imputations that one of the descendants of the tribe was also descended from some lesser group. For an ancient example of *kafā'a*, see *TMD* (Zah.) III, fol. 19a, discussing the marriage of the chief al-Ash'ath b. Qays of Kinda: "*wa-l-'ashrāfu lā yanālūna an yakūna akhwālu-hum ashrafa min a'māmi-him*," "the nobles do not permit their maternal relatives to be more noble than their paternal," a roundabout way of saying that they do not give their womenfolk in marriage to men of lesser station.

50. Cf. Bräunlich, "Beiträge," pp. 185-189.

51. I.H. 947.

52. On *ḥilf*, see Bräunlich, "Beiträge," p. 204; Chelhod, *Le Droit*, p. 381ff.; Ignaz Goldziher, *Muslim Studies*, 1, pp. 64-70; Nallino, "Sulla costituzione delle tribù arabe," pp. 76ff.

53. The best description of the *ḥaram* and its functions is provided by Serjeant, "Ḥaram and Ḥawṭah, the Sacred Enclave in Arabia." See also his "Two Tribal Law Cases (Documents) (Wāḥidī Sultanate, South-West Arabia)." For a descrip-

tion of a modern *ḥaram* functioning in the Maghreb, see W. Fogg, "A Moroccan Tribal Shrine and its Relation to a Near-by Tribal Market." See also Lammens, *Le Berceau de L'Islam*, pp. 60ff., on *ḥaram* and *ḥimā* (a pasturing reserve); Wellhausen, *Reste Arabischen Heidentums*, esp. pp. 84ff., on Mecca's *ḥaram*.

54. Cf. I.H. 640, where a captive siezed by the Meccans in battle and not subsequently ransomed by his tribesmen is taken outside the *ḥaram* to be executed. The *ḥaram* regulations might even include "sacred months," during which those tribesmen who participated in the cult were to desist from fighting one another even outside the *ḥaram*'s borders. Such a regime had, at least, arisen in pre-Islamic Mecca; but whether such arrangements were typical of all *ḥarams* or reflect the unusual size and influence of Mecca's *ḥaram* is difficult to say. See I.H. 30, 66, 424-425; Azraqi I, 115ff.

55. In a sense, of course, even the religious aristocracy ultimately relied for its power on warrior tribesmen allied to it, as the latter provided the means by which the *manṣib* could enforce his rule.

56. See, for example, the list in I.H. 50-56, or Ibn al-Kalbi, *Kitāb al-aṣnām*, infra. Cf. also Wellhausen, *Reste Arabischen Heidentums*, infra; Henri Lammens, "Les sanctuaires préislamites dans l'Arabie occidentale"; Toufic Fahd, *Le Panthéon de l'Arabie centrale à la veille de l'Hégire.*

57. On the role of law in pre-Islamic Arabian society, see the discussion in Section 4 below.

58. For a definition of the state, see below at note 59.

59. For our purposes the state can be defined as any *sovereign* political organization that (1) claims the exclusive right to adjudicate certain classes of disputes among its members in accordance with an established set of principles or laws; that (2) employs full-time military and administrative specialists to enforce its regulations and judgments; and that (3) in various ways binds subordinate individuals and groups to one another in associations that cut across ties of kinship. This definition is arbitrary, as all definitions of the state must be, and makes no claim to universal validity—that is, there may be other kinds of state. But in the Arabian context it seems to me that the moment when these three critical functions are beginning to be performed is the point at which we begin to sense the presence of a political structure that displays the centralized approach to order and social control that we normally associate with our common-sense notion of the "state." Whether the state, so defined, marks an advance to a "higher" level of social evolution, as the evolutionary theorists would view it, is not a question of particular concern to us here, although it is reasonable to assert that such a state would show a greater centralization of power than is attested in the tribal, prestate society of Arabia as we have so far described it. For some theoretical discussions on the "state" and how it may be defined, see Morton Fried, *The Evolution of Political Society*, infra, and Balandier, *Political Anthropology*, pp. 31ff.

60. On the use of this term in ancient South Arabia see Hermann von Wissmann, *Zur Archäologie und Antiken Geographie von Südarabien. Ḥaḍramaut, Qatabān und das 'Aden-Gebiet in der Antike*, p. 79 and notes.

61. On the monopolization of agricultural produce by the state in South Arabia, see Maria Höfner, "Die Kultur des vorislamischen Südarabien," pp. 22-23.

62. This part of our discussion must be recognized as very tentative because

the meaning of the terms *kabīr* and *qsd* is still not very clear, the strict systematizations of some scholars notwithstanding. I am indebted to Professor Jamme for awakening me to the great uncertainties surrounding this material.

63. Jacques Ryckmans, *L'Institution monarchique en Arabie méridionale avant l'Islam* (*Ma'īn et Saba*), p. 330.

64. The *qayls* were, of course, themselves all nobles, i.e., kinsmen from the ruling tribe.

65. See Joseph Halevy, "Les Arabes dans les Inscriptions Sabéenes"; Maria Höfner, "Die Beduinen in den vorislamischen arabischen Inschriften."

66. I.H. 80, 83, describes the grip in which Quṣayy held the tribe of Quraysh. It was firm and pervasive, including even a kind of tax, the *rifāda*, but suggests again (as above, Section 3 and note 51) that it was decidedly personal, not administrative, in character.

67. It is not clear whether in ancient Arabia the full "segmentary" structure came into play in such cases as a single homicide; that is, whether a murder involving a perpetrator from one major lineage A and a victim from another major lineage B automatically involved everyone in both lineages. It may have been so; but in more recent times the bedouin limit the retaliatory process to a group called the *khamsa* consisting of the victim's or perpetrator's children and grandchildren, his parents and grandparents, and the children and grandchildren of his parents and grandparents: that is, a kin group five generations deep with the victim or perpetrator at the center. Only the *khamsa* of the perpetrator is subject to retaliation, and only the *khamsa* of the victim is honor-bound to seek vengeance for his death; the other members of the respective tribes or lineages are unaffected by the affair. For an example of the *khamsa* system, see Musil, *The Manners and Customs of the Rwala Bedouins*; on the situation in ancient Arabia, see Caskel, "Der arabische Stamm," pp. 146-147, and Werner Reinert, *Das Recht in der altarabischen Poesie*, who suggest that the group called *rahṭ* in pre-Islamic times was the equivalent of the *khamsa* or vengeance group among the modern tribesmen.

68. The English term "honor" is used here solely in its meaning of prestige or reputation, not in the sense of integrity or ethically proper conduct. An example of this concern for honor rather than justice in pre-Islamic Arabia is found in I.H. 273: al-Walīd b. al-Mughīra, on his deathbed, charges his three sons with avenging his blood: "My blood lies on the Khuzā'a: don't let it remain uncompensated. I know they are innocent of it, but I fear that you may be ill spoken of because of it when I am dead." (Guillaume's translation, pp. 187-188.) The concept of honor and its overriding importance in Arabian tribal life is discussed by Édouard Farès, *L'Honneur chez les Arabes avant l'Islam. Étude de sociologie*, a work that should be better known. He argues (pp. 206ff.) that the elements of honor themselves constituted a system of laws among the Arabs—that is, a system of imposed constraints accompanied by sanctions. His opinion can be accepted without contradicting our assertion that there was no system of law in pre-Islamic North Arabia, however, because each view relies on a somewhat different definition of law, his being somewhat broader than ours and including under "law" all those traditional practices that we would view as

"custom." Our understanding of law, on the other hand, demands not only a system of constraints and sanctions, but also that the imposed constraints reflect some general principle of justice *independent of the differences in actual social power exercised by specific groups*. That is, there is a difference between "Thou shalt not kill" (a law) and "Thou shalt not kill anyone whose tribal backing is more powerful than yours" (an imposed constraint accompanied by a sanction—the threat of retaliation). In fact, however, the application of sanctions in Arabian society (and hence the effectiveness or even the existence of constraints) did not reflect the imposition of an abstract principle; retaliation was left to the aggrieved individual and his tribal backing to apply—if they could. The constraints imposed were thus directly reflective of an individual's or tribe's actual strength and ability to retaliate, and hence not a system of laws according to our understanding of the term.

Reinert, *Das Recht*, pp. 3-5, also argues that there existed something akin to an abstract concept of justice, but admits that the critical term for justice (*ḥaqq*) or just action almost always seems to have the meaning of "duty" or "claim" (to blood).

The case illustrated in Meir M. Bravmann, "The Community's Participation in the Punishment of Crime in Early Arab Society," in his *The Spiritual Background of Early Islam*, pp. 315-334, seems to me to be exceptional.

69. For the workings of the retaliatory system (*tha'r*), see Chelhod, *Le Droit*, pp. 265ff.; Henri Lammens, "Le Caractère religieux du ṯâr ou vendetta chez les Arabes préislamites," in *L'Arabie occidentale avant l'Hégire*, pp. 181-236; Walter M. Patton, "Blood-revenge in Arabia and Israel"; Michael J. L. Hardy, *Blood Feuds and the Payment of Blood Money in the Middle East*. The whole emphasis of the system is clearly not to punish the offender or to bring him to "justice" but to find a counter-victim of equal stature to the murdered man and, by killing him, to restore to the tribe as much honor as was taken away by the original murder. Multiple retaliations reflect the absence of any concept of reciprocity or balance in such calculations, the assumption being that several men of another tribe are needed to equal one of the aggrieved tribe—an opinion that clearly would not have found acceptance beyond the limits of one's own tribe. Cf. 'Amir b. al-Ṭufayl in Lyall (ed. and tr.), *The Dīwāns*, II, verse 22: "We slew of them a hundred in requital for an old man. . . ."; also Ṭufayl al-Ghanawī in Fritz Krenkow (ed. and tr.), *The Poems of Ṭufail ibn 'Auf al-Ghanawī and aṭ-Ṭirimmāḥ ibn Ḥakīm aṭ-Ṭā'yī*, XIV, verse 9. For the survival of double and triple vengeance in South Arabia until recent times, see Ettore Rossi, "Il diritto consuetudinario delle tribù Arabe del Yemen," under the practices called *taghūt*.

70. A need felt especially by individuals who had ties to both the offender and the victim, not infrequent in cases of crimes between members of the same tribe, lineage, or even extended family. On the kinds of concerns that led people in pre-Islamic Arabia to arbitrate disputes, see I.H. 275.

71. The importance of the idea of the restitution of tribal strength in blood-vengeance and blood-money customs is evident from the institution called "*ṣanā'a*" described in Austin Kennett, *Bedouin Justice. Laws and Customs among the Egyptian Bedouin*, p. 54. The fact that different tribes demanded—and re-

ceived—different amounts of blood-money according to their power and stature in cases of adjudication reveals that blood-money customs were not based on a principle of the intrinsic value of a human life or some such abstract principle; these inequities correspond to multiple retaliation in the blood-vengeance system, of which the blood-money system is essentially an extension. Cf. Kennett, infra, and Patton, "Blood-revenge," p. 715-716, for recent examples. For an ancient example, see I.H. 803, where we learn that a prominent clan of the B. Khuzā'a received double blood-money in arbitrated settlements. Indeed, even arbitration did not ensure that the party in whose favor judgment was made would not have to secure his due by force: cf. I.H. 284. On blood-money and adjudication in general, see also Chelhod, *Le Droit*, pp. 307ff.

72. Murād was later linked by Arab genealogists to the Madhḥij tribe; e.g., I.K./Caskel I, 61ff. and tables 258 and 271.

73. On Kinda, see Gunnar Olinder, *The Kings of Kinda of the Family of Ākil al-Murār*; Hermann von Wissmann, "Ḥimyar, Ancient History," pp. 486-489.

74. That is, not before their defeat and migration to South Arabia.

75. Irfan Kawar, "The Last Days of Salīḥ." For evidence of Roman and Byzantine efforts to utilize nomadic allies, see René Louis Victor Cagnat, *Inscriptiones Graecae ad Res Romanas Pertinentes* 3, no. 1136, 1247 ("*stratēgos nomadōn*").

76. The classic study of the Ghassānids is still Theodor Nöldeke, "Die Ghassânischen Fürsten aus dem Hause Gafna's," to which many important insights have been added by Irfan Kawar (Irfan Shahid) in his articles, "The Arabs in the Peace Treaty of A.D. 561"; "Arethas, Son of Jabalah"; "Ghassān and Byzantium: A New terminus a quo"; "Procopius on the Ghassānids"; and "The Last Days of Salīḥ." See also Ismā'īl R. Khālidī, "The Arab Kingdom of Ghassān: its origins, rise, and fall," and Roger Paret, "Note sur un passage de Malalas concernant les phylarques arabes."

77. On these, see Nöldeke, "Die Ghassânischen Fürsten," p. 18, and Kawar, "Procopius" (on their use as tribal allies); also Nöldeke, p. 11, and Kawar, "Arethas" (on their use in controlling rebellion). On the latter, see further Zachariah of Mitylene, *The Syriac Chronicle known as that of Zachariah of Mitylene*, p. 232.

78. Nöldeke, "Die Ghassânischen Fürsten," p. 47. For a Ghassānid *phylarch* over Palaestina Tertia, see Kawar, "Procopius," p. 86; over Palaestina Secunda, Provincia Arabia, and the Syrian *limes*, see Kawar, "Arethas."

79. Nöldeke collects the references to these, "Die Ghassânischen Fürsten," pp. 37-39. For the raid on al-Ḥīra, see Kawar, "Arethas" and his "Ghassān and Byzantium."

80. Nöldeke, "Die Ghassânischen Fürsten," p. 29.

81. For example, two brothers ruling in the northern Ḥijāz and elsewhere (as appanages?): Khālidī, "The Arab Kingdom of Ghassān"; Kawar, "Procopius" and "Arethas." The Byzantines also had other individuals of Arabian tribal origin serving as governors in appropriate districts besides the Ghassānids: e.g., a man of Judhām serving as governor (*'āmil*) of the Balqā' region (near 'Ammān), I.S. I/2, 31.

82. On al-Yamāma and its "king," Hawdha b. ʿAlī, see Elias S. Shoufani, *Al-Riddah and the Muslim Conquest of Arabia*, p. 28. On ʿUmān, see John Craven Wilkinson, "The Julandā of Oman."

83. The standard study of the Lakhmids is Gustav Rothstein, *Die Dynastie der Lahmiden in al-Ḥîra. Ein Versuch zur arabisch-persischen Geschichte zur Zeit der Sasaniden,* to be updated by reference to Meir J. Kister, "Al-Ḥīra. Some notes on its relations with Arabia." These form the basis of much of the following analysis.

84. Cf. Erich Bräunlich, *Bisṭām ibn Qais. Ein vorislamischer Beduinenfürst und Held*, first chapter, and Donner, "The Bakr b. Wā'il Tribes."

85. On the composition of the population of towns in this region, see Chapter IV, Section 4 below.

86. On tribal migration patterns in this region in recent times, see Carl Raswan, "Tribal Areas and Migration Lines of the North-Arabian Bedouins."

87. The territory of the latter two tribes extended well into upper Mesopotamia as well.

88. Cf. Ibn al-Faqih al-Hamadhānī, *Mukhtaṣar kitāb al-buldān*, p. 18; Tab. i/1933; also commentaries to Q. XXVIII: 57-59.

89. On weapons provided by the Sasanians or Lakhmids to their allies among the desert tribes, see accounts of the Dhū Qār episode, sources for which are cited in Donner, "The Bakr b. Wā'il Tribes."

90. E.g. Theophanes, *Chronographia*, p. 300 under A.M. 6104. Cf. Derwas Chitty, *The Desert a City*, pp. 156-157.

CHAPTER II

1. It appears that Mecca's sister city, al-Ṭā'if, was also beginning to evolve in this direction—perhaps because of its involvement in Mecca's commerce; see Henri Lammens, *La Cité arabe de Ṭāif à la veille de l'Hégire.* On Mecca's trade, see Henri Lammens, "La Meque à la veille de l'Hégire"; Henri Lammens, "La République marchande de la Mecque vers l'an 600 de notre ère"; Meir J. Kister, "Some Reports Concerning Mecca from Jāhiliyya to Islām," pp. 76ff.

2. The best treatments of Muḥammad's life are William Montgomery Watt's works, *Muhammad at Mecca, Muhammad at Medina,* and *Muhammad, Prophet and Statesman*; Maxime Rodinson, *Mohammed*; Muhammad Hamidullah, *Le Prophète de l'Islam*; Tor Andrae, *Mohammed, The Man and His Faith*; and Frants Buhl, *Das Leben Muhammeds*; note also the exhaustive compilation of sources by Leone Caetani, *Annali dell'Islam* of which the first volumes cover Muḥammad's career. The most detailed and careful synthesis on many points is that of Watt, whose work forms the starting point for all later efforts to elucidate Muḥammad's life, including the present study.

3. I.H. 203-204: Abū Jahl (of Makhzūm) opposes Muḥammad because of the rivalry between Makhzūm and ʿAbd Manāf, Muḥammad's lineage.

4. Robert Bertram Serjeant, "Ḥaram and Ḥawṭah, the Sacred Enclave in Arabia"; Robert Bertram Serjeant, "The Constitution of Medina."

5. The rise of a state concurrently with the development of the new religion of Islam is already suggested by Julius Wellhausen, *Reste Arabischen Heidentums*

(1897), p. 234: "With Islam, Arabian antiquity comes to an end. [The one] God triumphs over the multitude of lesser gods, the community in faith over the diversity of blood-groups, the unity of a theocratic state over the anarchy of tribes." The only attempt to examine the emergence of the state in any detail, however, is that of the anthropologist Eric Wolf, "The Social Organization of Mecca and the Origins of Islam." His essay, however, views the emergence of the Islamic state as the result of the political evolution of Meccan society instead of linking it to the appearance of Islam as an organizing ideology.

6. The concept of the *umma* underwent considerable evolution during Muḥammad's lifetime; cf. Rudi Paret, "Umma," *EI*(1); the discussions, in varying amounts of detail, in various biographies of Muḥammad; and the detailed study by Frederick Mathewson Denny, "*Ummah* in the Constitution of Medina."

7. E.g., Watt, *Medina*, pp. 238ff.; William Montgomery Watt, *Islamic Political Thought*, Edinburgh: University Press, 1968, pp. 9ff.

8. But see William Robertson Smith, *Lectures on the Religion of the Semites*, pp. 276-277 and p. 277, n. 1.

9. This development was linked to the rise of concepts of law and moral responsibility for one's actions; see below, Section 2.

10. The *ridda* wars (discussed below, section 5) show that at the time of Muḥammad's death there was still some resistance to the idea that the *umma* was a unified political entity; some of the rebels evidently felt that they could be Muslims without being part of the Medina-based *umma*, that is, they claimed to be able to establish new *ummas* of their own.

11. Q. III: 114 (Arberry's translation).

12. Q. VI: 68 (Arberry's translation).

13. See, for example, the case of two men of Thaqīf who upon embracing Islam sever all ties with their pagan kinsmen: I.H. 918.

14. Thus Abū Jahl, at the battle of Badr, reportedly exclaimed, "O God, destroy this morning him that more than any of us hath cut the ties of kinship and wrought that which is not approved": I.H. 445, Guillaume's translation p. 301.

15. Q. VII: 28 (Arberry's translation).

16. Q. XXX: 42-43 (Arberry's translation).

17. Q. XLII: 8 (Arberry's translation).

18. Q. XL: 13 (Arberry's translation).

19. Cf. Chapter I, Section 4.

20. Q. II: 174 (Arberry's translation).

21. Q. XVII: 35 (Arberry's translation).

22. Q. IV: 94-95 (Arberry's translation).

23. Watt, *Medina*, p. 267.

24. The difference becomes especially clear when we consider cases of accidental homicide. Under Islam the option of seeking vengeance against the manslaughterer is canceled; his tribe is simply responsible for paying some form of restitution to the dead person's kinsmen. The traditional approach would not have distinguished accidental from intentional homicide and therefore would have sought to deal with the manslaughterer just as it would have dealt with a murderer, that is, by seeking vengeance in the first instance.

25. Watt, *Medina*, p. 248. Note also the passage in I.S. VII/1, p. 3 (Waq—h—Ibrāhīm b. Muḥammad b. Shuraḥbīl al-ʻAbdarī < Muṣʻab b. Muḥammad b. Shuraḥbīl b. Ḥasana) in which Muḥammad is reported to have said, "The *ḥalīf* of a tribe is as one of them [*ḥalīf al-qawm min-hum*]." This may be a way of saying that the special status inherent in being a *ḥalīf* is canceled.

26. I.H. 342.

27. The revolutionary import of this shift in mentality can be fathomed by considering the many administrators sent out by Muḥammad to various tribes, a fuller discussion of which is found below in Section 3. In a number of cases these administrators were neither of the Quraysh, nor of the *anṣār* (either of which could have been seen, in accordance with pre-Islamic usage, as a new dominant tribe), nor of the tribe being administered. It is doubtful whether in pre-Islamic times tribesmen from one subject tribe, A, would have allowed members from another subject tribe B rather than those of the dominant tribe X to collect taxes in the name of the latter; an attempt to do so would have been viewed by tribe A as meddling by tribe B in affairs that were only of concern to A and X, or worse, as an indication that tribe A was subject not only to tribe X, but to tribe B as well. Muḥammad's appointment of administrators was possible only because the Muslims being administered had accepted, with Islam, the idea that Muḥammad's appointees had the same authority to regulate their lives as did Muḥammad himself, as long as the appointee was acting in accordance with the growing body of laws of the Islamic community. The ultimate impact of this notion can be appreciated by considering the case of an administrator such as al-Mughīra b. Shuʻba of the Thaqīf tribe, who after the Islamic conquest of Iraq was appointed governor over one of the garrison towns there—a post that put thousands of tribesmen from many different tribes under his direct command and administration.

28. I.H. 341-344. For examples of Muḥammad adjudicating disputes, see I.H. 777-778, 988.

29. Q. XLVIII: 10 (Arberry's translation).

30. This is not to suggest that no problems arose over the transfer of centralized authority upon Muḥammad's death; see below, Section 5.

31. Other political notions may well have been implicit in the teachings of early Islam, but the three selected for treatment here appear to me to have been the most important in preparing the way for the consolidation of the Islamic state and its expansion during the Islamic conquests. Another concept of some importance, especially during the conquests, was that of *jihād* or "holy battle"; clearly the knowledge that if one survived a battle he would receive booty, and that if he fell he would be rewarded with paradise, must have spurred faithful Muslims at least to greater efforts on the battlefield: cf. I.H. 445. The concept of fighting to the death for one's group was not essentially new to Arabia, however, for tribesmen had certainly fought and died for their tribes for many generations before the rise of Islam. What distinguished *jihād* from such active tribal solidarity and loyalty as tribesmen usually displayed was not, then, the idea of fighting for one's community, but rather the nature of the community for which one fought. *Jihād* certainly facilitated the expansion and, perhaps, even the cohesion of the Islamic community, but it is itself a product of the rise of

Islam, not a cause of it—a product, to be exact, of the impact of the new concept of *umma* on the old idea that one fought, even to the death, for one's community.

32. On Muḥammad's relations with the Jews of Medina, see Watt, *Medina*, pp. 192ff., and Arendt Jan Wensinck, *Muhammad and the Jews of Medina*. On his consolidation in Medina, see Watt, *Medina*, pp. 174ff., and Fred McGraw Donner, "Muḥammad's Political Consolidation in Western Arabia up to the Conquest of Mecca: A Reassessment."

33. Fred McGraw Donner, "Mecca's Food Supplies and Muḥammad's Boycott."

34. Cf. Elias S. Shoufani, *Al-Riddah and the Muslim Conquest of Arabia*, p. 27. We might wish to take the struggle for control of other settlements in the Ḥijāz as a fourth theme.

35. Donner, "Muḥammad's Political Consolidation."

36. I.H. 879.

37. I.S. I/2, 40.

38. I.H. 678.

39. I.H. 729. On the *aḥābīsh* see Muhammad Hamidullah, "Les 'Aḥābīsh' de la Mecque."

40. I.H. 763, 766, 771.

41. *Isaba*, s.n. "al-Ḍaḥḥāk b. Sufyān al-Kilābī." Muḥammad's marriage to Umm Ḥabība, daughter of the leader of Quraysh, Abū Sufyān, may also have had political overtones, although it took place before Abū Sufyān's conversion to Islam: Waq. 742. Cf. also the marriages described in I.H. 464-465; Tab. i/2134-2135; I.S. II/1, 64; and Tab. i/2141-2143, between Abū Bakr and a woman of the B. al-Ḥārith b. Khazraj. This is a subject that needs much more exploration.

42. E.g., the man from B. Kināna who wanted to use his share of booty from Tabūk to repay a favor: I.S. I/2, 48.

43. *TMD* (Zah.) XIII, fol. 254a: "*thumma qāla yā 'amra innī urīdu an ab'atha-ka 'alā jayshin fa-yughannina-ka llāhu wa yusallima-ka mā arghaba laka min al-māli raghbatan ṣāliḥatan. . . .*" Cf. variants in *TMD* (Zah.) XIII, fol. 246b, and Waq. 745.

44. Tab. i/2128.

45. On *ta'līf al-qulūb* see the discussion in Watt, *Medina*, pp. 348-353.

46. Yazīd b. Abī Sufyān reportedly received 100 camels and 40 *'ūqiyyas* (of silver): *TMD* (Zah.) XVIII, fol. 154b.

47. On *ta'līf al-qulūb* after Ḥunayn, see I.H. 880-881. Some of the money for "conciliation of hearts" appears to have come from the *ṣadaqa* tax; cf. Q.IX: 60, cited below pp. 70-71.

48. *Jawā'iz* to 'Abd al-Qays, I.S. I/2, 54; to Taghlib, I.S. I/2, 55; to Ḥanīfa, awards of 5 *'ūqiyyas* (of silver), I.S. I/2, 56; to Tamīm, awards of 12½ *'ūqiyyas*, I.S. I/2, 41; a cloak as award, I.S. I/2, 47; to al-Ruhāwiyūn of Madhḥij, awards of 12½ *'ūqiyyas*, I.S. I/2, 76.

49. I.H. 776, 777; Watt, *Medina*, pp. 124-125 on al-Ruhāwiyūn, compare I.S. I/2, 21-22 and 75-76; on the Ash'arīs, see *TMD* (Leningrad), fol. 221b.

50. I.H. 947.

51. I.S. I/2, 46, along with many other examples of this kind.

52. I.S. I/2, 24; cf. Watt, *Medina*, p. 111. This assumes that we accept Ibn

Sa'd's gloss of the critical word *si'āya* to mean *ṣadaqa*, "tax." It is possible that it may mean that Balī was put in charge of collecting taxes from the other tribes listed (interpreting *si'āya* to mean not "tax" but rather the verbal noun, "taxing" or "taxation").

53. I.S. I/2, 54.

54. As the Quraysh had tied their tribal allies to them by means of their profit-sharing arrangements called *īlāf.*

55. *TMD* (Zah.) IX, fol. 173a (—al-Zuhrī).

56. I.H. 895. 'Umar also contributed everything he owned: Waq. 991; *TMD* I, 414 (Waq.).

57. The same seems to have been true, on a more limited scale, for the Thaqīf. For a more detailed treatment of this subject, see below, Section 4.

58. *TMD* (Zah.) XIII, fol. 247b: "*fa-bāya'tu-hu 'alā l-'islāmi wa an yughfara lī mā taqaddama min dhanabī wa an ashraka fī l-'amri fa-fa'ala.*"

59. Watt, *Medina*, p. 84.

60. I.H. 680-684.

61. The B. 'Amīra b. Khufāf b. Imru' al-Qays b. Buhtha b. Sulaym. The political situation within Sulaym is even more difficult to determine than Watt, *Medina*, pp. 95-97 suggests, as can be appreciated by consulting I.D. 187-189, I.H.J. 261-264, and I.K./Caskel, tables 122-124. Another case of rivalries within a tribe providing the opportunity for Muḥammad to gain some influence is that of the Madhḥij: cf. Watt, *Medina*, pp. 119-120.

62. A similar process can be seen later in the Muslims' relations with the B. Bakr b. Wā'il: see below, Chapter IV, Section 4. More than the other themes of Muḥammad's career, his relations with many tribes still need detailed research; the material assembled by Watt, *Medina*, pp. 78-150, is a useful starting point but is far from exhaustive.

63. Cf. *Muhabbar* 317: the idol was located at al-'Ablā', four stages south of Mecca; its priests were of the B. Hilāl b. 'Āmir, a branch of Bajīla. A member of this branch, al-Ḥajjāj b. Khuwaylid, settled in Iraq and is said to have been among the *ashrāf* of al-Kūfa: Tab. i/2055, 2057. On relations of Bajīla and Khath'am, see I.K./Caskel II/45-46.

64. I.S. I/2, 78; I.H.J. 388. Neither I.H. nor Waq. appear to know of this episode. Cf. I.S. VI, 13; Watt, *Medina*, p. 121.

65. E.g., murder for political purposes: I.H. 548 (murder of Ka'b b. al-Ashraf); I.H. 714 (the case of Sallām b. Abī l-Ḥuqayq in Khaybar). Note, however, an account of Muḥammad's (unsuccessful) attempt to restrain his followers from killing an old man who had insulted him: I.H. 560.

66. There were, of course, some important differences between the methods used by Muḥammad to extend his influence and those that had been used by the Quraysh—notably, Muḥammad's use of force.

67. Q. IX: 34-35 (Arberry's translation).

68. Q. IX: 102-104 (Arberry's translation).

69. On taxes imposed on non-Muslims, see below, Section 4.

70. Q. LVIII: 12 (Arberry's translation).

71. Q. IX: 91 (Arberry's translation).

72. Q. IX: 34 (Arberry's translation).

73. Q. IX: 60 (Arberry's translation).

74. What is known is summarized by Watt, *Medina*, pp. 250ff., 368-372.

75. I.H. 777, 779; Waq. 690-691. An assessor was appointed to collect the annual share of the date crop due Medina.

76. See, for example, the case of B. Ṭayyi': *TMD* (Zah.) XI, fol. 238a (Sayf < Zābida b. 'Imrān al-Ṭā'ī < men of Ṭayyi').

77. Watt, *Medina*, p. 237.

78. Watt, *Medina*, p. 144.

79. Waq. 991.

80. Shoufani, *Al-Riddah*, pp. 44ff. Shoufani dates the dispatch of tax collectors to A.H. 10, but the date of early A.H. 11 is given in *TMD* (Zah.) XI, fol. 238b (I.S.—h—Waq.). Cf. Tab. i/1750 (I.I. < 'Abdullāh b. Abī Bakr).

81. See the collection of these treaties in I.S. I/2, 19 ff.

82. I.H. 955 (Guillaume's translation, p. 642).

83. Cf. also the *ḥimā* established at al-Muẓallala: I.S. I/2, 22. Other special pastures of this sort were established by 'Uthmān at al-Naqī', Rabadha, and Sharāf: Bal. *Ansab* V,38 (Waq.—Ma'mar—al-Zuhrī). Note also Waq. 577: "The only *ḥimās* are those of God and His Apostle (*lā ḥimā illā li-llāh wa li-rasūli-hi*)."

84. Bal. *Fut.* 65; Cf. text in I.S. I/2, 35-36.

85. I.S. I/2, 22, lines 6ff.

86. Watt provides a convenient list in *Medina*, pp. 366-368.

87. Cf. Chapter I, Section 4. The Lakhmids of al-Ḥīra, as we have seen, brought chiefs or families from nomadic groups to their city as hostages to ensure the good behavior of the rest of the tribe.

88. These "secular" alliances of the early period appear to give way to stricter Islamic control towards the end of Muḥammad's career.

89. I.H. 916-917; Waq. 966.

90. Compare the remark of 'Adī b. Ḥātim, cited above p. 33, for an idea of how much things had changed.

91. See below, Section 4.

92. On the duties of such agents see Watt, *Medina*, pp. 235-238. An example of agents raising taxes and troops (in this case for the campaign to Tabūk): Waq. 990-991.

93. E.g., Ubayy b. Ka'b sent to the B. Ghāmid with its delegation to teach them the Qur'ān: I.S. I/2, 77.

94. E.g., a delegation of two hundred men of al-Nakha' (part of Madhḥij) came to Muḥammad in A.H. 11 after having sworn allegiance to his governor in the Yemen, Mu'ādh b. Jabal: I.S. I/2, 77.

95. The detailed legal regulations of Islamic *fiqh* only developed, of course, much later.

96. I.S. I/2, 18 (< al-Zuhrī and others): "*fa-'ajāba ilā l-islāmi huwa wa akhū-hu jamī'an wa ṣaddaqa bi-l-nabī (ṣl'm) wa khallayā baynī wa bayna l-ṣadaqati wa bayna l-ḥukmi fī mā bayna-hum. . . .*"

97. I.S. I/2, 20. Abū 'Ubayda ordered that he be slapped in return, much to the disappointment of his captors, who hoped he would be killed or, at least,

that the offending hand would be cut off. The account may well be a later invention designed to emphasize the egalitarian character of Islam, or to explain why the proud Ghassānid chieftain ultimately turned coat and fled to the Byzantines. We cannot, however, simply assume the account to be a fabrication merely because it proved useful to later polemic; indeed, it may be a true account that survived precisely because of its very usefulness, which made it worth preserving. Furthermore, even if it could be proven to be a fabrication, the account retains a certain usefulness as evidence, since it suggests what a somewhat later generation thought was a likely scenario for the earlier period. Their understanding of prevailing conditions in the early period was admittedly not perfect, but it was probably much more perfect than our own.

98. Cf. Shoufani, *Al-Riddah*, pp. 10ff., for a summary of diverse opinions on this question.

99. Watt, *Medina*, p. 238.

100. I.H. 777, 779; *Amwal* 65.

101. I.S. I/2, 21.

102. I.S. I/2, 35-36; Bal. *Fut.* 64-65. *Amwal* 39 simply states that "the people of Najrān were the first to pay tribute (*jizya*)."

103. I.H. 965.

104. There was, of course, considerable rivalry between the *muhājirūn* and the *anṣār* themselves for primacy in the Prophet's affections—a rivalry that could at times work to the community's advantage as the two groups vied with each other in devotion, but one that could also lead to potentially dangerous tensions: cf. the incident at al-Muraysī' (I.H. 725ff.)

105. The exception to this pattern may be found in those individuals from tribes outside Medina who joined Muḥammad in the city and broke all ties with their original tribes—men such as al-Mughīra b. Shu'ba of Thaqīf, who left his native al-Ṭā'if (to escape vengeance for homicide) and became one of the Prophet's trustiest henchmen. In such cases, however, the converts actually settled in Medina and became for practical purposes members of the *anṣār* or *muhājirūn*; indeed, as we shall see, the term "*muhājirūn*" (settlers), was sometimes applied to them.

106. Watt, *Medina*, p. 104.

107. See below, pp. 79ff.

108. The relations of the Yemeni tribes with Muḥammad and the first successors represents a sizable field where detailed research is badly needed.

109. I.H. 965; Bal. *Fut.* 87.

110. I.S. I/2, 38: "*fa-ja'ala la-hum rasūlu llāhi (ṣl'm) al-hijrata fī dāri-him wa-qāla antum muhājirūna ḥaythu kuntum fa-rji'ū ilā amwāli-kum fa-raja'ū ilā bilādi-him.*"

111. I.S. I/2, 25.

112. Waq. 757 (h—Ibn Abī Sabra < Isḥāq b. 'Abdullāh b. Abī Ṭalḥa < Rāfi' b. Isḥāq < Zayd b. Arqam). Note that the use of the term *a'rāb* in this passage is similar to that found in the South Arabian inscriptions; cf. above, Chapter I, Section 4. On *bay'a 'arabiyya* and *bay'at hijra*, see Watt, *Medina*, pp. 85-86.

113. I.S. I/2, 41 (ak—I.K.—h—Abū Sha'b 'Ikrima b. Arbad al-'Absī and a number of B. 'Abs). Additional references to demonstrate that the term *muhājir* meant "settler" and was not simply an honorific status equivalent to one of the

Quraysh Emigrants: Waq. 1014; *TMD* (Zah.) V, fol. 265b (Abū Tāmir al-Mukhliṣ—ak—Aḥmad b. Sulaymān—h—al-Zubayr b. Bakkār), where *muhājirūn* (Quraysh Emigrants) is distinguished from *muhājirat al-'arab* (settlers of nomadic origin): *wa shahada [Khālidun] fatḥa Makkata wa dakhala fī muhājirati l-'arab fī muqaddimati rasūli l-lāhi (ṣl'm) Makkata wa dakhala l-Zubayru bnu l-'Awwāmi fī muqaddimati rasūli l-lāhi (ṣl'm) mina l-muhājirīna wa l-anṣāri min 'a'lā Makkata.* Muḥammad b. Ismā'īl al-Bukhārī, *al-Jāmi' al-Ṣaḥīḥ*, 2, p. 203, under *bāb ayyām al-jāhiliyya* (h—Abū l-Nu'mān—h—Abū 'Awāna < Bayān Abū Bishr < Qays b. Abī Ḥāzim) makes it clear that the term *muhājirūn* could refer to more than the Quraysh Emigrants. In it a woman meets Abū Bakr and asks, "Who are you?" He replies, "A man of the *muhājirūn*." "Which *muhājirūn*?" she inquires, to which Abū Bakr responds, "From Quraysh."

114. *Qurrā'*. I have adopted the old interpretation of the meaning of this term here, although the revised one proposed by M. A. Shaban, *Islamic History, A.D. 600-750 (A.H. 132)*, p. 23—that *qurrā'* meant "settled people"—is peculiarly suggestive in this context. On the term "*qurrā'*," see also G.H.A. Juynboll, "The Qurrā' in Early Islamic History," who adds his support to Shaban's interpretation. Though plausible, evidence for the reinterpretation remains very limited.

115. The phrase used is *lā islāma li-man lā hijrata lahu.*

116. I.S. I/2, 42.

117. I.S. I/2, 51; the terms used for nomadic and sedentary peoples are "*al-wabar*" and "*al-madar*" respectively.

118. The clearest exposition of this contrast in attitudes is provided by Toshihiku Izutsu, *Ethico-Religious Concepts in the Qur'ān.*

119. I.H. 743.

120. I.H. 1016.

121. Cf. I.H. 1013.

122. As the preceding description tries to suggest, however, these two decisions were probably made simultaneously as one.

123. *TMD* (Zah.) IX, fol. 170bff.

124. *TMD* (Zah.) IX, fol. 173b-174a (< al-Zuhrī).

125. The other was, by this account, Abū 'Ubayda b. al-Jarrāḥ, later a commander in Syria: *TMD* (Zah.) VIII, fol. 367b-368a (—al-Zubayr b. Bakkār).

126. I.H. 6-7; cf. I.H. 161.

127. *Iqd* III/248. The assumption operative here was that a group of tribesmen would only know the details of their own tribal genealogy, not those of other tribes, and hence could not conceal their identity under examination, as their ignorance of any tribe but their own would become evident.

128. His role as political adviser to Muḥammad may perhaps also be seen in his behavior during the incident at al-Ḥudaybiya, when he and Muḥammad alone of the troop of Muslims are initially satisfied with the terms of the truce. Is it possible that the whole episode of al-Ḥudaybiya was planned by Abū Bakr and Muḥammad? Cf. Donner, "Muḥammad's Political Consolidation."

129. Commonly called by the derogatory diminutive, "Ṭulayḥa" or "paltry Ṭalḥa," in Islamic tradition.

130. "Musaylima"—again the diminutive—to Islamic tradition.

131. The leaders of these movements were 'Uyayna b. Ḥiṣn and Khārija b. Ḥiṣn b. Hudhayfa, respectively.

132. Led by Mālik b. Nuwayra.

133. This tripartite characterization of the various movements is derived from Shoufani, *Al-Riddah*, pp. 96ff. See infra for the details of these *ridda* movements.

134. E.g., Shoufani, *Al-Riddah*, pp. 96ff.

135. This has traditionally been the question, however, to which Western historians have devoted the greatest attention.

136. I.S. IV/1, 94; *Isaba*, s.n.; *Isti'ab*, s.n.

137. I.S. IV/2, 72.

138. I.K./Caskel, s.n.; *Isaba*, s.n.

139. For details of various campaigns, see Shoufani, *Al-Riddah*, pp. 107-149.

140. Shoufani, *Al-Riddah*, p. 144. The Muslims' contacts with tribes living on the fringes of Syria and Iraq will be discussed in the chapters below devoted to the conquest of these localities.

141. Bal. *Fut.* 93. He was later granted another tract of land at al-Rayya by 'Umar.

142. *TMD* (Zaḥ) III, fol. 21b (—Waq.) and fol. 19b (—Shujā' b. 'Alī b. Shujā').

143. Shoufani, *Al-Riddah*, pp. 114, 118-119, 121-122, 125, 130, 134-135, 138-139. On B. Sakūn, see Bal. *Fut.* 100ff.

144. Shoufani, *Al-Riddah*, p. 144.

145. An old technique; as we have seen, the rulers of al-Ḥīra had used a similar tactic to keep subject tribes under control.

146. Bal. *Fut.* 104; cf. Bal. *Fut.* 101 on al-Nujayr.

147. Ya'qubi II, 139. Cf. Tab. i/1848 (Sayf <'Aṭiyya <Abū Ayyūb <'Alī and < al-Ḍaḥḥāk < Ibn'Abbās).

148. For further discussion of these taxes, see Chapter VI, Section 2.

CHAPTER III

1. For an excellent description of Syria's geography, see Eugen Wirth, *Syrien. Eine Geographische Landeskunde* (restricted to the modern Republic of Syria, i.e., the northern part of greater or geographical Syria).

2. E.g., Abū Bakr promises the Muslims that Syria will provide them with plenty to eat: *TMD* I/455.

3. For a study of urban life in Syria see Arnold Hugh Martin Jones, *The Cities of the Eastern Roman Provinces*, pp. 226-294.

4. See Werner Jaeger, *Early Christianity and Greek Paideia*.

5. See for example the inscriptions in René Louis Victor Cagnat (ed.), *Inscriptiones Graecae ad Res Romanas Pertinentes*, 3, nos. 1023; 1040; 1042; 1044; 1047; 1074; 1247. The last mentions "Hadrian and Sa'īd, sons of Mālik." The position of Greek in ancient Syria is curiously parallel to that of French in modern Syria; the many Syrian Antoinettes and Maurices often know hardly a word of French.

6. Chapter I, Section 1.

7. Syriac sources, interestingly, use the term "*'arabē*" for seminomads and call

full nomads "*ṭayyāyē*"—the latter term derived from the proper name of the North Arabian tribe of B. Ṭayyi'. Cf. Judah B. Segal, *Edessa, 'The Blessed City,'* p. 22.

8. Alexander Alexandrovich Vasiliev, "Notes on Some Episodes concerning the Relations between the Arabs and the Byzantine Empire from the Fourth to the Sixth Century," p. 309: ". . . Arabs formed the principal part of the local population [of Syria-Palestine]."

9. Robert Devreesse, *Le Patriarchat d'Antioche depuis la Paix de l'Eglise jusqu'à la conquête arabe.*

10. Especially after the conquest of Mecca and al-Ṭā'if and the battle of Ḥunayn in A.H. 8-9.

11. Waq. 989-990.

12. E.g., Waq. 200; Ibn 'Abd al-Ḥakam (the younger), *Futūḥ Miṣr*, p. 53; Bal. *Ansab* Reis. 598, p. 1211. Cf. Henri Lammens, "La Mecque à la veille de l'Hégire," and "La République marchande de la Mecque vers l'an 600 de notre ère."

13. On the prosperity of southern Syria, see Roger Paret, "Les Villes de Syrie du Sud et les routes commerciales d'Arabie à la fin du VIe siecle."

14. Bal. *Fut.* 129.

15. Shoufani, *Al-Riddah*, pp. 38ff.

16. On the *mi'rāj*, see Geo Widengren, *Muḥammad, the Apostle of God, and his Ascension*, pp. 96ff.

17. See, for example, Yaqut, s.n. "Ḥabrūn"; I.H.J. 422. On the B. al-Dār (al-Dāriyūn) see Chapter II, Section 3, and Section 3 below, under Judhām and Lakhm.

18. On the extent of Muḥammad's political control to the north of Medina, see below, Section 3.

19. Fred McGraw Donner, "Muḥammad's Political Consolidation in Western Arabia up to the Conquest of Mecca: A Reassessment," and above, Chapter II, Section 3.

20. See below, Section 3 under B. Ghassān.

21. On the chronology of the Persian Wars of Heraclius, see Andreas N. Stratos, *Byzantium in the Seventh Century, I: 602-634,* pp. 62-66, 104-117, 165ff.

22. It is interesting to recall that it was just this generation—by now entering full adulthood—that a few years later lived through the Islamic conquest of Syria. Does this help to explain their apparent passivity toward the new conquerors?

23. Theodor Nöldeke, "Die Ghassânischen Fürsten aus dem Hause Gafna's," p. 45; Leone Caetani, *Annali dell'Islam* II/2, p. 1113.

24. Philip Mayerson, "The First Muslim Attacks on Southern Palestine (A.D. 633-634)," p. 165.

25. Theophanes, *Chronographia,* p. 335 (A.M. 6123).

26. This interpretation runs counter to that proposed by some earlier writers, notably, Leone Caetani. In his *Annali*, II/1, pp. 409-413, Caetani argues forcefully that the campaign to Mu'ta cannot serve as evidence for Muḥammad's aspirations to extend his control into Syria and asserts (following Muir) that the Mu'ta campaign must be seen merely as an effort to erase an earlier defeat suffered by a group of Muslims at Dhāt al-Aṭlāḥ. But his logic is circular; he first constructs

a general argument that Muḥammad had no ambitions beyond the conquest of Mecca before the year A.H. 8/A.D. 630, on the grounds that there is no evidence of broader ambitions, and then rejects the Mu'ta campaign as evidence of broader ambitions because it does not conform to the general argument.

27. On Usāma's raid to al-'Araba: Tab. i/2108 (*qālū*) (=Mad.?).

28. *bināt al-aṣfar*: Waq. 992-993.

29. Waq. 995.

30. I.H. 984. On Dhāt al-Salāsil, see below.

31. E.g., the raid on Dhāt al-Aṭlāḥ, sent against the Quḍā'a tribes: I.H. 983; Tab. i/1601 (Waq.).

32. Cf. I.K./Caskel, s.v. " 'Uḏra b. Sa'd b. Huḏaim."

33. Waq. 1017.

34. I.H. 797.

35. On 'Udhra: I.S. I/2, 66-67 (Waq.—h—Isḥāq b. 'Abdullāh b. Nasṭās < Abū 'Amr b. Ḥurayth al-'Udhrī < his father); on Sa'd Hudhaym: I.S. I/2, 65 (Waq.—h—Muḥammad b. 'Abdullāh b. Akhī al-Zuhrī < Abū 'Umayr al-Ṭā'ī < Abū al-Nu'mān < his father). Cf. also accounts of delegations from Salāmān b. Sa'd Hudhaym, a tribe thought to be associated with B. 'Udhra: I.S. I/2, 67; cf. I.K./Caskel s.v. "Salāmān b. Sa'd Huḏaim."

36. Tab. i/1872 (Sayf < Abū 'Amr < Zayd b. Aslam); Tab. i/2082-2083 (Sayf < many authorities). Shoufani, *Al-Riddah*, p. 96, following Caetani, *Annali* II/1, p. 584, summarily dismisses these accounts as examples of Sayf's "careless statements," claiming them to be self-contradictory and unsupported by any other authorities. However, I.S. II/1, 115 mentions tax collectors being sent out to B. Sa'd Hudhaym in the beginning of A.H. 9/April, A.D. 630, an account related by an authority other than Sayf (a—Naṣr b. Bāb < al-Ḥajjāj b. Arṭāt < al-Ḥakam b. Miqsam < Ibn 'Abbās). The tradition describes a general dispatch of *muṣaddiqūn* to tribes of the Ḥijāz (Aslam, Ghifār, Sulaym, Muzayna, Juhayna, Fazāra, Kilāb, Ka'b, Dhubyān), including to the B. Sa'd Hudhaym. The B. 'Udhra, however, are not mentioned. Was this tax levy connected with the raid on Tabūk?

37. Assuming that a confusion with the general dispatch of tax agents at the beginning of A.H. 11/spring, A.D. 632 has not occurred, cf. above, Chapter II, Section 3.

38. I.K./Caskel II, 223 (s.v. "Balī b. 'Amr"); II, 358 (s.v. "Irāša b. 'Āmir").

39. On Mu'ta: I.H. 792ff.; Waq. 755ff.; I.S. II/1, 92-94; *TMD* I, 402-407. Cf. Theophanes, *Chronographia*, p. 335 (A.M. 6123); Nicephorus, *Opuscula Historica*, p. 23.

40. On Dhāt al-Salāsil: Waq. 770-771; cf. I.H. 984-985; I.S. II/1, 94-95.

41. I.H.J. 442-443; I.H. 492-499 and 504.

42. Tab. i/1687. On Dhāt al-Salāsil, see note 40.

43. *TMD* I, 405 (MbA—ak—WbM < IL < Abū 'l-Aswad < 'Urwa); *TMD* I, 406 (al-Qāsim b. 'Abdullāh b. al-Mughīra—h—Abū Uways—h—Ismā'il b. 'Uqba < Mūsā b. 'Uqba).

44. I.S. I/2, 24; above, p. 66. Cf. also I.S. I/2, 65-66 (Waq.—h—Abū Bakr b. 'Abdullāh b. Abī Sabra < Mūsā b. Sa'd < Ruwayfi' b. Thānī al-Balawī).

45. Tab. i/1930 (Sayf < Sahl b. Yūsuf < al-Qāsim b. Muḥammad).

46. Tab. i/1962 (Sayf < al-Ṣa'b b. 'Aṭiyya b. Bilāl < Sahm b. Minjāb < Minjāb b. Rāshid). Cf. *TMD* I/446 (I.S.—h—'Abd al-Ḥamīd b. Ja'far < his father): Abū Bakr appoints 'Amr governor over Balī, 'Udhra, and other Quḍā'a tribes he contacts—an account misplaced into the conquest of Syria. See the discussion above on 'Amr's governorship of Sa'd Hudhaym and other tribes.

47. I.K./Caskel II, 375-376 (s.v. "Laḫm"); II, 264 (s.v. "Ǧuḏām"); II, 53ff.

48. See note 39 above.

49. Waq. 990 reports this but denies its veracity.

50. E.g., I.H.J. 422-425 on Lakhm (one Badrī mentioned); I.H.J. 420-421 on Judhām (no early converts mentioned).

51. Tab. i/1687; I.H. 776, 777; I.S. I/2, 75.

52. I.H. 797; I.S. I/2, 21 contains a treaty between Muḥammad and this group that suggests that they were not merely allies of the Muslims, but had actually embraced Islam. Was the text later retouched? Cf. Watt, *Medina*, pp. 111-112.

53. I.H. 958; I.S. I/2, 18, 31, and 83. It is possible that this governor, certainly a Christian, turned to the rising Islamic state upon the Persian occupation of Syria because of the Muslims' comparatively favorable treatment of Christians; the Byzantines' reaction to his change of allegiance would then have occurred after their return to power in Syria.

54. I.H. 962-963, 975ff.; Tab. i/1740; Waq. 555-557; I.S. I/2, 82-83. On Judhām, see Watt, *Medina*, pp. 108-110.

55. Tab. i/2082 (Sayf < Abū Isḥāq al-Shaybānī < Abū Ṣafiyya al-Taymī and Sayf < Ṭalḥa < al-Mughīra and Sayf < M < Abū 'Uthmān); cf. above under 'Udhra and Sa'd Hudhaym.

56. Tab. i/1872-1873 (q—al-Sirrī al-Wālibī); cf. Tab. i/1880 (Sayf < Sahl b. Yūsuf < al-Qāsim b. Muḥammad).

57. I.K./Caskel II, 84ff.; II, 455 (s.v. "al-Qain b. Ǧasr"); I.H.J. 454.

58. Waq. 770-771.

59. E.g., I.H. 792, but not Waq. 760 or I.S. II/1, 93.

60. E.g., I.H.J. 454.

61. Tab. i/1872-1873 (Sayf < Abū 'Amr < Zayd b. Aslam and al-Sirrī). Cf. note 36.

62. I.K./Caskel II, 76ff. and II, 369 (s.v. "Kalb b. Wabara").

63. I.H.J. 434.

64. I.S. I/2, 68-69 (< I.K.) on "delegations" of one or two individuals; I.H.J. 457ff. On Diḥya b. Khalīfa al-Kalbī, reportedly sent as an envoy by Muḥammad to "Caesar", i.e. presumably to the Byzantine authorities in Syria, see I.H. 975ff.; Tab. i/1740ff. (< I.I.); I.S. IV/1, 184-185; *TMD* I/417 (several authorities).

65. I.S. II/1, 44-45, 64-65, 119-120; Waq. 1025ff.; *TMD* I, 385-386 (Waq.); *TMD* I, 422 (not Waq. or Sayf). Cf. Tab. i/1872 and *TMD* I, 432 (Sayf < Abū 'Amr < Zayd b. Aslam and al-Sirrī).

66. By Shoufani; see note 36 above.

67. *TMD* I, 405-406 (MbA—ak—WbM—h—IL < Yūnus b. Yazīd < al-Zuhrī). The other accounts, criticized by Shoufani, all derive from Sayf b. 'Umar's collections.

68. Tab. i/1872-1873 (al-Sirrī al-Wālibī).

69. Cf. above, pp. 98ff.

70. I.K./Caskel II, 35ff. and II, 273 (s.v. "Gassān").

71. On 'Āmila, see I.K./Caskel II, 156 s.v.; I.H.J. 420; *EI*(2), " 'Āmila."

72. Waq. 990.

73. *TMD* I, 392 (h—Abū Muḥammad al-Qāsim b. 'Abdullāh b. al-Mughīra al-Jawharī—h—Ismā'īl b. Ibrāhīm b. 'Uqba < Mūsā b. 'Uqba); cf. the section on B. Balī above for accounts claiming that his commander was of Balī.

74. I.S. I/2, 17.

75. Waq. 1051-1052. The party contacted was Ka'b b. Mālik, an *anṣārī* poet who was generally on good terms with Muḥammad, but who held back from participation in the Tabūk campaign and was subsequently disciplined by him: cf. Watt, *Medina*, index s.v. "Ka'b b. Mālik."

76. Waq. 1018-1019.

77. *TMD* I, 405-406 (*isnād*, see note 67).

78. I.K./Caskel II, 35ff. and II, 273.

79. Tab. i/1729 (Waq.); I.S. I/2, 72.

80. I.K./Caskel II, 470 (s.v. "Quḍā'a b. Mālik"); Bal. *Fut.* 144-145 on groups settled at Qinnasrīn, Aleppo.

81. *TMD* I, 392 (*isnād*, note 73).

82. I.K./Caskel II, 86 and II, 507 (s.v. "Salīḥ b. Hulwān"); I.H.J. 450.

83. The Ḍajā'ima are mentioned among the defenders of Dūmat al-Jandal against Khālid b. al-Walīd's efforts to subdue the town—the dating of which is, however, problematic.

84. I.K./Caskel II, 470 (s.v. "Quḍā'a b. Mālik"); II, 220 (s.v. "Bahrā' b. 'Amr"). On Bahrā' at Suwā and al-Muṣayyakh, see below, Section 6 and note 163.

85. I.H.J. 441. The delegation from Bahrā' that came to Muḥammad in A.H. 9 seems to have come from the Yemen, however, not from Syria, and must therefore represent a different (and little-known) branch of the tribe: Tab. i/1720 (Waq.); I.S. I/2, 66.

86. I.H. 792.

87. E.g., the members of Ṭayyi' (most of whom lived in the Najd) who had settled near Qinnasrīn: Bal. *Fut.* 145.

88. E.g., Tab. i/1740ff.

89. Waq. 1031.

90. Waq. 1031-1032; *TMD* I, 412 (MbA—ak—WbM < Muḥammad b. Muslim al-Zuhrī); I.H. 902; Yaqut s.v. "Ayla," "Maqnā," "Adhruḥ," "Jarbā' "; Bal. *Fut.* 59-60. The people of Maqnā were Jews, according to Bal. *Fut.* 60.

91. I.H. 958; I.S. I/2, 31.

92. *TMD* I, 396-397 (q—MbA—ak—WbM—h—a man of B. Salāmān < people of B. Salāmān); *TMD* I, 397 (MbA—q—WbM—ak—a man of Bahrā'). This somewhat weakens Caetani's claim that the Syrians were totally disaffected with the Byzantines and welcomed the Muslims as liberators: *Annali* II/2, p. 1052.

93. The attitude of towns toward the Muslims is not mentioned in the sources. In some cases we can infer what occurred; Taymā', for example, appears to have

remained loyal to Medina upon Muḥammad's death, for we find Islamic armies being stationed there before heading north to conquer Syria, and there is no record of a reconquest of the town. The argument from silence is always perilous in cases such as this, however, where the sources are so fragmentary. For Ayla, we have no data. Dūmat al-Jandal seems to have broken with Medina, but accounts of its relations with the Muslims are in general confused.

94. All these accounts are transmitted on the authority of Sayf b. 'Umar. This led Shoufani to assert that no "apostasy" took place in the northern Ḥijāz, and that the accounts of "apostasy" (*ridda*) there, like those about the extension of Muḥammad's control over the region, are merely fabrications of Sayf's. The basis of his argument is that such fabrications were intended to make the extent of Muḥammad's control in Arabia appear broader than it actually was, thereby justifying the conquest of previously unsubdued areas by Abū Bakr by portraying his expansion as reconquest or chastisement of rebels. As shown above, however, it is not so easy to brush aside the traditions that claim for Muḥammad a following and influence among the tribes of the northern Ḥijāz; and if this was indeed the case, it is difficult to see why Sayf should have wished to fabricate the story of an apostasy where none had occurred. More probably, events in the northern Ḥijāz were viewed as being of minor importance in comparison with the great rebellions of the Najd and eastern Arabia and so were not transmitted by most writers. They appear only in the collections of Sayf, who in general transmits accounts rich in material about the history of various tribes.

95. On Usāma's raid, see Shoufani, *Al-Riddah*, pp. 107-111. Tab. i/1851 (Sayf < Hishām b. 'Urwa < his father, and Sayf < Mūsā b. 'Uqba < al-Mughīra b. al-Akhnas, and Sayf < 'Amr b. Qays < 'Aṭā' al-Khurasānī) suggests that the purpose of the campaign was to raid the Quḍā'a tribes—i.e., those not already subjected? Some had already submitted; see above under B. Kalb, al-Qayn, 'Udhra, Sa'd Hudhaym, and Balī. Tab. i/1635 (h—'Abd al-Wārith b. 'Abd al-Ṣamad b. 'Abd al-Wārith—h—his father—h—Ābān b. 'Aṭṭār—h—Hishām b. 'Urwa < 'Urwa), furthermore, notes that some Quḍā'a tribesmen were among the allies of Muḥammad at the conquest of Mecca (perhaps, however, B. Juhayna?).

96. Tab. i/1894 (Sayf < T < Ḥabīb b. Rabī'a al-Asadī < 'Umāra b. Fulān al-Asadī).

97. 'Amr over the *'ulyā Quḍā'a* and al-Walīd over the *ḍāḥiya Quḍā'a*: Tab. i/2083 (Sayf).

98. Above, pp. 104-105.

99. Tab. i/1921 (Sayf); Tab. i/1930 (Sayf < Sahl b. Yūsuf < al-Qāsim b. Muḥammad); Tab. i/1963 (Sayf < al-Ṣa'b b. 'Aṭiyya b. Bilāl < Sahm b. Minjāb < Minjāb b. Rāshid). Shuraḥbīl seems to have been sent toward Dūmat al-Jandal but not to have reached it.

100. For a more detailed treatment of this problem, see Fred McGraw Donner, "The Arabic Sources for the Rise of Islam."

101. We can assume, of course, that many smaller communities in the Syrian deep south—Ayla, Ma'ān, etc.—were already under Islamic control.

102. See Section 6 of this chapter on the chronology of the early campaigns.

103. E.g., Kufi I, 98; Ya'qubi II, 133; *TMD* I, 443ff. (I.I.).

104. *TMD* I, 443-446 (I.I.); Ya'qubi II, 133; Tab. i/2079 (Mad.); Tab. i/2080 (Sayf < Mubashshir b. Fuḍayl < Jubayr b. Ṣakhr < his father). Cf. *TMD* I, 448 (h—Ismā'īl b. Abī Uways—h—Ismā'īl b. Ibrāhīm b. 'Uqba < Mūsā b. 'Uqba); *TMD* I, 453-454 (WbM—a—IL < Yūnus b. Yazīd < al-Zuhrī); Bal. *Fut.* 107-108; *TMD* (Zah.) V, fol. 223b-229b (many authorities).

105. Tab. i/2079 (Mad.); Tab. i/2079-2080 (I.I.); Tab. i/2080 (no *isnād*); Tab. i/2085-2086 (Sayf < Hishām b. 'Urwa); *TMD* I, 448; I.S. IV/1, 70 (Waq.).

106. Tab. i/2079 (Mad.); I.S. IV/1, 70 (Waq.).

107. Tab. i/2110-2113 (Sayf < MTMA). On Khālid's objectives in Iraq, see the discussion below, Chapter IV, Section 4.

108. Tab. i/2080 (*isnād*, note 104); Tab. i/2080-2083 (Sayf < Abū Isḥāq al-Shaybānī, and Sayf < T, and Sayf < AU).

109. Tab. i/2080-2083 (*isnād*, note 108) states that the Byzantines had rallied all the "outermost nomads" (*al-'arab al-ḍāḥiya*), among them B. Bahrā', Kalb, Salīḥ, Tanūkh, Lakhm, Judhām, and Ghassān.

110. Ibid.

111. Tab. i/2084-2085 (Sayf < Sahl b. Yūsuf, and Sayf < Mubashshir and AU < KU); Tab. i/2083-2084 (Sayf < Sahl b. Yūsuf < al-Qāsim b. Muḥammad).

112. Thus Michael Jan De Goeje, *Mémoire sur la conquête de la Syrie*, pp. 25-29. Cf. also the account of I.I. in *TMD* I, 466: 'Amr writes to Abū Bakr for reinforcements *after* the death of Khālid b. Sa'īd, upon which the caliph sends orders to Khālid b. al-Walīd to march from Iraq to Syria.

113. Excepting those accounts relating to Marj al-Ṣuffar, perhaps misplaced. Tab. i/2080-2083, however, describes Khālid as marching along the fringes of the desert to a point between al-Zayzā', Ābil, and al-Qasṭal (the first of which is in the Balqā' district); but this is followed by material that appears to belong to a description of the battle of Yarmūk.

114. So Tab. i/2086 (Sayf < 'Amr < al-Sha'bī); cf. Tab. i/2147 (Sayf < M < Abū 'Uthmān < Abū Sa'īd): 'Umar pardons Khālid b. Sa'īd and al-Walīd b. 'Uqba and allows them to join one of the other commanders in Syria, upon becoming caliph. *TMD* I, 448 (*isnād*, note 104): Abū Bakr removes Khālid b. Sa'īd from command and sends him to Dhū l-Marwa; cf. *TMD* I, 453-454 (*isnād*, note 104) in which Abū Bakr apparently removes Khālid from his command and sends Yazīd b. Abī Sufyān, his replacement, out to Dhū l-Marwa. Perhaps we can conclude from this that the remnants of the *jaysh al-bidāl* were integrated into Yazīd's army, whereas the disgraced commanders remained behind until pardoned by 'Umar. Cf. also Tab. i/2064 on al-Walīd b. 'Uqba's activities.

115. Tab. i/2107-2108.

116. *TMD* I, 446. Other accounts of al-Wāqidī simply list the three commanders without any indication of who proceeded first.

117. In this he is supported by one of WbM's accounts (*TMD* I, 453-454), by Bal. *Fut.* 107-108, and by *TMD* I, 460 (Ya'qūb b. Sufyān—h—Abū l-Yamān al-Ḥakam b. Nāfi'—h—Ṣafwān b. 'Amr < 'Abd al-Raḥmān b. Jubayr).

118. Especially Kufi I, 98 and 103, who gives the four commanders as Abū 'Ubayda, Shuraḥbīl b. Ḥasana, Yazīd b. Abī Sufyān, and Mu'ādh b. Jabal. No early source mentions Mu'ādh as a commander, but there is mention of him as a subordinate in Abū 'Ubayda's force some time later, after the conquest of Jerusalem (i.e., already in the third phase): *TMD* (Zah.) VII, fol. 381a (Abū Bakr b. 'Abdullāh b. Miryam < Ṣāliḥ b. Abī Mukhāriq). It therefore seems likely that he went to Syria, not as a commander, but as part of Abū 'Ubayda's army. Kufi's omission of 'Amr b. al-'Āṣ may stem from the fact that 'Amr was sent to Palestine, whereas the other commanders were sent to areas east of the Jordan. Kufi mentions 'Amr's force later, considering it to have been a reinforcement for the armies sent out earlier—thus agreeing with al-Madā'inī. It is interesting that another later source, Abū Ismā'īl al-Azdi al-Baṣrī's *Futūḥ al-Shām*, pp. 6-7, gives the same list of commanders as Kufi.

119. Most authorities, evidently themselves feeling unable to draw up a firm chronology from the data on the dispatch of the armies, simply state that Abū Bakr sent the four (or three) commanders to Syria, with no hint as to the sequence in which they marched: thus Ya'qubi II, 133; *TMD* I, 447 and 450 (Waq.); Bal. *Fut.* 107-108; Tab. i/2083-2084 (Sayf < Sahl b. Yūsuf < al-Qāsim b. Muḥammad); Eutychius, *Annales*, 2, p. 9.

120. *TMD* I, 447 (Waq.).

121. Ya'qubi II, 133. Cf. Bal. *Fut.* 108: Abū Bakr wished to place Abū 'Ubayda in charge, but he begged to be excused.

122. WbM in *TMD* I, 453; cf. AM in Bal. *Fut.* 108.

123. Ventures that took him to Egypt: Ibn 'Abd al-Ḥakam, *Futūḥ Miṣr*, p. 53; *TMD* (Zah.) XIII, fol. 246b ('Abd al-Wahhāb b. al-Ḥasan—ak—Abū Hawṣā'—s—Abū l-Qāsim b. Samī').

124. Tab. i/2078 and *TMD* I, 449, 449-450 (I.I.); Tab. i/2085-2086 (Sayf < Hishām b. 'Urwa); *TMD* I, 446 (Waq.); cf. Yaqut, s.v. "al-Mu'riqa"; Bal. *Fut.* 108.

125. Philip Mayerson, "The First Muslim Attacks on Southern Palestine (A.D. 633-634)."

126. Bal. *Fut.* 108; *TMD* I, 461-462 (WbM); *TMD* (Zah.) XIII, fol. 257b (Waq.). Cf. Eutychius, *Annales*, 2, pp. 10-11; he calls the village Tādūn and places the negotiations after the arrival of a large Byzantine army there. See also the anonymous *Chronicum Miscellaneum ad Annum Domini 724 Pertinens*, in Ernest Walter Brooks, *Chronica Minora*, 2, p. 148, which describes an engagement between the Byzantines and *ṭayyāyē* east of Gaza.

127. Tab. i/2107 (I.I.); Tab. i/2107-2108 (Mad.); cf. De Goeje, *Memoire*, pp. 22-24.

128. Tab. i/2078; *TMD* I, 449; *TMD* I, 449-450; Khalifa I, 86. Cf. Tab. i/2107; *TMD* I, 457 (mentions Yazīd only); Bal. *Fut.* 108 (I.I.?).

129. Tab. i/2110-2113 (Sayf < MTMA).

130. Tab. i/2107-2108 (Mad.); Bal. *Fut.* 108 (Waq.). The comment in Tab. that Abū Bakr assigned a district (*kūra*) to each commander—Palestine to 'Amr and 'Alqama b. Mujazziz, Jordan to Shuraḥbīl, Damascus to Yazīd, and Ḥimṣ to Abū 'Ubayda—seems to come from Sayf b. 'Umar (cf. *TMD* I, 545) and

reflects the situation in Syria somewhat later, after the battle of the Yarmūk. Mad. adds that some authorities think Shuraḥbīl was sent to Bostra.

131. *Ḍāḥiya Quḍā'a*, i.e., presumably the more southerly tribes of Quḍā'a? Tab. i/2084-2085 (Sayf < Sahl, Mubashshir and AU < KU).

132. Cf. note 128 for I.I.; Tab. i/2107-2108 (Mad.); Bal. *Fut.* 108 (Waq.) has him going to Damascus.

133. The locations of 'Araba and al-Dābiya have never been ascertained. Caetani, *Annali* II/2, pp. 1161-1171, tallies up an assumed identification of al-Dābiya with al-Dāthina near Gaza (following Nöldeke), and an account stating that 'Amr b. al-'Āṣ reinforced Yazīd, to conclude that Yazīd, like 'Amr, was active in southern Palestine rather than in the Balqā' district. Though this reconstruction is plausible, it is far from certain. We cannot be sure that 'Araba was the Wādī 'Araba and not some other place in Palestine, nor that al-Dābiya was in fact al-Dāthina. Even if the latter identification is correct, the account may be a fragment describing the battle near Gaza that AM or his sources erroneously included in his synthesis of the events of Yazīd's campaign. Finally, there is nothing to suggest that the battle took place before Yazīd's forces reached the Balqā'; the statement that 'Amr reinforced Yazīd could very well have originated in the later joint operations at Ajnādayn, and it is in any case contradicted by another account claiming that in cases of joint operations, 'Amr was to be in charge of prayer for the whole army, i.e., he was to command: *TMD* I, 447 (Waq.). Our object is not to dispose of Caetani's reconstruction as false, but to show that, though plausible, it is no more plausible than many other possible reconstructions one might create with the available data. Sources for this episode: Bal. *Fut.* 109 (AM and others); Tab. i/2108 (*qālū*); Theophanes, *Chronographia*, 1, p. 336. Cf. De Goeje, *Memoire*, p. 34; Mayerson, "The First Muslim Attacks," pp. 161-166. Theophanes is the source of the statement that the four armies were guided into Syria by Christian Arabs disgruntled with the Byzantine authorities for cutting off their stipend payments.

134. I.I. has all forces going to the Balqā'; Waq. does not mention Abū 'Ubayda going out at all; Mad. (in Tab. i/2107-2108) has him in al-Jābiya, the old Ghassānid capital, as does Kufi I, 132; Kufi I, 125 has him near Damascus. Note that he is later reported to have gone from al-Jābiya to Jerusalem to pray: *TMD* (Zah.) VII, fol. 381a. Caetani, *Annali* II/2, pp. 1171-1173, argues that Abū 'Ubayda was not present at all during the first phase of the conquests in Syria, and only arrived with the battles of Ajnādayn and Yarmūk; in his opinion, his presence was extrapolated back by eighth-century chroniclers wishing to diminish the apparent role of 'Amr b. al-'Āṣ and Yazīd b. Abī Sufyān in the conquests because of their close ties to Mu'āwiya, the first Umayyad caliph. Anti-Umayyad propaganda did circulate, but this seems farfetched.

135. Bal. *Fut.* 113 places it after the conquest of Bostra, i.e., in Phase II; cf. Yaqut, s.v. "Ma'āb"; Tab. i/2108 (Mad.?) makes it the first treaty in Syria and states explicitly that "it was a camp (*fusṭāṭ*), not a city (*madīna*)."

136. Kufi I, 124: *fa-bathth khayla-ka fī l-qurā wa fī l-sawād wa lā tuḥāṣirūna madīnatan min muduni-him ḥattā ya'tī-ka 'amrī*. Cf. *TMD* (Zah.) XVIII, fol. 157a (al-Muhājir—h—Abū 'l-'Āliya): Yazīd b. Abī Sufyān raiding the countryside.

137. Above, p. 113 and note 107.

138. In the case of Iraq, this included not only the tribal countryside, but a number of Arab towns as well. See below, Chapter IV, Sections 2 and 4.

139. Such is the wording of Bal. *Fut.* 107. Cf. Ya'qubi II, 133: *TMD* I, 450-451 (WbM—s—Abū 'Amr and others); *TMD* I, 453 (WbM—ak—Ṣafwān b. 'Amr < 'Abd al-Raḥmān b. Jubayr); Eutychius, *Annales* II, p. 9.

140. *TMD* I, 443-446 (I.I. < al-Zuhrī—h—Ibn Ka'b < 'Abdullāh b. Abī Awfā al-Khuzā'ī); *TMD* I, 453 (*isnād,* note 139); *TMD* I, 450-451 (WbM—s—Abū 'Amr and others). These suggest that the *ahl al-Yaman* and *ahl al-'Āliya* (people from the mountains, i.e., the 'Asīr district?) were the reinforcements.

141. Cf. especially Ya'qubi II, 133; Kufi I, 119; Bal. *Fut.* 108; Tab. i/2107-2108 (Mad.).

142. *TMD* I, 453 (*isnād,* note 139); *TMD* I, 450-451 (*isnād,* note 139)—both give 24,000. Bal. *Fut.* 108: 24,000. Kufi I, 132: 30,000. Sayf in Tab. i/2086-2088 lists the army at Yarmūk as 21,000 plus 6,000 reserves; cf. Tab. i/2090-2091.

143. Tab. i/2107-2108 and i/2079.

144. *TMD* I, 446; Kufi I, 123 states that he marched with nearly 6,000 men.

145. Bal. *Fut.* 108.

146. *TMD* I, 446.

147. Kufi I, 123.

148. Kufi I, 116; I, 103-104.

149. Kufi I, 98-99.

150. Kufi I, 116-119.

151. The account says that Khālid went back to Medina after the Ridda. *TMD* I, 450 (Waq—h—'Abdullāh b. Wābiṣa al-'Absī < his father < his grandfather).

152. *TMD* I, 461-462 (WbM < Yaḥyā < 'Abd al-Ḥamīd b. Ja'far < his father).

153. Khālid's military talents were apparent early on: see Watt, *Medina,* p. 25 for his role at Uḥud. On his campaigning in Iraq before his departure for Syria, see below, Chapter IV, Section 4.

154. The only early exception appears to be Waq., who mentions that Abū Bakr instructed Khālid to join the Muslims in Syria but says nothing of his desert march: *TMD* I, 447-448.

155. Only Bal. *Fut.* 249-250 places Khālid's departure from 'Ayn al-Tamr.

156. The following itineraries are given. *Ibn Isḥāq*: al-Ḥīra—'Ayn al-Tamr—Nuqayra—Qurāqir—Suwā/Tadmur—Ḥawwārīn—Marj Rāhiṭ/Qanāt Buṣrā (Tab. i/2121-2125; *TMD* I, 467-468, 469-470, 458, 460; Khalifa I, 86-87). *Sayf < MTMA etc.*: al-Ḥīra—Dūmat al-Jandal—Qurāqir—Suwā—Muṣayyakh Bahrā'/al-Quṣwāna—Suwā—al-Rummānatayn—al-Kathāb—Damascus—Marj al-Ṣuffar—Qanāt Buṣrā (Tab. i/2110-2113; *TMD* I, 463-464; cf. Tab. i/2113-2114). *al-Ṭabarī, anonymous*: al-Ḥīra—Ṣandawdā'—Muṣayyakh—al-Ḥuṣayd—Qurāqir—Suwā—Arak—Tadmur—Qaryatayn—Ḥuwwārīn—Quṣam—Marj Rāhiṭ/Ghūṭa (Tab. i/2108-2110). *al-Balādhurī, anonymous*: al-Ḥīra—'Ayn al-Tamr—Ṣandawdā'—Muḍayya / al-Ḥuṣayd—Qurāqir—Suwā—al-Kawāthil—Qarqīsiyyā'—Araka—Dūmat al-Jandal—Quṣam—Tadmur—Qaryatayn—Ḥuwwārīn—Marj Rāhiṭ—Thaniyyat al-Ghūṭa—Qanāt Buṣrā (Bal. *Fut.* 110-112; Kawāthil and Qarqīsiyyā' are said to come from Waq.). *Ibn A'tham al-Kūfī*: al-Ḥīra—al-Anbār—Ṣandawdā'—

Qurāqir—Kawāthil—Tadmur—Thaniyyat al-'Uqāb—Damascus (Kufi I, 132-142). *al-Ya'qūbī*: Iraq—'Ayn al-Tamr—al-Anbār—Tadmur—Ḥawrān. Some say: Ghūṭa—Thaniyyat al-'Uqāb—Ḥawrān—Buṣrā (Ya'qubi II, 133-134). *Sayf < A < Isḥāq b. Ibrāhīm < Ẓafar b. Dahī:* Qurāqir—Sūka—al-Ṣabā—Qaryatayn—al-Ḥiqār—al-'Arīr—Suwā (*TMD* I, 465-466; cf. Alois Musil, *Arabia Deserta*, pp. 559-560, on these place-names, based on very different readings derived from the Berlin manuscript of *TMD*). Also: Suwā—Muṣayyakh Bahrā'/al-Quṣwāna (Tab. i/2114). *Miscellaneous*: Iraq—al-Ḍumayr—al-Jābiya (*TMD* I, 460); al-Yamāma—'Ayn al-Tamr—Dūmat al-Jandal—Syria (*TMD* I, 448 and *TMD* (Zah.) V, fol. 277a-277b).

157. The main studies of Khālid's itinerary are found in De Goeje, *Memoire*, pp. 37-50; Caetani, *Annali* II/2, pp. 1220-1232; and Musil, *Arabia Deserta*, pp. 553-573. Wellhausen, *Prolegomena zur ältesten Geschichte des Islams*, prudently leaves out any discussion of the issue.

158. This is suggested by Musil in *Arabia Deserta*, pp. 559-560, and in *The Middle Euphrates*, pp. 283-314 (on Khālid's campaigns along the Euphrates). It is readily apparent that the sources have confused earlier material when the same or very similar episodes are recounted in different contexts—e.g., al-Muṣayyakh and the episode of Ḥurqūṣ b. al-Nu'mān (see note 163 below).

159. E.g., al-Ḥuṣayd or al-Muṣayyakh, which may be a place in either Syria or Iraq.

160. *TMD* I, 460 Ya'qūb b. Sufyān—h—Abū 'l-Yamān al-Ḥakam b. Nāfi'—h—Ṣafwān b. 'Amr < 'Abd al-Raḥmān b. Jubayr); *TMD* I, 497-498 (variant, same *isnād*); cf. Tab. i/2086-2089.

161. Caetani, *Annali* II/2, pp. 1214-1215 has drawn exactly the opposite conclusion: realizing the contradiction between the general statements to the effect that Khālid was hurried and the particulars of his many campaigns, he opted to favor the latter. As a result he includes in the march most of Khālid's exploits on the Euphrates north of al-Ḥīra, rejects as fabrications the statements that Khālid was hurried, and concludes that the march must have taken three months.

162. Several accounts give romanticized versions of the desert march, but the basic information is generally the same. *TMD* I, 466 and Tab. i/2113-2114 (Sayf < 'Ubaydallāh b. Muḥaffiz b. Tha'laba < Bakr b. Wā'il and Sayf < MT); Tab. i/2121-2125 (I.I.); *TMD* I, 467-468 (I.I.); *TMD* I, 469-470 (I.I.); Tab. i/2110-2113 (Sayf < MTMA); *TMD* I, 458-459 (h—Zubayr b. Bakkār—h—Mūsā b. 'Abdullāh) makes the desert march part of a march to Dūmat al-Jandal. *TMD* I, 465-466 (Sayf < A < Isḥāq b. Ibrāhīm < Ẓafar b. Dahī) gives a very confused list of stages on the six-day march. Kufi I, 136-138, makes the desert march fall between Qurāqir and Kawāthil; see note 163. Tab. i/2108-2110; Bal. *Fut.* 110-111; Ya'qubi II, 133-134.

163. I.I. places the raid on Bahrā' at Suwā: Tab. i/2122, *TMD* I, 467-468 and 469-470. Kufi I, 136-138, who places the desert march from Qurāqir to Kawāthil, mentions an engagement with the B. Tha'lib (an error for Taghlib?) at Kawāthil. Sayf < A places the raid at Muṣayyakh Bahrā' = al-Quṣwāna, perhaps combining accounts of a battle at al-Muṣayyakh or al-Quṣwāna (in Iraq?) with those of a skirmish with the Bahrā' on the march to Syria: Tab. i/2114, cf. Yaqut, s.v.

"al-Muṣayyakh." Anonymous traditions (Bal. *Fut.* 110-111, Tab. i/2108-2110) state that the raid and battle at Suwā led to the death of Ḥurqūṣ b. al-Nu'mān al-Bahrānī (i.e., of Bahrā'). But Ḥurqūṣ b. al-Nu'mān—now called al-Namirī—is also said to have been the name of the chief who led the B. al-Namir b. Qāsiṭ against Khālid's forces at al-Muṣayyakh "between Ḥawrān and al-Qalb" (Tab. i/2069-2072; cf. Chapter IV, Section 4). The traditionists have clearly confused actions in Iraq against the B. al-Namir b. Qāsiṭ with those during the march to Syria against Bahrā'; but to which of the events the leader al-Ḥurqūṣ or the place-name al-Muṣayyakh belongs it is impossible to say. The location of al-Muṣayyakh "between Ḥawrān and al-Qalb" does not help, for al-Qalb is unknown, and Ḥawrān could be either the district of that name in Syria (near the Bahrā' country) or the Wādī Ḥawrān in Iraq (near the al-Namir country). For good measure, we should note that Yaqut, s.v. "al-Muṣayyakh" mentions a place by this name in Syria, where Khālid is reported to have fought the B. Taghlib. al-Muḍayya in Bal. *Fut.* 110 is probably a scribal error for al-Muṣayyakh. Musil, *Middle Euphrates*, p. 303, identifies al-Muṣayyakh with the modern 'Ayn al-Arnab in Iraq, 115 km. northwest of al-Anbār, but gives no reasons for this identification.

164. Tab. i/2108-2110; Bal. *Fut.* 111-112; Ya'qubi II, 133-134; Khalifa I, 86-87 (I.I.). Kufi I, 140-144 gives an elaborated version, describing a fierce battle with a large number of Byzantines in the town, during which four sons of al-Ḥārith al-Sadūsī, who had accompanied Khālid's army from Iraq, were killed. The town was then occupied by the Muslims, who killed its military commander (*biṭrīq*).

165. In fact the desert march would have to fall between the Euphrates and the modern Sukhna, a distance of only about 75 km. This route was suggested by Caetani, *Annali* II/2, pp. 1220-1232, partly because he considered the accounts of Khālid's campaigning along the upper Euphrates to belong to his march to Syria. Musil, *Arabia Deserta*, pp. 555-556, with his usual generosity toward the Italian scholar, ridicules Caetani's proposal on the basis of his own unrivaled knowledge of local topography.

166. Bal. *Fut.* 110-111 calls both Qurāqir and Suwā wells of B. Kalb, but states that Bahrā' was camped at Suwā when Khālid arrived; *TMD* I, 467-468 (I.I.) calls Qurāqir a well of Kalb, but Suwā a well of Bahrā'.

167. On Kalb and Bahrā', see above, Section 3.

168. A variant, combining aspects of the first and second itineraries, would have Khālid march up to the Euphrates perhaps as far as Anāt, and then strike westward across the desert to Palmyra.

169. E.g., the route traced by René Mouterde and Antoine Poidebard, "La voie antique des caravans entre Palmyre et Hīt au IIe siècle après J.-C.," or the caravan route connecting Palmyra with the ancient Vologesias (on its location see Chapter IV, note 66); cf. Eric Herbert Warmington, *The Commerce between the Roman Empire and India*, pp. 85-86.

170. Roughly 500 km. from 'Ayn al-Tamr to Palmyra; roughly 250 km. from the Euphrates near Anāt to Palmyra.

171. Notably Bi'r al-Mulūṣī, Ābār al-Māṭ, and Qulbān al-Ruṭba in the upper reaches of the Wādī Ḥawrān. Could one of these be identified with Qurāqir or Suwā? For a description of Bi'r al-Mulūṣī and vicinity, see Musil, *Arabia Deserta*, pp. 63ff.

172. This itinerary is proposed by Musil, *Arabia Deserta*, pp. 553ff. As he states, the assumption that Dūmat al-Jandal is an error for Dūmat al-Ḥīra in the texts, made by De Goeje, *Memoire*, p. 15, is unwarranted.

173. It is difficult to see why Musil, *Arabia Deserta*, pp. 562-563, asserts that of the old authorities only Mad. mentions Khālid's presence at Palmyra; cf. note 164. Musil's claim that the reports of Khālid's activity in Palmyra stem from "the later relations of Khālid's descendants in Ḥomṣ with the settlements of Arak and Tadmur, in and about which they owned land," is unsubstantiated. On a later campaign to Palmyra, see Tab. i/2150-2155.

174. Musil, *Arabia Deserta*, pp. 555 and 569, considers this problem and suggests that the area northwest of Qulbān Qurājir was still occupied by Byzantine garrisons, so that Khālid could not advance there without fear of defeat. But was the same not true of Damascus, where Khālid ultimately entered Syria? Tab. i/2110-2113 (Sayf < MTMA) preserves an interesting account stating that it was Khālid's desire to emerge *behind* the Byzantine forces that were beginning to gather against the Muslims. How we interpret this statement depends, in part, on whether we opt for the Palmyra or for the Dūmat al-Jandal route.

175. Bal. *Fut.* 111; Tab. i/2108-2110; Khalifa I, 86-87 (I.I.). Ya'qubi II, 134 mentions at this point in the march some hard fighting at Ḥawrān: perhaps a hypercorrection for Ḥuwwārīn? The full name of the tribe is given by Bal. as B. Mashja'a b. al-Taym b. al-Namir b. Wabara b. Taghlib b. Ḥulwān b. 'Imrān b. al-Ḥāfī b. Quḍā'a. According to I.K./Caskel II, 403, they were affiliated with B. Kalb. Musil, *Arabia Deserta*, p. 563, identifies al-Quṣam with the Roman outpost named Casama, the modern Nabk (cf. René Dussaud, *Topographie historique de la Syrie antique et médiévale*, p. 264). Musil, *Arabia Deserta*, pp. 565-566 and 572, rejects the accounts of battles at Ḥuwwārīn and Qaryatayn because the chronology of the accounts is confused and because they require a detour from his reconstructed route of march. Why an additional 75 km. should have mattered when Khālid had gone, according to Musil's reconstruction, at least 300 km. farther than the direct route from Iraq to Syria requires, Musil does not explain.

176. See references in note 156 above. Places in the Ghūṭa mentioned are Thaniyyat al-'Uqāb and Marj al-'Adrawiyya (*TMD* I, 469-470). The lieutenants mentioned are Busr b. Abī Arṭāt al-'Āmirī and Ḥabīb b. Maslama al-Fihrī, both of Quraysh.

177. Mad. places the actual departure of troops in the beginning of A.H. 13 (Tab. i/2079); Bal. *Fut.* 107-108 puts it at Ṣafar, A.H. 13; I.I. states that Abū Bakr first sent out his call for troops upon his return from the pilgrimage of A.H. 12, i.e., during the last days of that year, so the departure of troops would have been some time into A.H. 13 (Tab. i/2079; Khalifa, I, 86; *TMD* I, 441, 449, 449-450).

178. E.g., *TMD* I, 467-468 (I.I.): 'Amr b. al-'Āṣ writes Abū Bakr after the death of Khālid b. Sa'īd, asking for reinforcements; Tab. i/2108-2110 (Mad.?); Tab. i/2086-2088 (Sayf); Tab. i/2110-2113 (Sayf < MTMA) has the Muslims facing the Byzantines at Wāqūṣa request reinforcements; *TMD* I, 447, 448 (Waq.); *TMD* I, 460 (al-Ḥakam b. Nāfi'—h—Ṣafwān b. 'Amr < 'Abd al-Raḥmān b. Jubayr); Kufi I, 132: Abū 'Ubayda facing Byzantine army at al-Jābiya, so Abū Bakr sends to Khālid to march from Iraq in support; Tab. i/2088-2089 (Sayf < Mubashshir, Sahl and AU < KU and AH): Abū Bakr's order sent when

the Muslims faced the Byzantines at Yarmūk in Syria. The exceptions are *TMD* I, 448 (Mūsā b. 'Uqba) and *TMD* (Zah.) V, fol. 277a-277b (IL—'Urwa), which say only that Abū Bakr's letter reached Khālid after al-Yamāma.

179. Departure placed in Rabī' II, A.H. 13: Tab. i/2108, Bal. *Fut.* 110. Reaches Syria in Rabī', A.H. 13: Tab. i/2088-2089 (*isnād*, note 178). Desert march in hot weather: Tab. i/2113-2114 (Sayf < MT and others).

180. Bal. *Fut.* 111-112; Tab. i/2108-2110.

181. In Brooks, *Chronica Minora* II, 148.

182. This chronology is developed with variations by Caetani, *Annali* II/2, pp. 1213-1220; De Goeje, *Memoire*, pp. 39-41; and Musil, *Arabia Deserta*, p. 563. Musil and Caetani refine it by attempting to resolve some of the apparent contradictions: Musil by contending that Rabī' and Ṣafar in the accounts refer not to the months so named in the lunar year, but to the seasons spring and autumn, and Caetani by contending that notices of Abū Bakr's pilgrimage refer not to the *ḥajj*, but to the *'umra* or lesser pilgrimage, which he made in Rajab, A.H. 12/ September-October, A.D. 633.

183. See Chapter IV, Section 4.

184. On the composition of Khālid's force: *TMD* I, 460; Tab. i/2110-2113; Tab. i/2114-2115; Tab. i/2088-2089; Tab. i/2108-2110; Bal. *Fut.* 110; Ya'qubi II, 133-134; Kufi I, 134; Tab. i/2121-2125; *TMD* I, 467-468, 469-470. On the Sadūsīs, see note 164 above. Other individuals mentioned, besides the guide from B. Ṭayyi', include a man of Muḥārib (Tab. i/2113, *TMD* I, 446), one of Azd (Kufi I, 139-140), two of Quraysh (note 176 above), one of Bajīla—a brother of Jarīr b. 'Abdullāh (Kufi I, 140), and al-Qa'qā' b. 'Amr of Tamīm (Yaqut, s.v. "al-Muṣayyakh"). The last is perhaps a misplaced tradition belonging to the Iraqi campaigns.

185. Bal. *Fut.* 110: 800 (or 600 or 500) men. Tab. i/2108-2110: 800 (or 500) men. *TMD* I, 460: 3,000 cavalry. Kufi I, 134: 7,000 cavalry. Tab. i/2114-2115: Khālid arrives at Wāqūṣa with 9,000 men. Tab. i/2090: Khālid arrives in Syria just before Yarmūk with 10,000 Iraqi reinforcements.

186. This did not, however, prevent earlier scholars from making such choices, mainly because they took the contextual traditions (i.e., those provided by systematizing transmitters to bolster their chronological schemes) to be as authoritative as the content traditions (i.e., those describing various events). De Goeje, Wellhausen, Caetani, and other writers dealing with the conquest of Syria generally favored the reconstruction put forth by Waq. and I.I., largely because the chronology of this reconstruction struck them as more plausible than that of Sayf. The approach followed here requires that we accept a greater measure of uncertainty in the chronology of the period. For a fuller discussion of this problem, see Donner, "The Arabic Sources." On the relationship of the Arabic to the non-Arabic sources, see pp. 142ff.

187. The actual content of their traditions about specific events is, of course, sometimes quite different.

188. Tab. i/2121-2125 (I.I.); *TMD* I, 484-485 (Waq.); *TMD* I, 485 (SbA); Ya'qubi II, 134. Cf. *TMD* I, 485 (Abū l-Ḥasan Muḥammad b. Aḥmad b. al-Qawās al-Warrāq); Bal. *Fut.* 112-113, which also places the conquest of Ma'āb at this time.

189. De Goeje, *Memoire*, pp. 50-61; Caetani, *Annali* III, pp. 22-24; Tāha al-Hāshimī, "Ma'rakat Ajnādayn: matā waqa'at, wa ayna waqa'at?"

190. These are collected by Caetani, *Annali* III, pp. 74-81. Cf. also Appendix A below.

191. Abū 'Ubayda, however, is not mentioned at the battle. This reflects Waq.'s conviction that he was only appointed upon the accession of 'Umar, which Waq. places after Ajnādayn.

192. Ajnādayn: Tab. i/2125-2126 (I.I.); Khalifa I, 87 (I.I.); *TMD*, 447, I, 482-483 (Waq.); *TMD* I, 483 (SbA and Ibn Jābir); Ya'qūbī II, 134. Cf. Bal. *Fut.* 113-114; *TMD* I, 481 (Abū l-Ḥasan b. al-Faḍl—ak—'Abdullāh b. Ja'far—ak—Ya'qūb); *TMD* I, 497 (WbM—h—al-Shaykh al-Umawī); *TMD* I, 484 (IL < Abū l-Aswad < 'Urwa); Tab. i/2126. *TMD* I, 480 dates both Ajnādayn and Faḥl to Dhū l-Qa'da A.H. 13. Kufi I, 142-145 gives a different account.

193. This account (Bal. *Fut.* 115) resembles the reconstructions of Sayf b. 'Umar < KU in the magnitude of the victory at Faḥl.

194. But note the absence of Yazīd b. Abī Sufyān's name.

195. This presents certain difficulties, for as noted above most accounts in this reconstruction describe 'Amr b. al-'Āṣ, not Khālid b. al-Walīd, as having been commander-in-chief at Ajnādayn. The problem of exactly when Khālid relinquished his command to Abū 'Ubayda fascinated De Goeje, who devoted a whole section of his *Memoire* (pp. 64-70) to the subject.

196. Faḥl: Tab. i/2145-2147 (I.I.); Khalifa I, 88 and I, 95 (I.I.); Tab. i/2155 (I.I.); *TMD* I, 482-483 (Waq.); *TMD* (Zah.) VIII, fol. 378b (Waq.); *TMD* (Zah.) XVIII, fol. 154b (Waq.). Note that Ya'qubi, SbA make no mention of Faḥl. Cf. Bal. *Fut.* 115 (Abū 'Ubayda said to be commander); *TMD* I, 481 (*isnād*, note 192) places Ajnādayn and Faḥl in A.H. 13; *TMD* I, 497 and I, 499 (WbM—h—al-Shaykh al-Umawī) places Faḥl in Dhū l-Qa'da, A.H. 13, but in the time of Abū Bakr; *TMD* I, 480 dates Faḥl to Dhū l-Qa'da, A.H. 13; *TMD* I, 450-451 (WbM—s—Abū 'Amr and others) places Faḥl after Ajnādayn, before Marj al-Ṣuffar and Damascus.

197. De Goeje, *Memoire*, pp. 48-49, places it east of Damascus. Theodor Nöldeke, "Zur Topographie und Geschichte des Damascenischen Gebiets und der Haurângegend," p. 425, note 3, places it near Tall Shaqḥabā just south-southwest of Kiswa. Caetani, *Annali* III, pp. 317ff., arrives at a similar conclusion. Dussaud, *Topographie historique*, p. 318, tentatively locates it near Khān Danūn, south of Damascus.

198. *TMD* (Zah.) VIII, fol. 378b; *TMD* I, 481; Bal. *Fut.* 118. In this he is followed by Ya'qubi II, 139 and by *TMD* I, 450-451 (WmB—s—Abū 'Amr and others).

199. Khalifa I, 88; *TMD* I, 481. Followed by AM, who places it twenty days after Ajnādayn: Bal. *Fut.* 118.

200. *TMD* I, 482.

201. Bal. Fut. 118; *TMD* I, 499 and I, 482 (SbA). Cf. Appendix B.

202. This is stated only by I.I. in Tab. i/2145-2147 and *TMD* I, 495.

203. Cf. Yaqut, s.v. "Barza"; Dussaud, *Topographie historique*, pp. 295-296 and Map IV.

204. Jean Sauvaget, "Esquisse d'une histoire de la ville de Damas," p. 443. Cf.

TMD I, 507 (WbM—a—Ṣafwān b. ʻAmr < ʻAbd al-Raḥmān b. Jubayr), which describes the place as *sūq maqsallāṭ*, and *TMD* I, 503, which says the commanders met at the oil market.

205. Damascus: Tab. i/2145-2147, i/2155; *TMD* I, 495; Khalifa I, 94 (all I.I.). *TMD* (Zah.) VIII, fol. 378b; *TMD* I, 481; Tab. i/2155; Bal. *Fut.* 130 (all Waq.). *TMD* I, 501-502; I, 494; I, 521 (all SbA). Yaʻqubi II, 140. Cf. Bal. *Fut.* 120-130; *TMD* I, 501 (MbA—h—Abū Bakr Marwān b. Muḥammad < Yaḥyā b. Ḥamza < Rashīd b. Dāūd al-Ṣanʻānī < Abū ʻUthmān al-Ṣanʻānī). *TMD* I, 496; Khalifa I, 94 (I.K.). *TMD* I, 493-494; I, 497; I, 499; I, 502-503; I. 507; I, 520 (WbM < al-Shaykh al-Umawī). *TMD* I, 503-506 (AM—h—Muḥammad b. Yūsuf b. Thābit < ʻAbbās b. Sahl b. Saʻd). *TMD* I, 509-512 (Abū Hudhayfa Isḥāq b. Bishr). *TMD* I, 495 (Abū Maʻshar and Maʻmar). *TMD* I, 496-497; I, 506-507 (Abū ʻUbayd). *TMD* I, 497 (Abū ʻUthmān Saʻīd b. Kathīr al-Miṣrī). Khalifa I, 94; *TMD* I, 499 (al-Walīd b. Hishām < his father < his grandfather). *TMD* I, 513; I, 506 (Abū Mushir). *TMD* I, 503 (Yazīd b. Marthad). Khalifa I, 94 (ʻAbdullāh b. al-Mughīra < his father). Kufi I, 157-161 supports Waq.'s chronology placing the fall of Damascus in Rajab A.H. 14, has the siege last for thirteen months.

206. Ḥimṣ: Khalifa I, 95; I, 99; *TMD* I, 526 (I.I.). *TMD* (Zah.) XVIII, fol. 154b; Bal. *Fut.* 130-131 (Waq.). Bal. *Fut.* 130 (AM). Yaʻqubi II, 141. Cf. Bal. *Fut.* 129-130; *TMD* I, 525-526 = Khalifa I, 99 (I.K.); *TMD* I, 526 = Khalifa I, 99 (ʻAbdullāh b. al-Mughīra). The traditions of SbA (in Bal. *Fut.* 132-133) only refer to the conquest of Ḥimṣ in the context of later activities in northernmost Syria that certainly must be dated after the battle of Yarmūk and thus support the reconstruction of KU on this point (see below). Similarly, SbA in Bal. *Fut.* 115-116 states that after the conquest of Damascus the Muslims' commanders were dispatched to various districts: ʻAmr b. al-ʻĀṣ to Palestine, Shuraḥbīl b. Ḥasana to "Jordan" (i.e., northern Palestine?), and Yazīd b. Abī Sufyān over the Damascus area. This is followed by an account of Shuraḥbīl's conquests in Tiberias and other northern Palestinian towns, including Acre and Tyre—events that almost certainly occurred only after the Yarmūk victory.

207. The text has "the cultivated districts (*sawād*) of Jordan": *TMD* I, 531-532 (WbM—ak—Ṣafwān < ʻAbd al-Raḥmān b. Jubayr).

208. *TMD* I, 535 (Abū Hudhayfa Isḥāq b. Bishr < SbA < old Syrian authorities); cf. *TMD* I, 539, and I, 541; Kufi I, 254-255; Tab. i/2165 (Sayf) on people of Najrān. Little additional information on the army's composition is gleaned from an examination of the names of individuals mentioned by this reconstruction as participants at Yarmūk, because most accounts are very general. A list of participants is provided as Appendix C.

209. Yarmūk: Tab. i/2347-2348 = *TMD* I, 531; Khalifa I, 100 (I.I.). Tab. i/2155 (Waq.). *TMD* I, 535-545; I, 529 (SbA). *TMD* (Zah.) XVI, fol. 88b (Abū Hudhayfa). Yaʻqubi II, 141. Cf. *TMD* I, 460-461 (al-Lālikāʼī < Ṣafwān b. ʻAmr < ʻAbd al-Raḥmān b. Jubayr?); *TMD* I, 527-528 (WbM, Abū Zurʻa, Yaʻqūb, Abū Maʻshar, I.K.)—all dates; *TMD* I, 531-532, 532-533, 534 (WbM < Ṣafwān b. ʻAmr < ʻAbd al-Raḥmān b. Jubayr); *TMD* I, 534 (WbM). Cf. Kufi I, 225-270, with many of the same details as the account of SbA.

210. *TMD* I, 544-545 (SbA); Yaʻqubi II, 141-142.

211. Unfortunately virtually nothing is known of any of these transmitters; even Sayf's life is essentially unknown.

212. The uncertainty in dating is seen in *TMD* I, 529, where Sayf transmits two different datings for the battle of Yarmūk. This suggests that Sayf himself was not responsible for the sequence or attempted datings, but was merely transmitting reconstructions elaborated by earlier scholars. In addition, we should note that the MTZMAS reconstruction (see below), also transmitted by Sayf, paints a very different picture of the conquest of Syria.

213. Caetani, *Annali* II/2, pp. 1124-1126, and III, pp. 177-178, follows Lammens in identifying Jilliq with the modern Jillīn on the Wādī al-Ḥarīr, an affluent of the Yarmūk. De Goeje, *Memoire*, pp. 55-56, equates it with Janīn in northern Palestine. Dussaud, *Topographie historique*, pp. 317-318 and 324, identifies it with al-Kiswa, 20 km. south-southeast of Damascus on the Nahr al-A'waj, a site he concludes to have been the former residence of the Ghassānids; cf. René Dussaud and Frédéric Macler, *Mission scientifique dans les régions désertiques de la Syrie moyenne*, pp. 39-41. The text of Tab. i/2086-2089 = *TMD* I, 548-549, states that the Byzantine army camped at *thaniyyat Jilliq bi-'a'lā Filasṭīn*, "in upper Palestine." Dussaud explains away the latter phrase as a later gloss added by a subsequent transmitter seeking to clarify the location of Jilliq, hence as not original or trustworthy.

214. Or Abū Rāqiṣ.

215. But see the estimates of the size of this force at the end of Chapter III, Section 6.

216. See the list of martyrs in Caetani, *Annali* III, pp. 593-598; cf. Appendix C below.

217. Cf. Tab. i/2100-2101.

218. Tab. i/2095-2099 = *TMD* I, 529 (Sayf < KU).

219. *TMD* I, 552. Another poem by a Tamīmī in Khālid's force verifies that the conquest of Bostra preceded Yarmūk and that Khālid's Iraqi contingent took part in it.

220. Cf. Appendix C. Yarmūk: Tab. i/2086-2088 = *TMD* I, 548-549 (Sayf < Mubashshir, Sahl, and AU < KU and AH). Tab. i/2090-2095 = *TMD* I, 546; Tab. i/2095-2099 = *TMD* I, 547; *TMD* I, 550; *TMD* I, 529; Tab. i/2100 (Sayf < AU < KU). Tab. i/2100-2101 (Sayf < Abū Umāma). Tab. i/2100 (Sayf < AU < his father). Tab. i/2147; Tab. i/2155; *TMD* I, 529.

221. Tab. i/2147 has al-Ṣuffar; *TMD* I, 513 has al-Ṣuffarīn. Cf. Tab. i/2104-2105 (Sayf): Abū Umāma relates a personal exploit at Marj al-Ṣuffar. On proposed identifications of this place, see above, note 197.

222. Tab. i/2147-2148. This is a curious statement, as one has the impression that 'Amr already was the commander for Palestine.

223. Dhū l-Kalā' is the name of one of the most powerful pre-Islamic South Arabian families: cf. I.K./Caskel II, 236, s.v. Are we dealing here with an individual of this name, or with a contingent from the tribe?

224. Damascus: Tab. i/2147-2148 = *TMD* I, 513-514; Tab. i/2150-2155 = *TMD* I, 514-518 (Sayf < AU < KU). Tab. i/2104-2105 (Sayf < Muṭarraḥ < al-Qāsim < Abū Umāma, Sayf < AU < Syrian authorities). *TMD* I, 496.

225. Tab. i/2150-2155 = *TMD* I, 514-518 (Sayf < AU < KU). Cf. *TMD* I,

518-519 (Sayf < KU?), citing a poem by al-Qa'qā' referring to "Dāray Sulaymān," which the editor glosses as the two *dārs* of Sulaymān in Damascus and Palmyra. But the poem is problematic, as al-Qa'qā', a member of Tamīm, was one of the Iraqi force that is said to have left Syria some time before.

226. One source mentions 80,000 cavalry on the Byzantine side.

227. The reasons for this move are not specified, but it could well have been intended to prevent reinforcements from reaching Baysān by way of Tiberias.

228. Faḥl: Tab. i/2150-2155 (Sayf < AU < KU); Tab. i/2156-2158, *TMD* I, 485-488 (Sayf < AU < AH).

229. Baysān, Tiberias: Tab. i/2156-2158; *TMD* I, 485-488 (Sayf < AU and AH). Tab. i/2158, i/2159. On treaty terms, see the discussion in Chapter V, Section 6.

230. Tab. i/2156-2158 has "Sumayr b. Ka'b"; *TMD* I, 485-488, "Bashīr b. Ka'b."

231. Tab. i/2389-2390 and i/2390-2391 (Sayf < KU?).

232. For his pedigree, see I.K./Caskel II, 513, and II, 532, and Tafel 236. Caskel notes a confusion between al-Simṭ and his son, Shuraḥbīl b. al-Simṭ and thinks that the latter was intended here.

233. Cf. I.K./Caskel II, 503 (s.v. "al-Sakūn"): Sakūn, once part of Kinda, had migrated from the Ḥaḍramawt to the region north of Ta'izz, losing most of their original ties to Kinda and becoming essentially an independent group.

234. Ḥimṣ: Tab. i/2390-2391 (Sayf < AU); cf. Tab. i/2391 (Sayf? < Abū l-Zahrā' al-Qushayrī < a man of his tribe); Tab. i/2391-2392 (Sayf? < *shaykhs* of B. Ghassān and Bal-Qayn); Tab. i/2392-2393.

235. This may be another reference to Theodore, the brother of Heraclius, mentioned above as one of the commanders at Yarmūk; presumably different from Tūdharā (also Theodore?), said to have been killed at Marj al-Rūm according to this reconstruction. As we shall see, the Greek sources also suggest that there were two Theodores active as commanders during these events: see pp. 145ff. The references to Ramla, one of the few new settlements established by the Muslims in Syria, is clearly anachronistic; perhaps the account uses Ramla to refer to Byzantine troops from Lydda (Diospolis), the main Byzantine town near the site of Ramla.

236. Ajnādayn, etc.: Tab. i/2390-2391 (Sayf < AU); Tab. i/2396-2398 (Sayf < AU and AH < KU); Tab. i/2398-2402.

237. This traditionist group is abbreviated MTZMAS. See the multiple *isnād* in Tab. i/2110-2113 = *TMD* I, 463, cited in note 238. If only one "M" is used in the abbreviation, it stands for Muḥammad b. 'Abdullāh.

238. Yarmūk: Tab. i/2110-2113 = *TMD* I, 463 (Sayf < A < Isḥāq b. Ibrāhīm < Ẓafar b. Dahī, Sayf < M < AU, Sayf < T < al-Mughīra, Sayf < M < 'Abd al-Raḥmān b. Siyāh al-Aḥmarī) (i.e., Sayf < MTMA); Tab. i/2114-2115 (Sayf < A < Isḥāq b. Ibrāhīm < Ẓafar b. Dahī); Tab. i/2089 = *TMD* I, 549-550 (Sayf < MTMA); *TMD* I, 474 (Sayf < MT); *TMD* I, 529 (Sayf < MTZ). Cf. *TMD* I, 476 (Sayf < Hishām b. 'Amr < his father); *TMD* I, 529 (Sayf); Tab. i/2155 (Sayf).

239. On this episode see below, Section 8. Tab. i/2498-2504.

240. *TMD* I, 500, and I, 508-509.

241. Tab. i/2108; Tab. i/2127; Tab. i/2144-2145; Tab. i/2145; Khalifa I, 87, and I, 100.

242. Cf. Fred McGraw Donner, "A Fragment of Ibn A'tham al-Kūfī's *Kitāb al-Futūḥ* dealing with the Caliphate of Abū Bakr." The reconstruction of Ibn A'tham is only given in bare outline here, for many of the specific details in it are similar to, and perhaps derived from, those given in reconstructions already discussed.

243. Kufi I, 132-161. Needless to say, the confusion that this narrative displays regarding the conquest of Damascus hardly inspires confidence in the general outlines of its chronological reconstruction.

244. Kufi I, 174-195.

245. Cf. above, note 208.

246. Kufi I, 195-294.

247. The main examples of this approach are, of course, De Goeje's *Memoire*, Wellhausen's *Prolegomena*, and Caetani's *Annali*. The main danger of this approach is that it presents an appearance of certainty where none really exists; another shortcoming is the frequent failure to consider the different kinds of sources available to the early systematizers such as Sayf, Waq. et al.

248. Later Byzantine chronicles (e.g., Cedrenus, Georgios Monachos) derive their information about the rise of Islam from Theophanes: cf. Wolfgang Eichner, "Die Nachrichten über den Islam bei den Byzantinern," p. 143. The only early Greek chronicle that seems to be independent of Theophanes for this subject, the *Istoria Syntomos* of Nicephorus, Patriarch of Constantinople (d. A.D. 828), contains an account of the events of these years that is of no assistance in understanding the chronology of the conquests, although it does shed some light on the Byzantine response to the conquest: *Opuscula Historica*, pp. 21-25.

249. Theophanes, *Chronographia*, p. 333 (A.M. 6122). Theophanes himself was apparently indebted to Syriac sources for some of his information: cf. Ann S. Proudfoot, "The Sources of Theophanes for the Heraclian Dynasty."

250. Elias bar Shīnāya, Bishop of Nisibis, *Opus Chronologicum*, pp. 126ff. (text), pp. 61ff. (translation), arranges his account according to the Islamic calendar, giving the Seleucid date corresponding to the start of each *hijra* year.

251. Michael the Syrian, *Chronique de Michel le Syrien*, 4, p. 414 (text), 2, p. 417 (translation). His account seems to have relied on the Greek chronicle of Theophanes for its general outlines.

252. The fragment is edited with translation in Brooks and Chabot, *Chronica Minora* 2 (=C.S.C.O., *Scriptores Syri*, III. 4) p. 75 (text), pp. 59-60 (translation) and edited and translated with commentary in Theodor Nöldeke, "Zur Geschichte der Araber im 1. Jahrhundert d. H. aus syrischen Quellen," pp. 76-82.

253. The reconstruction of I.I. and Waq. does seem to have been in circulation in Syria, for, as we have seen, it appears to have been followed by the Syrian scholar Sa'īd b. 'Abd al-'Azīz al-Tanūkhī. The uncertainties about the date of the Syriac fragment are especially great because it was written on the blank side of the first folio of another manuscript, doubtless by a later writer. But how much later?

254. The Greek text, of course, does not call them Muslims, but rather "Saracens" (*Sarakēnoi*) or "Arabs" (*Arabes*).

255. Presumably the same as the Bāhān of the Arabic sources.

256. Evidently not the same as Theodore, the emperor's brother. Is this the origin of the two forms Tadhāriq and Tūdharā in the Arabic sources?

257. This is suggested by Nöldeke, "Zur Geschichte der Araber," p. 81, note 2.

258. Theophanes, *Chronographia*, pp. 336-337 (A.M. 6125). The chronology is, however, confused: A.M. 6125 corresponds to A.H. 4-5/A.D. 625, but the events described (e.g., the death of Abū Bakr) belong to A.H. 13-14/A.D. 634-635 according to generally accepted chronological arrangements. To call the latter into question is possible but not very inviting.

259. Theophanes, *Chronographia*, pp. 337-338 (A.M. 6126).

260. Elias bar Shīnāya, Bishop of Nisibis, *Opus Chronologicum*, pp. 131-132 (text), pp. 63-64 (translation).

261. Michael the Syrian, *Chronique*, 4, p. 414 (text), 2, p. 417 (translation).

262. The manuscript mentions raids near "GBY...," which Nöldeke, "Zur Geschichte der Araber," p. 78, restores to "Damascus." But it is not clear whether the reference is speaking of a seizure of the town by the Muslims, and in any case the fragmentary word could much more plausibly be restored to "Gabīthā," "al-Jābiya."

263. This seems to be the implication of the radical source criticism being elaborated by Albrecht Noth, *Quellenkritische Studien zu Themen, Formen, und Tendenzen frühislamischer Geschichtsüberlieferung*.

264. Above, p. 133 and note 208. On Sulaym at Marj al-Ṣuffar, see the poem in Bal. *Fut.* 118.

265. The contrast with Iraq, where the *anṣār* were very prominent, is striking: cf. Chapter IV, Section 9.

266. E.g., Kufi I, 144 (supplying the Byzantines at Ajnādayn); Kufi I, 230-231 (*musta'riba* join the Byzantines before Yarmūk).

267. Above, p. 132. The alignment of much of Judhām and Lakhm on the Byzantine side is also reflected by the fact that 'Umar, when visiting Syria some time later, ordered that the booty (*ghanā'im*) be evenly distributed except that the B. Lakhm and Judhām were to be excluded from it: Ya'qubi II, 147.

268. For more on the tribal groups that may have been part of the Ghassānid confederation, see p. 187.

269. Unfortunately, virtually no individuals from these tribes are listed by name among the combatants on either side, so it remains impossible to ascertain along what lines the tribe may have divided itself. This can be done in the case of some Iraqi tribes; see Chapter IV, Section 2 for the comparison.

270. Tab. i/2392-2393 (Sayf? < Shaykhs of Ghassān and Bal-Qayn).

271. The chronological placement of the siege of Ḥimṣ depends, of course, upon which reconstruction one favors for the second phase.

272. The last is not as absurd as it may at first appear, if we accept the account describing Iraqi reinforcements sent to Syria to reinforce Abū 'Ubayda, cited in the next paragraph, and assume some chronological confusion—both of which

are possible. It is given in Tab. i/2395-2396 (Sayf < KU). For the others, see Khalifa I, 105 (h—Ubayy); Khalifa I, 105 (I.K.); Tab. i/2393-2394 (Sayf < AU and Jāriya); Ya'qubi II, 141-142; Kufi I, 218; Bal. *Fut.* 137, 144-150, 159. Cf. summary in Kamāl al-Dīn 'Umar b. Aḥmad Ibn al-'Adīm, *Zubdat al-ḥalab min ta'rīkh Ḥalab*, 1, pp. 25-29; Theophanes, *Chronographia*, p. 340 (A.M. 6128 and 6129), on the seizure of northern Syria and Antioch; Michael the Syrian, *Chronique* 4, p. 420 (text), 2, p. 426 (translation).

273. E.g., Bal. *Fut.* 164, on al-Darb (near Antioch?).

274. Tab. i/2393-2394 (Sayf? < AU and Jāriya); Ibn al-'Adīm, *Zubdat al-ḥalab*, pp. 25-29; Bal. *Fut.* 149; Tab. i/2498-2504 (Sayf < MTAS); Tab. i/2504 (Sayf < Zakariyyā' b. Siyāh < al-Sha'bī); Tab. i/2594 (Sayf).

275. For the rebellions of Antioch and Qinnasrīn, see Bal. *Fut.* 147, 159; Bal. *Fut.* 144-145.

276. His departure for Constantinople, however, only occurred after the Muslims had seized Edessa some time later, as part of the conquest of the Jazīra province. Waq. states that Heraclius left Syria in the year after Yarmūk, in Sha'bān (i.e., of A.H. 16), going from Antioch to Constantinople: Tab. i/2155. But I.I. dates Heraclius's withdrawal to Constantinople to A.H. 15, and Sayf agrees with Waq. in dating to it A.H. 16: Tab. i/2394.

277. Tab. i/2396 (Sayf? < Abū l-Zahrā' and 'Amr b. Maymūn); Tab. i/2395 (Sayf < Abū l-Zahrā' al-Qushayrī < a man of B. Qushayr); Tab. i/2395-2396 (Sayf? < KU).

278. Bal. *Fut.* 147; Khalifa I, 105 (I.K.) says that Khālid b. al-Walīd accompanied him.

279. Bal. *Fut.* 139 (Hishām b. 'Ammār < al-Awzā'ī) dates his activity at Qinnasrīn to A.H. 16, at Jerusalem to A.H. 17.

280. Above, Section 7.

281. Khalifa I, 105 (I.K.); Tab. i/2404; Ya'qubi II, 146-147; Kufi I, 289-290; Bal. *Fut.* 138-139. Cf. Tab. i/3401? But see Bal. *Fut.* 139 (h—al-Qāsim b. Sallām—h—'Abdullāh b. Ṣāliḥ < al-Layth b. Sa'd < Yazīd b. Abī Ḥabīb): 'Umar sends Khālid b. Thābit al-Fahmī at the head of an army from al-Jābiya to Jerusalem.

282. Bal. *Fut.* 158.

283. Kufi I, 294 says he went to Damascus and camped at the al-Jābiya gate. *TMD* (Zah.) XII, fol. 354a states that he camped at al-Jābiya but visited Damascus during his stay in Syria.

284. Tab. i/2404-2405 ('Adī b. Suhayl); Tab. i/2504 (Sayf < Zakariyyā' b. Siyāh < al-Sha'bī); Tab. i/2498-2504 (Sayf < MTAS).

285. Tab. i/2404; Ya'qubi II, 141-142, 147; Tab. i/2515 (Sayf < AU and AH and al-Rabī' b. al-Nu'mān); Tab. i/2524-2525 (Sayf < al-Mujālid < al-Sha'bī); Tab. i/2523-2524 (Sayf < Abū Ḍamra and Abū 'Amr < al-Mustawrid < 'Adī b. Suhayl); *TMD* (Zah.) XII, fol. 355b (Waq.); Kufi I, 290-296; Tab. i/2523 (s—AU and AH and al-Rabī'a). According to Ya'qubi, 'Umar ordered the booty to be evenly distributed except that the B. Lakhm and Judhām were to be excluded because they had backed the Byzantines.

286. On the debate over how many visits 'Umar made to Syria and the dating

of them and the plague, see Tab. i/2516 (Abū Ma'shar); Tab. i/2520 (Sayf); Tab. i/2513-2514 (Sayf < AH and AU and al-Rabī' b. al-Nu'mān); Bal. *Fut.* 139-140; Ya'qubi II, 150-151; *TMD* (Zah.) XII, fol. 335b (Waq.); Tab. i/2515 (Sayf < AU, AH, al-Rabī'); *TMD* I, 553-559 (many authorities); Bal. *Ansab* Reis. 598, p. 594; *TMD* I, 494 (WbM); Tab. i/2521 (Sayf). The plague and drought are usually dated to A.H. 18, but some traditions claim that on one of his visits to Syria 'Umar got as far as a place called Sargh and then turned back because he learned that the plague was rampant in Syria; the *'ām Sargh* is equated, however, with A.H. 17, which suggests that the plague occurred in that year. Once again, the various chronological schemes are contradictory and uncertain. Cf. Tab. i/2511 (I.I.); Tab. i/2511-2513 (I.I.); Tab. i/2516-2518 (I.I.); Kufi I, 310-317; Tab. i/2516 (I.I.); Khalifa I, 109 (I.I.); *TMD* I, 555 (Abū Ma'shar). Elias bar Shīnāya, Bishop of Nisibis, *Opus Chronologicum* p. 132-133 (text), p. 64 (translation), dates the plague to A.H. 17. Theophanes, *Chronographia*, p. 339 (A.M. 6127), says that 'Umar stayed in Jerusalem for two years.

287. On Jews: Tab. i/2402-2403 (I.I.? < Sālim b. 'Abdullāh); Ya'qubi II, 147. Most sources simply speak of the people of Jerusalem—presumably Christians—making a treaty with the Muslims: Kufi I, 296; Khalifa I, 105 (I.I.—a—Muḥammad b. Ṭalḥa b. Rukāna < Sālim b. 'Abdullāh b. 'Umar); Tab. i/2405-2407 (Sayf < KU). Cf. Tab. i/2408 (Sayf < AU, AH). Theophanes, *Chronographia*, p. 339 (A.M. 6127): Sophronius, high priest of Jerusalem, receives terms for all of Palestine. Michael the Syrian, *Chronique*, 4, pp. 419-420 (text), 2, p. 425 (translation) says Sophronius made a treaty forbidding Jews to live in Jerusalem.

288. Tab. i/2409-2410 (Anas b. Mālik); Tab. i/2408-2409 (Rajā' b. Ḥaywā')—with many fanciful details; Tab. i/2408 (Abū Miryam, *mawlā* of Salāma); Tab. i/2522-2523 (Sayf < Hishām b. 'Urwa < 'Urwa); Tab. i/2407 (Sayf < KU). Cf. also the references in note 287.

289. Theophanes, *Chronographia*, p. 342 (A.M. 6135). On Jerusalem in the early Islamic cult, see above, Section 2. Cf. Elias bar Shīnāya, Bishop of Nisibis, *Opus Chronologicum*, p. 133 (text), p. 64 (translation): 'Umar enters Jerusalem in A.H. 17.

290. As used here, Palestine includes some of the area called al-Urdunn (Jordan) by the Arabic sources, which refers not only to Transjordan but also to the area between the River Jordan and the Mediterranean, i.e., northern Palestine.

291. The choice depends upon which reconstruction of the second phase one selects; see Section 7, above.

292. Bal. *Fut.* 139-140 (h—al-Qāsim b. Sallām—h—'Abdullāh b. Ṣāliḥ < al-Layth b. Sa'd < Yazīd b. Abī Ḥabīb); Tab. i/2396-2402 (Sayf < AU, AH < KU); Bal. *Fut.* 116 (Abū Ḥafṣ al-Dimashqī < SbA < several including Abū Bishr). Cf. Tab. i/2090 and *TMD* I, 545 (Sayf): is the reference to 'Amr and 'Alqama as commanders in Palestine under Abū Bakr a misplaced reference to conditions under 'Umar?

293. Ya'qubi II, 147-148; 'Amr asks 'Umar for permission to march. Khalifa I, 114; *TMD* (Zah.) XVI, fol. 350b (WbM—h—IL < Yūnus < Ibn Shihāb): 'Umar orders 'Amr to march. Tab. i/2404 (Sayf? < KU); Tab. i/2410 (Sayf < AU, AH).

294. Bal. *Fut.* 115-116 (h—Ḥafṣ b. ʿUmar al-ʿUmarī < al-Haytham b. ʿAdī, and Abū Ḥafṣ al-Dimashqī < SbA). Cf. above, Section 7.

295. Bal. *Fut.* 142; others say ʿAmr. b. al-ʿĀṣ conquered ʿAsqalān.

296. See above, Section 7. Elias bar Shīnāya, Bishop of Nisibis, *Opus Chronologicum*, p. 133 (text), p. 65 (translation), states that Muʿāwiya took Caesarea in A.H. 19. Theophanes, *Chronographia*, pp. 341-342 (A.M. 6133) also speaks of the fall of Caesarea to Muʿāwiya after a seven-year siege.

297. Tab. i/2396-2402 (Sayf < AU, AH < KU); Tab. i/2407-2408 (Abū Ṣafiyya < shaykh of B. Shaybān); Bal. *Fut.* 140-142 (Waq. and others); Khalifa I, 112-113 (I.K., I.I.); Kufi I, 318-322; Yaʿqubi II, 51.

298. The rebellious activity of the Jarājima (Mardaites) in this region several decades later attests to the fact that the Muslims' real control here was still quite limited: e.g., Bal. *Fut.* 159ff.

299. Bal. *Fut.* 128 (SbA) describes how the Byzantines restored their control over some coastal towns; Tab. i/2594 (Sayf) describes how Heraclius raided Egypt and Syria by sea. But see Theophanes' statement (p. 338, A.M. 6126) that the Muslims "seized the districts of Phoenicia and settled there."

300. Bal. *Fut.* 132-133.

301. Bal. *Fut.* 126 (SbA).

302. Bal. *Fut.* 127-128.

303. Bal. *Fut.* 144-145 on Salīḥ; Bal. *Fut.* 164 on Ghassān, Tanūkh, Iyād.

CHAPTER IV

1. As used here, the word Iraq refers to the districts historically known as Babylonia and Khuzistān, bounded on the southeast by the Persian Gulf, on the northeast by the Zagros foothills, on the north and northwest by the line of bluffs running from the vicinity of Takrīt on the Tigris to near ʿAnā on the Euphrates, and on the southwest by the fringes of the Syrian and Arabian deserts. Our use of the word Iraq thus specifically excludes the northern part of the modern Republic of Iraq, which is here called Mesopotamia or the Jazira (al-Jazīra).

2. Geographical and climatic data for Iraq are conveniently summarized in the Great Britain Admiralty War Staff, Intelligence Division, *A Handbook of Mesopotamia*, 1 pp. 1ff.

3. Hans Jörg Nissen, "Südbabylonien in parthischer und sasanidischer Zeit," pp. 84-85. The older eastern channel flowed by the ancient city of Bābil (Babylon).

4. For a detailed description of the medieval course see Maximilian Streck, *Die alte Landschaft Babylonien nach den arabischen Geographen*, pp. 175-333 (with lengthy descriptions of Samarrā, al-Madā'in, and Wāsiṭ); Guy Le Strange, *Lands of the Eastern Caliphate*, chapters 2, 3, and 4; *EI*(2) articles "Didjla" and "al-Baṭīḥa"; Ernst Herzfeld and Friedrich Sarre, *Archaeologische Reise im Euphrat- und Tigris-Gebiete*, 1, pp. 60ff; Jean-Maurice Fiey, "Topography of al-Madā'in," esp. map on p. 37.

5. Bal. *Fut.* 292-293, and references in preceding note. See further, Robert M. Adams and Hans J. Nissen, *The Uruk Countryside*; George Martin Lees and

N.L. Falcon, "The Geographical History of the Mesopotamian Plains." Lees and Falcon attempted to explain the flooding and gradual spread of the marshes by postulating a gradual subsidence of the whole of southern Iraq due to geographical conditions. This thesis has, however, generated much debate. For a recent discussion, see Curtis E. Larsen, "The Mesopotamian Delta Region: A Reconsideration of Lees and Falcon."

6. Adams and Nissen, *Uruk Countryside*, passim; Nissen, "Südbabylonien," passim.

7. Le Strange, *Lands*, p. 27; Adams and Nissen, *Uruk Countryside*, pp. 59-60, 63; Great Britain Admiralty, *Handbook of Mesopotamia*, 1, pp. 113-114; *EI*(2) "al-Baṭīḥa." The extended political turmoil of the late Sasanian period cannot have helped matters, as it would have hindered drainage and levee-building operations.

8. Arrian, *Anabasis* VII.21; Appian, *Bella Civilia* II.153; cited in Alois Musil, *The Middle Euphrates*, pp. 279-280.

9. John Hansman, "Charax and the Karkheh."

10. Descriptions of the course of the Tigris through the marshes: Streck, *Die alte Landschaft*, passim; Le Strange, *Lands*, pp. 26-28; *EI*(2) "al-Baṭīḥa"; *EI*(2) "Didjla."

11. The modern Euphrates channel near the southern edge of the marshes is a more recent feature. Cf. *EI*(2) "Furāt"; William Willcocks, "Mesopotamia: Past, Present, and Future," pp. 11-12. That a clear channel had existed in ancient times is suggested by the presence of a major international trade route through this region in the first centuries A.D. This route, which sustained the last flowering of the city of Uruk as a way station between Charax Spasinu (later Mayshān, Maysān) and the Mediterranean, apparently followed the Euphrates for part of its length. For the remainder of the route, goods were carried overland by Palmyrene merchants (presumably from some point upstream on the Euphrates via their city to the Mediterranean). Other references indicate, however, that the Palmyrene caravans began to carry their goods overland directly to Charax; this suggests that the Euphrates channel through the marshes may already have become impassable before the end of the Palmyrene kingdom in the 270s A.D. Cf. Nissen, "Südbabylonien," pp. 83-84.

12. See maps reproduced in A. Sūsa, *al-'Irāq fī l-khawāriṭ al-qadīma*, no. 12 (from al-Balkhī, d. A.H. 322/A.D. 934); no. 16 and 18 (al-Istakhrī, d. 340/951); no. 22 (Ibn Ḥawqal, d. 367/977); no. 23 (al-Maqdisī, d. 375/985); no 27 (al-Jayhānī, d. 4th/10th century); and no. 30 (al-Idrīsī, d. 560/1164).

13. Cf. Adams and Nissen, *Uruk Countryside*, p. 62; for a good description of the marshes see Wilfred Thesiger, *The Marsh Arabs* and "Marsh Dwellers of Southern Iraq."

14. George Babcock Cressey, "The Shatt al-Arab Basin," p. 449.

15. Herzfeld and Sarre, *Archaeologische Reise*, 1, pp. 57-58.

16. Le Strange, *Lands*, p. 239.

17. Cressey, "The Shatt al-Arab Basin," pp. 449 and 452.

18. William Willcocks, *Irrigation of Mesopotamia*, p. 34; Lees and Falcon, "Geographical History," p. 35; Le Strange, *Lands*, pp. 233, 242.

19. Herzfeld and Sarre *Archaeologische Reise*, 1, p. 245.

20. Based on Streck, *Die alte Landschaft*, pp. 24-38; Le Strange, *Lands*, pp. 65-69 and 57-61; Musil, *Middle Euphrates*, pp. 267-283. Cf. *EI*(2) "al-Anbār"; map appended to Willcocks, "Mesopotamia," following p. 104; Herzfeld and Sarre, *Archaeologische Reise*, 1, pp. 53-63; Adams and Nissen, *Uruk Countryside*, passim; Nissen, "Südbabylonien," passim; Robert M. Adams, *Land behind Baghdad: A History of Settlement on the Diyala Plains*, pp. 76ff., and "Agriculture and Urban Life in Early Southwestern Iran"; Ernst Herzfeld, *Geschichte der Stadt Samarra*, pp. 7-16.

21. *EI*(2) "Didjla"; Herzfeld and Sarre, *Archaeologische Reise*, 1, pp. 61-63; Herzfeld, *Samarra*, p. 76; Streck, *Die alte Landschaft*, pp. 33-38; Le Strange, *Lands*, pp. 57-62; Adams, *Land behind Baghdad*, pp. 76-80.

22. Adams, *Land behind Baghdad*, pp. 80-82.

23. The only vestiges of irrigation works in this region dating from the Sasanian period are the remains of a channel running from west to east near the middle of the marshes. This channel apparently did not survive into the Islamic period. See Adams and Nissen, *Uruk Countryside*, pp. 62-63.

24. The extensive traces of irrigation works still visible just west of al-Baṣra appear to be of Abbasid construction: Lees and Falcon, "Geographical History," p. 35.

25. Adams, "Agriculture and Urban Life," p. 116; Nina Viktorovna Pigulevskaja, *Les Villes de l'état iranien aux époques parthe et sassanide*, p. 163.

26. *Sabkha nashshāsha za'iqa hashshāsha.*

27. Muḥammad b. 'Imrān al-Marzubānī, *Nūr al-qabas*, p. 172; Bal. *Ansab* Reis. 598, p. 995 (Mad. < Abū Bakr al-Hudhalī); Tab. i/2539 (Sayf < MTMA).

28. Louis Massignon, "Explication du plan de Kûfa (Iraq)," pp. 349-350. On the legal status of lands in Iraq, see Chapter V, Section 5 and note 93.

29. On rice in this period, see Adams, "Agriculture and Urban Life," p. 118; Adams and Nissen, *Uruk Countryside*, p. 62. On sugar, see Pigulevskaja, *Les Villes*, p. 163. Note, however, that Pigulevskaja's statement is based on Le Strange, which refers to a later period. For crops in the Islamic period, see Husam Qawam el-Samarraie, *Agriculture in Iraq during the Third Century A.H.*, pp. 79ff.

30. See Eugen Wirth, *Agrargeographie des Irak*, pp. 131-163.

31. The best concise description in English of the way of life of the modern marsh dwellers is Thesiger, "Marsh Dwellers of Southern Iraq."

32. Analysis based on Adams, "Agriculture and Urban Life."

33. On use of Aramaic: Joseph Toussaint Reinaud, "Mémoire sur le commencement et la fin du royaume de la Mésène et de la Kharacène," p. 170; Jacob Neusner, *A History of the Jews in Babylonia* 5, p. 129; cf. Alois Musil, *Middle Euphrates*, p. 280.

On use of Persian: *EI*(1), "Maisān"; al-Mas'ūdī, *Tanbīh*, index, s.v. "Akrād."

On maritime trade: David Whitehouse, "Excavations at Sīrāf: Fifth Interim Report."

34. On Zoroastrianism, see Geo Widengren, *Die Religionen Irans*, pp. 243-245 and 283ff.; Robert Charles Zaehner, *Zurvan. A Zoroastrian Dilemma*, pp. 35-52; Alfons Gabriel, *Religionsgeographie von Persien*, p. 62. On town foundations with fire temples, see Ernst Herzfeld, "Khorasan. Denkmalsgeographische Studien

zur Kulturgeschichte des Islam in Iran," pp. 149-152; Pigulevskaja, *Les Villes*, p. 123.

35. Jérôme Labourt, *Le Christianisme dans l'empire perse sous la dynastie sassanide (224-632)*, pp. 306, 314-317, 326-329; Antoine-Jean Saint-Martin, *Récherches sur l'histoire et la géographie de la Mésène et de la Characène*, pp. 59-60; Artur Christensen, *L'Iran sous les Sassanides*, p. 262. Saint-Martin places Dastumaysān (Dasimaysan) west of al-Baṣra, which seems unlikely. On schools: Labourt, *Le Christianisme*, pp. 290-291; Fiey, "Topography of al-Madā'in," p. 35.

36. Michael G. Morony, "Religious Communities in Late Sasanian and Early Islamic Iraq," pp. 114-116; Labourt, *Le Christianisme*, pp. 217-219; Arthur Vööbus, "Reorganisierung der westsyrischen Kirche in Persien," infra; Jean-Maurice Fiey, *Jalons pour une histoire de l'Église en Iraq*, pp. 63-64, and his "Tağrīt," p. 301, "Topographie chrétienne de Mahozé," p. 413, and "Topography of al-Madā'in," pp. 34-35; also Musil, *Middle Euphrates*, p. 364.

37. Fiey, "Topography of al-Madā'in," pp. 10, 15, and map, p. 37. The *Gaon* may have been revered as the highest religious authority by Jewish communities as far away as northern Arabia: Israel Friedländer, "The Jews of Arabia and the Gaonate." The *Gaon* was suspended by Khosrau II in A.D. 590, however, and no new incumbent was appointed until after the Islamic conquest: Neusner, *History*, 5, p. 127.

38. On schools: Abraham Berliner, *Beiträge zur Geographie und Ethnographie Babyloniens im Talmud und Midrasch*, pp. 39, 43, 45-58. Cf. Pigulevskaja, *Les Villes*, p. 123 (Nahard'ā part of "Seleuceia").

39. On Jewish settlement: Geo Widengren, "The Status of Jews in the Sassanian Empire," pp. 117, 132 (on Pērōz Shāpūr); Labourt, *Le Christianisme*, p. 7; Berliner, *Beiträge*, infra; *EI*(1) "Maisān"; Neusner, *History*, 5, p. 129; Musil, *Middle Euphrates*, p. 280. Despite Musil's objections, the town of Pallūgtā' must have been near 'Aqōlā (al-Kūfa), because the troops who put down the rising there were dispatched from 'Aqōlā. On mixed towns, see Berliner, *Beiträge*, s.v.v. "Māḥōzē," "Matā Meḥasyā."

40. On *dihqāns*, see Peter Brown, *The World of Late Antiquity*, p. 166. On slaves and the agricultural labor force, see Pigulevskaja, *Les Villes*, pp. 141-150; Berliner, *Beiträge*, pp. 43-44; Julius Newman, *The Agricultural Life of the Jews in Babylonia between the years 200 C.E. and 500 C.E.*, p. 72. On *dastkart*: Pigulevskaja, *Les Villes*, 145-148.

41. *Jabalā Ṭayyi'*; today the region called Jabal Shammar after the tribe that has dominated it since the thirteenth century.

42. For a detailed description of the population of various Euphrates towns, see below, Section 4. On the B. Tanūkh, see Yaqut, s.v. "al-Ḥīra"; the presence of Tanūkh in Syria suggests that they were probably found settled all along the Euphrates: e.g., *Muruj* II, 82. On the geographical distribution of B. Kalb, see above, Chapter III, section 3. On the tribes of Bakr b. Wā'il, see Fred McGraw Donner, "The Bakr b. Wā'il Tribes and Politics in Northeastern Arabia on the Eve of Islam." On B. Tamīm and Ṭayyi', see I.K./Caskel, s.v.v.

43. Fiey, "Tağrīt," p. 302; Labourt, *Le Christianisme*, p. 218. On Jacobite dioceses among the B. Taghlib with seats at 'Anā on the Euphrates and at Jazīrat

Ibn 'Umar in Mesopotamia, see Jean-Maurice Fiey, *Les Dioceses du 'Maphrianat' syrien, 629-1860*, p. 58; cf. Musil, *Middle Euphrates*, p. 346.

44. *Arḍ al-'arab*: land of the bedouin, or of Arabic speakers? Tab. i/2469 (Sayf < T < Māhān); Ya'qubi II, 152.

45. See Chapter I, Section 4.

46. This is suggested by Meir J. Kister, "Al-Ḥīra—Some Notes on its Relations with Arabia."

47. See Fred McGraw Donner, "Mecca's Food Supplies and Muhammad's Boycott," p. 255, for Mecca's limited trade with Iraq.

48. Cf. Elias S. Shoufani, *Al-Riddah and the Muslim Conquest of Arabia*, p. 147.

49. On this route, see Alois Musil, *Arabia Deserta*, p. 550; on the strategic location of Dūmat al-Jandal, pp. 532ff.

50. Tab. i/2057 (Sayf < MTM and Sufyān); Tab. i/2021 (Sayf < 'Amr) does not mention Dūmat al-Jandal but states that 'Iyāḍ was between the Ḥijāz and al-Nabāj (on the road to al-Baṣra: Yaqut, s.v.) and was to march on Iraq via al-Muṣayyakh. Musil, *Arabia Deserta*, p. 549, believes that this would have required him to march via Dūmat al-Jandal in any case.

51. On the reduction of Dūma by Khālid and 'Iyāḍ jointly, see below. Cf. Tab. i/2035-2036, which names 'Iyāḍ as governor of Dūmat al-Jandal.

52. Some of Waq.'s sources suggest the return to Medina: Tab. i/2016, Bal. *Fut.* 340. On the question of whether Khālid went to al-Baḥrayn himself, or whether he merely sent reinforcements to assist the army there under al-'Alā' b. al-Ḥaḍramī, see the analysis in Shoufani, *Al-riddah*, pp. 131-134.

53. Eutychius, *Annales* 2, p. 9.

54. On the general problems of chronology for this period, see the discussion in Section 6 of Chapter III. 'Aqrabā' is dated to the end of A.H. 11 or beginning of A.H. 12 by the Arabic sources.

55. Shoufani, *Al-Riddah*, p. 119. But see *TMD* I, 450, which suggests that after the campaigns with Khālid during the *ridda* the bedouin contingents from B. 'Abs, Ṭayyi', and Asad that had fought alongside him returned to their home territories.

56. Ṭayyi': Ya'qūb b. Ibrāhīm Abū Yūsuf, *Kitāb al-kharāj*, pp. 141-142. Tamīm: Tab. i/2021 (Sayf < 'Amr < al-Sha 'bī). The problem of the role of Tamīm in the early conquests was raised by Julius Wellhausen, *Prolegomena zur ältesten Geschichte des Islams*, esp. pp. 12-15, 37-51, who pointed out that the historian Sayf b. 'Umar (d. before A.H. 193/A.D. 809), himself of Tamīm, presented the Tamīmī tribal tradition, which naturally portrayed the chiefs of the tribe in a heroic light and, by including them in the early conquests, attempted to erase their history of rebellion during the *ridda*, since it was claimed that the former *ridda* rebels were barred by Abū Bakr from joining Khālid's army. There is no question that we are at times dealing with a tribal tradition that exaggerates the role of the tribe, as for example Tab. i/2068-2069, where Tamīmī chiefs are listed as lieutenants over all the important towns and instrumental in all the important victories against Persian forces. But contra Wellhausen we cannot simply conclude that, because some branches of Tamīm rebelled against Medina during the *ridda*, all parts of the tribe rebelled. Final resolution of this issue will only emerge

after a painstaking examination of the activities of various lineages of B. Tamīm during the *ridda* and conquest periods.

57. Tab. i/2022-2023 (Sayf < T < al-Mughīra b. ʿUtayba). Cf. below, Section 7 where ʿĀṣim b. ʿAmr is said to have led a contingent to Iraq with the army of Saʿd b. Abī Waqqāṣ, that is, in phase three.

58. Bal. *Fut.* 242; cf. Bal. *Fut.* 244-245, where other authorities deny that Jarīr came to Iraq with Khālid.

59. Tab. i/2021 (Sayf).

60. A list of individuals mentioned is provided as Appendix D.

61. Tab. i/1886-1887.

62. See above, Chapter III, Section 6. The notice that Khālid marched to Syria with half his army (*al-nās*), leaving half (mostly dependents?) in Iraq, is provided by Ibn Isḥāq in Tab. i/2121-2125 and *TMD* I/467-468. Caetani, *Annali* II/2, 916, estimates the army at about 500 men.

63. The data on locations passed during Khālid's campaigning along the southern and central reaches of the Euphrates is so fragmented and vague that it has seemed advisable simply to summarize it without, in most cases, attempting to harmonize all details. The main attempts to reconcile the data are those of Wellhausen, *Prolegomena*, pp. 37-51; Caetani, *Annali* II/2, pp. 993-997; and Musil, *Middle Euphrates*, pp. 283-314 (appendix VII). Musil criticizes Caetani's reconstructions relentlessly and frequently with good reason, but his own attempted reconstructions, although plausible, can be accepted only if we assume that his many correlations of ancient and modern toponyms are valid. In fact both Musil and Caetani approach the sources with the assumption that a definitive, detailed itinerary can be reconstructed from the fragmentary accounts available; but it seems more realistic to accept the likelihood that, though the general outlines of the itinerary will be fairly clear, a certain measure of uncertainty will always remain in matters of detail.

64. Khālid at al-Ubulla: Bal. *Fut.* 241-242 (AM), 340; Khalifa I, 85 (h—ʿAwn b. Kahmas b. al-Ḥasan—a—ʿImrān b. Ḥaydar—h—Muqātil < Quṭba b. Qatāda al-Sadūsī); Kufi I, 92. But al-Ṭabarī himself (Tab. i/2025-2026) asserts that the conquest took place under ʿUtba and that accounts of it were displaced into Khālid's campaign. It is possible, as Musil suggests (*Middle Euphrates*, p. 286), that the town was conquered once by Khālid, retaken by the Sasanians after Khālid's departure, and had to be reconquered by ʿUtba. There are other traditions relating to the conquest of al-Ubulla, however, that seem to be misplaced: thus Khalifa I, 85 (al-Walīd b. Hishām) and Bal. *Fut.* 242 assert that after Khālid conquered al-Baṣra (i.e., al-Ubulla?) he raided the alluvium of Iraq as far as Kaskar and Zandaward. But it is difficult to believe that Khālid should have plunged over 175 km. into the heart of Persian territory with his small force before the Arab tribes along the Euphrates were completely subdued—and far easier to believe that the account may be the memory of some later campaign launched into Kaskar (perhaps really from the new al-Baṣra) after the main Sasanian armies had been defeated and the alluvium was open to invasion. Cf. also Tab. i/2025, which states that after the battle of Dhāt al-Salāsil (in Iraq) Khālid dispatched Maʿqil b. Muqarrin al-Muzanī to sack al-Ubulla, suggesting that Khālid had not conquered it after all.

65. Tab. i/2023-2036 (many accounts, all < Sayf); Bal. *Fut.* 242; Tab. i/2018 (I.K. < AM and Abū l-Khaṭṭāb Ḥamza b. ʿAlī); Khalifa I, 85 (gives *Nahr al-Marra*).

66. On al-Ubulla: Le Strange, *Lands*, pp. 47-48; Jean-Maurice Fiey, *Assyrie chrétienne*, 3, p. 276; *EI*(1) "al-Obolla"; S. A. Nodelman, "A Preliminary History of Characene." On Nahr al-Mar'a: Fiey, *Assyrie chrétienne*, 3, pp. 278-279; Yaqut, s.v., cites al-Sājī stating that Khālid made a treaty with the people of Nahr al-Mar'a for 10,000 dirhams at the time of his descent on al-Baṣra and cites al-Balādhurī stating that Khālid took its castle by treaty. Cf. Hans Heinrich Schaeder, "Ḥasan al-Baṣri. Studien zur Frügeschichte des Islam," pp. 36-37.
On al-Madhār: Le Strange, *Lands*, pp. 42-43; Fiey, *Assyrie chrétienne*, 3, pp. 253-254 discusses proposed location (near modern al-ʿUzayr?). Yaqut, s.v., places it four days from al-Baṣra in the direction of Wāsiṭ and cites al-Balādhurī, who states that ʿUtba b. Ghazwān, after conquering al-Baṣra, marched on Furāt, then on al-Madhār whose *marzubān* he defeated, and then on Dastumaysān (the district around al-Ubulla: Le Strange, *Lands*, p. 80; *EI*(1) "al-Obolla"). In view of this tradition we might wonder whether the accounts of Khālid's activity in al-Madhār are not misplaced references to later campaigns under ʿUtba b. Ghazwān, as may be the case with al-Ubulla.
On al-Walaja: Otto Blau, "Altarabische Sprachstudien—II," p. 337, identifies it with ancient Vologesias, but Theodor Nöldeke, "Zur Orientalischen Geographie," p. 98, rejects this on the grounds that Ullays was the ancient Vologesias and that al-Walaja was farther south. Musil, *Middle Euphrates*, pp. 111 and 293, identifies al-Walaja with a site near modern ʿAyn Zāhik, about 50 km. southeast of al-Ḥīra, on the basis of Tab. i/2230, which states that al-Walaja was separated from al-Qādisiyya by a flood-plain (*fayḍ*).
On Ullays: Nöldeke, "Zur Orientalischen Geographie," pp. 96-97, identifies it with Vologesias, near modern Kafīl and notes the existence of another Ullays near al-Anbār. Pauly-Wissowa, *Real-Encyclopädie der Classischen Altertumswissenschaften*, "Neapolis" (no. 17) concludes that the location of Neapolis = Ullays = Vologesias = Ālu-eššu (?) is still uncertain, but near al-Ḥīra. Cf. Musil, *Middle Euphrates*, p. 288. André Maricq, "Vologésias, l'emporium de Ctesiphon," identifies Vologesias with Valāshābād = Sābāṭ, 5 km. from al-Madā'in, but makes no identification with Ullays. Yaqut, s.v., mistakenly places Ullays north of al-Ḥīra, but a perusal of his account shows that he himself does not know its location and merely repeats the account of its location given by al-Balādhurī's report of Khālid's activity there. But he shows that several places that, to judge from the conquest accounts, lay near Ullays, were located, not north of al-Ḥīra, but south of it (al-Walaja, al-Ḥafīr). Cf. Tab. i/2029, i/2029-2030.

67. Bal. *Fut.* 243 and I.D. 231 describe one of the Arab notables of the town, Iyās b. Qabīṣa al-Ṭā'ī, as the Sasanians' governor (*ʿāmil*) in al-Ḥīra, but other sources state that Iyās, who had served in this capacity for about nine years following the deposition of the last Lakhmid ruler, was himself removed from office and replaced by the Persian al-Azādhbih: Tab. i/1038; *Muruj* II, 80; *Muhabbar*, 360. Cf. Yaqut, s.v. "Darb al-Kilāb"; Artur Christensen, *L'Iran sous les Sassanides*, p. 447; Gustav Rothstein, *Die Dynastie der Laḫmiden in al-Ḥîra*, pp. 121-122.

68. Tab. i/2038-2039 (Sayf < M); Tab. i/2044-2045 (Sayf < al-Ghuṣn b. al-Qāsim < a Kinānī) places annual tax at 190,000 dirhams; Khalifa I, 86 (Yaḥyā b. Zakariyya b. Abī Zā'ida < his father < al-Sha'bī) places tax at 90,000 dirhams; Bal. *Fut.* 243; Tab. i/2019 (I.K. < AM and Abū l-Khaṭṭāb Ḥamza b. 'Alī); Tab. i/2041; Din. 112; Kufi I, 93.

69. Tab. i/2019 (I.K. < AM and Abū l-Khaṭṭāb Ḥamza b. 'Alī) states that Bāniqyā paid 1,000 dirhams and a *taylasān*; Tab. i/2049-2050 (Sayf); Tab. i/2050-2053 (Sayf < MT and Sufyān); Bal. *Fut.* 244, mentions traditions claiming that Jarīr b. 'Abdullāh al-Bajalī reduced Bāniqyā for Khālid, but it seems likely that he only came to Iraq later: see below, Section 6.

70. On al-Anbār: Tab. i/2076-2077 (Mad.); Tab. i/2059-2061; Tab. i/2062 (Sayf < MTMZ). Market towns: Tab. i/2062-2077 (Mad.); Bal. *Fut.* 246, "Sūq Baghdād." On 'Ayn al-Tamr: Tab. i/2062 (Sayf < MTMZ); Tab. i/2076-2077 (Mad.); Tab. i/2063-2064 (Sayf); Bal. *Fut.* 246-248. On Ṣandawdā': Bal. *Fut.* 110.

71. There is much confusion between the latter two names; instead of Quṭba we sometimes find Suwayd b. Quṭba b. Qatāda, and at times Quṭba is called "al-'Ijlī." As both are said to have been active around al-Ubulla it is impossible to discern whether we are dealing with two (or three!) individuals whose activities have become conflated by the traditionists, or whether we are reading of one individual whose name was given variously.

72. Tab. i/2016 (Mad.); Kufi I, 90; Din. 111-112.

73. Kufi I, 88-90; Din. 111-112. Cf. Bal. *Fut.* 241-242. Kufi considers Suwayd b. Quṭba to have been a cousin of al-Muthannā (of Shaybān) and a member of B. Sadūs (of B. Dhuhl); Din., of B. 'Ijl.

74. Tab. i/2018 (Mad.); the account also mentions Madh'ūr b. 'Adī al-'Ijlī. Cf. Bal. *Fut.* 241: al-Muthannā raids, Madh'ūr asks Abū Bakr to appoint him commander of raids on the Persians, Abū Bakr instructs them to join Khālid.

75. Bal. *Fut.* 241; cf. Tab. i/2021 (Sayf < A), who mentions these chieftains as allies of Khālid but makes no mention of prior activity by them. Bal. *Fut.* 241-242 (AM): Suwayd b. Quṭba al-Dhuhlī, or according to authorities other than AM, Quṭba b. Qatāda al-Dhuhlī.

76. Or Suwayd b. Quṭba.

77. See references in notes 64, 65, and 68 above.

78. The one exception is Mad.'s statement that al-Muthannā was sent to raid the market town called Sūq Baghdād, evidently above al-Anbār (see note 70). But another tradition claims that al-Muthannā remained behind in al-Ḥīra when Khālid marched north: Din. 112. There are also scattered references to individuals from B. Dhuhl or B. Shaybān in Khālid's forces during his later operations on the upper Euphrates but no indication that more than perhaps a few men of these tribes accompanied him: e.g., Tab. i/2072-2073: a Shaybānī sent as messenger to Abū Bakr after victory at al-Thanī.

79. The term describing the bedouin is *'arab al-ḍāḥiya*. Cf. E. A. Belyaev, *Arabs, Islam, and the Arab Caliphate*, p. 91, on use of this term in Mecca. Tab. i/2029-2030 (Sayf < al-Muhallab, Z, and 'Abd al-Raḥmān b. Siyāh).

80. Tab. i/2031-2035 (Sayf < Muḥammad b. Ṭalḥa and M). The B. 'Ijl, Ḍubay'a b. Qays b. Tha'laba, Taymallāt b. Tha'laba (all branches of Bakr b. Wā'il) and

the B. 'Anaza b. Asad b. Rabī'a together formed a confederation called "al-Lahāzim." Except for those parts of 'Ijl that backed the Muslims, the Lahāzim seem to have opposed early Islam, not only at Ullays but also in al-Baḥrayn, where they supported the rebellion of al-Ḥuṭam during the *ridda*. For further details, see Donner, "The Bakr b. Wā'il Tribes."

81. For details of this lineage analysis see Donner, "The Bakr b. Wā'il Tribes." It is of course possible that this lineage rivalry coincided with religious divisions within the tribe as well, but generally little evidence is available on the religious affiliations among lineages of B. Shaybān.

82. See above, Section 2 and note 41.

83. His name is sometimes given as 'Abd al-Masīḥ b. 'Amr. Bal. *Fut.* 243; Tab. i/2038-2039 (Sayf); Tab. i/2019 (AM and I.K.); Tab. i/2044-2045 (Sayf); Khalifa I, 86; Din. 112; I.D. 285; cf. Rothstein, *Laḫmiden*, pp. 20ff., and Henri Charles, *Le Christianisme des arabes nomades sur le limes et dans le désert syro-mésopotamien aux alentours de l'Hégire*, p. 55, where the Azd are considered part of the 'Ibād. Note also Tab. i/2197 (Sayf < MTZ): 'Abd al-Masīḥ serves as a guide for the Muslims at the "battle of Buwayb."

84. Bal. *Fut.* 243; Tab. i/2019 (AM and I.K.); I.D. 213; I.K./Caskel, s.v. "Hāni' b. Qabīṣa."

85. 'Adī's brothers Zayd and 'Amr are also mentioned, and all were apparently sons of 'Adī b. 'Adī "al-Maqtūl," killed at Dhū Qār, although the names clearly do not work out. Tab. i/2044-2045; Tab. i/2040; Tab. i/2038-2039 (Sayf); *Aghani* XX, 134, 136-137.

86. He took refuge in the "castle of B. Māzin" in al-Ḥīra; was he then a member of B. Māzin, and if so, of which B. Māzin—of Shaybān or of Azd? Tab. i/2038-2039 (Sayf < M < Abū 'Uthmān and Sayf < T < al-Mughīra and Sayf < Baḥr < his father).

87. *Amwal* 39. Cf. Yaqut, s.v. "al-Ḥīra," who states that the Tanūkh lived in the Euphrates district and formed one of the three "categories" of the population of al-Ḥīra. Rothstein, *Laḫmiden*, p. 20, suggests that the Christian Arabs ('Ibād) included some of Tamīm; p. 28, suggests that Tanūkh were the real founders of al-Ḥīra.

88. Rothstein, *Laḫmiden*, p. 20. The Lakhmids (B. Marīna) continued to live in al-Ḥīra for some time; cf. the story about Sa'd b. Abī Waqqāṣ and the daughter of the last Lakhmid ruler related in *Muruj* II, 79ff.

89. Tab. i/2038-2039 (Sayf); Bal. *Fut.* 62; Bal. *Fut.* 244 (I.K.); Yaqut, s.v. "Dūmat al-Jandal." Yaqut places Dūmat al-Ḥīra some distance from al-Ḥīra proper, but his account of its location is vague. Since Dūmat al-Jandal seems to have been at this time the main town of B. Kalb, it is possible that "Dūmat al-Ḥīra" was simply an expressive way of saying the Kalb quarter in al-Ḥīra, as Musil suggests (*Arabia Deserta*, p. 544).

90. Bal. *Ansab* I, 26. Cf. the accounts of the battle of Dhū Qār.

91. Tab. i/2059-2061; cf. Charles, *Le Christianisme*, p. 58.

92. Yaqut, s.v. "al-Ḥīra."

93. See the lists provided in Bal. *Fut.* 247-248 and Tab. i/2063-2064; Tab. i/2121-2124 (I.I).

94. *Aghani* XX, 134.

95. The name is given variously: ʿAqqa b. Abī ʿAqqa, ʿAqqa b. Qays, ʿUqba b. Abī Hilāl al-Namirī. Tab. i/2121-2124 (I.I.); *TMD* I/467-470 (I.I.); Tab. i/2062; Tab. i/2063-2064 (Sayf); Bal. *Fut.* 248; Yaʿqubi II, 133-134, says he commanded a Sasanian garrison and says he was beheaded.

96. Tab. i/2062, i/2074-2075 (Sayf).

97. Bal. *Fut.* 110.

98. Michael Jan De Goeje, *Mémoire sur la conquête de la Syrie*, pp. 15ff. rejects the notion that Khālid made such a detour from his Iraqi campaigns and takes references to Dūmat al-Jandal to be errors for Dūmat al-Ḥīra. Wellhausen, *Prolegomena*, p. 47, note 3, supports the notion that Khālid went to Dūmat al-Jandal.

99. On Khālid's march to Syria, see Chapter III, Section 6.

100. The best reconstruction of the relations between Dūmat al-Jandal and the Islamic state, during both Muḥammad's lifetime and the age of the conquests, is provided by Musil, *Arabia Deserta*, pp. 531-553. He effectively destroys Caetani's sweeping assertion that Khālid never set foot there after Muḥammad's death (*Annali* II, pp. 988-992).

101. Tab. i/2021 (Sayf < A); Tab. i/2064 (Sayf).

102. Since it is not clear exactly when the Dūma campaign took place relative to other events in the early conquest, and since Khālid's arrival in Iraq may have occurred considerably earlier than the departure of the Islamic armies for Syria, it is possible that the Dūma campaign took place before the Syrian armies were yet in the field. Hence Khālid's force may have been the only one readily available to serve as reinforcement for the Muslims already at Dūmat al-Jandal.

103. Tab. i/2064 (Sayf); Bal. *Fut.* 62 (al-ʿAbbās < ʿAwāna b. al-Ḥakam); Tab. i/2076-2077 (Mad.); Cf. Tab. i/2065 (*qālū), TMD* I, 448 (Ismāʿīl b. Ibrāhīm b. ʿUqba < Mūsā b. ʿUqba), and *TMD* (Zah.) V, fol. 277a-277b (IL—h—Abū l Aswad < ʿUrwa), which places Khālid's campaign in the context of his later march to Syria.

104. So at least Bal. *Fut.* 62 (al-ʿAbbās b. I.K.) and Bal. *Fut.* 63 (ʿAmr b. Muḥammad b. al-Nāqid < ʿAbdullāh b. Wahb al-Miṣrī < Yūnus al-Aylī < al-Zuhrī); Musil summarizes the traditions about Ukaydir's contacts with Muḥammad. Generally, however, the question of Dūmat al-Jandal's relations to Muḥammad still needs much clarification.

105. This is suggested by Musil, *Arabia Deserta*, p. 551.

106. Tab. i/2065 (*qālū*) and Tab. i/2065-2066 (*qālū*). These sources also provide the names of several tribal chiefs who headed the contingents from these tribes: Ibn Wabara b. Rūmānis al-Kalbī; Wadīʿa al-Kalbī with Kalb and Bahrāʾ; Ibn al-Ḥidrijān with the Ḍajʿam; Ibn al-Ayham (i.e., Jabala b. al-Ayham?) with groups of Ghassān and Tanukh.

107. Tab. i/2076-2077 (Mad.); Tab. i/2065-2066 and i/2066-2067 (*qālū*); *TMD* (Zah.) V, fol. 277a-277b (IL—h—Abū l-Aswad < ʿUrwa); Bal. *Fut.* 62 (h—al-ʿAbbās b. I.K. < his father < his grandfather); Bal. *Fut.* 62-63 (Waq.); Bal. *Fut.* 63 (*isnād*, note 104). A romantic epic was woven about the story of Laylā bint al-Jūdī, who according to *Aghani* XVI, 95 was the daughter of the "king" of Damascus and was captured there, not at Dūma: see Musil's discussion, *Arabia Deserta*, pp. 548-549.

108. Tab. i/2066-2067 (*qālū*). The question of Tamīmī participation in the early conquests still needs clarification, however; see note 56 above.

109. Tab. i/2076-2077 (Mad.): Khālid returns and camps in al-Ḥīra in A.H. 12; Tab. i/2066-2067 (*qālū*): Khālid returns after a stay in Dūma.

110. See the examination of Khālid's possible itineraries above in Chapter III, Section 6, which shows that the march to Syria probably did not proceed via the upper Euphrates.

111. *TMD* I/467-468 (I.I.); Ya‘qubi II, 133-134 links this to the defeat of B. al-Namir under Hilāl b. ‘Aqqa (above, p. 184).

112. Tab. i/2068-2069 places this at al-Ḥuṣayd (see note 114); cf. Tab. i/2020 (AM < al-Mujālid < al-Sha‘bī), recounting the treaty Khālid made with the people of al-Madā'in—apparently a misplaced tradition referring to a later treaty?

113. The place-names and names of the chieftain from the raid on al-Namir are very confused. Kufi I, 134-136 and Tab. i/2069-2072 state that the chief was al-Ḥurqūṣ b. al-Nu‘mān al-Namirī, and the latter states that the raid took place at al-Muṣayyakh. But both names recur in accounts of Khālid's battle against the Bahrā' during his desert march; cf. above, Chapter III Section 6 and note 163. Other accounts associate al-Muṣayyakh with the defeat of the B. Taghlib; cf. following note.

114. Tab. i/2072-2073 for the quotation; Tab. i/1976-1977 (AM < Abū Ma‘shar and others) and Kufi I, 134-136; Ya‘qubi II, 133-134; Tab. i/2108-2110 (*qīla*) mentions al-Ḥuṣayd and al-Muṣayyakh (see preceding note) as localities involved; Tab. i/2068-2069, mentioning al-Ḥuṣayd and al-Khanāfis; Bal. *Fut.* 110-11, mentioning al-Muḍayya (an error for al-Muṣayyakh?) and al-Ḥuṣayd. See Chapter III, note 163.

115. Bal. *Fut.* 110-111, raid on Qarqīsiyyā'; Tab. i/2072-2073, raid at al-Thanī and al-Zumayl, identified by Musil with sites near Jabal al-Bishrī (*Middle Euphrates*, pp. 312-313); Kufi I/135; Yaqut, s.v.v. "al-Zumayl," "al-Bishr."

116. Above, Chapter III Section 6. It is important to recall that we cannot determine whether the operations on the upper Euphrates took place before the operation against Dūmat al-Jandal or after it.

117. Tab. i/2121-2125 (I.I.); cf. Tab. i/2110-2113 (Sayf < MTMA), where the Anṣārī, ‘Umayr b. Sa‘d, is said to have taken the booty-fifth back to Medina.

118. The transmitters in question are the group MTZMAS passed on by Sayf b. ‘Umar; see Chapter III Section 7 and note 237. On the question of tribal oral traditions, see Fred McGraw Donner, "The Arabic Sources for the Rise of Islam." It was in part traditions such as these that led Wellhausen to condemn all of Sayf b. ‘Umar's accounts as unhistorical, but this judgment seems exaggerated.

119. Din. 112; Bal. *Fut.* 110; Tab. i/2108-2109 (*qīla*). Din. and Tab. say that he was left at Ṣandawdā' after Khālid subdued its inhabitants. Din. vocalizes his name ‘Amr b. Ḥazm.

120. Tab. i/2088-2089 (Sayf < Mubashshir, Sahl, AU < KU and AH); Tab. i/2110-2113 (Sayf < MTMA); Tab. i/2108-2109 (*qāla*); Tab. i/2115-2121 (Sayf < MTM); Tab. i/2121-2125 (I.I.); *TMD* I, 467-468, 469-470 (I.I.); Kufi I, 134; Ya‘qubi II, 133; Khalifa I, 90; Bal. *Fut.* 110. Tab. i/2115-2121 states that al-Muthannā's force included individuals of B. ‘Ijl, Dhuhl, Tamīm, Aslam, and

Muzayna; also perhaps Ḍirār b. al-Azwar of B. Mālik b. Tha'laba (Asad), but on him cf. I.K./Caskel II, 242: died at al-Yamāma?

121. Tab. i/2115-2121 (Sayf < MTM). Tab.'s comment on i/2121 is clearly derived from this account.

122. This is suggested by Caetani, *Annali* III, p. 134.

123. Tab. i/2115-2121 (Sayf < MTM); Tab. i/2160-2161 (Sayf < Sahl b. Yūsuf < al-Qāsim b. Muḥammad); Tab. i/2161-2162 (Sayf < al-Mujālid < al-Sha'bī); Tab. i/2162 (Sayf < Sahl and Mubashshir, and < al-Mujālid < al-Sha'bī); Ya'qubi II, 142.

124. E.g., Din. 113.

125. The composition of the army is discussed in detail below.

126. Din. 113; Bal. *Fut.* 250-251; *Muruj* II, 307 (Waq.); Kufi I, 162-165.

127. Tab. i/2166 (Sayf < MTZ); Tab. i/2167-2168 (Sayf < al-Ṣalt b. Bahrām < Abū 'Imrān al-Ju'fī); Tab. i/2168-2170 (Sayf < MTZ); Bal. *Fut.* 250-251; Khalifa I, 92-93 (Bakr < I.I.); Ya'qubi II, 142-143. Some of these accounts may include misplaced material from later raids. Most of the places named are described by Yaqut as being in this region, but in some cases his description is clearly derived from the conquest accounts themselves and hence cannot be taken as verification of the toponym's location. Bārusmā, according to Yaqut, Ya'qubi, and Sayf, was in the *sawād* (cultivated area) of Baghdad, but I.I. in Khalifa I, 92-93 places it near al-Ḥīra. Khalifa also says that a column of troops was sent to Nahr Jūbara, which Yaqut describes as a well-known river near al-Baṣra (Yaqut, s.v. "Nahr al-Ijjāna"), but it is possible that the place raided was Jawbar, near Baghdad (Yaqut, s.v.) and the name hypercorrected to the more familiar one by Khalifa's sources.

128. Tab. i/2174-2176 (Sayf < MTZ); Tab. i/2180-2181 (I.I.); Tab. i/2180 (Sayf < al-Mujālid < 'Aṭiyya); Tab. i/2180 (Sayf < al-Mujālid and 'Aṭiyya < al-Naḍr); Khalifa I, 93 (I.I.); other sources, see Appendix E.

129. Tab. i/2156, giving the datings of Waq. (A.H. 13) and I.I. (A.H. 14).

130. E.g., Tab. i/2181 (I.I.); Tab. i/2080 (Sayf < a man < Abū 'Uthmān al-Nahdī).

131. Tab. i/2164 (Sayf); Bal. *Fut.* 250-251; Din. 113; Kufi I, 165. The figures for casualties at the battle of the Bridge are of little assistance; some take the total size of the army up to 9,000 men: e.g., Tab. i/2180 (Sayf < a man < Abū 'Uthmān al-Nahdī).

132. Such a list has been compiled as Appendix E.

133. A list of martyrs is found in Caetani, *Annali* III, pp. 161-171.

134. This is especially true of the lists of martyrs. This bias is well illustrated in accounts of the *ridda* wars; cf. Shoufani, *Al-Riddah*, p. 129.

135. Appendix E, numbers 12-17.

136. Appendix E, numbers 1-11.

137. Appendix E, number 26.

138. Appendix E, numbers 21-25.

139. Caetani, *Annali* III, pp. 166-171. Cf. Waq. I, 350, which states that seventy of the *anṣār* were martyred at the battle of the Bridge.

140. Further data on the composition of al-Muthannā's force is analyzed below.

On ʻIjl, see p. 191 above: ʻUtayba b. al-Nahhās al-ʻIjlī a subordinate of al-Muthannā.

141. Tab. i/1283 (Sayf < Muḥammad b. Nuwayra, T,Z, ʻAṭiyya); Tab. i/2188 (Sayf < al-Mujālid < al-Shaʻbī and Sayf < ʻAṭiyya); Tab. i/2188-2189 (Sayf < MA); Tab. i/2201 (I.I.); Din. 114; I.K./Caskel II, 240 ("Ḍabba b. Udd"), II, 486 ("Ribʻī b. ʻĀmir b. Khālid"), II, 345 ("Khathʻam"), II, 380 ("Maʻbad b. Zurāra"). The last named, father of the man who led the 4,000 Tamīmīs, had been a chief of the B. Dārim on the eve of Islam.

142. On the location of these tribes see I.K./Caskel, s.v. "Qays b. al-Nās (ʻAilān)"; " ʻĀmir b. Ṣaʻṣaʻa"; "Ǧadīla"; "Fahm b. ʻAmr"; " ʻAdnān"; "Bağīla."

143. The details of this complicated episode are confused in the sources. Tab. i/2185-2187 (Sayf < ʻAṭiyya and Sayf < Sufyān al-Aḥmarī < al-Mujālid < al-Shaʻbī); Tab. i/2200-2201 (I.I.); Yaʻqubi II, 142-143; I.K./Caskel II, 258, s.v. "Ǧarīr b. ʻAbdullāh al-Bağalī."

144. Kufi I, 171; cf. below, Section 7 (on Bajīla at al-Qādisiyya) and Tab. i/2221-2222 (Sayf < MTZ): with al-Muthannā in Iraq were 2,000 Bajīla under Jarīr b. ʻAbdullāh.

145. E.g., Tab. i/2197 (Sayf < MTZ); Tab. i/2198 (Sayf < Ḥamza b. ʻAlī b. al-Muḥaffiz < a man of Bakr b. Wāʼil); Tab. i/2185-2187 (Sayf < ʻAṭiyya and Sayf < Sufyān al-Aḥmarī < al-Mujālid < al-Shaʻbī); Bal. *Fut.* 253 (AM). Cf. possibly *Muruj* II, 310-311 (Waq.?).

146. Tab. i/2187 (Sayf < ʻAṭiyya and Sayf < Sufyān al-Aḥmarī < al-Mujālid < al-Shaʻbī); Tab. i/2200-2201 (I.I.); Tab. i/2187-2188 (Sayf < ʻAṭiyya and al-Mujālid). Cf. Tab. i/2196 (Sayf < MT); Tab. i/2202-2203 (Sayf < MTZ).

147. Din. 114; for Mikhnaf's lineage see I.K./Caskel II, 407, s.v. It is of course possible that two different forces of Azd tribesmen were involved.

148. The Azd confederation of the early Islamic period consisted of two main divisions, the Azd ʻUmān and the Azd Shanūʼa or Azd al-Sarāt. The origin of the Azd tribesmen in the forces in question here is not specified in the sources, but, since both possible leaders (ʻArfaja and Mikhnaf) came from clans of Azd native to the Sarāt region, it seems likely that the tribesmen they led also came from this district. Cf. I.K./Caskel, s.v. "Bāriq"; "Ġāmid b. ʻAbdullāh"; also I.D. 282-283, 289; I.H.J. 367; *Isaba*, s.v. " ʻArfaja b. Harthama."

149. E.g., *Muruj* II, 310-311; Yaʻqubi II, 142.

150. See above, Section 4 and note 58.

151. E.g., Tab. i/2187 (Sayf < ʻAṭiyya and Sayf < Sufyān al-Aḥmarī < al-Mujālid < al-Shaʻbī); Tab. i/2202-2203 (Sayf < MTZ); Tab. i/2201 (I.I.). Cf. *Muruj* II, 311; Khalifa I, 98; Kufi I, 171-173.

152. Tab. i/2202-2203 (Sayf < MTZ) (misplaced?); Tab. i/2203-2206 (Sayf < ʻUbaydallāh b. Muḥaffiz); Tab. i/2201 (I.I.); Tab. i/2199-2200 (Sayf < ʻAṭiyya b. al-Ḥārith); Tab. i/2206-2209 (Sayf < MTZ) (misplaced?); Din. 115-116; Yaʻqubi II, 121; Bal. *Fut.* 254. Cf. Tab. i/2215 (Sayf < Khulayd b. Dhafra < his father): al-Muthannā sets up garrisons on the edge of the alluvium. Tab. i/2190 (Sayf < MA): al-Namir and Taghlib still Christians.

153. References to "Buwayb": Tab. i/2184-2185 (Sayf < MTZ and Sayf < Abū Isḥāq al-Shaybānī); Tab. i/2187 (Sayf < ʻAṭiyya and Sayf < Sufyān al-Aḥmarī < al-

Mujālid < al-Sha'bī); Tab. i/2190 (Sayf < MA); Tab. i/2191-2192 (Sayf < MT); Tab. i/2193 (Sayf < 'Ubaydallāh b. Muḥaffiz < his father Muḥaffiz b. Tha'laba); Tab. i/2196 (Sayf < MT); Tab. i/2199-2200 (Sayf < 'Aṭiyya b. al-Ḥārith); Din. 114-115; Bal. *Fut.* 253 (Sayf); Bal. *Fut.* 254; *Muruj.* II, 310-311.

154. E.g., Tab. i/2191-2192 (Sayf < MT).

155. Din. 115-116.

156. Tab. i/2182-2183 (Sayf < MTZA); Tab. i/2187 (Sayf < 'Aṭiyya and < al-Mujālid according to his *isnād*).

157. Tab. i/2202 (I.I.); Khalifa I, 90; Tab. i/2393 (Sayf < AU? and Jāriya).

158. Most of the traditions about "Buwayb" are transmitted by the MTZMAS group (cf. note 153 above). The account in Bal. *Fut.* 253-254 derives from Sayf's collection and hence probably also goes back to MTZMAS. The synthetic account in Din. 115-116, provided without any *isnād*, ends with verses a more complete version of which is found in one of Sayf's traditions (Tab. i/2199-2200), so Sayf was evidently one of Din.'s sources as well. It is noteworthy that the three traditions that do not come from MTZMAS, and which ascribe important activities to al-Muthannā, all originate with men from the B. Rabī'a (of which al-Muthannā's tribe, B. Shaybān, was a part): Tab. i/2185 (from a Shaybānī), Tab. i/2198 (from a man of B. Bakr), Tab. i/2193. The last mentioned is a pro-Taghlib tradition. The importance of the tribal origins of these traditions is highlighted by Bal. *Fut.* 254, where he states with his usual candor, "The Muslims were led, according to the Bajīla, by Jarīr . . . (of Bajīla), and according to the Rabī'a, by al-Muthannā (of Shaybān—Bakr—Rabī'a). . . ." That al-Muthannā's reputation was tarnished by the defeat at the Bridge is suggested by Kufi I, 278, evidently based on a Bajīla tradition, in which a Bajīla chief gloats over the victory at Jalūlā' in which the Bajīla played a prominent part: "Blessed be al-Muthannā; if only he had lived to see this day!" The implication is that the Jalūlā' victory was sufficient to erase the defeat at the Bridge.

159. On the process by which the *ayyām* tales were constructed, see Werner Caskel, "Aijām al-'Arab. Studien zur altarabischen Epik."

160. Tab. i/2190 (Sayf < MA); Tab. i/2192 (Sayf < MT).

161. Found in Bal. *Fut.* 253. Cf. Khalifa I, 90, which states simply that al-Muthannā had raided in the area around al-Kūfa.

162. Such an assemblage of participants in the transitional phase is provided as Appendix F.

163. Cf. above at note 152: raids on al-Namir and Taghlib, who were Christian. Tab. i/2192 (Sayf < MT): Anas b. Hilāl al-Namirī and Ibn Mirdā al-Fihrī al-Taghlibī join al-Muthannā, who exhorts Anas also to attack the Persians "even if you are not of my religion."

164. *Isaba*, s.v. "Suhayl b. 'Adī al-Azdī." As he was an ally (*ḥalīf*) of B. 'Abd al-Ashhal (of al-Aws), he may have been resident in Medina before Islam.

165. See the accounts in Tab. i/1984, 1985, and 1988 (all Sayf < T < 'Ikrima and Sahl < al-Qāsim b. Muḥammad).

166. Tab. i/2183 (Sayf < Muḥammad b. Nuwayra and T, Z, and 'Aṭiyya).

167. Ya'qubi II, 143; Tab. i/2202 (I.I.); Kufi I, 171-173; *Muruj* II, 309-311; *TMD* (Zah.) VII, fol. 84b (h—Khalifa).

168. Tab. i/2216 (Sayf < Sahl b. Yūsuf < al-Qāsim b. Muḥammad); Tab. i/2216-2217 (Sayf < MTZ); and references in note 167.

169. The tribes from whom the levies were drawn are discussed below.

170. Tab. i/2202 (I.I.); Tab. i/2219-2220 (Sayf < MT, Sahl < al-Qāsim); Tab. i/2221-2222 (Sayf < MT < Māhān and Sayf < Z); Kufi I, 173-174; Bal. *Fut.* 225; *Muruj* II, 312. On al-'Udhayb as the camp to which wounded Muslims repaired during the battle of al-Qādisiyya: Tab. i/2317-2319 (Sayf < MTZ and Sayf < Ibn Makhāriq < a man of Ṭayyi'). On the location of Zarūd see Ulrich Thilo, *Die Ortsnamen in der altarabischen Poesie*, p. 116 and map B. Although the general picture of Sa'd's passage across the Najd is the same, there is much disagreement among the sources over exact locations. Tab. i/2202 states that Sa'd wintered at Sharāf; Tab. i/2221-2222 states that the levies gathered at al-Ḥazn and al-Basīṭa; Bal. *Fut.* 235 says that Sa'd camped at al-Tha'labiyya and that the troops gathered there; *Muruj* II, 312 has Sa'd camping at Zubāla and Sirāf (evidently a misvocalization of Sharāf). All these sites are located in the central Najd, on or near the Mecca/al-Kufa road.

171. Tab. i/2221-2222 (Sayf < MT < Māhān and Sayf < Z); Bal. *Fut.* 255; Kufi I, 174; Tab. i/2202 (I.I.).

172. Tab. i/2226-2227 (Sayf < Abū 'Amr < Abū 'Uthmān al-Nahdī); Tab. i/2347 (I.I.); Kufi I, 174; Bal. *Fut.* 258; *TMD* I, 531 (I.I.). Her name is also given as Salmā bint Ḥafṣa. Bal. says she was of B. Taymallāt b. Tha'laba (a branch of Bakr b. Wā'il); Kufi says of Tamīm.

173. Tab. i/2265-2266 (Sayf < MTZAS and Sayf < al-Mujālid); Khalifa I, 101-102 (Sharīk < 'Ubayda < Ibrāhīm).

174. The low figure comes from Tab. i/2236-2237 (Muḥammad b. 'Abdullāh b. Ṣafwān al-Thaqafī < Umayya b. Khālid < Abū 'Awāna < Ḥuṣayn b. 'Abd al-Raḥmān < Abū Wā'il); the high, from Kufi I, 201. A selection of other guesses is provided in Khalifa I, 101-102.

175. E.g., Rustam hands over a clod of earth to the Muslims when he rejects their demand that he embrace Islam, symbolizing that the land would soon change hands. Tab. i/2239-2244 (Sayf < 'Amr < al-Sha'bī); Tab. i/2236-2237 (isnad, note 174); Tab. i/2267 (Sayf < al-Naḍr < Ibn al-Rufayl < his father); Tab. i/2267-2269 (Sayf < TZAS and al-Mujālid); Tab. i/2269-2274 (Sayf < MTZA); Tab. i/2274-2277 (Sayf < Abū 'Uthmān al-Nahdī); Tab. i/2277-2278 (Sayf < al-Naḍr < Ibn al-Rufayl < his father); Tab. i/2278 (Sayf < al-Mujālid < al-Sha'bī and Sayf < S); Tab. i/2279 (Sayf < 'Ubayda < Shaqīq); Tab. i/2291-2292 (Sayf < MTZ); Din. 120; Ya'qubi II, 121-122; Bal. *Fut.* 257.

176. Tab. i/2231-2235 (Sayf < 'Abdullāh b. Muslim al-'Uklī and Sayf < al-Miqdām b. Abī l-Miqdām < his father < Karib b. Abī Karib al-'Uklī); Tab. i/2244-2245; Tab. i/2258-2260 (Sayf < Muḥammad b. Qays < Mūsā b. Ṭarīf); Tab. i/2261-2264 (Sayf < Abū 'Amr < Abū 'Uthmān al-Nahdī); Tab. i/2264-2265 (Sayf < Muḥammad b. Qays < Mūsā b. Ṭarīf); Khalifa I, 101-102 (Sharīk < 'Ubayda < Ibrāhīm); Bal. *Fut.* 255 (Waq.); Bal. *Fut.* 257; Kufi I, 196-200.

177. On the reinforcements, see the discussion of army composition, below. On the sheep and camels, see Bal. *Fut.* 255 (Waq.).

178. On the organization of the army: Tab. i/2223-2225 (Sayf < 'Amr < al-Sha'bī); Tab. i/2265-2266 (Sayf < MTZS and Sayf < al-Mujālid); Tab. i/2298 (Sayf < MTZ); Tab. i/2353 (I.I.); Kufi I, 201-202.

179. Traditions of this sort are traceable to many tribes of later prominence in al-Kūfa—not merely the B. Tamīm, whose chauvinistic traditions led Wellhausen to cast aspersions on the credibility of everything transmitted by Sayf b. 'Umar, but also to the B. Asad, B. Thaqīf, and others. The fact that many of these traditions from tribes other than Tamīm were also transmitted by Sayf suggests that he was not so much interested in glorifying his tribe, as Wellhausen suggested, as in conveying the tribal traditions he or his informants had collected because of the information they provided about the conquests. We cannot, then, dismiss so lightly as biased all accounts transmitted by Sayf; each account must, rather, be examined in the light of its origins and judged on its own merits. Cf. note 56 above.

180. For a more detailed attempt to reconstruct the course of the battle, see Sayyid Muhammad Yusuf, "The Battle of al-Qādisiyya." Caetani, *Annali* III, p. 710, thinks the description of the three-day battle followed by a night of fighting is an exaggeration and is not found in any early sources. But it is found in Sayf's accounts, in a tradition of al-Madā'inī (Khalifa I, 102), in Kufi I, 202-206 (who, though not very early, seems to rely on I.I. and Waq.), and in *Muruj* II, 314. The idea of a three-day battle is hardly absurd when we recall that much time was probably consumed in the individual combats between champions while the two armies cheered their men on. The battle of Ṣiffīn during the First Civil War, after all, is commonly said to have sputtered on in this fashion for a month.

181. Khalifa I, 102 ('Awāna < Ḥusayn < Abū Wā'il); Din. 123; Bal. *Fut.* 259; Kufi I, 212.

182. E.g., *Muruj* II, 312: 90,000 men.

183. Tab. i/2261-2264 (Sayf < 'Ubayda < Shaqīq); Tab. i/2355-2358 (I.I. < Ismā'īl b. Abī Khālid, *mawlā* of Bajīla < qays b. Abī Ḥāzim al-Bajalī); Khalifa I, 101-102 ('Awāna < Ḥusayn < Abū Wā'il and Bakr < I.I.); Bal. *Fut.* 255 (Waq.); Kufi, I, 173.

184. Above, p. 200.

185. Tab. i/2216-2218 (Sayf < MT)

186. Tab. i/2218-2219 (Sayf < MT, al-Mustanīr, Ḥanash). Ḥanash is referred to in the preceding tradition as "al-Nakh'ī"; al-Nakha' is a section of Madhḥij.

187. Tab. i/2219 (Sayf < 'Ubayda < Ibrāhīm); Tab. i/2219-2220 (Sayf < MT, Sahl < al-Qāsim).

188. On the genealogical issue see I.K./Caskel II, 282, s.v. "Hilāl b. 'Āmir b. Ṣa'ṣa'a" and I, Tafel 92.

189. Tab. i/2221-2222 (Sayf < MT < Māhān and Sayf < Z); I.K./Caskel II, 486, s.v. "ar-Ribāb."

190. Kufi I, 173. According to this account, however, the Asadīs were sent out by 'Umar to join Sa'd after he had left Medina, rather than being levied by him en marche. The two Tamīmī chiefs are said to have been 'Āṣim b. 'Amr and 'Āṣim b. Zurāra. The latter is otherwise unknown, but the former is frequently mentioned in the conquest accounts, including in those about Khālid b.

al-Walīd's campaigning in Iraq, in which he is said to have participated (above, Section 4). Is it possible that Kufi has mistakenly used his name here? Or did 'Āṣim return to the Najd some time after Khālid's campaign to gather new contingents from Tamīm, with which he joined Sa'd's force?

191. Tab. i/2220-2221 (Sayf < Muḥammad b. Sūqa < a man); Tab. i/2221 (Sayf < MT < Māhān and Sayf < Z). On Mu'āwiya b. Ḥudayj (or b. Khadīj?) see I.K./Caskel II, 413, s.v.

192. Kufi I, 173. As Sulaym was part of Qays, this group may have been part of the unidentified Qaysites from the Najd just mentioned.

193. Mentioned in Din. 119-120; but cf. Tab. i/2222 (Sayf < MZ < Māhān), which has al-Ash'ath coming from Medina at the head of 700 Yemenites to join Sa'd at Sharāf. Cf. also Tab. i/2216-2218 (Sayf < MTZ): 2,300 Yemenites including al-Nakha' march with Sa'd from Medina. Note, however, that al-Ash'ath and al-Ashtar are mentioned in accounts of the battle of Yarmūk in Syria: Bal. *Fut.* 135-137; *TMD* I/544; *TMD* (Zah.) XVI, fol. 88b. I.K./Caskel II, 381, s.v. "Ma'dīkarib b. Qays" states that al-Ash'ath's participation at Yarmūk (as well as at al-Qādisiyya) was celebrated in later poetry in order to make his reputation among South Arabian chieftains equal to that of Qays b. Makshūḥ al-Murādī, who did fight in both.

194. Tab. i/2303-2306 (Sayf < MT); Tab. i/2318-2320 (Sayf < MTZ); Tab. i/2320-2321 (Sayf < al-Mujālid < al-Sha'bī); Tab. i/2321 (Sayf < Jakhdab b. Jar'ab < 'Iṣma al-Wābilī); Tab. i/2321 (Sayf < 'Amr b. al-Rayyān < Ismā'īl b. Muḥammad b. Sa'd); Tab. i/2322 (Sayf < Abū Kibrān al-Ḥasan b. 'Uqba); Tab. i/2349-2350 (I.I.); Tab. i/2351-2353 (I.I.); Tab. i/2355-2358 (I.I. < Ismā'il b. Abī Khālid, *mawlā* of Bajīla < Qays b. Abī Ḥāzim al-Bajalī); Tab. i/2367-2368 (Sayf < MTZM); Tab. i/2498-2504 (Sayf < MTZS); Din. 119-120; Ya'qubi II, 144-145; Bal. *Fut.* 256 (Waq.?); Bal. *Fut.* 256 (al-'Abbās b. al-Walīd < al-Narsī < al-Sha'bī); Kufi I, 173, 201, 210-211; *Muruj* II, 313-314; Khalifa I, 101-102. A few accounts put Qays b. Makshūḥ in command of one force. Kufi I, 201 puts the number of Syrian reinforcements at 20,000. I.S. V, 390 states that 'Umar sent Qays to Iraq and makes no mention of Syria.

195. Tab. i/2223-2225 (Sayf < 'Amr < al-Sha'bī), 500 men (?); Tab. i/2349-2350 (I.I.), 400 men direct from Medina; Khalifa I, 102 (I.I.), 400 men; Bal. *Ansab* Reis. 598, p. 1212, 600 men; Din. 120, 1,000 men; Bal. *Fut.* 256 (Waq.?), 800 or 400 men; Khalifa I, 102 (Ibn Zarī' < Ḥajjāj < Ḥamīd b. Hilāl < Khālid b. 'Umayr), 1,500 men. Cf. Bal. *Fut.* 256 (no *isnād*); Ya'qubi II, 146; Tab. i/2351-2353 (I.I.).

196. On the composition of forces in southern Iraq, see below, Section 8.

197. Kinda: Tab. i/2335 (Sayf < al-Mujālid < al-Sha'bī). Bajīla: Tab. i/2355-2358 (I.I. < *isnād*, note 183); Bal. *Fut.* 267 (Muḥammad b. al-Ṣabbāḥ < al-Bazzāz < Qays b. al-Haytham); the first is obviously a Bajīla tribal tradition.

198. A list of martyrs for al-Qādisiyya is found in Caetani, *Annali* III, pp. 688-690.

199. This material is assembled as Appendix G.

200. For those involved at al-Madā'in, see Appendix H. The accounts of some raids into the alluvium during the first phase and transitional phase may in some

cases belong here; cf. above, notes 64, 66, 112, and 127. Sources for raids and siege of al-Madā'in: Tab. i/2358-2359 (I.I.); Tab. i/2419-2454 (Sayf < various authorities); Khalifa I, 103-104 (Mad., Waq., and others); Din. 126-127; Ya'qubi II, 123; Bal. *Fut.* 263-264 (various authorities); Kufi I, 212-213.

201. Sources for Jalūlā': Tab. i/2456 (I.I.); Tab. i/2456 (Sayf < Ismā'īl b. Abī Khālid < Qays b. Abī Ḥāzim); Tab. i/2456-2457 (Sayf < al-Walīd b. 'Abdullāh b. Abī Ṭayba al-Bajalī); Tab. i/2460-2462 (Sayf < 'Ubaydallāh b. Muḥaffiz < his father); Tab. i/2458 (Sayf < MTMAS); Tab. i/2458-2460 (Sayf < 'Uqba b. Makram < Biṭān b. Bishr); Tab. i/2463-2464 (Sayf < MTMAS and al-Walīd b. 'Abdullāh and al-Mujālid and 'Uqba b. Mukram); Tab. i/2464-2465 (Sayf < 'Amr < al-Sha'bī); Tab. i/2465 (Sayf < MTMS); Tab. i/2465-2466 (Sayf < Zuhra and Muḥammad b. 'Amr); Tab. i/2578-2579 (Waq. and Abū Ma'shar); Din. 127-129; Kufi I, 272-278; Khalifa I, 107-109; Bal. *Fut.* 264 (Waq.); Bal. *Fut.* 264 (no *isnād*); Bal. *Fut.* 265 (I.K.); Ya'qubi II, 151. The participants at Jalūlā' are tabulated in Appendix J.

202. *Isaba*, s.v. "Ḥumayda b. al-Nu'mān" (< Sayf).

203. On the position of Sulaym during the *ridda*, see Shoufani, *Al-Riddah*, pp. 80, 138-139.

204. He married al-Ash'ath's sister during the *ridda*: I.S. V, 390; I.S. VIII, 105.

205. On 'Amr b. Ma'dīkarib and the rebellion in Yemen: Shoufani, *Al-Riddah*, pp. 88-95; on 'Āmir b. Ṣa'ṣa'a, pp. 119, 125; on Ghaṭafān, pp. 114-115, 118-119. Parts of Ghaṭafān were later to join the Muslims against the B. Ḥanīfa at the battle of 'Aqrabā', however.

206. Tab. i/2174-2176 (Sayf < MTZ). Since Sayf or his authorities date the Yarmūk to Jumāda II, A.H. 13, the Bridge works out to Sha'bān, A.H. 13. Sayf also dates "Buwayb" to A.H. 13; Tab. i/2199-2200 (Sayf < 'Aṭiyya b. al-Ḥārith).

207. A.H. 14: Tab. i/2289 (Sayf < MTZ); Tab. i/2377; *Muruj* II, 313. A.H. 15: Tab. i/2349; Tab. i/2377; Khalifa I, 102; *Muruj* II, 319-320 (I.I., Mad., *ahl al-Kūfa*). A.H. 16: Tab. i/2377, *Muruj* II, 319-320 (Waq.).

208. Ya'qubi II, 123; Din. 126-127.

209. Tab. i/2456 (Sayf and I.I.); Bal. *Fut.* 264 (Waq.); *TMD* (Zah.) VII, fol. 84b-85a ('Abdullāh b. Ja'far—h—Ya'qūb b. Sufyān—h—Ibn Bukayr—h—al-Layth).

210. Ya'qubi II/151.

211. Tab. i/2578-2579 (Waq. and Abū Ma'shar).

212. Tab. i/2381-2382 ('Umar b. Shabba < Mad. < al-Naḍr b. Isḥāq al-Sulamī < Quṭba b. Qatāda al-Sadūsī); Din. 116-117; Bal. *Fut.* 341.

213. Khalifa I, 95-96 (Mad.) and I, 128; Tab. i/2381-2382 (*isnād*, note 212). Cf. I.K./Caskel II, 577, s.v. " 'Utba b. Ghazwān" and Bal. *Fut.* 342-343 (I.I.).

214. References, notes 212 and 213 above. Yaqut, s.v. "al-Baṣra," claims that 'Utba had been with Sa'd b. Abī Waqqāṣ in central Iraq, and that 'Umar ordered Sa'd to send 'Utba to southern Iraq after Sa'd's victory at al-Qādisiyya. Given what can be determined of the composition of Sa'd's and 'Utba's armies, however, it seems improbable that 'Utba's force was originally part of Sa'd's. Cf. Bal. *Fut.* 345, Tab. i/2377 (Sayf), and Tab. i/2380 (Sayf < MTMA), which have 'Utba marching from al-Madā'in (read Medina?); also I.S. VII/1, pp. 1-3 (Waq.),

which also claims 'Utba was with Sa'd at al-Qādisiyya. Is it possible that these traditions presenting 'Utba in al-Kūfa are due to a confusion between 'Utba and al-Mughīra b. Shu'ba, who is also said to have been there and later was in command in southern Iraq? Cf. *TMD* (Zah.) XVII, fol. 34b (Abū Nu'aym al-Ḥāfiẓ) (Waq.).

215. Tab. i/2377-2378 ('Umar b. Shabba < Mad. < AM < al-Mujālid < al-Sha'bī); Bal. *Fut.* 341.

216. Tab. i/2377-2378 (*isnād*, note 215); Tab. i/2384-2385; Din. 116-117; Yaqut, s.v. "al-Baṣra"; Bal. *Ansab* Reis. 598, p. 1189 ('Abdullāh b. Ṣāliḥ < 'Abduh b. Sulaymān < I.I.); I.S. VII/1, pp. 1-3 (Waq.—h—Ibrāhīm b. Muḥammad b. Shuraḥbīl al-'Abdarī < Muṣ'ab b. Muḥammad b. Shuraḥbīl); *TMD* (Zah.) XVII, fol. 38b (Ismā'īl b. 'Īsā al-'Aṭṭār—a—Isḥāq b. Busr).

217. Tab. i/2385 (Dāūd b. Abī Hind); Tab. i/2385 (al-Sha'bī).

218. Tab. i/2377-2378 (*isnād*, note 215). On the settlement of al-Baṣra, see below, Chapter V, Section 2.

219. Tab. i/2377-2378 (*isnād*, note 215); Tab. i/2378-2380 (Muḥammad b. Bashshār < Ṣafwān b. 'Īsā al-Zuhrī < 'Amr. b. 'Īsā Abū Na'āma al-'Adawī < Khālid b. 'Umayr and Shuways Abū l-Ruqqād) mentions 4,000 *asāwira* under "Ṣāḥib al-Furāt" being defeated by 'Utba; Tab. i/2384-2385 (Mad. < Abū Ismā'īl al-Hamdānī) (AM < al-Mujālid < al-Sha'bī); Tab. i/2385 (Bashīr b. 'Ubaydallāh), read "Abū Bakra" for "Abū Bakr"; Tab. i/2385 (Dāūd b. Abī Hind); Tab. i/2385 (al-Sha'bī); Tab. i/2385 ('Abāya b. 'Abd 'Amr); Tab. i/2386 (Abū l-Malīḥ al-Hudhalī); Tab. i/2387 (al-Muthannā b. Mūsā b. Salama b. al-Muḥabbaq < his father < his grandfather); Khalifa I, 95-96 (Mad.) says 'Utba waited several months in the vicinity of al-Ubulla before launching any raids on it; Khalifa I, 96-97 (several authorities); Khalifa I, 98; Khalifa I, 101 (Mad.< al-Naḍr b. Isḥāq < Qatāda) (al-Walīd b. Hishām < his father < his grandfather); Bal. *Fut.* 341; Bal. *Fut.* 341-342 (al-Walīd b. Ṣāliḥ < Marḥūm al-'Aṭṭār < his father < Shuways al-'Adawī); Bal. *Fut.* 342 (Mad. < Jahm b. Ḥassān); Bal. *Fut.* 342-343 ('Abdullāh b. Ṣāliḥ al-Muqri' < I.I.); Bal. *Fut.* 344 (Rawḥ b. 'Abd al-Mu'min < Wahb b. Jarīr b. Ḥāzim < his father); Bal. *Fut.* 344 ('Abdullāh b. Ṣāliḥ < 'Abda < I.I.); Bal. *Fut.* 376; Ya'qubi II, 121; Yaqut, s.v. "al-Baṣra" (q—'Awāna b. al-Ḥakam); *TMD* (Zah.) XVII, fol. 38a-38b (Zakariyya al-Minqārī—h—al-Aṣma'ī—h—Salama b. Bilāl < Abū Rajā' al-'Uṭāridī); I.S. VII/1, 1-3 (*isnād*, note 216) mentions defeat of *ṣāḥib al-Madhār* by 'Utba and says he returned to Medina because he was unhappy over being subordinated to Sa'd b. Abī Waqqāṣ.

220. Such a list is provided as Appendix K.

221. Tab. i/2388 (Mad.). Nāfi', as noted above, was put in charge of al-Ubulla by 'Utba.

222. Tab. i/2384-2385 ('Umar b. Shabba < Mad. < Abū Ismā'īl al-Hamdānī and AM < al-Mujālid < al-Sha'bī).

223. I.H.J., 389; *TMD* (Zah.) XVII, fol. 39b (Ismā'īl b. 'Īsā al-'Aṭṭār—a—Isḥāq b. Busr).

224. Tab. i/2388 (Mad.). He and 'Utba married sisters.

225. Tab. i/2380 (Sayf < MTMA); Tab. i/2534-2537 (< MTMA).

226. Appendix K, numbers 14-17.

227. E.g., Ya'qubi II, 124. Sayf's authorities state that Abū Sabra b. Abī Ruhm of the B. 'Āmir b. Lu'ayy served as governor for the rest of the year in which 'Utba died, and that 'Abd al-Raḥmān b. Sahl served as governor in the year following, so that al-Mughīra only became governor the second year after 'Utba's death, serving as governor that year and the year following. The majority of traditions pass over this in silence. According to this account, al-Mughīra was sent north to al-Kūfa and was then called back by 'Umar to govern al-Baṣra a second time after the governorship of Abū Mūsā al-Ash'arī. *TMD* (Zah.) XVII, fol. 39b-40a (Sayf); Tab. i/2498 (Sayf < al-Mujālid < 'Amir).

228. E.g., Tab. i/2534-2537 (Sayf < MTMA); Tab. i/2561-2564 (Abū Zayd < Mad.).

229. Khalifa I, 101 (al-Walīd b. Hishām < his father < his grandfather) (Mad. < al-Naḍr b. Isḥāq < Qatāda); Khalifa I, 105 (al-Walīd b. Hishām); Bal. *Fut.* 376; Bal. *Fut.* 376-377 (AM and Waq.); Kufi II, 5. Tab. i/2534-2537, i/2540-2541, and i/2554-2555 (Sayf < MTMA) put the start of the campaigns against al-Aḥwāz in the time of 'Utba b. Ghazwān and state that two forces participated in its conquest: one from central Iraq, including al-Nu'mān b. Muqarrin al-Muzanī, Jarīr b. 'Abdullāh al-Bajalī, and other heroes; and a second sent by 'Utba, in which chiefs of Tamīm were prominent. This contradicts other accounts transmitted by MTMA and by other authorities, according to which the reinforcements from central Iraq and the cooperation of two armies occurred at the time of the Tustar campaign. It seems likely that the accounts have been misplaced by MTMA in the context of al-Aḥwāz.

230. Bal. *Fut.* 376-377 (AM and Waq.); Kufi II, 5; Bal. *Fut.* 377-378; *TMD* (Leningrad), fol. 256b ('Alwān < a man < al-Ḥasan).

231. Bal. *Fut.* 379. Cf. Le Strange, *Lands*, p. 242, for location.

232. Din. 130-131; Tab. i/2551-2552 (Sayf < MTMA); *TMD* (Leningrad), fol. 256b ('Abdullāh b. Ja'far—h—Ya'qūb—h—'Ammār b. al-Ḥasan—h—'Alwān). Cf. note 229 above.

233. Kufi II, 11; Bal. *Fut.* 379 (Rawḥ b. 'Abd al-Mu'min < Ya'qūb < Abū 'Aṣim al-Rāmhurmuzī). The people of Rāmhurmuz later rebelled and had to be resubdued; cf. Tab. i/2542 and i/2554 (Sayf < MTMA).

234. Tab. i/2561-2564 (h—Abū Zayd < Mad.); Tab. i/2564-2566 (Sayf < MTA and Dithār Abū 'Umar < Abū 'Uthmān); Tab. i/2567-2568 (Sayf < MTM and Abū 'Amr and Abū Sufyān); Tab. i/2556-2557 (Sayf < MTMA); Din. 132-133; Bal. *Fut.* 378 (Abū 'Ubayd al-Qāsim b. Sallām < Marwān b. Mu'āwiya < Ḥumayd al-Ṭawīl < Ḥabīb < Khālid b. Zayd al-Muzanī); Bal. *Fut.* 378, 382 (no *isnād*); Kufi II, 7.

235. A list of these is provided as Appendix L. The names of those who came as part of the reinforcements from central Iraq have been omitted from this list.

236. For what is known, see Shoufani, *Al-Riddah*, pp. 85-87 and 131-134. On the reinforcements: Tab. i/2382-2383 ('Umar b. Shabba < Mad. < 'Īsā b. Yazīd < 'Abd al-Malik b. Hudhayfa and Muḥammad b. al-Ḥajjāj < 'Abd al-Malik b. 'Umayr); Bal. *Fut.* 341. As noted above, however, (Section 6), great confusion surrounds 'Arfaja's activities after his quarrel with Jarīr b. 'Abdullāh and the B. Bajīla. The timing of 'Arfaja's arrival as reinforcement is also rather

7. Tab. i/2369 (probably Sayf < MTMZ).

8. The most detailed study of the technological question of armaments and transport is Donald Routledge Hill, "The Role of the Camel and the Horse in the Early Arab Conquests," in V. J. Parry and M. E. Yapp (eds.), *War, Technology, and Society in the Middle East*, pp. 32-43. Most of the references to large contingents of cavalry in the Muslims' forces come from relatively late sources: e.g., Kufi I, 123, who tells of 3,300 cavalry from Quraysh, 1,700 cavalry from Sulaym, and 200 horsemen of Murād at al-Qādisiyya. Older references that mention horses (e.g., those in notes 152 and 162 to Chapter III) are generally quite vague and give no indication of the size or importance of the cavalry contingents.

9. Kufi I, 89 on investitures, etc.

10. E.g., Tab. i/2332 (Sayf < al-Walīd b. ʿAbdullāh b. Abī Ṭayba < his father) or *TMD* I, 535-545 (*isnād*, note 4 above), at the Yarmūk.

11. Tab. i/2331 (Sayf < al-Mustanīr b. Yazīd < his authorities): standard of al-Nakhaʿ. Bal. *Fut.* 109: Abū Bakr assigns standards. Kufi I, 254: standard of *muhājirūn*, etc.

12. *Wa aqbala ilayhi l-nāsu qabīlatan baʿda ukhrā*: Kufi I, 294.

13. Cf. Tab. i/2090-2095 (Sayf < AU < KU); Tab. i/2223-2225 (Sayf < ʿAmr < al-Shaʿbī); Tab. i/2298 (Sayf < MTZ); Tab. i/2329; Kufi I, 254; *TMD* I, 532-533 (al-Walīd—ak—Ṣafwān < ʿAbd al-Raḥmān b. Jubayr); *TMD* I, 535-545 (Abū Hudhayfa Isḥāq b. Bishr < SbA < old Syrian authorities). In addition to *qalb, muqaddima, maysara, maymana, ṭalīʿa, al-rajl, al-rajjāla, al-khayl, al-sāqa, katība* and *kardūs*, the following terms appear: *rukbān*, "riders"; *rumāt* or *murāmiya*, "archers" (or "slingers"?); *aṣḥāb al-ḥajf*, "swordsmen"; *nabīd*, "bowmen" (?); *al-rimāḥ*, "spears(men), lance(rs)"; *al-ʿudda* (?). Also mentioned are *ahl al-rāyat*, "people of the banners," i.e., commanders (?); *ahl al-najadāt*, "champions"(?); *ahl al-ḥafāʾiẓ* (?). On some of these terms see Harold Glidden, "A Note on Early Arabian Military Organization," and Hill, "The Role of the Camel." It seems unlikely that all the units described in the latter article were primarily cavalry.

14. E.g., the unit reportedly led by ʿĀṣim b. ʿAmr al-Tamīmi during the siege of al-Madāʾin and environs, which included individuals from many tribes: Tab. i/2431-2434 (Sayf).

15. Tab. i/2223-2225 (Sayf < ʿAmr < al-Shaʿbī); Tab. i/2327-2328 (Sayf < ʿAmr b. Muḥammad b. Qays < ʿAbd al-Raḥmān b. Jaysh); Tab. i/2331 (Sayf < A).

16. Tab. i/2223-2225 (*isnād* in note 15 above) on "chain of command."

17. *lam yuwalli min-hum aḥadan*: Tab. i/2223-2225 (Sayf < ʿAmr < al-Shaʿbī).

18. Tab. i/2327-2328 (Sayf < A < ʿAbd al-Raḥmān b. Jaysh); Din. 135; Ṭalḥa and ʿAmr b. Maʿdīkarib al-Zubaydī are specifically mentioned by ʿUmar as untrustworthy for command positions.

19. Tab. i/2412-2413 (no *isnād*). For fuller information on the *ʿaṭā'* system, see Section 3. Unfortunately, almost nothing is known about the stipend system in Syria.

20. Tab. i/2451 (Sayf < al-Mujālid < al-Shaʿbī).

21. Cf. Tab. i/2360 (I.I. < Ismāʿīl b. Abī Khālid, *mawlā* of Bajīla < Qays b. Abī Ḥāzim al-Bajalī); Tab. i/2380-2381 (Sayf < MTMA); Tab. i/2481-2482 (Sayf < MTMAS); Tab. i/2484 (h—Muḥammad b. ʿAbdullāh b. Ṣafwān—h—Umayya b. Khālid—h—Abū ʿAwāna < Ḥuṣayn b. ʿAbd al-Raḥmān); Tab. i/

2483 (Sayf < MT and their colleagues); Tab. i/2484-2485 (Sayf < Makhlad b. Qays < his father < al-Nusayr b. Thawr); Tab. i/2485-2486 (Sayf < MTMAS); Tab. i/2497 (Sayf < MTMAS); Khalifa I, 109 (Abū Muḥsin < Ḥuṣayn < Abū Wā'il); Din. 124; Yaqut, s.v. "al-Kūfa."

22. Tab. i/2497 (Sayf < MTMAS).

23. Tab. i/2482 (Sayf < MTMAS).

24. Tab. i/2486-2487 (Sayf < Makhlad b. Qays < a man of Asad); Tab. i/2482 (Sayf < MTMAS).

25. Kufi I, 213-214.

26. Chapter IV, Section 7.

27. Yaqut, s.v. "al-Kūfa."

28. Tab. i/2360 (I.I. < Ismā'īl b. Khālid, *mawlā* of Bajīla < Qays b. Abī Ḥāzim al-Bajalī); Din. 124.

29. E.g., Tab. i/2484 (h—Muḥammad b. 'Abdullāh b. Ṣafwān—h—Umayya b. Khālid—h—Abū 'Awāna < Ḥuṣayn b. 'Abd al-Raḥmān); Tab. i/2484 (Sayf < Makhlad b. Qays < his father < al-Nusayr b. Thawr); Khalifa I, 109 (Abū Muḥsin < Ḥuṣayn < Abū Wā'il); Yaqut, s.v. "al-Kūfa."

30. Tab. i/2499 (Sayf < MTMAS) on rotation of troops.

31. Tab. i/2487-2488; Tab. i/2488 (MTMAS).

32. E.g., Yaqut, s.v. "al-Kūfa"; Bal. *Fut.* 276; Ya'qubi II, 151.

33. See Muhammad 'Ali Mustafa, "Preliminary Report on the Excavations in Kūfa during the Third Season"; also Kāẓim al-Janābī, *Takhṭīṭ madīnat al-Kūfa.*

34. Yaqut, s.v. "al-Kūfa"; Bal. *Fut.* 276.

35. From Tab. i/2488-2490 (Sayf < MTMAS). Cf. al-Janābi, *Takhṭīṭ*, pp. 75-78; Louis Massignon, "Explication du plan de Kûfa (Irak)."

36. Tab. i/2490 (Sayf < MTMAS); Yaqut, s.v. "al-Qawādis."

37. Tab. i/2490 (Sayf < Khulayd b. Dhafra al-Namarī < his father).

38. Yaqut, s.v. "al-Kūfa."

39. Bal. *Fut.* 276-277 (Wahb b. Baqūya al-Wāsiṭī < al-Sha'bī), repeated in Yaqut, s.v. "al-Kūfa."

40. Note especially the passage in Ya'qubi II, 157, where a list of governors includes those for al-Kūfa and *Maysān* (rather than al-Kūfa and al-Baṣra). Had al-Baṣra been in existence, the term *'āmil 'alā l-Baṣra* would probably have been used, rather than "governor of Maysān."

41. Khalifa I, 97 (several authorities); Bal. *Ansab* Reis. 598, p. 1188.

42. Bal. *Ansab* Reis. 598, pp. 1188-1189 (h—I.S. and 'Abdullāh b. Abī Shayba—h—Wakī' < Abū Na'āma (?) < Khālid b. 'Umayr), repeated in Yaqut, s.v. "al-Baṣra" (no *isnād*).

43. Bal. *Ansab* Reis. 598, p. 1189; Yaqut, s.v. "al-Baṣra."

44. Tab. i/2380-2381 (Sayf < MTMA).

45. Yaqut, s.v. "al-Baṣra."

46. Tab. i/2537-2550 (Sayf < MMA).

47. Tab. i/2380-2381 (Sayf < MTMA); Tab. i/2487-2488.

48. See Chapter IV, Section 1.

49. Abu Muḥammad 'Abdullāh b. Muslim Ibn Qutayba, *al-Ma'ārif*, p. 566.

50. Preserved in Tab. on the authority of Sayf < MTMAS, etc.

51. Tab. i/2496 (no *isnād*). The figure 1,500 occurs here in passing; the first

rādifa seems to have been left out in the passage cited in note 52, which lists the payment granted to other *rawādif.*

52. Tab. i/2412-2413 (no *isnād*). This account is clearly misplaced; 'Umar could not have established the stipends for the *ahl al-Qādisiyya* and for those coming to Iraq even later before the battle had taken place, which is what the placement of this tradition implies.

53. Tab. i/2616 (Sayf). "share" = *naṣīb*; cf. below, Section 5, for a discussion of this term.

54. E.g., in Bal. *Fut.* 452 (I.S.—h—Waq.—h—'Ubaydallāh b. 'Umar < Jahm b. Abī Jahm), which indicates that those at al-Qādisiyya received 2,000 or 1,500 dirhams; in another place (Bal. *Fut.* 456) we read that Sa'd (b. Abī Waqqāṣ?) assigned a pay level of 2,000 dirhams to those who were readers of the Qur'ān, but that 'Umar retracted this assignment.

55. Ya'qubi II, 153. It is possible, of course, that this tradition is a vehicle for tribal chauvinism.

56. Tab. i/2496 (no *isnād*)—similar especially as regards the organization it necessitated in both al-Kūfa and al-Baṣra, on which see below.

57. Din. 117-118; cf. Tab. i/2538 (Sayf < MTMA?).

58. Cf. Tab. i/2490-2491 (Sayf < MTMAS).

59. Tab. i/2852-2853 (Sayf < MT): *inna ahl al-Kūfa qad iḍṭaraba amru-hum wa ghuliba ahl al-sharaf min-hum wa l-buyūtāt wa l-sābiqa wa l-qudma wa l-ghālib 'alā tilka l-bilād rawādif radafat wa a'rāb laḥiqat. . . .*

60. Tab. i/2633 (Sayf < MMT): *alḥaqa-hum bi-'ahl al-Qādisiyya.*

61. See below, p. 234.

62. Tab. i/2538 (Sayf < MTMA?).

63. Tab. i/2412-2413 (no *isnād*).

64. Cf. above, Section 2.

65. 'Umar Riḍā Kaḥḥāla, *Mu'jam qabā'il al-'arab*, s.v. "al-'Ibād."

66. Tab. i/2607 (Sayf < MTMAS).

67. Tab. i/2609 (Sayf?). He was Qarīb b. Ẓafar al-'Abdī.

68. Tab. i/2922 (Sayf < 'Aṭiyya < Yazīd al-Faq'asī).

69. Yaqut, s.v. "al-Kūfa."

70. Tab. i/2490-2491 (Sayf < MTMAS).

71. This supports, in a general way, Hinds's suggestion that the newcomers lived on the outskirts of the city and the early settlers lived near the city center, but clearly the division cannot be taken to have been too sharp. Cf. Martin Hinds, "Kûfan Political Alignments and Their Background in the Mid-Seventh Century A.D."

72. Tab. i/2490-2491 (Sayf < MTMAS).

73. Tab. i/2490-2491 (Sayf < MTMAS). The function of the *masjid* as a kind of tribal center is suggested by the fact that when 'Umar wished to raise an army, he sent an envoy to al-Kūfa to visit the *masājid ahl al-Kūfa* soliciting volunteers.

74. Tab. i/2842 (Sayf < al-Ghuṣn b. al-Qāsim < 'Awn b. 'Abdullah and Sayf < al-Mughīra b. Maqsam < '*ulamā*' of al-Kūfa); cf. Bal. *Ansab* V, p. 31.

75. Tab. i/2495 (Sayf < MTZMAS).

76. Tab. i/2495 (Sayf < MTZMAS); cf. Julius Wellhausen, "Die religiös-politischen Oppositionsparteien im alten Islam," p. 58, note 1.

77. Al-Ḥamrā' are usually considered to be Persian knights; cf. Wellhausen, "Oppositionsparteien," p. 58, note 1. See also Bal. *Ansab* IVA, p. 216; Bal. *Fut.* 280; Yaqut, s.v. "Najrān" on *ḥamrā' al-Daylam*. But it is conceivable that the references at times are to tribesmen of Azd or Lakhm; cf. 'Izz al-Dīn Ibn al-Athīr al-Jazarī, *al-Lubāb fī tahdhīb al-ansāb*, s.v. "Aḥmarī," and Kaḥḥāla, *Mu'jam qabā'il al-'arab*, s.v. "al-Ḥamrā'."

78. E.g., Tab. i/2491 (Sayf < MTMAS): a *dihqān* of Hamadhān in al-Kūfa.

79. Bal. *Ansab* Reis. 598, p. 594; cf. Tab. i/2595 (Waq.).

80. Cf. Ṣāliḥ Aḥmad al-'Alī, "Khiṭaṭ al-Baṣra," esp. pp. 288ff.; Massignon, "Explication du plan de Baṣra (Irak)."

81. Excluded from consideration here, of course, are the campaigns in Sistān, Khurasān, etc., which occurred at a later time.

82. Compare Appendix M (Nihāwand) with Appendices G, H, and J.

83. Especially Tab. i/2642-2645 (h—Ya'qūb b. Ibrāhīm and 'Amr b. 'Alī—h—'Abd al-Raḥmān b. Mahdī—h—Ḥammād b. Salama < Abū 'Imrān al-Jawnī < 'Alqama b. 'Abdullah al-Muzanī < Ma'qil b. Yasār). Acceptance of such misplacement somewhat blunts the specific criticisms of Albrecht Noth in "Iṣfahān-Nihāwand. Eine quellenkritische Studie zur frühislamischen Historiographie."

84. See Appendices N and O.

85. Tab. i/2223-2225 (Sayf < A < al-Sha'bī); cf. Nicolaus Fries, *Das Heereswesen der Araber zur Zeit der Omaijaden nach Ṭabarī*, p. 17.

86. Tab. i/2496.

87. Bal. *Fut.* 384-385.

88. Tab. i/2596 (I.I.)

89. Cf. above, Section 2.

90. Bal. *Fut.* 264; Din. 124; Kufi II, 68, states that Jarīr b. 'Abdullāh, who established the garrison, was in Ḥulwān, not Jalūlā'.

91. Tab. i/2497 (Sayf < MTMAS).

92. Tab. i/2596, for Kaskar province.

93. A thorough examination of this problem belongs to the domain of Islamic law and is outside the scope of this study. For a fuller discussion of the issues involved, see Werner Schmucker, *Untersuchungen zu einigen wichtigen bodenrechtlichen Konsequenzen der islamischen Eroberungsbewegung*, and the older but still stimulating treatment by Daniel C. Dennett, *Conversion and the Poll Tax in Early Islam*.

94. Bal. *Fut.* 265-266 (al-Ḥusayn b. Aswad < Yazīd b. Abī Ḥabīb); cf. Ya'qubi II, 152; *TMD* I, 579-580 (Abū 'Ubayd al-Qāsim b. Sallām—h—Hushaym b. Bashīr—a—al-'Awwām b. Ḥawshab < Ibrāhīm al-Taymī); *TMD* I, 548-549 (Abū 'Ubayd—h—Abū l-Aswad < IL < Yazīd b. Ḥabīb).

95. Tab. i/2372 (Sayf < MTZM). Later the kinds of land that made up the *ṣawāfī* were systematized and listed, but it is clear that all types are lands that would have been left vacant by their landlords when the ruling power fled. Cf. Qudāma b. Ja'far al-Kātib al-Baghdādī, *Kitāb al-kharāj*, part seven, pp. 35-36.

96. *marākiz*—i.e., that which they had conquered by means of their arms?

97. Bal. *Ansab* V, pp. 39-43 (h—'Abbās b. Hishām < his father < AM); cf. Kufi II, 170-172 (most detailed account); Tab. i/2850-2856 (numerous traditions);

Tab. i/2915-2921 (Waq.—h—Shaybān < al-Mujālid < al-Sha'bī); Tab. i/2907-2914 (Sayf < MT); Kufi II, 173-175.

98. Cf. above, Section 3.

99. Bal. *Fut.* 253 (AM).

100. Tab. i/2376 (Sayf < A < 'Āmir): *qadra mā yaqūtu-hu wa lā shaṭaṭ.*

101. Bal. *Fut.* 267-268 (al-Ḥusayn < Jarīr and al-Walīd b. Ṣāliḥ < Jarīr b. Yazīd b. Jarīr b. 'Abdullāh < Jarīr b. 'Abdullāh).

102. Kufi I, 288.

103. Bal. *Fut.* 267-268 (*isnād*, note 101, above). Sometimes convincing people to withdraw their claim to land was not easy; see the anecdote about Umm Kurz in Bal. *Fut.* 267.

104. Tab. i/2471 (Sayf < Muḥammad b. Qays < al-Mughīra b. Shibl).

105. Tab. i/2376 (Sayf < A < 'Āmir); Ṭalḥa and Rabbīl b. 'Amr were also granted land, whereas Abū Mufazzir received *dār al-fīl* (in al-Kūfa or al-Madā'in?).

106. Bal. *Ansab* Reis. 598, p. 431.

107. Bal. *Ansab* Reis. 598, p. 402; cf. Yaqut, s.v. "al-Baṣra." This grant is probably not to be considered among those in the alluvium, the *sawād.*

108. Yaqut, s.v. "al-Baṣra."

109. Bal. *Fut.* 273-274 (al-Ḥusayn and 'Amr b. Nāqid < Mūsā b. Ṭalḥa, and 'Abdullāh b. Ṣāliḥ al-'Ijlī < al-Sha'bī, and Shaybān b. Farrūkh < Mūsā b. Ṭalḥa, and al-Walīd b. Ṣāliḥ < Mūsā b. Ṭalḥa); Tab. i/2376 (Sayf < A < 'Āmir); *TMD* I, 580 (Abū Bakr b. Abī Shayba—nah—Ḥamīd b. 'Abd al-Raḥmān < Ḥanash < Muṭarrif); *TMD* I, 593 (Wakī' < Sufyān < 'Amir).

110. Tab. i/2376 (Sayf < A < 'Āmir).

111. E.g., Yaqut, s.v. "al-Baṣra." Cf. Bal. *Ansab* Reis. 598, pp. 430-431 for several references to *dūr* owned by al-Zubayr b. al-'Awwām in various cities including al-Baṣra.

112. Tab. i/2469 (Sayf < T < Māhān); cf. note 115 below.

113. This annual redivision of land held in common is suggestive of the tenure called *mushā'* in Ottoman Syria.

114. Tab. i/2468-2469 (Sayf < T < Māhān): "That [land that had belonged to the dynasty of Kisrā] was *ṣāfiya*, between Ḥulwān and Iraq; and 'Umar was content with the *sawād* of the *rīf.*"

115. Tab. i/2538-2540 (Sayf < MTMA): "so [the caliph] granted as *qaṭī'a* those lands of Kisrā between the Tigris and al-Hajar, dividing it among them."

116. *TMD* I, 557-558 (MbA—h—Mudrik b. Abī Sa'd < Yūnus b. Maysara b. Ḥalbas).

117. Bal. *Fut.* 123.

118. Bal. *Fut.* 147; Yaqut, s.v. "Ḥalab."

119. Bal. *Fut.* 150.

120. Bal. *Fut.* 127.

121. Bal. *Fut.* 133; the phrase used is *hariba qawmun min naṣārā l-Lādhiqiyya.* They were later to return under a treaty with the Muslims.

122. E.g., see Tab. i/2405-2407 (Sayf? < KU), which suggests the emigration by Byzantines from Jerusalem.

123. E.g., Aleppo: Yaqut, s.v. "Ḥalab"; Bal. *Fut.* 147. Damascus: Tab. i/2159 (Sayf < KU?); Khalifa I, 94 ('Abdullāh b. al-Mughīra).

124. Bal. *Fut.* 123.

125. See above, Section 5. Schmucker, *Untersuchungen*, pp. 86-87, points out that the *ṣulḥ* and *'anwa* traditions for Syria (and Mesopotamia and Iran) are more consistent than those for Iraq and thinks that the theory may first have been worked out in Iraq and then applied to the other provinces. Even in Syria, however, the accounts about the status of lands in some of the towns (e.g., Damascus) are self-contradictory.

Treaty accounts for Syria. Damascus: Khalifa I, 94 ('Abdullāh b. al-Mughīra < his father); *TMD* I, 503-506 (AM—h—Muḥammad b. Yūsuf b. Thābit < 'Abbās b. Sahl b. Sa'd); *TMD* I, 509-512 (Abū Hudhayfa Isḥāq b. Bishr); Bal. *Fut.* 121; *TMD* I, 502; Tab. i/2150-2155 (Sayf?); *TMD* I, 563-574. *Bostra*: Bal. *Fut.* 112. *Ba'labakk*: Khalifa I 99 (Ibn al-Mughīra < his father); *TMD* I, 526 (same). *Ḥimṣ*: Tab. i/2391-2392 (Sayf? < *shaykhs* of Ghassān and Balqayn); Yaqut, s.v. "Ḥimṣ" (AM, Waq.); Khalifa I, 99 (I.K.); cf. Bal. *Fut.* 131 (on *khiṭaṭ*). *Tiberias*: Tab. i/2159 (Sayf). *Lydda*: Tab. i/2405-2407 (Sayf? < KU). *Jerusalem*: Tab. i/2405-2407 (Sayf? < KU).

126. Bal. *Fut.* 131; Yaqut, s.v. "Ḥimṣ" (Waq. and others).

127. Tab. i/2159 (Sayf? < KU). Cf. Tab. i/2405-2407 (Sayf? < KU): commanders in Palestine, 'Alqama b. Ḥakīm and 'Alqama b. Mujazziz, took up residence in al-Ramla and Jerusalem respectively with the troops that were with them.

128. Tab. i/2407 (Sayf? < KU).

129. Perhaps because Jews had been excluded from other Syrian towns, e.g., from Jerusalem? Bal. *Fut.* 127.

130. *TMD* (Zah.) XII, fol. 245a.

131. *TMD* (Zah.) IV, fol. 90b.

132. Bal. *Fut.* 144.

133. It can only be hoped that careful archaeological work will someday partly offset this paucity of material in the literary sources.

134. Bal. *Fut.* 152 (h—Abū Ḥafṣ al-Shāmī < Muḥammad b. Rāshid < Makḥūl). The weighty implications of this tradition for later legal discussions, however, behooves us to handle it with caution.

135. *arāda qismat al-'arḍ*: Bal. *Fut.* 151-152 (h—Hishām b. 'Ammār—h—Yaḥyā b. Ḥamza < Tamīm b. 'Aṭiyya < 'Abdullāh b. Qays al-Hamdānī). Cf. Tab. i/2524-2525 (Sayf < al-Mujālid < al-Sha'bī), which includes among 'Umar's main objectives the distribution of *fay'* (immovable booty, i.e., lands?), dwellings, and booty, the organization of border posts and military commands, and the determination of military pay (*'aṭā'*) and rations (*rizq*). Cf. also *TMD* I, 553-559.

136. *TMD* (Zah.) VII, fol. 56a; fol. 63a (I.S.—ak—Waq.—h—Muḥammad b. Ṣāliḥ < al-Zubayr b. al-Mundhir). Cf. Khalīfa I, 106.

137. Bal. *Fut.* 178; cf. Yaqut, s.v. "al-Mudaibir."

CHAPTER VI

1. See Chapters I and II above.

2. Tab. i/2082 (Sayf < Sahl b. Yūsuf < al-Qāsim b. Muḥammad). Cf. above, Chapter III, Section 3.

3. Bal. *Ansab* V, p. 28 (h—Muḥammad b. Ḥātim b. Maymūn—h—al-Ḥajjāj < al-'A'war < Ibn Jurayj < 'Aṭā' < Ibn 'Abbās).

4. Tab. i/2216; Bal. *Ansab* Reis. 598, p. 598 (Mad. < Muḥammad b. Ṣāliḥ < 'Abd al-Malik b. Nawfal b. Musāḥiq); Bal. *Ansab* Reis. 598, p. 692: Abū 'Ubayda appointed over *ṣadaqa* by 'Umar (but where?); Tab. i/2211: *kataba* [*'Umar*] *ilā 'ummāl al-'arab 'alā l-kuwar wa l-qabā'il.*

5. As we are told happened under the caliph 'Uthmān. On *ṣadaqa*: Bal. *Ansab* V, p. 28 (I.S. < Waq. < Muḥammad b. 'Abdullāh < al-Zuhrī); Bal. *Ansab* V, p. 29 (I.S. < Waq. < Ibn Abī Sabra < his authorities); Bal. *Ansab* Reis. 598, p. 588 (h—Salama b. al-Saqr al-Ḍabbī < 'Abdullāh b. Ṣuhayb < Ismā'īl b. Abī Khālid < Qays b. Abī Ḥāzim).

6. Tab. i/2508; Bal. *Ansab* V, p. 31 (I.S. < Waq. < Ma'mar < Jābir < al-Sha'bī); Tab. i/2843 (Sayf < MT); Tab. i/2840 (Sayf < MT); Tab. i/2812 (Sayf < al-Qāsim b. al-Walīd < al-Musayyib b. 'Abd Khayr < 'Abdullāh b. 'Ukaym). The last describes the post as *'āmil* over the Rabī'a, the "genealogical" grouping among which the B. Taghlib, al-Namir, and some other tribes of the Jazīra were classified.

7. Cf. Bal. *Ansab* V, p. 26 (I.S. < Waq. < Muḥammad b. 'Abdullah < al-Zuhrī); Bal. *Ansab* V, p. 28 (I.S. < Waq. < 'Abdullāh b. Ja'far < Umm Bakr < her father); Bal. *Ansab* V, p. 29 (I.S. < Waq. < Ibn Abī Sabra < his authorities); Bal. *Ansab* Reis. 598, p. 588 (*isnād*, note 5 above).

8. See above, Chapter II, Section 4.

9. Ya'qubi II, 147. Ya'qubi II, 142 has a variant account in which Jabala objects to paying the *jizya* as well because it was a tribute paid only by the *'ulūj*, "scum"—a reference, most probably, to the settled peasant population that did manual labor and was traditionally despised by arrogant warrior nomads such as Jabala.

10. Tab. i/2497 (Sayf < MTMAS). Cf. Ya'qubi II, 152: 'Umar levies tax (*jizya*) on tradesmen of all crafts.

11. Cf. above, Chapter IV, Section 7. On making contact with tribes at wells in the Najd to raise recruits: Tab. i/2221 (Sayf < MT < Māhān, and Sayf < Z); cf. also Tab. i/2216-2217.

12. Cf. above, Chapter V, Section 1.

13. E.g., the case of the Thaqaf' amirs in southern Iraq; see above, Chapter IV, Section 8.

14. As noted above, the composition of the armies for the various phases of the campaigns in Syria cannot be determined with sufficient clarity to state whether or not the same pattern obtained there as well. It seems likely, however, that the Quraysh predominated in the early phases in Syria, as the *anṣār* and Thaqīf did in the early phases in Iraq.

15. See above, Chapter IV, Section 7.

16. The exact relation of this stratum to the ruling elite in the first few years after Muḥammad's death needs further clarification.

17. On this, see the discussion in Chapter II, Section 2.

18. Tab. i/2563; Tab. i/2497 (Sayf < MTMAS); Ya'qubi II, 153-154; Tab. i/2494-2495 (Sayf < 'Umar b. 'Ayyāsh < Abū Kathīr); Tab. i/2261 (Sayf < Abū 'Amr < Abū 'Uthmān al-Nahdī); Tab. i/2463 (Sayf < MTMAS, al-Walīd b. 'Abdullāh, al-Mujālid, 'Uqba b. Makram); Bal. *Fut.* 457-458.

19. Ya'qubi II, 153-154.

20. Tab. i/2324.

21. The little that is known about these lands is described above, Chapter V, Section 5.

22. On army organization, see Chapter V, Section 1.

23. See above, Chapter IV, Section 6.

24. Bal. *Fut.* 268.

25. On Jarīr's background, see above, Chapter IV, Section 6.

26. Cf. Tab. i/2369 for another possible reference to *ta'līf al-qulūb.*

27. *TMD* (Zah.) III, fol. 19b (ak—Shujā' b. 'Alī b. Shujā'—ak—'Abdullāh b. Manda ?); fol. 21b (h—Waq.—ak—Ibrāhīm b. Ismā'īl b. Abī Ḥabība < Dāūd b. al-Ḥuṣayn).

28. *TMD* I, 531 (I.I.); Tab. i/2347; Bal. *Fut.* 258. Cf. above, Chapter IV, Section 7.

29. Above, Chapter V, Section 5.

30. For an example of this practice on the eve of the First Civil War see Tab. i/2907ff. (Sayf < MT), which describes a disastrous audience held by 'Uthmān's governor in al-Kūfa. A parallel case is mentioned by P. Salzman, "Political Organization among Nomadic Peoples," pp. 129-130, who describes the changing authority enjoyed by chiefs of the Tuareg under the impact of French colonial administration. The Tuareg chiefs had little power over their fellow tribesmen until the French used them as official spokesmen for their tribes, after which the status and power of the chiefs increased dramatically.

31. On the docile posture of the *ashrāf* of the garrison towns of Iraq, see any account of their role in the rebellion of Ḥujr b. 'Adī, the martyrdom of al-Ḥusayn b. 'Alī at Karbalā', or other social disturbances.

32. The importance of the function of "distributor of surplus" in the nascence of social ranking is stressed by Elman R. Service, *Primitive Social Organization,* pp. 143ff. See above, Chapter V, Section 4, for a discussion of the *'irāfa.*

33. Kufi II, 44.

34. Tab. i/2327-2328.

35. *'An lā yasta'mila-hu*: Ya'qubi II, 129-130.

36. *Wa amara an lā yuwallā shay'an wa an yustashāru fī l-ḥurūb*: I.S. V, p. 390.

37. *Wa lam yuwalli min-hum aḥadan*: Tab. i/2223-2225 (Sayf < A < al-Sha'bī).

38. Above, Chapter II, Section 4.

39. Bal. *Fut.* 457-458.

40. *A'rābī jilf* is the phrase employed: Bal. *Ansab* V, 30 (AM). Many other accounts exist in which the nomad bumpkin (*a'rābī*), fresh from the desert, is the butt of jokes among the settled tribesmen of the garrison towns.

41. Quotation from Kufi, *Kitāb al-Futūḥ* (Bankipore MS), fol. 1b. Cf. Abū Bakr's statement (fol. 3a, top); also the statement by al-Ash'ath b. Qays al-Kindī in *TMD* (Zah.) III, fol. 21a (I.S.—ak—Waq. < Khālid b. al-Qāsim < Zur'a b. 'Abdullāh < Ziyād b. Labīd).

42. *ḥattā lā tartaddu a'rābiyyan*: Tab. i/2858-2860 (Sayf < 'Aṭiyya < Yazīd al-Faq'asī); cf. Tab. i/2896 (Sayf < al-Qa'qā' b. al-Ṣalt < a man < Kulayb b. al-Ḥalḥal < al-Ḥalḥal b. Dhurrī).

43. 'Utba seems to have come originally from the B. Māzin b. Manṣūr, a

branch of the Qays b. 'Aylān grouping—and an essentially nomadic group. But he had apparently long lived in Mecca, where he was an ally (*ḥalīf*) of the B. Nawfal of Quraysh before Islam. He converted early to Islam, and migrated to Medina sometime during the year A.H. 1 (William Montgomery Watt, *Muhammad at Medina*, pp. 3, 6). He was evidently considered among the Meccan Emigrants (*muhājirūn*) as Muḥammad teamed him up with one of the *anṣār* when he established his "blood-brotherhood" system (*mu'ākhāt*) designed to help provide for needy *muhājirūn* in the trying first years after the *hijra* (I.S. III/2, 101). Although genealogically he was a member of the nomadic B. Qays b. 'Aylān, he was for practical purposes a Meccan townsman.

44. Bal. *Fut.* 343; Bal. *Ansab* Reis. 598, p. 1189; Ya'qubi II, 123-124; Yaqut, s.v. "al-Baṣra"; Tab. i/2386 (Mad.). The terms used in these passages are *ahl al-wabar* and *ahl al-madar.*

45. Cf. *Isaba*, s.v. "Mujāshi' b. Mas'ūd"; I.S. V, p. 34.

46. Cf. above, Chapter II, Section 2.

47. Or perhaps also *kharāj*, "tax." It is clear from the earliest citations using these terms that both *jizya* and *kharāj* originally meant simply "tax," and had not yet acquired the restricted meanings "poll tax" and "land tax" respectively that they bore in later times. Cf. Daniel C. Dennett, *Conversion and the Poll Tax in Early Islam.* The term "*kharāj*," though sometimes found in early sources (e.g., Tab. i/2371), does not seem to have been frequently used in the earliest period, and may only have come into common use during the Umayyad period.

48. *fa-man asra'a ilā l-hijrati, asra'a bi-hi l-'aṭā': Amwal*, p. 223 (no. 547). This passage is cited and differently interpreted by Miklos Muranyi, *Die Prophetengenossen in der frühislamischen Geschichte*, p. 48, who thinks the passage means that the earlier a member of the Meccan Emigrants made his *hijra* to Medina, the greater his *'aṭā'*. The text, however, does not speak of the size of the stipend, but rather asserts that one had to settle in order to be eligible for it—and the sooner the better.

49. *Fa-'inna-kum bi-l-ḥijāzi bi-ghayri dāri maqāmin, wa qad wa'ada-kum Allāhu 'azza wa jalla kunūza Kisrā wa Qayṣar*: Kufi I, 123; cf. *Muruj* II, 307 (Waq.).

50. Bal. *Fut.* 150; Bal. *Fut.* 178; cf. above, Chapter V, Section 6.

51. See, for example, the case of the thief Ḥukaym b. Jabala, who went out into the districts of Fārs "behind the army" after its return and plundered at will. He was locked up by the governor of al-Baṣra on 'Uthmān's orders, after the *ahl al-dhimma* and *ahl al-qibla* (i.e., non-Muslims and Muslims) together complained to the caliph about his depredations: Tab. i/2922 (Sayf < 'Aṭiyya < Yazīd al-Faq'asī).

52. Above, Chapter V, Sections 5 and 6. We must remember, also, that nomadic tribesmen despise the peasantry; it is therefore difficult to imagine that many of them would have been eager to adopt the peasant life.

53. This was noted already by Henri Lammens, "Études sur le règne du Calife Omaiyade Mo'awiya Ier," p. 30.

54. Cf. above, Introduction. The latter thesis depends upon the assumption that the trans-Arabian commerce in luxuries had in fact shifted north during the years preceding the conquest—an assumption that is exceedingly difficult to verify.

55. Bal. *Ansab* Reis. 598, p. 598 (Mad. < Muḥammad b. Ṣāliḥ < 'Abd al-Malik b. Nawfal b. Musāḥiq).

EPILOGUE

1. Tab. i/2141: *li-man hādha l-'amr? . . . hal li-l-'anṣāri fī hādha l-'amri naṣībun?*
2. I.S. VII/1, p. 3 (Waq.—h—Ibrāhīm b. Muḥammad b. Shuraḥbīl al-'Abdarī < Muṣ'ab b. Muḥammad b. Shuraḥbīl b. Ḥasana).
3. Bal. *Ansab* Reis. 598, p. 693.
4. See above, pp. 249-250.
5. Rudolf Veselý, "Die Anṣār im ersten Bürgerkriege (36-40 d. H.)."

APPENDICES

NOTE TO THE APPENDICES

Most of the appendices consist of lists of individuals mentioned in connection with a specific event or belonging to a specific group. These lists form the basis for some of the analysis carried out in Chapters III, IV, and V and are referred to in the notes to those chapters. The order in which individuals are listed is not strictly systematic; an attempt has been made, however, to group individuals from the same family or tribal group together, and individuals who played a major role in events, or who are mentioned very frequently in the sources for those events, are generally placed toward the beginning of the list. In some cases, all members of a specific tribe are grouped under a common heading; in others, where such grouping by tribe was for one or another reason less practical, the tribal affiliation of various individuals is given in parentheses after their proper name.

In Appendix J and Appendix O, the material to be tabulated did not lend itself to listing individuals, but suggested a somewhat different treatment. In these cases, separate accounts dealing with the subjects at hand are listed.

The lists make no claim to be exhaustive, particularly with regard to documentation, as many additional references could certainly be culled from a wide variety of sources not consulted for this study. It seems probable, however, that most new material that would be found in this way would merely reinforce the general picture already drawn, rather than altering it significantly. The lists, then, although not exhaustive, can claim to be fairly representative of the collective information that could be found if all sources were scrutinized.

APPENDIX A. AJNĀDAYN

QURAYSH

1. Nu'aym b. 'Abdullāh al-Nahhās al-'Adawī:	
martyred at Ajnādayn	Khalifa I/87 (I.I.); Tab. i/2126; Bal. *Fut*. 113-114
martyred at Mu'ta (?)	Bal. *Fut*. 113-114 (I.K.)
martyred at Yarmūk (?)	Bal. *Fut*. 113-114 (others)
killed; same as Nu'aym b. Ṣakhr al-'Adawī (?)	Kufi I/147-148
2. Hishām b. al-'Āṣ b. Wā'il al-Sahmī:	
martyred at Ajnādayn	Khalifa I/87 (I.I.); Tab. i/2126; Kufi I/147-148
martyred at Ajnādayn or Yarmūk	Bal. *Fut*. 113-114.
3. Salama b. Hishām b. al-Mughīra al-Makhzūmī:	
martyred at Ajnādayn	Tab. i/2126; Kufi I/147-148
martyred at Ajnādayn or Marj al-Ṣuffar	Bal. *Fut*. 113-114
4. al-Ḥārith b. Hishām b. al-Mughīra al-Makhzūmī (brother of no. 3):	
martyred	Bal. *Fut*. 113-114
5. 'Abdullāh b. al-Zubayr b. 'Abd al-Muṭṭalib b. Hāshim:	
martyred	Bal. *Fut*. 113-114
6. 'Amr b. Sa'īd b. al-'Āṣ b. Umayya:	
martyred	Bal. *Fut*. 113-114
7. Ābān b. Sa'īd b. al-'Āṣ b. Umayya (brother of no. 6):	
martyred	Kufi I/147-148; Bal. *Fut*. 113-114; Azdi 91-92
mentioned in battle	Azdi 87
8. Ṭulayb b. 'Umayr b. Wahb b. 'Abd b. Quṣayy:	
martyred	Bal. *Fut*. 113-114
9. 'Ikrima b. Abī Jahl b. Hishām al-Makhzūmī:	
martyred	Bal. *Fut*. 113-114
10. Sa'īd b. al-Ḥārith b. Qays b. 'Adī al-Sahmi:	
martyred	Bal. *Fut*. 113-114

11. al-Ḥārith b. al-Ḥārith b. Qays b. 'Adī al-Sahmī (brother of no. 10): martyred	Bal. *Fut.* 113-114
12. al-Ḥajjāj b. al-Ḥārith b. Qays b. 'Adī al-Sahmī (brother of no. 10): martyred	Bal. *Fut.* 113-114
13. Tamīm b. al-Ḥārith b. Qays b. 'Adī al-Sahmī (brother of no. 10): martyred	Bal. *Fut.* 113-114
14. Habbār b. al-Aswad b. 'Abd al-Asad al-Makhzūmī: martyred	Tab. i/2126
15. Hudhayfa b. Ghānim: martyred	*Isaba*, s.n.
16. Khālid b. al-Walīd al-Makhzūmī: mentioned	Ya'qubi II/134; Bal. *Fut.* 113-114; *TMD* I/481; Kufi I/142-145; Azdi 87ff.
17. 'Amr b. al-'Āṣ: mentioned	Khalifa I/87 (I.I.); *TMD* I/482-483 (Waq.); *TMD* I/481; Azdi 89
18. Yazīd b. Abī Sufyān: mentioned; commands right wing	*TMD* I/481; Kufi I/145
19. Abū 'Ubayda b. al-Jarrāḥ: mentioned	Azdi 89
20. Mu'ādh b. Jabal: commands right flank	Kufi I/145; Azdi 89-91
21. Khālid b. Sa'īd b. al-'Āṣ: commands *kamīn*	Kufi I/145
22. Sa'īd b. Zayd b. 'Amr b. Nufayl: commands cavalry	Azdi 90-91
23. Sa'īd b. 'Āmir b. Khidhyam: commands left flank	Kufi I/145; Azdi 90-91

AZD

24. Habbār b. Sufyān al-Azdī: martyred (Caetani, *Annali* III/77, considers him of Makhzūm-Quraysh, seems to conflate him with no. 14.)	Kufi I/147-148; Azdi 92
25. 'Abdullāh b. 'Amr b. Ṭufayl Dhū l-Nūr al-Dawsī: martyred	Kufi I/147-148; Azdi 92
26. 'Amr b. Ṭufayl b. 'Amr al-Dawsī:	

martyred at Ajnādayn or Yarmūk — Bal. *Fut.* 114

27. Jundab b. ʿAmr al-Dawsī: martyred — Bal. *Fut.* 113-114

ANṢĀR

28. al-Ḥārith b. Aws b. ʿAtīk al-Khazrajī: martyred — *Isaba*, s.n.; *Istiʿab*, s.n.

29. Qayẓī b. Qays b. Lūdhān al-Awsī: martyred — *Isaba*, s.n.
(N.B. Tab. i/2126: no members of Anṣār mentioned to us among martyrs at Ajnādayn.)

TAMĪM

30. Shuraḥbīl b. Ḥasana (*ḥalīf* of Quraysh): mentioned; over left wing — *TMD* I/481; Kufi I/145; Azdi 87ff.

31. Maʿbad b. ʿAmr al-Tamīmī: martyred at Ajnādayn or Faḥl — *Isaba*, s.n.

32. Saʿīd b. ʿAmr al-Tamīmī: martyred — *Isaba*, s.n.

JUMAḤ

33. ʿAbd al-Raḥmān b. Ḥanbal al-Jumaḥī: mentioned; messenger to Abū Bakr — Azdi 93

MASHJAʿA

34. al-Yaʿqūb b. ʿAmr b. Ḍurays al-Mashjaʿī: martyred — Azdi 92

ASAD

35. Ḍirār b. al-Azwar al-Asadī: martyred — *Isaba*, s.n.

APPENDIX B. MARJ AL-ṢUFFAR

1. Khālid b. Sa'īd b. al-'Āṣ b. Umayya (*Quraysh*): killed in battle	Bal. *Fut.* 118; Khalifa I/88 (al-Walīd b. Hishām)
2. Umm Ḥakam bint al-Ḥārith b. Hishām al-Makhzūmī (*Quraysh*): wife of preceding; fought in battle	Bal. *Fut.* 118; *TMD* I/482 (SbA and Ibn Jābir)
3. 'Amr b. Sa'īd b. al-'Āṣ (*Quraysh*): killed	Khalifa I/88 (al-Walīd b. Hishām)
4. al-Faḍl b. 'Abbās (*Quraysh*): killed	Khalifa I/88 (al-Walīd b. Hishām)
5. 'Ikrima b. Abī Jahl (*Quraysh*): killed	Khalifa I/88 (al-Walīd b. Hishām)
6. Ābān b. Sa'īd (*Quraysh*): killed	Khalifa I/88 (al-Walīd b. Hishām)
7. Khālid b. al-Walīd (*Quraysh*): commander	Khalifa I/88, *TMD* I/481 (I.I.); Ya'qubi II/139.
commander; defeats 20,000 Byzantines with no losses	Kufi I/150
8. B. Mālik b. Khufāf of *Sulaym*: witnessed Marj al-Ṣuffar	Bal. *Fut.* 118
9. B. 'Amīra b. Khufāf of *Sulaym*: not present at Marj al-Ṣuffar	Bal. *Fut.* 118
10. Fourteen men of *Quraysh*, one *Anṣārī* killed	*TMD* I/481 (I.I.)
11. 4,000 Muslim casualties	Bal. *Fut.* 118

APPENDIX C. PARTICIPANTS AT YARMŪK

(reconstructions of I.I., Waq., SbA, Sayf < MTZMAS, Sayf < KU, etc.)

1. Abū ʻUbayda b. al-Jarrāḥ (*Quraysh*):	
commander	*TMD* I/529 (SbA)
commander of quarter of army	*TMD* I/535-536 (SbA)
commander	Yaʻqubi II/141
commander	Khalifa I/100 (I.I.)
reinforcement (*ridʼ*)	*TMD* I/543
mentioned	Tab. i/2086 = *TMD* I/548-549 (Sayf < KU)
mentioned	Tab. i/2090-2095 = *TMD* I/546 (Sayf < KU)
messenger to Heraclius before defeat of Khālid b. Saʻīd	Tab. i/2103 = *TMD* I/475 (Sayf < MTA)
commanded those who had abandoned Khālid b. Saʻīd	Tab. i/2090-2095 (Sayf < KU)
supervised collection and distribution of booty	*TMD* I/550 (Sayf < KU)
2. ʻAmr b. al-ʻĀṣ (*Quraysh*):	
commander of quarter of army	*TMD* I/535 (SbA)
mentioned	*TMD* I/460-461; *TMD* I/542
mentioned	Tab. i/2086-2089 = *TMD* I/548-549 (Sayf < KU)
mentioned	Tab. i/2090-2095 = *TMD* I/546 (Sayf < KU)
3. Yazīd b. Abī Sufyān (*Quraysh*):	
commander of quarter of army	*TMD* I/535 (SbA)
mentioned	*TMD* I/460-461
in left wing of army	Tab. i/2090-2095 (Sayf < KU)
messenger to Heraclius before defeat of Khālid b. Saʻīd	Tab. i/2103 = *TMD* I/475 (Sayf < MTA)
mentioned	Tab. i/2086-2089 = *TMD* I/548-549 (Sayf < KU)
mentioned	Tab. i/2090-2095 = *TMD* I/546 (Sayf < KU)
4. Shuraḥbīl b. Ḥasana (*ḥalīf* of *Quraysh*):	
commander of quarter of army	*TMD* I/535 (SbA)
mentioned	*TMD* I/543 (SbA); *TMD* I/460-461
in right wing of army	Tab. i/2090-2095 (Sayf < KU)

mentioned	Tab. i/2086-2089 = *TMD* I/548-549 (Sayf < KU)
mentioned	Tab. i/2090-2095 = *TMD* I/546 (Sayf < KU)
5. Qiyātha b. Ashyam (*Kināna*):	
commanded left wing; "Qiyātha b. Usāma al-Kinānī"	*TMD* I/535 (SbA)
mentioned in fighting	*TMD* I/541-542
in left wing of army; commanded vanguard (*ṭalā'i'*); "Qubāth b. Ashyam"	Tab. i/2090-2095 (Sayf < KU)
among messengers to Medina with news of victory	*TMD* I/550 (Sayf < KU)
6. Khālid b. al-Walīd (*Quraysh*):	
commanded cavalry	*TMD* I/535 (SbA); *TMD* I/537-538 (SbA); *TMD* I/540ff. (SbA)
commander of army (?)	*TMD* I/460-461 (Ṣafwān b. 'Amr < 'Abd al-Raḥmān b. Jubayr)
commanded foreguard (*muqaddima*)	Ya'qubi II/141
mentioned; commander (?)	Tab. i/2101-2102 (Sayf < 'Amr b. Maymūn)
called in as reinforcement	Tab. i/2086-2089 = *TMD* I/548-549 (Sayf < KU)
mentioned	*TMD* I/550 (Sayf < KU)
mentioned	Tab. i/2095-2099 (Sayf < KU)
mentioned	Tab. i/2090-2095 = *TMD* I/546 (Sayf < KU); Tab. i/2100 (Sayf < KU); Tab. i/2089 = *TMD* I/545-550 (Sayf < MTMA)
7. Hāshim b. 'Utba b. Abī Waqqāṣ (*Quraysh*):	
commanded infantry (*rajjāla*)	*TMD* I/535 (SbA)
mentioned	Bal. *Fut.* 135-137
commanded one of contingents from Iraq	Tab. i/2090-2095 (Sayf < KU)
8. Abū Sufyān (*Quraysh*):	
mentioned; exhorts Muslims	*TMD* I/536-537 (SbA)
exhorts Muslims	Tab. i/2095-2099 (Sayf < KU)
mentioned	Tab. i/2090-2095 (Sayf < KU)
watches battle with *shaykhs*	*TMD* I/550 (Sayf < KU)
9. 'Ikrima b. Abī Jahl (*Quraysh*):	
martyred at Yarmūk	Khalifa I/100 (I.I.)
with reinforcements; mentioned	Tab. i/2086-2089 = *TMD* I/548-549 (Sayf < KU); Tab. i/2090-2095 = *TMD* I/546 (Sayf < KU)

mentioned; subcommander (?)	Tab. i/2095-2099 (Sayf < KU); *TMD* I/547 (Sayf < KU)
among commanders of those who had abandoned Khālid b. Sa'īd	Tab. i/2090-2095 (Sayf < KU)
vows to fight to death	Tab. i/2100 (Sayf < AU)
wounded in battle	Tab. i/2100 (Sayf < AU); Tab. i/2101 (Sayf < AU < Khālid)
10. 'Amr b. Sa'īd b. al-'Āṣ (*Quraysh*):	
martyred	Khalifa I/100 (I.I.)
wounded	Tab. i/2101 (Sayf < AU < Khālid)
11. Ḥabīb b. Maslama al-Fihrī (*Quraysh*):	
mentioned	Bal. *Fut.* 135-137
among commanders of those who had abandoned Khālid b. Sa'īd	Tab. i/2090-2095 (Sayf < KU)
12. al-Ṣimṭ b. al-Aswad (*Kinda*):	
noted for valor	Bal. *Fut.* 135-137
in right wing of army	Tab. i/2090-2095 (Sayf < KU)
13. Abū l-A'war b. Sufyān (*Sulaym*):	
exhorts Sulaym	*TMD* I/542 (SbA)
among commanders of those who had abandoned Khālid b. Sa'īd	Tab. i/2090-2095 (Sayf < KU)
14. Jundab b. 'Amr b. Ḥumama (*Azd*):	
addresses Azd; "Jundab b. 'Amr b. Jahma"	*TMD* I/539-540 (*qālū*)
in right wing of army	Tab. i/2090-2095 (Sayf < KU)
wounded	Tab. i/2101 (Sayf < AU < Khālid)
15. Mu'ādh b. Jabal al-Khazrajī (*Anṣār*):	
commanded right wing	*TMD* I/535-536 (SbA)
in single combat	*TMD* I/538 (SbA)
16. Qays b. Hubayra (al-Makshūḥ) (*Madhḥij*):	
subcommander of cavalry	*TMD* I/536-537 (SbA)
mentioned	Bal. *Fut.* 135-137
17. Sa'īd b. Zayd b. 'Amr b. Nufayl (*Quraysh*):	
mentioned in core force (*qalb*)	*TMD* I/542 (SbA)
mentioned	*TMD* I/537-538 (SbA); *TMD* I/543 (SbA)
18. 'Abd al-Raḥmān b. Mu'ādh b. Jabal (*Anṣār*):	
mentioned	*TMD* I/538 (SbA)

19. al-Ḥajjāj b. ʿAbd Yaghūth al-Zubaydī (*Madhḥij*):	
mentioned among Zubayd	*TMD* I/539 (SbA)
20. al-ʿAbbās b. Sahl b. Saʿīd (*Anṣār*):	
mentioned	*TMD* I/539 (SbA)
21. Khawla bint Thaʿlaba (wife of preceding) (*Anṣār*):	
mentioned	*TMD* I/539 (SbA)
22. ʿAmr b. Baḥr:	
mentioned	*TMD* I/539 (SbA)
23. ʿAmr b. al-Ṭufayl al-Dawsī (*Azd*):	
killed in intense fighting around Azd contingent	*TMD* I/539-540 (SbA)
24. Abū Hurayra (*Azd*):	
exhorts Azd	*TMD* I/540 (SbA)
mentioned	*TMD* I/543 (SbA)
25. Umm Ḥabība bint al-ʿĀṣ (*Quraysh*):	
mentioned among women fighting	*TMD* I/543 (SbA)
26. al-Musayyib (father of Saʿīd) (*Quraysh*):	
mentioned	*TMD* I/543-544
27. al-Ashtar al-Nakhaʿī (*Madhḥij*):	
mentioned among Muslims pursuing Byzantines to al-Thaniyya after Yarmūk	*TMD* I/544
mentioned	*TMD* (Zah) XVI/fol. 88b (Abū Hudhayfa)
28. Hind bint ʿUtba (*Quraysh*):	
mentioned; came to Syria with her husband, Abū Sufyān	Bal. *Fut.* 135-137
29. al-Ashʿath b. Qays (*Kinda*):	
mentioned	Bal. *Fut.* 135-137
30. Āmir b. Abī Waqqāṣ al-Zuhrī (*Quraysh*):	
martyred	Bal. *Fut.* 135-137
31. Jabala b. al-Ayham (*Ghassān*):	
sided with *Anṣār*, then returned to Byzantine side	Bal. *Fut.* 135-137
32. Ḥayyāsh b. Qays al-Qushayrī (*Ka ʿb b. Rabīʿa*):	
mentioned; "Ḥubāsh b. Qays"	Bal. *Fut.* 135-137
33. ʿUbāda b. al-Ṣāmit (*Anṣār*):	
mentioned (episode with Jabala b. al-Ayham, no. 31)	Bal. *Fut.* 135-137

34. Ḥudhayfa b. al-Yamān (*Ghaṭafān*):	
in delegation bringing news of Yarmūk victory to ʿUmar	Yaʿqubi II/141
35. Saʿīd b. ʿĀmir b. Khidhyam (*Quraysh*):	
mentioned; sent to Abū ʿUbayda by ʿUmar as reinforcement	Khalifa I/100 (IK)
36. ʿAbdullāh b. Sufyān b. ʿAbd al-Asad (*Quraysh*):	
martyred	Khalifa I/100 (IK)
37. Saʿīd b. al-Ḥārith b. Qays (*Quraysh*):	
martyred	Khalifa I/100 (I.I.)
38. Juwayriyya bint Abī Sufyān (*Quraysh*):	
wounded among women fighting	Tab. i/2100-2101 (Sayf < Abū Umays al-Qāsim b. ʿAbd al-Raḥmān < AU)
39. al-Qaʿqāʿ b. ʿAmr (*Tamīm*):	
subordinate commander	Tab. i/2095-2099 (Sayf < KU)
commanded one of Iraqi contingents	Tab. i/2090-2095 (Sayf < KU)
40. al-Ḥārith b. Hishām (*Quraysh*):	
subordinate commander(?)	Tab. i/2095-2099 (Sayf < KU); *TMD* I/574 (Sayf < KU)
vows to fight to death	Tab. i/2100 (Sayf < KU)
messenger to Heraclius before defeat of Khālid b. Saʿīd	Tab. i/2103 (Sayf < MTA)
41. Jaraja (George):	
Byzantine, joins Muslims	Tab. i/2095-2099 (Sayf < KU); *TMD* I/547 (Sayf < KU)
42. ʿAlqama:	
mentioned as commander of one of five armies at Yarmūk (?)	*TMD* I/546 (Sayf < KU)
43. Madhʿūr b. ʿAdī (*ʿIjl*):	
mentioned as commander of one of Iraqi contingents	Tab. i/2090-2095 (Sayf < KU)
44. ʿIyāḍ b. Ghanm al-Fihrī (*Quraysh*):	
mentioned as commander of one of Iraqi contingents	Tab. i/2090-2095 (Sayf < KU); *TMD* (Zah) XIII, fol. 407b
45. Ziyād b. Ḥanẓala	
mentioned as commander of one of Iraqi contingents	Tab. i/2090-2095 (Sayf < KU)

46. Diḥya b. Khalīfa (*Kalb*):	
mentioned among commanders of those abandoning Khālid b. Sa'īd	Tab. i/2090-2095 (Sayf < KU)
47. Imra' al-Qays:	
among commanders of those who abandoned Khālid b. Sa'īd	Tab. i/2090-2095 (Sayf < KU)
48. Yazīd b. Yuḥannas:	
among commanders of those who abandoned Khālid b. Sa'īd	Tab. i/2090-2095 (Sayf < KU)
49. Suhayl:	
among commanders of those who abandoned Khālid b. Sa'īd	Tab. i/2090-2095 (Sayf < KU)
50. 'Abd al-Raḥmān b. Khālid b. al-Walīd (*Quraysh*):	
among commanders of those who abandoned Khālid b. Sa'īd	Tab. i/2090-2095 (Sayf < KU)
51. Ṣafwān b. Umayya (*Quraysh*):	
among commanders of those who abandoned Khālid b. Sa'īd	Tab. i/2090-2095 (Sayf < KU)
52. Sa'īd b. Khālid (*Quraysh*?):	
among commanders of those who abandoned Khālid b. Sa'īd	Tab. i/2090-2095 (Sayf < KU)
killed at Marj al-Ṣuffar, before Yarmūk	Tab. i/2110-2113 = *TMD* I/463 (Sayf < MTMA)
53. Ibn Dhī l-Khimār:	
among commanders of those who abandoned Khālid b. Sa'īd	Tab. i/2090-2095 (Sayf < KU)
54. 'Umar b. Mukhashsha b. Khuwaylid:	
in right wing	Tab. i/2090-2095 (Sayf < KU)
55. Khālid b. Sa'īd (*Quraysh*):	
in right wing	Tab. i/2090-2095 (Sayf < KU)
wounded, but not known where he died afterwards	Tab. i/2101 (Sayf < AU < K)
56. 'Abdullāh b. Qays (Abū Mūsā [*al-Ash'arī*?]):	
in right wing	Tab. i/2090-2095 (Sayf < KU)
57. 'Amr b. 'Abasa (*Sulaym*):	
in right wing	Tab. i/2090-2095 (Sayf < KU)

58. Dhū l-Kalā' (family of Yemeni origin):	
in right wing	Tab. i/2090-2095 (Sayf < KU)
59. Mu'āwiya b. Ḥudayj (or Khadīj?) (*Kinda*):	
in right wing	Tab. i/2090-2095 (Sayf < KU)
60. 'Amr b. Fulān (*Shaybān*?):	
in right wing	Tab. i/2090-2095 (Sayf < KU)
61. Laqīṭ b. 'Abd al-Qays b. Bajra (*ḥalīf* of *Fazāra*):	
in right wing	Tab. i/2090-2095 (Sayf < KU)
62. al-Zubayr:	
in left wing, commands *kardūs*	Tab. i/2090-2095 (Sayf < KU)
63. Ḥawshab Dhū Ẓulaym (*Hamdān*);	
in left wing	Tab. i/2090-2095 (Sayf < KU)
64. Qays b. 'Amr b. Zayd b. 'Awf (*Hawāzin, ḥalīf* of *Anṣār*):	
in left wing	Tab. i/2090-2095 (Sayf < KU)
65. 'Iṣma b. 'Abdullāh (*Asad, ḥalīf* of *Anṣār*):	
in left wing	Tab. i/2090-2095 (Sayf < KU)
66. Ḍirār b. al-Azwar (*Asad*):	
in left wing	Tab. i/2090-2095 (Sayf < KU)
vows to fight to death	Tab. i/2100 (Sayf < AU)
wounded	Tab. i/2101 (Sayf < AU < K)
messenger to Heraclius before defeat of Khālid b. Sa'īd	Tab. i/2103 = *TMD* I/475 (Sayf < MTA)
67. Masrūq b. Fulān:	
in left wing	Tab. i/2090-2095 (Sayf < KU)
68. 'Utba b. Rabī'a b. Bahz (*ḥalīf* of *B. 'Iṣma*):	
in left wing	Tab. i/2090-2095 (Sayf < KU)
69. Jāriya b. 'Abdullāh (*Ashja', ḥalīf* of *Anṣār*):	
in left wing	Tab. i/2090-2095 (Sayf < KU)
70. Abū l-Dardā' (*Anṣār*):	
qāḍī at Yarmūk	Tab. i/2090-2095 (Sayf < KU)
71. 'Abdullāh b. Mas'ūd (*Hudhayl, ḥalīf* of *Quraysh*):	
over booty division (*aqbāḍ*)	Tab. i/2090-2095 (Sayf < KU)
72. Abū Jandal b. Suhayl (*Quraysh*):	
sent with news of victory	*TMD* I/550 (Sayf < KU)
messenger to Heraclius before defeat of Khālid b. Sa'īd	Tab. i/2103 = *TMD* I/475 (Sayf < MTA)
73. 'Amr b. 'Ikrima (*Quraysh*):	
wounded	Tab. i/2100 (Sayf < AU); Tab. i/2101 (Sayf < AU < K)

74. Salama b. Hishām (*Quraysh*):	
wounded	Tab. i/2101 (Sayf < AU < K)
75. Ābān b. Sa'īd (*Quraysh*):	
wounded at Yarmūk	Tab. i/2101 (Sayf < AU < K)
76. Habbār b. Sufyān (*Quraysh*):	
wounded at Yarmūk	Tab. i/2101 (Sayf < AU < K)
died at Ajnādayn (?)	I.S. IV/1, 100
77. Ṭulayb b. 'Umayr b. Wahb of B. 'Abd (*Quraysh*):	
wounded at Yarmūk	Tab. i/2101 (Sayf < AU < K)
78. al-Ṭufayl b. 'Amr (*Azd*):	
wounded at Yarmūk	Tab. i/2101 (Sayf < AU < K)
79. Hishām b. al-'Āṣ (*Quraysh*):	
wounded at Yarmūk	Tab. i/2101 (Sayf < AU < K)

APPENDIX D. MEMBERS OF KHĀLID'S ARMY IN IRAQ

1. Ḥanẓala b. al-Rabīʻ b. Rabāḥ al-Usayyidī (*Tamīm*):	
witnesses treaty	Tab. i/2049-2050 (Sayf)
witness; involved in tax affairs	Tab. i/2055 (Sayf)
subordinate commander	Bal. *Fut.* 246
"Kātib al-Nabī"	Tab. i/2346 (Sayf < MT)
scribe for Prophet	*Isaba*, s.n.
2. Ḍirār b. al-Azwar (*Asad*):	
subordinate commander at al-Ḥīra	Tab. i/2038-2039 (Sayf)
one of commanders on "frontier"	Tab. i/2052
mentioned	Kufi I/93
at al-Ḥīra battle	Bal. *Fut.* 245
died fighting in al-Yamāma during *ridda* wars	Bal. *Fut.* 245 (Waq.)
died fighting in al-Yamāma	IS VI/45 (Waq.)
3. Jarīr b. ʻAbdullāh (*Bajīla*):	
witnesses treaty; "al-Ḥimyarī"	Tab. i/2049-2050 (Sayf)
supervises tax of two villages: "al-Ḥimyari"	Tab. i/2051-2052 (Sayf?)
witnesses treaty	Tab. i/2055 (Sayf)
one of commanders over *sawād* of al-Ḥīra	Tab. i/2057-2058 (Sayf)
witnesses treaty; "al-Bajalī"	Kufi I/95
came to Iraq twice	Bal. *Fut.* 242-247 (Waq., AM)
came to Iraq once, under ʻUmar I, A.H. 13	Bal. *Fut.* 242-247 (others)
4. Rāfiʻ b. (Abi) ʻAmr b. Jābir al-Sunbusī (*Ṭayyi'*):	
guides Khālid into Iraq	Tab. i/2022-2023 (Sayf)
guides Khālid from Iraq into Syria	IS VI/44-45
at Dhāt al-Salāsil raid; according to Khalīfa b. Khayyāṭ, not same as guide	*Isaba*, s.n.
guides Khālid from Iraq into Syria (desert march)	Tab. i/2122-2125 (I.I.)
	Bal. *Fut.* 110-111
	Kufi I/136-138
	Tab. i/2110-2113 (Sayf)
	Tab. i/2113-2114 (Sayf)

	TMD I/458-459 (al-Zubayr b. Bakkār)
	TMD I/469-470 (I.I.)
5. al-Qa'qā' b. 'Amr (brother of no. 6) (*Tamīm*):	
sent by Abū Bakr to reinforce Khālid	Tab. i/2021 (Sayf)
witnesses truce	Tab. i/2049-2050 (Sayf)
one of commanders on "frontier"	Tab. i/2052
witness: involved in tax affairs	Tab. i/2055 (Sayf)
left in charge of al-Ḥīra by Khālid	Tab. i/2057-2058 (Sayf)
in charge of al-Ḥīra	Tab. i/2068-2069 (Sayf)
leads force at al-Ḥuṣayd	Tab. i/2068-2069 (Sayf)
leads force at al-Ḥuṣayd	Yaqūt, s.v. "al-Ḥuṣayd"
remains in Dūma when Khālid returns to al-Ḥīra	Tab. i/2066-2067
with Khālid on desert march to Syria	Yaqūt, s.v. "al-Muṣayyakh"; Tab. i/2114 (Sayf)
6. 'Āsim b. 'Amr (brother of no. 5) (*Tamīm*):	
subordinate commander	Tab. i/2022-2023 (Sayf)
individual combat at al-Madhār	Tab. i/2027-2028 (Sayf)
at battle of Dūma	Tab. i/2066-2067 (Sayf?)
at battle of Firāḍ	Tab. i/2074-2075 (Sayf)
7. Uṭṭ b. Abī Uṭṭ of B. Sa'd b. Zayd Manāt (*Tamīm*):	
over taxes of village	Tab. i/2051-2052
commander over part of *sawād* of al-Ḥīra	Tab. i/2057-2058 (Sayf)
8. al-Aqra' b. Ḥābis (*Tamīm*):	
commanded Khālid's foreguard after al-Qa'qā' (no. 5)	Tab. i/2057 (Sayf)
a noble of Tamīm	I.H. 933
captures an enemy at Dūma	Tab. i/2065-2066
9. al-Zibriqān b. Badr of B. Sa'd b. Zayd Manāt (*Tamīm*):	
left in charge of al-Anbār by Khālid	Tab. i/2062 (Sayf?)
in charge of al-Anbār	Tab. i/2068-2069 (Sayf)
a noble of B. Sa'd (Tamīm)	I.H. 933
early convert; did not apostasize, kept B. Sa'd from joining *ridda*.	IS VIIA/24

10. A'bad b. Fadakī al-Sa'dī (*Tamīm*):	
subordinate commander for al-Qa'qā' b. 'Amr (no. 5)	Tab. i/2068-2069 (Sayf)
11. Abū Laylā b. Fadakī (brother of no. 10) (*Tamīm*):	
subordinate commander	Tab. i/2068-2069 (Sayf)
12. Rabī'a b. 'Isl (*Tamīm*):	
one of commanders over *sawād* of al-Ubulla	Tab. i/2057-2058 (Sayf)
of 'Amr b. Yarbū'-Tamīm	I.K. /Caskel II/479 and table 68
13. 'Abdullāh b. 'Abd Shams (brother of no. 3) (*Bajīla*):	
killed at Tadmur during Khālid's raid	Kufi I/140
14. Jābir b. Ṭāriq al-Aḥmasī (*Bajīla*):	
witness	Tab. i/2055 (Sayf)
"Jābir b. Abī Ṭāriq al-Aḥmasī"	IS VI/23
15. al-Ḥajjāj b. Dhī l-'Unuq (*Bajīla*):	
witness; involved in tax affairs (?)	Tab. i/2055 (Sayf)
one of commanders over *sawād* of al-Ḥīra	Tab. i/2057-2058 (Sayf)
noble of Bajīla	I.K./Caskel II/291 and table 223
16. 'Adī b. Ḥātim (*Ṭayyi'*):	
subordinate commander	Tab. i/2022-2023 (Sayf)
individual combat at al-Madhār	Tab. i/2027-2028 (Sayf)
"Al-Ṭā'ī"	IS VI/13
leader of those sections of Ṭayyi' that did not join *ridda*	Tab. i/1887
17. Suwayd b. Muqarrin (brother of nos. 18, 19) (*Muzayna*):	
in charge of taxes (jizā')	Tab. i/2029 (Sayf)
tax agent for Nistār (?)	Tab. i/2051-2052 (Sayf?)
commander over part of *sawād* of al-Ḥīra and al-Ubulla (?) (mentioned twice)	Tab. i/2057-2058 (Sayf)
among companions who settled in al-Kūfa	Khalīfa b. Khayyāṭ, *Ṭabaqat*, p. 287
18. Ma'qil b. Muqarrin (brother of nos. 17, 19) (*Muzayna*):	
led conquest of al-Ubulla; Tab. says it occurred in A.H. 14	Tab. i/2025-2026 (Sayf?)
his family converted to Islam early	IS VI/11

19. Ḍirār b. Muqarrin (brother of nos. 17, 18) (*Muzayna*):	
at fighting for al-Ḥīra	Tab. i/2038-2039 (Sayf)
one of commanders on "frontier"	Tab. i/2052
one of commanders over *sawād* of al-Ḥīra	Tab. i/2057 (Sayf)
20. al-Ṣabāḥ b. Fulān (*Muzayna*):	
sent as messenger to Abū Bakr	Tab. i/2072-2073 (Sayf?)
21. Bilāl b. al-Ḥārith (*Muzayna*):	
part of Khālid's force from Iraq in Syria	Tab. i/2114-2115 (Sayf < Isḥāq b. Ibrāhīm < Ẓafar b. Dahī)
22. Hishām b. al-Walīd al-Makhzūmī (*Quraysh*):	
witnesses treaty	Tab. i/2049-2050 (Sayf)
witness	Tab. i/2055 (Sayf)
Khālid's brother	I.H. 273
23. al-Walīd b. 'Uqba (*Quraysh*):	
sent as messenger to Abū Bakr	Tab. i/2064 (Sayf)
24. Ḍirār b. al-Khaṭṭāb al-Fihrī (*Quraysh*):	
subordinate commander at al-Ḥīra	Tab. i/2038-2039 (Sayf)
one of commanders on "frontier"	Tab. i/2052ff.
went to Syrian front	IS VIIB/128-129
25. 'Umayr b. Ri'āb b. Muhashshim b. Sa'īd b. Sahm b. 'Amr (*Quraysh*):	Bal. *Fut.* 248
dies at 'Ayn al-Tamr	I.H. 785
26. 'Iyāḍ b. Ghanm al-Fihrī (*Quraysh*):	
among Iraqis coming with Khālid to reinforce Syrians	Tab. i/2500 (Sayf < MTAS)
27. Bashīr b. Sa'd Abū l-Nu'mān b. Bashīr (*Anṣār*):	
subordinate commander; dies at 'Ayn al-Tamr	Bal. *Fut.* 244, 248
28. Mālik b. 'Abbād (*Aws-Anṣār*):	
guide	Tab. i/2022-2023 (Sayf)
of Aws-Anṣār	I.K./Caskel II/384 and table 177
29. 'Amr b. Ḥarām (*Anṣār*):	
left over al-Ḥīra when Khālid departs for Syria; " 'Amr b. Ḥazm"	Din. 112
left over Ṣandawdā' when Khālid departs for Syria	Bal. *Fut.* 110

30. ‘Urwa b. Ja‘d al-Bāriqī (*Azd*): sent by al-Qa‘qā‘ as subordinate commander of the Azd	Tab. i/2068-2069 (Sayf) IS VI/21
31. ‘Amr b. al-Ṭufayl b. Dhū l-Nūn (*Azd*): sent as messenger to Abū ‘Ubayda during desert march	Kufi I /139-140
32. Shurayḥ b. ‘Āmir b. al-Qayn of B. Sa‘d Bakr (*Hawāzin*): lieutenant over al-Khurayba near al-Ḥīra	Bal. *Fut.* 241-242, 340 (AM)
33. Busr b. Abī Ruhm (*Juhayna*): one of commanders on the "frontier"	Tab. i/2052
34. Muhriz b. Quraysh (or Ḥarīsh?) (*Muhārib*): a guide for Khālid in desert march	Tab. i/2113 and *TMD* I/466 (Sayf < ‘Ubaydallāh b. Muḥaffiz < Bakr b. Wā'il)
35. ‘Uwaym (or ‘Uwaymir?) b. Kāhil (or Kāhīn?) (*Aslam*): left in charge of ‘Ayn al-Tamr when Khālid goes to Dūma	Tab. i/2065
36. ‘Iṣma b. ‘Abdullāh of B. al-Ḥārith b. Ṭarif (*Ḍabba*): at battle of al-Ḥuṣayd	Tab. i/2068-2069 (Sayf?)
37. al-Nusayr b. Daysam b. Thawr (*‘Ijl*): subordinate commander of Ḍubay‘a-‘Ijl	Bal. *Fut.* 248 I.K./Caskel II/453 and table 160
38. Sa‘īd, Qays, al-Ḥajjāj, and Sā'ib bb. al-Ḥārith al-Sadūsī (*Dhuhl*): killed at Tadmur during Khālid's raid	Kufi I/140
39. al-Hudhayl al-Kāhilī (*Asad*?): messenger to Abū Bakr	Tab. i/2041 (Sayf)
40. ‘Abdullah b. Wathīma al-Naṣrī: supervises tax affairs	Tab. i/2051-2052
41. Sālim b. Naṣr: guide	Tab. i/2022-2023 (Sayf)
42. Zirr b. Kulayb: messenger	Tab. i/2025 (Sayf)
43. Ma‘qil b. al-A‘shā b. al-Nabbāsh: commander? individual combat at al-Madhār	Tab. i/2027-2028 (Sayf)

44. Sa'īd b. al-Nu'mān:	
subordinate commander (?)	Tab. i/2029 (Sayf)
45. Azdād:	
witness; involved in tax affairs	Tab. i/2055 (Sayf)
46. Mālik b. Zayd:	
witness; involved in tax affairs	Tab. i/2055 (Sayf)
47. Khālid b. Wāshima:	
one of commanders over *sawād* of al-Ḥīra	Tab. i/2057-2058 (Sayf)
48. Ḥasaka al-Ḥabaṭī:	
one of commanders over *sawād* of al-Ubulla	Tab. i/2057-2058 (Sayf)
rejects Sayf's assertion; "al-Ḥanẓalī"	*Isaba*, s.v.
49. al-Ḥusayn b. Abī Bakr:	
one of commanders of *sawād* of al-Ubulla	Tab. i/2057-2058 (Sayf)
50. Shajara b. al-A'azz:	
at battle of al-Firāḍ	Tab. i/2074-2075 (Sayf)
51. 'Amr b. Ziyād b. Ḥudhayfa b. Hishām b. al-Mughīra:	
dies at 'Ayn al-Tamr	Din. 112

APPENDIX E. CENTRAL IRAQ—SECOND PHASE

1. Abū 'Ubayd b. Mas'ūd (*Thaqīf*):	
appointed commander	Tab. i/2160-2161 (Sayf < Sahl b. Yūsuf < al-Qāsim b. Muhammad)
commander	Tab. i/2161-2162 (Sayf < Mujālid < al-Sha'bī)
commander	Tab. i/2164 (Sayf < MTZ)
commander	Din. 113
commander	Ya'qubi II/142
commander	Bal. *Fut.* 250-251
commander	Khalifa I/92-93 (Bakr < I.I.)
commander at al-Namāriq	Tab. i/2166 (Sayf < MTZ)
commander at al-Namāriq	Tab. i/2167-2168 (Sayf < al-Ṣalt b. Bahrām < Abū 'Imrān al-Ju'fī)
commander at al-Saqāṭiya	Tab. i/2168-2170 (Sayf < MTZ)
commander at Barūsmā; killed at battle of Bridge	Khalifa I/92-93 (Bakr < I.I.)
battle of Bridge	Tab. i/2174-2176 (Sayf < MTZ)
killed at Bridge	Tab. i/2178-2180 (Sayf < al-Naḍr b. al-Sirrī < al-Agharr al-'Ijlī)
killed at Bridge	Bal. *Fut.* 251-252 (perhaps from Abu 'Ubayd al-Qāsim b. Sallām < Qays b. Abī Hāzim; cf. Bal. *Fut.* 252)
killed at Bridge	Din. 113
killed at Bridge	Ya'qubi II/142
commander	*Muruj* II/307 (Waq.)
commander	Kufi I/164-165
2. al-Jabr b. Abī 'Ubayd (son of no. 1) (*Thaqīf*):	
at Bridge	Tab. i/2177-2180 (Sayf < al-Naḍr b. al-Sirrī < al-Agharr al-'Ijlī)
at Bridge	Tab. i/2181 (I.I.)
at Bridge	Kufi I/168-169
killed at Bridge	Bal. *Fut.* 252
subcommander at Bridge—"Abū al-Jabr b. Abī 'Ubayd"	Khalifa I/93 (Bakr < I.I.)
3. Wahb b. Abī 'Ubayd (son of no. 1) (*Thaqīf*):	
at Bridge	Kufi I/169
4. Mālik b. Abī 'Ubayd (son of no. 1) (*Thaqīf*):	
at Bridge	Kufi I/169

5. ‘Abdullāh b. Mas‘ūd b. ‘Amr b. ‘Umayr (brother of no. 1) (*Thaqīf*):	
subcommander at Bridge	Khalifa I/93 (Bakr < I.I.)
6. Abū Qays b. Ḥabīb b. Rabī‘a b. ‘Amr b. ‘Umayr (*Thaqīf*):	
subcommander at Bridge	Khalifa I/93 (Bakr < I.I.)
7. Qays b. Ḥabīb (*Thaqīf*):	
killed at Bridge	Din. 113
8. al-Ḥakam (brother of no. 1) (*Thaqīf*):	
killed at Bridge	Din. 113
killed at Bridge	Bal. *Fut.* 261-252
9. Abū Miḥjan b. Ḥabīb (cousin of no. 1) (*Thaqīf*):	
led cavalry at Bridge	Din. 113
at Bridge	Kufi I/169
at Bridge	Bal. *Fut.* 252
10. ‘Abdullāh b. Marthad (*Thaqīf*):	
at Bridge	Tab. i/2177-2180 (Sayf < al-Naḍr b. al-Sirrī < al-Agharr al-‘Ijlī)
at Bridge	Kufi I/169
11. a man of Thaqīf	
at Bridge	Tab. i/2174-2176 (Sayf < MTZ)
12. Sa‘d b. ‘Ubayd *ḥalif* of b. Fazāra (*Ansār*):	
among Muslims with Abū ‘Ubayd	Tab. i/2160-2161 (Sayf < Sahl b. Yūsuf < al-Qāsim b. Muḥammad)
with Abū ‘Ubayd	Tab. i/2161-2162 (Sayf < Mujālid < al-Sha‘bī)
with Abū ‘Ubayd	Tab. i/2162 (Sayf < Sahl b. Yūsuf and Mubashshir)
with Abū ‘Ubayd	Tab. i/2164 (Sayf < MTZ)
with Abū ‘Ubayd	Tab. i/2159-2160 (Sayf < MTZ)
regrets fleeing after battle of Bridge	Kufi I/273
13. Salāṭ b. Qays of B. ‘Adī b. al-Najjār (Khazraj) (*Anṣār*):	
among Medinans with Abū ‘Ubayd (or no. 2)	Tab. i/2160-2161 (Sayf < Sahl b. Yūsuf < al-Qāsim b. Muḥammad)
with Abū ‘Ubayd	Tab. i/2161-2162 (Sayf < Mujālid < al-Sha‘bī)
with Abū ‘Ubayd	Tab. i/2162 (Sayf < Sahl b. Yūsuf and Mubashshir)
with Abū ‘Ubayd	Tab. i/2164 (Sayf < MTZ)
with Abū ‘Ubayd	*Muruj* II/307-308 (Waq.)

with Abū 'Ubayd	Bal. *Fut.* 250-251 (same as Tab.)
killed	Din. 113
with Abū 'Ubayd	Kufi I/164-165
at Bridge	Kufi I/168-170
at Bridge	Tab. i/2177-2180 (Sayf < al-Naḍr b. al-Sirrī < al-Agharr al-'Ijlī)
at Bridge	Bal. *Fut.* 251
14. 'Abdullāh b. Zayd b. al-Ḥusayn al Khaṭmī (*Anṣār*):	
fled after battle of Bridge	Tab. i/2176 (Sayf < MTZ)
fled after battle of Bridge	Tab. i/2177-2180 (Sayf < al-Naḍr b. al-Sirrī < al-Agharr al-'Ijlī)
fled after battle of Bridge	Tab. i/2181 (I.I.)
15. 'Abdullāh b. Yazīd al-Khaṭmī (or al-Thaqafī?) (*Anṣār*):	
at Bridge	Khalifa I/93 (Bakr < I.I.)
16. Mu'ādh b. Ḥusayn "al-Kātib" (*Anṣār*):	
fled after battle of Bridge	Tab. i/2182 (I.I.)
fled after battle of Bridge	Kufi I/170
17. Abū Zayd (*Anṣār*):	
killed at Bridge	Bal. *Fut.* 252 (AM)
18. al-Muthannā b. Ḥāritha of B. Hind (*Shaybān*):	
with Abū 'Ubayd in march from Medina	Tab. i/2162 (Sayf < Sahl and Mubashshir)
comes to Medina	Tab. i/2160 (Sayf < Sahl b. Yūsuf < al-Qāsim b. Muḥammad)
comes to Medina	Tab. i/2161 (Sayf < Mujālid < al-Sha'bī)
comes to Medina	Kufi I/162
with Abū 'Ubayd in march from Medina	Ya'qubi II/142
in Iraq, not in Ḥijāz	Din. 113
led cavalry at al-Namāriq	Tab. i/2166 (Sayf < MTZ)
led cavalry at al-Namāriq	Tab. i/2167-2168 (Sayf < al-Ṣalt b. Bahrām < Abū 'Imrān al-Ju'fī)
in Kaskar; sent to raid Bārusmā, near al-Madā'in	Tab. i/2168-2170 (Sayf < MTZ)
in Kaskar; sent to raid Zandaward	Khalifa I/92-93 (Bakr < I.I.)
at Bridge	Tab. i/2177-2180 (Sayf < al-Naḍr b. al-Sirrī < al-Agharr·al-'Ijlī)
at Bridge	*Muruj* II/307-308
at Bridge	Din. 113
at Bridge	Khalifa I/93 (Bakr < I.I.)

at Bridge	Kufi I/168-169
at Bridge	Bal. *Fut.* 252
wounded at Bridge	Tab. i/2180 (Sayf < a man < Abū 'Uthmān al-Nahdī)
wounded at Bridge	Tab. i/2180 (Sayf < Mujālid and 'Aṭiyya)
withdraws to Ullays area after Bridge	Tab. i/2181 (I.I.)
19. Maṭar b. Fiḍḍa of B. Taymallāt (*Qays b. Tha'laba*):	
at al-Namāriq	Tab. i/2167-2168 (Sayf < al-Ṣalt b. Bahrām < Abū 'Imrān al-Ju'fī)
at al-Namāriq	Tab. i/2166 (Sayf < MTZ)
at al-Namāriq	Kufi I/165
20. Madh'ūr (*'Ijl*):	
at Bridge	Tab. i/2174-2176 (Sayf < MTZ)
21. 'Āṣim b. 'Amr of Usayyid (*Tamīm*):	
in Kaskar; raids Jūbara	Khalifa I/92-93 (Bakr < I.I.)
in Kaskar; raids Nahr Jūbara	Tab. i/2168-2170 (Sayf < MTZ)
at Bridge	Tab. i/2174-2176 (Sayf < MTZ)
22. Aktal b. Shammāḥ al-'Uklī (*Tamīm*):	
at al-Namāriq	Tab. i/2166 (Sayf < MTZ)
23. 'Urwa b. Zayd "al-Khayl" (*Ṭayyi'*):	
in Kaskar; raids al-Zawābī	Khalifa I/92 (Bakr < I.I.)
in Kaskar	Bal. *Fut.* 250-251
at Bridge	Bal. *Fut.* 252
at Bridge	Din. 113
at Bridge	Khalifa I/93 (Bakr < I.I.)
24. al-Zubayd (*Ṭayyi'*):	
at Bridge, but not part of army	Bal. *Fut.* 252
25. al-Kalaj (*Ḍabba*):	
at Bridge	Khalifa I/93 (Bakr < I.I.)
at Bridge	Tab. i/2174-2176 (Sayf < MTZ)
26. 'Amr b. al-Haytham b. al-Ṣalt b. Ḥabīb (*Sulaym*):	
led left wing at al-Namāriq	Tab. i/2166 (Sayf < MTZ)
" 'Amr b. al-Ṣalt al-Sulamī"—at Bridge	Khalifa I/93 (Bakr < I.I.)
27. Maslama b. Aslam b. Ḥuraysh	
with Abū 'Ubayd in march from Medina	*Muruj* II/307-308 (Waq.)
28. Wāliq b. Jidāra:	
led right wing at al-Namāriq	Tab. i/2166 (Sayf < MTZ)
in Kaskar; raids Zawābī	Tab. i/2168-2170 (Sayf < MTZ)

29. Ubayy:	
at al-Namāriq	Tab. i/2166 (Sayf < MTZ)
at al-Namāriq	Tab. i/2167-2168 (Sayf < al-Ṣalt b. Bahrām < Abū ʻImrān al-Juʻfī)
30. al-Qāsim:	
at al-Namāriq	Tab. i/2167-2168 (Sayf < al-Ṣalt b. Bahrām < Abū ʻImrān al-Juʻfī)
31. Abū Zaʻbal:	
takes captives at Zandaward	Tab. i/2168-2170 (Sayf < MTZ)

APPENDIX F. CAMPAIGNS IN CENTRAL IRAQ—TRANSITIONAL PHASE

1. al-Muthannā b. Ḥāritha (*Shaybān*):

at Ullays; Jarīr and others sent to reinforce him	Tab. i/2182-2183 (Sayf < MTZ, ‘Aṭiyya)
at Buwayb; he requests Jarīr and ‘Iṣma to meet him	Tab. i/2184-2185 (Sayf < MTZ)
at Buwayb; Jarīr to meet him	Tab. i/2185 (Sayf < Abū Isḥāq al-Shaybānī)
urges Jarīr, ‘Iṣma to hurry	Tab. i/2185-2187 (Sayf < ‘Atiyya) and (Sayf < Sufyān al-Aḥmarī < Mujālid < al-Sha‘bī)
reinforced by men of ‘Amr, Ḍabba, Hanẓala, ‘Abd al-Qays	Tab. i/2188-2189 (Sayf < MA)
aided by Christians of B. Taghlib and al-Namir	Tab. i/2190 (Sayf < MA)
organization of his army	Tab. i/2191 (Sayf < MT)
Buwayb battle	Tab. i/2192 (Sayf < MT)
‘Iṣma, Jarīr support him	Tab. i/2197 (Sayf < MTZ)
commanding at Buwayb; divides spoils	Tab. i/2198 (Sayf < Hamza b. ‘Alī b. Muḥaffiz < a man of Bakr b. Wā’il)
Jarīr refuses to reinforce him; al-Muthannā dies	Tab. i/2200-2202 (I.I.)
after Buwayb, raids *sawād*; sends others on raids, including Jarīr	Tab. i/2202-2203 (Sayf < MTZ)
raids *sawād*, al-Anbār, etc.	Tab. i/2203-2206 (Sayf < ‘Ubaydallāh b. Muḥaffiz < his father)
raids around al-Anbār, sends B. ‘Ijl to raid Taghlib	Tab. i/2206-2207 (Sayf < MTZ)
makeup of his army at Buwayb; raids al-Anbār, Takrīt	Tab. i/2207-2208 (Sayf < MTZ)
sets up garrison near Kufa, waits for reinforcements	Tab. i/2215 (Sayf < Khulayd b. Dhafra < his father)
disputes command in Iraq with Jarīr; ‘Umar sends Sa‘d	Khalifa I/98
joins Jarīr’s army; they defeat Persians at Buwayb	Din. 114-115
raids a market town and al-Anbār	Din. 115-116

remained in Iraq after defeat at battle of Bridge	Bal. *Fut.* 253 (AM)
commanded at Nukhayla, according to Rabī'a	Bal. *Fut.* 254 (Sayf)
disputes command in Iraq with Jarīr; 'Umar sends Sa'd	Kufi I/171-174
Jarīr joins him; they defeat Mihrān	*Muruj* II/310-311
authorities disagree over whether Jarīr or al-Muthannā commanded	*Muruj* II/311
2. Jarīr b. 'Abdullāh (*Bajīla*):	
'Umar sends him to reinforce al-Muthannā; Bajīla gathered by him	Tab. i/2182-2183 (Sayf < MTZ, 'Aṭiyya)
al-Muthannā asks his support	Tab. i/2184-2185 (Sayf < MTZ)
al-Muthannā asks his support	Tab. i/2185 (Sayf < Abū Isḥāq al-Shaybānī)
Jarīr reinforces al-Muthannā	Tab. i/2185-2187 (Sayf < 'Aṭiyya) and (Sayf < Sufyān al-Aḥmarī < Mujālid < al-Sha'bī)
supports al-Muthannā at Buwayb	Tab. i/2192 (Sayf < MT)
supports al-Muthannā; addresses Bajīla on special spoil	Tab. i/2197 (Sayf < MTZ)
refuses to reinforce al-Muthannā; defeats Mihrān	Tab. i/2200-2202 (I.I.)
sent by al-Muthannā to raid Maysān after al-Muthannā's victory at Buwayb	Tab. i/2202-2203 (Sayf < MTZ)
'Umar sends him over *sawād*; disputes command with al-Muthannā; 'Umar sends Sa'd	Khalifa I/98
commands forces; joined by al-Muthannā; Mihrān defeated	Din. 114-115
disputes leadership of Bajīla with 'Arfaja; commands Muslim forces, victories at Madhār and al-Nukhayla	Ya'qubi II/142-143
offers to fight in Iraq if Bajīla is given one-fourth of booty	Bal. *Fut.* 253 (AM)
sent to Iraq after Bridge	Bal. *Fut.* 253 ('Affān b. Muslim < al-Sha'bī)
according to Bajīla, commanded at al-Nukhayla, killed Mihrān	Bal. *Fut.* 254 (Sayf)

sent to Iraq after Bridge	Kufi 110-111
disputes command with al-Muthannā; Sa'd sent	Kufi 111-112
sent to al-Ubulla, then to al-Madā'in; Marzubān killed, joins al-Muthannā at Buwayb	*Muruj* II/310-311
authorities disagree over whether Jarīr or al-Muthannā commanded	*Muruj* II/311
3. 'Arfaja b. Ḥarthama al-Bāriqī (*Azd*):	
replaced by Jarīr as leader of Bajīla; goes to Syria	Tab. i/2185-2187 (Sayf < 'Aṭiyya) and (Sayf < Sufyān al-Aḥmarī Mujālid < al-Sha'bī)
leads group of Azd to reinforce al-Muthannā	Tab. i/2187-2188 (Sayf < 'Aṭiyya, Mujālid)
with Azd at Buwayb; valor	Tab. i/2196 (Sayf < MT)
goes to al-Baṣra after it was settled, leaves Bajīla	Tab. i/2200-2202 (I.I.)
sent by al-Muthannā to raid Persian garrisons	Tab. i/2202-2203 (Sayf < MTZ)
4. Mikhnaf b. Sulaym (*Azd*):	
under Jarīr with 700 Azdīs	Din. 114-115
5. 'Abdullāh b. Sulaym (*Azd*):	
mentioned in battle of Buwayb	Din. 114-115
6. 'Amr b. 'Abd al-Masīḥ b. Buqayla (Azd):	
guided al-Nusayr (no. 43), then returned to al-Ḥīra	Tab. i/2197 (Sayf < MTZ)
7. Group of Azd (*Azd*):	
sent by 'Umar to Iraq	Bal. *Fut.* 253 (AM)
8. al-Mu'annā (b. Ḥāritha) (brother of no. 1) (*Shaybān*):	
commanded cavalry at Buwayb	Tab. i/2191 (Sayf < MT)
9. Mas'ūd b. Ḥāritha (brother of no. 1?) (*Shaybān*):	
killed at Buwayb	Tab. i/2196 (Sayf < MT)
killed at Buwayb	Din. 114-115
killed at Buwayb	Bal. *Fut.* 254 (Sayf)
"al-Mas'ūd" commanded infantry at Buwayb?	Tab. i/2191 (Sayf < MT)
10. al-Nu'mān b. 'Awf b. al-Nu'mān (*Shaybān*):	
commanded wing at Buwayb	Tab. i/2207-2208 (Sayf < MTZ)

11. Maṭar (*Shaybān*):	
commanded one wing at Buwayb	Tab. i/2207-2208 (Sayf < MTZ)
12. Bashīr b. al-Khaṣāṣiyya al-Sādusī (*Dhuhl*):	
left in charge of al-Ḥīra by al-Muthannā after Buwayb	Tab. i/2202-2203 (Sayf < MTZ)
"Bashīr"—commanded wing of al-Muthannā's army at Buwayb	Tab. i/2191 (Sayf < MT)
13. Madh'ūr (b. 'Adī) (*'Ijl*):	
commanded one wing of al-Muthannā's army at Buwayb	Tab. i/2184-2185 (Sayf < MTZ) and (Sayf < Abū Isḥāq al-Shaybānī)
commanded *rid'* (reserves?)	Tab. i/2191 (Sayf < MT)
14. Muḍārib (*'Ijl*):	
sent by al-Muthannā to raid Taghlib after Buwayb	Tab. i/2206-2207 (Sayf < MTZ)
15. Furāt b. Ḥayyān of B. Dulaf b. Sa'd (*'Ijl*):	
al-Muthannā's lieutenant over al-Anbār; sent to raid Taghlib and al-Namir	Tab. i/2206-2207 (Sayf < MTZ)
raids Taghlib and al-Namir	Tab. i/2207-2208 (Sayf < MTZ)
of B. 'Ijl; had been Abū Sufyān's guide to Syria	I.D. 208
16. 'Utayba b. al-Nahhās of B. Dulaf b. Sa'd (*'Ijl*):	
raids Taghlib and al-Namir	Tab. i/2206-2207 (Sayf < MTZ)
raids Taghlib and al-Namir	Tab. i/2207-2208 (Sayf < MTZ)
most notable 'Ijlī in Kūfa	I.D. 208
17. Group of 'Ijl (*'Ijl*):	
mentioned at Buwayb	Tab. i/2192 (Sayf < MT)
18. 'Iṣma b. 'Abdullāh of B. 'Abd b. al-Ḥārith (*Ḍabba*):	
sent to aid al-Muthannā	Tab. i/2182-2183 (Sayf < MTZ, 'Aṭiyya)
joins al-Muthannā; commands vanguard at Buwayb	Tab. i/2184-2185 (Sayf < MTZ) and (Sayf < Abū Isḥāq al-Shaybānī)
cooperated with Jarīr and al-Muthannā	Tab. i/2197 (Sayf < MTZ)
sent against Persian garrisons by al-Muthannā	Tab. i/2202-2203 (Sayf < MTZ)
19. Ibn al-Ḥawbar (*Ḍabba*):	
put in charge of one group of Ḍabba at Buwayb by al-Muthannā	Tab. i/2188-2189 (Sayf < MA)
assisting al-Muthannā	Tab. i/2192 (Sayf < MT)

uncertain; he appears to have been sent to aid 'Utba but may not have reached southern Iraq before 'Utba's death.

237. *TMD* (Zah.) XVII, fol. 44a (Abū Mūsā Ismā'īl al-Baṣrī—h—al-Thawrī < Sufyān b. 'Uyayna); *TMD* (Zah.) XVII, fol. 38b (Ismā'īl b. 'Īsā al-'Aṭṭār—h—Isḥāq b. Busr); I.S. VII/1, 1-3 (*isnād*, note 216 above).

238. The MTZMAS group. Of the numerous accounts mentioning eight members of Tamīm, all but one come from the group MTMA via Sayf b. 'Umar. The one tradition not explicitly derived from MTMA has no *isnād*, but as it appears in Bal. *Fut.* 384-385, it could also derive from Sayf's collections since al-Balādhurī did use them.

239. Bal. *Fut.* 376.

240. *TMD* (Zah.) XVII, fol. 38a-38b (Zakariyya al-Minqarī—h—al-Aṣma'ī—h—Salama b. Bilāl < Abū Rajā' al-'Uṭāridī).

241. Tab. i/2377-2378 (Sayf and Mad.), 'Utba sent to found al-Baṣra in A.H. 14; Tab. i/2377, al-Baṣra founded in A.H. 14 (Waq. Mad.), or A.H. 16 (Sayf); *TMD* (Zah.) XVII, fol. 38a-38b (*isnād* in note 240), al-Ubulla conquered in Rajab or Sha'bān, A.H. 14/August-October, A.D. 635; Yaqut, s.v. "al-Khurayba," (Ḥamza), al-Baṣra founded A.H. 14.

242. Unfortunately not specified: Tab. i/2569; Tab. i/2542.

243. Muhammad Abdulhayy Shaban, *Islamic History, A.D. 600-750 (A.H. 132). A New Interpretation*, p. 28.

CHAPTER V

1. On such theories, see Introduction.

2. Tab. i/2182-2183 (Sayf < Muḥammad b. Nuwayra, T, Z, 'Aṭiyya); Tab. i/2185-2187 (Sayf < 'Aṭiyya and Sufyān al-Aḥmarī < al-Mujālid < al-Sha'bī); Tab. i/2187-2188 (Sayf < 'Aṭiyya and al-Mujālid); Tab. i/2218 (Sayf < Ḥanash al-Nakha'ī < his father and others).

3. There were migrations of whole sections of tribes, of course, but only after the completion of the military conquest. See Sections 3 and 5 below.

4. Tab. i/2362-2363 (Sayf < Sulaymān b. Bishr < Umm Kathīr, wife of Hammām b. al-Ḥārith al-Nakha'ī), women at al-Qādisiyya; *TMD* I, 535-545 (Abū Hudhayfa Isḥāq b. Bishr < SbA < old Syrian authorities), women at Yarmūk; Kufi I, 253-254, women at Yarmūk; Tab. i/2197 (Sayf < MTZ), at "Buwayb"; Tab. i/2451 and Tab. i/2456 (Sayf < 'Amr < al-Sha'bī), at al-Madā'in; Tab. i/2121-2125 (I.I.), with Khālid b. al-Walīd in Iraq; Kufi I, 223, 224, at Ḥimṣ; Kufi I, 145, at Ajnādayn; Tab. i/2216-2218 (Sayf < TM), with Sa'd b. Abī Waqqāṣ.

5. Tab. i/2363 (Sayf < 'Aṭiyya b. al-Ḥārith); cf. Tab. i/2363-2364 (Sayf < MTM). This is all the more striking in a society with a marked preference for tribal endogamy.

6. Tab. i/2375 (Sayf < Ash'ath b. Siwār < Abū l-Zubayr < Jābir). It is possible, of course, that the "people of the book" in question were nonetheless Arabs, that is, Christian or Jewish Arab tribesmen who were fighting along with Arabian Muslims.

20. al-Mundhir b. Ḥassān b. Ḍirar (*Ḍabba*):	
put in charge of another group of Ḍabba at Buwayb by al-Muthannā (cf. no. 12)	Tab. i/2188-2189 (Sayf < MA)
with Jarīr at Nukhayla; they dispute Mihrān's armor	Tab. i/2200-2202 (I.I.)
disputes with Jarīr	Ya'qubi II/143
disputes with Jarīr	Bal. *Fut.* 254 (Sayf)
disputes with Jarīr: "Ḥassān b. al-Mundhir . . ."	*Muruj* II/310-311
disputes with Jarīr (placed in al-Qādisiyya accounts)	Kufi I/202-203
21. al-Kalaj (*Ḍabba*):	
raids Persian garrisons after Buwayb	Tab. i/2202-2203 (Sayf < MTZ)
22. Ḥiṣn b. Ma'bad b. Zurāra b. 'Udas (*Tamīm*):	
killed Mihrān, some say	Bal. *Fut.* 254 (Sayf)
23. al-Ḥuṣayn b. Ma'bad b. Zurāra (*Tamīm*):	
led 1,000 Tamīmīs to Medina; sent to Iraq under Jarīr	Din. 114-115
24. 'Amr b. Abī Sulmā al-Hujaymī (*Tamīm?*):	
left in charge (at al-Anbār?) as al-Muthannā raided	Tab. i/2206-2207 (Sayf < MTZ)
25. Rib'ī b. 'Āmir b. Khālid b. al-'Anūd (*'Amr-Tamīm*):	
led group of B. 'Amr; sent to reinforce al-Muthannā	Tab. i/2188-2189 (Sayf < MA)
26. 'Āmir b. Khālid (cf. preceding) (*'Amr-Tamīm?*):	
prowess at Buwayb battle	Tab. i/2196 (Sayf < MT)
27. Ibn Mirdā al-Fihrī (*Taghlib*):	
Christian; joins al-Muthannā at Buwayb	Tab. i/2190 (Sayf < MA)
joins al-Muthannā at Buwayb	Tab. i/2192 (Sayf < MT)
28. 'Abdullāh b. Kulayb b. Khālid (*Taghlib*):	
Christian; joins al-Muthannā at Buwayb	Tab. i/2190 (Sayf < MA)
29. Group of Taghlib youths (*Taghlib*):	
join Muslims at Buwayb	Tab. i/2193 (Sayf < 'Ubaydullāh b. Muḥaffiz < his father < Muḥammad b. Tha'laba)

30. Anas b. Hilāl (*al-Namir*):	
Christian; joins al-Muthannā at Buwayb	Tab. i/2190 (Sayf < MA)
joins al-Muthannā	Tab. i/2192 (Sayf < MT)
brings group of al-Namir; sent to Iraq under Jarīr	Din. 114-115
31. Khālid b. Hilāl (brother of preceding?) (*al-Namir?*):	
killed at Buwayb	Tab. i/2196 (Sayf < MT)
32. Hilāl b. 'Ullafa al-Taymī (*Taym al-Ribāb*):	
sent to raid Dastimaysān by al-Muthannā after Buwayb	Tab. i/2202-2203 (Sayf < MTZ)
33. 'Urwa b. Zayd "al-Khayl" (*Ṭayyi'*):	
prowess at Buwayb battle	Tab. i/2196 (Sayf < MT)
mentioned at Nukhayla battle under Jarīr	Din. 114-115
34. 'Adī b. Ḥātim (*Ṭayyi'*):	
sent to Iraq under Jarīr in command of group of Ṭayyi'	Din. 114-115
35. Ghālib b. 'Abdullāh al-Laythī (*Kināna*):	
led group of Kināna to reinforce al-Muthannā	Tab. i/2187-2188 (Sayf < 'Aṭiyya) and (Sayf < al-Mujālid)
backs al-Muthannā at Buwayb; valor	Tab. i/2196 (Sayf < MT)
36. Busr b. Abī Ruhm (*Juhayna*):	
commanded wing of al-Muthannā's army at Buwayb	Tab. i/2191 (Sayf < MT)
"Busr . . . al-Juhanī"	Tab. i/2292-2294 (Sayf < MTZ)
37. 'Abdullāh b. Dhī l-Sahmayn (*Khath'am*):	
leads group of Khath'am to 'Umar; sent to reinforce al-Muthannā in Iraq	Tab. i/2188 (Sayf < Mujālid) and (Sayf < 'Aṭiyya)
38. Rib'ī or Shabath b. Rib'ī (*Ḥanẓala*):	
led group of Ḥanẓala who join al-Muthannā	Tab. i/2188-2189 (Sayf < MA)
39. Abū Miḥjan (*Thaqīf*):	
fled from Ullays after Bridge	Tab. i/2182-2183 (Sayf < MTZ, 'Aṭiyya)
40. Qurṭ b. Jammāḥ (*'Abd al-Qays*):	
led group of 'Abd al-Qays to Iraq after 'Umar's call	Tab. i/2188-2189 (Sayf < MA)
mentioned at Buwayb	Bal. *Fut.* 254 (Sayf)

41. Bishr b. Munqidh (*Hamdān*):	
claimed to have been with al-Muthannā during campaigns	Kufi II/10
42. Ḥudhayfa b. Miḥṣan al-Ghalfānī	
commanded front-guard under al-Muthannā at Buwayb	Tab. i/2207-2208 (Sayf < MTZ)
"al-'Alqā'ī"	*Isaba*, s.n.
43. al-Nusayr:	
commanded right wing of al-Muthannā's army at Buwayb	Tab. i/2184-2185 (Sayf < MTZ) and (Sayf < Abū Isḥāq al-Shaybānī)
commanded vanguard for al-Muthannā's army at Buwayb	Tab. i/2191 (Sayf < MT)
brought captured supplies to families of Buwayb troops	Tab. i/2197 (Sayf < MTZ)
44. 'Āṣim:	
commanded detachment of al-Muthannā's army at Buwayb	Tab. i/2184-2185 (Sayf < MTZ) and (Sayf < Abū Isḥāq al-Shaybānī)
45. 'Ikrima:	
carried Buwayb booty to 'Umar	Tab. i/2198 (Sayf < Ḥamza b. 'Alī b. Muḥaffiz < a man of Bakr b. Wā'il)
46. Zayd:	
sent by al-Muthannā to raid Taghlib after Buwayb	Tab. i/2206-2207 (Sayf < MTZ)

APPENDIX G. BATTLE OF AL-QĀDISIYYA

BAJĪLA

1. Jarīr b. 'Abdullāh al-Bajalī:	
led Bajīla at al-Qādisiyya	Tab. i/2221-2222 (Sayf < MTZ, Māhān)
led right wing	Tab. i/2353 (I.I.)
criticizes Sa'd in poem	Tab. i/2361-2362 (Sayf < al-Miqdām b. Shurayḥ al-Ḥārithī < his father)
present at battle	Bal. *Ansab* Reis. 598/1212
present with al-Muthannā	Din. 119-120
leads Bajīla in attack	Din. 122, 123
present with 600 Bajīla	Kufi I/173
present at battle	Kufi I/196
leads Bajīla in first attack	Kufi I/210
mentioned	*Muruj* II/313
mentioned	Tab. i/2288 (Sayf < al-Qāsim b. al-Walīd al-Hamdānī < his father < Abū Nimrān)
performs heroics	Din. 123
2. 'Āmir b. 'Abāda Abū Iyās:	
present at battle	IS VI/136
3. Qays b. Abī Ḥāzim:	
present; Bajīla one-fourth of Muslims	Tab. i/2355-2358 (I.I. < Ismā'īl b. Abī Khālid, *mawlā* of Bajīla < Qays b. Abī Ḥāzim)
4. Miscellaneous:	
2000 Bajīla in battle	Tab. i/2221 (Sayf < MTZ, Māhān)
mention Bajīla	Tab. i/2298 (Sayf < Ismā'īl b. Abī Khālid < Qays b. Abī Ḥāzim)
mention Bajīla	Tab. i/2322 (Sayf < al-Walīd b. 'Abdullāh b. Abī Ṭayba < his father)
Bajīla important in battle	Din. 122

ṬAYYI'

5. 'Adī b. Ḥātim:	
led Ṭayyi', with Muthannā	Tab. i/2221-2222 (Sayf < MTZ, Māhān)
6. Bujayr al-Ṭā'ī:	
possibly present; poem	*Muruj* II/317-319

ASAD

7. Ṭalḥa b. Khuwaylid al-Faq'asī:	
raids Persian camp before battle of al-Qādisiyya	Tab. i/2261-2264 (Sayf < Abū 'Amr < Abū 'Uthman al-Nahdī)
harasses Persians	Tab. i/2258-2260 (Sayf < Muḥammad b. Qays < Mūsā b. Ṭarīf)
sent to reconnoiter	Tab. i/2264-2265 (Sayf < Muḥammad b. Qays < Mūsā b. Ṭarīf)
mentioned	Tab. i/2291-2292 (Sayf < MTZ)
assists Bajīla; commanding a *katība*(?)	Tab. i/2298 (Sayf < MTZ)
mentioned for valor	Tab. i/2307-2308 (Sayf < MTZ)
mentioned	Tab. i/2327-2328 (Sayf < 'Amr b. Muḥammad b. Qays < 'Abd al-Raḥmān b. Jaysh)
mentioned for valor	Tab. i/2329-2330 (Sayf < al-Naḍr < Ibn al-Rufayl < his father < Ḥumayd b. Abī Shajjār)
mentioned	Tab. i/2331 (Sayf < A)
sent to reconnoiter	Din. 119
heroics	Bal. *Fut.* 258-259
with 800 horsemen	Kufi I/173
mentioned	Kufi I/196
part of core of Sa'd's army	Kufi I/201-202
mentioned with B. Asad	*Muruj* II/313; II/316
8. Ḥammād b. Mālik al-Wālibī:	
commands infantry	Tab. i/2225 (Sayf < A < al-Sha'bī)
assists B. Bajīla	Tab. i/2298 (Sayf < MTZ)
mentioned for valor	Tab. i/2307-2308 (Sayf < MTZ)
mentioned for valor	Tab. i/2325-2326 (Sayf < Mujālid < al-Sha'bī) and (Sayf < A < al-Sha'bī)
mentioned	Tab. i/2331 (Sayf < A)
9. Qays b. Hubayra:	
mentioned at al-Qādisiyya	Tab. i/2261-2264 (Sayf < Abū 'Amr < Abū 'Uthmān al-Nahdī)
raids Persians before battle	Tab. i/2264-2265 (Sayf < Muḥammad b. Qays < Mūsā b. Ṭarīf)
mentioned	Tab. i/2291-2292 (Sayf < MTZ)
mentioned in battle	Tab. i/2329-2330 (Sayf < al-Naḍr < Ibn al-Rufayl < his father < Ḥumayd b. Abī Shajjār)
10. Ḍirār b. al-Azwar al-Asadī:	
mentioned (misplaced?)	Bal. *Fut.* 259
11. Ghālib b. 'Abdullāh:	
mentioned	Tab. i/2291-2292 (Sayf < MTZ)

mentioned	Tab. i/2292-2294 (Sayf < MTZ)
single combat	Tab. i/2295-2297 (Sayf < MTZ)
assists Bajīla	Tab. i/2298 (Sayf < MTZ)
mentioned	Tab. i/2331 (Sayf < A)
mentioned; called "al-Laythī"	Tab. i/2331-2335 (Sayf < 'Abdullāh b. Muslim al-'Uklī) and (Sayf < al-Miqdām b. Abī l-Miqdām < his father < Karib b. Abī Karib al-'Ukli)
single combat	*Muruj* II/312
12. Ḥanẓala b. Rabī'a "Dhū l-Ḥājib":	
killed at al-Qādisiyya	Khalifa I/102 (Abū l-Ḥasan)
13. al-Rabbīl b. 'Amr b. Rabī'a al-Wālibī:	
assists Bajīla; "Zabīl"	Tab. i/2298 (Sayf < MTZ)
mentioned for valor	Tab. i/2307-2308 (Sayf < MTZ)
mentioned for valor	Tab. i/2325-2326 (Sayf < Mujālid < al-Sha'bī) and (Sayf < A < al-Sha'bī)
14. Ibn al-Hudhayl al-Kāhilī:	
mentioned in mop-up after al-Qādisiyya	Tab. i/2345-2346 (Sayf < MMT)
15. Mas'ūd b. Mālik:	
mentioned	Tab. i/2329-2330 (Sayf < al-Naḍr < Ibn al-Rufayl < his father < Ḥumayd b. Abī Shajjār)
16. 'Abdullāh b. Sinān b. Jarīr al-Asadī *thumma* al-Ṣaydāwī:	
native of al-Ḥīra? kills al-Nu'man b. Qabīṣa and joins Muslims	Tab. i/2350 (I.I.)
17. Abū l-Hayyāj Ibn Mālik al-Asadī:	
messenger to Medina	Tab. i/2369 (Sayf < MTZM)
18. Asad Abū l-Mawt al-Asadī (?):	
kills elephant	Kufi I/204
19. Ten brothers of B. Kāhil b. Asad:	
mentioned	Tab. i/2328-2329 (Sayf < Qudāma al-Kāhilī < his authority) but cf. Tab. i/2333
20. Miscellaneous:	
3,000 Asadīs conscripted by Sa'd at Zarūd	Tab. i/2221-2222 (Sayf < MTZ, Māhān)
mentioned 500 of B. Asad	Tab. i/2299-2301 (Sayf < MTZ)
B. Asad attacks Persians second after Bajīla	Tab. i/2332 (Sayf < al-Walīd b. 'Abdullāh b. Abī Ṭayba < his father)
800 horsemen under Ṭalḥa b. Khuwalid	(see no. 7, Ṭalḥa b. Khuwaylid)

TAMĪM

21. ʿĀsim b. ʿAmr al-ʿAmrī al-Tamīmī:	
commands Muslim rear-guard	Tab. i/2223-2225 (Sayf < A < al-Shaʿbī)
sent to lower Euphrates	Tab. i/2234 (Sayf < ʿAbdullāh b. Muslim al-ʿUklī) and (Sayf < al-Miqdām b. Abī l-Miqdām < his father < Karib b. Abī Karib al-ʿUklī)
mentioned; a chief	Tab. i/2236 (Sayf < Mujālid, A, S)
in delegation to Persians	Tab. i/2243 (Sayf < A < al-Shaʿbī)
raids Persians	Tab. i/2258-2260 (Sayf < Muḥammad b. Qays < Mūsā b. Ṭarīf)
commands detachment	Tab. i/2265-2266 (Sayf < MTZA) and (Sayf < Mujālid, S)
mentioned	Tab. i/2287 (Sayf < MTZ)
mentioned	Tab. i/2291 (Sayf < MTZ)
mentioned	Tab. i/2292-2294 (Sayf < MTZ)
single combat	Tab. i/2295-2297 (Sayf < MTZ)
defeats elephants	Tab. i/2300-2301 (Sayf < MTZ)
mentioned for valor	Tab. i/2307-2308 (Sayf < MTZ)
chosen to attack elephants	Tab. i/2324-2325 (Sayf < MTZ)
chosen to attack elephants	Tab. i/2325-2326 (Sayf < Mujālid < al-Shaʿbī)
mentioned	Tab. i/2329-2330 (Sayf < al-Naḍr < Ibn al-Rufayl < his father < Ḥumayd b. Abī Shajjār)
mentioned	Tab. i/2331-2332 (Sayf < A, al-Naḍr)
mentioned	Tab. i/2345-2346 (Sayf < MTM)
sent with 400 to assist Saʿd	Kufi I/173
in delegation to Persians	Kufi I/196
mentioned in delegation	Yaʿqubi II/143-144
mentioned	*Muruj* II/132
22. al-Qaʿqāʿ b. ʿAmr (brother of preceding):	
led front-guard of Syrians at al-Qādisiyya	Tab. i/2306 (Sayf < MT)
single combat	Tab. i/2309 (Sayf < al-Qāsim b. Sulaym b. ʿAbd al-Raḥmān al-Saʿdī < his father)
heroics	Tab. i/2318-2320 (Sayf < MTZ)
in front-guard of Syrians (not in command)	Tab. i/2320-2321 (Sayf < Mujālid < al-Shaʿbī)
chosen to attack elephants	Tab. i/2324-2325 (Sayf < MTZ)

chosen to attack elephants	Tab. i/2325-2326 (Sayf < Mujālid < al-Sha'bī)
mentioned	Tab. i/2329-2330 (Sayf < al-Naḍr < Ibn al-Rufayl < his father < Ḥumayd b. Abī Shajjār)
mentioned	Tab. i/2331-2332 (Sayf < A, al-Naḍr)
leads Tamīm in first attack	Tab. i/2332 (Sayf < al-Walīd b. 'Abdullāh b. Abī Ṭayba < his father)
mentioned	Tab. i/2335-2337 (Sayf < MTZ)
mentioned; chief	Tab. i/2338-2339 (Sayf < MTZ)
mentioned	Tab. i/2345-2346 (Sayf < MTM)
heroics	Tab. i/2307-2308 (Sayf < MTZ)
poem stressing valor	Tab. i/2361-2362 (Sayf < al-Miqdām b. Shurayḥ al-Ḥārithī < his father)
mentioned	*Muruj* II/313-314; II/316; II/318
witnessed conquests of Damascus and Iraq	*Isaba*, s.v. "al-Qa'qā' b. 'Amr"
23. Nadhīr b. 'Amr (brother of two preceding?):	
mentioned	Tab. i/2231-2235
24. al-Mughīra b. Zurāra b. al-Nabbāsh al-Usayyidī:	
in delegation to Persians	Tab. i/2241 (Sayf < A < al-Sha'bī)
mentioned	Tab. i/2236 (Sayf < A, Mujālid, S)
mentioned?	Tab. i/2291-2292 (Sayf < MTZ)
25. 'Āṣim b. Zurāra al-Tamīmī (brother of preceding?):	
sent by Umar to reinforce Sa'd, with 700 men	Kufi I/173
26. Rabī' b. Bilād al-Sa'dī (Sa'd—Tamīm?):	
mentioned	Tab. i/2292-2294 (Sayf < MTZ)
27. Jaz' b. Mu'āwiya al-Sa'dī al-Tamīmī:	
mentioned	Tab. i/2245 (Sayf < A < al-Sha'bī)
of Sa'd-Tamīm	*Isaba*, s.n. "Jaz' b. Mu'āwiya"
28. 'Abdullāh b. Ḥābis al-Tamīmī:	
mentioned	Kufi I/204-206
29. Sawād b. Mālik:	
over vanguard of army	Tab. i/2225 (Sayf < A < al-Sha'bī)
raids for livestock	Tab. i/2244 (Sayf < A < al-Sha'bī)
raids Persians	Tab. i/2258-2260 (Sayf < Muḥammad b. Qays < Mūsā b. Ṭarīf)
commands Muslim vanguard	Tab. i/2265-2266 (Sayf < MTZA) and (Sayf < Mujālid, S)

mentioned	Tab. i/2309 (Sayf < al-Qāsim b. ʿAbd al-Raḥmān al-Saʿdī < his father)
30. Zuhra b. Ḥawiyya b. ʿAbdullāh b. Qatāda al-Saʿdī al-Tamīmī:	
mentioned pursuing Persians	Tab. i/2355-2358 (I.I. < Ismāʿīl b. Abī Khālid, *mawlā* of Bajīla < Qays b. Abī Ḥāzim al-Bajalī)
led front-guard in battle	Tab. i/2231-2235 (Sayf < ʿAbdullāh b. Muslim al-ʿUklī) and (Sayf < al-Miqdām b. Abī l-Miqdām < his father < Karib b. Abī Karib al-ʿUklī)
led front-guard in battle	Tab. i/2265-2266 (Sayf < MTZA) and (Sayf < Mujālid, S)
in delegation to Persians	Tab. i/2267-2269 (Sayf < al-Naḍr < Ibn al-Rufayl < his father)
subcommander at al-Qādisiyya	Tab. i/2267 (Sayf < TZAS and Mujālid)
mentioned	Tab. i/2287 (Sayf < MTZ)
mentioned	Tab. i/2288 (Sayf < al-Qāsim b. al-Walīd al-Hamdānī < his father < Abū Nimrān)
pursues Persians	Tab. i/2338-2340 (Sayf < MTZ)
pursues Persians	Tab. i/2341 (Sayf < S)
pursues Persians	Tab. i/2342 (Sayf < al-Barmakān and Sayf < Mujālid < al-Shaʿbī)
pursues Persians	Tab. i/2342-2343 (Sayf < ʿAbīd < ʿIṣma)
pursues Persians	Tab. i/2345-2346 (Sayf < MTM)
sent on raids	Khalifa I/101-120 (Sharīk < ʿUbayda < Ibrāhīm)
kills Rustam?	Khalifa I/102 (Abū l-Ḥasan)
led front-guard in battle	Tab. i/2223-2225 (Sayf < A < al-Shaʿbī)
forage expedition	Bal. *Fut.* 257-258
31. Salmā bint Ḥafṣa al-Tamīmiyya:	
Muthannā b. Ḥāritha al-Shaybānī's wife; Saʿd marries her on former's death	Kufi I/174
32. Ribʿī b. ʿĀmir:	
in delegation to Persians	Tab. i/2269-2274 (Sayf < MTZA)
exhorts troops	Tab. i/2292-2294 (Sayf < MTZ)
in delegation to Persians	Yaʿqubi II/144
campaigned in Syria, then in Iraq	*Isaba*, s.n. "Ribʿī b. ʿĀmir"
of Usayyid-Tamīm	I.K. /Caskel II/486 and Table 83

33. Nu'aym b. 'Amr b. 'Attāb al-Yarbū'ī (of B. Riyāḥ—Yarbū'—Tamīm):	
fought with al-Qa'qā' b. 'Amr	Tab. i/2307-2308 (Sayf < MTZ)
34. 'Attāb b. Nu'aym b. 'Attāb al-Yarbū'ī (of B. Riyāḥ—Tamīm):	
fought with al-Qa'qā' b. 'Amr	Tab. i/2307-2308 (Sayf < MTZ)
35. 'Amr b. Shabīb b. Zinbā' b. al-Ḥārith b. Rabī'a (of B. Riyāḥ—Tamīm):	
fought with al-Qa'qā' b. 'Amr	Tab. i/2307-2308 (Sayf < MTZ)
36. Ḥanẓala b. al-Rabī' "Kātib al-Nabī":	
mentioned in battle	Tab. i/2345-2346 (Sayf < MTM)
37. Miscellaneous:	
4,000 of Tamīm and al-Ribāb join Sa'd at Zarūd	Tab. i/2221 (Sayf < MTZ, Māhān)
Tamīmīs of indeterminate lineage oppose Persians before Sa'd arrives	Tab. i/2245 (Sayf < A < Al-Sha'bī)

MADHḤIJ:

38. 'Amr b. Ma'dīkarib al-Zubaydī (of B. Munabbih—Zubayd the Younger?):	
arrives in Medina commanding B. Munabbih	Tab. i/2218-2219 (Sayf < MT, al-Mustanīr, Ḥanash)
harasses Persians, raids	Tab. i/2258-2260 (Sayf < Muḥammad b. Qays < Mūsā b. Ṭarīf)
harasses Persians, raids	Tab. i/2261-2264 (Sayf < Abū 'Amr < Abū 'Uthmān al-Nahdī)
sent to reconnoiter	Tab. i/2264-2265 (Sayf < Muḥammad b. Qays < Mūsā b. Ṭarīf)
among "ahl al-najda"	Tab. i/2291-2292 (Sayf < MTZ)
mentioned in battle	Tab. i/2295-2297 (Sayf < MTZ)
mentioned in battle	Tab. i/2297 (Sayf < Ismā'īl b. Abī Khālid < Qays b. Abī Ḥāzim)
heroics	Tab. i/2322-2323 (Sayf < al-Miqdām al-Ḥārithī < al-Sha'bī)
fought at al-Qādisiyya	Tab. i/2355 (I.I.)
killed Rustam?	Khalifa I/102 (Mad.)
fought at al-Qādisiyya	Din. 122
in delegation to Persians	Bal. *Fut.* 257

heroics	Bal. *Fut.* 257-258
killed Rustam?	Bal. *Fut.* 259
joins Sa'd with 500 men	Kufi I/173
mentioned	Kufi I/196
commands right wing	Kufi I/201-202
heroics	Kufi I/204-206
leads an attack	Kufi I/210
mentioned	*Muruj* II/314-316
39. al-Ashtar al-Nakha'ī:	
arrives with Syrian force	Din. 119-120
did not witness al-Qādisiyya	Tab. i/2101 (Sayf < al-Mustanīr b. Yazīd b. Arṭāt b. Juhaysh)
40. Zayd and Arṭāt bb. 'Abdullāh al-Nakha'ī:	
led attacks; killed	Din. 122
41. Durayd b. Ka'b al-Nakha 'ī:	I.S. I/2, 77
had standard of al-Nakha'	Tab. i/2331 (Sayf < al-Mustanīr b. Yazīd < his authorities)
42. al-Aswad al-Nakha'ī:	
"I witnessed al-Qādisiyya"	Tab. i/2355 (I.I. < 'Abd al-Raḥmān b. al-Aswad al-Nakha'ī < his father)
43. Abu Sabra b. Dhu'ayb:	
arrives in Medina commanding B. Ju'fi, Jaz', Zubayd, Anas Allāt, and others	Tab. i/2218-2219 (Sayf < MT, al-Mustanīr, Ḥanash)
44. Yazīd b. al-Ḥārith al-Ṣuḍā'ī:	
arrives in Medina commanding B. Ṣudā', Janb, Musliyya	Tab. i/2218-2219 (Sayf < MT, al-Mustanīr, Ḥanash)
45. Qays b. Hubayra b. 'Abd Yaghūth al-Murādī (cf. next following):	
commanded one wing of Syrian reinforcements	Tab. i/2302-2306 (Sayf < MT)
arrives with Syrians	Tab. i/2318-2320 (Sayf < MTZ)
mentioned	Tab. i/2330-2331 (Sayf < 'Ubaydallāh b. 'Abd al-'A'lā < 'Amr b. Murra)
mentioned; "Qays b. 'Abd Yaghūth"	Tab. i/2335-2337 (Sayf < MTZ)
mentioned	Din. 122, 123
poem by him	Din. 125
arrives from Syria with 700 men	Bal. *Fut.* 256 (Waq.?)
46. Qays b. Makshūḥ al-Murādī:	
arrives leading 700 men from Syria	Tab. i/2320-2321 (Sayf < Mujālid < al-Sha'bī)
arrives leading 300 men from Syria	Tab. i /2321 (Sayf < Jakhdab b. Jar'ab < 'Iṣma al-Wābilī)

arrives with Syrians	Tab. i/2322 (Sayf < Abū Kibrān al-Ḥasan b. ʻUqba)
arrives with 700 from Syria	Tab. i/2349-2350 (I.I.)
arrives before battle	Tab. i/2351-2353 (I.I.)
commanded right wing	Tab. i/2353 (I.I.)
arrived leading 1,000 men from Syria	Din. 119-120
fought at al-Qādisiyya; or, according to others, he arrived only after battle	Bal. *Fut.* 258-259
joins Saʻd with 400 men; "al-Makshūḥ al-Murādī"	Kufi I/173
arrives from Syria with 700	Bal. *Fut.* 256 (al-ʻAbbās b. al-Walīd < al-Narsī < al-Shaʻbī)
47. Kathīr b. Shihāb al-Ḥārithī:	
killed Jālīnūs; "al-Ḥārithī"	Bal. *Fut.* 259
killed Jālīnūs	Khalifa I/102 (Mad.)
leader of Madhḥij in Kufa	*Isaba*, s.n. "Kathīr b. Shihāb"
48. Miscellaneous:	
Among the 2,300 Yamanis who came to Medina were al-Nakhaʻ b. ʻAmr; half of these go to Syria, half to Iraq with Saʻd b. Abī Waqqāṣ	Tab. i/2216-2218 (Sayf < MTZ); also Tab. i/2218 (Sayf < Ḥanash al-Nakhaʻī < his father)
4 men of al-Nakhaʻ	Tab. i/2307 (Sayf < Mujālid < al-Shaʻbī)
B. al-Nakhaʻ attacks	Tab. i/2331-2332 (Sayf < al-Naḍr, and Sayf < A)
B. al-Nakhaʻ attacks	Tab. i/2332 (Sayf < al-Walīd b. ʻAbdullāh b. Abī Ṭayba < his father)
B. al-Juʻfī participated in battle of al-Qādisiyya	Tab. i/2334 (Sayf < Muḥammad b. Jarīr al-ʻAbdī < ʻĀbis al-Juʻfī < his father)
B. Murād among those coming from Syria	Tab. i/2367-2368 (Sayf < MTZM)

BĀHILA

49. Salmān b. Rabīʻa al-Bāhilī:	
commands detachment	Tab. i/2225 (Sayf < A < al-Shaʻbī)
mentioned	Tab. i/2344 (Sayf < Yūnus b. Abī Isḥāq < his father and others)
invaded Syria, then Iraq	Bal. *Fut.* 259 (Aḥmad b. Salmān al-Bāhilī < his authorities)
heroics	Bal. *Fut.* 259 (Waq.)

50. ʻAbd al-Raḥmān b. Rabīʻa al-Bāhilī "Dhū l-Nūr" (brother of preceding?):	
judge for Saʻd's army	Tab. i/2225 (Sayf < Mujālid < al-Shaʻbī)
mentioned	Tab. i/2344 (Sayf < Yūnus b. Abī Isḥāq < his father < witnesses)

KINDA

51. Shuraḥbīl b. al-Simṭ b. Shuraḥbīl al-Kindī:	
over right wing; fought *ahl al-ridda*	Tab. i/2223-2225 (Sayf < A < al-Shaʻbī)
commanded a wing	Tab. i/2265-2266 (Sayf < MTZA) and (Sayf < Mujālid, S)
present at al-Qādisiyya	Tab. i/2287 (Sayf < MTZ)
present at al-Qādisiyya; replaced in lineup by Zuhra	Tab. i/2288 (Sayf < al-Qāsim b. al-Walīd al-Hamdānī < his father < Abū Nimrān)
pursues Persians	Tab. i/2338-2339 (Sayf < MTZ)
pursues Persians	Tab. i/2345-2346 (Sayf < MTM)
commanded right wing	Din. 120-121
mentioned; tribal chief	Din. 122
in delegation to Persians	Kufi I/196
52. al-Ashʻath b. Qays al-Kindī:	
joins Saʻd with 700 Yamanis at al-Sharāf	Tab. i/2222 (Sayf < MZ, Māhān); cf. i/2335 (Sayf < Mujālid < al-Shaʻbī)
mentioned	Tab. i/2236 (Sayf < A, Mujālid, S)
mentioned (later time)	Bal. *Ansab* Reis. 498/1212
arrives from Syria	Din. 119-120
in delegation to Persians	Bal. *Fut.* 257
exhorts Kinda to aid Asad	Tab. i/2300-2301 (Sayf < MTZ)
commanded 700 Kinda at al-Qādisiyya	Tab. i/2235 (Sayf < Mujālid < al-Shaʻbī)
of B. Muʻāwiya b. Kinda	I.H.J. 425
53. Muʻāwiya b. Ḥudayj al-Sakūnī:	
co-commander of 400 of B. Sakūn during formation of Saʻd's army in Medina	Tab. i/2220-2221 (Sayf < Muḥammad b. Sūqa < a man)
of Sakūn	I.H.J. 429
54. Ḥusayn b. Numayr al-Sakūnī:	
co-commander of 400 of B. Sakūn during formation of Saʻd's army in Medina	Tab. i/2220-2221 (Sayf < Muḥammad b. Sūqa < a man)
"*ṣāḥib ḥiṣār Makka*"	I.H.J. 429

AL-RIBĀB

55. Hilāl b. ʿUllafa al-Taymī (of Taym b. ʿAbd Manāt—"Taym al-Ribāb"): killed Rustam	I.D. 115
at battle of al-Qādisiyya	Tab. i/2335-2337 (Sayf < MTZ)
killed Rustam	Tab. i/2337 (Sayf < ʿAṭiyya < ʿAmr b. Salama)
killed Rustam	Tab. i/2340 (Sayf < al-Naḍr < Ibn al-Rufayl < his father)
mentioned	Tab. i/2338 (Sayf < MTZ)
killed Rustam	Tab. i/2355-2358 (I.I. < Ismāʿīl b. Abī Khālid, *mawlā* of Bajīla < Qays b. Abī Ḥāzim al-Bajalī
helped kill Rustam	Khalifa I/102 (Mad.)
helped kill Rustam	Bal. *Fut.* 259
killed Rustam; "Hilāl b. ʿAlqama al-ʿUqaylī"	Kufi I/211-212
killed Rustam; "Hilāl b. ʿAlqama of Taym al-Ribāb"	*Muruj* II/317-318
56. al-Mustawrid (b. ʿUllafa al-Taymī) (brother of preceding): commanded al-Ribāb	Tab. ii/2245 (Sayf < A < al-Shaʿbī)
57. Mālik b. Rabīʿa b. Khālid al-Taymī *thumma* al-Wāthilī: leads raid (foraging)	Tab. i/2245 (Sayf < A < al-Shaʿbī)
58. Qirfa b. Zāhir al-Taymī *thumma* al-Wāthilī:	
in delegation to Persians	Tab. i/2269-2274 (Sayf < MTZA)
in delegation to Persians	Yaʿqubi II/144
59. al-Musāwir b. al-Nuʿmān al-Taymī *thumma* al-Rubayʿī: leads raid (foraging)	Tab. i/2245 (Sayf < A < al-Shaʿbī)
60. al-Mundhir b. Ḥassān al-Ḍabbī:	
in delegation to Persians	Kufi I/196
a leader in army core	Kufi I/201-202
(misplaced—in Appendix C)	(Kufi I/202-203)
61. Miscellaneous:	
4,000 of Tamīm and al-Ribāb join Saʿd's army; 1,000 of them from al-Ribāb (?)	Tab. i/2221 (Sayf < MTZ, Māhān)

BAKR B. WĀ'IL

62. al-Muʿannā b. Ḥāritha al-Shaybānī: mentioned	Tab. i/2236 (Sayf < A, Mujālid, S)

mentioned	Tab. i/2226-2227 (Sayf < Abū 'Amr < Abu 'Uthmān al-Nahdī)
63. Ibrāhīm b. Ḥāritha al-Shaybānī:	
in delegation to Persians	Kufi I/196
commands one wing of army with an 'Ijlī	Kufi I/201-202
in attack at al-Qādisiyya	Kufi I/210
64. 'Utayba:	
Among *ahl al-'Iraq* sent by al-Muthannā to Medina	Tab. i/2221-2222 (Sayf < MTZ, Māhān)
65. Furāt b. Ḥayyān al-'Ijlī:	
Among *ahl al-'Iraq* sent by al-Muthannā to Medina	Tab. i/2221-2222 (Sayf < MTZ, Māhān)
mentioned	Tab. i/2236 (Sayf < A, Mujālid, S)
in delegation to Persians	Kufi I/196
66. Madh'ūr b. 'Adī al-'Ijlī:	
in delegation to Persians	Tab. i/2269-2274 (Sayf < MTZA)
in delegation to Persians	Ya'qubi II/144
67. al-Muḍārib b. Yazīd al-'Ijlī:	
in delegation to Persians	Tab. i/2269-2274 (Sayf <MTZA)
in delegation to Persians	Ya'qubi II/144
68. 'Ilbā' b. Jaḥsh al-'Ijlī:	
single combat	Tab. i/2310 (Sayf < al-Ghuṣn < al-'Alā' b. Ziyād, Qāsim b. Sulaym < his father)
commands one wing of army; "al-Shaybānī"	Kufi I/201-202
69. 'Alī b. Jaḥsh al-'Ijlī:	
in attack	Kufi I/210
70. Ma'bad b. Murra al-'Ijlī:	
in delegation to Persians	Tab. i/2269-2274 (Sayf < MTZA)
71. al-Hazhāz b. 'Amr al-'Ijlī:	
commands one wing of army	Tab. i/2303-2306 (Sayf < MT)
72. Bashīr b. al-Khaṣāṣiyya al-Dhuhlī (of Sadūs—Dhuhl):	
left in charge of al-Muthannā b. Ḥāritha's army upon al-Muthannā's death	Tab. i/2221-2222 (Sayf < MTZ, Māhān)
73. Maṭar b. Fiḍḍa (of Taymallāt b. Qays b. Tha'laba):	
Sharīf and *sayyid*; captured Khāqān al-Fārsī at al-Qādisiyya	*Iqd* III/280
74. Miscellaneous:	
al-Muthannā's force consists of 6,000 of B. Bakr, 2,000 other Rabī'a tribesmen	Tab. i/2221-2222 (Sayf < MTZ, Māhān)

AZD

75. ʻArfaja b. Harthama al-Bāriqī al-Azdī:	
in delegation to Persians	Tab. i/2269-2274 (Sayf < MTZA)
in delegation to Persians	Yaʻqubi II/144
76. Ḥumayḍa b. al-Nuʻmān b. Ḥumayḍa al-Bāriqī:	
headed 700 *ahl al-Sarawāt* including B. Bāriq, Alma and Ghāmid	Tab. i/2216-2218 (Sayf < MTZ)
77. Mikhnaf b. Sulaym:	
mentioned	Din. 123
78. Zuhayr b. Sulaym:	
single combat	Din. 123
79. Miscellaneous:	
attack of B. Azd important to course of battle	Din. 122
700 Azd (see above) among Saʻd's core force of 4,000 marching from Medina	Tab. i/2216-2218 (Sayf < MTZ)

THAQĪF

80. al-Mughīra b. Shuʻba al-Thaqafī:	
mentioned	Tab. i/2236 (Sayf < A, Mujālid, S)
in delegation to Persians	Tab. i/2236-2237 (Muḥammad b. ʻAbdullāh b. Ṣafwān al-Thaqafī < Umayya b. Khālid < Abū ʻAwāna < Ḥuṣayn b. ʻAbd al-Raḥmān < Abū Wāʼil)
in delegation to Persians	Tab. i/2267 (Sayf < TZAS, Mujālid)
in delegation to Persians	Tab. i/2269-2274 (Sayf < MTZA)
in delegation to Persians	Tab. i/2274-2277 (Sayf < Abū ʻUthmān al-Nahdī)
in delegation to Persians	Tab. i/2277-2278 (Sayf < al-Nahdī < Ibn al-Rufayl < his father)
in delegation to Persians	Tab. i/2278 (Sayf < Mujālid < al-Shaʻbī and < S)
in delegation to Persians	Tab. i/2279 (Sayf < ʻUbayda < Shaqīq)
mentioned	Tab. i/2351-2353 (I.I.)
mentioned with 1,000 men from southern Iraq	Din. 119-120
mentioned with 400 men	Khalifa I/101-102 (I.I.)

in delegation to Persians	Ya'qubi II/144
mentioned	Ya'qubi II/145
mentioned	Bal. *Fut.* 256
in delegation to Persians	Bal. *Fut.* 257
81. Abū Miḥjan al-Thaqafī:	
romantic tale	Tab. i/2312-2317 (Sayf < MTZ and Ibn Mikhrāq < a man of Ṭayyi')
romantic tale	Tab. i/2353-2355 (I.I. < 'Abdullāh b. Abī Bakr)
mentioned	Tab. i/2288 (Sayf < al-Qāsim b. al-Walīd al-Hamdānī < his father < Abū Nimrān)
romantic tale	Bal. *Ansab* Reis. 598/1267 (no *isnad*)
romantic tale	Bal. *Fut.* 258
romantic tale	Din. 121-122
romantic tale	Kufi I/207-209
romantic tale	*Muruj* II/314-316

SULAYM

82. Khath'am b. Abdullāh al-Sulamī:	
reinforces Sa'd with 1,000	Kufi I/173
83. Four sons of Khansā' (poetess of Sulaym):	
killed at al-Qādisiyya	Kufi I/206-207

QURAYSH, ANṢĀR

84. Hāshim b. 'Utba b. Abī Waqqāṣ:	
commanded force from Syria	Tab. i/2303-2306 (Sayf < MT)
arrives from Syria	Tab. i/2320-2321 (Sayf < Mujālid < al-Sha'bī)
arrives from Syria	Tab. i/2321 (Sayf < Jakhdab b. Jar'ab < 'Iṣma al-Wābilī)
arrives from Syria	Tab. i/2321 (Sayf < 'Amr b. al-Rayyān < Ismā'īl b. Muḥammad b. Sa'd)
arrives from Syria	Tab. i/2322 (Sayf < Abū Kibrān al-Ḥasan b. 'Uqba)
arrives from Syria	Din. 120, 121.
arrives from Syria with 10,000 men	Kufi I/211
arrives from Syria with 6,000 men	*Muruj* II/313-316

85. ʻIyāḍ b. Ghanm al-Fihrī:	
commanded Syrians	Tab. i/2349-2350 (I.I.)
commanded 1,000 Syrians who reinforced Zuhra in pursuit of Jālīnūs	Tab. i/2355-2358 (I.I. < Ismāʻīl b. Abī Khālid, *mawlā* of Bajīla < Qays b. Abī Ḥāzim al-Bajalī)
86. Khālid b. ʻUrfuṭa al-ʻUdhrī, *ḥalīf* of B. Zuhra:	
second in command	Tab. i/2223-2225 (Sayf < A < al-Shaʻbī)
second in command	Tab. i/2287 (Sayf < MTZ)
second in command; disliked by army	Tab. i/2288 (Sayf < al-Qāsim b. al-Walīd al-Hamdānī < his father < Abū Nimrān)
disliked by army	Tab. i/2289 (Sayf < MTZ)
in pursuit of Persians	Tab. i/2338 (Sayf < MTZ)
commanded whole army; *ḥalīf* of B. Umayya b. ʻAbd Shams	Tab. i/2353 (I.I.)
second in command over army	Bal. *Fut.* 258
pursues Persians	Bal. *Fut.* 259
second in command	*Isaba*, s.n. "Khālid b. ʻUrfuṭa"
87. Saʻd b. ʻUbayd al-Qāriʼ al-Anṣārī:	
killed at al-Qādisiyya	Tab. i/2366 (Sayf < Ṭalḥa, al-Muhallab) and (Sayf < at-Naḍr b. al-Sirrī < Ibn al-Rufayl b. Maysūr)
killed at al-Qādisiyya	Bal. *Fut.* 262
88. Ḍirār b. al-Khaṭṭāb al-Fihrī al-Qurashī:	
in fighting at al-Qādisiyya	Tab. i/2335-2337 (Sayf < MTZ)
of B. Fihr of Quraysh	*Isaba*, s.n. "Ḍirār b. al-Khaṭṭāb"
89. al-Walīd b. ʻAbd Shams:	
mentioned	Tab. i/2231-2235 (Sayf < ʻAbdullāh b. Muslim al-ʻUklī and al-Miqdām b. Abī l-Miqdām < his father < Karib b. Abī Karib al-ʻUklī)
died during *ridda* in al-Yamāma	Bal. *Fut.* 91
of Makhzūm-Quraysh	I.K. /Caskel II/586 and table 23

MISCELLANEOUS

90. Saʻd b. Nimrān *al-Hamdānī*:	
among those coming from Syria	Tab. i/2320-2321 (Sayf < Mujālid < al-Shaʻbī)
B. Hamdān arrived from Syria	Tab. i/2367-2368 (Sayf < MTZM)

91. ʻAbdullāh b. Dhī l-Sahmayn *al-Khathʻamī*:	
commanded *rukbān* for Saʻd	Tab. i/2225 (Sayf < A < al-Shaʻbī)
mentioned in attack	Tab. i/2329-2330 (Sayf < al-Naḍr < Ibn al-Rufayl < his father < Ḥumayḍ b. Abī Shajjār)
mentioned	Tab. i/2335-2337 (Sayf < MTZ)
92. Bishr b. Rabīʻa *al-Khathʻamī*:	
claims to have been at al-Qādisiyya	I.D. 306
claims to have been at al-Qādisiyya	I.H.J. 391
in Syria?	*Isaba*, s.n. "Bishr b. Rabīʻa"
93. Ibn Dhī l-Burdayn *al-Hilālī*:	
in attack	Tab. i/2329-2330 (Sayf < al-Naḍr < Ibn al-Rufayl < his father < Ḥumayḍ b. Abī Shajjār)
in battle	Tab. i/2335-2337 (Sayf < MTZ)
94. Bishr b. ʻAbdullāh *al-Hilālī*:	
leads 1,000 of Qays—ʻAylān in Saʻd's army	Tab. i/2218-2219 (Sayf < MT, al-Mustanīr, Ḥanash)
95. Bukayr b. ʻAbdullāh *al-Laythī*:	
led raid on al-Ḥīra	Tab. i/2331-2335 (Sayf < ʻAbdullāh b. Muslim al-ʻUklī, al-Miqdām b. Abī Miqdām < his father < Karib b. Abī Karib al-ʻUklī)
kills Persians notable in raid	Khalifa I/101-102 (Sharīk < ʻUbayda < Ibrāhīm)
96. Ghālib b. ʻAbdullāh *al-Laythī*:	
commander	Tab. i/2331-2335 (Sayf < ʻAbdullāh b. Muslim al-ʻUklī, al-Miqdām b. Abī Miqdām < his father < Karib b. Abī Karib al-ʻUklī)
97. Qays b. Ḥidhyām b. Jurthuma (of B. Nahd—Layth—Quḍāʻa?):	
mentioned in battle	Tab. i/2295-2297 (Sayf < MTZ)
98. Saʻd b. ʻUmayla *al-Fazārī* (Ghaṭafān—Qays):	
messenger to Medina	Tab. i/2339-2340 (Sayf?)
messenger to Medina	Tab. i/2366 (Sayf < T, al-Muhallab) and (Sayf < al-Naḍr b. al-Sirrī < Ibn al-Rufayl b. Maysūr)
1,000 of B. Hawāzin accompany Saʻd from Medina	Tab. i/2216—2217 (Sayf < MTZ)
99. Rabīʻa b. ʻUthmān b. Rabīʻa of B. Naṣr b. Muʻāwiyā b. Bakr b. *Hawāzin*:	
first to kill a Persian at al-Qādisiyya	Bal. *Fut.* 261 (I.K.)

100. al-Aʿraf b. al-Aʿlam *al-ʿUqaylī*:	
single combat at al-Qādisiyya	Tab. i/2310 (Sayf < al-Ghuṣn < al-ʿAlāʾ b. Ziyād and al-Qāsim b. Sulaym < his father)
101. al-Ḥarīth b. Ẓabyān b. al-Ḥārith (of B. Taym al-Lāt?):	
mentioned	Tab. i/2303-2306 (Sayf < MT)
102. Ḥamala b. Juwayya *al-Kinānī*:	
mentioned	Tab. i/2236 (Sayf < A, Mujālid, S)
103. al-Nuʿmān b. Muqarrin *al-Muzanī*:	
mentioned	Tab. i/2236 (Sayf < A, Mujālid, S)
mentioned	Tab. i/2239 (Sayf < T < Bint Kaysān al-Ḍabbiyya)
mentioned	Tab. i/2239 (Sayf < A < al-Shaʿbī)
in delegation to Persians	Yaʿqubi II/144
104. Busr b. Abī Ruhm *al-Juhanī*:	
mentioned	Tab. i/2236 (Sayf < A, Mujālid, S)
in delegation to Persians	Tab. i/2269-2274 (Sayf < MTZA)
exhorts troops	Tab. i/2292-2294 (Sayf < MTZ)
mentioned in battle	Tab. i/2345-2346 (Sayf < MTM)
in delegation to Persians; "Bishr b. Abī Ruhm"	Yaʿqubi II/144
105. Qurṭ b. Jammāḥ *al-ʿAbdī*:	
kills Rustam?	Bal. *Fut.* 259
106. al-Ḥuṣayn b. Maʿbad *al-Hanẓalī*:	
commander of Hanẓala	Tab. i/2245 (Sayf < A < al-Shaʿbī)
107. al-Shabba *al-Hanẓalī*:	
commander of Hanẓala	Tab. i/2245 (Sayf < A < al-Shaʿbī)
108. Ḥudhayfa b. Miḥṣan al-ʿAlqāʾī:	
in delegation to Persians	Tab. i/2269-2274 (Sayf < MTZA)
mentioned	Tab. i/2291-2292 (Sayf < MTZ)
in delegation to Persians	Yaʿqubi II/144
"al-ʿAlqāʾī"	*Isaba*, s.n. "Ḥudhayfa b. Miḥṣan"
109. Shaddād b. Ḍamʿaja:	
leads 600 from Ḥaḍramawt and al-Ṣadīf to Saʿd's army in Medina	Tab. i/2218-2219 (Sayf < MT, al-Mustanīr, Ḥanash)
110. ʿAmr b. Wabara:	
commanding Quḍāʿa (in al-Muthannā's army)	Tab. i/2221-2222 (Sayf < MTZ, Māhān)
111. ʿAbdullāh b. al-Muʿattam:	
commanded right wing	Tab. i/2223-2225 (Sayf < A < al-Shaʿbī)
112. Ḥumayṣa:	
mentioned	Tab. i/2258-2260 (Sayf < Muḥammad b. Qays < Mūsā b. Ṭarīf)
speaks with al-Juʿfī branch of Madhḥij	Tab. i/2334 (Sayf < Muḥammad b. Jarīr al-ʿAbdī < ʿĀbis al-Juʿfī < his father)

113. Zāhir:	
mentioned	Tab. i/2231-2235 (Sayf)
114. 'Adī b. Suḥayl:	
mentioned	Tab. i/2236 (Sayf < A, Mujālid, S)
115. 'Utārid b. Ḥājib:	
mentioned	Tab. i/2236 (Sayf < A, Mujālid, S)
mentioned	Tab. i/2345-2346 (Sayf < MTM)
116. al-Ḥārith b. Ḥassān:	
mentioned	Tab. i/2236 (Sayf < A, Mujālid, S)
117. al-Nu'mān:	
in delegation to Persians	Tab. i/2239-2244 (at 2239) (Sayf < A < al-Sha'bī)
118. Ibn al-Nābigha:	
mentioned	Tab. i/2245 (Sayf < A < al-Sha'bī)
119. al-Ḥusayn b. Niyār:	
mentioned	Tab. i/2245 (Sayf < A < al-Sha'bī)
120. al-A'war b. Bishāma:	
mentioned aiding preceding	Tab. i/2245 (Sayf < A < al-Sha'bī)
121. al-Aswad b. Yazīd:	
mentioned	Tab. i/2258-2260 (Sayf < Muḥammad b. Qays < Mūsā b. Ṭarīf)
122. al-Shammākh, al-Ḥuṭay'a, Aws b. Maghrā', 'Abda b. Ṭabīb:	
poets	Tab. i/2291-2292 (Sayf < MTZ)
123. Anas b. 'Abbās:	
commanded rear-guard of Syrian reinforcements	Tab. i/2303-2306 (Sayf < MT)
124. al-A'war b. Quṭba:	
poem praising lone palm	Tab. i/2317-2319 (Sayf < MTZ) and (Sayf < Ibn Makhāriq < man of Tayyi')
125. Salmān, 'Abd al-Raḥmān:	
mentioned	Tab. i/2345-2346 (Sayf < MTM)
126. Anas b. al-Ḥulays:	
sent as messenger to Medina	Tab. i/2368 (Sayf < MTZM)
127. Qays b. Khuraym:	
in battle line-up	Din. 121
128. Shu'ba b. Murra:	
in delegation to Persians	Ya'qubi II/144
129. 'Awwām b. 'Abd Shams:	
kills Rustam?	Bal. *Fut.* 259

APPENDIX H. PARTICIPANTS AT SIEGE OF AL-MADĀ'IN

1. Sa'd b. Abī Waqqāṣ (*Quraysh*):	
marches himself on al-Madā'in	Tab. i/2419 (Sayf < MMAS)
mentioned at Bahurasīr	Tab. i/2424-2425 (Sayf < MTMAS, al-Naḍr)
seizes Bahurasīr with force	Tab. i/2426-2427 (Sayf < MTM)
seizes Bahurasīr with force	Tab. i/2427 (Sayf < al-Miqdām b. Shurayḥ al-Ḥārithī < his father)
at Madā'in al-Quṣwa	Tab. i/2431-2434 (Sayf)
marches from al-Qādisiyya to al-Ḥīra, across Euphrates, to al-Madā'in	Khalifa I/103 (Mad)
2. Khālid b. 'Urfuṭa (*ḥalīf* of Umayya of *Quraysh*):	
sent by Sa'd in command of force to al-Madā'in	Tab. i/2355-2361 (I.I. < Ismā'īl b. Khālid, *mawlā* of Bajīla < Qays b. Abī Ḥāzim al-Bajalī)
mentioned among those sent to al-Madā'in by Sa'd	Tab. i/2420 (Sayf < MMAS)
commanded vanguard to al-Madā'in	Bal. *Fut.* 263 ('Abbās b. Hishām < 'Awāna b. al-Ḥakam)
3. 'Iyāḍ b. Ghanm al-Fihrī (*Quraysh*):	
sent by Sa'd to al-Madā'in	Tab. i/2355-2361 (I.I. < Ismā'īl b. Abī Khālid, *mawlā* of Bajīla < Qays b. Abī Ḥāzim al-Bajalī)
4. Hāshim b. 'Utba b. Abī Waqqāṣ (*Quraysh*):	
in foreguard of army sent to al-Madā'in	Tab. i/2355-2361 (I.I. < Ismā'īl b. Abī Khālid, *mawlā* of Bajīla < Qays b. Abī Ḥāzim al-Bajilī)
sent by Sa'd to al-Madā'in and Bābil	Tab. i/2420 (Sayf < MMAS)
sent ahead from Bābil by Zuhra (no. 6)	Tab. i/2422-2424 (Sayf < al-Naḍr b. al-Sirrī < Ibn al-Rufayl < his father)
mentioned at Bahurasīr	Tab. i/2424-2425 (Sayf < MTMAS, al-Naḍr)
5. Ḍirār b. al-Khaṭṭāb (*Quraysh*):	
at Bahurasīr	Tab. i/2431 (Sayf < MTMAS)
of Muḥārib-Quraysh	I.K. /Caskel II/242 and table 34
6. Zuhra b. Hawiyya (*Tamīm*):	
commanded left wing of force sent to al-Madā'in by Sa'd	Tab. i/2355-2361 (I.I. < Ismā'īl b. Abī Khālid, *mawlā* of Bajīla < Qays b. Abī Ḥāzim al-Bajalī)

sent by Sa'd to "al-Milṭāṭ" (later site of al-Kūfa), then to al-Madā'in	Tab. i/2419 (Sayf < MMAS)
sent via Bābil to al-Madā'in	Tab. i/2422-2424 (Sayf < al-Naḍr b. al-Sirrī < Ibn al-Rufayl < his father)
mentioned at Bahurasīr	Tab. i/2424-2425 (Sayf < MTMAS, al-Naḍr)
wounded or killed at Bahurasīr	Tab. i/2428 (Sayf < al-Naḍr b. al-Sirrī < Ibn al-Rufayl < his father)
sent to Nahrawān by Sa'd	Tab. i/2444 (Sayf < MMAS, 'Uqba, Abū 'Umar)
pursues Persians from al-Madā'in to Nahrawān	Tab. i/2445 (Sayf < al-Naḍr b. al-Sirrī < Ibn al-Rufayl < Rufayl b. Maysūr, his father)
among Sa'd's men	Khālifa I/103 (Mad.)
7. Abū Nubāta Nā'il b. Ju'sham al-A'rajī (*Tamīm*):	
heroics at Bābil	Tab. i/2422-2424 (Sayf < al-Naḍr b. al-Sirrī < Ibn al-Rufayl < his father)
8. al-Qa'qā' b. 'Amr (*Tamīm*):	
at crossing of Tigris	Tab. i/2436 (Sayf < Badr b. 'Uthmān < Abū Bakr b. Ḥafṣ b. 'Umar)
heroics at crossing	Tab. i/2437 (Sayf < Abū 'Umar Dithār < Abū 'Uthmān al-Nahdī)
9. 'Āṣim b. 'Amr (brother of no. 8) (*Tamīm*):	
leads a force in attack at Madā'in al-Quṣwa	Tab. i/2431-2434 (Sayf)
at crossing of Tigris	Tab. i/2436-2437 (Sayf < Badr b. 'Uthmān < Abū Bakr b. Ḥafṣ b. 'Umar)
10. al-Rubayl b. 'Amr (brother of no. 8?) (*Tamīm*):	
at crossing of Tigris	Tab. i/2436-2437 (Sayf < Badr b. 'Uthmān < Abū Bakr b. Ḥafṣ b. 'Umar)
11. Ibn al-Mukhāriq b. Shihāb (*Tamīm*):	
minor heroics at al-Madā'in	Tab. i/2442-2443 (Sayf < 'Aṭiyya, A, Dithār Abū 'Umar) and (Sayf < S)
of 'Amr-Tamīm	I.K. /Caskel II/426 and table 82
12. al-Nu'mān b. Muqarrin (*Muzayna*):	
put in charge of *kharāj* of Euphrates by Sa'd	Tab. i/2455-2456 (Sayf < Muḥammad b. Kurayb < Nāfi' b. Jubayr)
13. Suwayd b. Muqarrin (*Muzayna*):	
put in charge of *kharāj* of Tigris by Sa'd.	Tab. i/2455-2456 (Sayf < Muḥammad b. Kurayb < Nāfi' b. Jubayr)

14. 'Amr b. 'Amr b. Muqarrin (*Muzayna*):	
in charge of booty (*aqbāḍ*) at al-Madā'in	Tab. i/2444 (Sayf < MMAS, 'Uqba, Abū 'Umar)
in charge of booty	Tab. i/2454 (Sayf < MTMAS)
in charge of booty	Tab. i/2451 (Sayf < al-Mujālid < al-Sha'bī)
15. Salmān b. Rabī'a (*Bāhila*):	
in charge of dividing spoils (*al-qism*) at al-Madā'in	Tab. i/2451 (Sayf < al-Mujālid) al-Sha'bī)
in charge of dividing spoils of	Tab. i/2454 (Sayf < MTMAS)
Bāhila	I.K. /Caskel II/509 and table 137
16. Jahl (*'Ijl*):	
mentioned at Madā'in al-Quṣwa	Tab. i/2431-2434 (Sayf)
17. Bashīr b. al-Khaṣāṣiyya al-Sadūsī (*Dhuhl*):	
carried "fifth" of al-Madā'in	Tab. i/2454 (Sayf < MTMAS)
of B. Sadūs-Dhuhl	I.K. /Caskel II/225 and table 153
18. men of al-Taym (*Taymallāt b. Tha'laba*):	
mentioned at Madā'in al-Quṣwa	Tab. i/2431-2434 (Sayf)
19. al-Kalaj (*Ḍabba*):	
mentioned at Madā'in al-Quṣwa	Tab. i/2431-2434 (Sayf)
20. Khunaysh (?) b. Fulān (*Asad*):	
brought news of al-Madā'in victory	Tab. i/2454 (Sayf < MTMAS)
21. a man (*Ṭayyi'*):	
drowned in crossing river to al-Madā'in	Din. 126-127
"Salīl b. Yazīd b. Mālik al-Sinbisī"; killed	Bal. *Fut.* 263-264 ('Abbās b. Hishām < 'Awāna b. al-Ḥakam) and (Abū 'Ubayda Mu'ammar b. al-Muthannā < Abū 'Amr b. al-'Alā')
22. Jarīr b. 'Abdullāh (*Bajīla*):	
commanded right wing of force	Tab. i/2358-2359 (I.I. < Ismā'īl b. Abī Khālid, *mawlā* of Bajīla < Qays b. Abī Ḥāzim al-Bajalī)
23. 'Amr b. Ma'dīkarib al-Zubaydī (*Madhḥij*):	
mentioned crossing Tigris	Kufi I/213
24. Kathīr b. Shihāb al-Sa'dī (*Madhḥij*):	
among leaders in Zuhra's (no. 6) force at Bābil	Tab. i/2422-2424 (Sayf < al-Naḍr b. al-Sirrī < Ibn al-Rufayl < his father)
of B. al-Ḥārith-Madhḥij	I.K. /Caskel II/370 and table 261

25. *ghulām (B. al-Ḥārith b. Ka'b)*:	
mentioned at Madā'in al-Quṣwa	Tab. i/2431-2434 (Sayf)
26. Mālik b. Ka'b (*Hamdān*):	
mentioned at Madā'in al-Quṣwa	Tab. i/2431-2434 (Sayf)
27. Gharqada al-Bāriqi (*Azd*):	
mentioned crossing Tigris	Tab. i/2437 (Sayf < Abū 'Umar Dithār < Abū 'Uthmān al-Nahdī)
28. Zuhayr b. Sulaym (*Azd*):	
kills Persian leader	Bal. *Fut.* 262
29. Shuraḥbīl b. al-Simṭ (*Kinda*):	
appointed lieutenant over al-Madā'in by Sa'd	Tab. i/2360-2361 (I.I. < Ismā'īl b. Abī Khālid, *mawlā* of Bajīla < Qays b. Abī Ḥāzim al-Bajalī)
sent to Bābil, then al-Madā'in	Tab. i/2420 (Sayf < MMAS)
mentioned at Madā'in al-Quṣwa	Tab. i/2431-2434 (Sayf)
30. Bukayr b. 'Abdullāh al-Laythī:	
among leaders in Zuhra's (no. 6) force at Bābil	Tab. i/2422-2424 (Sayf < al-Naḍr b. al-Sirrī < Ibn al-Rufayl < his father)
31. men of B. Wallād:	
mentioned at Madā'in al-Quṣwa	Tab. i/2431-2434 (Sayf)
32. Thaqīf of B. 'Adī b. Sharīf:	
minor heroics at al-Madā'in	Tab. i/2442 (Sayf < MTM)
33. al-Halqām b. al-Ḥārith al-'Itkī:	
mentioned crossing Tigris	Kufi I/213
34. Abū Mufazzir al-Aswad b. Quṭba:	
at Bahurasīr (anecdote)	Tab. i/2429-2431 (Sayf < Simāk b. Fulān al-Hujaymī < his father and Muḥammad b. 'Abdullāh < Anas b. al-Ḥulays)
at Madā'in al-Quṣwa	Tab. i/2431-2434 (Sayf)
35. Ḥammāl b. Mālik:	
crossing Tigris	Tab. i/2436-2437 (Sayf < Baḍr b. 'Uthmān < Abū Bakr b. Ḥafṣ b. 'Umar)
36. 'Abdullāh b. al-Mu'attam:	
sent to al-Madā'in by Sa'd	Tab. i/2420 (Sayf < MMAS)
mentioned at Bābil	Tab. i/2421
37. Sa'd b. Mālik:	
appointed over *ṣalāt* and *ḥarb* of al-Madā'in by Sa'd	Tab. i/2455-2456 (Sayf < Muḥammad b. Kurayb < Nāfi' b. Jubayr)
with Sa'd's army	Khālifa I/104 (Maslama < Dāūd b. Abī Hind < al-Sha'bī)
38. Hilāl b. 'Ullafa:	
with Sa'd at al-Madā'in	Khalifa I/104 (Mad < 'Alī b. Ḍiyāl < Ḥamīd b. Hilāl)

APPENDIX J. JALŪLĀ'

1. Sa'd b. Abī Waqqāṣ sends 12,000 men to Jalūlā':
   over the front-guard: al-Qā'qā' b. 'Amr
   over the right wing: Si'r b. Mālik
   over the left wing: 'Amr b. Mālik b. 'Utba
   over the rear-guard: 'Amr b. Murra al-Juhanī
   (Tab. i/2456-2457 [Sayf < al-Walīd b. 'Abdullāh b. Abī Ṭayba al-Bajalī < his father])
2. Sa'd sends 12,000 men to Jalūlā':
   commander: 'Amr b. Mālik b. 'Utba b. Uhayl b. 'Abd Manāf b. Zuhra
   front-guard: al-Qa'qā' b. 'Amr
   reinforcements: Qays b. Makshūḥ, Ṭulayḥa, 'Amr. b. Ma'dīkarib, Ḥujr b. 'Adī
   (Tab. i/2460-2462 [Sayf < 'Ubaydallāh b. Muḥaffiz < his father])
3. Sa'd sends 12,000 men to Jalūlā':
   commander: Hāshim b. 'Utba b. Abī Waqqāṣ
   right wing: Ḥujr b. 'Adī al-Kindī
   cavalry: 'Amr b. Ma'dīkarib
   infantry: Ṭulayḥa b. Khuwaylid
   mentioned: Jarīr b. 'Abdullāh
   (Bal. *Fut.* 264)
4. Sa'd sends force to Jalūlā':
   commander: 'Amr b. Mālik b. Najāba b. Nawfal b. Wahb b. 'Abd Manāf b. Zuhra
   right wing: Ḥujr b. 'Adī
   left wing: Zuhayr b. Juwiyya
   cavalry: 'Amr b. Ma'dīkarib
   infantry: Ṭulayḥa b. Khuwaylid
   (Din. 127-128)
5. 12,000 troops sent to Jalūlā':
   commander: Hāshim b. 'Utba
   including: prominent *anṣār*, prominent *muhājirūn*, bedouin who had rebelled during *ridda* and those who had not
   (Tab. i/2458 [Sayf < MTMAS])
6. Sa'd sends force to Jalūlā':
   commander: Hāshim b. 'Utba
   right wing: Jarīr b. 'Abdullāh al-Bajalī
   left wing: Ḥujr b. 'Adī al-Kindī
   wings (?): Makshūḥ al-Murādī
   cavalry: 'Amr b. Ma'dīkarib (in center, according to Kufi I/277)
   infantry: Ṭalḥa b. Khuwaylid al-Asadī

Sent as reinforcements:
al-Mundhir b. Ḥassān al-Ḍabbī
Hishām b. 'Utba b. Abī Waqqāṣ (?)

Mentioned:
Sa'd b. 'Ubayd al-Anṣārī
'Awwām and Zuhayr bb. 'Abd Shams
Jābir b. Ṭāriq al-Nakha'ī
'Ubayd b. 'Amr al-Bajalī
(Kufi I/271-278)

7. Heroics by al-Qa'qā' b. 'Amr al-Tamīmī
(Tab. i/2458-2460 [Sayf < 'Uqba b. Makram < Biṭān b. Bishr]
Tab. i/2463 [Sayf < MTMAS, al-Mujālid, 'Uqba, al-Walīd b. 'Abdullāh])

8. B. 'Abs at al-Madā'in during Jalūlā' campaign
(Tab. i/2643-2644 [Sayf < MTMAS, al-Mujālid, 'Uqba, al-Walīd b. 'Abdullāh])

APPENDIX K. ARMY IN SOUTHERN IRAQ—SECOND PHASE

1. Suwayd b. Quṭba (*Dhuhl*):	
present in al-Ubulla area under Khālid b. al-Walīd	Bal. *Fut.* 340
raiding al-Ubulla area; ʻUmar sends ʻUtba b. Ghazwān	Bal. *Fut.* 341
informs ʻUmar of Persian weakness in southern Iraq; ʻUmar orders him to join ʻUtba	Din. 116
1a. Quṭba b. Qatāda al-Sadūsī (*Dhuhl*):	
present in al-Ubulla area under Khālid (or no. 1)	Bal. *Fut.* 340
raids al-Ubulla	Tab. i/2381-2382 (ʻUmar < Mad < al-Naḍr b. Isḥāq al-Sulamī < Quṭba b. Qatāda al-Sadūsī)
present at ʻUtba's siege of al-Ubulla	Tab. i/2384-2385 (ʻUmar b. Shabba < ʻAlī < Abū Ismāʻīl al-Hamdānī) and (AM < Mujālid b. Saʻīd < al-Shaʻbī)
2. Shurayḥ b. ʻĀmir of B. Saʻd b. Bakr (*Hawāzin*):	
according to some, left by Khālid as lieutenant in al-Ubulla (or no. 1)	Bal. *Fut.* 340
sent by ʻUmar to southern Iraq; killed campaigning	Tab. i/2381-2382 (ʻUmar < Mad < al-Naḍr b. Isḥāq al-Sulamī < Quṭba b. Qatāda al-Sadūsī)
sent by ʻUmar to Iraq; killed campaigning	Khalifa I/95-96 (Mad)
3. ʻUtba b. Ghazwān of B. Māzin b. Manṣūr (*Qays-ʻAylān*):	
sent from al-Madā'in to southern Iraq	Tab. i/2380 (Sayf < MTMA)
sent to southern Iraq from Medina with 500 men	Tab. i/2377-2378 (ʻUmar b. Shabba < Mad < AM < Mujālid < al-Shaʻbī)
sent from al-Madā'in to southern Iraq	Tab. i/2377 (Sayf)
sent from northern Iraq to southern Iraq	Bal. *Fut.* 345

sent by 'Umar to be his representative when no. 1 raids	Bal. *Fut.* 341
sent with 300 men; 500 levies raised en route	Tab. i/2377-2378 (*isnād* above)
sent with 300 men	Tab. i/2384-2385 ('Umar b. Shabba < Mad < AM < Mujālid < al-Sha'bī) and (Sayf)
sent to southern Iraq with 2,000 men; joined by Suwayd, conquers al-Ubulla	Din. 116-117
comes to al-Baṣra with 5,000 men	Tab. i/2540 (Sayf < MTMA)
sent to southern Iraq	Tab. i/2378-2380 (Muḥammad b. Bashshār < Ṣafwān b. 'Isā al-Zuhrī < 'Amr b. 'Īsā Abū Na'āma al-'Adawī < Khālid b. 'Umayr and Shuways Abū l-Ruqqād)
sent to southern Iraq	Tab. i/2382-2383 ('Umar < Mad < 'Īsā b. Yazīd < 'Abd al-Malik b. Ḥudhayfa and Muḥammad b. al-Ḥajjāj < 'Abd al-Malik b. 'Umayr)
conquers al-Ubulla, Dastumaysān	Tab. i/2385 ('Abāya b. 'Abd 'Amr)
conquers Dastumaysān	Tab. i/2386 (Abū l-Malīḥ al-Hudhalī)
conquers Dastumaysān; sends Mujāshi' (no. 16) to take al-Furāt; decides to return to Medina	Tab. i/2386 ('Alī b. Zayd)
same as preceding	Tab. i/2386 ('Abd al-Raḥmān b. Jawshan)
sent after death of Shurayḥ (no. 2); conquers al-Ubulla; lieutenants take al-Furāt, Maysān, Dastumaysān, Abarqubādh	Khalifa I/95-96 (Mad)
goes to Iraq with ca. 40 men	Yaqut, s.v. "al-Baṣra"
marches from central Iraq with 800 men, conquers al-Ubulla, al-Furāt	Yaqut, s.v. "al-Baṣra" ('Awāna b. al-Ḥakam)
conquered al-Ubulla, al-Furāt, Dastumaysān, Abarqubādh	Bal. *Fut.* 344 (Rawḥ b. 'Abd al-Mu'min < Wahb b. Jarīr b. Ḥāzim < his father)
sent to Iraq, conquers al-Ubulla	Khalifa I/96 (Muslim and Ḍaḥḥāk < Sawāda b. Abī l-Aswad < Qatāda)

sent to Iraq, conquers al-Ubulla	Khalifa I/96 (Marḥūm b. 'Abd al-'Azīz < his father < Khālid b. 'Umayr al-'Adawī)
captures al-Ubulla	Bal. *Fut.* 341
conquers al-Ubulla	Khalifa I/97 ('Abdullāh b. 'Awf < al-Ḥasan)
in southern Iraq	Khalifa I/97 (Ghadar < Shu'ba < 'Aqīl b. Ṭalḥa < Qabīṣa)
conquered al-Ubulla	Din. 117-118
'Umar sends him to Kuwar Dijla, al-Ubulla, Abarqubādh, Maysān—conquered	Ya'qubi II/143
conquers al-Ubulla; lieutenants take other places; he returns to 'Umar	Bal. *Fut.* 342 (Mad < Jahm b. Ḥassān)
conquers al-Ubulla; A.H. 14 returns to Medina, puts al-Mughīra in charge until al-Mujāshi' (no. 16) returns from al-Furāt	*TMD* (Zah.) XVII/fol. 38a-38b (Zakariyya al-Minqarī—h—al-Aṣma'ī—h—Salama b. Bilāl < Abū Rajā' al-'Uṭāridī)
marches to southern Iraq with 800 men	*TMD* (Zah) XVII/fol. 386 (Ismā'īl b. 'Īsā al-'Aṭṭār—h—Isḥāq b. Busr)
sent to Iraq with 800 men; captures al-Ubulla, Madhār Dastumaysān, Abarqubādh	Bal. *Fut.* 342-343 and Bal. *Ansab* Reis. 598/1189 ('Abdullāh b. Ṣāliḥ al-Muqri' < I.I.)
returns to Medina, leaves Mujāshi' (no. 16) in charge	Ya'qubi II/145-146
returns to Medina, leaves Mujāshi' in charge and al-Mughīra (no. 8) second	Khalifa I/98
4. Qasāma b. Zuhayr al-Māzinī (*Qays-'Aylān*):	
present at conquest of al-Ubulla	Tab. i/2384-2385 ('Umar b. Shabba < 'Alī < Abū Ismā'īl al-Hamdānī and AM < Mujālid < al-Sha'bī)
5. Nāfi' b. al-Ḥārith b. Kalada (*Thaqīf*):	
put in charge of al-Ubulla after 'Utba's conquest	Tab. i/2384-2385 ('Umar b. Shabba < 'Alī < Abū Ismā'īl al-Hamdānī and AM < Mujālid < al-Sha'bī)
present at al-Ubulla siege	Tab. i/2385 (Bashīr b. 'Ubaydallāh)
among 270 present at conquest of al-Ubulla	Tab. i/2385 (al-Sha'bī)
sent by 'Utba to inform 'Umar of Dastumaysān victory	Tab. i/2385 ('Abāya b. 'Abd 'Amr)

messenger after Dastumaysān victory	Tab. i/2386 (Abū l-Malīḥ al-Hudhalī)
one of 'Utba's in-laws, came with him to Iraq	Tab. i/2388 (Mad)
messenger after conquest of al-Ubulla	Bal. *Fut.* 341
messenger after conquest of al-Ubulla; assigned a *khiṭṭa* in al-Baṣra	Din. 117-118
at conquest of al-Ubulla; had one of first houses (*dār*) in al-Baṣra	Yaqut, s.v. "al-Baṣra" ('Awāna b. al-Ḥakam)
6. Abū Bakra (*Thaqīf*):	
present at al-Ubulla siege ("Abu Bakr")	Tab. i/2385 (Bashīr b. 'Ubaydallāh)
among 270 men at conquest of al-Ubulla	Tab. i/2385 (al-Sha'bī)
in-law of 'Utba (no. 3), came with him to Iraq	Tab. i/2388 (Mad)
with 'Utba at conquest of al-Ubulla	Yaqut, s.v. "al-Baṣra" ('Awāna b. al-Ḥakam)
7. Rabī'a b. Kalada b. Abī l-Ṣalt (*Thaqīf*):	
among 270 men at conquest of al-Ubulla	Tab. i/2385 (al-Sha'bī)
8. al-Mughīra b. Shu'ba (*Thaqīf*):	
among 270 men at conquest of al-Ubulla	Tab. i/2385 (al-Sha'bī)
left as second in command when 'Utba leaves; conquers Abazqubādh	Tab. i/2386 ('Ali b. Zayd)
same as preceding, except conquers *ahl Maysān*	Tab. i/2386 ('Abd al-Raḥmān b. Jawshan)
puts down rising of *ahl Maysān*	Tab. i/2386-2387 (Qatāda)
made governor of Baṣra after 'Utba's death, after Abū Sabra (no. 29)	Tab. i/2498 and i/2388 (Sayf < Mujālid < 'Āmir)
conquered Maysān, Dastumaysān, Abazqubādh, and banks of Tigris as subordinate of 'Utba (no. 3)	Khalifa I/95-96 (Mad)
left as second in command on 'Utba's departure	Bal. *Fut.* 342 (Mad < Jahm b. Ḥassān)
left as second in command on 'Utba's departure	Bal. *Fut.* 342-343 ('Abdullāh b. Ṣāliḥ al-Muqri' < I.I.)

left as second in command; defeats Persians at Maysān; 'Umar puts him in command	Ya'qubi II/145-146
'Umar places him in command over southern Iraq	Bal. *Fut.* 343
left as second in command on 'Utba's departure; 'Umar places him in command; governed it A.H. 15, 16, and 17	*TMD* (Zah) XVII/fol. 38a-38b (Zakariyya al-Minqari—h—Asma'ī—h—Salama b. Bilāl < Abū Rajā' al-'Uṭāridī)
raids Maysān, suppresses revolt at Abazqubādh	Bal. *Fut.* 344 ('Abdullāh b. Ṣāliḥ al-Muqri' < I.I.)
left as second in command; victory at Abazqubādh; 'Umar puts him in command	Khalifa I/98
left in command by 'Utba; raids, conquers Maysān	Din. 118
conquers Maysān; suppresses rebellion at Abazqubādh	Bal. *Fut.* 344 (Rawḥ b. 'Abd al-Mu'min < Wahb b. Jarīr b. Ḥāzim < his father)
conquered Dastumaysān and Nahr Tīrā	Khalifa I/101 (al-Wālid b. Hishām < his father < his father)
conquered Nahr Tīrā by force	Khalifa I/101 (Mad < al-Naṣr b. Isḥāq < Qatāda)
9. Arda bint al-Ḥārith b. Kalada (*Thaqīf*):	
present at battle against *ahl Maysān*	Tab. i/2386-2387 (Qatāda)
married to Shibl b. Ma'bad al-Bajalī (no. 20)	Tab. i/2388 (Mad)
at conquest of al-Ubulla; "Azda bint al-Ḥārith"	Yaqut, s.v. "al-Baṣra" ('Awāna b. al-Ḥakam)
10. Ṣafiyya bint al-Ḥārith b. Kalada (*Thaqīf*):	
married to 'Utba (no. 3)	Tab. i/2388 (Mad)
11. Ziyād b. Abīhi (*Thaqīf*):	
among those accompanying inlaws of 'Utba in Iraq	Tab. i/2388 (Mad)
ghulām of Thaqīf, taken as scribe by Abū Mūsā, then al-Mughīra	Din. 118
at conquest of al-Ubulla; divided spoils at al-Furāt	Yaqut, s.v. "al-Baṣra"
12. Anas b. Mālik (*Anṣār*):	
one of 10 *Anṣār* accompanying Abū Mūsā to Iraq	Din. 118

13. al-Barā' b. Mālik (*Anṣār*):	
one of 10 *Anṣār* accompanying Abū Mūsā to Iraq	Din. 118
14. 'Abdullāh b. Dharr (*Muzayna*):	
present at Maysān	Khalifa I/97 (al-Walīd b. Hishām < his father < Ibn 'Awn < his father < Arṭubān)
15. Ma'qil b. Yasār (*Muzayna*):	
had one of first houses (*dār*) in al-Baṣra	Yaqut, s.v. "al-Baṣra"
of Muzayna	*Isaba*, s.n. "Ma'qil b. Yasār"
16. Mujāshi' b. Mas'ūd (*Sulaym*):	
among 270 men at conquest of al-Ubulla	Tab. i/2385 (al-Sha'bī)
of B. Sulaym	*Isaba*, s.n. "Mujāshi' b. Mas'ūd"
sent by 'Utba against al-Furāt; on 'Utba's departure, left in command	Tab. i/2386 ('Abd al-Raḥmān b. Jawshan)
same as preceding	Tab. i/2386 ('Alī b. Zayd)
same as preceding	*TMD* (Zah) XVII/fol. 38a-38b (Zakariyya al-Minqarī—h—al-Aṣma'ī—h—Salama b. Bīlāl < Abū Rajā' al-'Uṭāridī)
sent by 'Utba against al-Furāt	Khalifa I/95-96 (Mad)
sent by 'Utba against al-Furāt	Bal. *Fut.* 342 (Mad < Jahm b. Ḥassān)
led vanguard in 'Utba's conquest of al-Furāt; left in command on 'Utba's departure	Bal. Fut. 342-343 ('Abdullāh b. Ṣāliḥ al-Muqri' < I.I.)
married to 'Utba's sister al-Khuḍayrā'	Bal. *Ansab* Reis. 598/1189 ('Abdullah b. Ṣāliḥ < 'Abduh b. Sulaymān < I.I.)
left in charge by 'Utba; 'Umar replaces him with al-Mughīra b. Shu'ba	Ya'qubi II/145-146
'Umar replaces him with al-Mughīra b. Shu'ba	Bal. *Fut.* 343
left in charge by 'Utba; 'Umar replaces him with al-Mughīra b. Shu'ba	Khalifa I/98
17. Abū Miryam (*Balī*):	
Among 270 men at conquest of al-Ubulla	Tab. i/2385 (al-Sha'bī)
"Abū Miryam al-Ḥanafī"	Bal. *Fut.* 379

18. ʻArfaja b. Harthama al-Bāriqī (*Azd*):	
sent to reinforce ʻUtba in southern Iraq	Tab. i/2382-2383 (ʻUmar < Mad < ʻĪsā b. Yazīd < ʻAbd al-Malik b. Ḥudhayfa and Muḥammad b. al-Ḥajjāj < ʻAbd al-Malik b. ʻUmayr)
sent to reinforce ʻUtba in southern Iraq (from al-Baḥrayn); "Harthama b. ʻArfaja"	Bal. *Fut.* 341
19. Abū Mūsā (*Ash'ar*):	
ordered by ʻUmar to al-Baṣra	Din. 118
reconquered Dastumaysān and Nahr Tīrā after rebellions	Khalifa I/101 (al-Wālid b. Hishām < his father < his father)
20. Shibl b. Maʻbad (*Bajīla*):	
among 270 men at conquest of al-Ubulla	Tab. i/2385 (al-Shaʻbī)
of Bajīla; he and his son the only Bajīla in al-Baṣra	I.H.J. 389
in-law of ʻUtba (no. 3), came with him to Iraq	Tab. i/2388 (Mad)
only Bajalī in al-Baṣra	*TMD* (Zah) XVII/fol. 39b (Ismāʻīl b. ʻĪsā al-ʻAṭṭār—ak—Isḥāq b. Busr)
21. Abū Jarbā' ʻĀsim b. al-Dulaf of B. Ghaylān b. Mālik b. ʻAmr (*Tamīm*):	
in charge of encampment (*inzāl*) at al-Baṣra	Tab. i/2380-2381 (Sayf < MTMA)
22. Sulma b. al-Qayn (*Tamīm*):	
sent by ʻUtba to Manādhir and Dastumaysān area (cf. Appendix L, no. 36)	Tab. i/2534-2537 (MTMA)
23. Ḥarmala b. Murayṭa (*Tamīm*):	
sent by ʻUtba to Manādhir and Dastumaysān area (cf. Appendix L, no. 37)	Tab. i/2534-2537 (MTMA)
24. Anas b. Ḥujayra (*Yashkur*):	
present at conquest of Dastumaysān	Tab. i/2385 (ʻAbāya b. ʻAbd ʻAmr)
25. Shuways al-ʻAdawī:	
"I was at the conquest of al-Ubulla and al-Furāt"	Bal. *Fut.* 341-342 (al-Wālid b. Ṣāliḥ < Marḥūm al-ʻAṭṭār < his father < Shuways al-ʻAdawī)
26. al-Ḥajjāj:	
among 270 men at conquest of al-Ubulla	Tab. i/2385 (al-Shaʻbī)
27. ʻAbāya b. ʻAbd ʻAmr:	
"I witnessed the conquest of al-Ubulla with ʻUtba"	Tab. i/2385 (ʻAbāya b. ʻAbd ʻAmr)

28. Salama b. al-Muḥabbaq:	
"I witnessed the conquest of al-Ubulla"	Tab. i/2387 (al-Muthannā b. Mūsā b. Salama b. al-Muḥabbaq < his father < his father)
29. Abū Sabra:	
made governor of al-Baṣra briefly on 'Utba's death	Tab. i/2498 (Sayf < Mujālid < 'Āmir)
same as preceding	*TMD* (Zah.) XVII/fol. 39b-40a (Sayf)
30. Anas b. al-Shaykh b. al-Nu'mān:	
sent to 'Utba as messenger by 'Umar	Din. 117-118

APPENDIX L. ARMY IN SOUTHERN IRAQ—THIRD PHASE

(Does not include reinforcements from central Iraq)

1. al-Mughīra b. Shu'ba (*Thaqīf*):	
governor in southern Iraq two years, followed by Abū Mūsā	Tab. i/2388
governor after Abū Sabra	Tab. i/2498 (Sayf < Mujālid < 'Āmir)
governor before Abū Mūsā	Tab. i/2529-2530 (Ma'mar < al-Zuhrī < Ibn al-Musayyib)
replaced by Abū Mūsā	Tab. i/2531 (Sayf < MTMA)
governor after Abū Sabra, before Abū Mūsā	Tab. i/2550-2551 (Sayf < MMA)
knew some Persian	Tab. i/2559-2560 (Sayf < Abū Sufyān Ṭalḥa b. 'Abd al-Raḥmān < Ibn 'Īsā)
left in charge of al-Baṣra by 'Utba; raids Maysān, etc; confirmed by 'Umar	Din. 118
conquers Dastumaysān, Nahr Tīrā	Khalifa I/101 (al-Walīd b. Hishām < his father < his father)
conquers Nahr Tīrā	Khalifa I/101 (Mad < al-Naṣr b. Isḥāq < Qatāda)
makes pact with Aḥwāz	Khalifa I/105 (al-Walīd b. Hishām < his father < his father)
raids Sūq al-Aḥwāz	Bal. *Fut.* 376
2. Abū Bakra "Nufay' " (*Thaqīf*):	
accusation against al-Mughīra	Tab. i/2529-2530 (Ma'mar < al-Zuhrī < Ibn al-Musayyib)
accusation against al-Mughīra	Ya'qubi II/146
mentioned	Bal. *Fut.* 384-385
3. Nāfi' b. Kalada (brother of no. 2) (*Thaqīf*):	
accuses al-Mughīra	Tab. i/2529-2930 (Ma'mar < al-Zuhrī < Ibn al-Musayyib)
accuses al-Mughīra	Ya'qubi II/146
mentioned; "Nāfi' b. al-Ḥārith b. Kalada"	Bal. *Fut.* 384-385
4. Ziyād b. Abīhi (*Thaqīf*):	
acquits al-Mughīra	Tab. i/2529-2530 (Ma'mar < al-Zuhrī < Ibn al-Musayyib)
acquits al-Mughīra	Ya'qubi II/146
scribe for Abū Mūsā, then for al-Mughīra	Din. 118

5. Ḥajjāj b. ʿAtīq (*Thaqīf*):	
made governor of al-Furāt	Bal. *Fut.* 384-385
6. al-Sāʾib b. al-Aqraʿ of B. Yasār (*mawlā* of *Thaqīf*):	
accompanies Manjūf b. Thawr in taking Mihrajān Qadhaq	Din. 132-133
of B. Yasār of Thaqīf	I.D. 183
7. Abū Mūsā ʿAbdullāh b. Qays (*Ashʿar*):	
governor of al-Baṣra after al-Mughīra; or, before him	Tab. i/2388
governor after al-Mughīra	Tab. i/2498 (Sayf < Mujālid < ʿĀmir)
governor after al-Mughīra	Tab. i/2529-2530 (Maʿmar < al-Zuhrī < Ibn al-Musayyib)
sent to replace al-Mughīra	Tab. i/2531 (Sayf < MTMA)
at Rāmhurmuz, Tustar, then returns to al-Baṣra	Tab. i/2556-2557 (Sayf < MTMA)
with Kufans, opposes Persians in Khūzistān	Tab. i/2561-2564 (Abū Zayd < Mad)
at Susa; ordered back to al-Baṣra	Tab. i/2564-2566 (Sayf < MTA, Dithār Abū ʿUmar < Abū ʿUthmān)
sent by ʿUmar to assign *khiṭaṭ* for bedouin (*ʿarab*)	Din. 118
reconquered Dastumaysān, Nahr Tīrā (cf no. 1)	Khalifa I/101 (al-Walīd b. Hishām < his father < his father)
reconquered Aḥwāz (cf no. 1)	Khalifa I/105 (al-Walīd b. Hishām < his father < his father)
reconquered Nahr Tīrā, Aḥwāz	Bal. *Fut.* 376
conquered all Aḥwāz except Tustar, Susa, Manādhir, Rāmhurmuz	Bal. *Fut.* 376-377 (AM and Waq)
conquered Aḥwāz and districts except Manādhir, Rāmhurmuz, Susa, Tustar	Kufi II/5
campaigns at Manādhir	Bal. *Fut.* 377-378
conquers Susa (after Manādhir)	Bal. *Fut.* 378
conquers Susa	Bal. *Fut.* 378 (Abū ʿUbayd al-Qāsim b. Sallām < Marwān b. Muʿāwiya < Ḥumayd al-Ṭawīl < Ḥabīb < Khālid b. Zayd al-Muzanī)
conquers Surraq	Bal. *Fut.* 379
receives Kufan support in battling Persians at Tustar	Din. 130
receives Kufan support in battling Persians at Tustar	Bal. *Fut.* 380

after Tustar, sends men to take Mihrajān Qadhaq	Din. 132-133
surrounds, seizes Susa	Kufi II/6-7
makes treaty with Jundaysābūr	Bal. *Fut.* 382
conquers Rāmhurmuz (truce)	Bal. *Fut.* 379
conquers Tustar	*TMD* (Leningrad), fol. 256 b ('Abdullāh b. Ja'far—h—Ya'qūb—h—'Ammār b. al-Ḥasān—h—'Alwān (?))
campaigns at Manādhir	*TMD* (Leningrad), fol. 256 b (za'ama-'Alwān < a man < al-Ḥasān)
makes truce with people of Rāmhurmuz; later they rebel, he makes campaign again	Bal. *Fut.* 379 (Rawḥ b. 'Abd al-Mu'min < Ya'qūb < Abū 'Āṣim al-Rāmhurmuzī)
ally of part of 'Abd Shams (Quraysh), early Muslim	I.K./Caskel, s.n.
his sister married a member of Thaqīf	I.D. 185
8. Anas b. Mālik (*Anṣār*):	
among 29 who accompanied Abū Mūsā to Iraq	Tab. i/2531 (Sayf < MTMA)
in delegation to 'Umar after Tustar, etc.	Tab. i/2557 (Sayf < MTMA)
sent with Abū Mūsā to Iraq; 10 *anṣār* "like salt to food"	Din. 118
commanded whole army at Tustar	Din. 130
commanded horsemen of Abū Mūsā's army (only) at Tustar	Bal. *Fut.* 380
among *ṣulaḥā'* of Abū Mūsā's army (Khūzistān, Rāmhurmuz)	Kufi II/11
in delegation to 'Umar	*TMD* (Leningrad) fol. 257a (al-Ḥusayn b. Asad al-Tamīmi—h—Aḥmad b. Salm al-Kūfī < Naḍla)
9. 'Abd al-Raḥmān b. Sahl (*Anṣār?*):	
among Basrans at Tustar and Rāmhurmuz	Tab. i/2551-2552 (Sayf < MTMA)
(two listed, both *anṣārīs*, no mention of Iraq)	*Isaba*, s.n. "'Abd al-Raḥmān b. Sahl"
10. al-Barā' b. Mālik (*Anṣār*):	
among Basrans at Tustar and Rāmhurmuz	Tab. i/2551-2552 (Sayf < MTMA)
killed at Tustar siege	Tab. i/2554 (Sayf < MTMA)
sent with Abū Mūsā to Iraq	Din. 118

commanded right wing at Tustar; killed	Din. 130
commanded right wing at Tustar	Bal. *Fut.* 380
11. Sa'īd b. 'Amr (*Anṣār*):	
among *ṣulaḥā'* of Abū Mūsā's army	Kufi II/11
12. Sahl b. 'Adī al-Khazrajī (*Anṣār*):	
led Basrans at Rāmhurmuz and Tustar	Tab. i/2551-2552 (Sayf < MTMA)
at Rāmhurmuz, Tustar	Tab. i/2554 (Sayf < MTMA)
"al-Khazrajī"	*Isaba*, s.n. "Sahl b. 'Adī"
13. 'Āmir b. Qays (*Anṣār*):	
mentioned at Tustar siege	Tab. i/2555 (Sayf < MTMA)
of *Anṣār*	I.K./Caskel II/162 and Table 183
14. al-Barā' b. 'Āzib (*Anṣār*):	
commands wings at Tustar? (Kufan reinforcement?)	Kufi II/13
among *ṣulaḥā'* of Abū Mūsā's army	Kufi II/11
of *Anṣār*	I.K./Caskel II/224 and Table 180
15. Hishām b. 'Amr (*Quraysh*):	
among 29 accompanying Abū Mūsā to Iraq	Tab. i/2531 (Sayf < MTMA)
early Qurashī companion	*Isaba*, s.n. "Hishām b. 'Amr"
16. al-Nu'mān b. 'Adī b. Naḍla of Ka'b b. Lu'ayy (*Quraysh*):	
made governor of Kuwar al-Dijla	Bal. *Fut.* 384-385
emigrant to Abyssinia; 'Umar made him governor of Maysān	I.D. 86
made governor of Maysān by 'Umar	I.H. 786
17. Abū Sabra b. Abī Ruhm of B. Mālik b. Ḥisl b. 'Āmir b. Lu'ayy (Quraysh):	
appointed governor of southern Iraq before al-Mughīra	Tab. i/2498 (Sayf < Mujālid < 'Āmir)
governor before al-Mughīra	Tab. i/2550-2551 (Sayf < MMA)
leads army to relieve troops from Baḥrayn trapped in Fārs	Tab. i/2549-2550 (Sayf< MMA)
led army (Basrans and Kufans) at Rāmhurmuz, Tustar	Tab. i/2551-2552 (Sayf < MTMA)

in delegation to 'Umar after Tustar, etc.	Tab. i/2557 (Sayf < MTMA)
at Susa with army	Tab. i/2564-2566 (Sayf < MTZ, Dithār Abū 'Umar < Abū 'Uthmān)
goes to Jundaysābūr after Susa	Tab. i/2567-2568
18. Khālid b. Zayd (*Muzayna*):	
"I was at Susa"	Bal. *Fut.* 378 (Abū 'Ubayd al-Qāsim b. Sallām < Marwān b. Mu'āwiya < Ḥumayd al-Ṭawīl < Ḥabīb < Khālid b. Zayd al-Muzanī)
19. Bishr b. al-Muhaffiz (*Muzayna*):	
governor of Jundaysābūr	Bal. *Fut.* 384-385
"al-Muzanī"; companion	I.K./Caskel, s.n.
20. 'Āsim b. Qays b. al-Ṣalt (*Sulaym*):	
appointed governor over Manādhir by Abū Mūsā	Bal. *Fut.* 377-378
appointed governor over Manādhir by Abū Mūsā	Bal. *Fut.* 384-385
21. Naṣr b. al-Ḥajjāj (*Sulaym*):	
in Abū Mūsā's army at Tustar; expelled from Medina to Iraq because of an affair	Kufi II/15-18
22. Ḥāritha b. Badr (*Judhām*):	
sent to reconquer Surraq by Abū Mūsā; fails; later, made governor of Surraq	Bal. *Fut.* 379
23. Samura b. Jundab al-Fazārī (*Ghaṭafān*):	
appointed governor of Sūq al-Aḥwāz by Abū Mūsā	Bal. *Fut.* 377-378
appointed governor of Sūq al-Aḥwāz by Abū Mūsā	Bal. *Fut.* 384-385
"al-Fazārī"	I.D. 172
24. Ḥudhayfa b. al-Yamān al-'Absī (*Ghaṭafān*):	
among *ṣulaḥā'* of Abū Mūsā's army	Kufi II/11
Abū Mūsā puts him in charge of infantry at Tustar	Kufi II/13
commanded left wing of 'Ammār's force (Kufan reinforcements?)	Bal. *Fut.* 380
important in conquest of Iraq	*Isaba*, s.n. "Ḥudhayfa b. al-Yamān al-'Absī"

25. 'Abdullāh b. Bishr (*Hilāl*):	
mentioned at Tustar siege	Tab. i/2555 (Sayf < MTMA)
26. al-Ashras b. 'Awf (*Shaybān*):	
present at Tustar	Din. 131
present at Tustar	Bal. *Fut.* 380
27. Majza'a b. Thawr al-Sadūsī (*Dhuhl*):	
among Basrans at Rāmhurmuz and Tustar	Tab. i/2551-2552 (Sayf < MTMA)
killed at Tustar	Tab. i/2554 (Sayf < MTMA)
commanded left wing at Tustar; killed; "al-Bakrī"	Din. 130
commanded left wing of Abū Mūsā's army at Tustar; "al-Sadūsī"	Bal. *Fut.* 380
28. Manjūf b. Thawr al-Sadūsī (*Dhuhl*):	
sent by Abū Mūsā to take Mihrajān Qadhaq	Din. 132-133
"al-Sadūsī"; he and his son Suwayd were *sāda*	I.D. 212
29. Abū Miryam (*Ḥanīfa*):	
held *qaḍā'* of al-Baṣra? re-subdues Rāmhurmuz (new treaty)	Bal. *Fut.* 379
30. al-Aḥnaf b. Qays (*Tamīm*):	
in delegation to 'Umar after Tustar, etc.	Tab. i/2557 (Sayf < MTMA)
ruled all Tamīm of al-Baṣra	I.D. 152
31. Ghālib al-Wā'ili of B. al-'Amī (*Tamīm*):	
seizes Manādhir, Nahr Tīrā	Tab. i/2534-2537 (Sayf < MTMA)
over Manādhir	Tab. i/2538 (Sayf < MTMA)
at battle at Sūq al-Aḥwāz	Tab. i/2540-2541 (Sayf < MTMA)
32. Jaz' b. Mu'āwiya (*Tamīm*):	
sent out by Hurqūs (no. 33) after Aḥwāz victory to pursue Hurmuzān	Tab. i/2542-2545 (Sayf < MTMA)
at Tustar and Rāmhurmuz	Tab. i/2554 (Sayf < MTMA)
made governor of Surraq; uncle of al-Aḥnaf (no. 30)	Bal. *Fut.* 384-385
33. Hurqūs b. Zuhayr al-Sa'dī (*Tamīm*):	
conquers Sūq al-Aḥwāz	Tab. i/2540-2541 (Sayf < MTMA)
conquers Sūq al-Aḥwāz	Tab. i/2542-2545 (Sayf < MTMA)
at Rāmhurmuz, Tustar	Tab. i/2554 (Sayf < MTMA)

34. 'Āṣim b. 'Amr (*Tamīm*):	
in Basran army at Tustar, Rāmhurmuz	Tab. i/2551-2552 (Sayf < MTMA)
35. Kulayb b. Wā'il al-Kulaybī of B. al-'Amī (*Tamīm*):	
seizes Manādhir, Nahr Tīrā	Tab. i/2534-2537 (Sayf < MTMA)
over Nahr Tīrā	Tab. i/2538 (Sayf < MTMA)
at battle of Sūq al-Aḥwāz	Tab. i/2540-2541 (Sayf < MTMA)
36. Sulma b. al-Qayn, *muhājir* of B. 'Adawiyya of B. Ḥanẓala (*Tamīm*):	
sent by 'Utba to Manādhir, Dastumaysān area	Tab. i/2534-2537 (Sayf < MTMA)
over Manādhir (?)	Tab. i/2538 (Sayf < MTMA)
at Sūq al-Aḥwāz battle	Tab. i/2540-2541 (Sayf < MTMA)
at Rāmhurmuz, Tustar	Tab. i/2554 (Sayf < MTMA)
37. Ḥarmala b. Murayṭa, *muhājir* of B. 'Adawiyya of B. Ḥanẓala (*Tamīm*):	
sent by 'Utba to Manādhir, Dastumaysān area	Tab. i/2534-2537 (Sayf < MTMA)
over Nahr Tīrā	Tab. i/2538 (Sayf < MTMA)
at Sūq al-Aḥwāz battle	Tab. i/2540-2541 (Sayf < MTMA)
at Rāmhurmuz, Tustar	Tab. i/2554 (Sayf < MTMA)
38. Ḥasaka al-Habaṭī (*Tamīm*):	
mentioned at Tustar siege	Tab. i/2555 (Sayf < MTMA)
knight of Tamīm	I.D. 392
39. Ka'b b. Sūr of B. Laqīṭ, of B. Zuhrān b. Ka'b (*Azd*):	
among Basrans at Rāmhurmuz, Tustar	Tab. i/2551-2552 (Sayf < MTMA)
killed at Tustar	Tab. i/2554 (Sayf < MTMA)
held *qaḍā'* of al-Baṣra for 'Umar and 'Uthmān, died at Camel; of Azd-Shanū'a	I.D. 500
held *qaḍā'* of al-Baṣra for 'Umar; died at Camel (with Meccans)	I.H.J. 380
40. 'Arfaja b. Harthama al-Bāriqī (*Azd*):	
among Basrans at Rāmhurmuz and Tustar	Tab. i/2551-2552 (Sayf < MTMA)
41. 'Imrān b. Ḥuṣayn (*Khuzā'a*):	
among 29 accompanying Abū Mūsa to Iraq	Tab. i/2531 (Sayf < MTMA)
early companion; died in al-Baṣra	*Isaba*, s.n.

42. Shibl b. Ma'bad (*Bajīla*):	
accuses al-Mughīra	Tab.i/2529-2530 (Ma'mar < al-Zuhrī < Ibn al-Musayyib)
accuses al-Mughīra	Ya'qubi II/146
43. al-Ḥuṣayn b. Ma'bad (brother of no. 42?) (*Bajīla?*):	
among Basrans at Rāmhurmuz and Tustar	Tab. i/2551-2552 (Sayf < MTMA)
44. Muhājir b. Ziyād b. al-Diyār of Sa'd al-'Ashīra (*Madhḥij*):	
heroics at Manādhir	Kufi II/5
among Abū Mūsā's troops at Manādhir	Bal. *Fut.* 377-378
killed at Tustar among Abū Mūsā's troops; of Sa'd al-'Ashīra of Madhḥij	I.D. 238
commanded *muqaddima*, killed at Tustar; "al-Ḥarithī"	*TMD* (Leningrad) fol. 256b ('Alwān < a man < al-Ḥasar)
45. Rabī' b. Ziyād al-Ḥārithī (brother of no. 44) (*Madhḥij*):	
Abū Mūsā appoints him lieutenant of Manādhir; he subdues it	Bal. *Fut.* 377-378
conquers Kalbāniyya for Abū Mūsā	Bal. *Fut.* 382
appointed lieutenant after brother	*TMD* (Leningrad) fol. 256b (as above)
46. Bishr b. al-Munqidh (*Hamdān*):	
at Tustar (possibly part of Kufan force?)	Kufi II/10
47. Nāfi' b. Zayd (*Ḥimyar*):	
mentioned at Tustar siege	Tab. i/2555 (Sayf < MTMA)
48. Ḥudhayfa b. Miḥṣan al-'Alqā'ī	
among Basrans at Rāmhurmuz, Tustar	Tab. i/2551-2552 (Sayf < MTMA)
49. Zirr b. 'Abdullāh b. Kulayb al-Fuqaymī	
'Umar orders him to march on Jundaysābūr	Tab. i/2556 (Sayf < MTMA)
at Jundaysābūr and Nihāwand	Tab. i/2564-2566 (Sayf < MTA, Dithār Abū 'Umar < Abū 'Uthmān)
at Jundaysābūr	Tab. i/2567-2568 (Sayf < MTM, Abū 'Amr, Abū Sufyān)
50. al-Aswad b. Rabī'a "al-Muqtarib" of B. Rabī'a b. Mālik	
'Umar appoints him over *jund* of al-Baṣra	Tab. i/2556-2557 (Sayf < MTMA)

over Basrans at Susa; sent by Abū Sabra (no. 17) to Jundaysābūr	Tab. i/2564-2566 (Sayf < MTA, Dithār Abū ‘Umar < Abū ‘Uthmān)
‘Umar appoints him over *jund* of al-Baṣra	Tab. i/2556-2557 (Sayf < MTMA)
over Basrans at Susa; sent by Abū Sabra (no. 17) to Jundaysābūr	Tab. i/2564-2566 (Sayf < MTA, Dithār Abū ‘Umar < Abū ‘Uthmān)
51. Suwayb b. Math‘aba	
mentioned at Tustar siege	Tab. i/2555 (Sayf < MTMA)
52. Warqā’ b. al-Ḥārith	
mentioned at Tustar siege	Tab. i/2555 (Sayf < MTMA)
53. ‘Umar b. Surāqa	
in al-Baṣra; ‘Umar orders him to return to Medina	Tab. i/2556-2557 (Sayf < MTMA)
54. Abū Tamīmī	
killed at Tustar	Tab. i/2554 (Sayf < MTMA)
55. ‘Abdullāh b. ‘Āmir	
sent to reconquer Surraq by Abū Mūsā; succeeds	Bal. *Fut.* 379
56. Salma b. Rajā’	Din. 130
commanded infantry at Tustar	

APPENDIX M. PARTICIPANTS IN NIHĀWAND CAMPAIGN

1. al-Nu'mān b. Muqarrin (*Muzayna*):	
commanded Kufans; killed	Tab. i/2596-2598 (I.I.)
killed	Tab. i/2600-2605 (h—al-Rabī' b. Sulaymān—h—Asad b. Mūsā—h—al-Mubārak b. Faḍāla < Ziyād b. Jubayr < his father)
chosen by 'Umar to lead force against Nihāwand; at that time he was leading Kufans assisting in south Iraq	Tab. i/2612-2614 (Sayf < Abū Bakr al-Hudhalī
requests removal from tax collection duties and military action; made commander against Nihāwand: killed	Tab. i/2615 (Muḥammad b. 'Abdullāh b. Ṣafwān al-Thaqafī—h—Umayya b. Khālid—h—Abū 'Awāna < Ḥuṣayn b. 'Abd al-Raḥmān—q—Abū Wā'il)
commander at Nihāwand; numerous incidents	Tab. i/2615-2630 (Sayf)
treaty with people of "al-Māhayn"	Tab. i/2632-2633 (Sayf < MTM)
assigned to leadership by 'Umar	Bal. *Fut.* 302ff.
either in Medina or Kashkar, appointed commander by 'Umar	Bal. *Fut.* 303
commander at Nihāwand	Bal. *Fut.* 305 (IK < AM)
commander; killed	Ya'qubi II/156
was over *kharāj* of Kashkar; appointed commander	Din. 135-136; Kufi, II/40ff.
requests Kufans and Basrans to join him at al-Madā'in	Kufi II/41-42
killed	Kufi II/61
goes to Nihāwand	Tab. i/2647-2648 (Sayf < MTMAS)
2. Suwayd b. Muqarrin (brother of nos. 1, 3, 4) (*Muzayna*):	
mentioned	Tab. i/2596-2598 (I.I.)
takes standard when al-Nu'mān is killed	Tab. i/2615 (Muḥammad b. 'Abdullāh b. Ṣafwān al-Thaqafī—h—Umayya b. Khālid—h—Abū

	'Awāna < Ḥusayn b. 'Abd al-Raḥmān—q—Abū Wā'il)
over one wing at Nihāwand	Tab. i/2615-2630 (Sayf) (at 2618)
treaty witness, Māh Dīnār	Tab. i/2632-2633 (Sayf < MTM)
mentioned at Nihāwand	Din. 136
wounded, gives standard to Ḥudhayfa (no. 5)	Kufi II/50
3. Nu'aym b. Muqarrin (brother of nos. 1, 2, 4) (*Muzayna*):	
mentioned	Tab. i/2615-2630 (Sayf) at 2615
takes standard when al-Nu'mān falls in battle	Tab. i/2615-2630 (Sayf) at 2625
pursues defeated Persians	Tab. i/2615-2630 (Sayf) at 2626
made to camp in Hamadhān when it fell	Tab. i/2615-2630 (Sayf) at 2627-2628
witnesses treaty with people of Māh Dīnār	Tab. i/2632-2633 (Sayf < MTM)
takes standard when al-Nu'mān falls in battle	Tab. i/2648 (Sayf < MTMAS)
4. Ma'qil b. Muqarrin (brother of nos. 1, 2, 3) (*Muzayna*):	
mentioned; killed	Kufi II/50
5. Ḥudhayfa b. al-Yamān (*'Abs-Ghaṭafan*):	
"al-'Absī," ally of *anṣār*	Bal. *Fut.* 306-307
commanded Kufans until arrival of al-Nu'mān (no. 1); replaces al-Nu'mān on his death	Tab. i/2600-2605 (h—al-Rabī' b. Sulaymān—h—Asad b. Mūsā—h—al-Mubārak b. Faḍāla < Ziyād b. Jubayr < his father)
commanded Kufans until al-Nu'man arrived from Aḥwāz	Tab. i/2615-2630 (Sayf)(at 2615)
commanded one wing of army	Tab. i/2615-2630 (Sayf) (at 2618)
among 14 Kufans who "*sābaqu*"	Tab. i/2615-2630 (Sayf) (at 2619)
kept standard during battle	Tab. i/2615-2630 (Sayf) (at 2625)
treaty with people of al-Māhayn	Tab. i/2632-2633 (Sayf < MTM)
went to Nihāwand	Tab. i/2647-2648 (Sayf < MTMAS)
commander after al-Nu'mān's death	Bal. *Fut.* 302-303; 304-305; Din. 135-137; Kufi II/48, 40, 51, 52, 55
6. Simāk b. 'Ubayd (*'Abs-Ghaṭafān?*):	
he and other 'Abs present at Nihāwand (?)	Tab. i/2631-2632 (Sayf < Abū Ma'bad al-'Absī, 'Urwa b. al-Walīd < others)
mentioned	Bal. *Fut.* 305-306; Din. 137

7. Usāma b. Qatāda (*'Abs-Ghaṭafān?*):	
mentioned in al-Kūfa	Tab. i/2605-2608 (Sayf < MTMAS)
8. B. Asad, B. 'Abs (Ghaṭafān?) (*Asad, 'Abs*):	
mentioned in al-Kūfa	Tab. i/2605-2608 (Sayf < MTMAS)
9. Ṭalḥa (Ṭulayḥa) b. Khuwaylid (*Asad*):	
among companions sent against Persians	Tab. i/2596-2598 (I.I.)
in Medina to advise 'Umar on planning of Nihāwand campaign	Tab. i/2608-2610 (Sayf?) (at 2610)
at Nihāwand	Tab. i/2615-2630 (Sayf) (at 2617)
offers advice	Tab. i/2615-2630 (Sayf) (at 2621)
performs feat of "magic"	Tab. i/2630 (Sayf < Muḥammad b. Qays al-Asadī)
not to be trusted with command positions	Din. 135
made commander of al-Nu'mān's foreguard, over 4,000 men of al-Kūfa and al-Baṣra	Kufi II/42
mentioned	Kufi II/44, 57
10. al-Jarrāḥ b. Sinān (*Asad*):	
mentioned	Tab. i/2605-2608 (Sayf < MTMAS)
11. al-Qa'qā' b. 'Amr (*Tamīm*):	
commanded detachment at Nihāwand	Tab. i/2615-2630 (Sayf) at 2618 and 2621
pursued defeated Persians	Tab. i/2615-2630 (Sayf) at 2626
made to settle in Hamadhān when it is taken	Tab. i/2615-2630 (Sayf) at 2627-2728
witness to treaty with people of al-Māhayn	Tab. i/2632-2633 (Sayf < MTM)
pursued Persians fleeing from Nihāwand to Hamadhān	Tab. i/2648 (Sayf < MTMAS)
12. Ḥanẓala b. al-Rabī' "al-Kātib" al-Usayyidī (*Tamīm*):	
among 14 Kufans who "*sābaqū*"	Tab. i/2615-2630 (Sayf) at 2619
13. Ṭarīf b. Sahm of B. Rabī'a b. Mālik (*Tamīm*)	
messenger to 'Umar after victory at Nihāwand	Tab. i/2615-2630 (Sayf) at 2627
14. Rib'ī b. 'Āmir (*Tamīm*)	
sent by 'Umar to 'Abdullāh b.	Tab. i/2615-2630 (Sayf) at 2615

'Abdullāh (no. 39) to raise troops to join al-Nu'mān	
among 14 Kufans who "*sābaqū*"	Tab. i/2615-2630 (Sayf) at 2619
15. 'Urwa b. Zayd "al-Khayl" (*Tayyi'*)	
heroics; with 300-odd men of Ṭayyi'; mentioned also *qabā'il Ṭayyi'*	Kufi II/53
16. Bashīr b. al-Khaṣāṣiyya al-Sadūsī (*Dhuhl*):	
among 14 Kufans who "*sābaqū*"	Tab. i/2615-2630 (Sayf) at 2619
17. Mujāshi' b. Mas'ūd (*Sulaym*):	
sent to Aḥwāz by 'Umar, thence to Nihāwand	Tab. i/2615-2630 (Sayf) at 2616
commanded rear-guard of army at Nihāwand	Tab. i/2615-2630 (Sayf) at 2618
18. Sāriya b. Zunaym (Zanīm?) (*Kināna)*:	
foils attempted Persian ambush	Kufi II/58
19. Bukayr (*Qays-'Aylān*):	
heroics	Kufi II/55-56
20. Mālik (*Qays-'Aylān*):	
heroics	Kufi II/55-56
21. 'Abdullāh b. 'Umar b. al-Khaṭṭāb (*Quraysh*):	
among companions	Tab. i/2596-2598 (I.I.)
sent by 'Umar among Medinans	Tab. i/2600-2605 (h—al-Rabī' b. Sulaymān—h—Asad b. Mūsā—h—al-Mubārak b. Faḍāla < Ziyād b. Jubayr < his father)
among Medinans sent to reinforce the *ahl Nihāwand*	Tab. i/2615-2630 (Sayf) at 2618
22. 'Uqba b. 'Amr (*Anṣār*):	
among 14 Kufans who "*sābaqū*"	Tab. i/2615-2630 (Sayf) at 2619
of Khazraj-Anṣār?	I.K./Caskel II/573 and table 188
23. 'Amr b. Bilāl b. al-Ḥārith (*Anṣār*):	
left in charge of al-Māhayn	Tab. i/2647-2650 (Sayf < MTMAS)
of Khazraj-Anṣār	I.K./Caskel II/172 and table 189
24. Muḥammad b. Maslama (*Anṣār*):	
sent by 'Umar to raise troops for Nihāwand campaign; returns to Medina	Tab. i/2605-2608 (Sayf < MTMAS)

25. al-Mughīra b. Shu'ba (*Thaqīf*):	
mentioned	Tab. i/2596-2598 (I.I.)
sent as envoy to Persians	Tab. i/2600-2605 (h—al-Rabī' b. Sulaymān—h—Asad b. Mūsā—h—al-Mubārak b. Faḍāla < Ziyād b. Jubayr < his father)
among Medinans sent to reinforce *ahl Nihāwand*	Tab. i/2615-2630 (Sayf) at 2618
among 15 Kufans who "sābaqū"	Tab. i/2615-2630 (Sayf) at 2619
mentioned	Tab. i/2622, 2625
fourth in command order; " 'Umar wrote to the Kufans to reinforce al-Nu'mān—they did, including al-Mughīra"	Bal. *Fut.* 302-303; Bal. *Fut.* 303; Din. 135
command left wing at Nihāwand	Bal. *Fut.* 305 (I.K. < AM)
fifth in command order	Kufi II/148
26. al-Sā'ib b. al-Aqra' (*mawlā* of *Thaqīf*):	
scribe; sent by 'Umar to Iraq	Tab. i/2598; Kufi II/40ff.
returns (to Medina?)	Tab. i/2615-2630 (Sayf) (at 2615)
after Nihāwand, plunder and booty given to al-Sā'ib, who was *ṣāḥib al-aqbāḍ*	Tab. i/2615-2630 (Sayf) (at 2627)
placed in charge of booty by 'Umar	Bal. *Fut.* 304-305 (al-Qāsim b. Sallām < al-Sā'ib b. al-Aqra')
mentioned	Din. 135
in charge of booty (*maghānim*)	Din. 138
"al-Tamīmī" (?)	Kufi II/41
in charge of booty	Kufi II/59-61
of B. Yasār of Thaqīf; brings news of Nihāwand victory to 'Umar	I.D. 183
27. Maḥmūd b. Zukār (or Rukād) (*Khath'am*):	
mentioned; strongman	Kufi II/45
28. Jarīr b. 'Abdullāh (*Bajīla*):	
mentioned	Tab. i/2596-2598 (I.I)
among 14 Kufans who "*sābaqū*"	Tab. i/2615-2630 (Sayf) (at 2619)
third in command order	Bal. *Fut.* 302-303 (I.I.); Din. 135; Kufi II/48
exhorts Muslims in battle	Kufi II/57
witness to treaty with *ahl al-Māhayn* (or no. 28a?)	Tab. i/2632-2633 (Sayf < MTM)

28a. Jarīr b. Abdullāh (*Ḥimyar*):	
among 14 Kufans who "*sābaqū*"	Tab. i/2615-2630 (Sayf) (at 2619)
treaty witness (?) (cf. no. 28?)	Tab. i/2632-2633 (Sayf < MTM)
29. 'Amr b. Ma'dīkarib al-Zubaydī (*Madhḥij*):	
mentioned	Tab. i/2696-2598 (I.I.)
at Nihāwand (?) (" 'Amr")	Tab. i/2615-2630 (Sayf) (at 2617)
offers advice	Tab. i/2615-2630 (Sayf) (at 2621)
not to be trusted with command positions	Din. 135
30. Qays b. Makshūḥ al-Murādī (*Madhḥij*):	
mentioned	Tab. i/2596-2598 (I.I.)
"Qays b. Hubayra"; asked by al-Nu'mān to head 4,000 men as a kind of second foreguard behind Ṭalḥa (no. 9); one of warriors in Syria	Kufi II/43
"Qays b. Hubayra"; kills an elephant	Kufi II/53
31. *fursān* B. Madhḥij (*Madhḥij*):	
mentioned	Kufi II/57
32. Abū Mūsā (*Ash'ar*):	
to march with Basrans to Nihāwand	Tab. i/2600-2615 (h—al-Rabī' b. Sulaymān—h—Asad b. Mūsā—h—al-Mubārak b. Faḍāla < Ziyād b. Jubayr < his father)
marches with one-third of Basrans to al-Kūfa, then to Nihāwand	Din. 135
same as preceding, done on 'Alī's suggestion	Kufi II/39
'Umar asks him to send one-third of Basrans to join one-third of Kufans for Nihāwand campaign	Kufi II/41
33. Sa'īd b. Qays (*Hamdān*):	
among 14 Kufans who "*sābaqū*"	Tab. i/2615-2630 (Sayf) at 2619
34. Abū 'Uthmān al-Nahdī (*Nahd*):	
carries news of victory at Nihāwand to 'Umar	Bal. *Fut.* 304 (Shaybān < Abū 'Uthmān al-Nahdī)
35. al-Ash'ath b. Qays (*Kinda*):	
among 14 Kufans who "*sābaqū*"	Tab. i/2615-2630 (Sayf) at 2619
fifth in command at Nihāwand	Bal. *Fut.* 302-303; Din. 135

fourth in command	Kufi II/48
commanded right wing at Nihāwand	Bal. *Fut.* 305 (I.I. < AM)
36. Wa'il b. Ḥujr (*Kinda*):	
among 14 Kufans who "*sābaqū*"	Tab. i/2615-2630 (Sayf) at 2619
37. al-Aqra' b. 'Abdullāh (*Ḥimyar*):	
among 14 Kufans who "*sābaqū*"	Tab. i/2615-2630 (Sayf) at 2619
38. Qarīb b. Zafar (*'Abd al-Qays*):	
messenger to 'Umar	Tab. i/2609 (Sayf?)
returns (to Medina) (?)	Tab. i/2615-2630 (Sayf) (at 2615)
39. 'Abdullāh b. 'Abdullāh b. 'Itbān	
lieutenant over al-Kūfa for Sa'd b. Abī Waqqāṣ; Nihāwand occurred during his time	Tab. i/2605-2608 (Sayf < MTMAS)
Sa'd's lieutenant over al-Kūfa	Tab. i/2615-2630 (Sayf) (at 2615)
40. Zirr b. Kulayb:	
messenger from 'Umar to al-Nu'mān (in S. Iraq?)	Tab. i/2611-2614 (Sayf < Abū Bakr al-Hudhalī)
ordered to reinforce Nihāwand army from Iṣbahān	Tab. i/2615-2630 (Sayf) (at 2616-2617)
41. al-Muqtarib al-Aswad b. Rabī'a:	
sent as messenger from Umar to al-Nu'mān (no. 1)	Tab. i/2611-2614 (Sayf < Abū Bakr al-Hudhalī)
ordered to reinforce Nihāwand army from Iṣbahān	
42. Salama b. al-Qayn:	
'Umar orders him to reinforce Nihāwand army from Iṣbahān	Tab. i/2615-2630 (Sayf) at 2616-2617
43. 'Amr b. Abī Salama al-'Anazī:	
among *ahl Nihāwand*	Tab. i/2615-2630 (Sayf) at 2617
44. Ḥarmala b. Murayṭa:	
'Umar wrote him to reinforce *ahl Nihāwand*; among troops in Iṣbahān?	Tab. i/2615-2630 (Sayf) at 2616-2617
45. Ibn al-Hawbar:	
among 14 Kufans who "*sābaqū*"	Tab. i/2615-2630 (Sayf) at 2619
46. 'Amīr b. Maṭar:	
among 14 Kufans who '*sābaqū*"	Tab. i/2615-2630 (Sayf) at 2619
47. al-Nusayr b. Thawr:	
holds Marj al-Qal'a with a group of 'Ijl and Ḥanīfa; these tribes did not fight at	Tab. i/2647-2648 (Sayf < MTMAS)

Nihāwand, but did share in Nihāwand booty for their services holding fortress	
holds fortress at Marj al-Qal'a	Tab. i/2615-2630 (Sayf) at 2628
48. Ja'far b. Rāshid:	
speaks to Ṭalḥa (no. 9), who performs magic feat	Tab. i/2630 (Sayf < Muḥammad b. Qays al-Asadī)
49. 'Abdullāh b. Dhī l-Sahmayn:	
witnesses treaty with people of al-Māhayn	Tab. i/2632-2633 (Sayf < MTM)
50. Bukayr b. Shidākh:	
sent as scout	Kufi II/44
51. Bisṭām b. 'Amr:	
mentioned	Kufi II/56
52. 'Amr b. Thubī:	
offers military advice	Tab. i/2615-2630 (Sayf) at 2620
53. 'Abdullāh b. Ma'dūd:	
mentioned	Kufi II/49

APPENDIX N. IṢBAHĀN

1. 'Abdullāh (b. 'Abdullāh b. 'Itbān):	
sent to Iṣbahān by 'Umar; joined by men from Nihāwand army. Sent by 'Umar to join Suhayl b. 'Adī in Kirmān	Tab. i/2638-2640 (*qālū*)
2. 'Abdullāh b. Warqā' (*Asad*):	
heroics; commanded one wing of army of 'Abdullāh b. 'Abdullāh (no. 1)	Tab. i/2638-2640 (*qālū*)
witnessed treaty with Iṣbahān	Tab. i/2641 (Sayf < MTMAS)
"Abdullah b. Budayl b. Warqa' al-Khuzā'ī" came from al-Baṣra	Kufi II/69
" 'Abdullāh b. Budayl" effected conquest of Iṣbahān	Bal. *Fut.* 312; 312-313 (Ibn Sa'd < I.I.)
" 'Abdullāh b. Budayl" and his troops joined by forces of Abū Mūsā; together they take Iṣbahān	Bal. *Fut.* 313
" 'Abdullah b. Budayl b. Warqā' " conquered Iṣbahān	Ya'qubi II/157
3. 'Iṣma b. 'Abdullāh b. 'Ubayda b. Sayf b. 'Abd al-Ḥārith:	
commanded one wing of army of 'Abdullāh b. 'Abdullāh	Tab. i/2638-2640 (*qālū*)
witnessed treaty with Iṣbahān	Tab. i/2641 (Sayf < MTMAS)
4. Abū Mūsā ('Abdullāh b. Qays) (*Ash'ar*):	
comes from Aḥwāz area to join Muslims at Iṣbahān	Tab. i/2638-2640 (*qālū*)
came as reinforcement to Muslims at Iṣbahān	Tab. i/2640 (Sayf < al-Mubārak b. Faḍāla and others < al-Ḥasan < Asīd b. al-Mutashammis)
came from al-Baṣra via Aḥwāz; commander at Iṣbahān	Kufi II/68-71
at Iṣbahān, defeats Persians; Bal. says this refers to Qum	Bal. *Fut.* 312 (Ibn Sa'd < Bashīr b. Abī Umayya)
joins " 'Abdullāh b. Budayl" (no. 2) in conquest of Iṣbahān	Bal. *Fut.* 313
witnessed treaty with Iṣbahān	Tab. i/2641 (Sayf < MTMAS)

5. al-Nu‘mān b. Muqarrin (*Muzayna*):	
commanded Iṣbahān army	Tab. i/2641 (Ma‘qul b. Yasār)
commanded Iṣbahān army (‘Umar places him in command when he observes his piety)	Tab. i/2642-2645 (h—Ya‘qūb b. Ibrāhīm and ‘Amr b. ‘Alī—h—‘Abd al-Raḥmān b. Mahdī—h—Ḥammād b. Salama < Abū ‘Imrān al-Jawnī < ‘Alqama b. ‘Abdullāh al-Muzanī < Ma‘qil b. Yasār)
6. al-Mughīra b. Shu‘ba (*Thaqīf*):	
envoy for al-Nu‘mān b. Muqarrin to Persians	Tab. i/2642-2645 (Ya‘qūb b. Ibrāhīm and ‘Amr b. ‘Alī—h—‘Abd al-Raḥmān b. Mahdī—h—Ḥammād b. Salama < Abū ‘Imrān al-Jawnī < ‘Alqama b. ‘Abdullāh al-Muzanī < Ma‘qil b. Yasār)
7. al-Ash‘ath b. Qays (*Kinda*):	Tab. i/2642-2645
8. (‘Abdullāh?) Ibn ‘Umar	Tab. i/2642-2645
9. Ibn al-Zubayr (*Quraysh*):	Tab. i/2642-2645
10. ‘Amr b. Ma‘dīkarib (*Madhḥij*):	Tab. i/2642-2645
11. Ḥudhayfa	Tab. i/2642-2645
12. al-Aḥnaf b. Qays (*Tamīm*):	
"whose name was al-Ḍaḥḥāk b. Qays al-Tamīmī"	Bal. *Fut.* 312
commanded vanguard of Abū Mūsā's army	Bal. *Fut.* 313
13. al-Sā'ib b. al-Aqra‘:	
left in charge of Iṣbahān	Tab. i/2638-2640 (*qālū*)
left in charge of Iṣbahān	Bal. *Fut.* 312

APPENDIX O. HAMADHĀN, RAYY, QŪMIS, JURJĀN, ṬABARISTĀN

1. Anonymous account in Bal. *Fut.* 309:
   al-Mughīra b. Shu'ba marched against Hamadhān with Jarīr b. 'Abdullāh in his vanguard (or, according to a variant, he sent Jarīr against Hamadhān). After the town was taken, al-Mughīra left Kathīr b. Shihāb al-Ḥārithī in charge of it.
2. Sayf b. 'Umar considers the campaign against Hamadhān, Rayy, Qūmis, Jurjān, and Ṭabaristān as a continuation of the Nihāwand campaign led by al-Nu'mān b. Muqarrin, etc. New names mentioned in these accounts are:
   'Iṣma b. 'Abdullāh al-Ḍabbī: at Hamadhān (Tab. i/2649-2651)
   Muhalhal b. Zayd al-Ṭā'ī: at Hamadhān (Tab. i/2649-2651)
   Simāk b. Makhrama al-Asadī: at Hamadhān (Tab. i/2649-2651)
   Simāk b. Kharsha al-Anṣārī: at Hamadhān (Tab. i/2649-2651)
   at Rayy (Tab. i/2655)
   Bukayr b. Qays al-Hamdānī: at Hamadhān (Tab. i/2649-2651)
   sent to Adharbayjān (Tab. i/2655)
   Yazīd b. Qays al-Hamdānī: "confirmed over Hamadhān by Nu'aym" (Tab. i/2649-2651, 2653)
   al-Muḍārib al-'Ijlī: messenger to Medina after conquest of Rayy (Tab. i/2655)
   'Utba b. al-Nahhās al-Bakrī: sent to Medina with "fifth" of booty (Tab. i/2655);
   sent to Qūmis (Tab. i/2656-2657)
   witness, Ṭabaristān (Tab. i/2659-2669)
   Abū Mufazzir: sent with fifth (Tab. i/2655)
   Sawād b. Quṭba al-Tamīmī: witness, Ṭabaristān (Tab. i/2659-2660)
   Hind bint 'Amr al-Murādī: witness, Ṭabaristān (Tab. i/2659-2660)
3. Anonymous account in Ya'qubi II/157:
   Abū Mūsā al-Ash'arī took Iṣṭakhr in A.H. 23
   'Abdullāh b. Budayl al-Khuzā'ī took Hamadhān and Iṣbahān
   Qurẓa b. Ka'b al-Anṣārī took Rayy
4. Anonymous account in Kufi II/62-68:
   Kufi considers the expedition against Rayy as a separate force of 10,000 men from al-Kūfa, under the command of 'Urwa b. Zayd "al-Khayl" al-Ṭā'ī. Other participants include:
   Suwayd b. Muqarrin al-Muzanī
   Simāk b. 'Ubayd al-'Absī
   Shibl b. Ma'bad al-Bajalī—single combat
   Zakāt b. Muṣ'ab of 'Abd al-Qays—in charge of *jizya* of Rayy
   B. Ṭayyi'—mentioned
   After taking Rayy, these troops, augmented by 300 reinforcements from al-Kūfa, marched to Qum and Kāshān. Hamadhān and Rayy placed before Iṣbahān. Jarīr b. 'Abdullāh ordered to reinforce Muslims at Hamadhān.

BIBLIOGRAPHY

The following list is essentially restricted to sources and studies cited in the notes to the present volume and makes no attempt to include all works treating the rise of Islam. In alphabetizing, the article al- has been disregarded.

TRADITIONAL SOURCES (ARABIC)

Abū 'Ubayd al-Qāsim b. Sallām. *Kitāb al-amwāl.* Edited by Muḥammad Khalīl Harrās. Cairo: Maktabat al-Kullīyāt al-Azhariyya, 1968.

Abū Yūsuf, Ya'qūb b. Ibrāhīm. *Kitāb al-kharāj.* Cairo: Maktabat al-Salafiyya, A.H. 1352 (A.D. 1933-1934).

al-Azraqī, Abū l-Walīd Muḥammad b. 'Abdullāh. *Kitāb akhbār Makka.* Edited by Ferdinand Wüstenfeld. Leipzig: F. A. Brockhaus, 1858 (=*Chroniken der Stadt Mekka*, vol. 1).

al-Bakrī, Abū 'Ubayd 'Abdullāh. *Mu'jam mā ista'jama l-Bakrī.* Edited by Ferdinand Wüstenfeld. Göttingen: Dieterich, 1876-1877 (*Das Geographische Wörterbuch des Abu 'Obeid 'Abdallah . . .*). Partly translated by F. Wüstenfeld. "Die Wohnsitze und Wanderungen der arabischen Stämme, aus der Vorrede des Abu 'Obeid el-Bekrí zu seinem geographischen Wörterbuche." *Abhandlungen der Gesellschaft der Wissenschaften zu Göttingen* 14 (1868-1869), pp, 93-172.

al-Balādhurī, Aḥmad b. Yaḥyā. *Ansāb al-ashrāf.* MS, Reisülkuttap 597 and 598, housed in Sülemaniye Kütüphanesi, Istanbul.

———. *Ansāb al-ashrāf* I. Edited by Muḥammad Ḥamīdullāh. Cairo: Dār al-Ma'ārif, 1959.

———. *Ansāb al-ashrāf* IVA. Edited by Max Schloessinger and M. J. Kister. Jerusalem: Magnes Press, 1971.

———. *Ansāb al-ashrāf* V. Edited by Shlomo. D. F. Goitein. Jerusalem: University Press, 1936.

———. *Futūḥ al-buldān.* Edited by Michael Jan de Goeje. Leiden: E. J. Brill, 1866 (*Liber expugnationis regionum . . .*). Translated by Philip Khuri Hitti and Francis Clark Murgotten. *The Origins of the Islamic State.* New York: Columbia University Press, 1916 and 1924.

al-Baṣrī, Muḥammad b. 'Abdullāh Abū Ismā'īl al-Azdī. *Ta'rīkh futuḥ al-Shām.* Edited by 'Abd al-Mun'im 'Abdullāh 'Āmir. Cairo: Mu'assasa Sijill al-'Arab, 1970.

al-Bukhārī, Muḥammad b. Ismā'īl. *al-Jāmi' al-ṣaḥīḥ.* Bulāq(?), n.d., 4 vols.

al-Dīnawarī, Abū Ḥanīfa Aḥmad b. Dāūd. *al-Akhbār al-ṭiwāl.* Edited by 'Abd al-Mun'im 'Āmir and Jamāl al-Dīn al-Shayyāl. Cairo: Dār Iḥyā' al-Kutub al-'Arabiyya, 1960.

al-Diyārbakrī, Ḥusayn b. Muḥammad. *Ta'rīkh al-khamīs fī aḥwāl anfas nafīs.* Cairo: Maṭba'at al-Wahbiyya, 1866. Reprinted Beirut: Mu'assasa Sha'bān, 1970.

Eutychius, Patriarch of Alexandria (=Sa'īd b. al-Biṭrīq). *Annales.* Edited by

L. Cheikho, B. Carra de Vaux, and H. Zayyat. 2 vols., Beirut: Catholic Press, 1906-1909. (=*Kitāb al-ta'rīkh al-majmū' 'alā l-taḥqīq wa l-taṣdīq*) (=Corpus Scriptorum Christianorum Orientalium, Scriptores Arabici, series 3, vol. 7).

al-Hamadhānī, Ibn al-Faqīh. *Mukhtaṣar kitāb al-buldān*. Edited by M. J. de Goeje. Leiden: E. J. Brill, 1885.

Ibn 'Abd al-Barr, Yūsuf b. 'Abdullāh. *al-Istī'āb fī ma'rifat al-aṣḥāb*. 4 vols. Cairo: Maṭba'at al-Sa'āda, A.H. 1328 (A.D. 1910). Reprinted Beirut: Dār Ṣādir, n.d. (ca. 1960). In margins of Ibn Ḥajar, *al-Iṣāba*.

Ibn 'Abd al-Ḥakam (the younger). *Futūḥ Miṣr*. Edited by Charles C. Torrey. New Haven: Yale University Press, 1922 (Yale Oriental Series, Researches, 3).

Ibn 'Abd Rabbihi, Aḥmad b. Muḥammad. *al-'Iqd al-farīd*. Edited by Muḥammad Sa'īd al-'Iryān. Cairo: al-Maktaba al-Tijāriyya al-Kubrā, n.d. Reprinted 8 vols. in 4, Beirut: Dār al-Fikr, 1953.

Ibn al-'Adīm, Kamāl al-Dīn 'Umar b. Aḥmad. *Zubdat al-ḥalab min ta'rīkh Ḥalab*. Edited by Sāmī al-Dahhān, 1. Damascus: Institut Français de Damas, 1951.

Ibn 'Asākir, Abū l-Qāsim 'Alī b. al-Ḥasan b. Hibatullāh. *Ta'rīkh madīnat Dimashq* I. Edited by Ṣalāḥ al-Dīn al-Munajjid. Damascus: al-Majma' al-'Ilmī al-'Arabī, 1951.

———. *Ta'rīkh madīnat Dimashq*. MS, Ẓāhiriyya Library, Damascus. 19 vols.: 1-5 = Ta'rīkh 1-5; 6 = Ta'rīkh 113; 7-19 = Ta'rīkh 6-18.

———. *Ta'rīkh madīnat Dimashq* MS, Asiatic Museum, Leningrad. Arabic no. 202.

Ibn A'tham al-Kūfī, Abū Muḥammad Aḥmad. *Kitāb al-futūḥ*. Edited by Muḥammad 'Abd al-Mu'īd Khān, Maḥāmid 'Alī al-'Abbāsī, and Sayyid 'Abd al-Wahhāb Bukhārī. 8 vols. Hyderabad: Dā'irat al-Ma'ārif al-'Uthmāniyya, 1968-1975.

———. *Kitāb al-futūḥ*. MS no. 2290B, Khuda Bakhsh Oriental Public Library, Patna, India (falsely attributed to al-Wāqidī under title *Kitāb al-ridda*).

Ibn al-Athīr al-Jazarī, 'Izz al-Dīn. *al-Lubāb fī tahdhīb al-ansāb*. 3 vols. Beirut: Dār Ṣādir, n.d.

Ibn Durayd, Abū Bakr Muḥammad b. al-Ḥasan. *al-Ishtiqāq*. Edited by Ferdinand Wüstenfeld. Göttingen: Dieterischen Buchhandlung, 1854.

Ibn Ḥabīb, Muḥammad, *Kitāb al-muḥabbar*. Edited by Ilse Lichtenstadter. Hyderabad: Dā'irat al-Ma'ārif al-'Uthmāniyya, 1942.

Ibn Ḥajar al-'Asqalānī, Aḥmad b. 'Alī. *al-Iṣāba fī tamyīz al-ṣaḥāba*. 4 vols. Cairo: Maṭba'at al-Sa'āda, A.H. 1328 (A.D. 1910). Reprinted Beirut: Dār Ṣādir, n.d. (ca. 1960).

Ibn Ḥazm al-Andalusī, Abū Muḥammad 'Alī b. Aḥmad b. Sa'īd. *Jamharat ansāb al-'Arab*. Edited by 'Abd al-Salām Muḥammad Hārūn. Cairo: Dār al-Ma'ārif, 1971.

Ibn Hishām, 'Abd al-Malik. *al-Sīra al-nabawiyya*. Edited by Ferdinand Wüstenfeld. (*Das Leben Muhammeds* . . .). 2 vols. Göttingen: Dieterischen Buchhandlung, 1858-1860. Translated by Alfred Guillaume. *The Life of Muhammad*. London: Oxford University Press, 1955.

Ibn Isḥāq, Muḥammad. *Kitāb ḥurrāb al-Basūs bayna Bakr wa Taghlib*. MS, Tehrān University, no. 2134 (fols. 122b-202b).

Ibn al-Kalbī, Hishām b. Muḥammad. *Jamharat al-nasab*. Reduced to tables and notes by Werner Caskel and Gert Strenziok. 2 vols. Leiden: E. J. Brill, 1966.

———. *Kitāb al-aṣnām*. Edited by Aḥmad Zakī Pasha. Cairo: 1914. Reprinted Cairo: al-Dār al-Qawmiyya li-l-Ṭibā'a wa l-Nashr, 1965. Translated by Nabīh Amīn Fāris. *The Book of Idols*. Princeton: Princeton University Press, 1958 (Princeton Oriental Studies, vol. 14).

Ibn Qutayba al-Dīnawarī, Abū Muḥammad 'Abdullāh b. Muslim. *al-Ma'ārif*. Edited by Tharwat 'Ukkāsha. Cairo: Dār al-Ma'ārif, 1969.

———. *'Uyūn al-akhbār*. Edited by Muḥammad 'Abd al-Qādir Ḥātim. 4 vols. Cairo: Dār al-Kutub, 1924-1930. Reprinted 1963.

Ibn Sa'd, Muḥammad, *Kitāb al-ṭabaqāt al-kabīr*. Edited by Eduard Sachau et al. 9 vols. Leiden: E. J. Brill, 1904-1940.

al-Iṣfahānī, 'Alī b. al-Ḥusayn Abū l-Faraj. *Kitāb al-aghānī*. Vols. 1-20. Būlāq, A.H. 1284-1285 (=A.D. 1867-1869); vol. 21. Leiden: E. J. Brill, A.H. 1306 (=A.D. 1888-1889); Index. Leiden: E. J. Brill, 1900.

Khalīfa b. Khayyāṭ al-'Uṣfūrī, Abū 'Umar Shabāb. *Kitāb al-ṭabaqāt*. Edited by Suhayl Zakkār. Damascus: Wizārat al-thaqāfa, 1966.

———. *Ta'rīkh*. Edited by Akram Ḍiyā' al-'Umarī. 2 vols. al-Najaf, 1967.

Krenkow, Fritz, ed. and trans. *The Poems of Ṭufail ibn 'Auf al-Ghanawī and aṭ-Ṭirimmāḥ ibn Ḥakīm al-Ṭā'yī*. London: Luzac, 1927 (Gibb Memorial Series, no. 25).

Lyall, Charles, ed. and trans. *The Dīwāns of 'Abīd ibn al-Abras, of Asad, and 'Āmir ibn al-Ṭufail, of 'Āmir ibn Ṣa'ṣa'a*. London: Luzac and Leiden: E. J. Brill, 1913 (Gibb Memorial Series, no. 31).

al-Marzubānī, Muḥammad b. 'Imrān. *Nūr al-qabas*. Edited by R. Sellheim. Wiesbaden: Steiner, 1964 (Bibliotheca Islamica, vol. 23, part 1).

al-Mas'ūdī, 'Alī b. Ḥusayn. *Murūj al-dhahab wa ma'ādin al-jawhar*. Edited by Yūsuf As'ad Dāghir. 4 vols. Beirut: Dār Ṣādir, 1965-1966.

———. *al-Tanbīh wa l-ishrāf*. Edited by M. J. de Goeje. Leiden: E. J. Brill, 1894. Reprinted Beirut, 1965.

al-Qalqashandī, Abū l-'Abbās Aḥmad. *Nihāyat al-'arab fī ma'rifat ansāb al-'Arab*. Edited by Ibrāhīm al-Ibyārī. Cairo, 1959.

Qudāma b. Ja'far, al-Kātib al-Baghdādī. *Kitāb al-kharāj*. Part 7 translated by A. Ben Shemesh, *Taxation in Islam*, 3. Leiden: E. J. Brill, 1965.

Sa'īd b. al-Biṭrīq. See Eutychius, Patriarch of Alexandria.

al-Ṭabarī, Muḥammad b. Jarīr. *Ta'rīkh al-rusul wa l-mulūk (Annales)*. Edited by M. J. de Goeje et al. 15 vols. Leiden: E. J. Brill, 1879-1901.

al-Tha'ālibī, Abū Manṣūr. *Ghurar akhbār mulūk al-Furs wa siyari-him*. Edited and translated by H. Zotenberg. Paris: Imprimerie Nationale, 1900 (*Histoire des Rois des Perses*).

al-Wāqidī, Muḥammad b. 'Umar. *Kitāb al-maghāzī*. Edited by Marsden Jones. 3 vols. Oxford: Oxford University Press, 1966.

Wüstenfeld, Ferdinand, ed. *Die Chroniken der Stadt Mekka*. 4 vols. Leipzig: F. A. Brockhaus, 1857-1861.

al-Ya'qūbī, Aḥmad b. Abī Ya'qūb. *Ta'rīkh al-Ya'qūbī.* 2 vols. Beirut: Dār Ṣādir and Dār Bayrūt, 1960.

Yāqūt al-Ḥamawī, Shihāb al-Dīn Abū 'Abdullāh. *Mu'jam al-buldān.* 5 vols. Beirut: Dār Ṣādir and Dār Bayrūt, 1957.

NON-ARABIC SOURCES

Brooks, Ernest Walter, I. Guidi, and Jean-Baptiste Chabot (eds. and trs.). *Chronica Minora.* 3 vols. Paris: E Typographeo Reipublicae, 1903-1905 (=Corpus Scriptorum Christianorum Orientalium, Scriptores Syri, series 3, vol. 4).

Cagnat, René Louis Victor. *Inscriptiones Graecae ad Res Romanas Pertinentes.* 4 vols. Paris: E. Leroux, 1906-1927.

Chronicum Miscellaneum ad Annum Domini 724 Pertinens. In Ernest Walter Brooks et al. *Chronica Minora,* 2.

Elias bar Shīnāya, Bishop of Nisibis. *Opus Chronologicum.* Edited by Ernest Walter Brooks. Translated by Jean-Baptiste Chabot. Paris: E Typographeo Reipublicae, 1910.

John, Bishop of Ephesus. *The Third Part of the Ecclesiastical History of John, Bishop of Ephesus.* Edited by William Cureton. Oxford: Oxford University Press, 1853. Translated by R. Payne Smith. *The Third Part* . . . . Oxford: Oxford University Press, 1860.

Michael the Syrian. *Chronique de Michel le Syrien.* Edited and translated by Jean-Baptiste Chabot. 4 vols. Paris: Academie des inscriptions et belles-lettres, 1899-1910. Reprinted Brussels: Culture et Civilisation, 1963.

Nicephorus, Patriarch of Constantinople. *Opuscula Historica.* Edited by Carolus de Boor. Leipzig: G. Teubner, 1880.

Pliny the Elder (C. Plinius Secundus). *Natural History.* Edited and translated by H. Rackham. 7 vols. London: W. Heinemann and Cambridge, Mass.: Harvard University Press, 1938-1956.

Schoff, Wilfred Harvey, trans. *The Periplus of the Erythraean Sea.* New York: Longmans, Green, and Co., 1912.

Theophanes. *Chronographia.* Edited by Carolus de Boor. Leipzig: B. G. Teubner, 1883. Reprinted Hildesheim: Georg Olms, 1963.

Zachariah of Mitylene. *The Syriac Chronicle known as that of Zachariah of Mitylene.* Translated by F. H. Hamilton and Ernest Walter Brooks. London: Methuen and Co., 1899.

STUDIES

Adams, Robert M. "Agriculture and Urban Life in Early Southwestern Iran." *Science* 136 (1962), pp. 109-122.

———. *Land behind Baghdad. A History of Settlement on the Diyala Plains.* Chicago: University of Chicago Press, 1965.

——— and Hans J. Nissen. *The Uruk Countryside.* Chicago: University of Chicago Press, 1972.

'Alī, Maḥmūd. "Tanqībāt fī l-Ḥīra." *Sumer* 2 (1946), Arabic pp. 29-32.

al-'Alī, Ṣāliḥ Aḥmad. "Khiṭaṭ al-Baṣra." *Sumer* 8 (1952), Arabic pp. 72-83, 281-302.

———. *al-Tanẓīmāt al-ijtimā'iyya wa l-iqtiṣādiyya fī l-Baṣra fī l-qarn al-'awwal al-hijrī*. Baghdad, 1953.

Altheim, Franz, and Ruth Stiehl. *Die Araber in der alten Welt*. 5 vols. Berlin: W. de Gruyter, 1964-1969.

al-Anṣārī, 'Abd al-Qaddūs. *Banū Sulaym*. Beirut: Dār al-'Ilm li-l-Malāyīn, 1971.

Andrae, Tor. *Mohammed, The Man and His Faith*. New York: Harper and Row, 1960. German original *Mohammed, Sein Leben und Sein Glaube*. Göttingen: Vandenhoeck und Ruprecht, 1932.

'Arabī, 'Abd al-Raḥmān. *L'Islam et la guerre à l'époque du prophète Mahomet* (thèse, Lausanne). Ambilly: Coopérative "Les Presses de Savoie," 1954.

Asad, Talal. "The Beduin as a Military Force: Notes on Some Aspects of Power Relations between Nomads and Sedentaries in Historical Perspective." In Cynthia Nelson, ed. *The Desert and the Sown—Nomads in the Wider Society*. Berkeley: Institute of International Studies, 1973.

Ashkenazi, Touvia. "La tribu arabe: ses elements." *Anthropos* 41-44 (1946-1949), pp. 657-672.

———. *Tribus semi-nomades de la Palestine du Nord*. Paris: Librarie Orientaliste Paul Geuthner, 1938.

Aswad, Barbara. "Social and Ecological Aspects in the Formation of Islam." In Louise Sweet, ed. *Peoples and Cultures of the Middle East*, 1. Garden City, N.Y.: Natural History Press, 1970, pp. 53-73.

Awad, Mohamed. "Settlement of Nomadic and Semi-Nomadic Tribal Groups in the Middle East." *International Labour Review* 79 (1959), pp. 25-56.

Bacon, Elizabeth E. "Types of Pastoral Nomadism in Central and Southwest Asia." *Southwestern Journal of Anthropology* 10 (1954), pp. 44-68.

Balandier, Georges. *Political Anthropology*. New York: Vintage Books, 1970. French original *L'Anthropologie politique*. Paris: Presses Universitaires, 1967.

Baneth, D.Z.H. "What did Muḥammad mean when he called his religion "Islam"?—The Original Meaning of Aslama and its derivatives." *Israel Oriental Studies* 1 (1971), pp. 183-190.

Becker, Carl Heinrich. "Die Ausbreitung der Araber." In his *Islamstudien* 1. Leipzig, 1924, pp. 66-145. Reprinted Hildesheim: Georg Olms, 1967. English translation. "The Expansion of the Saracens." appears as chapters 11 and 12 of the *Cambridge Medieval History*. Edited by H. M. Gwatkin et al. Vol. 2. Cambridge: Cambridge University Press, 1913. Reprinted 1967.

Belyaev, E. A. *Arabs, Islam, and the Arab Caliphate in the Early Middle Ages*. London: Pall Mall Press, and Jerusalem: Israel Universities Press, 1969. Russian original *Araby, islam i arabskii Khalifat v rannee srednevekov'e*. 2nd ed. Moscow, 1966.

Berliner, Abraham. *Beiträge zur Geographie und Ethnographie Babyloniens im Talmud und Midrasch*. Berlin: J. Gordeanczyk and Co., 1884.

Berque, Jacques. "Qu'est-ce qu'une tribu nord africaine?" In *Évantail de l'histoire vivante, hommage à Lucien Febvre*. Paris: Armand Colin, 1953, pp. 261-271.

Blau, Otto. "Altarabische Sprachstudien." *ZDMG* 25 (1871), pp. 525-592, and "Altarabische Sprachstudien—II." *ZDMG* 27 (1873), pp. 295-363.

Blunt, Lady Anne. *Bedouin Tribes of the Euphrates*. New York: Harper and Brothers, 1879.

de Boucheman, Albert. *Matérial de la vie bédouine; recueilli dans le désert de Syrie (tribus des Arabes Sba'a)*. Damascus: Institut Français de Damas, 1935.

———. "Note sur la rivalité de deux tribus moutonnières de Syrie. Les Mawâlî et les Hadîdyîn." *Revue des études islamiques* 7 (1934), pp. 9-58.

———. *Sukhné. Une petite cité caravanière*. Damascus: Institut Français de Damas, n.d. (ca. 1938).

Bousquet, Georges Henri. "Observations sur la nature et les causes de la conquête arabe." *Studia Islamica* 6 (1956), pp. 37-52.

———. "Quelques remarques critiques et sociologiques sur la conquête arabe et les théories émises à ce sujet." In *Studi Orientalistici in Onore de Giorgio Levi della Vida*, 1. Roma: Istituto per l'Oriente, 1956, pp. 52-60.

Bowen, Richard LeBaron, Jr., and Frank P. Albright. *Archaeological Discoveries in South Arabia*. Baltimore: Johns Hopkins Press, 1958.

Bräunlich, Erich. "Beiträge zur Gesellschaftsordnung der arabischen Beduinenstämme." *Islamica* 6 (1934), pp. 68-111 and pp. 182-229.

———. *Bisṭām ibn Qais. Ein vorislamischer Beduinenfürst und Held*. Leipzig: E. Pfeiffer, 1923.

Bravmann, Meir M. *The Spiritual Background of Early Islam*. Leiden: E. J. Brill, 1972.

Brown, Peter. *The World of Late Antiquity*. London: Harcourt, Brace, Jovanovich, 1971.

Buhl, Frants. *Das Leben Muhammeds*. Leipzig: Quelle und Meyer, 1930. Danish original *Muhammeds Liv med en Indl edning om Forholdene i Arabien för Muhammeds Optraeden*. Copenhagen: Gyldendalske Boghandels Forlag, 1903.

Butzer, Karl W. "Der Umweltfaktor in der grossen arabischen Expansion." *Saeculum* 8 (1957), pp. 359-371.

Cadoux, H. W. "Recent Changes in the Course of the Lower Euphrates." *Geographical Journal* 28 (1906), pp. 266-277.

Caetani, Leone. *Annali dell'Islam*. 10 vols. Milan: U. Hoepli, 1905-1926.

———. *Studi di Storia Orientale*. 3 vols. Milan: U. Hoepli, 1911-1914.

Cahen, Claude. *Der Islam, I: Vom Ursprung bis zu den Anfängen des Osmanenreiches*. Frankfurt am Main: Fischer, 1968.

Cambridge History of Islam. Edited by P. M. Holt, A.K.S. Lambton, and B. Lewis. 2 vols. Cambridge: Cambridge University Press, 1970.

Cambridge Medieval History. Edited by H. M. Gwatkin et al. 8 vols. New York: Macmillan Co., 1911-1936.

Canard, Marius. "L'expansion arabe: le problème militaire." In *L'Occidente e l'Islam nell'Alto Medioevo* 1 (Settimane di Studio del Centro Italiano di Studi sull'Alto Medioevo, 12, 2-8 April 1964), Spoleto, 1965, pp. 37-63.

Caskel, Werner. "Aijām al-'Arab. Studien zur altarabischen Epik." *Islamica* 3 (1930), fascicule 5 (Ergänzungsheft), pp 1-99.

———. "Die alten semitischen Gottheiten in Arabien." In S. Moscati, ed. *Le*

Antiche Divinità Semitiche. Rome: Universita di Roma, Centro di Studi Semitici, 1958, pp. 95-117.

———. "Der arabische Stamm vor dem Islam und seine gesellschaftliche und juristische Organisation." In *Atti del Convegno Internazionale sul tema: Dalla Tribu allo Stato (Roma, 13-16 aprile 1961)*. Rome: Accademia Nazionale dei Lincei, 1962, pp. 139-149. (*Atti* No. 54).

———. *Die Bedeutung der Beduinen in der Geschichte der Araber*. Köln and Opladen: Westdeutscher Verlag, 1953.

———. "Die einheimischen Quellen zur Geschichte Nord-Arabiens vor dem Islam." *Islamica* 3 (1927), pp. 331-341.

———. *Lihyan und Lihyanisch*. Köln and Opladen: Westdeutscher Verlag, 1954.

Caton-Thompson, Gertrude, and Elinor Wight Gardner. "Climate, Irrigation, and Early Man in the Hadramawt." *Geographical Journal* 93 (1939), pp. 18-38.

Charles, Henri. *Le Christianisme des arabes nomades sur le limes et dans le désert syro-mésopotamien aux alentours de l'Hégire*. Paris: Bibliotheque de l'Ecôle des Hautes-Études, 1936. (Sciences religieuses, vol. 52).

———. *La Sedentarisation entre Euphrate et Balik. Note d'ethnosociologie*. Beirut: Imprimerie Catholique, 1942.

———. *Tribus moutonnières du Moyen-Euphrate*. Damascus: Institut Français d'Études Arabes, n.d. (ca. 1937).

Chelhod, Joseph. *Le Droit dans la société bédouine*. Paris: Marcel Riviere, 1971.

Chitty, Derwas. *The Desert a City*. Oxford: Blackwell's, 1966.

Christensen, Artur. *L'Iran sous les Sassanides*. Copenhagen: Munksgaard, 1936.

Cleveland, Ray L. "Zur'Landes- und Völkerkunde von Dhofar." *Bustān* 7 (1966), pp. 41-44.

Cole, Donald Powell.*Nomads of the Nomads. The Āl Murrah Bedouin of the Empty Quarter*. Chicago: Aldine, 1975.

Constantelos, Demetrios J. "The Moslem conquests of the Near East as revealed in the Greek sources of the seventh and eighth centuries." *Byzantion* 42 (1972), pp. 325-357.

Cressey, George Babcock. "The Shatt al-Arab Basin." *Middle East Journal* 12 (1958), pp. 448-460.

Cunnison, Ian G. "History and Genealogies in a Conquest State." *American Anthropologist* 59 (1957), pp. 20-31.

De Goeje, Michael Jan. *Mémoire sur la conquête de la Syrie*. 2nd ed. Leiden: E. J. Brill, 1900.

———. *Mémoire sur le Fotouho's-Scham attribué à Abou Ismaïl al-Baçri*. Leiden: E. J. Brill, 1864.

Dennett, Daniel C. *Conversion and the Poll Tax in Early Islam*. Cambridge, Mass.: Harvard University Press, 1950.

Denny, Frederick Mathewson. "The Meaning of *Ummah* in the Qur'ān." *History of Religions* 15 (1975), pp. 34-70.

———. "*Ummah* in the Constitution of Medina." *Journal of Near Eastern Studies* 36 (1977), pp. 39-47.

Devreesse, Robert. *Le Patriarchat d'Antioche depuis la Paix de l'Eglise jusqu'à la conquête arabe*. Paris: J. Gabalda et Cie., 1945.

Dickson, Harold R. P. *The Arab of the Desert. A Glimpse into Badawin Life in Kuwait and Sau'di Arabia*. London: George Allen and Unwin, 1949.

Dillemann, Louis. *Haute-Mésopotamie orientale et pays adjacents*. Paris: P. Geuthner, 1962.

Doe, Brian. *Southern Arabia*. London: Thames and Hudson, 1971.

Donner, Fred McGraw. "The Arabic Sources for the Rise of Islam." (forthcoming)

———. "The Bakr b. Wā'il Tribes and Politics in Northeastern Arabia on the Eve of Islam." *Studia Islamica* 29 (1980), pp. 5-38.

———. "A Fragment of Ibn A'tham al-Kūfī's *Kitāb al-Futūḥ* dealing with the Caliphate of Abū Bakr." (forthcoming)

———. "Mecca's Food Supplies and Muḥammad's Boycott." *Journal of the Economic and Social History of the Orient* 20 (1977), pp. 249-266.

———. "Muḥammad's Political Consolidation in Western Arabia up to the Conquest of Mecca: A Reassessment." *Muslim World* 69 (1979), pp. 229-247.

Dostal, Walter. "The Evolution of Bedouin Life." In F. Gabrieli, ed. *L'Antica Società Beduina*. Rome: Università di Roma, Centro di Studi Semitici, 1959, pp. 11-34.

———. "Zur Frage der Entwicklung des Beduinentums." *Archiv für Völkerkunde* 13 (1958), pp. 1-14.

Doughty, Charles M. *Travels in Arabia Deserta*. 2 vols. 3rd ed. New York: Boni and Liveright, Inc., 1923.

Dussaud, René, and Frédéric Macler. *Mission scientifique dans les régions désertiques de la Syrie moyenne*. Paris: Imprimerie nationale, E. Leroux, 1903.

Dussaud, René. *La Pénétration des Arabes en Syrie avant l'Islam*. Paris: P. Geuthner, 1955.

———. *Topographie historique de la Syrie antique et médiévale*. Paris: P. Geuthner, 1927.

Ebert, Charles H. V. "Water Resources and Land Use in the Qaṭīf Oasis of Saudi Arabia." *Geographical Review* 55 (1965), pp. 469-509.

Eichner, Wolfgang. "Die Nachrichten über den Islam bei den Byzantinern." *Der Islam* 23 (1936), pp. 133-162, pp. 197-244.

Encyclopaedia of Islam. 1st ed. Edited by M. T. Houtsma et al. 4 vols. Leiden: E. J. Brill, 1913-1934; 2nd ed. Edited by H.A.R. Gibb et al. Leiden: E. J. Brill, 1960-.

Eph'al, I. " 'Arabs' in Babylonia in the Eighth century B.C." *Journal of the American Oriental Society* 94 (1974), pp. 108-115.

Fahd, Toufic. *Le Panthéon de l'Arabie centrale à la veille de l'Hégire*. Paris: P. Geuthner, 1968.

Farès, Édouard. *L'Honneur chez les Arabes avant l'Islam. Étude de sociologie*. Paris: Adrien-Maisonneuve, 1932.

Fernea, Robert A. *Shaykh and Effendi. Changing Patterns of Authority among the El Shabana of Southern Iraq*. Cambridge, Mass.: Harvard University Press, 1970.

Field, Henry, and John Bagot Glubb. *Yezidis, Sulubba and Other Tribes of Iraq and Adjacent Regions*. Menasha, Wisconsin: Banta, 1943.

Fiey, Jean-Maurice. *Assyrie chrétienne*. 3 vols. Beirut: Dar al-Mashriq, 1965-1968.
———. *Les Dioceses du 'Maphrianat' syrien, 629-1860*. Dissertation, Dijon, 1972.
———. *Jalons pour une histoire de l'Église en Iraq*. Louvain and Washington: Corpus Scriptorum Christianorum Orientalium, 1970.
———. "Tağrīt." *L'Orient syrien* 8 (1963), pp. 289-342.
———. "Topographie chrétienne de Mahozé." *L'Orient syrien* 12 (1967), pp. 397-420.
———. "Topography of al-Madā'in." *Sumer* 23 (1967), pp. 3-38.
Fisher, William Bayne. *The Middle East. A Physical, Social, and Regional Geography*. 5th ed. London: Methuen and New York: E. P. Dutton, 1963.
Fogg, W. "A Moroccan Tribal Shrine and its Relation to a Near-by Tribal Market." *Man* 40 (1940), pp. 100-104 (item no. 124).
Fortes, Meyer, and E. E. Evans-Pritchard, eds. *African Political Systems*. Oxford: Oxford University Press, 1940. Reprinted 1967.
Fraenkel, Siegmund. "Das Schutzrecht der Araber." In Carl Bezold, ed. *Orientalische Studien Theodor Nöldeke*, 1. Giessen: A. Töpelmann, 1906, pp. 293-301.
Fried, Morton H. *The Evolution of Political Society*. New York: Random House, 1967.
———. "On the Concepts of 'Tribe' and 'Tribal Society.' " *Transactions of the New York Academy of Science* 28, no. 4, series 2 (1966), pp. 527-540.
———, ed. *Readings in Anthropology*. 2 vols. New York: Thomas Y. Crowell, 1959.
Friedländer, Israel. "The Jews of Arabia and the Gaonate." *Jewish Quarterly Review* 1 (1910-1911), pp. 249-252.
Fries, Nicolaus. *Das Heereswesen der Araber zur Zeit der Omaijaden nach Ṭabarī*. Tübingen, 1921.
Funk, Salomon. *Die Juden in Babylonien, 200-500*. Berlin: M. Poppelauer, 1902.
Gabriel, Alfons. *Religionsgeographie von Persien*. Vienna: Hollinek, 1971.
Gabrieli, Francesco, ed. *L'Antica Società Beduina*. Rome: Università di Roma, Centro di Studi Semitici, 1959.
———. *Muhammad and the Conquests of Islam*. New York and Toronto: McGraw-Hill, 1968.
Glidden, Harold. "A Note on Early Arabian Military Organization." *JAOS* 56 (1936), pp. 88-91.
Glubb, J. C. [read John Bagot]. "The Bedouins of Northern 'Iraq [read Northern Arabia]." *Journal of the Royal Central Asian Society* 22 (1935), pp. 13-31.
Goldziher, Ignaz. *Muslim Studies*. 2 vols. London: George Allen and Unwin, Ltd., 1967. German original *Muhammedanische Studien*. 2 vols. Halle: Max Niemeyer, 1889-1890.
Great Britain Admiralty War Staff, Intelligence Division. *A Handbook of Mesopotamia*. 4 vols. n.p., 1916-1917.
Grohmann, Adolf. *Arabien*. Munich: C. H. Beck, 1963 (= *Handbuch der Altertumswissenschaften*, III.1.3.4)
Halévy, Joseph. "Les Arabes dans les inscriptions Sabéenes." *Revue sémitique d'épigraphie et d'histoire ancienne* 7 (1899), pp. 146-157.
Hamidullah, Muhammad. "Les 'Aḥābīsh' de la Mecque." In *Studi Orientalistici*

in Onore di Giorgio Levi della Vida, 1. Rome: Istituto per l'Oriente, 1956, pp. 434-447.

———. *Le Prophète de l'Islam*. 2 vols. Paris: Vrin, 1959.

Hansman, John. "Charax and the Karkheh." *Iranica Antiqua* 7 (1967), pp. 21-58.

Hardy, Michael J. L. *Blood Feuds and the Payment of Blood Money in the Middle East*. Leiden: E. J. Brill, 1963.

al-Hāshimī, Ṭāha. "Ma'rakat Ajnādayn: matā waqa'at wa ayna waqa'at?" *Majallat al-Majma' al-'Ilmī al-'Irāqī* 2 (1951), pp. 69-102.

Henninger, Joseph. "La religion bédouine préislamique." In F. Gabrieli, ed. *L'Antica Società Beduina*." Rome: Università di Roma, Centro di Studi Semitici, 1959, pp. 115-140.

Herzfeld, Ernst. *Geschichte der Stadt Samarra*. Hamburg: Eckardt und Messtorff, 1948.

———. "Hatra." *Zeitschrift der Deutschen Morgenländischen Gesellschaft* 68 (1914), pp. 655-676.

———. "Khorasan. Denkmalsgeographische Studien zur Kulturgeschichte des Islam in Iran." *Der Islam* 11 (1921), pp. 107-174.

——— and Friedrich Sarre. *Archaeologische Reise im Euphrat- und Tigris-Gebiete*. 4 vols. Berlin: D. Reimer, 1911-1920.

Hess, J. J. *Von den Beduinen Innern Arabiens—Erzählung/Lieder/Sitten und Gebräuche*. Zürich, 1938.

Higgins, Martin J. *The Persian War of the Emperor Maurice (582-602). Part I, The Chronology, with a Brief History of the Persian Calendar*. Washington: The Catholic University of America Press, 1939.

Hill, Donald Routledge. "The Role of the Camel and the Horse in the Early Arab Conquests." In V. J. Parry and M. E. Yapp, eds. *War, Technology, and Society in the Middle East*. London: Oxford University Press, 1975.

Hinds, Martin. "Kûfan Political Alignments and Their Background in the Mid-Seventh Century A.D." *International Journal of Middle East Studies* 2 (1971), pp. 346-367.

Höfner, Maria. "Die Beduinen in den vorislamischen arabischen Inschriften." In Francesco Gabrieli, ed. *L'Antica Società Beduina*. Roma: Centro di Studi Semitici, Università di Roma, 1959, pp. 53-68.

———. "Die Kultur des vorislamischen Südarabien." *Zeitschrift der deutschen morgenländischen Gesellschaft* 99 (1945-1949), pp. 15-28.

———. "War der sabäische Mukarrib ein 'Priesterfürst' ? " *Wiener Zeitschrift für die Kunde des Morgenlandes* 54 (1957), pp. 77-85.

Hurgronje, Christiaan Snouck. "Sa'd ès-Suwênî, ein seltsamer Walî in Ḥadhramôt." *Zeitschrift für Assyriologie* 26 (1912), pp. 221-239.

Ingrams, William Harold. *A Report on the Social, Economic, and Political Conditions of the Hadramaut*. London: Colonial Office, 1936.

Irons, William. "Livestock Raiding among Pastoralists: An Adaptive Interpretation." *Papers of the Michigan Academy of Science, Arts, and Letters* 50 (1965), pp. 393-414.

Izutsu, Toshihiku. *Ethico-Religious Concepts in the Qur'ān*. Montreal: McGill University Press, 1966.

Jacob, Georg. *Altarabisches Beduinenleben*. Berlin, 1897. Reprinted Hildesheim: Georg Olms, 1967.

Jaeger, Werner. *Early Christianity and Greek Paideia*. Cambridge, Mass.: Belknap Press of Harvard University Press, 1961.

Jamme, Albert. "Le panthéon sud-arabe préislamique d'après les sources épigraphiques." *Le Muséon* 60 (1947), pp. 55-147.

———. *Sabaean Inscriptions from Maḥram Bilqis (Marib)*. Baltimore: Johns Hopkins University Press, 1962.

al-Janābī, Kāẓim. *Takhṭīṭ madīnat al-Kūfa*. Baghdad: al-Majma' al-'Ilmī al-'Irāqī, 1967.

Jaussen, Antonin. *Coutumes des Arabes au pays de Moab*. Paris: J. Gabalda, 1908. Reprinted Paris: Maisonneuve, 1948.

——— and Raphaël Savignac. *Coutumes des Fuqarâ*. Paris: E. Leroux, 1914 (= *Mission archéologique en Arabie, supplement au volume II*).

Jones, Arnold Hugh Martin. *The Cities of the Eastern Roman Provinces*. Oxford: Clarendon Press, 1971.

Jones, J.M.B. "The Chronology of the *Maghāzī*—a textual survey." *Bulletin of the School of Oriental and African Studies* (University of London) 19 (1975), pp. 245-280.

Juynboll, G.H.A. "The Qurrā' in Early Islamic History." *Journal of the Economic and Social History of the Orient* 16 (1973), pp. 113-129.

Kaḥḥāla, 'Umar Riḍā. *Mu'jam qabā'il al-'arab*. 3 vols. Beirut: Dār al-'Ilm li-l-Malāyīn, 1968.

al-Kasab, Nafi Nasser. *Die Nomadenansiedlung in der Irakischen Jezira*. Tübingen: Selbstverlag des Geographischen Instituts der Universität Tübingen, 1966.

Kawar, Irfan. "The Arabs in the Peace Treaty of A.D. 561." *Arabica* 3 (1957), pp. 181-213.

———. "Arethas, Son of Jabalah." *Journal of the American Oriental Society* 75 (1955), pp. 205-216.

———. "Ghassān and Byzantium: A New terminus a quo." *Der Islam* 33 (1958), pp. 145-158.

———. "The Last Days of Salīḥ." *Arabica* 5 (1958), pp. 145-158.

———. "Procopius on the Ghassānids." *Journal of the American Oriental Society* 77 (1957), pp. 79-87.

Kennett, Austin. *Bedouin Justice. Laws and Customs among the Egyptian Bedouin*. Cambridge: Cambridge University Press, 1925. Reprinted London: Frank Cass and Co. Ltd., 1968.

Khālidi, Ismā'īl R. "The Arab Kingdom of Ghassān: its origins, rise, and fall." *Moslem World* 46 (1956), pp. 193-206.

Kirchhoff, Paul. "The Principles of Clanship in Human Society." *Davidson Journal of Anthropology* (1955). Reprinted in Morton H. Fried, ed. *Readings in Anthropology*, 2. 2nd ed. New York: Crowell, 1968, pp. 370-381.

Kister, Meir J. "Al-Ḥīra—Some Notes on Its Relations with Arabia." *Arabica* 15 (1968), pp. 143-169.

———. "Mecca and Tamīm (Aspects of their Relations)." *Journal of the Economic and Social History of the Orient* 8 (1965), pp. 113-163.

Kister, Meir J. "Some Reports Concerning Mecca from Jāhiliyya to Islam." *Journal of the Economic and Social History of the Orient* 15 (1972), pp. 61-93.

Labourt, Jérôme. *Le Christianisme dans l'empire perse sous la dynastie sassanide (224-632).* 2nd ed. Paris: V. Lecoffre, 1904.

Lammens, Henri. *L'Arabie occidentale avant l'Hégire.* Beirut: Imprimerie Catholique, 1928.

———. *Le Berceau de l'Islam. L'Arabie occidentale à la veille de l'Hégire, Vol. I: Le climat—Les bédouins.* Rome: Pontificium Institutum Biblicum, 1914.

———. "*La Cité arabe de Ṭāif à la veille de l'Hégire.*" Beirut: Imprimerie Catholique, 1922.

———. "Études sur le règne du Calife Omaiyade Mo'awiya Ier." *Mélanges de l'Université Saint-Joseph* (Beirut) 1-3 (1906-1908).

———. "La Mecque à la veille de l'Hégire." *Mélanges de l'Université Saint-Joseph* (Beirut) 9 (1924), pp. 97-439.

———. "La République marchande de la Mecque vers l'an 600 de notre ère." *Bulletin de l'Institut Égyptien,* 5e serie 4 (1910), pp. 23-54.

———. "Les sanctuaires préislamites dans l'Arabie occidentale." *Mélanges de l'Université Saint-Joseph* (Beirut) 11 (1926), pp. 39-173.

Larsen, Curtis E. "The Mesopotamian Delta Region: A Reconsideration of Lees and Falcon." *Journal of the American Oriental Society* 95 (1975), pp. 43-57.

Leeds, Anthony, and Andrew P. Vayda, eds. *Man, Culture and Animals. The Role of Animals in Human Ecological Adjustments.* Washington: American Association for the Advancement of Science, 1965 (publication no. 78).

Lees, George Martin, and N. L. Falcon. "The Geographical History of the Mesopotamian Plains." *Geographical Journal* 118 (1952), pp. 24-39.

Le Strange, Guy. *Lands of the Eastern Caliphate.* Cambridge: Cambridge University Press, 1905. Reprinted London: Frank Cass and Co. Ltd., 1966.

Lewis, Bernard. *The Arabs in History.* Revised ed. London: Hutchinson & Co. Ltd, 1958. Reprinted New York: Harper and Row, 1960.

Maricq, André. "Vologésias, l'emporium de Ctesiphon." *Syria* 36 (1959), pp. 264-276.

Massignon, Louis. "Explication du plan de Baṣra (Irak)." *Westöstliche Abhandlungen Rudolf Tschudi zum 70. Geburtstag.* Edited by Fritz Meier. Wiesbaden: Otto Harrassowitz, 1954, pp. 154-174.

———. "Explication du plan de Kûfa (Irak)." *Mélanges Maspéro* 3. Cairo: Institut Français d'Archeologie Orientale, 1940, pp. 337-360.

Matthews, Charles S. "Bedouin Life in Contemporary Arabia." *Rivista degli Studi Orientali* 35 (1960), pp. 31-61.

Mayerson, Philip. "The First Muslim Attacks on Southern Palestine (A.D. 633-634)." *Transactions and Proceedings of the American Philological Association* 95 (1964), pp. 155-199.

Menasce, R. "L'Église mazdéenne dans l'empire sassanide." *Cahiers d'histoire mondiale* 5 (1955), pp. 554-565.

Mitchell, R. C. "Recent tectonic movement in the Mesopotamian plains." *Geographical Journal* 123 (1957), pp. 569-571.

Montagne, Robert. "Contes poétiques bédouins (recueillis chez les Šammar de

Ğezīré)." *Bulletin d'études orientales* (de l'Institut Français de Damas) 5 (1935), pp. 33-120.

———. *La Civilisation du désert. Nomades d'Orient et d'Afrique.* Paris: Hachette, 1947.

———. "Notes sur la vie sociale et politique de l'Arabie du Nord." *Revue des études islamiques* 6 (1932), pp. 61-79.

Morony, Michael G. "Religious Communities in Late Sasanian and Early Islamic Iraq." *Journal of the Economic and Social History of the Orient* 17 (1974), pp. 113-135.

Moscati, Sabatino. *The Semites in Ancient History. An inquiry into the settlement of the Beduin and their political establishment.* Cardiff: University of Wales Press, 1959.

Mouterde, René, and Antoine Poidebard. "La voie antique des caravans entre Palmyre et Hīt au IIe siècle après J.-C." *Syria* 12 (1931), pp. 101-114.

Muir, Sir William. *The Caliphate: its Rise, Decline and Fall.* London: The Religious Tract Society, 1898. Reprinted Beirut: Khayats, 1963.

al-Munajjid, Ṣalāḥ al-Dīn. *A'lām al-ta'rīkh wa l-jughrāfiyā 'inda l-'Arab.* Beirut: Mu'assasa al-turāth al-'arabī, 1959.

Muranyi, Miklos. *Die Prophetengenossen in der frühislamischen Geschichte.* Bonn: Selbstverlag des Orientalischen Seminars der Universität Bonn, 1973.

Murphy, Robert F., and Leonard Kasdan. "The Structure of Parallel Cousin Marriage." *American Anthropologist* 61 (1959), pp. 17-29.

Musil, Alois. *Arabia Deserta.* New York: American Geographical Society, 1927 (Oriental Explorations and Studies, no. 2).

———. *The Manners and Customs of the Rwala Bedouins.* New York: American Geographical Society, 1928 (Oriental Explorations and Studies, no. 6).

———. *The Middle Euphrates.* New York: American Geographical Society, 1927 (Oriental Explorations and Studies, no. 3).

———. *The Northern Ḥeğâz.* New York: American Geographical Society, 1926 (Oriental Explorations and Studies, no. 1).

———. *The Northern Neğd.* New York: American Geographical Society, 1928 (Oriental Explorations and Studies, no. 5)

———. *Palmyrena.* New York: American Geographical Society, 1928 (Oriental Explorations and Studies, no. 4).

Mustafa, Muhammad 'Ali. "Preliminary Report on the Excavations in Kūfa during the Third Season." *Sumer* 19 (1963), pp. 36-65.

Nallino, C. A. "Sulla costituzione delle tribù arabe prima dell'islamismo." In *Raccolta di scritti editi e inediti* 3. Rome: Istituto per l'Oriente, 1941, pp. 64-86 (written in 1893).

Nau, François. *Les Arabes chrétiens de Mésopotamie et de Syrie du VIIe au VIIIe Siecle.* Paris: Imprimerie Nationale, 1933.

Nelson, Cynthia, ed. *The Desert and the Sown—Nomads in the Wider Society.* Berkeley: Institute of International Studies, 1973.

Neusner, Jacob. *A History of the Jews in Babylonia.* 5 vols. Leiden: E. J. Brill, 1965-1970.

Newman, Julius. *The Agricultural Life of the Jews in Babylonia between the years 200 C.E. and 500 C.E.* London: Oxford University Press, 1932.

Nielsen, Ditlef. *Handbuch der altarabischen Altertumskunde.* Copenhagen: Nyt Nordisk Forlag, Arnold Busck, 1927.

Nieuwenhuijze, Christoffel Anthonie Olivier van. *Sociology of the Middle East. A Stocktaking and Interpretation.* Leiden: E. J. Brill, 1971.

Niewenhuise, G. "The *umma*, an Analytic Approach." *Studia Islamica* 10 (1959), pp. 5-22.

Nissen, Hans Jörg. "Südbabylonien in parthischer und sasanidischer Zeit." *Baghdader Mitteilungen* 6 (1973), pp. 79-86.

Nodelman, Sheldon A. "A Preliminary History of Characene." *Berytus* 13 (1960), pp. 83-121.

Nöldeke, Theodor. "Die Ghassânischen Fürsten aus dem Hause Gafna's." *Abhandlungen der königlichen Akademie der Wissenschaften zu Berlin.* 1887, 2, pp. 1-63.

———. "Die Traditionen über das Leben Muhammeds." *Der Islam* 5 (1914), pp. 160-170.

———. "Zur Geschichte der Araber im 1. Jahrhundert d. H. aus syrischen Quellen." *Zeitschrift der Deutschen Morgenländischen Gesellschaft* 29 (1875), pp. 76-98.

———. "Zur Orientalischen Geographie." *Zeitschrift der Deutschen Morgenländischen Gesellschaft* 28 (1874), pp. 93-102.

———. "Zur Topographie und Geschichte des Damascenischen Gebiets und der Haurângegend." *Zeitschrift der Deutschen Morgenländischen Gesellschaft* 29 (1875), pp. 419-444.

Noth, Albrecht. "Iṣfahān-Nihāwand. Eine quellenkritische Studie zur frühislamischen Historiographie." *Zeitschrift der Deutschen Morgenländischen Gesellschaft* 118 (1968), pp. 274-296.

———. *Quellenkritische Studien zu Themen, Formen, und Tendenzen frühislamischer Geschichtsüberlieferung.* Bonn: Selbstverlag des Orientalischen Seminars der Universität Bonn, 1973.

Obermeyer, Jacob. *Die Landschaft Babylonien im Zeitalter des Talmuds und des Gaonats.* Frankfurt am Main: Kaufmann, 1929.

Olinder, Gunnar. *The Kings of Kinda of the Family of Ākil al-Murār.* Lund: C.W.K. Gleerup, 1927.

Oppenheim, Max Adrian Simon von. *Die Beduinen.* 4 vols. Leipzig and Wiesbaden: Otto Harrassowitz, 1939-1968. Vols. 3, 4 edited by Werner Caskel.

Ostrogorsky, George. *History of the Byzantine State.* Revised ed. New Brunswick: Rutgers University Press, 1969.

Paret, Roger. "Note sur un passage de Malalas concernant les phylarques arabes." *Arabica* 5 (1958), pp. 251-262.

———. "Les Villes de Syrie du Sud et les routes commerciales d'Arabie à la fin du VIe siecle." *Akten des XI. Internationalen Byzantinisten-Kongresses, München 1958.* Munich: C. H. Beck, 1960, pp. 438-444.

Patai, Raphael. "The Structure of Endogamous Unilineal Descent Groups." *Southwestern Journal of Anthropology* 21 (1965), pp. 325-350.

Patton, Walter M. "Blood-revenge in Arabia and Israel." *American Journal of Theology* 5 (1901), pp. 703-731.

Pauly, August Friedrich von, and G. Wissowa. *Paulys Real-Encyclopädie der Classischen Altertumswissenschaften.* Revised ed. by G. Wissowa. Stuttgart: J. B. Metzler, 1894-1963, with supplements.

Peppelenbosch, P.G.N. "Nomadism on the Arabian Peninsula—A General Appraisal." *Tijdschrift voor economische en sociale Geografie* 59 (1968), pp. 335-346.

Pernice, Angelo. *L'Imperatore Eraclio.* Florence: Galletti e Cocci, 1905.

Peters, Emrys. "The Proliferation of Segments in the Lineage of the Bedouin of Cyrenaica (Libya)." *Journal of the Royale Anthropological Institute* 90 (1960), pp. 29-53. Reprinted in L. Sweet, ed. *Peoples and Cultures of the Middle East,* 1. Garden City, N.Y.: Natural History Press, 1970, pp. 363-398.

Pigulevskaja, Nina Viktorovna. *Les Villes de l'état iranien aux époques parthe et sassanide.* Paris and The Hague: Mouton, 1963.

Proudfoot, Ann S. "The Sources of Theophanes for the Heraclian Dynasty." *Byzantion* 44 (1974), pp. 367-439.

Qāsim, 'Awn al-Sharīf. *Diblūmāsiyyat Muḥammad.* Khartum: Dār al-Ṭibā'a, Jāmi'at al-Kharṭūm, n.d. (ca. 1965).

Raswan, Carl. *Black Tents of Arabia.* New York: Creative Age Press, 1935. Reprinted New York: Farrar, Straus & Giroux, 1971.

———. "Tribal Areas and Migration Lines of the North-Arabian Bedouins." *Geographical Review* 20 (1930), pp. 494-502.

Ratjens, Carl. "Kulturelle Einflüsse in Südwest-Arabien von den ältesten Zeiten bis zum Islam, unter besonderer Berücksichtigung des Hellenismus." *Jahrbuch für Kleinasiatische Forschung* 1 (1950-1951), pp. 1-42.

Reinaud, Joseph Toussaint. "Mémoire sur le commencement et la fin du royaume de la Mésène et de la Kharacène." *Journal asiatique* 18 (1861), pp. 161-262.

Reinert, Werner. *Das Recht in der altarabischen Poesie.* Dissertation, Köln, 1963.

Rhodokanakis, Nikolaus. "Die Bodenwirtschaft im alten Südarabien." *Anzeiger der kaiserlichen Akademie der Wissenschaften in Wien,* Philologische-Historische Klasse 53 (1916), pp. 173-204.

Rice, David Talbot. "Ḥīra." *Journal of the Royal Central Asiatic Society* 19 (1932), pp. 254-268.

———. "The Oxford Excavations at Hira." *Ars Islamica* 1 (1934), pp. 51-74.

Rodinson, Maxime. "Bilan des études mohammadiennes." *Revue historique* 229 (1963), pp. 169-220.

———. "The Life of Muhammad and the Sociological Problem of the Beginnings of Islam." *Diogenes* 20 (1957), pp. 28-51.

———. *Mohammed.* New York: Vintage Books, 1974. French original *Mahomet.* 1st ed. Paris: Club français du livre, 1961.

Rosenfeld, Henry L. "The Social Composition of the Military in the Process of State Formation in the Arabian Desert." *Journal of the Royal Anthropological Institute* 95 (1965), pp. 75-86 and pp. 174-194.

Rossi, Ettore. "Il diritto consuetudinario delle tribù Arabe del Yemen." *Rivista degli Studi Orientali* 23 (1948), pp. 1-36.

Rothstein, Gustav. *Die Dynastie der Lahmiden in al-Ḥîra. Ein Versuch zur arabisch-persischen Geschichte zur Zeit der Sasaniden.* Berlin: Reuther, 1899.

Rowton, M. B. "Autonomy and Nomadism in Western Asia." *Orientalia* 42 (1973), pp. 247-258.

———. "Enclosed Nomadism." *Journal of the Economic and Social History of the Orient* 17 (1974), pp. 1-30.

———. "The Physical Environment and the Problem of the Nomads." In Jean Robert Kupper, ed. *XVe Rencontre assyriologique International (1966).* Paris: Société d'Éditions "Les Belles Lettres," 1967, pp. 109-121.

———. "Urban Autonomy in a Nomadic Environment." *Journal of Near Eastern Studies* 32 (1973), pp. 201-215.

Rutter, Eldon. "The Habitability of the Arabian Desert." *Geographical Journal* 76 (1930), pp. 512-515.

Ryckmans, Gonzague. *Les Réligions arabes préislamiques.* 2nd ed. Louvain: Publications Universitaires, 1951.

Ryckmans, Jacques. *L'Institution monarchique en Arabie méridionale avant l'Islam (Ma'în et Saba).* Louvain: Publications Universitaires, 1951.

Sachau, Eduard. "Der erste Chalife Abu Bekr." *Sitzungsberichte der königlichen Preussischen Akademie der Wissenschaften* 43 (1903), pp. 16-37.

Safar, Fuad. *Wâsiṭ: The Sixth Season's Excavations.* Cairo: Institut Français d'Archeologie Orientale, 1945.

Sahlins, Marshall D. "Segmentary Lineage: An Organization of Predatory Expansion." *American Anthropologist* 63 (1961), pp. 322-345.

———. *Tribesmen.* Englewood Cliffs, N.J.: Prentice-Hall, 1968.

Saint-Martin, Antoine-Jean. *Récherches sur l'histoire et la géographie de la Mésène et de la Characène.* Paris: Imprimerie Royale, 1838.

Salzman, Philip C. "Political Organization among Nomadic Peoples." *Proceedings of the American Philosophical Society* 111 (1967), pp. 115-131.

El-Samarraie, Husam Qawam. *Agriculture in Iraq during the Third Century A.H.* Beirut: Librarie du Liban, 1972.

Saunders, John Joseph. "The Nomad as Empire Builder: A Comparison of the Arab and Mongol Conquests." *Diogenes* 52 (1965), pp. 79-103.

Sauvaget, Jean. "Esquisse d'une histoire de la ville de Damas." *Revue des études islamiques* 8 (1934), pp. 421-480.

Schaeder, Hans Heinrich. "Ḥasan al-Baṣrī. Studien zur Frühgeschichte des Islam." *Der Islam* 14 (1924), pp. 1-75.

Schmucker, Werner. *Untersuchungen zu einigen wichtigen bodenrechtlichen Konsequenzen der islamischen Eroberungsbewegung.* Bonn: Selbstverlag des Orientalischen Seminars der Universität Bonn, 1972.

Segal, Judah B. *Edessa and Harran.* London: School of Oriental and African Studies, University of London, 1963.

———. *Edessa, 'The Blessed City'.* Oxford: Clarendon Press, 1970.

———. "Mesopotamian Communities from Julian to the Rise of Islam." *Proceedings of the British Academy* 41 (1955), pp. 109-139.

Serjeant, Robert Bertram Y. "The Constitution of Medina." *Islamic Quarterly* 8 (1964), pp. 3-16.

———. "Ḥaram and Ḥawṭah, the Sacred Enclave in Arabia." In Abdurrahman Badawi, ed. *Mélanges Taha Husain*. Cairo: Dār al-Maʻārif, 1962, pp. 41-58.

———. "Saint Sergius." *Bulletin of the School of Oriental and African Studies* (University of London) 22 (1959), pp. 574-575.

———. *The Saiyids of Ḥaḍramawt*. London: School of Oriental and African Studies, University of London, 1957.

———. "Two Tribal Law Cases (Documents) (Wāḥidī Sultanate, South-West Arabia)." *Journal of the Royal Asiatic Society* (1951), pp. 33-47 and pp. 156-169.

Service, Elman R. *Primitive Social Organization*. New York: Random House, 1962.

Seyfarth, Wolfgang. "Nomadenvölker an den Grenzen des spätrömischen Reiches." In *Das Verhältnis von Bodenbauern und Viehzüchtern in Historischer Sicht*. Berlin: Akademie-Verlag, 1968, pp. 207-213 (Deutsche Akademie der Wissenschaften zu Berlin, Institut für Orientforschung, Veröffentlichung Nr. 69).

Sezgin, Fuat. *Geschichte des arabischen Schrifttums*. 5 vols. Leiden: E. J. Brill, 1967-1975.

Shaban, Muhammad Abdulhayy. *Islamic History, A.D. 600-750 (A.H. 132). A New Interpretation*. Cambridge: Cambridge University Press, 1971.

Shoufani, Elias S. *Al-Riddah and the Muslim Conquest of Arabia*. Toronto: University of Toronto Press, and Beirut: Arab Institute for Research and Publishing, 1972.

Smith, William Robertson. *Kinship and Marriage in Early Arabia*. London: A. and C. Black, 1903. Reprinted Boston: Beacon Press, n.d. (ca. 1965).

———. *Lectures on the Religion of the Semites. The Fundamental Institutions*. 2nd ed. London: A. and C. Black, 1894. Reprinted New York: Schocken Books, 1972.

Spencer, Robert F. "The Arabian Matriarchate: An Old Controversy." *Southwestern Journal of Anthropology* 8 (1952), pp. 478-502.

Spooner, Brian. *The Cultural Ecology of Pastoral Nomads*. Reading, Mass.: Addison-Wesley, ca. 1975.

Stein, Lothar. *Die Šammar-Ǧerba. Beduinen im Übergang vom Nomadismus zur Sesshaftigkeit*. Berlin: Akademie-Verlag, 1967.

Stratos, Andreas N. *Byzantium in the Seventh Century, I: 602-634*. Amsterdam: Adolf M. Hakkert, 1968.

Streck, Maximilian. *Die alte Landschaft Babylonien nach den arabischen Geographen*. Leiden: E. J. Brill, 1900-1901.

Sūsa, Aḥmad. *al-ʻIrāq fī l-khawāriṭ al-qadīma*. Baghdad, 1959.

Sweet, Louise E. "Camel Pastoralism in North Arabia and the Minimal Camping Unit." In Anthony Leeds and Andrew P. Vayda, eds. *Man, Culture, and Animals. The Role of Animals in Human Ecological Adjustments*. Washington: American Association for the Advancement of Science, 1965, pp. 129-152.

———. "Camel Raiding of North Arabian Bedouin: A Mechanism of Ecological Adaptation." *American Anthropologist* 67 (1965), pp. 1132-1150.

Sweet, Louise E., ed. *Peoples and Cultures of the Middle East.* 2 vols. Garden City, N.Y.: Natural History Press, 1970.

Teixidor, Javier. "The Kingdom of Adiabene and Hatra." *Berytus* 17 (1967-1968), pp. 1-12.

———. "Notes hatréennes." *Syria* 43 (1966), pp. 91-97.

Thesiger, Wilfred. *Arabian Sands.* Harmondsworth: Penguin Books, 1964. Originally London: Longmans, Green, 1959.

———. "The Badu of Southern Arabia." *Journal of the Royal Central Asian Society* 37 (1950), pp. 53-61.

———. *The Marsh Arabs.* London: Longmans, 1964.

———. "Marsh Dwellers of Southern Iraq." *National Geographic Magazine* 113 (February, 1958), pp. 204-239.

Thilo, Ulrich. *Die Ortsnamen in der altarabischen Poesie.* Wiesbaden: Otto Harrassowitz, 1958.

Les Tribus nomades et seminomades des états du Levant placés sous mandat français. Beirut, 1930.

Vasiliev, Alexander Alexandrovich. *History of the Byzantine Empire, 324-1453.* 2nd English ed., revised. 2 vols. Madison, Wisconsin: University of Wisconsin Press, 1952.

———. "Notes on Some Episodes concerning the Relations between the Arabs and the Byzantine Empire from the Fourth to the Sixth Century." *Dumbarton Oaks Papers* 9-10 (1955-1956), pp. 303-316.

Veccia-Vaglieri, Laura. "The Patriarchal and Umayyad Caliphs." in P. M. Holt et al., eds. *The Cambridge History of Islam,* 1. Cambridge: Cambridge University Press, 1970, pp. 57-103.

Veselý, Rudolf. "Die Anṣār im ersten Bürgerkriege (36-40 d.H.)." *Archiv Orientální* 26 (1958), pp. 36-58.

Vidal, Federico S. *The Oasis of al-Hasa.* Dhahran: Arabian American Oil Co., 1955.

Vööbus, Arthur. "Reorganisierung der westsyrischen Kirche in Persien." *Oriens Christianus,* 4th series, 15 (1967), pp. 106-111.

Von Grunebaum, Gustav E. *Classical Islam: A History, 600 A.D.-1258 A.D.* Chicago: Aldine, 1970. German original *Der Islam in seiner klassischen Epoche, 622—1258.* Zürich and Stuttgart, Propyläen Verlag, 1966.

———. "The First Expansion of Islam: Factors of Thrust and Containment." *Diogenes* 53 (1966), pp. 64-72.

———. "The Nature of Arab Unity before Islam." *Arabica* 10 (1963), pp. 5-23.

Warmington, Eric Herbert. *The Commerce between the Roman Empire and India.* Cambridge: Cambridge University Press, 1928.

Watt, William Montgomery. *Muhammad at Mecca.* Oxford: Clarendon Press, 1953.

———. *Muhammad at Medina.* Oxford: Clarendon Press, 1956.

———. *Muhammad, Prophet and Statesman.* Oxford: Clarendon Press, 1961.

Wellhausen, Julius. *Prolegomena zur ältesten Geschichte des Islams.* Berlin: Reimer, 1899. (= *Skizzen,* 6:1.)

———. "Die religiös-politischen Oppositionsparteien im alten Islam." *Abhand-*

lungen der königlichen Gesellschaft der Wissenschaften zu Göttingen, Phil.-Hist. Klasse, new series, 5 no. 2 (1901), pp. 1-99.

———. *Reste Arabischen Heidentums*. 2nd ed. Berlin: Reimer, 1897. Reprinted Berlin: W. de Gruyter, 1927, 1961. (= *Skizzen*, 3.)

———. *Skizzen und Vorarbeiten*. 6 vols. Berlin: Reimer, 1884-1899.

Wensinck, Arent Jan. *Muhammad and the Jews of Medina*. Freiburg: Klaus Schwarz, 1975. Dutch original *Mohammed en de Joden te Medina*. Leiden: E. J. Brill, 1908.

Whitehouse, David. "Excavations at Sīrāf: First Interim Report." *Iran* 6 (1968), pp. 1-22.

———. "Excavations at Sīrāf: Fifth Interim Report." *Iran* 10 (1972), pp. 63-87.

———. "Excavations at Sīrāf: Sixth Interim Report."*Iran* 12 (1974), pp. 1-30.

———. "Sīrāf: A Sasanian Port." *Antiquity* 45 No. 180 (1971), pp. 262-266.

Widengren, Geo. *Muḥammad, the Apostle of God, and his Ascension*. Uppsala: A. B. Lundequistska and Wiesbaden: Otto Harrassowitz, 1955.

———. *Die Religionen Irans*. Stuttgart: Kohlhammer, 1965.

———. "The Status of Jews in the Sassanian Empire." *Iranica Antiqua* 1 (1961), pp. 117-162.

Wilkinson, John Craven. "The Julandā of Oman." *Journal of Oman Studies* 1 (1975), pp. 97-108.

Willcocks, William. *Irrigation of Mesopotamia*. 2nd ed. London: E and F. N. Spon, Ltd., and New York; Spon & Chamberlain, 1917.

———. "Mesopotamia: Past, Present, and Future." *Geographical Journal* 35 (1910), pp. 1-17.

Wirth, Eugen. *Agrargeographie des Irak*. Hamburg: Selbstverlag des Instituts für Geographie und Wirtschaftsgeographie der Universität Hamburg, 1962 (Hamburger Geographische Studien, 13).

———. *Syrien. Eine Geographische Landeskunde*. Darmstadt: Wissenschaftliche Buchgesellschaft, 1971.

Wissman, Hermann von. "Bauer, Nomade, und Stadt im islamischen Orient." In R. Paret, ed. *Die Welt des Islam und die Gegenwart*. Stuttgart: W. Kohlhammer, 1962, pp. 22-63.

———. "Ḥimyar, Ancient History." *Le Muséon* 77 (1964), pp. 429-499.

———. *Zur Archäologie und Antiken Geographie von Südarabien. Ḥaḍramaut, Qatabān und das 'Aden-Gebiet in der Antike*. Istanbul: Nederlands Historisch-Archaeologisch Instituut in Het Nabije Oosten, 1968 (Uitgaven van Nederlands Historisch-Archaeologisch Instituut te Istanbul, 24).

Wolf, Eric. "The Social Organization of Mecca and the Origins of Islam." *Southwestern Journal of Anthropology* 7 (1951), pp. 329-356.

Wüstenfeld, Ferdinand. "Die Wohnsitze und Wanderungen der arabischen Stämme." See al-Bakrī, Abū 'Ubayd 'Abdullāh.

Yusuf, Sayyid Muhammad. "The Battle of al-Qādisiyya." *Islamic Culture* 19 (1945), pp. 1-28.

Zaehner, Robert Charles. *Zurvan. A Zoroastrian Dilemma*. Oxford: Clarendon Press, 1955.

INDEX OF TRADITIONISTS MENTIONED IN NOTES AND APPENDICES

This list provides the names of traditionists mentioned in the Notes and Appendices; for traditionists mentioned in the text, see main index. Citations are by chapter and note number (e.g., II: 48) or by appendix and entry number (e.g., D 17). In alphabetizing, the article *al-* has been disregarded.

Ābān b. 'Aṭṭār, III: 95.
'Abāya b. 'Abd 'Amr, IV: 219; K 3 , 5, 24, 27.
al-'Abbās, IV: 103.
al-'Abbās b. Hishām b. Muḥammad al-Kalbī, IV: 104, 107; V: 97; H 2, 21.
'Abbās b. Sahl b. Sa'd, III: 205; V: 125.
al-'Abbās b. al-Walīd, IV: 194; G 46.
'Abda, IV: 219.
'Abd al-'Azīz (father of Marḥūm b. 'Abd al-'Azīz al-'Aṭṭār), IV: 219; K 3, 25.
'Abd al-Ḥamīd b. Ja'far, III: 46, 152.
'Abd al-Malik b. Ḥudhayfa, IV: 236; K 3, 18.
'Abd al-Malik b. Nawfal b. Musāḥiq, VI: 4, 55.
'Abd al-Malik b. Qarīb al-Aṣma'ī, *see* al-Aṣma'ī, 'Abd al-Malik b. Qarīb.
'Abd al-Malik b. 'Umayr, IV: 236; K 3, 18.
'Abd al-Raḥmān b. al-Aswad b. Yazīd al-Nakha'ī, G 42.
'Abd al-Raḥmān b. Jawshan, K 3, 8, 16.
'Abd al-Raḥmān b. Jaysh, V: 15, 18; G 7.
'Abd al-Raḥmān b. Jubayr, III: 117, 139, 140, 142, 160, 178, 204, 207, 209; V: 13; C 6.
'Abd al-Raḥmān b. Mahdī, V: 83; N 5, 6.
'Abd al-Raḥmān b. Siyāh al-Aḥmarī, III: 238; IV: 79.
'Abd al-Ṣamad b. 'Abd al-Wārith, III: 95.
'Abd al-Wahhāb b. al-Ḥasan III: 123.
'Abd al-Wārith b. 'Abd al-Ṣamad b. 'Abd al-Wārith, III: 95.
'Abduh b. Sulaymān, IV: 216; K 16.
'Abdullāh b. Abī Awfā al-Khuzā'ī, III: 140.
'Abdullāh b. Abī Bakr, II: 80; G 81.
'Abdullāh b. Abī Shayba, V: 42.
'Abdullāh b. Abī Ṭayba al-Bajalī, V: 10; G 4, 20, 22, 48: J 1.
'Abdullāh b. 'Awf, K 3.
'Abdullāh b. 'Awn, *see* Ibn 'Awn, 'Abdullāh.
'Abdullāh b. Ja'far, III: 192, 196; IV: 209, 232; VI: 7; L 7.
'Abdullāh b. Manda, VI: 27.
'Abdullāh b. al-Mughīra al-'Abdī, III: 205, 206; V: 123, 125.
'Abdullāh b. Muslim al-'Uklī, IV: 176; G 11, 21, 30, 89, 95, 96.
'Abdullāh b. Qays al-Hamdānī, V: 135.
'Abdullāh b. Ṣāliḥ al-'Ijlī, V: 109.
'Abdullāh b. Ṣāliḥ al-Muqri', III: 281, 292; IV: 216, 219; K 3, 8, 16.
'Abdullāh b. Ṣuhayb, VI: 5, 7.
'Abdullāh b. 'Ukaym, VI: 6.
'Abdullāh b. Wābiṣa al-'Absī, III: 151.
'Abdullāh b. Wahb al-Miṣrī, IV: 104, 107.
'Ābis al-Ju'fī, G 48, 112.
Abū l-'Āliya, III: 136.
Abū 'Amr, III: 36, 61, 65, 139, 140, 142, 196, 198, 285; IV: 172, 176, 234; V: 18; G 7, 9, 38, 62; L 49.
Abū 'Amr b. al-'Alā', H 21.
Abū 'Amr b. Ḥurayth al-'Udhrī, III: 35.
Abū 'Āṣim al-Rāmhurmuzī, IV: 233; L 7.
Abū l-Aswad, Muḥammad b. 'Abd al-Raḥmān b. al-Aswad b. Nawfal, III: 43, 192; IV: 103, 107; V: 94.
Abū 'Awāna, II: 113; IV: 174, 175; V: 21, 29; G 80; M 1, 2.
Abū Ayyūb, II: 147.
Abū Bakr al-Hudhalī, IV: 27; M 1, 40, 41.
Abū Bakr b. 'Abdullāh b. Abī Sabra, *see* Ibn Abī Sabra, Abū Bakr b. 'Abdullāh.
Abū Bakr b. 'Abdullāh b. Miryām, III: 118.

GENERAL INDEX

The following index lists all personal names found in the text, notes, and appendices, all place names found in the text and notes, and a number of subject entries (for example, "taxation"). Because Arabic personal names sometimes appear in conflicting forms in different texts, it has proven impossible to provide authoritative forms for many of them, and the entries should not be taken as such. In alphabetizing, the Arabic article *al-* and the abbreviation *b.*, "son of," are ignored.

Badāt canal, 163
Badr, 62, 63, 77, 104, 135, 202
Baghdad, 277
Bāhān, 131, 132, 140
Bahrā' (tribe), 108, 110, 122, 123, 187, 307
al-Baḥrayn, 85, 86, 177, 216, 230, 233, 267, 331
Bahurasīr (Veh-Ardashīr), 209
Bajāla (tribe?), 228
Bajīla (tribe), 68, 78, 88, 175, 178, 196, 197, 200, 201, 207-209, 215, 219, 221-223, 228, 235, 242, 260, 297, 314
Bakhtnaṣṣar, *see* Nebuchadnezzar
Bakr b. 'Abd Manāt (clan of Kināna), 67
Bakr b. Wā'il (tribe), 16, 19, 24, 25, 44, 86, 170, 171, 180, 183, 184, 188, 213, 330, 331
Ba'labakk, 112, 124, 132, 133, 141, 142, 146
al-Balādhurī, 118, 124, 158
Balī (tribe), 66, 88, 103-105, 109-111, 132, 147, 148, 207, 215, 219, 304
Balikh river, 185
Bālis, 246, 266
Balqā', 101, 103, 105, 107, 110, 115, 116, 141, 292, 307
Bal-Qayn (tribe), *see* al-qayn
Bāniqyā, 180
Ba'quba, 163
al-Barā' b. 'Āzib al-Anṣārī, 422
al-Barā' b. Mālik al-Anṣārī, 416, 421-422
Baradā river, 247
Barbīsamā, 163
Bāriq (clan of Azd), 196, 200, 205
Bārusmā, 163, 192
Barza, 131, 136
Bashīr b. Ka'b, 138, 318
Bashīr b. Ka'b b. Ubayy al-Ḥimyarī, 136
Bashīr b. al-Khaṣāṣiyya al-Dhuhlī, 203, 383, 398, 407, 431
Bashīr b. Sa'd Abū l-Nu'mān al-Anṣārī, 372
al-Basīṭa, 337
Basmā, 180
al-Baṣra, 160, 164, 165, 215-217, 232, 237, 239, 240, 243-245, 264, 277; foundation of, 213, 217; migration to, 232-233, 236; settlement of, 229-230
al-Bathaniyya, 137
al-Baṭīḥa, 158
bay'a 'arabiyya, 79
bay'at hijra, 79
Baysān (Beth Shan), 112, 130, 134, 137, 139, 146
Bayt Jibrīn, 129
Bayt Lihyā, 131
Beirut (Berytus), 92, 112, 154
Beroe, *see* Aleppo
Beth Shan, *see* Baysān
Bihqubād, 180
Bilāl, 139
Bilāl b. al-ḥārith al-Muzanī, 372
Biqā' (Coele-Syria), 95, 132-133
Bi'r Ma'ūna, 67
Bi'r al-Mulūṣī, 312
Bishr b. 'Abdullāh al-Hilālī, 206, 402
Bishr b. al-Muḥaffiz al-Muzanī, 423
Bishr b. Munqidh al-Hamdānī, 386, 426
Bishr b. Rabī'a al-Khath'amī, 402
Bisṭām b. 'Amr, 435
biṭrīq, 44, 115
blood feud, blood vengeance, 40, 58, 59, 72
booty, 47, 65, 80, 267, 271; as factor in conquests, 5-7; attraction of, 97; Syrian, divided by 'Umar, 151
Bostra (al-Buṣrā), 51, 95, 96, 112, 117, 123, 124, 129, 135, 140, 141, 145, 146
Bridge, battle of, 174, 175, 192-195, 197-200, 202, 208, 211, 219, 220, 260
Bujayr al-Ṭā'ī, 387
Bukayr b. 'Abdullāh al-Laythī, 402, 408
Bukayr b. Qays al-Hamdānī, 438
Bukayr al-Qaysī, 431
Bukayr b. Shīdākh, 435
Buqayla (clan of Azd), 183
bureaucracy, *see* administrators
Busr b. Abī Arṭāt al-'Āmirī, 313
Busr b. Abī Ruhm, 373, 385, 403
al-Buṣrā, *see* Bostra
Buwayb, battle of, 198-200, 211
Byzantines, Byzantine Empire, 4, 8, 41-45, 48, 73, 89, 92, 110, 172, 222, 223, 249, 266, 267, 269, 271; agents in Ḥijāz, 109; campaigns in Iraq, 203; in Mesopotamia, 169; resistance to conquests, 111-112, 114-116, 126, 128-150; response to early Islamic raids, 132-134; tribal allies of, 98-101, 103, 105-108, 113, 117, 129,

Michael the Syrian, 144, 146
migration, tribal, 3-7; to Iraq, 226-245; to Syria, 245-250; causes, 267-268
Mihrajān Qadhaq, 216
Mihrān, 198
Mikhnaf b. Sulaym al-Azdī, 197, 382, 399
Milḥān b. Zayyār al-Ṭā'ī, 132
militias, 29
Milṭāṭayn, 180
Mīnās, 149
mi'rāj, 97
monarchy, South Arabian, 37-38
Monophysites, Monophysitism, 94, 95, 249. *See also* Christianity
monotheism, 52, 56, 60, 61, 97
monsoon, 11
Moses, 52
Mosul, 227, 229, 239, 257
Mount Hermon, 91
Mu'ādh b. Ḥusayn al-Anṣārī, 377
Mu'ādh b. Jabal al-Khazrajī, 151, 152, 298, 358, 363
mu'ākhāt, 352
al-Mu'annā b. Ḥāritha al-Shaybānī, 203, 382, 397-398
Mu'āwiya (clan of Kinda), 139
Mu'āwiya b. Abī Sufyān, 139, 153, 154, 235, 247, 248, 266, 274-277
Mu'āwiya b. Ḥudayj al-Sakūnī, 207, 367, 396
Mu'āwiya b. Khadīj, 367
al-Mudaibir, 248
Muḍar (confederation), 178, 207, 232
al-Muḍārib b. Yazīd al-'Ijlī, 383, 398, 438
al-Muḍayya, 333
Mudlij (tribe), 67
al-Mughīra b. Shu'ba al-Thaqafī, 73, 176, 207, 212, 214-217, 264, 299, 341, 399-400, 414-415, 419, 432, 437, 438
al-Mughīra b. Zurāra al-Tamīmī, 391
al-Muhājir b. Abī Umayya, 87
Muhājir b. Ziyād b. al-Diyār, 426
muhājirūn, 77-80, 82, 83, 86, 88, 118, 119, 126, 178, 191-195, 202, 223. *See also* Quraysh
Muhalhal b. Zayd al-Ṭā'ī, 438
al-Muhallab b. 'Uqba al-Asadī, 139
Muḥallim (tribe), 24
Muḥammad, the Prophet, 8, 76-82, 86, 87, 89, 90, 96-99, 118, 135, 187, 201, 202, 237, 251-253, 256-258, 260, 261, 263, 265, 269, 273, 277; early career, 52-55; teachings and their political import, 55-62; political consolidation in Medina, 62-75; relations with northern Ḥijāz and southern Syria, 101-111; death, 82, 264
Muḥammad b. 'Abdullāh, 139, 140
Muḥammad b. Maslama al-Anṣārī, 431
Muḥārib (tribe), 228, 235, 314
Muhriz b. Ḥarīsh, 373
Muhriz b. Quraysh, 373
Mujāshi' b. Mas'ūd al-Sulamī, 214, 264, 416, 431
mukarrib, 14, 38
Munabbih "the elder" = Zubayd (clan of Madhḥij), 205, 206
munākh, 235
al-Mundhir b. Ḥassān al-Ḍabbī, 195, 384, 397, 410
muqaddima, 224
muqātila, 221-223, 229, 231, 238, 244
al-Muqtarib al-Aswad b. Rabī'a, 434
Murād (clan of Madhḥij), 42, 119, 207, 209, 211
murāmiya, 344
al-Muraysī', 299
Mu'riqa road, 115
Murra (clan of Dhuhl), 24
al-Musāwir b. al-Nu'mān al-Taymī, 397
Musaylima, *see* Maslama b. Ḥabīb
al-Musayyakh, 333
al-Musayyib, 364
mushā', 348
Musliya (clan of Madhḥij), 206, 211
al-Muṣṭaliq (tribe), 64
al-Mustawrid b. 'Ullafa, 397
Mu'ta, 101, 103, 105-110
al-Muthannā b. Ḥāritha al-Shaybānī, 87, 174-176, 181-183, 189-195, 197-200, 202, 203, 223, 261, 377-378, 380-381
al-Muthannā b. Lāḥiq al-'Ijlī, 182
al-Muẓallala, 298
Muzayna (tribe), 16, 74, 79, 87, 119, 126, 179, 201, 207, 215, 217-219, 228, 229, 254, 303, 334

al-Nabāj, 327
Nabataeans, 95
nabīd, 344

Sajāḥ, 85, 183
Sakūn (clan of Kinda), 88, 139, 147, 206, 209
Salama b. Hishām b. al-Mughīra al-Makhzūmī, 357, 368
Salama b. al-Muḥabbaq, 418
Salama b. al-Qayn, 434
Salāmān b. Sa'd Hudhaym (clan), 303
Salāṭ b. Qays al-Anṣārī, 376-377
Salīḥ (tribe), 43, 44, 108, 110, 154, 187, 307
Sālim b. Naṣr, 373
Sallām b. Abī l-Ḥuqayq, 297
Salmā, 36
Salmā bint Ḥafṣa/Khaṣafa al-Tamīmiyya, 203, 337, 392
Salma b. Rajā', 427
Salmān b. Rabī'a al-Bāhilī, 395, 407
Samaritans, 43, 151
Samosata, *see* Shimshāṭ
Samura b. Jundab al-Fazārī, 423
Ṣan'ā', 36
ṣanā'a, 291
al-Ṣandawdā', 121, 180, 185
sāqa, 224
al-Ṣaqallār, 132
Ṣaqallār b. Mikhrāq, 137
al-Saqāṭiya, 192
al-Sarāt, 68, 195-197, 200, 201, 204-206, 211, 219, 254
Sāriya b. Zunaym al-Kinānī, 431
Ṣarṣar canal, 163, 165
Sasanians, Sasanian Empire, 8, 41-48, 73, 87, 89, 99, 100, 107, 158, 168, 222, 223, 241, 253, 266, 267, 269, 271; weakness of, as cause for conquests, 4-7; irrigation works of, 163, 164, 167-169; tribal allies of, 189-190; resist conquests, 174, 175, 179, 181-185, 188-191, 203, 204, 209, 210, 213, 215, 218
sawād, 163, 209, 210, 230
Sawād b. Mālik, 391-392
Sawād b. Quṭba al-Tamīmī, 438
al-Sayb b. Ḥāritha, 191
Ṣaydā (Sidon), 112, 154
Sayf b. 'Umar, 115, 134, 137, 139, 140
al-Saylaḥān, 203
Scythopolis, *see* Baysān
Second Civil War, 26, 275, 277
sedentarization, *see* settlement
Seleuceia-Ctesiphon, *see* al-Madā'in
seminomads, 16-20; social relations among, 24, 26-28; political relations among, 29-34, 45, 46; in Syria, 94-96, 116-118, 147, 148; in Iraq, 170-172. *See also* nomads
Sergius, 115
Sergius, Saint, 286
settlement, of nomads by Muslims, 77-80, 227-228, 265-267; in Iraq, 226-245; in Syria, 151-152, 245-250
Shabath b. Rib'ī, 385
al-Shabba al-Ḥanẓalī, 403
Shaddād b. Ḍam'aja, 206, 403
Shajara b. al-A'azz, 374
al-Shammākh, 404
Shanas al-Rūmī, 138
Shaqīq, 203
Sharāf, 203, 298, 339
sharaf (pl. *ashrāf*), *sharīf*, 14, 30, 35, 37, 42, 261. *See also* aristocracy
al-Sharāt, 110
Shaṭṭ al-'Arab, 162
Shaybān (tribe), 24, 25, 46, 87, 171, 174, 178, 181-183, 185, 188-192, 195, 199, 200, 203, 208, 209, 217, 219, 223, 261, 330
Shibl b. Ma'bad al-Bajalī, 215, 417, 426, 438
Shimshāṭ (Samosata), 150
Shu'ba b. Murra, 404
Shuraḥbīl b. Ḥasana, 86, 111, 114-116, 118, 119, 129-131, 134-137, 139, 140, 152, 153, 359, 361-362
Shuraḥbīl b. al-Simṭ al-Kindī, 396, 408
Shurayḥ b. 'Āmir, 213, 373, 411
Shustar, *see* Tustar
Shuways, al-'Adawī, 417
si'āya, 297
Sidon, *see* Ṣaydā
Simāk b. Kharsha al-Anṣārī, 438
Simāk b. Makhrama al-Asadī, 438
Simāk b. 'Ubayd al-'Absī, 429, 438
Simeon Stylite, Saint, 286
al-Simṭ b. al-Aswad al-Kindī, 132, 139, 150, 363
Sinai, 115
Si'r b. Mālik, 409
slaves (*'abīd*), 193, 195, 219, 243, 271
Sophronius, 322
sources, non-Arabic, 142-146
South Arabia, South Arabian kingdoms,

Library of Congress Cataloging in Publication Data

Donner, Fred McGraw, 1945-
The early Islamic conquests.

Bibliography: p.
Includes indexes.
1. Islamic Empire—History—622-661. I. Title.
DS38.1.D66 909'.09767101 80-8544
ISBN 0-691-05327-8 AACR2